# THE FUTURE OF MUSEUM AND GALLERY DESIGN

*The Future of Museum and Gallery Design* explores new research and practice in museum design. Placing a specific emphasis on social responsibility, in its broadest sense, the book emphasises the need for a greater understanding of the impact of museum design in the experiences of visitors, in the manifestation of the vision and values of museums and galleries, and in the shaping of civic spaces for culture in our shared social world.

The chapters included in the book propose a number of innovative approaches to museum design and museum-design research. Collectively, contributors plead for more open and creative ways of making museums, and ask that museums recognize design as a resource to be harnessed towards a form of museum making that is culturally located and makes a significant contribution to our personal, social, environmental, and economic sustainability. Such an approach demands new ways of conceptualizing museum and gallery design, new ways of acknowledging the potential of design, and new, experimental, and research-led approaches to the shaping of cultural institutions internationally.

*The Future of Museum and Gallery Design* should be of great interest to academics and postgraduate students in the fields of museum studies, gallery studies, and heritage studies, as well as architecture and design, who are interested in understanding more about design as a resource in museums. It should also be of great interest to museum and design practitioners and museum leaders.

**Suzanne MacLeod** is Professor of Museum Studies at the University of Leicester, UK.

**Tricia Austin** is a design researcher and Course Leader at Central Saint Martins, University of the Arts, UK.

**Jonathan Hale** is Professor in the Department of Architecture and Built Environment at the University of Nottingham, UK.

**Oscar Ho Hing-Kay** is Associate Professor in the Department of Cultural and Religious Studies at the Chinese University of Hong Kong.

## Museum Meanings

Series Editors: Richard Sandell and Christina Kreps

Museums have undergone enormous changes in recent decades; an ongoing process of renewal and transformation bringing with it changes in priority, practice and role as well as new expectations, philosophies, imperatives and tensions that continue to attract attention from those working in, and drawing upon, wide-ranging disciplines.

*Museum Meanings* presents new research that explores diverse aspects of the shifting social, cultural and political significance of museums and their agency beyond, as well as within, the cultural sphere. Interdisciplinary, cross-cultural and international perspectives and empirical investigation are brought to bear on the exploration of museums' relationships with their various publics (and analysis of the ways in which museums shape – and are shaped by – such interactions).

Theoretical perspectives might be drawn from anthropology, cultural studies, art and art history, learning and communication, media studies, architecture and design and material culture studies amongst others. Museums are understood very broadly – to include art galleries, historic sites and other cultural heritage institutions – as are their relationships with diverse constituencies.

The focus on the relationship of the museum to its publics shifts the emphasis from objects and collections and the study of museums as text, to studies grounded in the analysis of bodies and sites; identities and communities; ethics, moralities and politics.

### *Also in the series:*

**Museum as Process**
*Translating Local and Global Knowledges*
*Edited by Raymond Silverman*

**Museums, Moralities and Human Rights**
*Richard Sandell*

**Critical Practice**
*Artists, Museums, Ethics*
*Janet Marstine*

**The Future of Museum and Gallery Design**
*Purpose, Process, Perception*
*Edited by Suzanne MacLeod, Tricia Austin, Jonathan Hale and Oscar Ho Hing-Kay*

www.routledge.com/Museum-Meanings/book-series/SE0349

# THE FUTURE OF MUSEUM AND GALLERY DESIGN

## Purpose, Process, Perception

*Edited by Suzanne MacLeod, Tricia Austin, Jonathan Hale and Oscar Ho Hing-Kay*

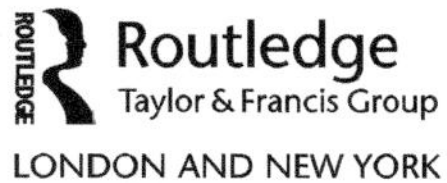


LONDON AND NEW YORK

First published 2018
by Routledge
2 Park Square, Milton Park, Abingdon, Oxon OX14 4RN

and by Routledge
711 Third Avenue, New York, NY 10017

*Routledge is an imprint of the Taylor & Francis Group, an informa business*



*British Library Cataloguing-in-Publication Data*
A catalogue record for this book is available from the British Library

*Library of Congress Cataloging-in-Publication Data*
A catalog record for this book has been requested

ISBN: 978-1-138-30732-2 (hbk)
ISBN: 978-1-138-56820-4 (pbk)
ISBN: 978-1-315-14948-6 (ebk)

Typeset in Bembo
by Apex CoVantage, LLC

# CONTENTS

*Illustrations* *viii*
*Acknowledgements* *xii*
*About the contributors* *xiii*

Introduction: the future of museum and gallery design 1
*Suzanne MacLeod, Tricia Austin, Jonathan Hale and Oscar Ho Hing-Kay*

**PART I**
**Purpose: social responsibility, cultural specificity and museum making** **9**

1 An ethical future for museum and gallery design: design as a force for good in a diverse cultural sector 13
*Suzanne MacLeod*

2 Zen and the art of museum maintenance 29
*Oscar Ho Hing-Kay*

3 On the importance of 'And': museums and complexity 34
*Elaine Heumann Gurian*

4 The designer's role in museums that act as agents of change 45
*Tricia Austin*

5 Cities as exhibition spaces: illuminated infrastructure in the smart city 59
*Dave Colangelo*

6 Representations of Chinese civilisation: exhibiting Chinese art in Republican China 71
*Pedith Chan*

7 The museum and multivalences of place 86
*Laura Hourston Hanks*

8 A site for convergence and exchange: designing the twenty-first-century university art museum 100
*Timothy J. McNeil*

**PART II**
**Process: collaboration, experimentation and participation 117**

9 Examining process in museum exhibitions: a case for experimentation and prototyping 121
*Kathleen McLean*

10 Designing and programming in 'baggy' space: a case study of the Oriel Wrecsam People's Market project 132
*Sarah Featherstone and Jo Marsh*

11 Collective creativity in the art museum 147
*Mette Houlberg Rung*

12 Placing citizens at the heart of museum development: Derby Silk Mill – Museum of Making 160
*Tony Butler, Hannah Fox and Suzanne MacLeod*

13 New approaches to universal design at The Gateway Arch National Park 175
*Bill Haley and Oriel Wilson*

14 Experimental exhibition models: curating, designing and managing experiments: a case study from the Humboldt Lab Dahlem 189
*Annette Loeseke*

15 From the 'field' to the 'wilderness': translation and creation in curating socially engaged arts 200
*Sipei Lu*

16 Unboxing history exhibitions: experience design in museum practice 213
*Clare Brown*

17 Untangling exhibition narratives: towards a bridging of design research and design practice 225
*Jona Piehl and David Francis*

18 Beyond the museum: a comparative study of narrative structures in films and museum design 239
*Tom Duncan*

**PART III**
**Perception: embodiment, experience and narrative** **255**

19 Yaji garden: art under the sky 259
*Tsong-Zung Chang and Shiming Gao*

20 Screening times: dioramas at the Shanghai Film Museum 277
*Linda Johnson*

21 Displaying and interpreting industrial pollution: a study of visitor comments on 'When the South Wind Blows' 288
*Hsu Huang and Chia-Li Chen*

22 Spatial meaning-making: exhibition design and embodied experience 304
*Maja Gro Gundersen and Christina Back*

23 The fear of popcorn: drawing inspiration from Hollywood for curating suspenseful exhibitions 317
*Ariane Karbe*

24 The Yellow Box and its rhetoric of display: exhibiting Chinese art in a museum 328
*Vivian Ting*

25 From body to body: architecture, movement and meaning in the museum 340
*Jonathan Hale and Christina Back*

Top 20 principles for the future of museum and gallery design 352

Afterword 354
*Adrian Cheng*

*Index* *356*

# ILLUSTRATIONS

## Figures


6.1 Entrance to the 1935 *Shanghai Exhibition* 79
6.2 A view of fan paintings displayed at the *Shanghai Exhibition*, 1935 80
6.3 A view of the hall of calligraphy and painting on the first floor of the *Shanghai Exhibition*, 1935 81
6.4 A set of bronze objects displayed at a temple in Beijing, 1915 82
6.5 Bronze objects installed inside tailor-made temple-like stands at the History Museum of China, 1927 83
7.1 The Novium, Chichester 89
7.2 The Pier Arts Centre, Stromness, Orkney 93
7.3 Zinc fin wall of new 'shed' building at The Pier Arts Centre, Stromness, Orkney 94
8.1 The Baggins End Domes, UC Davis, California 101
8.2 Robyn Martin's 1967 M.F.A. Thesis Project, the *Bird*, UC Davis Art Department 104
8.3 'Imagine! Three Museum Designs Revealed'. Community members take part in the selection process for a new University Art Museum 108
8.4 Museum plan Jan Shrem and Maria Manetti Shrem Museum of Art, UC Davis, California 110
8.5 Crowds during the opening of the Jan Shrem and Maria Manetti Shrem Museum of Art captured by local community sketch-crawler Pete Scully 113
10.1 Anonymous protest poster in response to the proposed Oriel Wrecsam People's Market development 139
10.2 Marking key corners of the existing People's Market building 141
10.3 Nolli plan of Wrexham's historic core with images of arcades 142
11.1 'Skyen', Statens Museum for Kunst, 2015 152
11.2 'MatchSMK', Statens Museum for Kunst, 2011 157
12.1 Derby Silk Mill, Derby, UK 161

12.2 Maker-in-Residence co-production workshop, Derby Silk Mill 170
13.1 General Arrangement plan showing the replica covered wagon and associated complex interpretative media components, The Gateway Arch National Park in St Louis, Missouri, USA 180
13.2 Plan showing access for wheelchairs avoiding any potential overlap, The Gateway Arch National Park in St Louis, Missouri, USA 181
13.3 Drawing showing the three standard locations for large-print graphic captions, The Gateway Arch National Park in St Louis, Missouri, USA 183
13.4 Drawing showing the optimal articulation of touchscreen units to maximise usability for wheelchair users, The Gateway Arch National Park in St Louis, Missouri, USA 184
13.5 The Universal Design Group and Haley Sharpe Design review exhibit prototypes for usability and access, the Gateway Arch National Park in St Louis, Missouri, USA 187
15.1 Nanting Research students at the Guan Temple of Lineage, Nanting, China, 2015 204
15.2 Entrance to the Nanting section of the 'The Civil Power', Minsheng Art Museum, Beijing, 2015 206
17.1 Exhibition view of 'Defining Beauty', British Museum, 2015 226
17.2 The narrative structure in three acts, 'Defining Beauty', British Museum, 2015 228
17.3 Expressing the plot in diagrammatic form, 'Defining Beauty', British Museum, 2015 229
17.4 Comparison of sequential wall colour structure and text based three-act structure, 'Defining Beauty', British Museum, 2015 230
17.5 Graphic language in the British Museum and in 'Defining Beauty', 2015 231
18.1 Bal's three-level model of narrative theory for the exhibition 'Botticelli Reimagined', Victoria and Albert Museum, 2016 242
18.2 An excerpt from Sergei Eisenstein's analysis of sequence in *The Film Sense* 1938 245
18.3 Diagram comparing the narrative structure of the film *Run Lola Run* and the visitor experience at Vischering Castle, Germany 248
18.4 Site plan of Vischering Castle, Germany 249
19.1 Copy by Feng Chengsu (c. 627–50) of Jin-dynasty (265–420) calligrapher Wang Xizhi's (c. 303–61) original calligraphic masterpiece Lantingji xu (Preface to the Anthology of the Orchid) 261
19.2 *Dwelling in the Fuchun Mountains*, by Huang Gongwang (1269–1364) 266
19.3 Zheng Li (b. 1964), *Downstream*, 2016 267
19.4 Installation view of *Illuminated Presence* featuring photographs and artefacts by Yeh Wei-Li (b. 1971), and painting by Yeh Shih-Chiang (1926–2012) 268
19.5 The South Gate to Heaven, and boulder calligraphy, at Mount Tai 270
19.6 Photograph of contemporary *yaji* gathering and landscape at Jia Yuan Hall in Suzhou, China, 2016 274
21.1 Floor plan of 'When the South Wind Blows: The Documentary Photographs of Taixi Village', National Museum of Natural Science, Taiwan, 2014 290

21.2 Photograph of Mei-Chue Chen and her husband, 'When the South Wind Blows: The Documentary Photographs of Taixi Village', National Museum of Natural Science, Taiwan, 2014 293
21.3 Photograph of Cai Cai-feng and Su Wei, 'When the South Wind Blows: The Documentary Photographs of Taixi Village', National Museum of Natural Science, Taiwan, 2014 294
22.1 'Imprints of War – Photography from 1864', National Museum of Photography, Royal Danish Library, Copenhagen, 2014 305
22.2 'Imprints of War – Photography from 1864', National Museum of Photography, Royal Danish Library, Copenhagen, 2014, installation view 307
22.3 'Imprints of War – Photography from 1864', National Museum of Photography, Royal Danish Library, Copenhagen, 2014, installation view 307
23.1 Private collector Franz Fromm with son Paco and daughters Luisa and Zoila, c. 1906 323
24.1 Bed platform, 'The Yellow Box: Contemporary Calligraphy and Painting in Taiwan' exhibition, Taipei Fine Arts Museum, 2004–5 335
25.1 '101 Danish Poets', Royal Danish Library, Copenhagen, 2014 349

## Colour plates

1 People and place: using interpretive design to map people and place
2 Imagining a central hub from which visitors might go off to explore stories around the Tower of London in the places they unfolded
3 Imagining the potential for a range of emotional responses to story and site at the Tower of London
4 A framework for the Ethical Treatment of the subject of prisoners, punishment and torture at the Tower of London
5 Ars Electronica Center, Linz, Austria
6 *In The Air, Tonight* (2014–2016), Public Visualization Studio
7 *The Illuminated River*, 'Current', Leo Villareal with Lifschutz Davidson Sandilands and Future\Pace
8 Lace pattern façade detailing, Nottingham Contemporary, UK
9 Turner Contemporary, Margate, UK
10 The Leaf, Henning Larsen. Competition entry for the Jan Shrem and Maria Manetti Shrem Museum of Art, UC Davis, California
11 The Slant, WORKac. Competition entry for the Jan Shrem and Maria Manetti Shrem Museum of Art, UC Davis, California
12 The Grand Canopy, SO – IL and Bohlin Cywinski Jackson. Winning design for the Jan Shrem and Maria Manetti Shrem Museum of Art, UC Davis, California
13 Oriel Wrecsam People's Market exploded axonometric drawing
14 '22 Skies' by Filip Vest, 'Mix it up', Statens Museum for Kunst, 2015
15 'MatchSMK', permanent collection, Statens Museum for Kunst, 2011
16 Working through the display considerations of objects with young people, Derby Silk Mill, 2013
17 A bridge-building workshop with Leach Colour, Derby Silk Mill, 2016

18 Statue of Dred and Harriet Scott outside the St Louis Old Courthouse
19 The first room of the exhibition 'Botticelli Reimagined', V&A Museum, 2016
20 The exhibition 'Luther and the Princes', Hartenfels Castle, Torgau, Germany, 2015
21 Street Angel, *Malu tianshi* (1937) diorama, Shanghai Film Museum, 2014
22 Bai Yang diorama, Shanghai Film Museum, 2014
23 Ruan Lingyu and Hu Die diorama, Shanghai Film Museum, 2014
24 Slideshow of photographs of Taixi residents holding photographs of relatives lost to cancer, 'When the South Wind Blows: The Documentary Photographs of Taixi Village', National Museum of Natural Science, Taiwan, 2014
25 'The Yellow Box: Contemporary Calligraphy and Painting in Taiwan' exhibition, Taipei Fine Arts Museum, 2004–5
26 Movable viewing frames, 'The Yellow Box: Contemporary Calligraphy and Painting in Taiwan' exhibition, Taipei Fine Arts Museum, 2004–5
27 'Treasures' devised by the Russian artist Andrey Bartenev, Royal Danish Library, Copenhagen, 2012
28 'Everything you can think of is true – the dish ran away with the spoon', curated by Robert Wilson, Royal Danish Library, Copenhagen, 2008–9
29 'The Original Kierkegaard', Royal Danish Library, Copenhagen, 2013

## Tables

1.1 Positive and negative characteristics of the interpretation of prisoners, punishment and torture at the Tower of London 24
21.1 Comments from the South Wind Exhibition: categories and percentages 296

# ACKNOWLEDGEMENTS

The activities which preceded this book were enabled by the kind support of the University of Leicester, K11 Art Foundation, Hong Kong University, Leisure and Cultural Services Department (LCSD) in Hong Kong, and UK Trade and Investment (now DIT). We are particularly grateful to Clare Hudson, Adrian Cheng, Florian Knothe, Shing-wai Chan, Richard Parry, Carmen Ho, Priscilla Kong, Grace Tan, Regina Zhang, Robin Clarke, Lars Nittve, Wang Wei, Julien de Casabianca, Yongwoo Lee, Eve Tam and all the speakers, workshop hosts and participants in *The Future of Museum and Gallery Design*, Hong Kong, 2015. Since then, a great deal of time has been spent looking at the wide range of papers, selecting the most representative, inviting additional researchers and practitioners to contribute to this book and working with Routledge and all the contributors to develop the book proposal and manuscript. We are particularly grateful to those colleagues who submitted papers which were not eventually taken forward for their time and goodwill – some of those papers are now thankfully being published elsewhere. We are grateful to Marc Stratton, Dominic Shyrane and Heidi Lowther at Routledge for their support and efforts to ensure that the book was as strong as possible. To the three anonymous reviewers of the proposal, thank you for your insightful comments; we hope that you can see where they positively impacted the final book. We are grateful to the University of Leicester and Central Saint Martins, University of the Arts London who provided funding for colour images and final copy editing, and to Bob Ahluwalia for his work on the images and general support in the final stages of drawing the manuscript together. We would like to say a particular thank you to the Museum Meanings Series Editors, Richard Sandell and Christina Kreps, and also to the wide range of colleagues and students with whom we have discussed the project over the last few years. We hope it is a useful contribution to the increasingly dynamic field of museum design research. Finally and as always, love and thanks to Jocelyn, Allan, Lee and Frances.

# ABOUT THE CONTRIBUTORS

**Tricia Austin** is a Design Researcher, PhD Supervisor and the Course Leader of MA Narrative Environments in the Spatial Practices Programme at Central Saint Martins, University of the Arts London. She has convened several international conferences, most recently Chaos at the Museum, infiltrating the urban fabric, 2016 in Buenos Aries. Tricia was the UK lead on EU-PA, a European project to develop culture-led city regeneration methodologies, involving multiple stakeholders and producing exemplar case studies. Tricia has lectured in Europe, Asia and South America and led a number of collaborative projects with universities and governmental organisations across the world.

**Christina Back**, Architect MAA, is exhibition co-ordinator and head of exhibition design at the Royal Library and the National Museum of Photography, Denmark. She holds a master's degree in architecture from the Royal Danish Academy of Fine Arts' School of Architecture in Copenhagen and has worked with spatial design within exhibition, installation and performance since 1998. She works with an interdisciplinary mode of expression based on abstraction, focusing her work on exploring the embodied and multisensory exhibition encounter and the potential of exhibitions as a spatial interpretive medium.

**Clare Brown** is an exhibition designer with 20 years of experience creating exhibitions for large-scale history and culture museums in New York City and Washington, DC. She served as Chair and Program Head of the Master of Arts in Exhibition Design program at the Corcoran School of the Arts and Design at George Washington University from 2012 to 2017. She is currently Chief of Design at the Smithsonian Institution, National Museum of American History. Clare has a background in Cultural Anthropology, Theater Design, Museum Studies, and is completing doctoral research in Exhibition/Experience Design at Central Saint Martins in London.

**Tony Butler** became Executive Director of Derby Museums in January 2014. Prior to that, Tony was director of the Museum of East Anglian Life for nine years. He repositioned the organisation as a social enterprise and led a major capital development programme involving the restoration of a Queen Anne mansion and associated buildings. In 2011 he founded the Happy Museum Project to create an international community of practice to explore how museums could contribute to a society in which well being and environmental sustainability were its principle values. Happy Museum has supported 22 UK museums to develop projects which build mutual relationships with audiences and steward the future as well as the past. Tony read History and Welsh History at Aberystwyth University and has an MA in Museology from University of East Anglia. He was the Fellow for Museums on the Clore Leadership Programme in 2007–08 and Fellow of the National Arts Strategies chief executive programme in the United States. He is a Fellow of the Museums Association, Director of Mission Models Money and is trustee of Kids in Museums.

**Pedith Chan**, PhD (2009) at SOAS, University of London, is an Assistant Professor for the Cultural Management Programme, Faculty of Arts, Chinese University of Hong Kong. Her publications include a monograph (*The Making of a Modern Art World*, BRILL, 2017) and articles on modern and contemporary Chinese art.

**Tsong-Zung Chang** is independent curator, guest professor of China Academy of Art in Hangzhou, China, and director of Hanart TZ Gallery in Hong Kong. He has been active in curating Chinese exhibitions since the 1980s: as co-curator of 2008 Guangzhou Triennial, 'Farewell to Post-Colonialism', and co-curator of Shanghai Biennale 2012. Current active projects include *Jia Li Hall*, a series of researches on Confucian rites and aesthetics; *West Heavens*, Sino Indian exchange in art and social thought; *Yaji Garden* (a project relating to the *Yellow Box Projects*), which investigates Chinese aesthetic space and culture of connoisseurship for contemporary practices; and *Inter-Asia School*, which organised the 'Inter-Asia Biennale Forums' in 2014 and 2016 at the Taipei Biennial, Shanghai Biennial, Kwangju Biennale and Kochi-Muziris Biennale.

**Chia-Li Chen** is Professor and Director of the Graduate Institute of Museum Studies at the Taipei National University of the Arts, Taiwan. She is also the Editor-in-Chief of *Journal of Museum and Culture*. Her research interests focus on three main areas: the engagement of people with disabilities/mental illnesses and their representation in museums; visitor studies; and museums and human rights issues. She is the author of *Museums and Cultural Identities: Learning and Recollection in Local Museums in Taiwan* (VDM Publishing House), *Wound on Exhibition: Notes on Memory and Trauma* (Artco Publisher, Taiwan), and *From Margin to Representation: The Museum and Cultural Rights* (National Taiwan University Press).

**Adrian Cheng** is the art pioneer who founded the K11 Art Foundation (KAF), a non-profit art foundation in China to incubate young contemporary artists and curators, and to promote public art education. By providing young emerging artists and curators with a local, regional and international platform to gain greater public awareness, Adrian is the new generation to represent the contemporary Chinese art scene. Adrian is a Board Member of the West Kowloon Cultural District Authority, and Member of the M+ Board and M+ Acquisitions Committee. He is also a Board Member of the Public Art Fund of New York and MoMA PS1, Trustee of Royal Academy of Arts, Board Director of the National Museum of China Foundation, Director of CAFAM Funds of the Central Academy of Fine Arts, Visiting Committee of the Department of Asian Art at The Metropolitan Museum of Art, Member of

International Circle of Centre Pompidou, Member of TATE's International Council, Board Member of Asia Art Archive and Trustee of Design Trust. In 2013, he set up an annual Master of Arts degree full scholarship programme in collaboration with Central Saint Martins. He is among the ArtReview Power 100 list of the contemporary art world's most powerful figures for three consecutive years since 2014, reaching #54 in 2016.

**Dave Colangelo** is Assistant Professor of Digital Culture at Portland State University and Director, North America, of the Media Architecture Institute. He holds an MA in Cultural Studies from Goldsmiths College, University of London and a PhD in Communication and Culture from Ryerson and York Universities. His research is centred upon the impact of digital media on art, curation, architecture and scholarship. His work as a media artist (with Public Visualization Studio), working primarily with large-scale public projections, urban screens and media architecture, and has been presented at the International Symposium for Electronic Art and the Biennale of Architecture and Urbanism.

**Tom Duncan** is an architect and exhibition designer for museums and heritage sites. He combines professional practice with academic research and teaching and is a PhD candidate at the University of Leicester, School of Museum Studies. His research investigates how the contemporary museum master plan can combine the spatial qualities of architecture with the experiential and storytelling qualities of the visitor experience. Based in Berlin, Germany, he is a founding partner, together with Noel McCauley, of the studio Duncan McCauley, working for clients such as the Victoria and Albert Museum in London and the State Museums of Berlin.

**Sarah Featherstone** is an architect and co-director of London-based practice Featherstone Young. She is interested in the way people shape their environment and how architecture can stimulate, rather than dictate, activity and social interaction. Her practice has won many awards including RIBA awards for The Dellow Centre for homelessness, SERICC Crisis centre and Ty Hedfan, a new house in Wales. Sarah studied architecture at Kingston University, the Architectural Association and the Bartlett, UCL, and currently teaches at Central St Martins. She has been an external examiner at a number of universities and is currently on the Islington, Southwark and Camden Design Review panels.

**Hannah Fox** is the Project Director leading the redevelopment of Derby Silk Mill, site of the world's first factory, as the Museum of Making. Trained as a designer and photographer, Hannah's background is in developing cross-sector creative projects. Her passion is putting people at the heart of how places, products and services are co-designed to support community needs. Hannah travels widely, teaching human-centred design methodologies to people working in arts and culture. She is part of the National Arts Strategies Creative Community Fellowship, an international network of cultural and social entrepreneurs, and is a board member of FIGMENT, a global participatory arts programme.

**David Francis** is a writer and researcher who specialises in museums, zoos and botanic gardens. He is currently writing his PhD, which focuses on how narrative shapes the creation and reception of exhibitions in the museum. He has previously worked as an interpretation officer at the British Museum in the UK, and also as an evaluation researcher at Chester Zoo. He is currently working as Research Associate on the Big Picnic Project, a European-wide project about botanic gardens engaging the public on the topic of food security.

**Shiming Gao** is a curator and critic based in Hangzhou, China. He is currently the Vice President of China Academy of Art. He is also curator of many exhibitions and intellectual projects, including: *The Yellow Box: Contemporary Art and Architecture in Chinese Space*, 2006; *Reversing Horizons: Artist Reflections of the Hong Kong Handover 10th Anniversary*, 2007; *Revival of the Countryside: Special Project of Sao Paulo Architectural Biennial*, 2007; *Farewell to Post-colonialism: the Third Guangzhou Triennial*, 2008; *Rehearsal: the 8th Shanghai Biennale*, 2010; *Reflecta: the First West Bund Biennale for Architecture and Contemporary Art*, 2013; *Inter-Asia Biennial Forum (Taipei, Shanghai, Kochi)*, 2014; *Renjian Thoughts Forum: Reports of Asian Social Thought Movements*, 2014; *Forums in Motion: BANDUNG/Third World 60 Years*, 2015; *Shan Shui: A Manifesta*, 2016; *The Future Media/Art Manifesta*, 2017.

**Maja Gro Gundersen** holds an MA in art history and media science from Aarhus University. From 2010–13 she worked with the production and layout of exhibitions at the Royal Danish Library and the National Museum of Photography, and in 2014–15 she conducted research on exhibition design. She has been a guest teacher at the Danish National School of Theatre and Contemporary Dance, Department of Scenography, and currently runs a small exhibition space, Kvadrat16, in Copenhagen together with artist Birgitte Støvring.

**Elaine Heumann Gurian** is consultant/advisor/speaker/teacher to museums, universities, associations, and governments worldwide. She was deputy director of the US Holocaust Memorial Museum and National Museum of the American Indian following service as Deputy Assistant Secretary at the Smithsonian. She has received fellowships from the Georgia O'Keeffe Museum, the Exploratorium, and the Fulbright program. Routledge published her book, *Civilizing the Museum*, in 2006. Most of her writings are now available at www.egurian.com. Elected to many offices in AAM and ICOM/CECA, Gurian was named to AAM's Centennial Honor Roll in 2006 and presented its Distinguished Service award in 2004. Gurian is a founder of the Museum Group, an association of US independent museum consultants.

**Jonathan Hale** is an architect and Professor of Architectural Theory at the University of Nottingham. His research interests include phenomenology and the philosophy of technology; the relationship between architecture and the body; and embodied experience in museums and exhibitions. Recent publications include a monograph for the Routledge series *Thinkers for Architects* on the philosopher Maurice Merleau-Ponty (2017). Previous co-edited books include *Museum Making: Narratives, Architectures, Exhibitions* (Routledge 2012) and *Rethinking Technology: A Reader in Architectural Theory* (Routledge 2007). He is currently Head of the research group Architecture, Culture and Tectonics (ACT), and was founding Chair of the Architectural Humanities Research Association (AHRA).

**Bill Haley** is the company founder of Haley Sharpe Design Ltd (**hsd**). His enthusiasm for outstanding design and understanding of the museum and heritage sector, prompted him to form **hsd** with fellow director, Alisdair Hinshelwood, in 1983. Under their direction, the company grew from a small UK-based agency, to an international design and planning consultancy with an unrivalled track record in the creation of dynamic arts, cultural and museum environments. Through first-hand experience on various high profile US-based projects, Bill now advocates for a universal design approach to exhibition development, which draws upon social constructs of disability.

**Laura Hourston Hanks** is Associate Professor and Senior Tutor in the Department of Architecture and Built Environment at the University of Nottingham, where she teaches across the undergraduate and postgraduate programmes. Her research interests include contemporary museum design, the architectural expression of identities and issues of narrative place making. She has published chapters in *Architecture and the Canadian Fabric* and *Museum Making: Narratives, Architectures, Exhibitions*, which she also co-edited (MacLeod, Hourston Hanks and Hale, Routledge, 2012). Notable among her other publications are *Museum Builders II* (John Wiley and Sons, 2004), and contributions to *Architectural Design, arq: Architectural Research Quarterly* and *Curator: The Museum Journal.*

**Oscar Ho Hing-Kay** specialises in the practice and critical studies of cultural management, particularly in the areas of visual arts, museum management and curatorship. He was formerly Exhibition Director at the Hong Kong Arts Centre, Senior Research Officer at the Home Affairs Bureau of the Hong Kong Government, and Founding Director of Museum of Contemporary Art in Shanghai. He is currently Programme Director of the MA in Cultural Management at the Chinese University of Hong Kong.

**Hsu Huang** is an associate curator at the National Museum of Natural Science in Taiwan. He has been working in the Department of Exhibitions as a planner and researcher, and has conducted and designed many exhibitions in the past 20 years including 'When the South Wind Blows – the Documentary Photography of Taixi Village'. Hsu Huang has also been the Editor-in-Chief of the academic journal *Museology Quarterly* since 2011. His research interests focus on relationships between knowledge and space, and the social responsibility of museum exhibitions.

**Linda Johnson** is a graduate of the MA Museum Studies programme at Leicester University. Linda trained originally as a lawyer with an LLB (Hons) from Warwick University (1978), an MPhil in Criminology from Cambridge University (1982) and a PhD in Social Sciences from Brunel University (1990). She qualified as a Solicitor in 1981 and worked as a Law Lecturer and Senior Lecturer at Hong Kong University (1986–1995) and at the University of Hertfordshire (1996–2000) before moving permanently to Shanghai in 2000. She has owned and operated a store and gallery in Shanghai since then, specialising in Mao Period propaganda art and contemporary design. Since 2011 Linda has also convened the Chinese Film Group for the Royal Asiatic Society in Shanghai.

**Ariane Karbe** is an independent curator, based in Berlin. She holds an MA in Social and Cultural Anthropology (University of Bayreuth) and trained as a scriptwriter at the Filmschool Hamburg Berlin. Her current PhD research at the School of Museum Studies, University of Leicester, investigates how dramaturgic tools used for writing exciting film scripts could be adapted for curating (exciting) exhibitions.

**Annette Loeseke** is Lecturer in Museum Studies at New York University Berlin. Her research interests include museums as public (political) space, visitor studies, and reception-centred curatorial formats. A scholar-in-residence at Cornell University, Ithaca, New York, in summer 2015, she worked on intercultural exhibition models. She has carried out numerous visitor studies at museums in Berlin, London, Shanghai and Amsterdam, and worked as visiting lecturer at universities in Berlin, Heidelberg, Hildesheim, Moscow and Amsterdam (Reinwardt Academy). Annette holds a PhD in art history from the University of Bonn; she studied art history in Freiburg, Munich and Paris, and cultural management in London.

**Sipei Lu** is a PhD researcher of Museum Studies at the University of Leicester in the UK. Her writing and curatorial projects investigate art's engagement with Chinese society and what agency art institutions and curating have in this process. Her recent projects include the 'Water System Museum', a socially engaged art project undertaken in collaboration with A4 Art Museum, Chengdu (2015). Lu served as a guest researcher at Times Museum, Guangzhou (2015) and also translated *Active Withdrawals: the Life and Death of Institutional Critique* (Jilin Publishing Group/Black Dog Publishing, 2016).

**Suzanne MacLeod** is Professor of Museum Studies at the University of Leicester where she has worked in a range of roles since 1997. She has published widely around museum architecture and design and has a particular interest in design forms and processes and how they might be harnessed towards positive social and organisational impacts by progressive museums. She undertakes research with museum and design partners and is currently working on a book titled *Design for Creative Lives*. Previous publications include *Reshaping Museum Space*; *Museum Making* (with Jonathan Hale and Laura Hanks); and *Museum Architecture: A New Biography*.

**Jo Marsh** has worked as a freelance artist, curator and facilitator since 2009. In 2011 she won the Leeds-based Woolgather Art Prize with her socially engaged project 'With Love from the Artist', and received funding from Arts Council of Wales in 2013 and 2014 to build and tour her portable sculpture-gallery, WanderBox. In 2014 Jo came into post as learning and engagement officer at Oriel Wrecsam, delivering an extensive off-site programme for the gallery; in January 2017 Jo became Creative Director for Oriel Wrecsam and is designing new programmes which hold socially engaged practice and civic responsibility at heart.

**Kathleen McLean,** principal of museum consulting firm Independent Exhibitions, was creative director for concept, design, and reinstallation of the Oakland Museum of California's galleries, 2008–2012, and Director, Center for Public Exhibitions and Programs, Exploratorium, 1994–2004. McLean has created award-winning exhibitions and programs for museums of history, art, and science, focusing on social issues and public response. She is author of *The Convivial Museum* (2010), *Visitor Voices in Museum Exhibitions* (2007), and *Planning for People in Museum Exhibitions* (1994). McLean was selected for AAM's 2006 Centennial Honor Roll: one of 100 professionals who made significant contributions to American museums over the last century.

**Timothy J. McNeil** is the Director of the UC Davis Design Museum and a Professor of Design at the University of California Davis. With over 25 years of experience developing exhibition, signage, and interpretive environments, his research and practice seeks to define exhibition design in relation to the curatorial process, and the contribution this multidisciplinary design field makes to meaningful audience engagement. McNeil's award-winning design research has been featured in multiple publications and he is a frequent speaker both nationally and internationally on museum and design issues.

**Jona Piehl** is a graphic designer and design researcher. She recently completed her PhD in which she examined the roles of graphic design in exhibition narratives. Prior to her doctorate she led the graphic design team of the London-based exhibition design consultancy Land Design Studio where she worked on projects for clients such as the Victoria and Albert Museum, the Natural History Museum London, English Heritage and Miraikan/Tokyo. She teaches on the MA Narrative Environments and the BA Culture, Criticism and Curation at Central Saint Martins/University of the Arts London.

**Mette Houlberg Rung** has a background in art history and holds a PhD from Leicester University. For the past 15 years she has been working in museums in Denmark and the UK. Currently she holds a position as art interpreter and researcher at Statens Museum for Kunst (National Gallery of Denmark). Her research areas include museology, visitor studies and aesthetic experiences. She is also engaged in planning, designing and producing temporary exhibitions where her main focus areas are the narrative structure, interpretative materials and user experiences within the exhibition.

**Vivian Ting** is the Head of Historical Research at the Design and Cultural Studies Workshop. She was trained as a historian at the Chinese University of Hong Kong where she developed an interest in the study of objects and connoisseurship. This interest was developed during her PhD degree in Museum Studies at the University of Leicester. She has taught Museum Studies and Material Culture Studies in universities, and been involved in many contemporary curatorial projects. Her research looks at how to cultivate a global vision of cultural appreciation in the exhibition context.

**Oriel Wilson** has been part of the interpretative and development teams at Haley Sharpe Design Ltd for over 15 years. Completing the University of Leicester Museum Studies Masters, she went on to hold curatorial posts in several London museums, including the Museum of London Docklands. Since joining **hsd**, she has led the interpretative development of many leading museum and heritage attractions. Particular interests include narrative storytelling in regenerated urban and maritime landscapes and the role of museums in suburban place-making.

# INTRODUCTION

## The future of museum and gallery design

*Suzanne MacLeod, Tricia Austin, Jonathan Hale and Oscar Ho Hing-Kay*

As we draw the chapters together for this book in spring 2017, strange things are happening in museums in our home countries, the UK and China. In the UK, already large museums are planning expansions, seemingly only able to survive in a state of perpetual growth. We have seen examples of collections being moved from museums in the north of the country to London, reducing the cultural resource for audiences in one location whilst simultaneously fuelling even more expansion in the capital (Ellis-Petersen 2017). Flagship Heritage Lottery Fund projects, part of the growth in new museums and updating and expansion of many established museums which took place across the country around the millennium, are under threat of closure as their funding is cut, and it is assumed that they can operate in just the same way as large London-based museums where tourism and corporate sponsorship now dominate (Newbould 2017). In extreme cases, these museums only continue to survive as a result of the energy, ingenuity and vision of their leaders. And once iconic exhibits and displays such as Launchpad in London's Science Museum, which offered free educational fun to families for almost 30 years, have been replaced by high-budget displays with big business sponsors and placed behind a paywall (Macrae and Payne 2015; Garrard 2016). This is happening elsewhere in the country as the notion of charging for access to public collections gains greater traction in the face of cuts in public funding and a lack of alternative vision.

In China, the context is different but the shape of museum development is equally worrying. The recent drive to expand the number of museums in the country has progressed at such a rate that it is ahead of the building of collections, content, trained personnel and, most importantly, a sense of why the arts and culture might benefit people in China and provide an important addition to their cultural lives. New museums stand empty, some abandoned and, in places, large cultural developments have been frozen as the vast resources needed for their continuation have dried up. In addition to the government-funded museums, an increasing number of museums are being built and run by developers as they have, in Ou Ning's words, 'come to realize that building museums is an effective means of obtaining land and marketing the adjacent residential projects with attractive cultural packages' (2014: 120). The scale of growth and investment has made China a magnet for architects, designers and a whole range of international consultants who see an opportunity to win new contracts, without always thinking deeply about the needs of audiences or the specific and varied context within which they are working (Ibid.). Whilst these observations are not new – critics have been citing similar examples internationally for many years – the realities they describe continue to unfold around us, seemingly unchallenged.

The impetus for much of this activity, of course, is economic. Museums are the archetypal malleable institution; they have come to speak of civilisation, modernity, democracy and economic prosperity (regardless of the realities), and any self-respecting international city must now be home to museums and galleries of international quality, ideally on a waterfront site. Conceived as a draw for tourists, at times they are built with only this in mind, while in other cases local museum services are harnessed in a bid to generate city brands and tempt inward investment, as we can see in the way that Manchester is currently being marketed to international travellers. At one level these may be perfectly reasonable uses for culture and museums (as the ultimate malleable institution, museums have the capacity to be many things to many people simultaneously); nonetheless, the power and force of these economic drives does push museum developments in specific directions, towards commerce, towards income generation and often, in design terms, towards the bland uniformity of the generic. These tendencies are not benign. As Richard Sennett reminds us, human feelings of exclusion and indifference are not only tied to the march of capitalism and its processes, but to the physical built forms capitalism produces (Sennett 2000). Conceived from such a high level, these developments ignore the realities of life as it is lived and, far from silent and inactive, they erode community, belonging and care for others.

Disappointingly, design is often blamed for these ills, as those working in museums are puzzled by the museum that gets built or as budgets are doubled as a result of the pressure on designers to create something new and iconic. Rarely do those involved in cultural developments – museum professionals, design professionals, politicians and funders – stand back to consider how their project is being shaped by economic and political forces, to question design decisions from the perspective of the politics of space and the vastly differentiated experiences and often competing claims of the people who occupy the locale, or to ask how the investment might connect more fully with an integrated, comprehensive plan for community development, the production of empowering social relations, or the creation of moments of clarity, connection and openness in an increasingly homogenised and socially fragmented world. Whilst the progress of museums designed as disconnected icons feels unstoppable and way beyond the control of people working in and for the cultural sector, it is also clear that more interesting forms of museum making are happening in places where it clearly *is* possible to generate a greater sense of social intent, stronger institutional identities and community connections, and where the users of arts and culture (actual and potential) are a significant part of the design process. In these examples, design and designed forms are recognised as a significant resource for socially purposeful museums.

It is within this context of massive museum investment which far too often fails to strive to meet its full social potential, that discussions about the future of museum design have flourished over the last 15 years. Driven by a desire to acknowledge the opportunities socially driven museums and galleries miss when they fail to think deeply about design and seeking to release design from the narrow and bureaucratic commercial and economic constraints museums place around it and, instead, recognise design processes and a design sensibility as having significant contributions to make to the shaping of museum experiences which can enrich the lives of citizens in whole variety of ways, an international, dynamic and connected network of 'museum design thinkers' has emerged. Supported by research teams at the Universities of Leicester, Nottingham, Central Saint Martins and the Chinese University of Hong Kong, researchers from across museums, design and academia are working together to build networks, share resources and ideas and, importantly, offer new research and knowledge which might inform alternatives to the dominant, economically led modes of museum making. This work has taken on an interesting urgency in various cultural contexts in recent years and months as political unrest and turmoil have made clear the need for privileged public institutions such as museums to harness the opportunities they have to shape our social world in ways which benefit the many, not just a privileged few.

*The Future of Museum and Gallery Design* has emerged directly from this set of interactions and collaborations, the result of the enthusiasm and conviction of those involved that design can, if allowed and if approached in very specific ways, play a fundamental role in the reshaping of museums and galleries of genuine interest and relevance to the lives of not just established museum audiences (which, as we know, represent a very narrow segment of society), but also to the lives of a far greater range of people. The project began as a conference in Hong Kong – a large gathering of experts interested in sharing their ideas, learning from others and exploring new possibilities. As with all the work previously undertaken by network participants, the conference attracted academics, museum professionals, architects, artists and designers of varied career ages and from diverse contexts. As a group, we represented 16 different countries.

The location of the conference in Hong Kong was pivotal to establishing connections between design research groups and individuals from across the world, an opportunity which continues to positively impact those involved. Over the course of three days, we established some common ground, discussed research and research-led practice, shared something of the differences of our cultural contexts and what that might mean for museum development, and took part in an active programme of workshops, visits and performances. Many of us left Hong Kong with a very clear sense of some of the fundamental cultural differences between, for example, Europe and Asia which must, particularly in China, be allowed to impact museum development. Since then, a number of researchers and practitioners who were unable to take part in Hong Kong have joined the conversation by contributing important chapters to this volume.

One of the activities worked through at the conference involved a large-scale pyramid game where participants were asked to write down their top hopes and principles for the future of museum and gallery design. The hundreds of response cards were then reduced down to our Top 20 Principles through a process of group discussion and debate. The Principles, which are reproduced at the back of this book, were not necessarily surprising but did get straight to the heart of some of the key challenges for design in museums today. At the top of our list were visitors and the need to place visitors and their specific needs at the centre of the design process. It remains incredibly rare for museum architects and designers to establish a consistent focus on visitors and generate new design methods and strategies which can channel knowledge from and about visitors and the broader society into the physical solutions produced. The pull of museum conventions, the formality and commercialism of the client/consultant relationship and the formality of museums and galleries themselves mean that design is still, in the main, focused around objects in cases and the communication of curatorial knowledge. Within this inherently conservative sector, participatory innovations are all the more impressive and our entire group of some 150 conference participants were united around the desire to learn from these innovations and seek new routes to inclusive forms of museum design.

More than this, the principle of placing visitors first also pointed to a small but powerful number of projects which do not simply reach out to draw visitors and their expertise into the museum – to encourage participation – but which begin from community. An outward focus which demands that museums involve themselves with a whole range of issues and challenges in the locale, in these museums citizens and their needs provide the very rationale for the institution and resources and programmes are shaped accordingly. This Principle placed pressure on museum designers to familiarise themselves with studies of leading-edge practice and particularly the vast bodies of research about museum learning and the social impacts of culture as a route to generating experimental design processes and appropriate spatial and social forms. Only through the development of a specialist focus on *design for the cultural sector* will design fully embrace the social aims and ambitions of many in the arts and culture sectors. Such a focus on others also demands that both designers and museum professionals relinquish control and let go of some of their professional preferences. In one sense feeling like familiar territory, these ideas are significantly under-developed and under-utilised in museum design.

Second in our list and directly linked to the desire for new spatial and social forms was collaboration. Seemingly obvious, collaboration not only pointed to an interest in team-based approaches to exhibition making which have been prioritised sporadically in museums since the 1960s and '70s as well as more recent participatory and experimental approaches, but also to deep-seated feelings within our group around two key issues: the continued holding of design at arm's length in museums *and* recognition of design as a significantly under-utilised resource. For many of the design professionals at the conference, the high importance of this Principle reflected their sense that design is rarely allowed to be a full collaborator in the process of making museums. Still a process which prioritises curatorial knowledge and museum knowledge above all else, discussions made clear both the need for more in-depth engagements with what a genuine process of collaboration entails, and a need for all those involved in the production of museums and galleries to open up to an understanding of design as a resource laden with potential to make a significant contribution to arts and culture. This Principle placed pressure on museum personnel and all those with a vested interest in museum design to broaden their understanding and educate themselves about the skills, qualities and roles of the excellent, socially engaged designer. A design approach that gives a voice to a wider range of potential participants within the design process itself will also produce outcomes where all the constituent elements of the designed environment – from the physical to the virtual – can become active agents in creation of inclusive visitor experiences.

A number of other Principles linked directly to notions of collaboration and the need for improved processes: a plea for non-hierarchical approaches to museum making which value and take concrete steps to build on the knowledge of diverse stakeholders; the need for the sharing of practical and tested processes of participatory design and co-design; the need for risk-taking and experimentation; the need for all involved in museum making to look beyond museums for their inspiration; and the need for our community of design thinkers to be strategic, visible, connected and organised. All of these ideas were underpinned by a sophisticated understanding of visitor experience as owned by visitors themselves and created through diverse forms of action and interaction with the institution and its resources. Included in the Principles, then, was a plea for museums to trust their visitors and recognise the role of museum makers as one of creating opportunities to access new ways of knowing – moments in our lives when we might, even momentarily, understand the experience of someone else or suddenly see the world differently. Implicit within this Principle was an awareness of the need for museums to free themselves from the desire to create exhibitions full of information and to, rather, open themselves up to creating spaces full of complexity, opportunity and possibility. Research was identified as playing an important role here and museum makers were challenged to find ways to make use of, direct and consolidate the growing body of museum design research through their practice.

A number of the Principles related specifically to the experiences of museum users inside the built, physical museum. Perhaps unsurprisingly in light of the identities of those involved in the conference, these echoed recent research in visitor experience and perception. The Principles captured the need for museum design to work hard to appeal to all the senses in recognition of the embodied nature of all our experiences and our increasing understanding of sensory perception and emotion in processes of cognition. They called for design solutions which prioritise movement and action in recognition of the centrality of movement to the museum experience and action to human meaning-making processes. In a world where society is retreating further into the private spheres of family and individuality, participants recognised the need for an emphasis on museums which seek to enable social interaction and which are varied as a result of their willingness to encourage and celebrate difference.

Linked to all of these priorities, *The Future of Museum and Gallery Design* was tasked with finding new ways to break down the formality of museums and embed the arts and culture more fully in everyday life. In relation to this last Principle, of seeking physical solutions to embedding museums and galleries more effectively in everyday life, were others which expressed a desire for museums built at a human scale and which involve themselves in real human processes such as engendering curiosity or increased and empathetic awareness of other people and places. Across all of these discussions, there was a very clear sense that by driving forward innovations in museum design of the kind suggested here, design itself could be a driver for transformation and democratisation not just at the level of the museum but in society more broadly.

## The future

*The Future of Museum and Gallery Design*, then, is not about gizmos or digital technologies; it isn't about predicting what museums will be like in the future or about a radical form of museum making that we seek to promote. Rather, our focus is on the future role of museum design in a broader and far more complex process of museum making, both within museums themselves and across the broader physical and social landscape. This approach acknowledges cultural context, seeks positive social impacts, and pays attention to the vast array of people who need to be involved in the production of museums readdressing the balance between museum professionals, funders, designers, architects, researchers and, most importantly, the far wider range of people who will, ideally, use the museum as part of their daily lives and in whose lives and locale the museum might be regarded as a force for good. Here, our concerns are with the ways in which design, often outsourced and held at arm's-length from the organisation, is integrated and allowed to come closer to the museum as organisation.

We are concerned then, with the ways in which design is conceptualised and seek to expand limiting notions of design as a technical process of display or building, to a far more expansive notion of design as a significant strategic resource to be harnessed by museums in their drive to shape truly visitor-centred experiences and institutions which have the potential to positively impact the larger society. These are ambitious aims which give full credit to the skills of the excellent designer and the importance of the physical, designed forms of museums not just in individual visitor experiences but also in the tangible manifestation of organisational vision and values (consciously or unconsciously) in the wider world.

We began our discussions in Hong Kong with a series of questions and we pose them again here. How can design be harnessed to create the social, life-affirming spaces full of possibility and opportunity for all that our public museums and galleries should be? How can we construct them in such a way that they might open up opportunities for moments of insight, learning, sociality, wellbeing, reflection, empathy and political empowerment at a time when our lives are shaped so much by the agendas of big business and when politics seems more and more disconnected from daily life? What kinds of design processes and what kinds of designers are needed for such an ambitious aim? And what is at stake if we fail to recognise design and designed forms as key resources in the drive to produce located, dynamic and empowering cultural spaces of direct interest and use to a diverse range of people?

For the contributors to *The Future of Museum and Gallery Design*, the answers to these questions are likely to be found in the sharing of ideas and the generation of new forms of research-led design and design-led research. Across the three parts of the book, a series of approaches and case studies are introduced which speak to all of the themes above and which also provide a sense of the range, diversity and creativity of museum design research and practice at the current time. Here we have purposefully sought to include the voices of early career researchers and practitioners alongside more established voices.

Although the chapters are varied in their approaches and span a range of cultural contexts, a number of themes recur. First is the belief in museums as sites full of potential to offer something fundamental to diverse individuals in a complex social world. Museums here are encouraged to shake off established conventions, to recognise design as a process which demands an ethical prioritisation of others, and to open themselves up to new spatial and social forms. Second is the belief in design as a strategic resource which can be channelled towards the empowering of citizens. Implicit here is a critique of the tendency to always reach for tried and tested solutions or for references and solutions from the world of commerce, and a belief in the social value of making things together, through collaboration, experimentation and participation. Design here utilises the museum as a site for exploration, visitor-centred participatory experimentation which draws on the collective creativity of all those involved and, as a result, builds diversity into the very heart of strategic design processes.

Third, and finally, colleagues are giving a great deal of thought to how increasingly sophisticated understandings of processes of human perception, the narrative tendencies of human beings and the possibilities embedded in new research around the embodied processes of human cognition can be drawn into museum design and museum design research, as a route to creating empowering and impactful experiences at the level of the individual. There are interesting synergies here between research in China focusing around the idea of the 'yellow box' and how museum makers might reimagine a museum space where Chinese traditions and ways of seeing might flourish, and research in Europe exploring phenomenological approaches to museum making.

All of the museum design research described above demands input from users, from designers, from architects, from a range of academics as well as from museum professionals if it is to really move our understanding forward and impact our ability to shape museums in new and wholly democratic ways. As well as demanding cross-sectoral collaboration, recognition that design must be research led and research must be design led demands the production of new creative methodologies. Interestingly, these new ways of working have the potential to blur previously distinct boundaries between design and curation, between design and research, and between museums and everyday life. Such an approach to museum design is dependent on the testing and open sharing of findings and on small-scale experimentation with users. It demands openness and generosity on the part of all involved and a shared desire to ensure that museums genuinely support the only political project which really matters: the lives of ordinary people. This is the future of museum and gallery design.

## References

Ellis-Petersen, H. (2017) 'V&A to Open New Galleries for Photos Acquired from Bradford Museum', *The Guardian*, 5 April 2017. Online. Available HTTP: www.theguardian.com/artanddesign/2017/apr/05/va-to-open-new-galleries-for-photos-acquired-from-bradford-museum. Accessed 6 May 2017.

Garrard, C. (2016) 'With Entry Charges and Oil Sponsorship, the Science Museum Has Lost Its Way', *The Guardian*, 17 October 2016. Online. Available HTTP: www.theguardian.com/science/political-science/2016/oct/17/with-entry-charges-and-oil-sponsorship-the-science-museum-has-lost-its-way. Accessed 9 August 2017.

Macrae, F. and Payne, T. (2015) 'Anger After Science Museum Which Has Been Free Since 2001 Announces it is to Start Charging Families to Use Launchpad Gallery', *Daily Mail*, 1 August 2015. Online. Available HTTP: www.dailymail.co.uk/news/article-3181962/Anger-Science-Museum-free-2001-announces-start-charging-families-use-Launchpad-gallery.html#ixzz4gHy5ijSb. Accessed 6 May 2017.

Newbould, D. (2017) 'Future of Closure-threatened New Art Gallery Walsall Debated in Parliament', *Walsall Advertiser*, 2 January 2017. Online. Available HTTP: www.walsalladvertiser.co.uk/8203-future-of-closure-threatened-new-art-gallery-walsall-debated-in-parliament/story-30063923-detail/story.html. Accessed 6 May 2017.

Ning, O. (2014) 'Shrine of Knowledge, Palace of Aesthetics, or Theatre of History: Museum Design in China', in Chiu, M. (ed.) *Making a Museum in the 21st Century*, New York: Asia Society, pp. 119–28.

Sennett, R. (2000) 'Capitalism and the City', Lecture at *cITy: Data on the City Under the Conditions of Information Technology*, 11 November 2000, ZKM_Karlsruhe. Online. Available HTTP: http://on1.zkm.de/zkm/stories/storyReader$1513. Accessed 7 May 2017.

# PART I

# Purpose

## Social responsibility, cultural specificity and museum making

### Introduction

Part I focuses on the larger Purpose of museum design and draws together a diverse range of chapters from researchers and practitioners in China, Hong Kong, the UK and the United States. All of the chapters in Part I point towards the potential for making museums in ways which respond to their locale and raise related questions of personal, social and environmental sustainability. Importantly, all of the chapters in Part I work to overcome false divisions between the built, physical world and our social experience, recognising that designed forms, design process and a design sensibility have diverse social effects and possibilities, both positive and negative. A number of the chapters concern themselves with how design can be harnessed towards the needs and desires of citizens, rather than the advancement of corporate power. Museums and galleries here are constantly evolving public events, diverse social and civic spaces animated through inhabitation and use as well as sites for social production, not least the creation of empowering forms of cultural experience and citizenship. In this analysis, design is an enabler, directed towards the creation of opportunities for action and transformation.

In Chapter 1, Suzanne MacLeod argues that museums have yet to effectively draw design into their strategies to reposition themselves as socially purposeful institutions. Through a detailed exploration of a research project undertaken with Historic Royal Palaces (HRP) in the UK, she sets forward the case for an ethics of museum design as a route to demanding deep reflection and consideration of design choices. The chapter both illustrates a research-led process which sought to provide HRP with an ethical framework for design and interpretation at the Tower of London, and begins to sketch the characteristics of an emerging ethics of museum design. Design here is an as yet under-utilised resource to be harnessed by museums as a route to new social, civil and spatial forms.

The focus on ethical practices, processes and outcomes is picked up in Chapter 2 in a short and provocative piece of writing from Oscar Ho Hing-Kay, one-time founding director of MOCA Shanghai and now professor at the Chinese University of Hong Kong. Ho questions the usefulness of museums in the context of China and in light of the often heavy-handed use of culture in top-down economic processes. Pointing instead to the lived cultural experiences and objects of Hong Kong residents, and to the spontaneous cultural productions of young protestors during the Umbrella Movement in Hong Kong in 2014, Ho sets forward a challenge to museum makers in Asia to develop far more sophisticated approaches to representing and enabling this lived experience of culture as a route to generating sites of genuine significance and relevance to the lives of local people.

In Chapter 3, Elaine Heumann Gurian continues the focus on relevance, introducing the notion of complexity and setting out a vision for the future of museums which prioritises plurality of political perspectives and supports citizens towards more thoughtful, civil and open-ended discussions of pressing contemporary issues. Driven by the current political climate in the United States and the evident danger of simplified and polarised argument which is coming to characterise political behaviour, Gurian begins to imagine a new form of museum design which rather than prioritising specific narratives and experiences for specified target audiences embraces the challenge of museums for all and the need for complexity in complex democratic societies which aspire to democracy and equality. Museums here are, importantly, intentional, subtle resisters – rather than collaborators – in a world becoming more autocratic.

The next pair of chapters in Part I shifts our focus beyond the institutional space of the museum in order to explore the potential for museum making processes in the city. In Chapter 4, Tricia Austin explores the potential for exhibition making as a social process and takes us through an important review of approaches to exhibition making in the public realm, from high-art interventions to artist-led critiques of museums as institutions, digital projects to which users can contribute content and the 'illusive practice' of genuine co-curation. Reviewing the relationships between the genesis of notions of co-curation and co-design and introducing a project undertaken as part of her research and teaching practice, Austin makes a strong case for socially motivated designers to be acknowledged as creative strategists, social mediators, user-centred enablers, inventive storytellers and experts in engaging audiences.

Dave Colangelo picks up Austin's focus on exhibitionary strategies in the city in Chapter 5 to explore the potential of massive media – large urban digital screens – in offering citizens something more than an endless barrage of products and marketing. Exploring the scope for the participatory practices of museums to impact the urban scale and experience of urban life, and focusing on the potential in massive media to memorialise culture in new ways and experiment with new ways of being social and civic, Colangelo asks how the utopian and emancipatory qualities of the Situationist International, who argued that citizens should be able to reconfigure the infrastructures of the city, might be captured in the curating of massive media and deliver audiences to critical and creative encounters with art, the city and each other. Of particular note here is the potential for massive media to generate new forms of public space, take an active part in creating a shared sense of democratic debate and open up opportunities for the nurturing of perceptual acuity as well as collective and individual intelligences.

In Chapter 6 we return to China, though this time looking back to the first decades of the twentieth century, to explore the introduction of European modes of exhibition and display to Asia. In a chapter which speaks directly to Oscar Ho Hing-Kay's contribution above as well as Tsong-Zung Chang and Shiming Gao's chapter in Part III, Pedith Chan considers the ways in which new museological standards introduced to China through the 1935 *Shanghai Exhibition* changed traditional display conventions and expected viewing practices in China, despite their reinterpretation through key Chinese concepts. Drawing attention to the history of museum making in China, Chan highlights the importance of contemporary discussions about museum design in that context and makes clear the need for museum design researchers to seek far more located, culturally specific approaches to museum making.

The final two chapters in Part I return our focus to contemporary modes of museum making and the need for deep analysis – in order to better understand the physical forms of museums and galleries and the varied roles they seek to play – and, importantly, confident new modes of museum making, if museums and galleries are genuinely to generate new forms of civic and social expression. In Chapter 7, Laura Hourston Hanks explores the strategies used by a series of architects in the representation and manifestation of place in the visitor experience. Recognising that a close focus on place has emerged as a key strategy utilised by museum architects, Hanks explores both the potential and limits of a situated approach to architectural development through a number of recent architectural projects in the UK. The chapter draws our attention to the importance of spirit of place in future museum making whilst simultaneously questioning the specific ways in which this genius loci is harnessed and expressed.

Locality is also of great significance in our final chapter in Part I, though in a very different way. In Chapter 8, Timothy J. McNeil takes us back to 1970s California to reveal the inspirations for and deep thinking involved in generating inclusive design approaches in the building of the new Jan Shrem and Maria Manetti Shrem Museum of Art at the University of California, Davis. McNeil takes us through the user-centred design process developed at the museum, revealing how the process of making the new museum was leveraged as an opportunity for community debate and interaction. The project stands as one of a small number of museum architectural projects which have genuinely sought to move beyond the established conventions of architectural development. McNeil captures the learning for museums and for design from this process. The project is an important example of how a clear articulation of intent and desired social impact can lead, in the right hands, not only to a new and vital museum but also to multiple positive impacts in the lives of diverse people.

# 1

# AN ETHICAL FUTURE FOR MUSEUM AND GALLERY DESIGN

## Design as a force for good in a diverse cultural sector

*Suzanne MacLeod*

### Abstract

Chapter 1 argues that museums have yet to effectively draw design into their strategies to reposition museums as socially purposeful institutions. As a route towards this, the chapter argues for an ethics of museum design and suggests that museums need to wrest control of design from the political and economic drivers that often shape it. Such an approach recognises the ways in which the processes and built forms of museums are implicated in an unequal and divided social world. Developed through a detailed case study from the Tower of London, the chapter also poses a larger question. Could we, it asks, if led by the values and visions of cultural organisations and their desire to impact our creative lives in diverse ways, shape a more explicitly differentiated cultural landscape of wider relevance to peoples' everyday experience?

### Introduction

In 2010 I undertook a series of interviews with museum professionals, all of whom had been involved in leading capital developments in UK museums, the building of new museums or the expansion and renovation of existing museums. At that time, discussions mainly focused on process. Were design processes making use of the wide range of expertise available from stakeholders, including audiences? Or were architects, designers and institutions being swept through such projects in order to get them completed on time with little opportunity to think deeply about the decisions they were taking and the various social, environmental or economic impacts (positive and negative) those decisions might have? The landscape was mixed as one might have expected, but what emerged from the interviews and a desk-based research process that took place alongside, was the observation that an approach to design which prioritised a deep consideration of sense of place in recognition of the importance of place to belonging and identity; harnessed diverse expertise through stakeholder participation in design as a route to social relevance and use; recognised that capital development is an opportunity for reflection on and building of organisational identity; and utilised new and more sophisticated models for measuring social, environmental and economic sustainability as key factors of success beyond the simple formulation of completion within budget offered potential routes towards socially purposeful ways of making museums (MacLeod 2011).

The research made a claim for ethical museum making; a form of museum design which responded to and prioritised the public-facing missions and ambitions of museums, galleries and heritage sites and which acknowledged that cultural organisations should have a duty to the broader society to set some standards and ambitions for public life and the future of our shared social world. All of this research and discussion was, of course, undertaken in full recognition of the enormity of these projects, the bureaucratic constraints that local governments, funders and institutions placed on such projects and, importantly and unfortunately, the political and economic agendas that would push and pull cultural developments, sometimes to such an extent that they would become unrecognisable to the professionals within.

At the time, and in recognition of the politics of space and the centrality of space to the ongoing transformation of museums and galleries, part of this desire to utilise capital builds to generate a discussion of ethical design in museums and galleries was to seek a route towards the manifestation of the human and social values of cultural organisations physically in our surroundings as a challenge to the commercialism that, in the main, shapes our environments and life experiences and continues to diminish our civic and social lives (Crouch 2011). Increasingly however, we see this same commercialism shaping museums and galleries. They share the same shiny, attention-seeking architecture of shopping centres and bright, produce-laden interiors of department stores. Since then, the ethics of museum design continues to be a minor question in our sector; ethics codes, even of design groups, tend not to relate to the physical thing designed and built, the opportunities to generate empowering encounters built into (or out of) them or the design processes and methodologies used, but rather to ethical business practices and ethical behaviours towards clients (Till 2009: 180). As a result, large amounts of funding continue to be spent on museum developments, but without the fine-grained and open discussion of the ethics of design that the social scale and impact of these spaces deserves.

Since 2010, I have been involved in a number of projects with cultural partners around particular aspects of design, and ethics continues to emerge as a necessary frame within which to think about the potential of museum design, if allowed, to make a significant contribution to the cultural sector's social ambitions. This chapter draws these ideas and activities together through a discussion of what an ethics of museum design might entail, and why the development of an ethics of museum design could be a game-changing addition to the cultural sector. The discussion is developed through a single project undertaken with Historic Royal Palaces (HRP), the Research Centre for Museum and Galleries in the School of Museum Studies at the University of Leicester (RCMG) and Berlin-based exhibition design studio Duncan McCauley (DMC), as a mechanism for exploring the ways in which an ethics of museum design, as a responsibility, an outlook and a process rather than a specific set of guidelines, might be worked through. The chapter contains a clear challenge to design researchers, design practitioners and cultural organisations to 'think together' about the various roles of museums and galleries, the physical, material and embodied nature of all human experience and the urgency of opening up new ways of making vital, valued and socially impactful spaces for culture in an increasingly commercialised, homogenised and divided social world.

## 'Design is as moral as a hammer': from caricatures of museum design to complexity, purpose and ethics

Design is a complex and competitive field. It is also a field in which caricatures – poor, ludicrous imitations of reality – abound. These over-simplifications of design and designed forms complicate the ways in which cultural organisations engage with design and negatively influence expectations of, and approaches to, investment in the physical infrastructure of museums. For example, design in museums continues to be discussed as the object of the designer, a view fuelled not just by the reductive words and images which architects and architectural critics place between us and design in museums (images of people-less galleries, images of spectacular forms with a distant and blurry world around them, reductive stories of what specific architectural forms represent), but also by anecdotes of architects who will not waver from their vision. Whilst the caricatures come from somewhere (the examples are often real enough) and the images and words have their uses (selling an idea or enabling us to make sense of a complex architectural form), they also work to mask the complexity of capital projects, the diverse range of people involved in capital projects and the ways in which decisions come to be taken. Most significantly perhaps, such ideas and practices impact design decisions; they continue to separate our social and physical worlds, ensuring that the social impacts of design and designed forms remain out of reach and, in museums and galleries at least, beyond detailed discussion.

A few studies *have* sought to trace how decisions are taken on such projects and reveal the ways in which cultural projects are implicated in the wider social world. For example, Paul Jones (2011) has explored the role of iconic architecture in state-led projects, an area where museums feature strongly. Investigating how culture and urban space are mobilised in the production of surplus value, Jones reveals the ways in which museums today are drawn into a direct relationship to economic elites and their struggles for power. Interestingly, this kind of research is often undertaken from outside museums and museum studies, and there remains a paucity of internal reflection on and analysis of the social implications and impacts of design decisions in museums. There are also a number of studies which, contrary to the mass of projects in the cultural sector which rightly seek to illustrate the value of culture, point to the complicity of cultural projects in so many social ills such as the draining of scarce resources, environmental degradation, social segregation and the creation of spaces which lead to the production of passivity, uncritical nostalgia and a valuing of icons, spectacle and consumerism (Janes 2009; Harvey 2000; Glendinning 2010). Museums generally don't claim that they want to generate passivity, nostalgia or a celebration of consumerism, yet we rarely question the decisions taken on museum projects (about either process or form) and how they might be complicit in such social processes.

How, then, do we differentiate between projects? Where are the amazing examples of low-cost, effective cultural spaces which prioritise social relationships, encourage debate and are activated through the inhabitation and action of diverse groups of people? Could we, if led by the values and visions of cultural organisations and their desire to impact our creative lives in diverse ways (by opening up, variously, opportunities towards wellbeing, education and learning, political awareness, critical engagement with the world around us and understanding of others), shape a diverse and more explicitly differentiated cultural landscape of wider relevance to people's everyday experience? The question is too large to be dealt with in full here, and there will always be competing interests in all museum design projects which influence the decisions taken (though which, I would argue, need questioning and challenging), but a discussion about ethics can, nonetheless, open up the possibility of thinking and acting differently.

An emphasis on ethical design perhaps also explodes another caricature which is implicit in the discussion above and unfortunately still abounds in museums – that design is a technical process of display or, put more accurately, a specialist process of making a building, a display or some other physical entity. Of course, design does do this and in museums, where design is still, in the main, held at arm's-length from the organisation and contained within bureaucratic processes and practices, it is often reduced to exactly this. However, there are other ways in which design can be utilised as a resource by museums and approached in a much fuller, all-encompassing and potentially impactful sense, where it can be recognised as a social process.

In a recent issue of *RSA Journal*, the new-found status of design ('not just as a profession but as a deeper way of thinking about the world') was taken as the main topic of discussion (Taylor 2015: 5). Exploring the new management focus on design where the term 'design thinking' is used to refer to a hybrid approach driven by business and which uses design methods of brainstorming, decision-making, working with end users, prototyping and testing as a new route to innovation (Hunt 2015), a range of authors illustrated the potential contribution of design to a whole range of areas of social life from the economy to specific social problems such as reducing aggression in hospitals and the improvement of human-based services. With a common theme of design as strategy and a whole range of examples of how design is being utilised across increasingly diverse sectors and in increasingly diverse ways, the collection made clear the positive impact design is having in so many scientific, industrial and public contexts. Disappointingly, none of the examples were drawn from the cultural sector.

Similar ideas and practices do exist in the cultural sector, though they are certainly less mainstream and are thoroughly under-explored. For example, at Derby Museums in the UK (see Chapter 12 in this volume), where the organisation's mission is 'to inspire people of all backgrounds and interests to become part of a living story of world-class creativity, innovation and making', human-centred design is currently being utilised to transform the ways in which Derby Museums are made, position visitors and co-production at the centre of development, and reflect on the challenges faced by museums in becoming socially, environmentally and economically sustainable. Similarly, at Battersea Arts Centre in London, an iterative and participatory process of cultural production most often associated with theatre is being utilised to reimagine and transform a nineteenth-century town hall into a dynamic, embedded and vital hub for cultural engagement. Here, a 'scratch' process, dubbed 'Playgrounding', is allowing creative practice to shape the physical surroundings as a way of prioritising as well as formulating the values and ambitions of the organisation. Less obviously creative, perhaps, but no less impactful, the notion of 'service design' is also in use in the cultural sector and elsewhere in this volume other examples of design solutions developed through an integrated and ongoing design process are evident (see Chapter 13 on the St Louis Arch). Admittedly, this work is far from mainstream. Nonetheless, all of this activity is taking place in our sector and yet is rarely discussed at any level of detail.[1]

Many of these projects can be characterised as having a research-led or experimental methodology debunking yet another caricature, this time of the creative genius. Here, rather than a design brief being produced and a designer being commissioned to deliver the brief, projects are characterised by an ongoing collaborative process of dialogue, iteration, reflection, research and testing where the views and expertise of diverse groups of people matter. Also here perhaps, and not reducible to but certainly informed by the methodology, is an increased emphasis on real people, on human and bodily experience as well as a recognition that the shared endeavour is to shape a meaningful and enabling frame for action driven by the mission and values of the organisation and through which the organisation will be made manifest. To differing degrees, then, many of these projects begin to point to a more sophisticated understanding of the inseparability of our social and physical worlds.

Of course the landscape is varied as designers play with the imagery and spatial formations of museum space and as cultural institutions imagine and shape themselves in myriad ways. However, as we understand more about the ways in which the built environment of the museum is implicated in the social world and as museums and designers utilise a range of media in increasingly affective ways to *touch* us as visitors and make us *feel* (empathy, anger, sadness, happiness, confusion and so on), the need for an ethics of museum design becomes even more urgent. As Jamer Hunt (2015: 13) has argued, '[d]esign is as moral as a hammer'; design in itself is not ethical and is used by all sorts of agencies and industries to a whole range of positive and negative ends. If social, environmental, economic and individual impact matters, then, design needs to be considered within an ethical frame. In museums, that ethical frame might also open up new kinds of discussions which free us from the caricatures and default approaches to design and instead, open up the complexity of design as well as possibilities for new ways of working.

Here we might do well to learn from the writings of Emmanuel Levinas. For Levinas, ethics can be found in our interpersonal relations with others, in the moment of response. In our very subjectivity, he argues, we are dependent for our existence on others (past, present and future) and this debt entails a responsibility, always, to the other (Levinas 1969). Social existence then, incorporates the ethical and is 'the ultimate content of the utter particularity of the self and the other' (Morgan 2011: 10). There is an optimism in Levinas and an idea that if we put the needs of others before our own, we open the door to sociality, the varying particularities of everyday life and the possibility of reciprocity. It is for these reasons that theorists and practitioners in fields as diverse as medicine, social work, architecture and museums have turned to Levinas for something which might move beyond and resist power relations and notions of ownership and control, to seek instead a genuine focus on the hope of people-centred ethical practice (Till 2009; Rossiter 2011; Lynch 2011; Bennahum 2013).

## Prisoners, punishment and torture: the context, the 'puzzle' and harnessing interpretive museum design[2]

Historic Royal Palaces (HRP) is an independent charity with responsibility for six royal palaces in the UK: the Tower of London; Hampton Court Palace; Banqueting House, Whitehall; Kensington Palace; Kew Palace; and Hillsborough Castle. Since 1998, when it became an independent charity, HRP has been self-financing and has built a reputation for the development of a highly successful business model which incorporates large-scale reinvestment in the physical conservation of the palaces, enlightened management and a visitor-focused emphasis on witty, theatrical and enjoyable storytelling. Since 2005, visitor figures have risen by approximately 76% and HRP has been able to invest over £100 million in preserving the fabric and future of these important historic sites.[3]

Of all of these heritage sites, the Tower of London is arguably the most iconic. Built in the eleventh century as a fortress and a symbol of power by King William I, the Tower has housed a variety of institutions over its long history including the Royal Menagerie, the Royal Armouries, the Royal Mint and the Royal Observatory. It has been both a royal residence and for a long period up to the mid-twentieth century was used to hold prisoners considered to pose a particular threat to national security. Today, the Tower is a complex site covering some

12 acres and is home to the Crown Jewels, the Royal Armouries, and the Yeoman Warders as well as being part of HRP. In 2016–17, the site received 2.78 million visits.[4] A high proportion of visitors are from overseas and are part of time-limited, highly structured tours.

In the summer of 2012, HRP was grappling with visitor evaluation undertaken at the Tower, which had revealed that whilst visitors were satisfied with their experience overall, they expressed a wish for more (and perhaps more gory) interpretation around the themes of punishment and torture. In an approach which illustrated the openness of the organisation and the value it places against research, HRP approached RCMG to 'think with' HRP about how the organisation could meet the perceived needs of its visitors whilst also maintaining its desire to act ethically and position itself at the forefront of museum practice. By then, Alex Gaffikin, interpretation manager at HRP, had completed some preliminary research, visiting a range of heritage sites and looking at how those sites were positioned in the museum, heritage and visitor attraction sectors. Whilst there was at this stage a lack of clarity about what form interpretation at the Tower should take (Alex phrased this as 'the Tower needs to find its voice'), Alex and colleagues were very clear that although they wanted to be entertaining and provide an enjoyable day out, they did not want to be the kind of gory visitor experience which traded on horror and disgust, or a historic theme park where the drive to entertain might lead to a loss of focus on the history of the site and visitors' sense of authenticity.

A number of preliminary questions were occupying the minds of Alex and her team: How could the Tower incorporate more interpretation around themes of prisoners, punishment and torture? How could they generate an engaging experience around these themes without recourse to waxworks and horror? How could HRP forge its own identity for the Tower, one which would be ethically informed and potentially make a contribution to the ongoing development of museum and gallery practice? And how could HRP navigate the complexities of a shared site which offers visitors access to a range of historic places as well as varying organisations and collections, in order to generate a coherent visitor experience? HRP wanted a piece of research that would work through these dilemmas and provide a framework within which future interventions within the historic site could be made; to use research as a thinking process which could feed findings and principles into the broader, ongoing processes of exhibition making and interpretation. After some lengthy discussions, the research question was identified as: how might the Tower of London take forward their interpretation of stories of imprisonment, punishment and torture in ways that would take account of and reconcile (1) visitors' expectations, motivations and interests and (2) HRP's commitment to interpretive practice underpinned by ethical values and standards of museological and curatorial practice?

As the research plan developed, RCMG felt that the site-specific puzzle could be understood in relation to a suite of broader international scholarly and professional debates in the field, all of which could help to inform the research. The project was also recognised as an opportunity to explore how a design sensibility and interpretive design approach could be utilised as part of the research methodology in order to engage in a truly integrated way with both the physical and social aspects of the visitor experience. As a result, RCMG drew together a multi-disciplinary research team including interpreters, designers and academics with a range of expertise and skills relevant to the solving of the research puzzle and designed a methodology which would enable this range of skills and knowledge to impact the research process and findings.[5] All team members would work through all aspects of the methodology which would include:

- Site visits to establish the way in which the theme was currently interpreted and to begin to apply research-led master planning and interpretive design approaches to the site.
- Working papers which addressed themes connected to the puzzle and which would provide important underpinning knowledge for the project: (1) emotional and learning experiences; (2) narrative and embodiment; and (3) challenging histories.
- In-depth qualitative visitor research to supplement the existing visitor evaluations and provide a more fine-grained understanding of visitors' ideas and experiences at the Tower.
- A two-day workshop which would provide an opportunity for the research team to work through all of the data together and where we could place an emphasis on creative approaches and activities intended to ensure that the full range of knowledge and expertise in the team (academic skills and knowledge, 'designerly' skills and knowledge, the skills and knowledge of the museum practitioner) could impact the research findings.
- The testing of an 'ethical framework' with the wider HRP team as a route to refining the findings.

## Social biographies of space and embodied narrative experience

Two related ideas provided the research team with an important starting point for the project – *social biographies of space* and *embodied narrative experience*. *Social biographies of space* related to how we might understand the physical site of the Tower in ways which would get beyond simply dating or accrediting certain sections of the Tower to different periods, monarchs or functions. Reduced back to the deceptively simple premise that people shape spaces and spaces shape people (Lefebvre 1991), the team began from the assumption that all built environments can be understood as social and cultural productions constituent of social relations and active in the making of our social world. Here architecture and built forms are recognised as physical manifestations of deep structures of power that simultaneously embody human thought and have the capacity to impact on how people feel, think and act. Here then, social relations and social experience exist, and only exist, in and through space (Ibid.). Importantly, from this perspective, architecture or our built environment is all material forms (from the site to the built structures, layout, interior architecture and furniture to the objects, collections, exhibition hardware, interpretive approaches and media on display). Even more importantly, this material is produced, and can only be understood, through the multiple lives that have shaped and reshaped it constantly and in myriad ways over time.

From this perspective, the physical site can be recognised as an ongoing human and bodily production, produced through all sorts of ordinary practices and ways of being and active in so many aspects of our lives such as the production of relationships, identities and experiences as well as our understanding of past, present and future. At a historic site such as the Tower of London, this production is evident in layer upon layer of human existence that one can see from the moment of arrival at the site and in the infinite tiny traces of human inhabitation of the site. Here, the Tower can be viewed as a rich, experiential environment; both embedded with multiple biographies (latent narratives) of the people who lived, visited and died at the Tower and as a living, ongoing site of inhabitation and production with the potential to place us in time and in relation to others.

The research team was able to push all of this thinking further through a second underlying idea – *embodied narrative experience* – which related specifically to the detailed ongoing physical production of the site through the embodied and meaningful (meaning-making) experiences of present-day visitors. Here, the team drew on a number of well-established strands of research which tell us that human beings are constantly learning as they work to make sense of the world and that the feeling and sensing body is key to these human processes; to make sense of something is to be emotionally and sensorily engaged. Embedded in 'the flesh of the world' (Merleau-Ponty in Hale 2012: 198), we are continuously reaching out through our bodies and experiencing and building our understanding of the world through all sorts of interactions, including, and perhaps particularly at a heritage site, interactions with the physical site. This complex experience has to be active – lived or performed – to be a conscious experience. As Jonathan Hale (2012: 198) has noted, it is 'this gradually accumulating "history of interactions" between ourselves and our environment that helps to define what actually "shows up" in perception and counts for us as experience' and we will respond to the 'affordances' of the site based on our 'body schema' or repertoire of 'learned skills, routines and bodily capacities'. Finally, human beings are embodied narrative beings with a propensity to both seek out and generate narratives – stories about themselves and about others – from within the ongoing flow of experience and perception, as a way of building relationships and reaching out to create our shared social world (Ibid: 194).

Even though the various conceptualisations of learning or cognition in the texts reviewed varied and although new research is clearly needed in this area, a number of sources did draw attention to the importance of the physicality of the visitor experience in sense-making processes and the ways in which the physical, historic site provides a tangible link to the past which is immediate, exciting and real. For Bagnall, who studied visitors to two heritage sites, the physical, embodied nature of the visitor experience was identified as significant in promoting 'an emotional response which allows the imagination to be stimulated' (1996: 240) and where emotion and imagination were engendered by 'the physicality of the process of consumption' (2003: 87). Key to this emotional response is an 'emotional realism' whereby the feelings stimulated are 'real' and 'meaningful' (Ibid: 88). Importantly however, Bagnall noted that this process was underpinned by a dual demand for authenticity whereby visitors not only required access to the authenticity of the site but also to factual certitude; visitors needed 'information presented by the sites to be genuine, authentic, based in facts' (1996: 229). In her analysis of the research data, and in a way which chimed with our notion of *embodied narrative experience*, Bagnall highlighted the key role of memories, life histories, and personal and family narratives in enabling visitors to relate their experiences at the site, 'to a range of experienced and imagined worlds' (2003: 88). In addition to these findings and building on other research which has argued that at these sites we will connect to the lives of people in the past through issues which resonate emotionally across time (Abram 2002: 131), the team were reminded of the need to provide context and an element of the known, against which the challenge of new understanding or the 'unsettlement' of new knowledge and experience could be introduced.

Understanding the Tower (or any place) in this way as both laden with traces of past lives and the site for incredibly complex present-day meaning-making experiences, and recognising this process of social and spatial production as ongoing (a common and shared human experience across time), ensured that the research team could develop an integrated approach to both the physicality of the site and the experiences of present-day visitors.

## 'History where it happened'[6]: social biographies of space as a route to embodied narrative experiences

These ideas were given added importance through the early completion of the visitor research. At the Tower, visitor evaluations had given HRP a clear message that although visitors were highly satisfied with their visit overall, interpretation around themes of prisoners, punishment and torture did not meet their expectations. In order to find out more about the detail of visitors' perceptions, in-depth interviews were carried out and one accompanied visit was undertaken. The findings of the research were enlightening and although the majority of respondents could not articulate how their (already positive) experience could be improved, there was a striking consensus around two features of the visit that respondents found most enjoyable and which resonated strongly with the theory and research introduced above: *stories of people* and *connection to place*. Visitors made clear their desire for human stories, increased insight into the lives, experiences and motivations of key characters from the past and an understanding of connection to place, a sense of where, when and how the life experiences of people in the past unfolded at the Tower. The centrality of the physical site in these desires was evident. For example, visitors often picked out the small but memorable traces of earlier human inhabitation, such as the inscriptions in the Beauchamp Tower:

> Probably where we just came from was most memorable for me . . . the inscriptions I think. They were quite interesting . . . Just that it's actually there, somebody's taken the time to inscribe their name and their inscription. It kind of hits home that there were people imprisoned there.
>
> *(Hayley)*

The emotional pull of the site and the Tower's iconic status was clearly linked to visitors' sense of authenticity and the fact that they could feel a physical closeness to (and reduce their temporal distance from) people from the past:

> because you think of the people who stood in those same spots in different times. It's like a time machine, isn't it? . . . It's the thought that they were actually on that same spot all those years ago in completely different circumstances.
>
> *(Marion)*

Visitors often recalled and relished specific details linked to the story of an individual which enabled them to gain a feeling of shared experience with people from the past. For example, Katazyna noted:

> I also liked in the zoo part . . . the small notes of what people thought and did at that time, for example, I think an animal keeper, he felt sorry for animals and there was a small quotation that he said that it was like putting an intelligent man into prison or something like that. I don't expect a 17th century man to think that, you know. It was nice to see that quote.

This desire to imagine and make an emotional connection to real people from the past and feel the layers of history embedded in the environment of the Tower, also resulted in some dissatisfaction with the existing displays and a desire for more insight. Whilst a few enjoyed the object- and text-based displays in the White Tower, a number of visitors felt they detracted too much from the building itself:

> It did not feel like a castle actually. . . . What made it less special is that you could not imagine what happened inside the room . . . you cannot imagine yourself . . . the King was sitting here or eating here, the coronation, whatever it was inside that room you have no idea.
>
> *(Darius)*

In addition to wanting more stories about real people in the places they inhabited, visitors did not always have sufficient context to understand the role of the Tower as a place of torture, punishment and imprisonment.

> It says here 48 were tortured here but I want to know more – there's very little context. It's horrific and it's still happening today but I'd like to know more.
>
> *(Julie)*

As the research progressed, it became clear that context and deep analysis (understanding the motivations of perpetrators of violence, for example) were key to providing visitors with the necessary knowledge and understanding for emotionally rich experiences, as was the more obviously physical and emotional engagement with the atmosphere of the authentic site. The opposite of the approach taken at many museums and heritage sites today (where pared-back voices of people affected by trauma have often been used with single, highly emotive or resonant objects), here, and in a way which chimed with some of the findings in Bagnall's study, the visitor research was giving us clues that context and analysis mattered and, rather than being something we might associate with a didactic, less affective experience, may in fact be deeply entwined in our ability to make an emotional connection to the visit at a site such as the Tower. More fundamentally, this work enabled the team to acknowledge that biographies of space (authentic stories of people, told in the places they happened and linked to the physicality of the site and experience) are, at the Tower of London, key to the enabling of successful embodied narrative experiences.

As they worked through these ideas, the team were able to utilise interpretive design processes to begin to capture the need for an overarching structure at the site, plot where stories of people and place might come together, consider how a range of opportunities for diverse experiences and emotions might be mapped onto the site, and identify where (in a central hub in the White Tower, for example) more context and information might be provided (Plates 1–3). Far from intended as solutions for the Tower, this process was regarded as one of both beginning to imagine how the structure of the site could draw attention to biographies of space and support a diversity of embodied narrative experiences and ensure that the physicality of the site and its role in visitors' experiences remained central to the research.

## Ethical behaviour, ethical interpretation and the making of the institutional frame

The concerns of HRP not to be a historical theme park or to trade on horror and disgust connect very directly with a number of debates evident in the scholarly literature around the interpretation of difficult and challenging history. Whilst there is very little evidence about the motivations of people who visit sites of dark or difficult history, there is a large body of work around some of the ethical dilemmas faced by cultural organisations who interpret these pasts (MacLeod *et al.* 2014). At the heart of these debates sit concerns around the commodification, glorification, trivialising or sanitising of histories which include experiences of death and torture. Here there is, to some extent, a distinction to the Tower. At sites of mass death in the relatively recent past, or where the content explored relates directly to contemporary identity politics, clearly the ethical issues are acute. At the Tower, where the majority of the stories of prisoners, punishment, torture and execution date back to earlier centuries,[7] these questions are undoubtedly less sensitive, and certainly from observing the Yeoman Warders' tours around the site, it is clear that there is an appetite amongst visitors for more theatrical and gory stories. That said, as the visitor research illustrated, there is also a desire amongst visitors for more understanding, more context and more detail about human lives as a route to informed, engaging, human and respectful understandings of people and place. What also matters here, however, is the institutional frame of HRP; HRP's vision of itself and its sense of its mission or cause. As our social experience outside of work becomes more and more about consuming, how might HRP use its skills in experience development – the same skills used by multi-million-pound brands, supermarket chains and a whole range of visitor attractions – to provide something inviting and enjoyable, but also socially meaningful? How might it make a positive contribution to our shared social world?

Key to all of these discussions and far from straightforward was a sense of how HRP imagined its visitors reacting and behaving. If we return to the ideas of built forms and social production underlying the project, we are reminded that museums and cultural organisations are produced through use; this is actually where we will find the museum, in the dance between the social and the physical. The true (and always changing) museum is the accumulation of those myriad moments of experience and interaction produced within and around the physical forms, collections, exhibitions and displays, and it is this museum which becomes known to us and manifests the character of the institution through its majority use. How visitors behave then, how they occupy the site (movement, responses, (inter)actions and behaviours) will produce the Tower today and give tangible form to the organisation HRP. In this sense, the physical museum and the physical experience are identified as of great significance to the making and validating of the organisation. For HRP, the kinds of emotions, behaviours and actions it hopes to enable are a complex mix of enjoyable day out combined with learning about the past and, specifically in relation to the theme of prisoners, punishment and torture, ethical engagement with some of the more 'gory' content.

As one route to understanding more about what the voice of the Tower might be, the team drew across the research (site visits, working papers, visitor research and interpretive design) to critique the existing approaches to the interpretation of prisoners, punishment and torture at the Tower, though this was undertaken with a lightness of touch recognising that many of the displays were over 20 years old. The exercise resulted in some helpful observations. Some displays (the story of George, Duke of Clarence, for example, who reputedly drowned in a barrel of claret and whose stricken face looks back out at you from a barrel at the Tower today) were found to be quite literal, providing little in the way of information and generating immediate reactions (shock, laughter, repulsion) rather than any close sense of the individual or how and why events unfolded. Similarly, in places, the use of tableaux, such as the story of John Gerard, were recognised as reducing complex stories to a single moment of reconstruction. In these instances, the completeness of the image and the presentation of a frozen moment result in a flattening of our experience in a way which leaves little room to imagine who this person was and what he experienced at the Tower, cutting off opportunity to identify with Gerard or feel any sense of contemporary relevance. Also at play here perhaps is the reduction of the visitor to static observer. Rather than encouraging us to physically explore the space and experience story and space through our actions and sensory perception, the experience is limited to a static and rather distanced experience of looking.

This over-distancing of present-day visitors from the past and severing of opportunities to build some level of intimate identification with individuals from the past could also be located elsewhere. As became clear, this was not always unintentional. In the *Torture at the Tower* exhibition in the Wakefield Tower, the installation of authentic and replica instruments of torture in a space probably never used for torture combined with technical and factual text-based interpretation and the use of materials (such as Perspex) intended to create a sense of neutrality, result in a dislocated and emotionless display. Disconnected from the actual sites of torture and from any detailed insight into human experience, visitors are denied the opportunity to feel and imagine through the authenticity of story and site. The result of an institutional nervousness at the time of its making, *Torture at the Tower* had been intentionally constructed to protect visitors from any visceral grasp of the subject matter. Elsewhere, in spaces with a high degree of interpretive potential (the inscriptions in the Beauchamp Tower and the Traitor's Gate where so many prisoners were brought into the Tower by boat, for example) opportunities for connecting with the people who left their mark or whose lives played out in these spaces, were often missed or deadened by the use of sensorily bankrupt interpretation.

As the discussion unfolded, the team produced a table of what might be considered ethical and unethical interpretation within the institutional context of HRP (Table 1.1), an activity which contributed significantly, along with a half-day session with staff at the Tower which

**TABLE 1.1** Positive and negative characteristics of the interpretation of prisoners, punishment and torture at the Tower of London

| *Positive visitor experience* | *Negative visitor experience* |
|---|---|
| Paced with diversity of emotions | Relentless |
| Clear narrative | No schema, no frame in which to place experience (unclear or missing introduction and ending) |
| Understanding codes, clues, rules of engagement | Bland, one size fits all |
| Humour, enjoyment | Inauthentic |
| Unsettling, provocative but not 'shock for the sake of shock' | Confusing or misleading |
| Authentic, real experiences | Simplistic, focus on the moment of pain, not the full story |
| Real people and stories | Didactic |
| Accessible | Over themed or interpreted (close down opportunities for imagination or emotion) |
| Choices, free choice – includes choice to go further (more gore, more tech, more info) | |
| Nuanced, rich, complex experiences | No opportunity to go further |
| Space for imagination, reflection and down time | |

*Source*: Reproduced with the kind permission of RCMG.

tested and refined all of the findings, to the final conclusions of the research and the production of a *Framework for Ethical Interpretation at the Tower* (Plate 4). Both capture the need for an aligning of space and story in recognition of the embodied nature of narrative experiences and the agency of the authentic physical site and its social biography of space in those experiences. Linked to this, the *Framework* captures our need for structure and information in order to organise our visit and, potentially, to generate deep engagements at the site. The model captured the seriousness and ongoing nature of torture, as a reminder of the need for thoughtful and respectful interpretation and the need for a sense of purposefulness, a contemporary and socially motivated rationale for the telling of these stories today beyond entertainment and fascination. Context, complexity and opening access to the motivations, thoughts and feelings of those involved in punishment and torture at the Tower were acknowledged as of great importance in enabling the embodied meaning-making processes of visitors.

Finally, recognising that our embodied narrative experience is only ever our own embodied narrative experience and any sense of place will always be our own sense of place, the model repeated the well-established need to offer diverse routes into experience and captured the important point that this access should be offered on a physical and emotional (bodily) level, linked carefully to the physicality of the site. The framework both captured parameters within which interpretation might be developed (seriousness of torture, insight into human stories and motivations, etc.) *and* provided a number of characteristics of embodied narrative experiences for the Tower to explore (embodied, active, authentic). Most significantly, the research highlighted the need for colleagues at the Tower to harness the potential of the diversity of experiences that visitors will have as a route to creating environments full of possibility, rather than displays full of information.

## Conclusion

Thinking about the ethics of museum design at the Tower did a number of things. It enabled us to get close to the embodied experiences of visitors and think deeply about what visitors needed within the realms of what was possible at HRP. The process enabled us to understand more about the design decisions taken at the Tower in the past and why these approaches were no longer working for contemporary audiences. It also enabled us to think deeply (by drawing across all of the research at the workshop) about the identity and voice of the institution and the role of diverse actions in making the museum tangible, that is what HRP imagined visitors feeling, thinking and doing and how this majority use would make HRP and its ethical approach to museum making manifest. Importantly, approaching the research as ethically informed design, enabled us to think creatively with design, building a methodology which rather than segmenting design off, built interpretive design knowledge and a design sensibility into a wider process of research and development. Clearly this project was very particular and additional research is now needed to explore how a range of media might support opportunities for embodied engagements with space and story at the site.

Beyond the specifics of the Tower, the project pointed to a number of important characteristics of a future ethics of museum design. First, an ethics of museum design places a sustained and close focus on users, their lives, their needs and their agendas. Visitor research, a deep knowledge of learning as an ongoing human process of becoming, and a subtle understanding of the social value of everyday involvement in culture, are key here. However, Levinas also helps us to see the ethical response to others as a first philosophy, the foundation for human being. More research is needed to consider how such an awareness might de-centre professional knowledge (museum knowledge and design knowledge) and change the dynamics between all those involved in museum design.

Second, and recognising that design in and of itself is 'as moral as a hammer', an ethics of museum design demands that all those involved in shaping museums (museum professionals, architects, designers, politicians, publics) acknowledge the social aspects of space and commit to a prioritisation of the social over the formal. Only by researching and continually revisiting the relevance and involvement of built, designed forms and processes in the production of social relations and experiences can we begin to overcome entrenched divisions between our physical and social worlds and really begin to close the gap between museum design and everyday life.

Third, an ethical approach to museum design will necessitate a deep engagement with the set of values which constitute the institutional frame as a route to both refining that frame (is the focus really on others above all else?) and ensuring that these social intentions are made manifest in the possibilities for action and meaning-making built into the space. Overcoming the often fuzzy association between designed forms and organisational ambition, work here will be wholly directed towards placing organisational intent at the heart of the design process.

Such complex productions demand subtle, thoughtful and research-led ways of working. Fourth, then, projects will be characterised by meaningful reflection on decision-making, the posing of difficult questions, consideration of alternatives, and deep research to inform the direction of travel. Such an approach will draw widely on available knowledge, will value diverse ways of knowing and will be characterised by a non-hierarchical process of learning from and with others.

Finally, an ethics of museum design understands that our only aim is to contribute to the creative lives of diverse individuals, and so it seeks to build generous spaces open to diverse forms of appropriation and complete with structures to support varied contemporary creative and critical engagements with cultural resources and with each other. Here, concepts of slack or loose space (Franck and Stevens 2007) which offer themselves up for diverse forms of use and experience, as opposed to clearly defined spaces which force themselves onto visitors, seem particularly promising, though ongoing research is required to really probe the ways in which design can create sites of embodied experience which support the production of empowering social relationships, explore new ways of being civic and open up important moments of critical and creative action in an increasingly commercial, homogenous and divided world.

A key characteristic of this emerging ethics of museum design is that design is freed from bureaucratic and task driven constraints to make a significant, integrated and fundamental contribution to museum making that is not about commerce, not about brand (though a stronger sense of the values of the organisation will undoubtedly result) and not about disconnected visitor experiences. Rather, within an ethical framework, museums can be stronger and design can move into a new future as an equal and embedded partner in the development of physical museums which are fit for purpose. It is just possible that a more diverse cultural landscape, rooted in everyday life and with greater differentiation between museums, galleries and heritage sites, would occur as a result.

Design can be a vehicle for much of this work, not providing the answers, but providing creative methods and a testing ground for new ways of working, new approaches which might break the cycle of ever bigger and shinier museums. The cultural organisation, though, needs to lead, to be a significant voice for the public realm and expert in how arts and culture can enable our collective creative lives. It is leaders in cultural organisations who have the power to take up the challenge of thinking deeply about how the physical museum (site, building, layout, interior architecture and furniture, display and exhibition hardware, interpretive approaches and media) plays a role in mediating varied critical and creative experiences, actions, interactions and relations, how it can make organisational vision and values manifest physically in space and in our experience, and how such a kind of museum making might both act as a catalyst for cultural organisations to undertake a close reassessment of their goals and achievements *and* make a significant, ethical and responsible contribution to our shared social world.

## Acknowledgements

Thank you to Richard Sandell, Tricia Austin, Michael Day and Jocelyn Dodd, all of whom took the time to comment on earlier drafts of this chapter.

## Notes

1 For Battersea Arts Centre, see http://playgroundprojects.bac.org.uk/, accessed 26 April 2017. For Derby Silk Museum see http://derbysilkmill.tumblr.com/, accessed 26 April 2017.
2 Many of the best museum design studios would describe their practice as interpretive museum design, a recognition of the interpretive potential of design which includes a shift in emphasis from designed forms themselves, to a recognition that experience (all our experience) sits *between* us and the physical world. Interpretive museum design draws on what we understand about varying types of human experience (for example, perception, memory, emotion, imagination, kinaesthetic experience, spatial awareness, social interaction, awareness of others and so on) to create often media-rich environments which might stimulate or enable varying opportunities for action and meaning-making. For the interpretive designer, all of these ideas – undoubtedly and perhaps necessarily schematic – begin to provide clues about how interpretation and design can be approached to appeal to the logic, perception, emotion and sociality of human beings and to enable valued forms of social exchange and engagement to flourish. Challenging any notion of simply setting out objects for passive experience, such a starting point raises a whole host of questions about the knowledge and opportunities for action that we can add into such an experience. It also raises a whole series of ethical questions. That said, this approach to design is often harnessed in ways which do not exhibit an ethical stance. Interpretive design is not in itself an ethical approach.
3 Personal communication with Michael Day, CEO, HRP, 8 May 2017.
4 Personal communication with Michael Day, CEO, HRP, 8 May 2017.
5 The core team comprised Alex Gaffekin (HRP), Jocelyn Dodd, Richard Sandell, Ceri Jones and Suzanne MacLeod (RCMG), and Tom Duncan (DMC).
6 This has been the marketing strapline for HRP for many years.
7 The final execution took place at the Tower in 1941 and it was used as a prison up to the 1950s.

## References

Abram, R.J. (2002) 'Harnessing the Power of History', in Sandell, R. (ed.) *Museums, Society, Inequality*, London and New York: Routledge, pp. 125–41.

Bagnall, G. (1996) 'Consuming the Past', in Edgell, S., Hetherington, K., and Warde, A. (eds) *Consumption Matters: The Production and Experience of Consumption*, Oxford: Blackwell Publishers, pp. 227–47.

Bagnall, G. (2003) 'Performance and Performativity at Heritage Sites', *Museum and Society*, 1(2), pp. 87–103.

Bennahum, D.A. (2013) 'On First Reading Emmanuel Levinas', *Cambridge Quarterly of Healthcare Ethics*, 22(4), pp. 420–4.

Crouch, C. (2011) *The Strange Non-Death of Neoliberalism*, Cambridge: Polity Press.

Franck, K.A. and Stevens, Q. (eds) (2007) *Loose Space: Possibility and Diversity in Urban Life*, London and New York: Routledge.

Glendinning, M. (2010) *Architecture's Evil Empire? The Triumph and Tragedy of Global Modernism*, London: Reaktion Books.

Hale, J. (2012) 'Narrative Environments and the Paradigm of Embodiment', in MacLeod, S., Hourston Hanks, L., and Hale, J. (eds) *Museum Making: Narratives, Architectures, Exhibitions*, London: Routledge, pp. 192–200.

Harvey, D. (2000) *Spaces of Hope*, Edinburgh: Edinburgh University Press.

Hunt, J. (2015) 'Known Unknowns', *RSA Journal* (1), pp. 10–15.

Janes, R.R. (2009) *Museums in a Troubled World: Renewal, Irrelevance or Collapse*, London and New York: Routledge.

Jones, P. (2011) *The Sociology of Architecture*, Liverpool: Liverpool University Press.

Lefebvre, H. (1991) *The Production of Space* (trans. D. Nicholson-Smith), Oxford: Basil Blackwell.

Levinas, E. (1969) *Totality and Infinity* (trans. A. Lingis), Pittsburgh: Duquesne University Press.

Lynch, B. (2011) 'Collaboration, Contestation, and Creative Conflict: On the Efficacy of Museum/community Partnerships', in Marstine, J. (ed.) *The Routledge Companion to Museum Ethics: Redefining Ethics for the Twenty-First Century Museum*, London: Routledge, pp. 146–63.

MacLeod, S. (2011) 'Towards an Ethics of Museum Architecture', in Marstine, J. (ed.) *The Routledge Companion to Museum Ethics: Redefining Ethics for the Twenty-First Century Museum*, London: Routledge, pp. 379–92.

MacLeod, S., Sandell, R., Dodd, J., Duncan, T., Jones, C., and Gaffekin, A. (2014) *Prisoners, Punishment and Torture: Developing New Approaches to Interpretation at the Tower of London*, Leicester: RCMG. Online. Available HTTP: https://www2.le.ac.uk/departments/museumstudies/rcmg/publications/prisoners-punishment-and-torture. Accessed 29 April 2017.

Morgan, M.L. (2011) *The Cambridge Introduction to Emmanuel Levinas*, New York: Cambridge University Press.

Rossiter, A. (2011) 'Unsettled Social Work: The Challenge of Levinas's Ethics', *The British Journal of Social Work*, 41(5), pp. 980–5.

Taylor, M. (2015) 'Comment', *RSA Journal* (1), p. 5.

Till, J. (2009) *Architecture Depends*, Cambridge, MA: The MIT Press.

# 2

# ZEN AND THE ART OF MUSEUM MAINTENANCE

*Oscar Ho Hing-Kay*

## Abstract

Seduced by a fantasy of the economic potential of the cultural industries, Asian governments have dramatically increased their investment in building new museums in recent years. Copying models from the West, Ho argues that these new museums are irrelevant to the local cultural experience. Amidst such a frenzy of new museum construction, it is necessary to integrate creative expressions back into the community in order for the arts to serve the basic function of touching people's hearts. From a simple act of visiting the fishing village at Tai O to witnessing the creative explosion at the occupied zones during the Umbrella Movement in Hong Kong, one can find alternative platforms which reconfirm the wisdom of the Sixth Patriarch Huineng, an illiterate Cantonese known for bringing alive the call of Zen Buddhism for 'skipping the words and going directly into the heart'. It might be time to look back into the heart instead of the glamour and formality of building this institution called museum.

## Introduction

Since the turn of the twenty-first century, many Asian governments, charmed by the economic promises of cultural tourism and this vague but attractive thing called 'creative industries', began to launch a series of ambitious cultural projects, building museums, performing arts spaces and cultural districts with unprecedented zeal. This has been especially pronounced in regions such as Hong Kong, Taiwan, Singapore and more recently China, where governments are seeking new developmental possibilities to replace declining manufacturing industries. Suddenly they found culture and its industries a lifesaver amidst the frightening waves of economic calamities. This phenomenon of investing in culture through the massive investment in building new cultural venues and districts is particularly outstanding in China, where one gets the impression that the number of new museums built has outgrown the number of Starbucks opened.

In order to catch up with cultural developments in the West, in 2010 China launched an ambitious five-year plan to build some 3,500 museums. By the end of 2012, 3,589 museums were already built (Pan Xun 2013). The heavy-handedness of investment in Abu Dhabi's cultural district is also astonishing. Equally shocking but little known is the investment in some of the second-line Chinese cities. Take the Jianchuan Museum (樊建川博物館) Cluster in Chengdu, Sichuan, for example, where 15 new museums were built within a space of 500 acres. In Hong Kong, while the West Kowloon Cultural District (WKCD) is suffering a long delay as a result of financial problems, the government made another announcement launching the building of the East Kowloon Cultural District. This new development comes on top of another ongoing large-scale project which will see the Central Police Station converted into another cultural district.

Having ignored the wellbeing of arts and culture for decades, Asian governments' 'suddenly cultured' behaviour has shocked the arts community and introduced a number of new problems. The absence of a balanced, healthy arts ecology and the continuous domination of a conservative, bureaucratic system of civil servants within the government-controlled cultural infrastructure make it nearly impossible to nurture professionals locally in the field of cultural management. The lack of local 'software' in the planning and running of these newly created cultural facilities remains one of the main blocks to any sustainable development.

Frequently, international brand-name architects are eagerly brought in to build a grand 'urban icon' before any vision, missions and mandates of the institutions are defined, if they are ever defined. In Hong Kong, for example, the closed-door decisions of the WKCD and government to add a new museum at WKCD featuring collections borrowed from the Beijing Palace in China, and the direct appointment of the architect for designing the museum were made only by the then chief secretary and a few senior members of the WKCD Board, without input from local art professionals and experts (Cheung, Chou and Ng 2017). In China, many of these grand architectural projects have remained vacant or inactive following their openings (Chung 2016). When I was working in Shanghai building the Museum of Contemporary Art, Shanghai was in the middle of a museum building fever with a plan to construct 100 museums within 10 years, in preparation for the upcoming grandeur of the World Expo. Within the cultural field, we had an insider joke saying that the lifespan of new museums in China is usually three years. After three years, if it does not die, it is a living dead.

## The vanity of being cultured

The design of a museum is strongly affected by the missions, objectives, types of exhibits in the displays, the activities planned of the institution and the image the museum wants to project. It requires vision, sensibility and knowledge in understanding arts and culture within the context of local heritage and cultural possibilities. It also demands knowledge of the cultural habits and expectations of its audiences. Unfortunately in most parts of Asia, at the senior level of the infrastructure, vanity, limited knowledge and, for some, a continuous inferiority complex retained from a colonized mindset make it impossible for these decision-makers to pay attention to local culture and to meet the cultural needs and expectations of the community, especially at a time when visiting tourists appear to be more important than local people. Partly instinct, partly because of unawareness of alternatives, decision-makers turn to trusting brand-name architects to design the museum without any open or deep discussion or reference to professional knowledge.[1]

Behind all these heavy investments and the inflated desire to become cultured, there is always this vague ambition of hoping to be a 'global city'. Within a global city, you need culture to attract the international creative class for the building of a creative economy. Of course it could easily trigger local criticism if the cultural official dares to say 'only global but not the local'. Subsequently the professional cliché 'global vision with local standing' has been commonly adopted. This was even the case in WKCD's report in defining the curatorial role of its art space M+, when the entire senior curatorial team except one is from Hong Kong (Home Affairs Bureau 2014). In reality, the local has always been missed out in this blind quest for the glory of being 'global'.

Before we talk about the design of a museum, maybe we should first think about what is this thing we call 'art' that is displayed in a museum. Amidst this absurd fever of building new museums without any sensible consideration of its content and its meaningfulness within the local context, it is time in Asia to critically review the definitions of museum, its format of presentation and its content.

## Ideal 'museum'

My ideal museum experience happened 15 years ago at Tai O, one of Hong Kong's oldest fishing villages on Lantou Island. A friend of mine was planning to set up a personal museum to preserve the local culture of Tai O and invited me to visit and to provide some advice. When I asked to view her collection, she took me for a walk along the Wing On Street, the main street of Tai O. It was a sunny, quiet weekday morning. One could smell the salty fragrance of the sea carried by the gentle breeze. As we walked and talked about the history of Tai O, she stopped suddenly and turned around to walk into a shady little house where an old lady was sitting. After knowing that I wanted to see some of the objects she had, she climbed up to her cupboard and took down a little vase. She started telling me the stories behind the vase, how her grandfather got this vase, what the family used it for and how it was passed on to her. The humble, ordinary vase was suddenly filled with intimate, historical memories connected to her and her family, and to the village.

We continued our visit and walked into a small grocery shop where an old man was practicing calligraphy while doing his business. During weekdays there was not much business. He took out some of his works and started explaining to me proudly the meaning of the poetry within his calligraphy. Opposite to his store was another small store where the owner made sculptures of Snow White and the Seven Dwarfs. Unable to make a truly handsome prince, he felt sorry for the loneliness of Snow White, and made an international call for a sculpture of a handsome prince to accompany Snow White. It was like walking within a cabinet of curiosity, where one wandered in a personal collection of memories, curiosity and imagination, where one could be free to appreciate the values of an object without adopting the vocabularies of the experts, and where one could construct and invent a world of one's own.

## The art of the ordinary and the necessary

The experience of such a 'museum visit' was outstanding for its intimacy and directness in linking with people and their histories, within a specific social and cultural context. I am not totally defying the existing museum where I can see some of the Old Masters' works, but it is equally important to look into other dimensions of cultural experience, at a time when we are drowning in this superficial trend of trying to be cultured by stuffing ourselves with brand names, grand museums, fanciful aesthetics and vocabularies from others. For a better look at ourselves, maybe we should retune our aesthetic to look into the ordinary, the art that is outside of those vocabularies we studied at school or read in an art magazine.

In 1989, I curated an exhibition titled *In Search of Art* with Dr David Clarke, where we asked people to send in objects that no longer served any particular function but they nevertheless still kept them just to look at. Along with submitting the objects, they needed to write a few lines explaining why they still kept them to look at. The outcome was fascinating. Those ordinary 'art objects' people brought in were frequently loaded with intimate stories such as 'this is the comb my grandma gave me before she died'; 'this paper pineapple is the most beautiful art in the world as it was meticulously made with one cent note by my boyfriend, who is now my husband'. Unable to get access to these intimate stories, which are the core values and meaning of these objects, the critics could only fall back into adopting vocabularies such as form, school, movement, critical content and contextual implications, missing the important and the very human part of the values of the objects and display. When collection and display of art become formally institutionalized, and the task of defining art has become the exclusive act of the 'professionals', such intimacy that composes the meaningfulness of art vanishes.

On the other hand, the desire to express oneself, not because of a conscious desire of 'making art', but as the result of an urge driven by a sense of necessity, is another powerful primal force through which cultural expressions are made. Starting in late September 2014, over one million people in Hong Kong participated in 79 days of demonstration. Seeking universal suffrage, the demonstrators, many of whom were university and high school students, occupied three central areas at Hong Kong Island and the Kowloon Peninsula. Such unprecedented political campaign for the Special Administration District of China was a collective expression of the frustration of the Hong Kong people over the unwillingness of the Central Government in fulfilling its promise of real universal suffrage following the signing of the Sino-British agreement for the return of Hong Kong to China.[2] At the occupied zones, villages of tents with facilities such as libraries, study rooms, shower rooms, garbage collection services, supplies centers and even a small farming area were organically set up.

During the long occupation period, the zones became an open platform where individuals, with or without formal artistic training, freely voiced out their wish and anger to criticize the failed promise and call for support and solidarity in fighting for real democracy. Not bounded by any preconceived ideas of what arts should be, they freely and spontaneously sought their own ways of creating expressions, from graphic work on paper, text on banner, to song, dance, digital installation, body painting, body gesture and religious rituals. Creative expressions blossomed at every corner of the occupied zones.

The dazzling creative expressions during the first phase of the occupation period of the Umbrella Movement was an outstanding example of when 'art', if we like to use this term, returns to the ordinary folks who were not threatened by the concept of 'art' and just made creative expressions out of necessity. The result, as demonstrated by the arts at the occupied zones of the Umbrella Movement, was overwhelming in its diversity and unbounded creative energies. During the 79 days of occupation, the organic growth of the creative expression and the continuous dialogues among 'resident and visiting artists' constructed the grandest museum Hong Kong has never seen.

## Directly to the heart

Designing a museum is culturally contextual, determined by the roles and functions of the museum, by its collection and the image it tries to communicate, and more importantly, by its 'meaningfulness' to the people the museum serves. At a time when Asian cities are passionately building new museums and cultural districts, we need to critically review possibilities outside these trends, adjust our aesthetics and look into the local and the ordinary. If museums want to survive and maintain some meaningful relevance to the people, this need for reflection is vital.

The Sixth Patriarch of Zen Buddhism Huineng, an illiterate Cantonese, is known for bringing alive the Zen Master Bodhidharma's call for 'skipping the words and going directly into the heart'. It might be time to take a different look into the heart of the people. At a time when art is made in the name of cultural industries, with the functions of pumping out glamour, big names and terminologies that no longer carry any meaning to the people, it cannot survive in this part of the world.

Before talking about designing and building museums, maybe there are some fundamental questions we need to address. If we were going to build a museum at Tai O, or amidst the blossoming creative expressions at the occupied zones of the Umbrella Movement, what kinds of forms could those museums take? Do we even need a museum at all? A long time ago there were people whose creative expressions, memories and communal bonds were all closely linked with the community and were fully integrated in their everyday lives, and there was no museum.

## Notes

1 The most recent example was the commissioning of an architect for the Palace Museum Hong Kong before any curatorial positioning of the Museum was made.
2 The Central Government offers one person one vote for the Chief Executive of Hong Kong, under the condition that the candidates are nominated by a committee strongly controlled by Beijing.

## References

Cheung, T., Chou, O., and Ng, N. (2017) 'Museum Critics Hit Out at "Very Bad" Displays', *South China Morning Post*, 11 January 2017.

Chung, S. (2016) 'Abandoned Architecture Marvels China's Largest Ghost Town', *CNN News*, 22 November 2016. Online. Available HTTP: http://edition.cnn.com/2016/04/04/architecture/china-ordos-ghost-town/. Accessed 9 May 2017.

Home Affairs Bureau (2014) *'On Recent Development of M+': Report to WKCD Committee of the Legislative Council*, Hong Kong: Home Affairs Bureau. Legco document CB(2)316/14–15(01).

Pan Xun (2013) 'Crazily Building Museums, Big But Useless', *Wanted Daily*, 8 June 2013. Online. Available HTTP: www.chinatimes.com/cn/newspapers/20130608001117-260306. Accessed 15 May 2017.

# 3

# ON THE IMPORTANCE OF 'AND'

## Museums and complexity

*Elaine Heumann Gurian*

### Abstract

In order to better prepare our citizens to have more thoughtful, civil and nuanced discussions of important contemporary problems, museums must create presentations that presume most contested issues are complex; recognize disputing parties hold only partial truth; and illustrate solutions as organic and never complete. To encourage civil debate, I am suggesting that museums, using complexity theory as justification, should add a new exhibition paradigm that does not resolve issues into a pre-determined message, is proactively multidisciplinary, and has embedded multiple worldviews without editorial judgement. This format would leave the outcome unsettled for the viewer who would need further reflection to come to a personal resolution.

### Introduction

In a world that is politically traumatized, the ideas explored in this chapter – museums' opportunities to promote nuance, complication, and approximation in their presentations, using complexity theory as a lens – might seem tangential and will not, by themselves, change things appreciably because much more than this is needed. What I am looking for is a lever that might allow museums to become intentional, subtle resisters – rather than collaborators – in a world becoming more autocratic. I will be referencing the current state of academic inquiry where theories of empathy, complexity and personalization are rampant and currently serve as structures to explain heretofore unexplainable phenomenon with non-predictable outcomes. I want to find out how we, in the museum world, can use complexity theory in our exhibition conventions by providing multiple avenues of exploration, adding continuously cumulative input, surveying a non-hierarchical multi-disciplinary intellectual landscape, enfranchising the individual visitor in self-exploration, and supporting non-conclusory outcomes. In simpler terms, I want to change exhibitions from institutionally controlled narratives to ones where the displayed object is decoupled from explicit explanations, but linked laterally to multi-varied avenues of exploration. Here, I also want to ask what this might mean for museum design.

## Habits of mind

I want to begin with some remarks about the political tilt to the right in most of our countries. I feel impelled to talk about the disquiet that the election of Donald Trump has caused me personally and many others in my birth country (Cohen 2016). I am an American Progressive, which makes me, when measured against other countries' political spectra, mildly center-left but further left than that in my own land. I ask myself, along with so many others, how did we get to this worrisome place? An explanation must center on voters, who when faced with uncertainty in what feels like an overly complex and ambiguous world chose simple explanations with a willingness to cede personal responsibility to a controlling figure even at the expense of their democracy, their personal knowledge of right and wrong, their expectations of civility, and their belief in facts as bedrocks of civil society. Headline-writing journalism, texting conventions and social media platforms, especially Twitter, have allowed us, the public, to practice and then accept simple messages and 'the slogan' as truth. More importantly, insidiously, is the rise of intentionally false news and our increasing acceptance of a flexible relationship to facts, in part, because 'simple' impedes investigation.

I hope that learning to accept complication will enhance our ability to empathize with the opposition's point of view and lead to a willingness to accommodate for it. It is the walking back from extreme posturing and simple, quick outcomes that allows for a pathway to messy compromise. I am arguing for ending 'winners and losers' as the only acceptable outcome to all issues and replacing it with complexity, nuance, thoughtfulness and empathy for others' perspectives.

I am stating the obvious when I assert that most societal questions are complicated, that each of the contrarian positions can offer some, but not all, answers and that to overhaul society's ills requires multiple small, and often seemingly unrelated, actions. To move peacefully ahead, we will need to tolerate unreconciled messy situations. And at the moment, no public presentations of issues, in any of our media systems, overtly welcomes mess of any kind. In an article titled 'Learning and Leading with Habits of Mind', Arthur L. Costa (2008: 38) has written:

> A great mystery about humans is that many times we confront learning opportunities with fear rather than mystery and wonder. We seem to feel better when we know rather than when we learn. We defend our biases, beliefs, and storehouses of knowledge rather than invite the unknown, the creative, and the inspirational. Being certain and closed gives us comfort, whereas being doubtful and open gives us fear.

And in a *New York Times* op-ed, TV personality Trevor Noah (2016) wrote:

> America, I've found, doesn't like nuance. Either black people are criminals, or cops are racist – pick one. It's us versus them. You're with us, or you're against us. This national mentality is fueled by the hysteria of a 24-hour news cycle, by the ideological silos of social media and by the structure of the country's politics.

To assist people in appreciating nuance and complexity, institutions in the public sphere should, I am advocating, move away from assertive simplicity and lead the way in changing information-processing expectations, demonstrating that problems are complicated, their solutions intertwined, estimated and cumulative. Simplified presentations may have helped get us into this political fix, and the presentation of complexity may help to get us out.

## Museums

This chapter is about museums, and since I am by nature an action person, I am suggesting that we have a role, nay an obligation, to aid in re-establishing a more complex and nuanced dialogue by revamping our conventions of language and content presentation so that audiences, while still trusting in our veracity, will learn to expect density in public dialogue. Nick Poole, a wonderful thinker on museums, has written:

> For centuries, the role of museums has been to digest complexity and express it as pattern. Whether it is a linear hang in an art museum, giving the impression of a coherent progression of art-historical movements or a social-historical display giving the impression of a singular 'community' with identifiably-shared beliefs and values – we are temples to the illusion of order and predictability in a complex and chaotic world.
>
> *(Poole 2014)*

We need to prepare for resistance, at the same time understanding that welcoming all means welcoming Trumpites as well. The stories we tell and the materials we show are, and should be, theirs as well as ours. Museum history is a continuous unsettled landscape with honorable actors on all sides. Collectively the more boisterous right and left actors now need to uneasily join with each other because current world events need new pathways. To quote Nick Poole again:

> For our museums, our galleries, libraries and archives to be relevant to this world, we have to be part of the solution. We must help people understand their collective responsibility for each other, to see that the answers to some of mankind's most urgent questions lie in a better understanding of our shared past.
>
> *(Poole 2012)*

Research shows that going from simple to complex is not automatic and requires training and experience. Researchers have found, even at the secondary school level:

> the university students tended to solve problems using statements that were reductive, assumed central control, described a single source of causality, were predictable, and focused on objects, while the complex systems experts tended to solve the problems with statements that considered the overall system, described de-centralized control and multiple causal factors, noted probabilistic nature of solutions, and were process oriented.
>
> *(Jacobsen 2017)*

More problematically, noted neurologist Susan Greenfield controversially argues that the outcomes of the current social media technology practices are reinforcing expectations toward simplicity in brain development:

> As a neuroscientist I am very aware that the brain adapts to its environment – if you're placed in an environment that encourages, say, a short attention span, which doesn't

> encourage empathy or interpersonal communication, which is partially addictive or compulsive . . . all these things will inevitably shape who you are.
>
> *(Rivett 2014)*

Under my proposals for museum presentations, visitors will find evidence, thoughtfulness, and attention to facts, where they exist, but will no longer come to expect easy answers. Hopefully, our audience will grow to expect cogency, complexity, creativity, non-conformity and overt dialogue. Following personal curiosity, each visitor will leave with their interest pathways at least partially fulfilled. The personalized quest is likely an essential part of the solution we seek because the technological world has emphasized the role of individual control or agency.

## Complexity theory

What is the philosophical underpinning for this approach? Academics looking at large data sets and the ubiquitous way society has used technology in the last half century have created a theory explaining the unpredictable nature of large interrelated events. There are overlapping explanatory systems variously called Complexity, Chaos, Network Theory and others as well. Whatever the title, each of these systems can be described as non-linear, non-hierarchical, fluid, porous and ever-changing. Causality seem to be unconnected but are not. Small events cumulate and patterns arise but the pattern is not necessarily predictable nor repeatable. These theories, looking at the 'butterfly effect' of small actions are contrary to the single massive 'big bang' model.

The current application of complexity theory shows up in many heretofore unrelated fields both in the sciences and humanities. Gratefully, I find that researchers have been exploring the need for integration of complexity theory in educational curriculum development and the organizational structure of not-for-profit organizations. In this chapter, I am linking the underlying assumptions of complexity theory to the delivery of content in museums and, in the context of *The Future of Museums and Gallery Design*, to museum design.

Think tanks like the New England Complexity Institute and the Santa Fe Institute have sprung up to investigate the integration of sociological phenomena with scientific data in the context of complexity theory. What researchers are doing is combining multiple measurements found in different and seemingly unrelated academic silos in order to illustrate that seemingly different ways of interpreting can be, and often are, related. It turns out, not surprisingly, that complexity theory is complex and potentially overused for all manner of applications in a multiplicity of fields. It is the current darling of the academic world. I have had a difficult time understanding it, but am convinced that grasping and then using parts of complexity theory will prove beneficial for museums.

## What is complexity theory and how is it different from complication?

Let me introduce a string of definitional quotes describing complexity theory so that much more knowledgeable people than I will help define the relevant bits. The *Business Dictionary* (2017) writes that complexity theory is a:

> Set of concepts that attempts to explain complex phenomenon not explainable by traditional (mechanistic) theories. It integrates ideas derived from chaos theory, cognitive psychology, computer science, evolutionary biology, general systems theory, fuzzy

> logic, information theory, and other related fields to deal with the natural and artificial systems as they are, and not by simplifying them (breaking them down into their constituent parts).
>
> It suggests that simple deterministic functions can give rise to highly complex and often unpredictable behavior, and yet this complexity can still exhibit surprising order and patterns. It may offer a synthesis of two competing perspectives on how organizations adapt to their environments, organizational adaptation and population ecology. Most tantalizing, perhaps, is the promise that complexity theory will lead us to understand how systems can learn more effectively and spontaneously self-organize into more structured and sophisticated forms that are better adapted to their environments.
>
> *(Levy 2000: 68)*

Helpfully there are those that think that small things could have big impacts:

> it is now commonly understood that in complex and dynamical systems, a small action may have interactions in the system that contribute to a significant and large-scale influence – the so-called 'butterfly effect'.
>
> *(Jacobsen 2017)*

To make understanding tougher, the word 'complicated', whose synonym in the past would have been 'complex', is now differentiated from complexity. As Larry Cuban, emeritus professor of education from Stanford and an educational blog writer, has written:

> A complicated system assumes expert and rational leaders, top-down planning, smooth implementation of policies, and a clock-like organization that runs smoothly. Work is specified and delegated to particular units.
>
> *(Cuban 2010)*

The same author has defined complexity as follows:

> Complex systems like criminal justice, health care, and schools, however, are filled with hundreds of moving parts, scores of players of varied expertise and independence yet missing a 'mission control' that runs all these different parts within an ever-changing political, economic, and societal environment. The result: constant adaptations in design and action.
>
> *(Cuban 2010)*

The words to remember in complexity theory are non-linear, non-hierarchical, produced by small events, creating unexpected patterns and often unpredictable as to outcome.

## Other philosophical assumptions

Part of the difficulty in applying complexity theory is that, although we understand that the soundbite is bad for us, complexity theory entails many, many variables. While we understand that academic silos need collapsing and cross-cutting influences, science is always looking for the 'elegance' in data to make complexity simple and large chaotic systems more understandable. Prior to the interest in complexity theory, Western thought most often relied on the following:

> the universe was rationalistic, deterministic and of clockwork order; effects were functions of causes, small causes (minimal initial conditions) produced small effects (minimal and predictable) and large causes (multiple initial conditions) produced large (multiple) effects. Predictability, causality, patterning, universality and 'grand' overarching theories, linearity, continuity, stability, objectivity, all contributed to the view of the universe as an ordered and internally harmonistic mechanism in an albeit complex equilibrium, a rational, closed and deterministic system susceptible to comparatively straightforward scientific discovery and laws.
>
> *(Morrison 2008: 19)*

We have all learned the scientific method which has at its heart repeatability and provability. And that methodology continues to be useful. Yet we, who have privileged rationality and the scientific method over faith and religion, have continued to understand that both rationality and faith continued to exist as unreconcilable methods of understanding the world. Complexity theory is not a replacement theory. Rather it is additive because it begins to explain those elements of real life that don't fit into either the scientific method or the faith-based view.

## What does a complex museum exhibition look like, and what might this mean for museum design?

So, what might a complex museum exhibition look like? The exhibition content, responding to complexity theory, will be multivariate and non-linear, and while there may be a curator-led contingent narrative, it will be defined as only one way to understand the exhibition. Like libraries, the system of use will be non-judgmental and filled with material that will seem tangential to some while not to others. Browsing will be, at baseline, a respected and supported activity. A visitor will be able to wander through a multiplicity of sources that are visual, tactile, verbal and so forth, and can personalize interests through surfing, combining and recombining – understanding that his/her idea trail will be unlike others. And there will be ways that the visitor can affect the exhibition and that effect will add to the cumulative ways the exhibition can be used by others.

Importantly, the creators of the exhibition will have intended it to be that way and their training in exhibition work will, of necessity, be enlarged to include complexity theory and its practical outcomes. The revolutionary part of training will be to encourage curators to enthusiastically embrace and present expertise other than their own even when it conflicts with the thesis they have developed. It will mean that curators will have become enthusiastic 'knowledge sharers' (Gurian 2010).

As for designers, while the variety of techniques, sometimes known as layering, are mostly known, what is not well understood is how to have multiple ways of accessing different lines of thought in the same exhibition at the same time without interfering with each visitor's individual quest. Nor have designers presented keys in the introduction that inform the audience of the many ways they might engage the exhibition without interfering with other avenues of presentation.

The exhibition in question may look substantially the same as it does today with a curatorial presentation that has a conclusory point of view in the forefront. However, that presentation, which I refer to as 'light framing', will be only one way to encounter the exhibition and will be available as an introductory offering. The audience will be encouraged to do something else if they wish. There will be a glossary of possibilities embedded in the orientation. The director, as a matter of policy, will demand that multiple modalities with differing points of view or simply raw data be overlaid on the exhibitions in forms (probably technical) that do not interfere with the frame but are just as easy and comfortable to use. The audience, rather than chastising themselves for not following the intended plot, will be encouraged to follow a personal quest or to dig deeper in some parts because of the availability of both visual storage and access to the internet for further exploration. Access to conflicting points of view will be expected.

There are already examples of all the relevant techniques somewhere. What is revolutionary (and needs a director's hand) is requiring that multiple avenues of exploration be decoupled from the curator's thesis yet embedded into the exhibition fabric itself. Organizationally, multiple staff might create parts of the same exhibition without having to compromise their interest or their positions. But it is important that each of the 'authors' follows a visual track that does not muddy the artistic direction of their colleagues.

There are obvious problems in this approach. If by multi-varied we mean keeping unrationalized, conflicting viewpoints simultaneously in mind, we might be creating intellectual overload that leads to viewer stasis rather than internal choice. However such a frozen phase might come about, it is not the outcome that is useful in a public education space. Practical experimentation is needed to see how to overcome this problem. It is imperative that in our experimentation, we use evaluation tools and mock-ups of ideas to figure out what modalities work simultaneously in complex exhibitions. Prototyping, openness, sharing, testing and ongoing change will all be expected in the process.

The outcome I am hoping for is that our visitors will take away not just specific content of interest, but will come to appreciate that all large ideas are complicated and are multi-faceted. In summary, I hope museum audiences will become more empathic and patient as citizens willing to see incremental change as useful, and trial and error as essential.

Is anyone in the museum community experimenting with exhibitions that fit within this model? I am happy to note that there are some exhibitions moving in this direction and some writers who are thinking about this model. I am hopeful that combining experimental exhibition technique with a coherent theory makes this growing direction less random, suggests new ways forward and continues the previous tradition of creating exhibition modalities based on theory.

## Background for museum learning theory

Over the past hundred years, museum educators have used selected learning theories, or portions thereof, as the rationale for embedding various new approaches into previously static exhibitions. The new techniques were justified as satisfying the needs of formerly underserved publics. For example, the use of interactive elements has been justified by accepting Howard Gardner's theory of multiple intelligences, and the use of tactility has been linked to Piaget and Jerome Bruner. Additionally, 'Behaviorism, cognitivism, and constructivism are the three broad learning theories most often utilized in the creation of instructional environments.

These theories, however, were developed in a time when learning was not impacted through technology' (Siemens 2005).

Similarly, the faith-based world has affected exhibition practice. A major influence has been the recognition of the spiritual nature of some of the objects created by indigenous peoples. Explanation of this has given rise to, for example, first person and multiple-voiced labels and the embedding of ceremony and protocols in the museum when objects are placed on view.

I am not suggesting that all learning theories and their exhibition cognates have been employed, but I am making the point that many exhibition conventions have theoretical underpinnings.

## Who is thinking this way?

The museum world has practitioners who have begun this complexity theory museum journey before me, and on whom I have relied in writing this chapter. I commend Nick Poole, Tony Bennett and Fiona Cameron as relevant theorists (Bennett 1988; Cameron and Mengler 2009; Poole 2012, 2014). Nick Poole, for example writes:

> there is a need for us to focus on what it would mean to provide a platform for contemporary audiences to reflect on the full chaos and complexity of our lived experience. Not just as a project or an exhibition, but for that to become what the word 'museum' means in the collective psyche.
>
> *(Poole 2014)*

I wish to thank the experimenters in the museum world. Most of these folks come from the collections and technology side of museum work. There are those who have worked with large databases of objects like Europeana and Google Art, and have worked in multiple ways to allow for public curation like Seb Chan and Piotr Adamczyk. But, in a 'shout-out' to museum folk I am mindful that my personal examples are unfortunately limited to Anglophone practitioners and mostly those who write papers. We need to continue to share examples of excellent work and excellent thinking.

Historically, there are on-site exhibition precursors that linked objects and a deeper access to information. 'Study storage' originating with Michael Ames (1992) at the Museum of Anthropology in Vancouver Canada and advancing to current, increasingly sophisticated incarnations is one of my favorites. Suze Anderson has written:

> For possibly the first time, the objects in our collection are not being sequestered away from the world and hidden within the safe space of the museum. . . . Not only are we inviting the public to interact with our collections in ways that have previously been impossible, we are asking the objects in our collection to take their place in a complex environment from which they have previously been quarantined.
>
> *(Anderson 2011)*

There are examples of audience involvement, like the 'talk-back' boards of the 1970s Boston Children's Museum, now further developed through co-creation and participatory exhibition theories expanded and promulgated by Nina Simon (2010). There are some current physical interactive technical exhibition examples known as 'media walls', such as 'The Wall' created by the Gibson Group and supported by the director Jette Sandahl, first in Te Papa and then as an out-of-doors version that is part of the Museum of Copenhagen. These emerging technical bulletin boards in an increasing number of places combine big databases and audience input in real time (Gibson Group 2017).

Outside of museum practice, there are internet platforms that should inspire us. My current favorite is the online system Pinterest, which allows for personal visual learning of a very complex and self-originated order. The web itself is, therefore, not only the progenitor of the simplistic soundbite but also of the large, non-judgmental accumulated data sets like Wikipedia and Flickr, created by the generosity of many. Watching how big online free databases operate and their complex and multiple uses is the closest example, I think, that museum practitioners can use now.

Let me reiterate the important elements of Complexity Theory, as applied by Joan Gallos for altering organizational structures, and reapply it to exhibition creation.

> First it is that multiple viewpoints from multiple academic pursuits using different criteria are all at play. Second the outcome cannot be predicted until one is immersed and that multiple outcomes are good. Third that the tension built into the uncertain outcome and the competition surrounding the process can be good. Fourth, in using it within organizations, rather than using top down organizational administration to solve and quiet problems, multiple outcomes are accepted and even hoped for. Organizational theory is to try not to clean this up but allow for tension and individual decision making within a set of competing ideas and data.
>
> *(Gallos 2006)*

## Expectations must be changed

To create exhibitions with such complexity, museum studies, exhibition design programs and individual museums themselves must change practice. Respect for strategies that provide multiple intellectual outcomes will need to be included in their training regimens. The programs that continue to teach the creation of the 'main message' and multi-level label writing formulas will need to broaden their offerings. The convention of label construction will need reinterpretation to accept multiple forms of information availability.

But while celebrating these experimentations, we should remind ourselves that most exhibitions remain curatorially controlled and intended to reach a single thematic conclusion. Museums, where we all work, are not easy to change, perhaps in part because many may be organically stuck in the organizational structures which align with the top-down business model. Making museums amenable to open-ended complex ideas probably requires a change in leadership style and structure. This is difficult but not impossible. Complexity theory and its implication in administrative make-up is being taught in some business and public administration graduate schools already, and some organizations are experimenting with altering their structure.

## Conclusion

I am hoping that from now on, we produce many exhibitions that do not resolve into some pre-determined message, are proactively multidisciplinary, and share multiple worldviews simultaneously without judgement. I am interested in leaving the outcome of visiting an exhibition unsettled, and in need of further reflection by the visitor. And I am suggesting that the opportunities for understanding embedded in such an exhibition are too many for any participant to absorb during a single visit, leaving them to pick and choose their own trajectory of discovery without guidance. I am not writing about designing multiple modalities toward one predetermined intellectual end, but rather suggesting that lack of resolution is a wholly acceptable outcome.

Museums, I am urging, need to help our citizens expect that real public problems are complex, that solutions are always approximate and unintended consequences can and do arise when least expected. We all need admiration for patience. We need new methods of discourse that includes respect for people who see other parts of the problem in starker terms than we do, because what they are seeing is also partially valid. If most of our exhibitions remain the syntheses of complicated subject matter formed into a single narrative, then what will be omitted is a presentation of conflicting partial truths and our audiences will not be challenged to reach their own nuanced understandings.

I am advocating for museums to add an important approach – complexity – to the previous standard ones we have relied on in presenting material to our publics: rationality, faith, emotion, aesthetics. In a world where dialogue is moving toward the shouting of slogans, let us use complexity theory to place our museums in the mix of institutions that provide civil dialogue. Indeed, how can we do less?

## Acknowledgements

An earlier version of this chapter was originally written for the MuseumNext conference and first delivered on 16 February 2017 at the Australian Centre for the Moving Image in Melbourne, Australia.

## References

Ames, M.M. (1992) *Cannibal Tours and Glass Boxes: The Anthropology of Museums*, Vancouver: University of British Columbia Press.

Anderson, S. (2011) 'Museum Objects and Complexity', *Museum Geek*. Online. Available HTTP: https://museumgeek.xyz/2011/06/08/museum-objects-and-complexity/. Accessed 10 January 2017.

Bennett, T. (1988) 'The Exhibitionary Complex', *New Formations*, 4(Spring) 73–102.

Business Dictionary (2017) 'What Is Complexity Theory?', *Business Dictionary*, Fairfax, VA: Webfinance Inc. Online. Available HTTP: www.businessdictionary.com/definition/complexity-theory.html. Accessed 10 January 2017.

Cameron, F. and Mengler, S. (2009) 'Emergent Metaphors for a Complex World: Complexity, Transdisciplinarity and Museum Collections Documentation', *Journal of Material Culture*, 14(2), pp. 189–218.

Cohen, R. (2016) 'Pax America is Dead', *New York Times*, 16 December 2016. Online. Available HTTP: www.nytimes.com/2016/12/16/opinion/trumps-chinese-foreign-policy.html?rref=collection%2Fcolumn%2Froger-cohen&action=click&contentCollection=opinion®ion=stream&module=stream_unit&version=latest&contentPlacement=1&pgtype=collection. Accessed 10 January 2017.

Costa, A. L. (2008) 'Describing the Habits of Mind', in Costa, A. L. and Kallick (eds) *Learning and Leading with Habits of Mind*, Alexandria, VA: ASCD, pp. 15–41.

Cuban, L. (2010) 'The Difference Between "Complicated" and "Complex" Matters', *Larry Cuban on School Report and Classroom Practice*. Online. Available HTTP: https://larrycuban.wordpress.com/2010/06/08/the-difference-between-complicated-and-complex-matters/. Accessed 15 January 2017.

Gallos, J.V. (2006) 'Reframing Complexity: A Four Dimensional Approach to Organizational Diagnosis, Development, and Change', in Gallos, J.V. (ed.) *Organization Development: A Jossey-Bass Reader*, San Francisco, CA: Jossey-Bass, pp. 344–62.

Gibson Group (2017) *Copenhagen Touch Wall*. Online. Available HTTP: www.gibson.co.nz/visitor-experiences/copenhagen-touch-wall. Accessed 28 May 2017.

Gurian, E.H. (2010) 'Curator From Soloist to Impresario', in Cameron, F. and Kelly, L. (eds) *Hot Topics, Public Culture, Museums*, Newcastle: Cambridge Scholars Publishing, pp. 95–111.

Jacobsen, M. (2017) 'Complex Systems and Education: Cognitive, Learning, and Pedagogical Perspectives', NECSI. Online. Available HTTP: www.necsi.edu/events/cxedk16/cxedk16_2.html. Accessed 14 January 2017.

Levy, D.L. (2000) 'Applications and Limitations of Complexity Theory in Organization Theory and Strategy', *Public Administration and Public Policy*, 79, pp. 67–88.

Morrison, K. (2008) 'Educational Philosophy and the Challenge of Complexity Theory', *Educational Philosophy and Theory*, 40(1) pp. 19–34.

Noah, T. (2016) 'Let's Not Be Divided. Divided People Are Easier to Rule', *New York Times*, 5 December 2016, Op-Ed. Online. Available HTTP: www.nytimes.com/2016/12/05/opinion/trevor-noah-lets-not-be-divided-divided-people-are-easier-to-rule.html. Accessed 10 January 2017.

Poole, N. (2012) 'Powering the Museum of Tomorrow', CIDOC Enriching Cultural Heritage, Helsinki, Finland. Online. Available HTTP: http://network.icom.museum/fileadmin/user_upload/minisites/cidoc/ConferencePapers/2012/poole-keynote.pdf. Accessed 10 January 2017.

Poole, N. (2014) 'Change', CODE | WORDS: Technology and Theory in the Museum. Online. Available HTTP: https://medium.com/code-words-technology-and-theory-in-the-museum/change-cc3b714ba2a4. Accessed 25 November 2014.

Rivett, G. (2014) 'Neuroscientist Warns Young Brains Being Re-wired by Technology', *ABC News*, 20 November 2014. Online. Available HTTP: www.abc.net.au/news/2014-11-20/neuroscientist-warns-young-brains-being-reshaped-by-technology/5906140. Accessed 20 November 2014.

Siemens, G. (2005) 'Connectivism: A Learning Theory for the Digital Age', *International Journal of Instructional Technology and Distance Learning*, 2(1). Online. Available HTTP: www.itdl.org/journal/jan_05/index.htm. Accessed 15 January 2017.

Simon, N. (2010) *The Participatory Museum*, Santa Cruz, CA: Museum 2.0.

# 4

# THE DESIGNER'S ROLE IN MUSEUMS THAT ACT AS AGENTS OF CHANGE

*Tricia Austin*

## Abstract

This chapter casts a critical eye over trends to engage audiences, beyond the museum walls, in collaborative co-curation. The chapter goes onto to examine recent parallel developments in co-design and explores the contribution of the designer to the success of outward-facing co-curation initiatives. It makes a case for designers to be acknowledged and deployed as creative strategists, social mediators, user-centred enablers, inventive storytellers and experts in engaging audiences, specifically in association with museums which act as agents of change in their sociogeographic context.

## Introduction

The museum as an agent of change in the social fabric of the city was one of the key trends identified in 'Museums in the Digital Age' (Arup 2014), a report compiled by Arup Foresight and Innovation. The Arup research team scan news sources and governmental statistics, and as a global organisation they call on their own internal architecture expertise and forecasting models to infer future trends. In this case, Arup's researchers envisaged how broad socio-economic, environmental and technological drivers of change might impact museums over the next 25 years. They suggested museums will increasingly engage audiences beyond the confines of the museum walls not only through digital communications but also through mobile exhibitions and temporary architecture. This will 'shift the notion of where and how museums can exist in the future' (Arup 2014).

The Arup article also suggests we are entering an era of 'collaborative curation', referring to a rising desire among audiences to shape their own cultural experiences, allowing for individually curated experiences and enabling the public to take greater control over both museum content and experiences. In the report, they speculated increased visitor participation will 'allow people themselves to reinvent the museum experience' (Arup 2014). Taken together, these two shifts signal the potential for museums to enhance their civic role as proactive agents of change working outside the museum walls collaborating with nearby stakeholders and communities, actively addressing pressing social and environmental issues. However, questions arise about how this role for museums is enacted. What skills, structures and strategies are needed to move towards open source, participatory models of exhibition making outside the museum, and how do these have a positive and sustainable impact on the locale?

This chapter casts a critical eye over the trends described above exploring their genealogy and scope. The text then looks at recent parallel developments in co-design and explores the contribution of the designer to the success of outward-facing co-curation initiatives. It argues that the traditional and somewhat entrenched view of the designer as a technician, resolving questions of display, is thoroughly outdated. It makes a case for designers to be acknowledged and deployed as creative strategists, social mediators, user-centred enablers, inventive storytellers and experts in engaging audiences, specifically in association with museums which act as agents of change in their sociogeographic context. In examining the relationship between co-curation and co-design, the chapter surveys a number of examples and concludes with a case study from Central Saint Martins (CSM). The case study project shows how user-centred, strategic design skills were pivotal for an exhibition-making team that developed a proposition for an exhibition platform and social space in the courtyard of Sidney Estate, Somers Town, a low-income district in north London. The partners on the project were the tenants; Origin Housing, which owns and runs Sidney Estate; a multidisciplinary design team from CSM, University of the Arts London; the Francis Crick Institute; and the Wellcome Trust.

## Reaching beyond the walls of the museum

This section discusses a range of recent exhibition making beyond museum walls exploring a variety of spaces and approaches used. The examples include museum-commissioned art installations, museum-related art practice, apps for historic trails, outreach, pop-ups, 'ubiquitous museology' and the 'comprehensive approach' some museums are taking in co-curating with local partners.

The word 'curation' has become somewhat ambiguous through over-use (Balzer 2015). The premise here is that curation implies a certain power that entitles the curator(s) to define the purpose and consequently the content of the exhibition. It follows that co-curation is shared decision-making about the purpose and what constitutes knowledge in an exhibition (Golding and Modest 2013). Two main questions will be addressed below. First, how curatorial authority is or is not shared, and amongst whom; second, in the context of working outside the museum, how the initiatives described can be said to be improving the material and social conditions in their surrounding communities.

In recent years, the walls of the museum have been 'pierced', 'dissolved' or extended in many different ways. There are, for example, specially curated art installations that take place on the skin of the museum, such as Biografias by artist Alicia Martin. The installation, part of the 2012 International Paper Biennale in The Hague, comprised hundreds of books appearing to cascade out of a second-storey window of the Meermanno Museum and landing on the ground outside. The piece was a very engaging dramatisation of the spatial threshold of the museum, and the huge tide of books was highly evocative. The piece was associated with the biennale theme but did not set out to address the specific social or economic issues of the particular street where it took place. As such, the installation extended the museum display space and expanded the curatorial agency of the expert festival and museum curators into the public realm. The critique is that although the festival provided thought-provoking and visually appealing installations, the approach perpetuates the tradition of art curation in the public realm by decision-makers from prominent cultural institutions, government or corporations, who treat the city as a blank canvas and provide 'high art' they agree is uplifting, inspirational or morally improving. It is suggested that by doing this they impose a particular set of sociopolitical values on the audience and the street (Hauser 1999; Golding and Modest 2013) rather than responding to the specific conditions of the place. This reasoning raises further questions about who should be deciding what is shown in public space and consequently discussions of the use, control and meaning of civic space.

Civic space can be taken to mean shared space, a place for citizens to enact their public lives. However, it has a profoundly complex history (Sennett 1993). Civic space can also be a source of inter-communal unrest (Gaffikin *et al.* 2010). Henri Lefebvre (1991) argues that space is not simply a matter of physical dimensions and material structures, but, being purposefully constructed by vested interests, spaces embody and enact political and social relations. For Lefebvre space is never neutral; it is conceived by planners, constructed by commercial entities, perceived and performed by users according to their cultural backgrounds and is often subverted by individuals and group spatial practices. Civic spaces are continually contested and conflicted. This suggests that cultural interventions in public spaces need to recognise and work from specific tensions of place and in doing so find a way to 'co-curate' among complex sets of stakeholders and users who may all have very different needs and aspirations for the structure, look, feel and use of the space.

An acknowledgement of this socio/spatial tension focused on deliberate interventions in specific public places can be seen in the work of artist Julien de Casabianca. In his 'Outings' project, Casabianca (2013-) 'releases' artworks into the urban environment and encourages others to follow his lead. He uses his mobile phone to photograph a figure in a painting in a museum. He then reproduces this, without specific permission, as a large-scale print and pastes it to the walls of backstreets, car parks, hoardings and the like. The contrast between the sumptuous historical images and dilapidated settings is extraordinarily striking. As part of the process, Casabianca shows interested passers-by and local residents, usually low-income, non-museum-visiting members of the public, how they too can use his techniques to create their own 'Outing'. As such he is encouraging a kind of co-curation that involves selection, appropriation and recontextualisation. The critique here is that the art in itself cannot change the material conditions that perpetuate poverty and inequality. The 'Outings' project may raise awareness but it is questionable as social activism, and furthermore the museum here is not acting deliberately as an agent of social change.

Turning to deliberate spatial strategies, museums are increasingly using digital geo-located mobile phone software applications (apps) to move beyond their walls into the city. One of the first examples is the award-winning Streetmuseum developed by the Museum of London in 2010. The free app enables users to overlay historic images of London at specific sites in the location and access text about the location's history. This is an immersive and resonant experience. Places can be visited in any order and people get instant access to information in situ in a way that was previously unavailable. Since Streetmuseum was launched, several geo-located apps have been developed on similar principles for urban quarters and heritage trails which use scannable QR codes to access text, image and video – for example City Insights (2017). The critique here is that the content is, like the first example above, an embodiment of the institution's, and by extension the curator's, view of history. Some apps such as the National

Trust app (2017) enable users to send images to friends via social media, which suggests a certain user-centred selection and clustering of content online akin to curation, though it remains a peer-to-peer communication outside the core curatorial process of the National Trust.

Some projects such as Makehistory (9/11 Memorial & Museum 2016–2017) use crowd-sourced content. Here, users can read citizens' personal accounts of their experiences of 9/11 online. However, contributions are framed and edited by the commissioning institution. This example begs the question: to what extent can content contribution be described as co-curation? It is argued here that content contribution is insufficient on its own to qualify as co-curation. This is because co-curation implies shared decision-making on the framing and purpose of the exhibition and the examples above were not devised or managed by the contributors. Furthermore, in relation to social impact, although all these apps offer the benefits of additional access to increased information, and despite the fact they may also develop new audiences, they do not function as significant tools for prompting dialogue among local residents, nor do they function as a means to change any material situation in the locale.

Co-curation outside the museum, sharing curatorial authority and making a material impact on people's lives is an elusive practice. To understand why co-curation and sharing curatorial authority has become such an important political goal for museums, it may be useful, for readers who are unfamiliar with the topic, to take a brief look at the lineage of the museum as agent of change. The oldest public museums dating back to the eighteenth century espoused a transformational educational role, albeit from a paternalistic, monological perspective (Bennett 1995). However, during the 1960s and 1970s an ambition emerged for museums to contribute proactively to social wellbeing, social inclusion and environmental conservation (Davis 1999). In Europe, the concept of the 'ecomuseum' emerged 'as an instrument of popular participation in regional planning and community development' (de Varine 2006). Over the same period in the United States, the practice of small community-based museums and art centres such the Studio Museum in Harlem and the Children's Art Workshop in New York (Newsom and Silver 1978) was 'appropriated' by larger museums and the term 'outreach' was coined. Outreach has become firmly embedded in many museums in the United States and Europe. However, very often, outreach forms part of an audience development strategy and is typically a didactic process of knowledge transmission rather than a collaborative approach that shares curatorial authority.

In the UK, the impetus towards museums as agents of change gathered pace in the 1980s. Despite outreach initiatives many museologists became increasingly concerned with combatting the perception of museums as remote from their local communities. Eilean Hooper Greenhill (2000) was one of the key theorists whose work in the 1980s and 1990s promoted a flood of critical debate and writing on the history and role of museums. Research on social inclusion became an important focus for museums (Sandell 1998) and surfaced questions about the role of museums that can be traced back to the mid-Victorian era. Mark O'Neill (2008) argues that historical research into the development of museums reveals a long-standing conflict between museums as instruments of social reform and museums as defenders of traditional values and hierarchies. He writes that in the late nineteenth century museums became detached from their foundations as instruments of social change and entered a long period when they catered only to an educated few. It was in 1979 that Margaret Thatcher's government, under the guise of challenging cultural elitism, reduced public funding for museums and imposed entry charges, and although subsequent Labour governments reinstated free entry to museums they too attempted to change museums, in their case, linking funding to accountability. So, for example, the Labour government formed a Social Exclusion Unit in 1997, the approach was enshrined in European objectives by 2000, and museum funding consequently became linked to audience development and social inclusion.

Government legislation has bred scepticism in some museums. Unfortunately, in some cases, top-down legislation has turned the process of the museum as agent of change into a tick-box exercise. Added to this, some museums have found community projects to be expensive and time-consuming. Dr Bernadette Lynch (2015), examining the progress of museums towards active social inclusion, writes that a number of challenges persist. She suggests management inertia and a lack of appetite for change has limited the potential for the museum as agent of change, and this has led to public participation being persistently perceived as peripheral.

Nevertheless, during this period debate and practices of co-curation have continued to emerge. For example, at a small scale, Deveron Arts (2007-), launched in 1995, developed the notion of 'the town as the venue' based in Huntly, Scotland. The curators, treating the town as a collaborative gallery, aim to balance local participation with international art practice and consequently became deeply involved with town planning and the economic sustainability of the area. Some national museums have also engaged with co-curation, for example the Science Museum London, which ran an international workshop on co-curation and the public history of science in 2010. Simultaneously, in the United States, Nina Simon (2010: 2) developed parallels between social media and exhibition making, suggesting the museum be seen as 'a platform that connects different users who act as content creators, distributors, consumers, critics and collaborators'. Simon also goes on to advocate visitor participation at many levels including governance and the sharing of decision-making about purpose and themes of exhibitions.

Participation and a level of co-curation are evident in the trend for pop-up temporary museum experiences that has grown in recent years. The Santa Cruz Museum of Art and History, where Nina Simon is director, describes their pop-ups as 'temporary exhibitions created by the people who show up to participate' (Santa Cruz Museum 2017). Simon explains that their pop-ups work by choosing a theme and location and inviting people to bring something on topic to share. The pop-up exhibitions take place in store fronts, parks, cafés, libraries and other social spaces and usually last just a few hours. Museums have also used pop-ups in other ways, for example to explore and develop their curatorial strategies, as a form of low-cost rapid prototyping of concepts and ways of creating ties with partner organisations and building community engagement (Center for the Future of Museums 2013). Some theorists have reservations about the terminology and practice of 'pop-up' since, because it is so closely associated with commercial strategies to pave the way for profit-oriented urban redevelopment processes, it is viewed as exploiting the museum as a regeneration tool (Harris 2015). However, others maintain that museum pop-ups, if conceived and driven by multiple stakeholder consensus and fuelled by user engagement and participation, can produce polyvocal challenges to top-down curating and urban planning processes (Kopke 2011).

Other, alternative approaches to exhibition making beyond the museum walls are emerging that treat the world itself as a museum. In the United States, since 2012 Michael Burns has been leading an initiative which aims to enable people to see the everyday world around them through a museum lens. Instead of using relatively expensive and short-lived pop-ups or mobile units, an existing site is chosen to investigate. Burns describes his initiative as 'Ubiquitous Museology' and suggests looking at shopping malls, for example, as history. He maintains that everyday place is an ideal site for informal learning, that it can be viewed as a richly layered collection. He advocates bringing specialists such as scientists, together with historians, business people and citizen-experts, to read their cities and rural landscapes (Burns 2017).

A report by the Institute of Museum and Library Services (Manjarrez and Fuller 2015) in the United States suggests equal partnerships, shared decision-making, institutional commitment, investment of resources and long-termism are key to effective co-curation and community revitalisation across multiple domains such as housing, economic development, public health and education. This 'comprehensive' approach reaches beyond audience development. The report cites examples of museums and libraries in the United States becoming partners in the physical revitalisation of blighted neighbourhoods, community building efforts and delivery of economic, educational and social programmes. The report describes, for example, Danville Science Center constructed in a disused railway station which was launched as part of a regeneration effort in partnership with the City of Danville, the State of Virginia and regional corporate stakeholders. This approach points to co-curation outside the museum as part of a larger urban, economic and political strategy. This approach seems to be promising, however, the scale of such initiatives is a challenge for communications and there may be a danger that such strategies might become too diffuse or be co-opted by powerful entities with other interests.

In the discussion of co-curation between museums as agents of change, visitors and local stakeholders, it is interesting to note that the role of the designer is rarely mentioned. The section below draws parallels to, and reveals synergies between, the fields of co-curation and co-design in their mutual pursuit of social justice.

## The evolution of co-design

In the last 30 years, design has expanded to become a strategic and socially enabling practice. This section argues that expertise in co-design is key to successful co-curated exhibition making for outward-facing museums wishing to act as agents of change.

Since its emergence in the Industrial Revolution, design has evolved in different directions. One direction, to produce the 'face' of products has become closely associated with a market-led approach, in other words producing products to sustain or expand a market, and a marketing approach driving an increase in customers or, in the case of museums, increasing audiences. In architectural design for example, 'starchitecture' has emerged as a brand opportunity for institutions and cities. Sometimes called 'the Bilbao effect', the commissioning of iconic buildings has proved irresistible to many museums as grand architectural schemes have multiplied across the world (Haynes 2014). This approach reinforces the idea that design is solely about technical and aesthetic feats (Till 2011).

Market-led design can obscure another thread of design practice reaching back to the Arts and Crafts movement in the nineteenth century. This tradition is based on a vision of an egalitarian world and can be traced through the twentieth century. Social purpose was taken as a guiding principle at the Bauhaus in the 1920s and 1930s and was rearticulated in a different form in the 1970s by Victor Papanek. Papanek (1985) connected product design, architecture and anthropology to advocate that design meet people's needs within the finite physical resources available in the world.

In the 1980s, the emphasis on how consumers used designed goods intensified. Industrial designer Bill Moggeridge pioneered human-centred design, in which design decisions are driven by an empathy with the people you are designing for. Moggeridge's work was inspired in part by Alvin Toffler's (1980) concept of the 'prosumer', which suggested the consumer can also be the producer. It is interesting to note how this notion resonates with discussions of co-curation where the audience co-develop an exhibition or event which they then also attend, as in the Santa Cruz Museum example.

Moggeridge co-founded IDEO in 1991, and the company helped to establish the process of design research and strategy as being of equal importance to the material outcome of design – a logo, a building and so on. This approach developed into the practice of 'design thinking', often described as a human-centred, empathetic approach to problem-shaping and problem-solving, as opposed to design being solely driven by technology or aesthetics. Design thinking advocates building 'what if' scenarios based on ideas generated from understanding the user. Designers immerse themselves in the situation they are investigating, first creating a large contextual frame, defining problems and opportunities, and then synthesising insights to generate multiple propositions. Here, design incorporates problem-solving activities, idea generation and the creation of meanings (Kimbell 2012). Design thinking advocates starting with a curious, open-minded, experimental approach focusing on discovery. It proceeds to invention and then an iterative process of prototyping, user testing, refining and making. Design thinking correlates to some degree with notions of co-curation since it advocates working with clients and users to achieve collective engagement and support the communication of shared values, and the subsequent triggering of transformation.

Design thinking also resonates with the 'knowledge-based economy' (European Commission 2000); the shift from an industrial manufacturing economy as primary economic driver to an information, service and communications economy. Rather than new products, the knowledge-based economy produces new ideas. Design thinking has thrived in the knowledge-based economy. Research from the Design Council, UK (Coldrick 2015) shows that design is the second largest sector in the UK economy, contributing £71.7 billion to the UK gross domestic product (GDP) in 2015. Design thinking has been taken up by many business schools. Some theorists express concerns that design thinking has been co-opted by commerce, as evidenced by formulaic design thinking courses sold online. Nevertheless, creative and purposeful design has emerged from design thinking, such as the service design, socially responsive design, participatory design and co-design approaches that have gathered pace since 2000.

Service design overtly shifts the focus of design from being about the development of material artefacts to the design of interactions between service providers and consumers (Service Design Network 2017). Service design emerged in the 1990s partly as a response to the service economy but also as an opportunity to shift systems of production and consumption towards environmental and social sustainability. Service design has been deployed in the public sector where it has been used to tackle organisational change in health and transport services. For example, the service design company Uscreates, based in London, applied a co-design approach with the Policy Lab at the Cabinet Office, the Work and Health Unit and service users to develop design-led approaches reimagining how people can be supported to manage their health conditions and stay in work. Service design looks for inventiveness and creativity among 'ordinary people' to solve daily life problems related to housing, food, ageing, transport and work, and develops collaborative services and business models helping to shape new forms of community and new ideas of locality. Service design would seem to offer a useful set of skills for museums working with local communities.

The term 'socially responsive design' emerged in the last 10 years (Melles *et al.* 2011). It envisages users and designers as real partners, and the whole process of design as an opportunity for evolving both the institution and the social groups around it. Design scholars Lorraine Gamman and Adam Thorpe (2016), who helped to coin the term, explain socially responsive design is a departure from socially responsible design in that it is driven by social issues, it aims to create positive social impact and social change and is enacted through co-design. Thorpe, Professor at CSM, UAL, is currently working in partnership with Camden Council and local residents exploring ways socially responsive design can mitigate against recent government funding cuts to public services and researching ways to combat obesity among local residents.

The term 'co-design' first appeared in the UK in 1971 (Sanders and Stappers 2008). Like co-curation, co-design implies sharing authority. The user assumes the role of expert in their area of experience. Co-designers work as mediators among partners, facilitating and designing workshops and communication networks. Co-designers also work as strategists envisioning the steps and impact of the design, and ideators generating concepts, visualising and catalysing ideas within transdisciplinary teams. However, just as in co-curation, questions arise about the cost of extensive co-design and the degree of authority each party has in the design steps: research, concept development, interpretation, experimentation, making and testing propositions.

Co-design for social innovation aims to benefit multiple stakeholders and empower communities. It shares many of the principles of the 'comprehensive' approach to museum-making mentioned earlier. Such projects are usually situated within social and community contexts, with multiple partners. Engagements are preferably long term, and new propositions may well challenge existing socioeconomic and political paradigms in order to bring about significant positive social change.

It is also interesting to note that a thread of architectural education and professional practice has also evolved user-centred approaches. Described as socially engaged architecture, this movement emerged from a critique of traditional architectural consultation processes which were perceived as top-down tokenism. Peer-to-peer urbanism or participatory urban activism developed in Scandinavia, the United States and Europe (Krivý and Kaminer 2013). In 2001, the Architecture Foundation in the UK published a book called *Creative Spaces/A Toolkit for Participatory Urban Design*. Since then, the efforts and debates in socially engaged architecture and urban design have produced a substantial body of critical writing.

Reflecting back on recent shifts in museum making and design, it is remarkable to see how each field is simultaneously pursuing participatory practice, albeit within their own spheres. It is suggested here that huge benefit could be produced by sharing expertise across fields. In particular, the theory and methodologies developed in co-design offer substantial support for developing practices of co-curation outside the museum. The following section presents an example of the integration of co-design and co-curation that aimed to make material difference to both the environment and residents' lives in Somers Town, London.

## Co-curation and co-design

The final part of this chapter describes the collaboration between MA Narrative Environments at Central Saint Martins (CSM), the Francis Crick Institute, the Wellcome Collection and Origin Housing Association in London. It demonstrates how designers can play a strategic and creative role in researching user needs and aspirations, and how they can provide creative direction for public engagement and mediation between different users, partners and stakeholders. It shows how designers take on the role of enablers through co-design workshops and how they interpret and translate ideas into visual and material structures that encourage and communicate user-generated stories and foster user-centred ownership. This case study also demonstrates how the design of narrative environments can be applied beyond the walls of museums in an urban context and how design here is underpinned by a conscious political and ethical stance. This project helps to envisage exhibition making of the future as content-driven, user-focused, socially responsive, creative practice capable of working with multiple partners outside the walls of the museum to affect positively the material and social conditions of nearby communities.

Local partnerships, as discussed above, were key to this project on the Sidney Estate in Somers Town, a deprived area bordered on the east by two of London's main railway stations, St Pancras and Kings Cross. The new multimillion-pound Francis Crick medical research institute has recently been built in Somers Town. The world-famous Wellcome Collection is a 10-minute walk further to the west and CSM is a five-minute walk to the north east of Somers Town. The area around Somers Town is undergoing huge regeneration with local government and international businesses moving in. Nevertheless, urban poverty and its associated problems persist in Somers Town, where the 30,000 population comprises a long-standing white, working-class community living alongside a large population of Bengali and Somali immigrant communities.

Much of the housing in Somers Town is owned and run by Origin Housing Association, a charitable business that started life regenerating the slums of Somers Town in 1928. Origin's mission is to provide housing and connect tenants to local resources. It is concerned in a broad sense with its tenants' wellbeing, aiming to offer good quality homes but also care and support services for the vulnerable; for example, it offers debt advice and assists its residents to find employment. At the time of the project, Origin was renovating its buildings raising the possibility of reconsidering physical changes to the courtyard of Sidney Estate.

In this case, trust and good communications were in place, and key workers at Origin Housing, the Crick and the Wellcome already knew each other. The three organisations had worked together before to address their missions. The mission of the Wellcome Collection is to explore the links between medicine, life and art, and it is part of the Wellcome Trust. In the Sidney Estate project, it wanted to reach local non-museum-going audiences. The mission of the Francis Crick Institute is to advance and disseminate medical research. As a new and not necessarily welcome neighbour it needed to build trust in, win acceptance from and provide benefits to its local community.

In 2015, the Wellcome, the Crick and Origin Housing conceived a public engagement project as part of the United Nations 'International Year of Light'. Their research at the Sidney Estate revealed the residents were unhappy with their bleak, under-used and poorly lit courtyard. They wanted the courtyard to be welcoming and comfortable, like 'an outdoor living room'. This was part of the tenants' overall wish to generate a greater sense of homeliness throughout the estate. Among the three organisations sufficient funding was available to implement a physical intervention. The Crick and the Wellcome had developed a craft workshop to teach or share skills around the theme of light, but they did not know how to interpret the idea of light into an outdoor living room. What forms would be appropriate to the place and the particular residents? What would be its scale, colour, density and material?

What process would create a sense of ownership? What would be its legacy? How could it be updated by residents over time? The three partners recognised they needed creative direction and invited CSM, as another nearby neighbour, to join the group and co-design a proposition.

A team of six students and a mentor from MA Narrative Environments (MANE 2005–17) joined the partnership. MANE has pioneered multidisciplinary co-design since its inception in 2003. On the course, architects, communication designers and curators work in small teams to create story-led spaces for cultural, commercial and community environments. Students are taught user-centred design and how to apply lateral, creative thinking, strategic planning and mediation skills. Many of them are particularly interested in being enablers and taking part in social innovation projects. The mission of CSM is to apply creative design thinking and practice to create a better world so the project appealed to the students, the course and the college as a whole.

Taking a step back, it is also important to recognise that although all four organisations in the partnership shared the same principle (i.e. to create a more sustainable, democratic world), there were additional drivers at play. UK government legislation, Section 106, requires property developers to contribute to improving the local area. The post of community engagement manager at the Crick was specified as part of contract Section 106 agreement with Camden Council when planning permission for the Crick was granted. UK government legislation also requires that science research grants include a communication strategy to non-scientists, which is another key reason for the Crick to invest in a public engagement team. As described earlier, museums including the Wellcome Collection have evolved outreach programmes as part of audience development strategies. Origin Housing seeks to provide tangible upgrades for its tenants. CSM seeks strategic partnerships with other local organisations to offer inclusive design briefs for students. Consequently, all partners had something to gain from working together. This was a promising project because it had all the basic requirements in place: sufficient funding, outward-facing policies in all organisations, key proactive employees, trusted partners, timely needs and opportunities, and expertise in public engagement.

The MANE student team of six comprised an exhibition designer, a spatial designer, an interior designer, an urban designer, a curator and a photographer. First, they met each partner to understand the partners' values and strategies. The student team quickly discovered that each stakeholder had slightly different priorities; for example, Origin was keen that the installation discourage anti-social behaviour and reinvigorate the sense of community; the Wellcome wanted a light installation that established a connection in people's minds to the Wellcome Collection; and the Crick wanted to give something back to the community. The MANE team realised they would be playing an important role mediating among the partners.

The students researched inspirational case studies and documented the physical affordances and limitations of the site as well as researching its history online. Over two months, they attended several 'On Light' events run by the partners in the courtyard where they met and talked to the tenants. They devised and ran a creative participatory workshop, piggybacking on these existing events. The aim of the workshop was to elicit residents' ideas about what constitutes a living room, its possible functions and the kinds of emotions residents would want to feel there. The design team prepared images, colour swatches, material samples and questions to engage and draw out responses from the residents. They acknowledged the tenants as experts on their own environment and tried to ensure they received input from a cross-section of the whole community. The team drafted a report and met with Origin, the Wellcome and the Crick to discuss their research insights. The student team recognised at that point that in addition to being mediators who could facilitate consensus among the partners, they were also a driving force who could develop a design direction that satisfied everyone's different goals.

The six-person team then divided into three pairs to evolve three different visual/material design propositions that would come in on budget. Producing more than one proposition is a typical design strategy that acknowledges that there is no one single correct solution but that exploring multiple options leads to a more satisfactory result. Through analysing the research information and drawing lateral connections, the students produced three creative directions and 3D models. These were presented to tenants and partner organisations for comments and recommended modifications. Finally, one of the three concepts, developed by Julie Howell and Zhongxi Liu, was selected by the tenants and partners.

In this example the Crick, Wellcome and Origin initiated the project, the tenants decided on the purpose and broad content, the designers interpreted the content, and all parties had an opportunity to modify the design interpretation. The tenants played a key decision-making role at the beginning, middle and end of the proposition development, differentiating the project from tick-box consultation or simple audience contribution. Nevertheless, the interpretation phase was conducted separately by the designers in the studio. This recognises that while citizens are experts in their own contexts, designers bring specific expertise in creative development. This method of co-design was appropriate to this project given its resource availability and timescale. Involving citizens in the creative steps of a co-design project is possible but needs considerable additional preparation and framing to be successful.

The creative process is part synthesis, part interpretation and part invention. It requires logical and associative thinking, imagination and skill in translation of words into material manifestation, discussed by Boland and Kollop (Kimbell 2012: 130): 'Designers do not just choose between alternatives but generate concepts'. The creative skill of the design team was, in this case, to look beyond a literal sitting room by employing a two-step process. The winning design team first settled on the theme 'Parlour Games' because it was playful and engaging and responded to residents' wishes to capture the social spirit and history of the living room. The MANE team then drilled down to one specific game, 'Pick-Up Sticks'. The team recognised the sticks could be scaled-up to the size of large poles offering sculptural potential to animate the space and the poles could also be used to support lighting. They planned to fit the poles with solar powered lights at the ends giving a warm glow in the evening and providing light at night for safe passage through the courtyard. The poles also lent themselves to seating of different kinds that would turn the courtyard into a convivial social space. The sticks also resembled images of DNA alluding to Crick and Watson's discovery of DNA in 1953, linking the installation to the new institute. Importantly the giant pick-up sticks were sufficiently large to allow two-dimensional images and text to be added. In other words, the poles presented an opportunity for residents to display their own images for temporary exhibitions recording their present-day experiences. The design team also identified the opportunity to use the poles to display the results of future workshops among the residents, the Crick and the Wellcome. Significantly, the project was planned to provide the material conditions for continuing shared activities.

Origin said they were particularly struck by the amount of thought and time and degree of care taken by the designers to understand the specific environment, its users and context and made a point that this approach was very successful compared to previous art and architectural schemes they had commissioned. They said the MANE process provided new ways for them to work with their tenants and that they really valued the insights gained during the process. The entire project was built around listening, building trust and developing a sense of ownership among the residents with a strategic view to enabling a more social, safer and welcoming environment, a framework for future workshops and physical means for residents to display content of their choice in their own space. Although all key factors were in place at the beginning of the project and the installation was agreed for late 2016, the scheme has been delayed due to a change in Origin's redevelopment plans. Even so, the process and proposition remain extremely useful as examples of a synthesis of long-term, creative and strategic co-design and co-curation. Returning to the overall discussion of the parallel threads of co-curation and co-design, there is a case to be made for museums to embrace the substantial expertise in and critical debate developed around co-design. 'Too often museums think of designers as the people in marketing who make the posters' (Buck 2016). Museums that act as agents of change are faced with a real opportunity to deploy designers as social mediators, user-centred enablers, experts in engaging audiences, creative strategists, inventive storytellers that deliver tangible results.

Nevertheless, questions remain. Close observation of processes of co-curation and co-design reveals there are many different levels of decision-making. Decision-making is not a one-off event. One decision leads to questions that require further decision-making. Can all stakeholders realistically work together at every stage of the process? There is also a question of aligning knowledge. How exactly does the citizen expert work with the professional expert? In a more pragmatic vein, what financial and organisational structures and strategies need to be developed to enable such complex long-term projects to be funded and sustained?

## Conclusion

Reflecting on the original question – what skills, structures and strategies are needed to move towards open source, participatory models of exhibition making outside the museum and how can these have a positive and sustainable impact on the locale? – there are some preliminary conclusions that can be made. First, while networking, research, collaboration and shared decision-making skills are needed by all participants, the particular skills that designers bring are those of mediation, strategic and creative direction and materialisation. These design skills enable groups to move past principles and policies to action and to bring partners' diverse goals into creative synthesis. Second, adopting this approach enables trusted partnerships to be built and good communications to be established across diverse organisations and pooling resources among several partners can provide necessary funding. Content contribution is not enough. Organisations need to share decision-making with the people who inhabit or use the space. Finally, all partners need to take a long-term view, not just in terms of longevity but in terms of sustainability and resilience.

## References

9/11 Memorial & Museum (2016–17) 'Make History', *The Memo Blog*. Online. Available HTTP: www.911memorial.org/blog/tags/make-history. Accessed 16 June 2016.

Arup (2014) *Museums in the Digital Age*, London: Arup. Online. Available HTTP: http://publications.arup.com/Publications/M/Museums_in_the_digital_age.aspx. Accessed 13 March 2016.

Balzer, D. (2015) *Curationism: How Curating Took Over the Art World and Everything Else*, London: Pluto Press.

Bennett, T. (1995) *The Birth of the Museum*, London: Routledge.

Buck, S. (2016) Personal Interview conducted on 17 April 2016.

Burns, M. (2012–17) *The Omnimuseum Project*. Online. Available HTTP: http://omnimuseum.org/. Accessed 13 April 2016.

Casabianca, J. (2013-) *Outings*. Online. Available HTTP: www.outings-project.org/#!about/c66t. Accessed 5 April 2016.

Center for the Future of Museums (2013) 'Pop-ups and Emerging Museums', Center for the Future of Museums Blog. Online. Available HTTP: http://futureofmuseums.blogspot.co.uk/2013/02/pop-ups-and-emerging-museums.html. Accessed 16 June 2016.

City Insights (2017) *City Insights*. Online. Available HTTP: http://city-insights.com/. Accessed 5 April 2016.

Coldrick, A. (2015) 'New Research Shows Design Contributes £71.7bn to UK Economy', *Design Council*. Online. Available HTTP: goo.gl/uWfznO. Accessed 11 February 2017.

Davis, P. (1999) *Ecomuseums: A Sense of Place*, London: Leicester University Press.

De Varine, H. (2006) 'Ecomuseology and Sustainable Development', *Museums & Social Issues: A Journal of Reflective Discourse*, 1(2), pp. 225–31.

Deveron Projects (2007-) *Deveron Arts*. Online. Available HTTP: www.deveron-arts.com/home/. Accessed 16 June 2016.

European Commission (2000) 'Presidency Conclusions'. Online. Available HTTP: goo.gl/9XRb6d. Accessed 11 February 2017.

Gaffikin, F. *et al.* (2010) 'Creating Shared Public Space in the Contested City: The Role of Urban Design', *Journal of Urban Design*, 15(4), pp. 493–513.

Gamman, L. and Thorpe, A. (2016) 'What is Socially Responsive Design and Innovation', in Fisher, F. and Sparke, P. (eds) *Routledge Companion to Design Studies*, London: Routledge, pp. 317–29.

Golding, V. and Modest, W. (eds) (2013) *Museums and Communities: Curators, Collections and Collaboration*, London: Bloomsbury.

Harris, E. (2015) 'Navigating Pop-up Geographies: Urban Space – Times of Flexibility, Interstitiality and Immersion', *Geography Compass*, 9(11), pp. 592–603.

Hauser, A. (1999) *The Social History of Art*, London: Routledge.

Haynes, G. (2014) 'Starchitects' Are Ruining Our Cities', *Vice*. Online. Available HTTP: www.vice.com/en_ca/article/gavin-haynes-starchitects-711. Accessed 5 February 2017.

Hooper Greenhill, E. *et al.* (2000) *Museums and Social Inclusion Group for Large Local Authority Museums: (GLLAM) Report*, Leicester: RCMG.

Kimbell, L. (2012) 'Rethinking Design Thinking: Part II', *Design and Culture*, 4(2), 129–48.

Kopke, J. (2011) 'The Denver Community Museum', *Curator: The Museum Journal*, 54(4) 339–402.

Krivý, M. and Kaminer, T. (2013) 'The Participatory Turn in Urbanism', *Footprint*, 13, pp. 1–6. Online. Available HTTP: http://footprint.tudelft.nl/index.php/footprint/article/view/766. Accessed 10 May 2017.

Lefebvre, H. (1991) *The Production of Space*, Oxford: Blackwell.

Lynch, B. (2015) *Our Museum: A Five-year Perspective From a Critical Friend*, London: Paul Hamlyn Foundation.

MA Narrative Environments (2005–17) *Narrative Environments*. Online. Available HTTP: www.narrative-environments.com. Accessed 5 February 2017.

Manjarrez, C. and Fuller, S. (2015) *Museums, Libraries and Comprehensive Initiatives: A First Look at Emerging Experience*, Washington, DC: Institute of Museum and Library Services.

Melles, G., *et al.* (2011) 'Socially Responsible Design: Thinking Beyond the Triple Bottom Line to Socially Responsive and Sustainable Product Design', *CoDesign*, 7(3/4), 143–54.

Museum of London (2010) *London Streetmuseum*. Online. Available HTTP: www.museumoflondon.org.uk/Resources/app/you-are-here-app/home.html. Accessed 5 April 2016.

National Trust (2017) 'Mobile Apps'. Online. Available HTTP: www.nationaltrust.org.uk/features/mobile-apps. Accessed 16 June 2016.

Newsom, B. and Silver, A. (1978) *The Art Museum as Educator: A Collection of Studies as Guides to Practice and Policy*, Berkeley: University of California Press.

O'Neill, M. (2008) 'Museums, Professionalism and Democracy', *Cultural Trends*, 17(4), 289–307.

Papanek, V. (1985) *Design for the Real World: Human Ecology and Social Change* (2nd edition), London: Thames and Hudson.

Sanders, E. and Stappers, P. (2008) 'Co-creation and the New Landscapes of Design', *Codesign*, 4(1), pp. 5–18.

Sandell, R. (1998) 'Museums as Agents of Social Inclusion', *Museum Management and Curatorship*, 17(4), 401–18.

Santa Cruz Museum of Art and History (2017) *Pop up Museum Santa Cruz Museum of Art and History*. Online. Available HTTP: https://santacruzmah.org/events/category/pop-up-museum/. Accessed 5 February 2017.

Sennett, R. (1993) *The Conscience of the Eye: The Design and Social Life of Cities*, London: Faber and Faber.

Service Design Network (2017) *Service Design Network*. Online. Available HTTP: www.service-design-network.org. Accessed 5 February 2017.

Simon, N. (2010) *The Participatory Museum*, Santa Cruz: Museum 2.0.

Till, J. (2011) *Spatial Agency: Other Ways of Doing Architecture*, London: Routledge.

Toffler, A. (1980) *The Third Wave*, New York: Morrow.

# 5

# CITIES AS EXHIBITION SPACES

## Illuminated infrastructure in the smart city

*Dave Colangelo*

### Abstract

Large-scale projections, urban screens, and media façades are transforming the communicative and expressive capacities of cities. Through overlapping lenses of infrastructure, geomedia, smart cities, play, and placemaking, this chapter critically analyzes a number of case studies, including two works of research-creation, that extend concepts of and possibilities for museum and gallery design to the city itself through communicative, illuminated infrastructure. I conclude that the focus of these initiatives should be on collective and individual perceptual acuity and expression, not on increased efficiency, profit, and control.

### Introduction

The Situationist International, and in particular, their resident architectural theorist, Constant, argued that the city should include modular and reconfigurable elements that citizens could control. Essentially, they believed that city should not be treated as a Corbusian machine for living, but as material for urban experiments that were necessarily temporary, emergent, ephemeral, transitory, and volatile (McDonough 2009). Guy Debord, the figurehead of the Situationists, went as far as suggesting that street lamps themselves be equipped with switches so that citizens could decide how they wanted their streets, neighbourhoods, and cities to be lit (Knabb 2006).

While the Situationist dream of a radically open city has not and will likely never come to fruition, the infrastructure of cities today, namely large-scale LED-equipped bridges and buildings have taken on greater capacities for ephemerality, reactivity, expressivity, and participation, changing the character of contemporary urban life and the nature of display culture. These conditions are expressive of the ongoing development of what Scott McQuire (2008) calls the media city, where feedback associated with urban structures through screens and devices large and small serve to reconstruct contemporary life, instituting new ways of memorializing and experiencing culture, and of being social and civic.

They have also expanded the possibilities for museums, galleries, corporations, and cities to extend their ability to engage citizenry and expand their publics. Take, for example, the lighting of the iconic Empire State Building in New York City. In the 1970s, the building was limited to a few colour changes a year due to the equipment and work required to reconfigure coloured filters on the spotlights that lit its upper reaches. This meant that the building would be lit in Christmas colours during the holidays and in patriotic hues during the Fourth of July, but for little else. In 2012, when a Philips Color Kinetics programmable LED lighting system was installed the building was suddenly capable of displaying an array of over 16 million colours in 'virtually limitless combinations', all at the push of a 'computer controlled' button (Philips 2012). What has followed is a much more varied program of colours on the building which includes lightings for Eid, Hanukkah, and even Argentinian Independence Day, along with participatory commercial promotions for Verizon which asked participants to vote to change the building's lights, tributes to the victims of the November 2015 Paris attacks, and special lightings for the elections which turn the building into a public data visualization (Colangelo and Davila 2011), tallying votes in real time. The Empire State Building is one glowing piece of civic infrastructure amongst many in the world that has been able to better reflect the diversity of its publics, the reality of its ownership and economic milieu, and the vicissitudes of time via its expressive façade. The lights of the Empire State Building have become an attraction in themselves, a central functional and iconic feature of the Empire State Building and New York City experience. Beyond the lights themselves, this is achieved via social media which serves as a digital, sharable didactic and through the working model of the building and its lights that greets visitors in the lobby.

Of course, the Empire State Building does not stand alone in this, and other cities around the world have their own iconic, illuminated, animated structures that function as civic exhibition spaces – beacons that connect people to the attractions they contain and to the city itself – and attractions unto themselves. The San Francisco-Oakland Bay Bridge glows with 'The Bay Lights', a generative art installation by artist Leo Villareal, producing organic patterns inspired by the waves below the bridge. The CN Tower in Toronto maintains its civic centrality and attracts visitors to its exhibits via changes to its LEDs nightly to commemorate national holidays, special events, causes, and concerns. More interestingly, and relevant to the discussion of museum and gallery design, smaller buildings such as the ARS Electronica Center building in Linz, Austria, and the Ryerson Image Centre in Toronto use their programmable, expressive façades to extend the reach and mandate of their buildings, housing new media art and photography, respectively, to display work by media artists, or allow the community to modify the colours via outreach programs and interfaces, drawing the gallery out into the city and vice versa (Plate 5).

These examples demonstrate the prevalence of public installations and experiences centred upon expressive illuminated infrastructure in our contemporary media cities (McQuire 2008), public works that are typically large-scale, networked, interactive, participatory, and digital. Commonly referred to as media architecture (Media Architecture Institute 2015) or as I have suggested, as massive media (Colangelo 2015) – *massive* because of their architectural scale and the breadth and depth of networks, digital and otherwise, that they engage, and *media* because of the incorporation of elements such as mobile phones, digital kiosks, recording devices, projection, sensors, and addressable LEDs – these sites invoke new expressive modes for citizens and cities. But do these represent, in any way, the utopian and emancipatory qualities outlined by the Situationists? How can the programing and curation of these sites deliver audiences to critical and creative encounters with art, the city, and each other within the challenges and constraints that come with producing complex and costly large-scale public works? How can they avoid becoming mere advertisements for cities and for art in general? How can they become sustainable and relevant as more permanent community resources and exhibition spaces; as infrastructure that is as essential, materially and symbolically, to our cities as pipes and electrical wires?

Using overlapping definitions and theoretical frameworks of infrastructure, geomedia, smart cities, play, and placemaking, which I will explain briefly in turn, I will categorize and critically analyze a number of case studies, including two works of research-creation (Chapman and Sawchuk 2012), that represent the extension of museum and gallery design to the city itself, while also extracting the various expectations, uses, and areas of contestation present in these sites today and into the future. This chapter argues that we should envision and evaluate the communicative, animated infrastructure of massive media as city-scale exhibition spaces which can develop perceptual acuity and collective and individual intelligence, not just increase efficiency and accelerate corporate surveillance and control, or amount to little more than civic and corporate advertising and branding. In this way, these illuminated, civic exhibition spaces should be seen as an emergent and important infrastructural category alongside sanitary, electrical, and sewage systems. Illuminated infrastructure should be seen as increasingly functional expressions of our communicative systems and key structures for the 'dialectic development of the social whole' (Stevens 2007: 196).

## Theoretical framework

An analysis of illuminated infrastructure as civic exhibition space first requires a working definition of infrastructure itself. While infrastructure might be seen as purely material, that is, as a mere collection of things, Bateson reminds us that 'things' can never be studied. Instead, 'What can be studied is always the relationship or an infinite regress of relationships' (Bateson 1978: 249). Thus, infrastructure must be seen as the relationships between things and the people that use them (Star 1999). Take, for example, the electrical wires that service our businesses and homes. To the city planner or electrician, these represent a vast system that must be planned and managed, whereas to the end user they remain invisible conduits that power coffee makers and light bulbs. Infrastructure is a set of relations that are unique to the situation in which they are substantiated. Furthermore, values are inscribed into technical systems and reproduced through their use and the associated infrastructure that are built and supported as a result. Take the example of the Grand Central Parkway in New York. Designed by Robert Moses in the 1960s, it was purposefully made too low for public transport to pass through so as to exclude lower-income people from the developments it connected to the city (Winner 1980). Extending this relational view of infrastructure, we can observe that the values and exclusionary relationships that are embedded within bridges exist crucially and perhaps more insidiously in digital networks. As Star (1999: 389) notes, 'there are millions of tiny bridges built into large-scale information infrastructures, and millions of (literal and metaphoric) public busses that cannot pass through them'. For example, if information about a city is only available in an iOS application, then only users with Apple smartphones can access it. Thus, infrastructure must be seen as value-laden and essentially relational, in digital and physical forms. While gallery and exhibition space is self-evidently relational, communicating ideas and suggesting relationships, it may not immediately appear to be value-laden.

Yet, one needs only to think of the efforts made by museums and art galleries to expand their publics through community outreach programs and extended hours to see that they are aware of structural barriers to participation.

Infrastructure, not unlike museum or gallery space, is also expressive and communicative. Amin (2014: 137) has studied the social life and sociality of urban infrastructure, noting that infrastructure is deeply implicated in the experience of 'community, solidarity and struggle for recognition'. Referring to his work in Brazilian favelas, Amin shows how provisional systems for waste removal and electricity reveal the centrality of identity formation and the relationship between citizen and city – here, citizens see themselves as city builders not by choice but by necessity. He notes that the social life of the city can in fact be read from the provision and use of its infrastructure. He proposes an 'anthropology of infrastructure' that foregrounds what he calls 'the urban backstage', which includes everything from roads, pipes, cables, broadband, and code, as well as the sociotechnical systems that they are a part of (Amin 2014: 139). Infrastructure, like exhibition and gallery design, in its relationality and its value(s), represents a site of struggle for both the practical and symbolic. Later in this chapter, I will address how the illuminated infrastructure of buildings and bridges extend the practical and symbolic struggles of the city to display culture in new ways.

Seemingly far from the rudimentary infrastructure of Brazil's favelas, but central to the making of urban functionality, sociality, and identity through infrastructure, is the idea and practice of the 'smart city', a concept that will be central to my analysis of illuminated infrastructure and public display culture. The smart city refers to the growing integration of technological infrastructure such as sensors, networked communication, and ubiquitous computing in cities to achieve greater efficiency in the delivery of various services. These might include street lights that sense light levels and turn on only when needed, such as when the presence of a vehicle or pedestrian is detected. Smart cities might also include algorithms that modulate traffic signals to reduce traffic or open data that allows citizens to track the arrival times of public transportation. In the YouTube video '2030: Smart City Life 360 View' (PhilipsLighting 2016), lighting technology company Philips predicts that street lighting will become 'an information highway' where 'connected streetlights stream data between millions of devices' providing citizens with WiFi, coordinating the flow of autonomous vehicles, sensing available parking spots, monitoring noise, and tracking air pollution.

While the smart city is built on ubiquitous networks, connected devices (otherwise known as the Internet of Things (IOT)), and various public and private interfaces and displays, it is also built on the willing participation, explicit or implicit, of local authorities and citizens. These participants might work together to reduce energy use, increase automation, and remove the friction associated with the urban experience, thus representing the relationality and expressivity of infrastructure described above. And, like all infrastructure, the infrastructure of the smart city is not without built-in values and biases. Adam Greenfield (2013) warns that the processes of the smart city represent a number of tricks and dead-ends that are concealed in order to serve the corporations that are heavily invested in promoting the products that create the smart city and the governments interested in maintaining law and order. For example, sensors that support driverless cars serve to reinforce car culture and the automobile industry, not to mention government and corporate surveillance, and do not necessarily reflect the best way forward for cities and citizens. Other dangers of the smart city lie in proprietary devices and software that may not necessarily represent citizens' best interests and instead benefit administrators, in the replication of top-down planning principles that were the downfall of modernist developments, and in the potential for purposeful inefficiency, such as with internet throttling for certain streaming services, that may push citizens and cities to purchase unnecessary equipment and services.

Public display culture via the illuminated infrastructure of massive media fit into this contentious concept of smart cities in the ways that they might act as communicative beacons for the workings of the various sensor networks that make up the smart city but also as communicative beacons for the myths of objectivity and progress that surround the concept. On the practical side they might, for example, display the total amount of energy used by the city over a certain period of time, indicate faster routes for travel, or alert drivers to parking lots that can accommodate them. These, of course, work in tandem with mobile ubiquitous media, both as a way to personally deliver this information, but as devices that gather information themselves to feed into the algorithms and analyses that drive these systems, together forming what Nana Verhoeff (2012) refers to as a composite dispositif, delivering citizens to certain messages and values through the confluence of semi-coordinated, location-sensitive screen messages.

Urban screens and LED façades can also be seen as providing incentives for citizens to voluntarily participate in actively reporting things like energy use, crime, transportation routes and times, and so on, so as to increase the reliability of such information. This, also, can constitute active participation in regimes of surveillance and practices of self-management. Taken together, the illuminated infrastructure of massive media can present environments that signify technological advancement, superior organization, and objectively maximal efficiency. The degree to which these goals might be achieved through illuminated infrastructure is a central matter of concern of this chapter.

Related to the smart city concept, and relevant to the analysis of illuminated infrastructure, is the growing emphasis on placemaking in cities. Placemaking has been, and continues to be, an important consideration in gallery and museum design, and is quite often related to the spaces around museums and galleries. My analysis will extend these considerations to the city itself. In the context of the city, placemaking, as noted by Project for Public Spaces (2017), 'refers to a collaborative process by which we can shape our public realm in order to maximize shared value'. This is achieved by enhancing the sociability, access, and comfort of public spaces. Placemaking initiatives often involve the coordination of practical improvements such as the provision of street furniture, expanded sidewalks, adequate lighting, and affordable retail spaces.

The concept and practice of placemaking emerged from earlier work by Jane Jacobs and William W. Whyte, who emphasized the importance of lively neighbourhoods and involved citizens in the creation of a sense of place. As they noted, these processes are 'essential for well-being and feelings of safety, security and orientation, and a remedy against feelings of alienation and estrangement' (quoted in Tomitsch 2016: 340). Furthermore, Krajina (2016) notes that placemaking also refers to how space is invested with 'routine and familiarity', such as with the ringing of a clock tower in a church courtyard or the regular passage of a subway car. In this way, the illuminated infrastructure of massive media as communicative infrastructure and public display culture holds promise for placemaking, depending of course on how these assemblages are planned, programmed, and deployed.

The related concepts of placemaking and the smart city are also wrapped up in changing notions of public space and the public sphere that allow for tactics and techniques of exhibition design to permeate into urban space. McQuire (2016) notes that the technologies and practices that are present in smart cities and illuminated infrastructure leads to a hybridized notion of public space and the public sphere that he calls 'geomedia'. For McQuire, this is a state defined by 'the convergence of media sectors, the ubiquity of digital devices and platforms, the everyday use of place-specific data and location-aware services, and the routinization of distributed, real-time feedback' (McQuire 2016: 19). These changes serve to reduce our reliance on traditional forms of information gathering, sociality, and discourse through media, such as the cinema, radio, newspapers, television, or even the museum, that were bound more closely to physical structures, environments, and devices. As such, 'contemporary processes of social interaction are being shaped less decisively by traditional modes of urban boundary formation, such as the hard infrastructure of the built environment' (McQuire 2016: 3).

In a way, through networked, illuminated displays, the hard infrastructure of the city is further softened, while at the same time revived as site of communicative consequence: it becomes expressive and constitutive of the increasing boundarylessness of information and identity in public space. As McQuire notes, 'as much as digital media enable *emancipation* from place, they have also become a key modality of contemporary *placemaking*' (2016: 6). That said, McQuire, like Greenfield, wonders if geomedia will lead to increasingly intense processes of scrutiny and micro-evaluation. There is a danger that geomedia such as the illuminated infrastructure of massive media might be complicit in 'aiding and abetting the commodification of the common' instead of developing social practices that 'might enable a reinvention of the urban' (McQuire 2016: 20) – and, I would suggest, of public display culture.

Finally, the concepts and values of play and participation are important considerations for an analysis of contemporary urban media and illuminated infrastructure as extended exhibition spaces for organizations and for the city itself. These concepts provide touchstones for the support, but also critique, of smart city and placemaking initiatives. Play, as Stevens (2007: 1) notes, is an important feature of good public spaces when it represents 'economically inefficient, impractical and socially unredemptive activities'. But play can also be deployed for other purposes. Stevens warns that 'The diversity, leisure and *jouissance* generated by urban life are constantly being reappropriated and exploited by governments and investors to serve instrumental ends of power and profit' (2007: 2). This can be seen in the example of the Empire State Building's Verizon promotion, which engaged citizens in a playful contest to change the lighting on the building based on the popularity of a football team.

Illuminated infrastructure, while providing a means by which play can occur in the urban sphere, can also quite easily be driven by the goal of capital and symbolic gain for particular groups. Participation, as an essential part of play and the urban experience, represents an extension of this problematic. While, as Bishop (2016: 145) states, participation, and participatory art in particular, 'aims to restore and realize a communal, collective space of shared social engagement', it often remains a tool of those in power, be it artists, curators, exhibition programmers, or corporations, to attract and manipulate audiences, often symbolizing delegated power and citizen control but never divesting it as such. Bishop argues that for something to be truly participatory it must seek to hand over the reins to the public it seeks to engage, and for this uncertain and precarious proxy for democracy to continually be performed and tested.

Media-related processes of play, participation, efficiency, comfort, and control are now built into the urban realm in a tapestry of individual and shared connections and infrastructures. In the case studies that follow, I will apply the concepts developed above to perform an analysis of the illuminated infrastructure of massive media as exhibition spaces that extend the reach of individuals, collectives, and organizations in critical, creative, and controversial ways.

## *In The Air, Tonight* and #RyeLights: exhibiting social dimensions in digitized urban space

Sociocultural expectations are framed by the separation and means of connections afforded by public spaces (Stevens 2007: 54). Illuminated infrastructure play an important function in expressing, engaging, defining, and redefining the social dimensions of urban space by modulating the distance and means by which other people are encountered, changing our characters, moods, and intensions, as well as our capacity and desires to respond to stimuli in public space. As such, display cultures of urban infrastructure such as the LED façades of buildings and other expressive architectural displays can engage directly in civic struggles and contests that are both practical and symbolic.

Take, for example, *In The Air, Tonight* (2014–2016), an installation that I created with my collaborators at Public Visualization Studio (2016) (Plate 6). This was a project that allowed participants to change the colour of a building in downtown Toronto, the Ryerson Image Arts Building, with tweets that contained the hashtag '#homelessness'. The results were visible locally but also online via a webcam. The project attempted to visualize, engage, and enable a hybrid, borderless public sphere centred upon the illuminated infrastructure of the building. The building, as communicative beacon, was an important transfer point that aimed to modulate the perceived distance between people interested in debates and conversations about an important civic issue, both in Toronto and around the world, while also amplifying the perceived efficacy of their actions. The ability to control a glowing building, up close or from afar, extended sociocultural expectations of what can and should happen in public discourse that extends beyond, yet is critically anchored to, the symbolic power of highly controlled, physically substantial, public infrastructure.

*In The Air, Tonight* has proven an effective proof of concept for a longer, more sustainable exhibition project that I have managed since 2015 called #RyeLights (2017). #RyeLights uses the same LED façade and its programmable capabilities to extend the ability to request lighting changes to the Ryerson University community. This is an important step in addressing the critiques of smart cities and participation which advocate for ongoing opening of so-called participatory and smart systems to the participating public, and represents a new mode of public display culture which extends engagement between institutions and their publics. Thus far, #RyeLights has facilitated lighting changes for a variety of groups promoting everything from relief for Syrian refugees to on-campus art installations, allowing the community to have their environment reflect their character, mood, or intentions while extending this to the less-bordered publics of online discourse through images of the building circulating on social media. In a recent pilot project, a group concerned with murdered and missing indigenous women made the building pulse red with tweets containing #MMIW (Shades of Our Sisters 2016), demonstrating the potential for this element of illuminated infrastructure to continue to function as an exhibition space of community engagement, representation, and concern.

#RyeLights presents us with a dense analytical transfer point for debates about public display culture, infrastructure, smart cities, play, participation, and placemaking. As infrastructure, it represents an example of infrastructure as a set of relations, instead of merely a thing. In fact, #RyeLights, and LED façades in general, in their ephemerality and changing forms and meanings, can be seen to draw our attention to the ways that other, more permanent elements of our physical and visual spaces of congregation and passage (such as bus shelters, roads, and alleyways) communicate their own values, affordances, and restrictions, albeit at a slower pace.

It is the rate of change available on such illuminated, animated infrastructures that makes the communicative capacity of infrastructure apparent. This rate of change also contributes to new routines and familiarity with the urban environment. With programs like #RyeLights we come to expect the same things from our physical environments that we do from most of the things in our contemporary world, including our galleries and museums: that we can change, modify, and essentially be in conversation with them.

The question for #RyeLights and similar infrastructure that allow for lighting requests, including the CN Tower in Toronto, the Empire State Building, the Calgary Tower, or the Morrison Bridge in Portland, Oregon, to name a few, is whether these structures reproduce exclusionary practices that deter and restrict the public from communicating in and through their physical environment, or if they are made to promote and foster the best interests of citizens. Unlike many corporately owned structures (i.e. Empire State Building), #RyeLights does aim to be an inclusive community resource first and foremost and does not accept lighting requests for commercial purposes. Yet, while #RyeLights provides citizens of the Ryerson community with the means to enhance sociability and access by granting and promoting lighting requests from the community, elements central to placemaking, and represents an element of spatial responsiveness central to smart city initiatives, it can also be seen as a means by which the school can promote itself by co-opting the participation of its own community members. Therein lies one trade-off of participation and the smart city with respect to illuminated infrastructure, and infrastructure in general: no matter how open these systems are, all outcomes of open, communicative, urban infrastructures are reflected through and captured by the owners and operators of the infrastructure, for better or worse, and are not necessarily transferred to the citizens that use and animate them. It is up to citizens and participants to go on to act to make the changes in awareness, in action, in policy, and in society that these causes promote, both in their own name and in the inescapable name of the infrastructure provider. What this speaks to more than anything is the responsibility that the builders and hosts of illuminated, communicative, architectural urban environments have to their communities.

## 'The Illuminated River': sensing the urban environment

While Richard Sennett argued that twentieth-century life in cities increased detachment while simultaneously increasing visibility, Eric Kluitenberg (2016: 75) adds that electronic media exacerbate this modern disorder, and mobile electronic media 'transfer this trend of electronic isolation to public space itself'. Given these conditions in cities, it is no surprise that cities are seeking symbolic and functional solutions through large-scale, digital public displays.

Recently, the City of London hosted a competition for coordinated lighting design for its primary bridges, from the Albert Bridge to the Tower Bridge (Sulcas 2016). Tellingly, almost all of the plans and proposals for the bridges had a conceptual focus on reclaiming connections to one another and to our environment, some things that have been lost, arguably, in the midst of rapid accelerations of urbanization and technological change. The proposals put forth by a number of artists and collaborations with architecture firms such as Diller Scofidio + Renfro reveal the underlying social character and symbolic potential of the infrastructure now and in these future visions, and extend public display culture which previously would have existed at the scale of the public square or monument (as in Trafalgar Square's 'The Fourth Plinth'), to the city itself.

Building on this sense of pervasiveness and scale, one group connected the lighting of the bridges with the natural rhythms of the tides. Amanda Levete, from London architecture firm AL_A, noted of their proposed approach: 'In the space of two hours, you see the tidal change; we want to remind people that their lives play out not in minutes and hours, but in the context of centuries, and the forces of nature' (Sulcas 2016). Another firm suggested creating light planes that are generated by data readings of the river's depth, flow and surface tension. Diller Scofidio + Renfro's proposal, titled 'Synchronizing the City: Its Natural and Urban Rhythms', sought to create curtains of falling water as screens for projections on each of the bridges along with floating platforms along the riverbanks for performance. Most notably, their plan included creating a 'night kiss' effect which when night falls on each bridge, a white vertical light will be produced, each at roughly 20 seconds apart due to the rotation of the earth. As they say, 'We're imagining the moment of the beams going up a bit like the chiming of Big Ben; a moment of urban consciousness' (Sulcas 2016). Furthermore, Diller notes, 'It's an opportunity to pay attention to the transition between day and night, and to evoke a collectivity that is missing in our urban lifestyle' (Sulcas 2016). The winning scheme by Leo Villareal (the artist who created The Bay Lights) with Lifschutz Davidson Sandilands and Future\Pace, also features site-specific illumination that reacts to the river and ambient light in the city (Plate 7).

While connectivity to one another, to the environment, and to the city are the conceptual goals of the artists and architects involved, the goals of planning commissions are more profit driven. As stated on 'The Illuminated River' (2016), the official website for the London bridge lighting initiative, the goals of the $24.8 million plan are clearly aligned with smart city and placemaking initiatives that primarily seek economic gain: to contribute to the international profile of London as a world city and a centre for creative industries, draw attention to what they call 'London's important and under-valued public realm', and 'provide more opportunities for Londoners and visitors to come together for outdoor celebrations'. As Hannah Rothschild, chairwoman of the Illuminated River Foundation notes, the transformation will be dramatic: 'Light, energy, beauty, commerce, at the flick of a switch' (2016).

With these examples, we are again able to see how infrastructure as public displays are much more than technical systems, but in fact a set of relations between people and things as well as a means by which values are imposed and shaped and social consciousness is formed. The various proposals noted above are explicit attempts at placemaking and enhancing the experience of the city – seeking to make the areas over and around the river a more attractive destination in the evening by extending sociability and comfort. While this may be achieved by some of the plans, each one lacks an important feature: the ability to maximize shared values through access and collaboration. With grand infrastructural gestures such as 'The Illuminated River', what rhetorical and operational openings are left for citizens? What kind of intelligence do these structures enable and symbolize in the so-called smart city other than the intelligence of the creative firms involved in their construction?

In the proposals described above, very little is left open for debate, contestation, or conversation. By creating visualizations of environmental cycles and changes, these large-scale expressions are stripped of any political or social content and become primarily ambient decorations. Citizens are not able to inhabit this space in any way; they merely witness it. In this sense, the city appears smart, but citizens are essentially shut out of gaining any more knowledge about their surroundings, given tokenistic elements of senses of collectivity by virtue of being able to do little more than gaze upon the same thing at the same time. If we are to envision (and accept) the city as an exhibition space for itself and its citizens, these structures must do more than this. Here we can refer to what McQuire calls the right to the digital city, which itself refers to Lefebvre's concept of 'the right to the city'. As McQuire (2016: 17) notes, the ability of a city's inhabitants to 'actively appropriate the time and space of their surroundings' was something that Lefebvre believed was crucial to creating and maintaining a modern conception of democracy. None of this comes into play in the various proposals put forward by the groups involved in 'The Illuminated River', and what we see replicated are some of the same top-down, authoritarian planning models that plagued many of the failures of modernism both in cities and in exhibition design. All of the proposals invoke passive spectatorship which reinforces the subject position of the citizen as witness to spectacle and not as an active node in a relational system.

While 'The Illuminated River' seeks to construct new social connections and 'make' place lost by way of the distractions of contemporary urban life, it also helps to mark or brand a city as a smart city, as sufficiently technologically advanced, thus performing a dual function of placemaking and smart city-making (at least, symbolically) that serves the agendas of cities in competitive globalized economies for resources, tourism, and talent. Unfortunately, trademarks (as opposed to landmarks) and branded spaces do little for actually existing democratic use of public space and take us away from the potential the city holds as a critical exhibition space. As Georgiou (2016) argues, the stakes for getting these projects right are now higher due to 'the dominant but fragile order of the postcolonial western metropolis, which is deeply connected, deeply diverse, and deeply divided'. It is especially at these large scales, the scale of the city, and in these fraught political times, that more effort must be made to open these spaces to public determination in order to reflect the need for connection between diverse publics. This requires careful community engagement, long-term capital planning, and strategic foresight that provides the respectful means and ends for participation.

## Discussion and conclusion

The illuminated infrastructure of massive media continue to expand our expectations for sociability, sensation, identity, and the possibilities for the city as exhibition space. While they expand our beliefs and attitudes about what and where publics and public spaces are, our connection to the urban environment, and to our own bodies, they are also bound up in processes of placemaking and smart city initiatives and can be co-opted as such to serve corporate interests instead of the needs of citizens. Furthermore, networked, expressive, digital infrastructure can be seen as important sites of collective contestation and perceptual training. As McQuire (2016: 16) notes, 'networked public space is today a vital laboratory for incubating and practicing the sociotechnical skills – which is to say, the new forms of communication, collaboration and cooperative action – needed for this complex task'. Illuminated, expressive, communicative, and networked infrastructure are important sites in our culture today, providing visible bridges between the real and virtual, and dramatizing, at their best, their inhabitation and contestation by a spatially and culturally diverse public and the organizations that serve them. As Kluitenberg (2016: 77) notes of digital public spaces, 'It is here that the sign of the real inscribed itself most vigorously' in our culture today. Culture now abhors the vacuum of virtuality, and communicative, illuminated infrastructure helps to fill in the gaps.

Overall, greater attention must be paid to these structures as essential infrastructure for shaping our experience of the complex dynamic between information and space, and between cultural institutions and publics. Animated, large-scale infrastructures of communication and expression can help us to develop perceptual acuity and collective and individual intelligence. The danger remains that these same infrastructures, due to the barriers to ownership and control and the structures of the urban planning system, are often deployed for the purposes of advancing efficiency, corporate surveillance, advertising, and city branding. McQuire (2016: 119–20) comments that 'urban planners need to reconsider their overly instrumental approaches to designing public spaces, and instead take the risk of building spaces whose purposes and intended uses remain loose and ambiguous'. The same can be said of the designers of museums and galleries that seek to occupy the urban realm. The illuminated infrastructure of massive media lends itself well to loose and ambiguous use in the way that it furnishes ephemerality through its digitality. At the same time, challenges exist in that a great deal of planning rules and permissions are required before these large-scale public expressions are approved and deployed. Furthermore, an 'open' system will not guarantee the bottom-up approaches and efforts that the Situationists once envisioned.

What we should expect from illuminated infrastructures are frameworks, guides, and hands-on education to allow people to engage with their complex systems and the dynamics of hybrid public spaces they produce. This requires sustained community engagement and long-term capital planning to allow for the training, programming, and curatorial leadership needed to open these spaces to their inhabitants. This is something that we are continually working on with the #RyeLights project, and hope to have technical frameworks and workshops in place soon to allow students and community members to propose and program the lights on the building themselves.

Finally, a fundamental change is needed in the way that artistic, expressive infrastructure is commissioned. In the case of 'The Illuminated River' in London, with money coming from philanthropic foundations, little to no input was solicited from citizens. Instead, in these cases, cities bend over backwards to welcome the high-profile influx of money and position the investment as part of smart city and placemaking initiatives without considering that these schemes do not necessarily make citizens feel more welcome, intelligent, empowered, or involved in their city. As Krajina (2016) warns, 'Ways in which different people seek, successfully or not, to construct a place of their own, will be one measure of mediated urbanity of our time'. Cities and the creative, cultural, and commercial institutions that serve them should take this into account and find creative ways to sustainably construct, fund, and program expressive civic infrastructure that places the citizen's right to the city at its core.

## References

Amin, A. (2014) 'Lively Infrastructure', *Theory, Culture & Society*, 31(7/8), 137–61.

Bateson, G. (1978) *Steps to an Ecology of Mind*, New York: Ballantine.

Bishop, C. (2016) 'Spectacle and Participation', in Pop, S., Toft, T., Calvillo, N., and Wright, M. (eds) *What Urban Media Art Can Do: Why When Where & How*, Stuttgart: avedition, pp. 145–54.

Chapman, O. and Sawchuk, K. (2012) 'Research-creation: Intervention, Analysis, and "Family Resemblances"', *Canadian Journal of Communication*, 37, pp. 5–26.

Colangelo, D. (2015) 'Curating Massive Media', *Journal of Curatorial Studies*, 4(2), 238–62.

Colangelo, D. and Davila, P. (2011) 'Public Data Visualization: Dramatizing Architecture and Making Data Visible', *International Symposium on Electronic Art*, Istanbul, Turkey, 14–21 September 2011. Online. Available HTTP: http://isea2011.sabanciuniv.edu/paper/public-data-visualization-dramatizing-architecture-and-making-data-visible. Accessed 19 February 2017.

Georgiou, M. (2016) 'Right to the City, or Compulsion to Connect?', *Mediapolis: A Journal of Cities and Culture*, 5(1). Online. Available HTTP: www.mediapolisjournal.com/2016/11/right-city-compulsion-connect/. Accessed 19 February 2017.

Greenfield, A. (2013) *Against the Smart City (The City is Here For You to Use Book 1)*, New York: Do Projects. Online. Available HTTP: www.amazon.com/Against-smart-city-here-Book-ebook/dp/B00FHQ5DBS. Accessed 3 September 2016.

Kluitenberg, E. (2016) 'Public Agency in Hybrid Space: In Search of Foundations for New Forms of Public Engagement', in Pop, S., Toft, T., Calvillo, N., and Wright, M. (eds) *What Urban Media Art Can Do: Why When Where & How*, Stuttgart: avedition, pp. 73–80.

Knabb, K. (2006) *Situationist International Anthology*, Berkeley: Bureau of Public Secrets.

Krajina, Z. (2016) 'Seeking Place in Mediated Urban Space', *Mediapolis: A Journal of Cities and Culture*, 5(1). Online. Available HTTP: www.mediapolisjournal.com/2016/11/seeking-place-in-mediated-urban-space/. Accessed 19 February 2017.

McDonough, T. (ed.) (2009) *The Situationists and the City*, London: Verso.

McQuire, S. (2008) *The Media City: Media, Architecture, and Urban Space*, London: Sage.

McQuire, S. (2016) *Geomedia: Networked Cities and the Future of Public Space*, Cambridge: Polity.

Media Architecture Institute (2015) *About*. Online. Available HTTP: www.mediaarchitecture.org/about/. Accessed 19 February 2017.

Philips (2012) *Press Information*. Online. Available HTTP: www.esbnyc.com/documents/press_releases/2012_05_09_Philips_Press_Release.pdf. Accessed 1 May 2014.

Philips Lighting (2016) *2030: Smart City Life 360 View*. Online. Available HTTP: www.youtube.com/watch?v=A1fcDP8L4gs&linkId=31181870. Accessed 19 February 2017.

Project for Public Spaces (2017) *What is Placemaking?* Online. Available HTTP: www.pps.org/reference/what_is_placemaking/. Accessed 19 February 2017.

Public Visualization Studio (2016) *In the Air, Tonight*. Online. Available HTTP: http://publicvisualizationstudio.co/projects/in-the-air-tonight. Accessed 19 February 2017.

Shades of Our Sisters (2016) *Glowing Red for #MMIW | 11/21/2016–11/23/2016*. Online. Available HTTP: www.blog.shadesofoursisters.com/post/153520700443/glowing-red-for-mmiw-11212016-11232016. Accessed 19 February 2017.

Star, S.L. (1999) 'The Ethnography of Infrastructure', *American Behavioral Scientist*, 43, 377–90.

Stevens, Q. (2007) *The Ludic City: Exploring the Potential of Public Spaces*, New York: Routledge.

Sulcas, R. (2016) 'London Bridges Are Lighting Up', *The New York Times*, 11 November 2016. Online. Available HTTP: www.nytimes.com/2016/11/11/arts/design/london-bridges-illuminated-river.html. Accessed 19 February 2017.

The Illuminated River (2016) *Aims*. Online. Available HTTP: http://illuminatedriver.london/ – _aims, 2016. Accessed 19 February 2017.

Tomitsch, M. (2016) 'Communities, Spectacles and Infrastructures: Three Approaches to Digital Placemaking', in Pop, S., Toft, T., Calvillo, N., and Wright, M. (eds) *What Urban Media Art Can Do: Why When Where & How*, Stuttgart: Avedition, pp. 339–47.

Verhoeff, N. (2012) *Mobile Screens: The Visual Regime of Navigation*, Amsterdam: Amsterdam University Press.

Winner, L. (1980) 'Do Artifacts Have Politics?', *Daedalus*, 109(1), 121–36.

#RyeLights (2017) *#RyeLights*. Online. Available HTTP: www.ryerson.ca/ryelights/. Accessed 19 February 2017.

# 6

# REPRESENTATIONS OF CHINESE CIVILISATION

## Exhibiting Chinese art in Republican China

*Pedith Chan*

### Abstract

This chapter looks at the curatorial arrangements and display methods of the 1935 *Shanghai Preliminary Exhibition of Chinese Art*, exploring how the concept of Chinese art was materialised, visualised, and exhibited. It examines how the first generation of museum professionals adopted newly introduced museum practices from Europe and America to create a visual narrative of Chinese civilisation and a new relationship between viewer and object mediated through the format of exhibition. It argues that despite the fact that the imported methods of display were altered to fit the needs of Chinese art objects, those methods also distorted the original viewing context of the objects. This argument needs to be acknowledged today as we search for modes of display and experience of relevance to the context of China.

### Introduction

Since the late nineteenth and early twentieth centuries in China, exhibition, as a new form of displaying cultural objects, has dominated the public presentation of nation, and has been used as an effective means for the construction of national identity on both local and international stages. The establishment of the Republic of China in 1912 fostered the transformation of the imperial collections of the Qing dynasty (1644–1912) into public national property, and this is perhaps one of the most crucial factors that has contributed to the emergence of an exhibition culture in China. Following the establishment of the Republic and fuelled by the flourishing exhibition culture introduced to China from Europe and America in the late nineteenth century, Chinese objects were reorganised and displayed in several local and overseas exhibitions, becoming a crucial means for cultural propaganda, playing a pivotal role in the construction of national identity, and enabling the dissemination of knowledge of Chinese art both internationally and within modern China.

Among those exhibitions of national treasure, the 1935 *Shanghai Preliminary Exhibition of Chinese Art* (hereinafter *Shanghai Exhibition*) and the 1935 *International Exhibition of Chinese Art* (hereinafter *International Exhibition*) were the most influential and comprehensive in terms of scale and selection of exhibits. As the first state-funded exhibition of Chinese art, the *Shanghai Exhibition* was launched in Shanghai and then travelled to the Royal Academy of Arts in London as the *International Exhibition* in late 1935. This chapter looks at the curatorial arrangements and the displaying methods of the *Shanghai Exhibition*, exploring how the concept of Chinese art was materialised, visualised, and exhibited. It also probes the curatorial rationale with the aim of examining how the first generation of museum professionals adopted newly introduced museum practices from Europe and America in order to create a visual narrative of Chinese civilisation and a new relationship between viewer and object mediated through presentation. It argues that despite the fact that the imported display methods and museum practices were altered to fit the needs of the Chinese art objects, those methods also distorted the original viewing context of the objects and the meanings attached to them, a finding which needs to be acknowledged today as we search for modes of display and experience specific to the context of China.

## From private to public

Introduced at the turn of the twentieth century, by the 1930s exhibitions were still a relatively new practice in China, bringing a new viewing experience to the public in various aspects of society, ranging from retail and education to the art world. As Mayching Kao (1972: 13–14) points out, in the Chinese art world the art exhibition was 'a new product of new era', playing a significant role in promoting art, educating the public and, in the process, democratising access to art and creating a new channel of communication between artists and audiences. The proliferation of art exhibitions, particularly in the 1930s which saw a surge in the number of art exhibitions in China, changed modes of viewing of art objects and the perception of art and Chinese civilisation in general. For the first time, historical objects and collectibles were classified under the category of 'art', being hung on walls or placed inside glass cabinets, displayed for the general public, and viewed by an international audience that was neither the owner of the objects nor had direct or personal connection with them. This was a sea change in the once-intimate relationship between art objects and their owners in imperial China, and it conferred art objects with new identities, bringing them from a private space to the public sphere and producing what Carol Duncan (1995) has described as a new ritualised space, which created new publics, shaped the viewing experience of those publics, and attached new meanings to objects.

In the 1930s and before the launch of the *International Exhibition*, the Royal Academy of Arts in London had organised several spectacular exhibitions on the art of foreign nations, including France, Italy, and Iran. The imperial collection of China had also caught the attention of international experts. In 1932, French Sinologist Paul Pelliot (1878–1945), together with British experts including George Eumorfopoulos and Percival David, proposed to organise an international exhibition of Chinese art in London by borrowing art objects from Chinese museums.[1] Considering it an opportunity to showcase China's glorious past to an international audience, the Nationalist government eventually made a deal with the British experts. However, before shipping the selected art objects to Britain, the Chinese government proposed organising a preliminary exhibition in Shanghai (Anon. 1934: 55–6; Na and Zhuang 2007: 38–9; Liu 2010: 7–8). Though this was not the first time Chinese art objects were displayed in a public space, it was the first large-scale state-funded exhibition which would showcase over 1,000 artefacts drawn mainly from the Palace Museum, a public museum established in 1925 from the royal collection of the Qing dynasty.

In 1934, the Chinese Organising Committee held a meeting in Nanjing, deciding that bronzes, ceramics and paintings were to form the principal exhibits and that, as requested by the British experts, only artefacts produced before 1800 would be sent to London (Anon. 1935b: 25). The selection of art objects was in the hands of a committee of experts from China and Britain, headed by Wang Shijie (1891–1981) (Liu 2010: 7–8; Guo 2011: 86), and it was believed that the purpose of the exhibition would be to demonstrate the grandeur of the Chinese civilisation to a worldwide audience and to garner sympathy and support for China's resistance to Japan, which had been pressing on Chinese territory with its occupation of Manchuria beginning in September 1931. Within this sociopolitical context, the *International Exhibition* was intended to cultivate a love of Chinese cultural heritage and regain China's leading position in Asia and on the international stage. Locally, the intention was to boost and enhance cultural nationalism and patriotism. As a result, the exhibition was targeted not only to a local audience but also an international one. Funded by the state, the project involved a group of intellectuals who believed that the adoption of Euro-American museum standards could modernise the nation and lay the foundation for the development of museum practices in modern China. Due to the lack of a formal exhibition venue for such a large-scale production in Shanghai, the committee decided to install the exhibition in the three-storey Western-style building, the Bank of China, the former German Club. Poy Gum Lee (or Li Jingpei 1900–1968), a renowned architect, was invited to design the exhibition (Anon. 1935a: 10).

The *Shanghai Exhibition* was held between 8 April and 5 May 1935. It achieved unprecedented success, attracting more than 60,000 visitors in its one-month run. It is intriguing that the rhetoric applied to frame the exhibition by Chinese and British experts and critics showed their different views on the Chinese art objects on display. While Western critics called the Chinese objects 'art treasures', Chinese media and experts framed the exhibits as 'national art treasures', with an emphasis on their national representation rather than their status as works of art. The framing of national affiliation suggests a growing conception in China that the artefacts were no longer imperial property but items of a national tradition collectively owned by the public (Guo 2011: 84–5). It also demonstrates how exhibitions on national culture and material objects from the past could be used in the present to generate a national spirit and imagine a new future.

The changing context of the previous royal collection also altered the meanings attached to the Chinese art objects, inevitably dictating the curatorial design of the *Shanghai Exhibition*. As Wang Chen-hua (2009) has argued, the transformation of the imperial collection from private to public property in the museum context changed the classification system employed to organise the royal collections of objects. Previously, the Qing imperial collections were classified and catalogued according to traditional classification systems of collectable or ritual objects, revealing the historical and symbolic meanings and functions attached to the objects.[2] These objects were arranged and displayed according to the physical places with in which they were stored, conferring on them meanings and significance (Wang 2009: 331). For example, the catalogues of painting and calligraphy compiled in the Qing dynasty show that all entries were grouped according to storage buildings. For instance, the portraits of emperors, empresses and sages were displayed and stored in the Hall of Southern Fragrance for ritual purposes, while the most significant calligraphic works by the Wang family were stored and displayed at Emperor Qianlong's residential halls. The objects' functions and significance were related to the physical context (Cheng, 2010: 134–56). However, when the Forbidden Palace of the Qing dynasty was transformed from private to public property, the royal collections underwent restructuring and reorganisation according to the newly introduced museum concept. The new concept of the museum not only conferred a new art status on the Chinese objects, but it also brought in a new way of constructing national history through displaying visual and material objects in public space.

Following the establishment of the first museum in China in 1883, the development of public museums became one of the crucial items in the Chinese government's agenda of nation-building. Supported by the Nationalist government, China underwent the first wave of a museum boom, aiming to showcase its achievements in various aspects of past and present times. In 1914, the Ministry of the Interior opened the Beijing Ancient Relics Exhibition Hall to display more than 70,000 pieces of the imperial collection of the Qing dynasty. By 1921, the Republic of China had 13 museums located in Beijing, Hubei, Shandong, Shanxi, Hebei, Jiangsu, Guangdong, and Yunnan. In 1925, part of the Forbidden City was opened to the public and served as a public museum. By 1937, there were 77 museums, 56 art galleries, and almost 100 repositories in China (Lu 2014: 62–88). In order to professionalise museum practices in China, in 1934 Ma Hen (1881–1955) and Fu Sinian (1896–1950) initiated the establishment of a Museum Association. In May 1935, perhaps catalysed by the organisation of the *Shanghai Exhibition*, the Museum Association of China was established with members from different sectors, including politicians and the cultural elite, such as Fu Sinian and Ye Gongchuo (1881–1968). At its inaugural meeting, four special committees were set up to oversee the following four main areas of museum development:

1 Conducting academic research on museology
2 Improving architectural designs of the museum, its displays and facilities
3 Building up a library of museum studies
4 Organising conferences.

These 'issues of interest' offer a glimpse at the social elite's understanding of the concept of the museum and their determination to impact museum development in modern China. A new word to denote museum (*bowuguan*) was created by combining the three Chinese characters *bo, wu, guan* and proposed for adoption. Both the launch of the Association and the invention of the new term suggest that the concept of museum and public exhibition were regarded as an immediate and important issue to be discussed among intellectuals.

## Systematic organisation of Chinese art objects

As most of the members of the Museum Association were also facilitators of the *Shanghai Exhibition*, such as Ye Gongchuo, Wu Hufan (1894–1968), Xu Beihong (1895–1953), and Deng Yizhe (1892–1973), the organisation of the exhibits and the installation of the Chinese art objects in the *Shanghai Exhibition* reflected to some extent how the first generation of modem intellectuals from different disciplines in China adopted and translated the newly introduced Euro-American museum practices. Ye Gongchuo was a high official of the Nationalist government, a collector, and scholar. Wu was a renowned connoisseur and artist, while Xu and Deng were active artists and art critics. Their views on the exhibition reflect how they adopted the exhibition culture to construct the material history of Chinese civilisation.

Adopting the traditional valuation of collectable objects, the committee divided the exhibits of the *Shanghai Exhibition* into four categories: calligraphy and painting, bronze, ceramics, and crafts, which were then organised for showcasing in seven halls at the Western-style building of China Bank (The Chinese Organising Committee, 1935). As described in great detail in an article published in the magazine *Shishi xunbao* (Anon. 1935b: 25–8), a visiting route was set to guide visitors, and all visitors were required to follow it. The exhibition route suggests a way to read the narrative of Chinese civilisation, starting from the two halls on the ground floor and then five halls on the first floor. On the ground floor there was a waiting room furnished with a folding screen and Qianlong emperor's imperial throne, before which sat a table belonging to Qianlong's minister Liu Yong. On top of the table, a few antiques were displayed (Ahai 1935: 14–15; Yizi 1935: 703–6). Unlike the categories showcased on the first floor, which were organised according to types and medium, the second hall on the ground floor displayed painting and calligraphy from the Ming to Qing dynasties as well as fans, jades, ancient books, and crafts, all clustered in a single room. On the first floor were five halls: one dedicated to calligraphy and painting from the Tang to Yuan dynasties, one for bronze artefacts, two for ceramics, and one for crafts including lacquer wares, jades, and ancient books (Anon. 1935b: 26–7; Ahai 1935: 14–15).

The sequence of the exhibits on the first floor, led by calligraphy, painting, and bronze, suggests the hierarchical order of art objects based on the Chinese traditional valuation of collectable objects. This order showed some slight differences from the printed exhibition catalogues, which organised the exhibits on display into four volumes, namely bronze, ceramics, painting and calligraphy, and crafts (The Chinese Organising Committee 1935). The order of the exhibition catalogue may be due in part to the intention of presenting different groups of objects in chronological order. Bronze was the most important ritual object in the bronze age of China. Pottery and ceramic dominated material culture in ancient China, while painting and calligraphy became the predominant art form and collectable items since the Tang dynasty. In the *Shanghai Exhibition*, however, recognising that the audience was mainly Chinese and so following Chinese tradition, the objects were organised hierarchically based on their perceived artistic value.

In an exhibition review, the author Ahai (1935: 14–18) offers his viewing experience of the exhibition in detail stating, for example, that in the first hall on the first floor, calligraphy and painting were arranged mostly in chronological order, though a few did not follow the rule, while the two halls showcasing ceramics from the Song to Qing dynasties grouped the pieces according to the kilns which produced them. The arrangement clearly illustrated a linear historical development of ceramics in China, from plain and monochrome to colourful and extensively decorated fine porcelains. Interestingly, however, as Fu Zhenlun (1936: 154), a historian and museum expert in Republican China pointed out, in the London exhibition, the British experts' lack of profound understanding of the cultural value of Chinese objects meant that they arranged ceramics from the same period by clustering those with similar colour together. The difference in classification shows two different approaches to arranging art objects, in this case ceramics, with the British looking at the artistic elements of the creation and the Chinese emphasising the source of production and history.

Ahai (1935: 16–17) pointed out that ceramic works were praised as the finest of crafts made in China in the eyes of foreigners, and the *Shanghai Exhibition* provided an invaluable opportunity to let visitors delve into the historical development of the category by juxtaposing representative ceramics from renowned kilns to allow visitors to make comparisons easily. For instance, Ahai stated he would consider a green dragon vase a fake if it were not displayed side by side with other ceramic wares. It was only through the chronological arrangement of the ceramics at the exhibition that Ahai could understand the historical and aesthetic significance as well as the authenticity of the green dragon vase. Ahai's viewing experience clearly shows that the systematic arrangement of the exhibits was well received by the audience, presenting a new perspective to understand the meanings and history of the Chinese objects.

The arrangement of the *Shanghai Exhibition* reflects how the newly introduced concept of the systematic display of art objects was interwoven with Chinese principles in space to tell a larger story of development, laying the foundation for the later production of museum exhibitions on Chinese culture. In the 1930s, museum practitioners were also working to professionalise their area of work. The Museum Association of China published research articles on museology in its periodical *Societal Journal of the Museum Association of China*. Important essays published in the journal at this time and which would have certainly allowed Chinese professionals to gain a better understanding of the curatorial rationale of the *Shanghai Exhibition* included 'On Museum and Nationalism' and 'The Changes in the Arrangement of Exhibits in Euro-American Art Museums' (Wang 1936: 14–6; Li 1935: 1–12).

In the article 'The Changes in the Arrangement of Exhibits in Euro-American Art Museums', the author Li Ruinian (1935: 1) argued that the establishment of museums in Europe and America served two purposes: educating the public about national histories and culture, and encouraging the continuous progression in art and culture. He lamented that despite ongoing museum developments in China, there was no similar institution. Therefore, it was necessary that Chinese museum professionals learn from Euro-American experience regarding organising exhibitions and managing public collections of art objects. With reference to the Euro-American experience in operating museums, Li (1935: 2–7) came up with the following nine exhibition arrangement methods:

1 Displaying all or selected objects together regardless of type or colour, such as the Musée de Louvre's Asian art collection.
2 Displaying objects on different floors: adopted by the Museum of Fine Arts, Boston, the method displays the most important exhibits on the second floor, while other relevant exhibits are on the first and third floors.[3]
3 Chronological order: the Pennsylvania Museum of Arts employs this arrangement as does the Boston Museum. The only difference is that the Pennsylvania Museum displays the important exhibits on the second floor in chronological order.
4 Highlighting important exhibits: in order to attract visitors' attention, selected precious exhibits would be displayed separately from other exhibits to highlight their importance. One gallery at the Fitzwilliam Museum adopted this method. Many museums followed suit, but this method is restricted by a museum's architectural structure.
5 Displaying on rotation basis, derived from the selective displaying method: the Freer Museum and the Musée de Luxembourg employ this method. The exhibits would be changed regularly.
6 Parallel displaying: paintings, sculptures, and crafts were displayed together.
7 Horizontal displaying: the Kunstgewerbe Museum applies this displaying method by grouping objects with similar functions together regardless of their provenance, dates, and quality.
8 Arranging based on artistic association/quality: this is a new curatorial strategy, which groups art objects based on their artistic connection. Museum Folkwang uses this idea to

arrange the exhibits. For instance, Neoclassicism would be put together with art objects from Hellenistic and Roman periods.

9 Encyclopedic arrangement: most history museums and museums of decorative arts adopt this strategy. For instance, the Hermitage Museum uses art objects including paintings, sculptures, and decorative arts as a mirror to reflect the history of French art in the past 300 years.

Li concluded that there were two important achievements in the Euro-American museum industry that the Chinese needed to consider. First, they applied advanced technology, such as lighting and fire prevention systems, to modernise museum facilities. Second, they adopted logical and systematic ways to arrange and display exhibits. These logical and systematic arrangement of exhibitions became the very task to which the museum professionals in modern China would now apply themselves.

Li's article gives us insight into the curatorial rationale of the above styles adopted by the committee of the *Shanghai Exhibition*. Undoubtedly, art objects were divided into four main categories, which were generally arranged in chronological order. The most important categories were located on the second floor. This curatorial logic was clear enough for visitors, such as Ahai, to understand. Unlike in European and American museums, exhibits of Chinese objects were put together based entirely on dates, creating a new way to understand the historical development of Chinese art objects. A visitor to the *Shanghai Exhibition* even exclaimed that he spent over four hours to visit the exhibition and could not help but admire the ancient artists and creators (Ahai 1935: 18). Since then, this systematic arrangement has been adopted by most of the large-scale museums, such as the Shanghai Museum and Palace Museum.

The exhibits on display at the *Shanghai Exhibition* allowed visitors the opportunity to make visual and conceptual connections between artistic traditions as well as with the past. The systematic arrangement of exhibitions became a new mode of displaying Chinese art objects and was well appreciated by visitors. For instance, a review of exhibitions held at the newly established Shanghai Museum in 1936 vividly describes the impact of the systematic display on the viewers. The author stated that when he saw the stone tools, he thought of the barbaric customs of the Neolithic people, while ancient paintings gave him a fuller understanding of the ranking system of paintings described in historical documents. The viewing experience could connect visitors to historical documents, so as to get a fuller understanding of the merits of works of art described in ancient texts. He emphasised that the systematic arrangement of the exhibits, the beautiful design of the exhibition halls, and the informative captions all offered an imaginative power to visitors through viewing (Anon. 1936: 10).

## Exhibiting Chinese civilisation

Although exhibitions were introduced only in the early twentieth century, displaying cultural objects is not a new practice in China. As discussed in Craig Clunas's *Superfluous Things* (2004: 40–74), the relationship between the owner and collectable objects was very intimate and interactive in Ming China, and this relationship determined the way of viewing as well as the physical context of displaying. The following discussion shifts from the subject of curatorial arrangement to the physical context in which art objects were viewed in Republican China, with the purpose of looking at how the new way of displaying art objects altered viewing practices and removed the indexical signs attached to the Chinese art objects.

As mentioned, although viewing cultural objects has a long history in China, it was not until the late nineteenth and early twentieth centuries that this practice was brought from the private space to the public domain. In the late nineteenth century, the Qing government actively participated in international expositions to present Chinese objects at the China pavilion through the format of exhibition. Within the limited space, selected cultural pieces, including art objects and commodities made in China, were showcased on stands or in glass cabinets. For instance, at the 1893 Chicago World's Fair, the 1905 St Louis World's Fair, and the 1915 Panama World's Fair, ceramics and refined crafts were displayed on stands, and Chinese-style glass cabinets and paintings were hung on walls, framed and mounted as Western-style paintings. The practice of displaying objects in glass cabinets was adopted immediately by different sectors in modern China. For instance, commodities were grouped and placed inside glass cabinets in the retail industry. Displaying (*chenlie*) became a fashionable marketing strategy not only in the commercial sector but also in academic and cultural sectors, creating a new and direct relationship between objects and viewers.

The *Shanghai Exhibition* is a case in point for showing how Chinese art objects were installed in the 1930s by following the newly introduced museum practices and displaying culture. As described by a visitor in an exhibition review published in the magazine *Shishi xunbao* (Anon. 1935b: 25–7), the setting of the exhibition was well planned. At the entrance a yellow banner with the title written in green was hung over the door (Figure 6.1). For the Chinese visitors, the colours denoted imperial ownership of the art objects on display, because yellow and green were restricted for use by the emperor in imperial China. The visitors would then enter the antechamber where painting catalogues published by the Palace Museum and other relevant books were on display. Behind the antechamber was an exhibition hall where ancient paintings and embroideries were showcased in cabinets and hung on copper rails. To avoid overweighting of the copper rails, the paintings mounted in the format of hanging scrolls were suspended by ribbons to tie the scroll ends. On the first floor, copper glass cabinets were used to showcase bronze wares, jades, fans, ceramics, and so on. Bilingual captions were placed alongside the exhibits in which the details of the artefacts were provided, such as date, artist, title, and provenance. Together with the informative bilingual catalogues published by the Chinese Organising Committee, visitors could get a comprehensive and fuller understanding of the historical development and cultural values of the national treasures. Since the paintings and calligraphy were not framed, wooden railings were placed on the floor to set the distance between the viewers and the exhibits for security purposes (Anon. 1935b: 27).

The installation methods of Chinese objects employed offer a trace of the connection between the displaying practices adopted by Chinese pavilions in the world fairs. In the world fairs, the Chinese organisers showcased Chinese objects by installing the objects on walls, stands or cabinets within a well-designed physical context with distinctive Chinese characteristics. For instance, paintings were hung densely on walls while three-dimensional objects were put inside glass cabinets. Signs of 'Chineseness' were suggested by decorative motifs, such as typical Chinese-style stands. The designs and installations of the world's fairs were appropriated in the exhibition culture and museum context in the 1920s. For instance, the History Museum of China used a tailor-made Chinese-style cabinet to display crafts. Objects, particularly three-dimensional art objects such as bronze and ceramic works, were protected and displayed in cabinets for both viewing and security purposes. The *Shanghai Exhibition* adopted the prevailing installation methods to hang paintings and calligraphy on walls and showcase bronze and ceramic works inside glass cabinets. Tailor-made display cabinets were manufactured in China and the cabinets for bronze objects were decorated with a cloud-like pattern – a typical Chinese decorative motif (Anon. 1935d: 11).

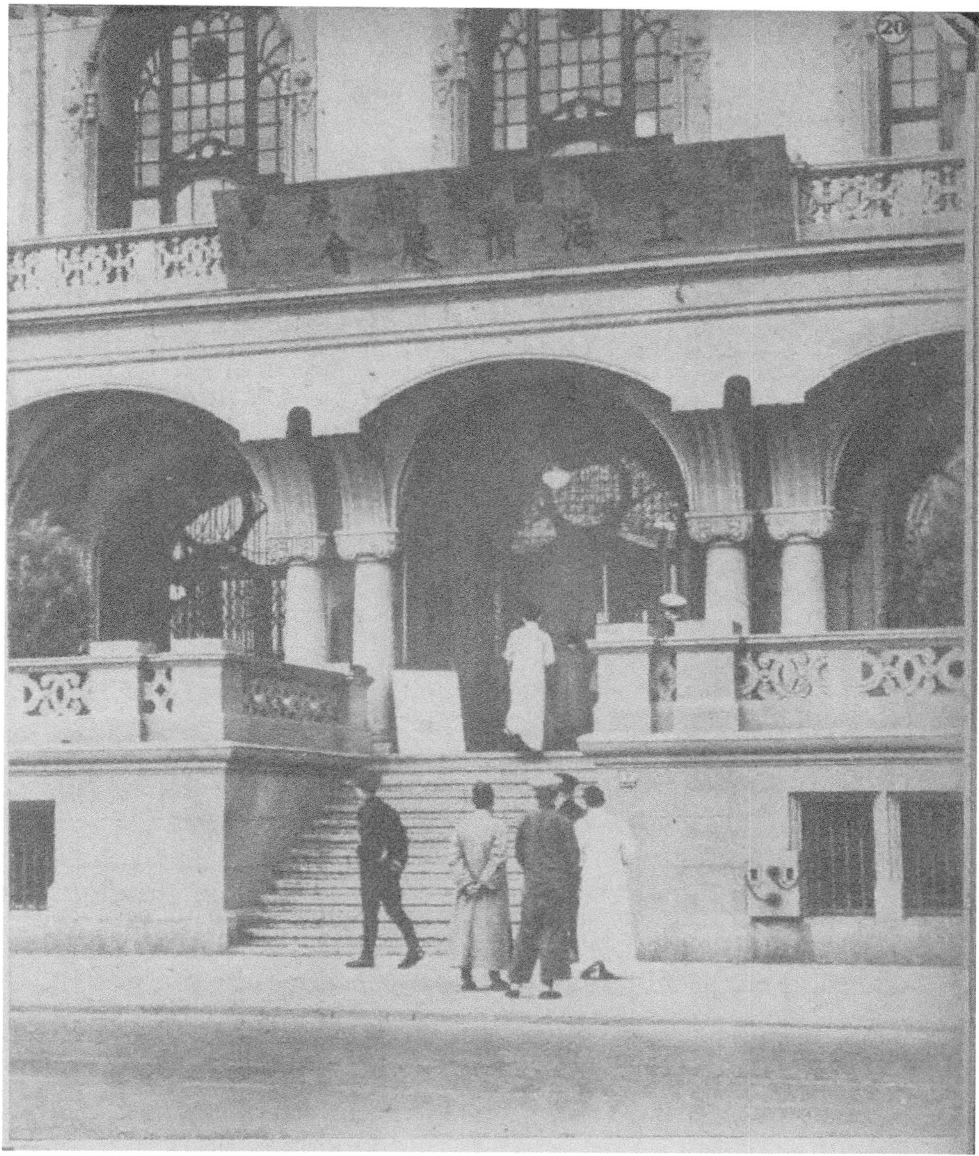

**FIGURE 6.1** The entrance of the *Shanghai Exhibition* (1935), *Zhonghua*

*Photo:* Quan Guo Bao Kan Suo Yin (CNBKSY)

Interestingly, the *Shanghai Exhibition* installed fans as three-dimensional objects and displayed them inside glass cabinets (Figure 6.2). In the early twentieth century, when exhibition culture was ubiquitously permeating society, fan-painting exhibitions flourished, particularly in the summer when the art form was in high demand. For instance, the Women's Art Association's exhibition placed a table to display fan paintings. An exhibition on fan painting even tried to appropriate a Western-style display by hanging fans on the wall in imitation of the

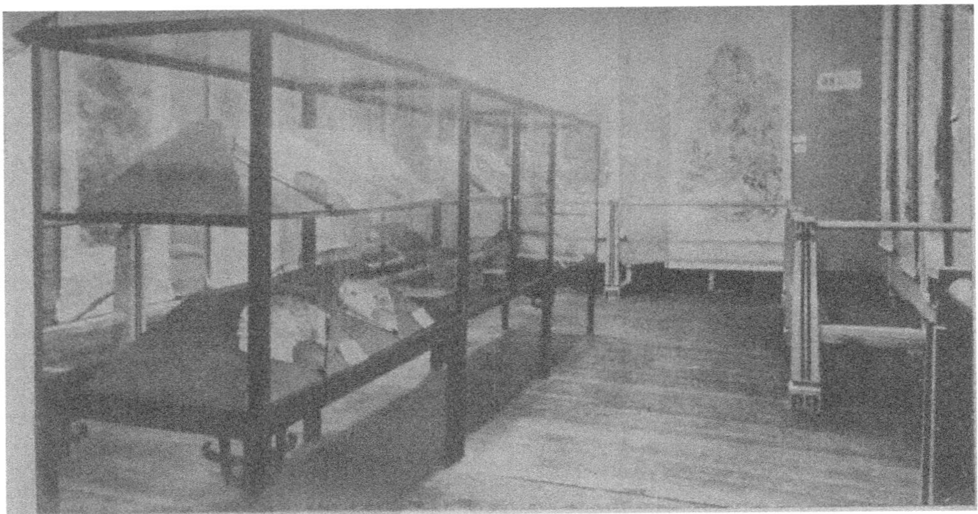

**FIGURE 6.2** A view of the fan paintings displayed at the *Shanghai Exhibition* (1935), *Zhonghua*

*Photo:* Quan Guo Bao Kan Suo Yin (CNBKSY)

mounting of oil paintings in Europe. Among these installation variations, the Committee of the *Shanghai Exhibition* chose to display fan paintings in cabinets.

Regarding hanging scrolls and handscrolls, formats particular in Chinese art, the Chinese Organising Committee decided to mount the hanging scrolls on the wall with an interval between each painting, while displaying the handscrolls on tables (Figure 6.3). It is interesting to note that the handscroll by Wang Ximeng was displayed differently in China and Britain. While a visitor complained that only a section of the handscroll by Wang Ximeng was opened at the *Shanghai Exhibition*, a visitor praised the British installation of the same handscroll, which was opened completely (Fu 1936: 153; Anon. 1935c: 155). The differences in the way of showing the handscrolls may reflect the fact that the British experts considered the scroll as an artwork, and thus thought it should be opened completely to show its artistic merits. However, for the Chinese experts, the handscroll was a national treasure that should thus be viewed by following the traditional viewing practice, namely, allowing the reader to view it section by section in a close and intimate setting.

This cultural difference is also evident in the installation of hanging scrolls. While hanging scrolls were suspended on copper rails in the Shanghai exhibition, the British experts framed and hung them on the wall. Obviously, the historically established format determined the way to install hanging scrolls in the *Shanghai Exhibition*. By looking at the visual documents of the Ming and Qing dynasty, it is not hard to find that hanging scrolls were hung in the central position of the room and were usually flanked by a pair of calligraphic works. In this regard, only a single or a few paintings were displayed in a private domestic context, so the format of hanging scrolls was designed purposely to fit the environment.

Another example is a painting titled *The Eighteen Scholars* from the Ming dynasty that depicts an elegant gathering in which a group of men of letters is viewing and appreciating a hanging scroll within an intimate distance. These examples show that the viewing context

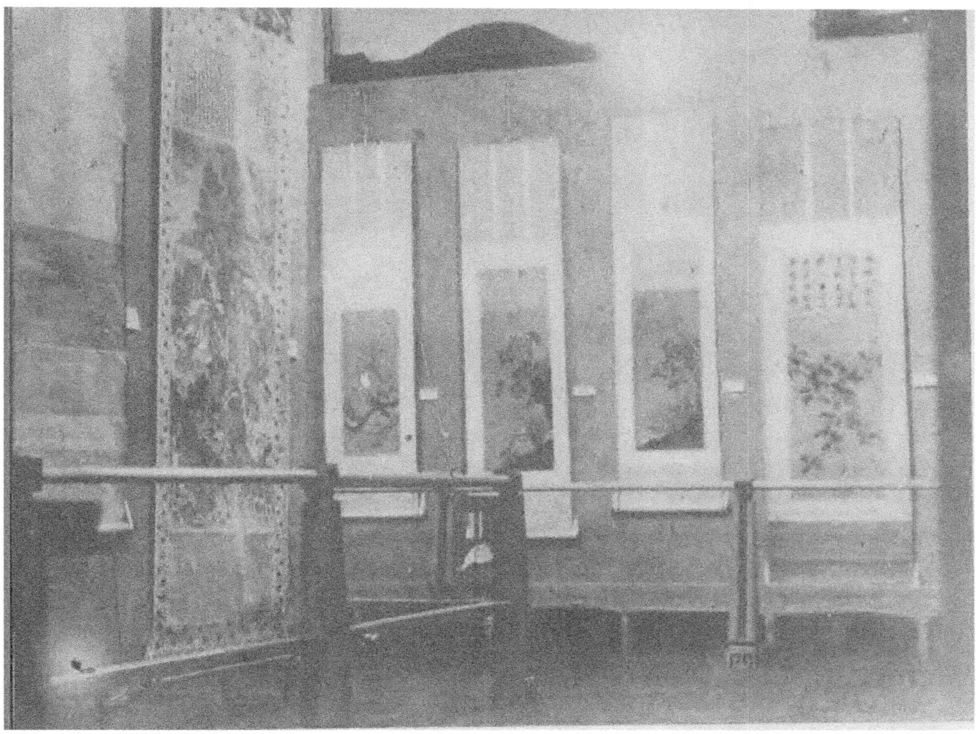

**FIGURE 6.3** A view of the exhibition hall of calligraphy and painting on the first floor, the *Shanghai Exhibition* (1935), *Shenbao yuekan*

*Photo:* Quan Guo Bao Kan SuoYin (CNBKSY)

has been changed from private to public, and from an intimate distance to a standardised distance set by museum experts, as was the complaint of a visitor at the *Shanghai Exhibition*, indicating the work was too far away to see the painting's details (Ahai 1935: 15). This newly suggested distance between the art objects and the audience to some extent altered the traditional viewing habit of Chinese painting, inevitably changing the meanings attached to the objects. In traditional practice, the intimate distance of viewing allows the audience to appreciate the details of the brushwork of a painting, which somehow dictates the artistic style of Chinese paintings with emphasis on nuanced details of the artistic language. As such, the new exhibiting practice to a large degree has offered a new distance that hinders the interpretation of the paintings, yet democratised the accessibility of Chinese painting and calligraphy as well as the viewing experience of the public.

If the viewing context of scrolls was altered in the exhibition context, the method for installing bronze objects changed the status of exhibits from ritual to secular. Bronze objects have been used as ritual vessels since the Shang dynasty, and hence were collected by those who possessed political power and wealth and consequently displayed them in a ritual context. In the Qing dynasty a considerable number of scholars collected and conducted research on bronze objects. They organised gatherings to display and appreciate the bronze objects together with like-minded friends. In this context, the audience was knowledgeable enough to understand the political and cultural value attached to the bronze objects (Brown 2011: 51–72). However, in the new exhibition context, the bronze objects were shown in a public space to the general public who might not have adequate knowledge about them. In this regard, to preserve the ritual value of the bronze objects, in the early twentieth century, some of these ritual objects were installed in a constructed ritual context with an attempt to help the audience to get a better understanding of their ritual and cultural meanings. For instance, an old photograph shows that a set of bronze objects were placed on an altar in front of a temple in Beijing in 1915. The religious context confers ritual value to the bronze objects (Figure 6.4). Similarly, the History Museum of China applied tailor-made display stands with a temple-like structure at the top to showcase bronze objects (Figure 6.5). As mentioned by a visitor to the History Museum of China, a pair of imperial jade seals was installed inside a tailor-made small pavilion, which illuminates the superiority of the objects (Du 1926: 75–6). However, in the *Shanghai Exhibition*, simple standardised museum cabinets and stands were used to display small and large bronze objects, respectively, which somehow removed their superior status. Only the sequence of the different categories provided a mechanism to illustrate their importance.

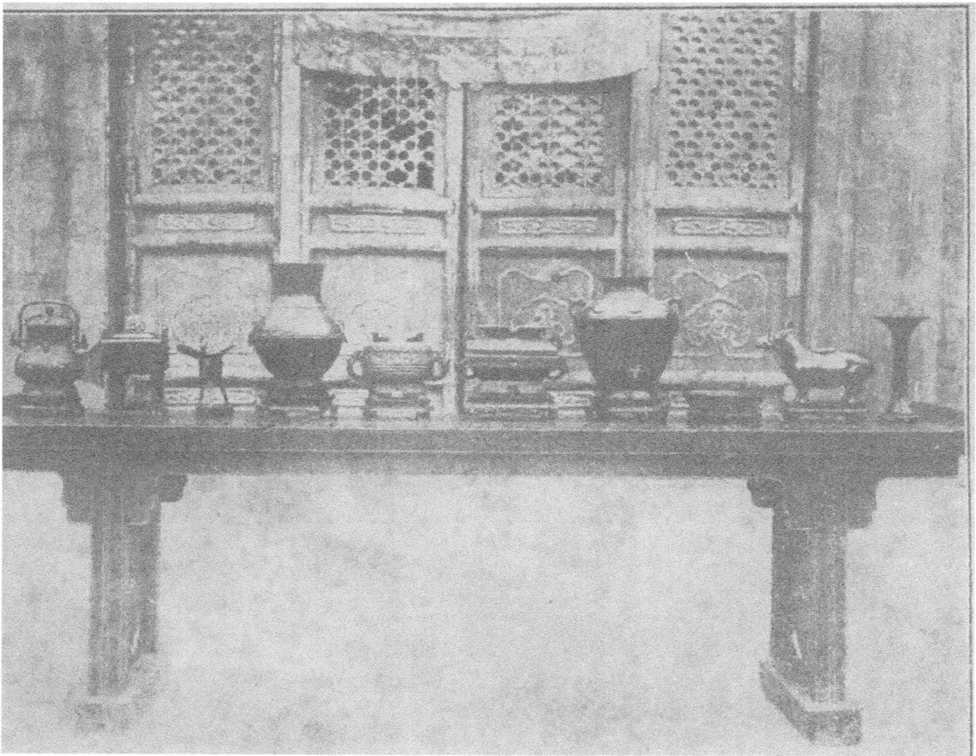

**FIGURE 6.4** A set of bronze objects displayed at a temple in Beijing in 1915 (1915), *Dongfang zashi*
*Photo:* Quan Guo Bao Kan Suo Yin (CNBKSY)

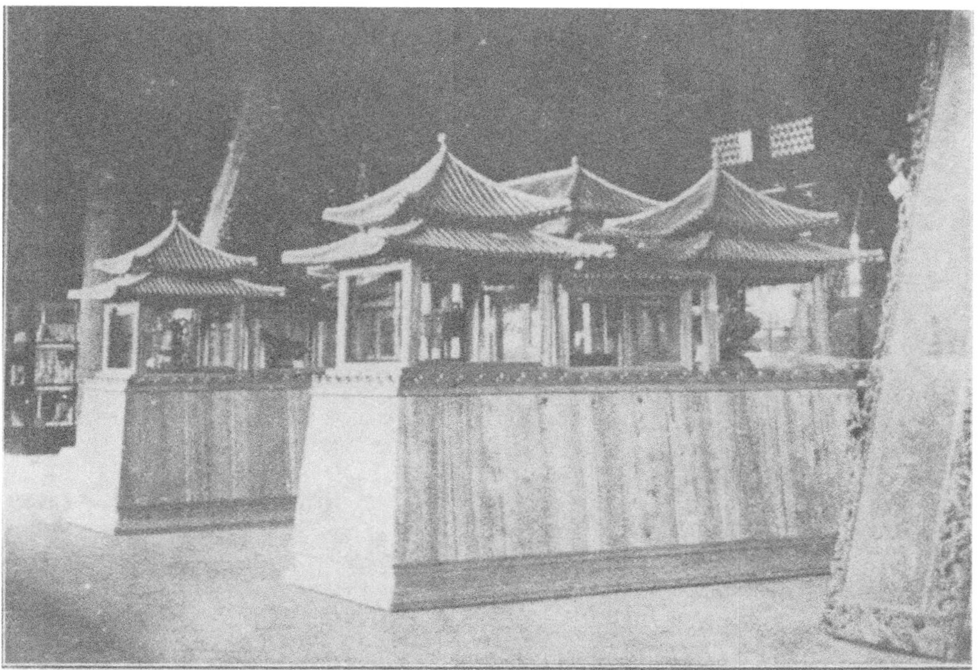

**FIGURE 6.5** Bronze objects were installed inside tailor-made temple-like stands at the History Museum of China (1927), *Guoli lishi bowuguang*

*Photo:* Quan Guo Bao Kan SuoYin (CNBKSY)

## Conclusion

The *Shanghai Exhibition* was incredibly well received and the exhibits were then shipped to London. Together with thousands of exhibits drawn from some 240 collections around the world, the *International Exhibition* was launched in London. Upon completion of the London exhibition, the Chinese national treasures were returned to China ready for an exhibition in Nanjing. The design and arrangement of the Nanjing exhibition was similar to the *Shanghai Exhibition*, dividing the art objects into four main categories, leading by the category of painting and calligraphy at seven exhibition halls, but a new exhibition hall was added to display photographs of the London exhibition (Chen 2003: 68–9).

The design and installation of the *Shanghai Exhibition* demonstrates how the newly introduced museum practices created a new viewing experience in China. These observations advance our understanding of the historical development of museum practices and exhibition culture in modern China. Applying a systematic arrangement and new installation of Chinese art objects, the Chinese Organising Committee of the exhibition offered an exemplified model to narrate Chinese civilisation, aspiring to professionalise museum practices in modern China. In the process of the transformation of the collectable objects from private ownership to public property, from displaying in private space to public domain, a new set of values was attached to the Chinese objects and a novel viewing experience of cultural artefacts was cultivated through the format of exhibition. Whilst all of these forms of viewing and exhibiting are located in time and place, a deeper understanding of where ideas about exhibition in China come from also opens up questions about the future of museum design and the potential for new ways of conceptualising, displaying and experiencing in museums fit for present-day China.

## Acknowledgements

I would like to thank Suzanne MacLeod, Vivian Ting, Eileen Lam, Yu-jen Liu and the anonymous reviewers for their helpful suggestions and comments, and the generous support from the Research Grants Council of the Hong Kong SAR, China (Project No. 154712) and the Shanghai Library.

## Notes

1 Established museums in China included the Palace Museum (1925), the National Museum (1914), the Academia Sinica (1928), the Henan Museum (1928), the Beijing Library (1909), and the Anhui Provincial Library (1913). Before launching the *International Exhibition of Chinese Art*, Chinese art experts in Europe had organised a few exhibitions on Chinese art. Those organisers, such as George Eumorfopoulos (1863–1939), Sir Percival David (1892–1964), Otto Kummel (1874–1964), and Robert Lockhar Hobson (1872–1941), had played significant roles in the development of the International Exhibition of Chinese Art. For more detail see Steuber (2006).

2 According the Qing catalogues of collectable objects, there were three main categories, including calligraphy and painting; ritual objects including bronze vessels, ceremonial attire, and cosmological apparatus; ink stones and historical currencies.

3 In Europe the second floor would be described as the first floor, the first floor would be described as the ground floor, and the third floor would be described as the second floor.

## References

Ahai (1935) 'Canguan lundun zhongguo yishu yuzhanhui guilai', *Tongxing yuekan*, 3(5), pp. 14–18.

Anon. (1934) 'Choubei zhong zhi lundun zhongguo yizhan', *Jiaoyu zhoukan*, 210–11, pp. 55–6.

Anon. (1935a) 'Canjia lundun yizhan guwu ding xiayue zhongxun xianxing zhanlan', *Shenbao*, 22 February 1935, p. 10.

Anon. (1935b) 'Lundun zhongguo yizhan shanghai yuzhan kaimu', *Shishi xunbao*, 29, pp. 25–8.

Anon. (1935c) 'Lundun zhongguo yishu zhanlanhui shanghai yuzhanhui', *Xueshu shijie*, 1(1), pp. 154–6.

Anon. (1935d) 'Yizhan yuzhanhui kaimuqi shangweiding', *Shenbao*, 13 March 1935, p. 11.

Anon. (1936) 'Xingjiang kaimu zhi shanghai bowuguan', *Liangyou*, 120, pp. 10–11.

Brown, S.J. (2011) *Pastimes: From Art and Antiquarianism to Modern Chinese Historiography*, Honolulu: University of Hawaii Press.

Chen, J.N. (2003) 'Hongdong ouzhou de zhongguo guobao zhan ji qi fengbo', *Dangan yu shixue*, 3, pp. 67–9.

Cheng, Y.W. (2010) *Tradition and Transformation: Cataloguing Chinese Art in the Middle and Late Imperial Eras*, Dissertation, University of Pennsylvania.

Clunas, C. (2004) *Superfluous Things: Material Culture and Social Status in Early Modern China*, Honolulu: University of Hawaii Press.

Du, J.D. (1926) 'Canguan lishi bowuguan ji', *Xuesheng zazhi*, 13(12), pp. 74–80.

Duncan, C. (1995) *Civilizing Rituals: Inside Public Art Museums*, London: Routledge.

Fu, Z.L. (1936) 'Zhongguo yishu guoji zhanlanhui can guanji', *Guoli beiping gugong bowuyuan niankan*, pp. 137–68.

Guo, H. (2011) 'Guobao zhilu: 1935–1936 nian lundun zhongguo yishu guoji zhanlanhui ji qi shanghai yuzhan', *Museum International*, 249, pp. 84–91.

Kao, M. (1972) *China's Response to the West in Art: 1898–1937*, Dissertation, Stanford University.

Li, R.N. (1935) 'Oumei bowuguan ji meishuguan chenliefa zhi yanjin', *Zhongguo bowuguan xiehui huibao*, 1(2), pp. 1–12.

Liu, N.N. (2010) 'Beijing gugong bowuyuan canjia lundun zhongguo yishu guoji zhanlanhui shiliao xuanji', *Minguo dangan*, 3, pp. 6–14.Lu, T. (2014) *Museums in China: Materialized Power and Objectified Identities*, London: Routledge.

Na, Z.L. and Zhuang, Y. (2007) 'Zao guonan yu Zhan guobao: 1935 nian lundun yizhan qinli', *Zijincheng*, 3, pp. 32–52.

The Chinese Organising Committee (ed.) (1935) *Illustrated Catalogue of Chinese Government Exhibits for the International Exhibition of Chinese Art in London*, Nanjing: The Chinese Organising Committee.

Wang, C.H. (2009) 'The Qing Imperial Collection, Circa 1905–25: National Humiliation, Heritage Preservation, and Exhibition Culture', in Wu, H. (ed.) *Reinventing the Past: Archaism and Antiquarianism in Chinese Art and Visual Culture*, Chicago: Harvard University, pp. 320–41.

Wang, Y.Q. (1936) 'Bowuguan yu minzu fuxing', *Zhongguo bowuguan xiehui huibao*, 2(1), pp. 14–16.

Yizi (1935) 'Lundun zhongguo yishu zhanlan: Shanghai yuzhanhui canguanji', *Xinren zhoukan*, 1(35), pp. 703–7.

# 7

# THE MUSEUM AND MULTIVALENCES OF PLACE

*Laura Hourston Hanks*

## Abstract

This chapter contends that an increasing exploration and privileging of *place* may well define one future direction in the making of museums and galleries, and it aims to explore current practice of such *enhanced situatedness* through a range of contemporary British architectural-exhibition designs. Narratives deployed by the design teams will be critiqued, particularly in respect to the notion of multivalency – having or being susceptible of many applications, interpretations, meanings or values. In particular, the chapter will differentiate between a *heterogeneous* mode of place multivalency, compared with an *integrated* approach, exploring the potential of these different applications in the experiences of diverse visitors.

## Introduction

> Museums and galleries, of course, no longer shun the outside world, the contingencies of its light and life.
>
> *(Caiger-Smith 2011: 38)*

Recent significant shifts in the political sphere are prompting the reframing of personal place identities. At a 'meta' scale, political events – most notably the referendum vote for Britain to leave the European Union and the subsequent triggering of Article 50, along with the US election victory for a 'populist' and protectionist administration – have been seen by many critics as challenges to the pervasiveness of globalisation and decades of dominance of centrist politics. These events have questioned long-standing national and international alliances and identities, and in so doing have set in train the entrenchment or reimagining of personal place identities. With the increasing questioning and potential fragmentation, or even dissolution, of supranational organisations, the national and local appear to be gaining ground, as evidenced by the Scottish Parliament's March 2017 majority motion giving the first minister authority to approach the UK government to request a new independence referendum. Within this fluctuating landscape, place and identities of place are taking on greater significance, and as a result the museum visitor may be attempting to re-assimilate their own biographical connections to and understandings of place. This chapter explores the possibility that an increasing exploration and privileging of *place* may define one future direction in the making of museums and galleries. Could such foregrounding of place identity and experience in museums be seen as a reaction to current pressures on visitors' own sense of geographical and cultural belonging?

This projected privileging of place would naturally lead to a greater degree of cultural specificity within the museum/gallery. The reassuringly familiar and inherently placeless 'pan-national' white/black box museum model has become increasingly scrutinized, with a concomitant intensified attention to *sitedness* in museum and exhibition design. As a litmus test of cultural consciousness, the museum is uniquely positioned, providing encounters with the unique object, the reality of its physical context, and with the people of that place and far beyond. Moving forward the visitor may be more attracted to a distinct experience of place in the museum, and in turn may be more engaged and even challenged by it.

As museum design evolves in the twenty-first century and museums and galleries often strive to make distinct offers to their visiting publics, audience experience may be increasingly inspired by *place identity*. Interpretive designers are being charged with an amplified social responsibility – to curate and enhance the 'site' of the museum in order to create both connections and collisions with visitors' own personal place identity constructs. This chapter aims to explore current practice of such *enhanced situatedness* through a range of contemporary British architectural exhibition designs: the Novium, Chichester; the Pier Arts Centre, Orkney; Nottingham Contemporary; and Turner Contemporary, Margate. Although these cases vary between complete new-builds, a new-build housing archaeological remains, and an extension to existing historic structures, all are significant museum or gallery commissions completed within the UK within the last decade and a half. They all demonstrate the conscious engagement with site propounded, and the possibilities and pitfalls for designers and the museum-visiting public of this enhanced situatedness both now and into the future.

Revealed and constructed narratives deployed by the design teams will be critiqued, particularly in respect to the notion of multivalency. Multivalent approaches are those having or being susceptible of many applications, interpretations, meanings or values, wherein, it may be argued, lie both their strengths and weaknesses. A number of affective moments of cross-scale, empathetic and sometimes multimedia narrative encounters with place will be interrogated to better understand their emotional and intellectual holds and to address their inherent dangers. Through scrutiny of the material 'stuff' of the place, the chapter will assess the various meanings, values and appeals – or *multivalences* – of place in these cases, and will consider the future directions and usefulness of such a sited approach to exhibition and museum making. It will be questioned how this approach can challenge and satisfy contemporary audiences, and remain relevant and revealing into the future. In particular, the chapter will differentiate between a *heterogeneous* mode of place multivalency and an *integrated* approach. Here, the former heterogeneous mode is shown to exhibit a number of independent, distinct responses to place at a series of bounded physical (and interpretive) locations across the site of the museum/gallery. Meanwhile, the latter, integrated, approach concerns itself with a single site vested with multiple or layered place meanings and interpretations. Overall, the chapter aims to expose and elucidate these strategic responses to place, and to point to their increasing potential in future museum and gallery making.

## Multivalency of place: a heterogeneous approach

A heterogeneous approach to multivalency of place is in evidence at two contemporary projects at either end of the British Isles: the Novium Museum in Chichester, West Sussex, and the Pier Arts Centre in Stromness, Orkney. The creative production of these independent moments, with their embedded memories, contemporary meanings and implicit guides to future practice, will be explored.

The Novium Museum, which opened in 2012, demonstrates a strong connection to its place in distinct ways at different points on the visitor journey. It is grounded in its context through the adoption of different, largely discrete, narrative approaches in different locations and galleries. The museum, sited in the heart of both Roman and twenty-first-century Chichester, has the remit to explore the history, people and places of Chichester and the surrounding district, and it provokes conversations across time and space between the museum building as artefact, the wider urban context and the many communities engaged with the museum. Keith Williams Architects chose to deploy a range of associative references, both constructed and construed, in an attempt to portray the story of Chichester's built heritage and lived experience through their design. Three rich extant buildings on or near the museum site form the basis of this approach.

Externally, on the museum's Tower Street façade, the architectural referencing of the cathedral's bell tower is most apparent. The bell tower, which terminates the southern vista of the street, has its origins in the fifteenth century and is the only extant separate bell tower in any English cathedral. The Novium's design clearly references this bell tower structure, with a taller extruded element to the north of the museum (Figure 7.1), the correspondence being emphasised by the layered façade, protruding at second floor tower level and in a frame around the entrance portal, but recessed elsewhere to create contrast and articulation of parts to whole; the dark strip glazing at first floor level below the tower; and the vertical slit window on the tower's street façade. However, the tower form is as concerned with proclaiming itself as deferring to its surroundings: '[a]t its northern end, the museum's main elevation incorporates a cubic turret to introduce variety and accent to the street scene and to announce the museum to both West Street and the approach from the city walls to the north' (Williams 2009: 145). A challenge with such referencing, largely met here, is to avoid a stultifying replay of past forms, and to instead see 'the museum itself [as] an artifact whose history can be read, provoking new institutional and urban narratives that evoke relationships between the past, present and future' (Norrie 2013: 137). Multiple design moves have been incorporated to make a single reference to a single form: the bell tower. As a centuries-old civic landmark, the bell tower is a part of the cognitive make-up or mental mapping of Chichester's residents, and an important physical and intellectual wayfinding monument for visitors (Lynch 1960: 78–82). Its referencing speaks to both these constituencies: drawing on the former's biographical memories and hence identity, and the latter's openness to new intellectual and visual stimuli, or 'information' (Prak 1977: 15).

The next location of interest in this heterogeneous approach to place apparent at the Novium is the main Roman bathhouse exhibition space. The unexpected discovery of extensive Roman remains beneath a car park in 1974 led to the conception of the museum and its eventual opening 38 years later. The museum building straddles a sizeable existent portion of a 1,300-square-metre Roman bathhouse complex, clearly visible in a deep archaeological pit, 'which now reveals the Roman remains, 1.5 metres below street level, enclosed by glass cases holding the bits and bobs dropped by the last bathers almost 2,000 years ago:

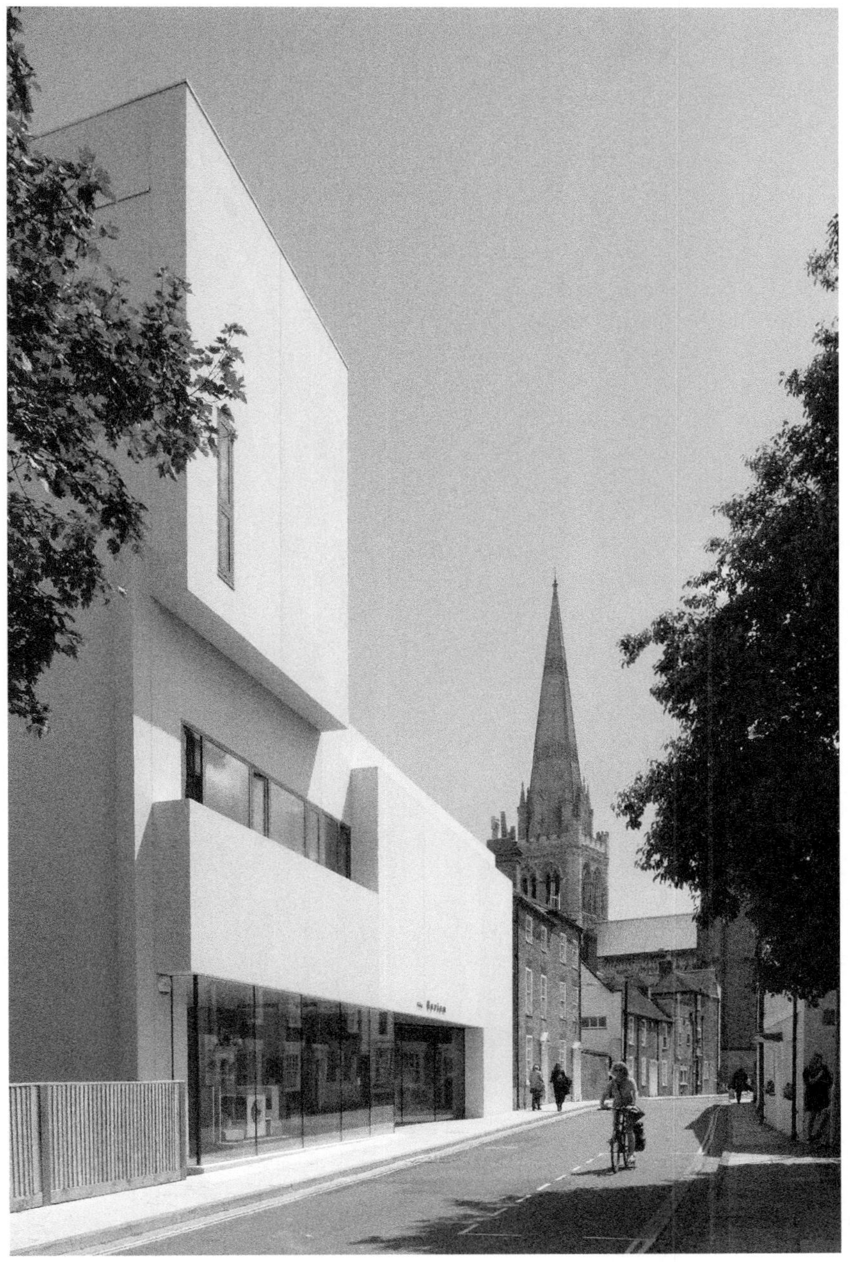

**FIGURE 7.1** The Novium Chichester's reconstituted stone-clad entry façade with distinctive tower element, by Keith Williams Architects

*Photo:* ACT 124 distributed under a CC-BY-SA-4.0 license

dress pins, ointment and oil jars, a regimental badge' (Kennedy 2012). The presence of these archaeological remains is congruent with the museum's overall objective to tell the story of Chichester and its people over the past 500,000 years, and self-evidently informed Keith Williams Architects' structural and overall design response, with the authentic materiality of the site connecting directly to its past narratives. Without interpretation, however, the remains are largely mute to the non-expert – creating a visitor experience akin, in Sverre Fehn's terms, to 'a dance around dead things' (Fehn 1992: 160).

So the design team incorporated a series of interpretive layers to reveal the past lives of the site. One element was a film projected onto the concrete back wall of the gallery space, which attempts to 'recreat[e] the glory days, when the city was an important and wealthy Roman base, with fountains, marble columns, statues and frescos' (Kennedy 2012: 2). Its mix of objective architectural information with reenactments of life in the Roman bathhouse allows the visitor direct insight to a particular projection of the narrative of life in the place, and encourages empathic connections, particularly between residents past and present. However, the familiarity of the Romans and their social life to contemporary audiences, as well as their wide geographic influence, also connects visitors from far beyond the city and region to the displays. Indeed, this portrayal of the city's former immigrants may resonate with contemporary immigrants.

The introduction of a dramatic narrative inevitably produces a more bounded experience, potentially less multiple and stimulating of the imagination. Supplementing this digital layer are the Roman artefacts themselves: many were found during excavation of the site, so they demonstrate a congruence or sameness between place and exhibition content. They are displayed in glass cases adjacent to the glazed banister overlooking the bathhouse remains, with the interpretative film playing in the background, thereby achieving a strong and internally integrated – if single-themed – relation to place. The overlaying of personal artefacts with in-situ structure and social dramatisation provides a compelling sited social agenda, connecting to the personal, civic and social identities of the twenty-first-century onlookers.

As its name implies, the 'Cathedral View' gallery on the museum's second floor similarly draws on the form of a specific surrounding historic building, Chichester Cathedral, again incorporating museum artefacts and interpretive layers. The cathedral on the skyline acts as exhibition artefact, given particular expression through a range of interpretive strategies. Via the glazed light box design, the cathedral is drawn into the narrative of the museum and the visitor becomes the assimilator of this urban display. As Giebelhausen asserts, albeit in a different context:

> the panoramic view furnishes a more detached and picturesque perception that turns the city itself into an exhibit to be consumed visually and from a distance. This perspective renders the viewer at once a reader and godlike: according to Michel de Certeau, '[i]t transforms the bewitching world by which one was "possessed" into a text that lies before one's eyes'.
>
> *(Giebelhausen 2003: 9)*

Indeed the best architect-curators are always attempting to set scenes, as at Carlo Scarpa's Castellvecchio, where '[t]he placing of the monument (Cangrande) was a fine example of one of the basic principles of the architect's museological work: the inseparable nature of the architecture and the staging' (Beltraimi and Zannier 2006: 14). Here in Chichester it is the city's key iconic monument which is being staged, ensuring a bond between the Novium and *Noviomagus Reginorum*,[1] and encouraging audience reflections on the power of place and belonging: 'Views through and beyond the building create shifting relationships of adjacency and scale that reinforce the dynamic relationship between movement and visual spectacle, creating ambiguity between the inside and outside and the museum and the city' (Norrie 2013: 173).

The methods of interpretation are multiple. An audio narration focuses primarily on Chichester Cathedral's medieval and modern history, encouraging the visitor to rest on the benches provided and drawing their gaze out into the city and story beyond the confines of the museum. Through this actual and imaginary gaze, the physical and conceptual gaps between the Novium and the city which it is 'curating' are narrowed, as is that between the contemporary audience and the former 'actors' on the city's stage. Another interpretive expression is simple, yet effective: the designers applied a transparent film with sketched silhouette of the cathedral to the glazing of this light-box viewing gallery in an attempt to create a dialogue between inside and out, institution and urban realm, museum and city, and present/future audiences with past residents, in order to re-contextualise the museum's collections in light of the surrounding civic context. Comparisons here abound, to Surrealism and Mannerism, the latter of which is not new to the work of Keith Williams. Indeed Kenneth Powell writes of the architect's 'mannerist leanings', and the shifting perspectives and plays of parallax here when trying to line up the real and the representational are a demonstration of this tendency (Powell in Williams 2009: 14). Here the visitor is encouraged to seek multiple physical, ocular perspectives, but cognitively the landscape is somewhat static, and in terms of a multivalency of applications, interpretations, meanings and values, the display appears to be finite.

A last interpretive strategy of *spoliation* sees the display of fragments. A range of masonry fragments, tiles, and other architectural elements from the cathedral precinct are displayed on the east wall facing the stairs, creating a high degree of coalescence between museum content, civic context and the critical interpretation. Most of the fragments are displayed in a similar orientation to their original positioning, strengthening this integration or lack of interpretive barrier, creating a dialogue across interior and exterior space. Against the west wall are a series of decorative chimney pots: with the sacred facing the secular; the civic, the domestic. The everyday here acts as a common lived entry point for visitors to the grander, civic narrative evoked by the cathedral. Despite this foray into life beyond the cathedral, the story here again is largely discrete and autonomous, fitting with the heterogeneous model of place experience.

The multivalency of approach at the Novium could be described as heterogeneous, as different moments of the visitor journey have individual, distinct relations or connections to place. In each instance, it is an extant historic monument which forms the subject (or object) of the connection: the bell tower and Chichester Cathedral remote from the site; and the Roman bathhouse located within the site itself. The design and curatorial approaches across the three sites vary greatly in material/media and interpretation, but all strengthen the museum's position as the latest addition to the 'crystallised history' of the interpretative terrain – or archaeological and architectural palimpsest – of Chichester (Geddes in Howard 2001: 151). All also encourage the notion of a continuous community, providing vignettes into the life of the place. And in drawing attention to this shared past, they implicitly question the coherence and direction of Chichester's contemporary society and civic life.

Another example of this heterogeneous approach may be seen at the Pier Arts Centre in Stromness, Orkney. The centre originally opened in 1979, and in 2005 a new £4.5 million extension was opened to house the collection of abstract art produced in the middle decades of the twentieth century. At its core are the early works of Hepworth and Nicholson, and by far the major part of the collection comes from painters and sculptors closely associated with St. Ives in Cornwall. As at the Novium, three historical structures have primarily informed the design's relation to its site. However, in this case rather than off-site references, they are the buildings of the centre itself: a pier, house and shed. The morphology of the town of Stromness evolved with '[t]he houses, built gable on to the sea, belong[ing] to merchants. . . [being] accompanied by such outbuildings and piers as were necessary to sustain their commerce', and this wider development is exemplified at the Pier Arts Centre site (Gillespie 2007: 34). The architects Reiach and Hall's response to the primary site conditions of 'pier', 'house' and 'shed' was to augment the distinctive spirit of place by retention, extension and addition: retention of the pier, extension of the existing streetscape and addition of another 'shed' to the pier (Figure 7.2).

Cramer and Breitling suggest that buildings are often used as 'bearers and points of orientation in individual collective memory', and as with the Roman remains in Chichester, the existent architecture here becomes both memory repository and connector to local people past and present (Cramer and Breitling 2007: 18). The piers have been at the heart of Stromness's social life for centuries, with fishermen and women exchanging news over the catch. They have also acted as viewing platforms for numerous and various 'performances', from the launch of the lifeboat to the traditional fisher-girls' tub racing. As such, these piers have become important sites of an individual yet shared past, and in this way, the existing pier at the Pier Arts Centre is a site of connectedness and can be understood as a material bridge to the past of the place. Such a site of community engagement is also highly appropriate for the current agenda of the Pier Arts Centre: to be an institution inclusive to and welcoming of all local community groups, as well as visitors from around the world. Such congruence between the site's community past and current social agenda is useful in promoting its acceptance and use.

In the original house building, which contains the entry, administration, library and meeting rooms along with the artist's studio and flat, biographical clues to the past are evident at the scales of room and detail. The first floor of the former merchant's house, which fronts on to the main street of the town, Victoria Street, has been given over to a display and meeting space. But through the retention of the still tarnished grate and fireplace, skirting boards, wooden panelling and domestic furniture, it reads very differently to the other gallery spaces, and its former life as a merchant's drawing room is clearly recalled. The art in this space is also hung as in a normal domestic interior, which heightens this connectivity to the past. More subtle and abstracted links between the existing and contemporary elements of the scheme can be seen with the mirroring of door widths – from old to new – across the plan and the use of small, deep-set openings into new from old, matching the exterior windows of the original building. The sensitive, vernacularly treated extension of the existing house perpetuates the urban identity of Stromness. However, a somewhat uncanny 'memoryscape' is created through the whitewashed façade and the at once familiar, yet distorted, positioning and proportions of the openings. This approach seems fitting, both resonating with visitors' memories of the streetscape and hinting at a new, edgier artistic and institutional agenda.

In the project's major design move, a contemporary 'shed' slides alongside the original shed gallery and – in the urban tradition – presents its gable end squarely to the harbour front. Reiach and Hall were strongly influenced by the surrounding vernacular light-industrial

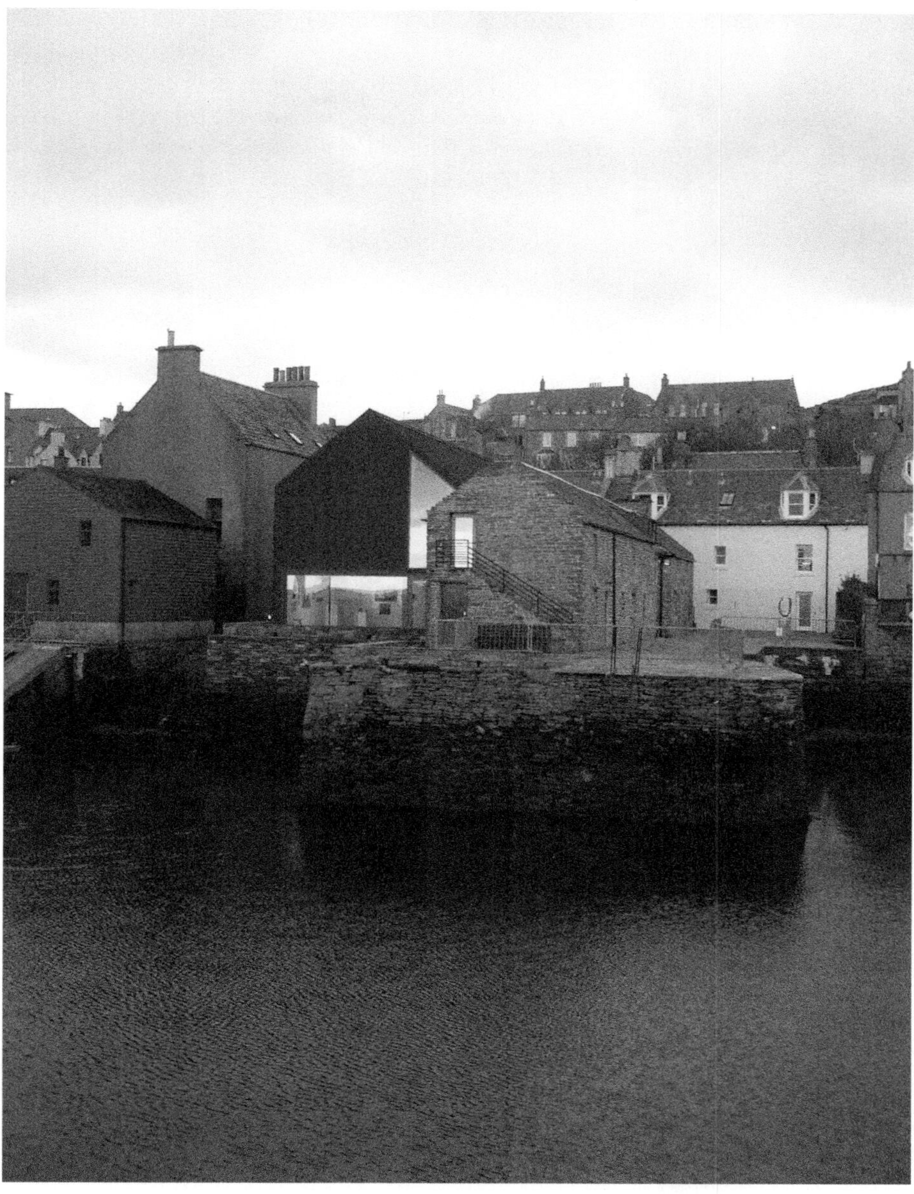

**FIGURE 7.2** The Pier Arts Centre, Stromness, Orkney

*Photo:* Author's own

morphology. With its pitched roof and chimneyless harbour-front gable end, the formal inspiration on the new pier building from adjacent sheds along the historic waterfront is literal. Traditional sheds along the harbour were of stone construction with raftered roofs, but Reiach and Hall favoured a steel frame with black patinated zinc cladding, which whilst evoking the black tarred roofs of the sheds is lightweight and contemporary. The new north-facing glazed façade is characterised by the repeating vertical zinc fins, which recall the rafters of the boat sheds but are now displaced to the elevation, and set up a rhythm, revealing and concealing the landscape to the passer-by (Figure 7.3). Where openings in the original sheds were kept to a minimum to protect against the sometime fierce elements, this solidity is replaced by transparency down the entire north-facing façade and a large swathe of the gable façade. Most

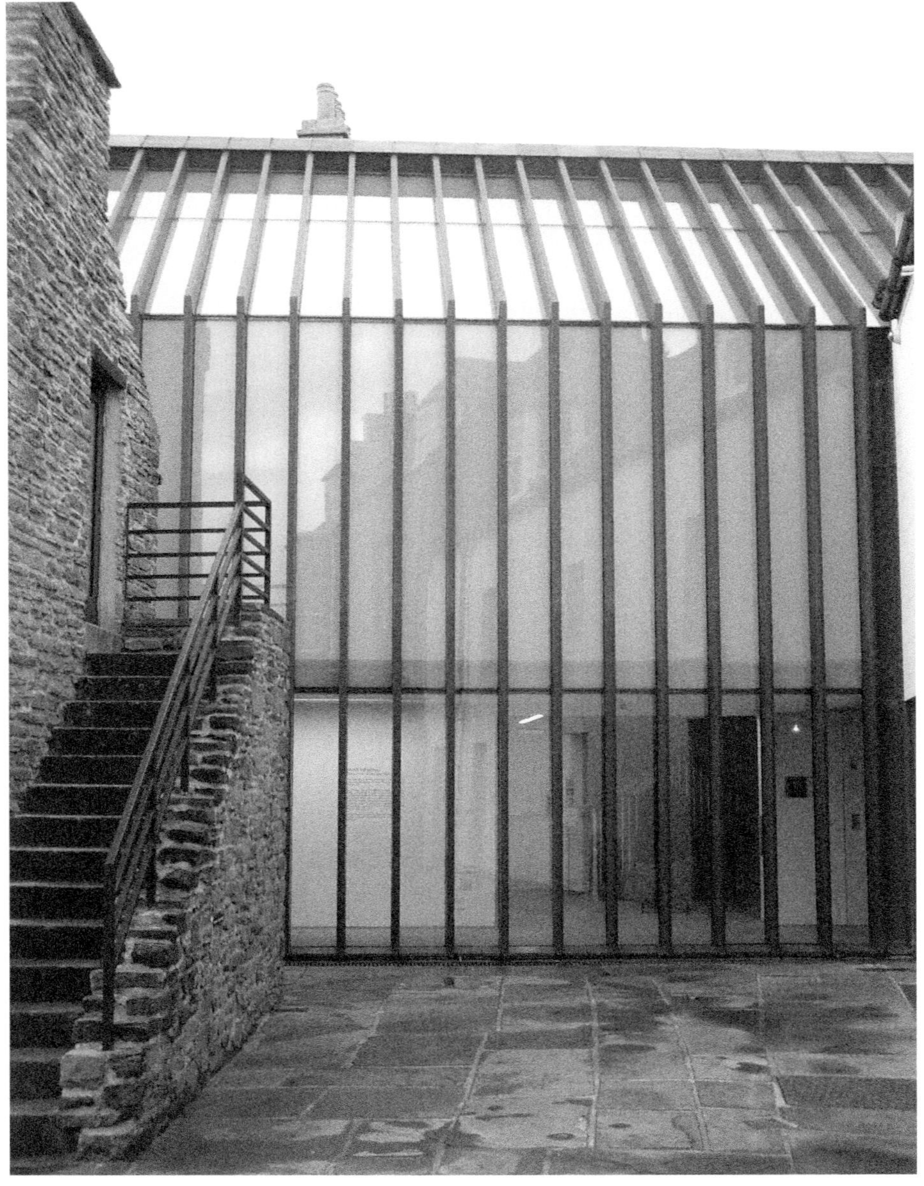

**FIGURE 7.3** Zinc fin wall of new 'shed' building contrasting with the stonework of the original

*Photo:* Author's own

clearly, this material displacement or inversion demonstrates the contemporary disregard for previously form-determining concerns of weather, but the glazing also reveals the workings of the building to the outside, expressing its public nature, in contrast to its previous private function. The design reads as simultaneously familiar yet unusual, industrial and closed yet cultural and open, vernacular yet progressive, and it is in these ambiguities that its appeal lies. This new building then practically acts as a conduit to both existing buildings, solving previous circulation issues at a stroke, and aesthetically acts as a conduit to the past.

In all, it appears that each of the three primary sites of pier, house and shed embody discrete and different meanings, values and appeals. In this way the Pier Arts Centre adheres to a heterogeneous approach to place.

## Multivalency of place: an integrated approach

The following contemporary British galleries demonstrate a different approach to place multivalency, with single 'sites' being invested with multiple, often cognate meanings. A compelling narrative of place, derived from a 'fragment' remote from the site, was influential in the design of Nottingham Contemporary by Caruso St. John, that opened in the Weekday Cross area of the city centre of Nottingham in 2009. The story begins much earlier than this, however, when construction work was underway in the city centre for a new Marks & Spencer's store in the 1930s and a time capsule was unearthed. Amongst other items, this included a small sample book of lace, labelled 'Mallet and Birkin, lace manufacturers, St. Mary's Gate, Nottingham', which had been buried under the then newly created Albert Street in 1847 (Matthews 2008). Being situated on the edge of the city's historic Lacemarket area and only a very short distance from the place of origin of the sample book, the architects chose to use one of the retrieved patterns to inform their façade design. In a material inversion, the design team decided to impress the up-scaled pattern from the lightweight, delicate lace sample onto large, solid and sculptural concave concrete panels, the resultant subtle patterning only revealing itself as the visitor nears the building. So, 'clad in verdigris scalloped panels pre-cast with a traditional lace pattern, over a pre-cast terrazzo base and capped with bands of gold anodized aluminium', the material treatment clearly references the fabric on which the urban quarter's prosperity lay (Harwood 2008: 96–7) (Plate 8).

This use of 'sited' detailing was a departure for the architects and a challenge for some of the building's users and reviewers, more used to the universalist model of twenty-first-century gallery design: '[i]nitially, this seems like one of those ubiquitous shallow gestures at contextualism (with the former lace mills nearby) which hide a slash and burn approach to urbanism' (Hatherley 2010: 111). However, the material narrative of place here is powerful: in its serendipitous story, site specificity, historic continuity, and abstracted and 'inverted' architectural resolution, not to mention its bravely unfashionable embrace of a decorative approach. This association and its challenges and potentials was not lost on the critics:

> Nottingham Contemporary seems to signify something unexpected, something pointed. While . . . other schemes try to wipe out the past, creating grinningly jolly containers for a perpetual present, here we have a visual amalgam of nineteenth-century industry – intricate patterns, made by underpaid workers on the inhuman machines of the nearby mills – and the twenty-first century's semi-automated, out-of-town industries, the non-aesthetic of containerisation and its windowless warehouses. It's a return of the

> repressed, the mechanical, the far from creative processes that occur in a real docklands. It's alone in daring to court such pessimistic associations, but it feels the least dated.
> *(Hatherley 2010: 111)*

Crucially though, as Hatherley alludes to here, this material meaning was allied with formal references to the nearby buildings of the lace industry. The architects themselves acknowledged, '[o]ne inspiration was the surrounding Lace Market, specifically the bold, elegant design of the warehouses that serviced the city's world famous trade in the 19th century' (Nottingham Contemporary 2017). The conceptual and physical *integration* between the inspiration from warehouse forms and the more intimate association of the delicate, *hand*-made, hand-selected and hand-buried lace sample, produces a compound response to place, which is at once coherent as well as evocative. A single site of the museum's façade conveys multiple – if related – meanings, values and appeals. This approach echoes that of warehouses and factories of the Industrial Revolution, which became the company's advertisement, as at Templeton's Carpet Factory in Glasgow, where 'the flamboyant glazed brick, vitreous enamel tiles, red brick and terracotta of the facade evoke[s] the rich Oriental-influenced patterns of the carpets the factory produced' (Clyde Waterfront 2017). The project therefore has multiple 'hooks' for contemporary, plural audiences: from empathetic connections to lace workers to 'pessimistic associations' with a repeating architecture of labour (Hatherley 2010: 111). Whilst not always easy, these aspects of the contemporary place experience are potentially meaningful to a more dispossessed current demographic, perhaps less practiced in the ritual of museum and gallery visiting. In this case at Nottingham Contemporary, the design evokes unknown individuals – the lace producers – but in the final case, a particular person is portrayed and their life remembered.

Maybe at the Turner Contemporary, opened in Margate in April 2011, we find the most compelling example of an integrated multivalency of place. The gallery was designed to 'celebrate . . . the Kentish resort's rich associations with the iconic English painter' (Ijeh, 2011: 21). Simply, as the gallery's website explains, 'Turner's connection with Margate was the founding inspiration for our organisation' (Turner Contemporary 2017a). Having first travelled to school in the coastal town at the age of 11, the English Romanticist landscape artist became a frequent visitor to the place in adult life, drawn by the quality of light, the sea and the skies over Thanet, which he declared to be 'the loveliest in all Europe' (Turner Contemporary 2017a). Indeed the east coast of Kent inspired over 100 of his works, including some of the most well-known seascapes. Another strong attraction to the place came in the form of Mrs. Booth, Turner's paramour and landlady of the Cold Harbour guest house at Rendezvous, where he stayed when visiting the town: 'He loved Margate for the sea, the skies, and his landlady Mrs Booth' (Turner Contemporary 2017a).

The gallery building, by David Chipperfield Architects, has intentionally been sited on the same spot as this original guest house, meaning that '[f]rom the entrance foyer and ground floor gallery, large expanses of glazing plunge epic views of the North sea – as they would have been seen by Turner himself – deep into the interiors' (Ijeh 2011: 21). In an empathic conjunction, '[f]rom the gallery, everyone will be able to see the fine views over the harbour that Turner saw, capturing the same unique light that inspired his works' (Turner Contemporary 2017a) (Plate 9). Here, then, a sited biographical narrative – or personal association with place – was the raison d'être of the Gallery's inception and exact location. As a result there is congruence between the place (Margate, and specifically the site of the former Cold

Harbour guest house), the museum building (in its siting and orientation in particular), and the museum's collection, which largely comprises works by Turner himself. The visitor experience draws on a historical landscape and memoryscape, and allows a rooted empathy or understanding between the observer (visitor) and the subject (Turner); with a shared vista or perspective across centuries. This phenomenological experience of Turner's life is an inclusive and affecting device, allowing easy physical, intellectual and emotional access to the building.

Light is a common currency between art and architecture, and in the case of Chipperfield in Margate, is appropriately the essence of the design: 'From the spacious naturally lit galleries to its opaque glass exterior, the building will absorb and reflect light to create a distinctive and inspirational building' (Chipperfield in Wood 2010: 5). Indeed, as the Gallery's Director Victoria Pomerey stated; 'It had to be a building that balanced architectural merit with function and flexibility as an exhibition space, and one that ideally made use of the legendary natural light' (Wood 2010: 2). This lighting landscape is variegated, interestingly determined by functional considerations and narratives of place:

> The double-height entrance hall window, ground floor events space with external terrace and first floor Clore learning studio all have large north-facing windows offering unrivalled views out to sea. These capture the ever-changing light conditions, reflecting the range of colours found in Turner's paintings. The three first floor gallery spaces are lit by natural 'maritime light' from the north-facing roof and sky lights. The balcony on this floor cantilevers out over the ground floor gallery, again giving spectacular sea views. The 'urban window' of the reception area, café and shop faces the town to connect the building with its surroundings. To emphasise the changing and dramatic effect of light outside the building, a white opaque glass façade has been used. This will also resist storm and wind damage, humidity and saline intrusion.
>
> *(Turner Contemporary 2017b)*

Just as light was probably the fundamental concern in Turner's work, with the artist himself stating, '[l]ight is therefore colour', so Chipperfield explained it as the gallery's 'primary material', expressing the design concept as 'light explains form' (Ijeh 2011: 21). Not only is there consonance between site, building and collection in this case, but the architect has also used the medium of light to draw a parallel between the prodigious output of the proclaimed Turner and the work of his own contemporary architectural practice. The architectural arrangement simultaneously sets up powerful biographically rooted views and carefully orchestrated interior lighting conditions in an integrated narrative of place. As such the site feels multivalent; having or being susceptible of many applications, interpretations, meanings or values.

## Conclusion

This chapter has explored the privileging of place in four contemporary museums and galleries built or substantially extended in the UK since 2005. It is apparent that in each case the design teams have been substantially influenced by genius loci. The manifold *sources* of place association utilised by the designers have been revealed, across sites, degrees of completeness, and types. The locations of the design cues range from distant, off-site inspirations (a small sample of Nottingham lace), site adjacent influences (Stromness's 'industrial' sheds), and on-site, congruent sources (Chichester's Roman bathhouse remains). Their completeness differs from the adaptive reuse of existing buildings, to instances where material fragments – or even material memories – provide the design muse. Finally, their types again span spectrums; from the material to the immaterial, and the formal – or 'physiological' – to the biographical – or 'anthropological'. So the sources of inspiration utilised by the architects is extremely diverse – from fragments of fabric to twelfth-century cathedrals.

Multivalence – or the quality or state of having many values, meanings, or appeals – is forwarded as a useful conceptual device to make sense of potential connections to site, and is found to be in evidence in the selected designs. It would appear that this approach does have many strengths (providing compelling, legible narratives; creating cohesion of intent across sites, buildings and collections; and allowing strong personal and community identification with place and therefore institution) but also weaknesses (artificial neatness; historical sanitisation; lost narratives; the privileging of particular epochs or moments; and the possible hegemony of the architect/curator). Beyond this, the chapter seeks to categorise two distinct design positions in relation to the multivalency of place: a *heterogeneous* approach and an *integrated* approach. In the former category, the museums and galleries exhibit multiple points of sitedness, each with single meanings. In the latter case of an integrated approach, a single site is found to evoke multiple meanings. Overall, the cases all promote the identities of their places; that much is clear. However, it might be argued that where the former, heterogeneous approach promotes clarity of intent and message, the latter promotes impact on a less intellectual, more emotive level.

Place currently informs the conception and design of museum experiences in many ways. Within a default modern condition of architectural universalism, with its globalised practices and agencies – and a similarly homogenised curatorial landscape – the museum is a site of real interest and significance. Culturally, a reaction to the dominant international art gallery aesthetic – be it black or white box – of *universal space*, seems inevitable. And socially and politically, a backlash against globalisation and supra-national organisations, and a seeming strengthening of national sovereignty and regionally devolved parliaments, may also point towards an increasing interest in – and projection of – local place associations. Such a shift offers significant opportunities to museum and exhibition designers, who – as we have seen – are already often deeply influenced by the spirit of place offered by the projects with which they engage. Such a distinct place identity offer may be an increasingly attractive proposition to museum visitors over the coming years and decades, and as such, may offer a way forward for curators and directors in terms of strengthening exhibition and institutional narratives, and continuing and extending community engagement. It at once orientates the outside visitor to the particularities of the new place, whilst strengthening the locals' comprehension of and affinity to their own place. In terms of speculation as to how this 'placed' or 'located' design approach may develop into the future, the adoption of a *multivalent approach*, 'susceptible of many applications, interpretations, meanings or values', suggests itself as one potential avenue. In creating an impactful, *multivalent* interpretation of place, the designer-curator may be able to embody the essence of genius loci in an open, creative and unique way.

## Acknowledgements

With very many thanks to the staff at the Novium, the Pier Arts Centre, Nottingham Contemporary and Turner Contemporary.

## Note

1 *Noviomagus Reginorum* was the Roman name for present-day Chichester.

## References

Beltraimi, G. and Zannier, I. (2006) *Carlo Scarpa: Architecture and Design*, New York: Rizzoli.

Caiger-Smith, M. (2011) 'Beyond the White Cube: A New Role for the Art Museum', *Architecture Today*, 219, pp. 38–44.

Clyde Waterfront (2017) 'Templeton's Carpet Factory'. Online. Available HTTP: www.clydewaterfront.com/clyde-heritage/glasgow-green/templeton's-carpet-factory. Accessed 11 March 2017.

Cramer, J. and Breitling, S. (2007) *Architecture in Existing Fabric: Planning, Design, Building*, Berlin: Ruksaldruck.

Fehn, S. (1992) *The Poetry of the Straight Line*, Helsinki: Museum of Finnish Architecture.

Giebelhausen, M. (ed.) (2003) *The Architecture of the Museum: Symbolic Structures, Urban Context*, Manchester and New York: Manchester University Press.

Gillespie, N. (2007) 'The Black House', in *The Pier Arts Centre*, Edinburgh: Sleeper.

Harwood, E. (2008) *Nottingham: City Guides (Pevsner Architectural Guides: City Guides)*, London: Yale University Press.

Hatherley, O. (2010) 'Jolly Containers for a Perpetual Present', *Tate Etc.* (20), pp. 106–11. Online. Available HTTP: www.tate.org.uk/context-comment/articles/jolly-containers-perpetual-present. Accessed 25 April 2017.

Howard, D. (2001) 'Lessons From History: Edinburgh', in Echenique, M. and Saint, A. (eds) *Cities for the New Millennium*, Spon Press: London & New York, pp. 145–54.

Ijeh, I. (2011) 'An Artist's Impression', *Building Magazine*, 8 April, pp. 20–1.

Kennedy, M. (2012) 'Chichester's New £7m Museum Displays Roman Past', *The Guardian*, 6 July 2012. Online. Available HTTP: www.theguardian.com/culture/2012/jul/06/chichester-museum-roman-past. Accessed 15 January 2013.

Lynch, K. (1960) *The Image of the City*, Cambridge, MA and London, England: The MIT Press.

Matthews, C. (2008) *Snottingham: Nottingham History Book*. Online. Available HTTP: www.nottingham contemporary.org/sites/default/files/Snottingham%20by%20Chris%20Matthews.pdf. Accessed 21 February 2013.

Norrie, H. (2013) *Urban Narratives: Museums and the City*. PhD diss., University of Melbourne.

Nottingham Contemporary (2017) 'Our Building'. Online. Available HTTP: www.nottinghamcontem porary.org/our-building. Accessed 9 February 2017.

Powell, K. (2009) 'Architecture of the Specific: The Romantic Rationalism of Keith Williams', in Williams, K.R. (ed.) *Keith Williams: Architecture of the Specific*, Mulgrave, Australia: The Images Publishing Group, pp. 10–19.

Prak, N. (1977) *The Visual Perception of the Built Environment*, Delft: Delft University Press.

Turner Contemporary (2017a) 'Turner and Margate'. Online. Available HTTP: www.turnercontempo rary.org/turner-and-margate. Accessed 23 January 2017.

Turner Contemporary (2017b) 'About'. Online. Available HTTP: www.turnercontemporary.org/about/gallery. Accessed 23 January 2017.

Williams, K.R. (2009) *Keith Williams: Architecture of the Specific*, Mulgrave, Australia: The Images Publish ing Group.

Wood, J. (2010) 'Contemporary History in the Making'. Online. Available HTTP: www.turnercontem porary.org. Accessed 9 February 2017.

# 8

# A SITE FOR CONVERGENCE AND EXCHANGE

## Designing the twenty-first-century university art museum

*Timothy J. McNeil*

### Abstract

Using the new Manetti Shrem Museum of Art at the University of California, Davis as a case study, this chapter argues that museum architecture should serve as a platform, facilitating programming and sustaining long-term community outreach. It demonstrates how a democratic, transparent, and public design process can be leveraged to create appropriate and responsive design solutions, craft a welcoming sense of place, shape pedagogical and educational experiences, and turn the museum into a site for inclusion and community engagement.

### Introduction

> Not a static shrine, but a constantly evolving public event.
>
> *(Idenburg* et al. *2013: 89)*

I'm going to take you back to 1972 and the City of Davis, California. Sustainable and communal living, farmers markets, the first officially dedicated bike lanes in the United States (started in 1967), and the Whole Earth Festival flourished in a climate of counterculture and 'back-to-the-land' Hippiedom that was emblematic of Northern California at the time. The activism, civic engagement, and a desire for a utopian style of living that flourished in 1970s Davis still runs deep in the community today.

The City and the University of California, Davis have a tradition of community-based architecture and social spaces. In 1972, the Domes housing co-operative was a radical, forward-thinking alternative for student housing (Figure 8.1). Designed and built by engineering professors and students, the Baggins End Domes were created using a collaborative design process. The prefabricated fiberglass shells, once lowered into place on site, addressed the student need for affordable housing and the advantages of a cooperative living lifestyle. The still thriving experimental community embraced the ideals of 'low-cost sharing' long before the advent of the gig economy and the likes of Airbnb.

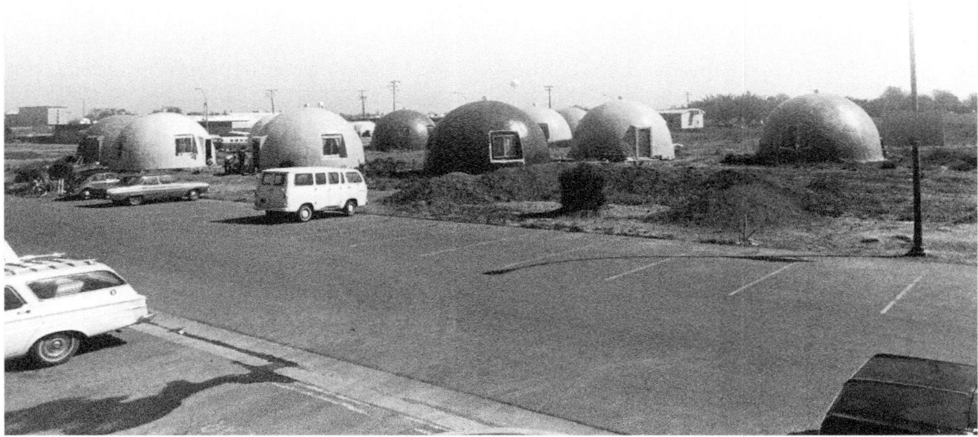

**FIGURE 8.1** Fabricated in the early 1970s by UC Davis engineering students as low-cost cooperative housing, the Baggins End Domes are still thriving today

*Photo:* Courtesy Special Collections, UC Davis Library Strategic Communications Records AR-031

As the university began another building project some four decades later, a similar question was posed: can the design of a new museum capture this same democratic ethos and shared experience? From the perspective of museums, significant progress has been made in recent decades to change the museum space into a more accessible and welcoming environment. I've worked with museums for nearly three decades as in-house design staff, contractor/consultant and as a design theorist and educator. Through these different lenses I've witnessed firsthand a greater focus on the visitor and their needs, and an openness to their participation in shaping the museum experience. Much of this is based on a genuine desire to be more inclusive; sometimes it is driven by other factors such as funding. While these forces are clearly for the better, these visitor-centric advances have often been achieved through programming, exhibition and education initiatives, while the design of the physical building and spaces have remained a few steps, even strides behind the trend toward participation. In this chapter, I will offer one case study that did embrace a user-centered design process, carrying on a Davis approach to architecture.

## Designing a museum for the twenty-first century

> The new museum won't be defined by architectural glamour or by a market-vetted collection, though it may have these. Structurally porous and perpetually in progress, it will be defined by its own role as a shaper of values, and by the broad audience it attracts.
>
> *(Cotter 2015: F10)*

Holland Cotter wonderfully describes the museum of the twenty-first century and challenges architects and museum planners to reconsider what influences museum design and the design process.

The Jan Shrem and Maria Manetti Shrem Museum of Art at the University of California, Davis is a privately funded entity that opened in November 2016. The museum will be the focus of this examination into the impact a democratic design process has on shaping a new university art museum. This case study will demonstrate how the design process – rather than the design implementation – was leveraged to create a forum for community engagement, inclusion and interaction. Frequently driven by advisory boards, funders, museum staff, architects and designers, the commissioning, planning and design of new museum buildings happens behind closed doors, kept under wraps and built by experts for experts. Staffing needs, spatial adjacencies, programming and industry standards determine the design of museum buildings. The manifestation of these factors as a built environment lies very much in the hands of the architects and senior staff, with a kind of 'if we build it they (the visitors) will come' attitude. But what about the intended audience? Can the community have a meaningful role in the design of a new museum and as a result, become vested in the outcome?

The following questions will be addressed:

- How can the design process play a role in creating a sense of place, shaping learning and enabling educational experiences, turning the museum into a site for community interaction?
- How can the design of the physical museum space promote social discourse, inclusion and education for a full spectrum of demographic audiences?
- How can the design create a unifying visual language that facilitates the balance between architectural form and visitor comfort?

Asserting that a democratic design process can be applied equally to private and non-university museum projects, the following assumptions underpin my argument:

- Museum as welcoming: responsive design solutions lead to accessible museum buildings and more inclusive visitor experiences.
- Museum as pedagogy: design thinking and making processes facilitate learning, exchange and community engagement.
- Museum as platform: architecture is a means to an end. The programming and outreach will sustain the museum in the long run.

These assumptions draw on my previous experience as a designer for the J. Paul Getty Museum at the Getty Center and Getty Villa in Los Angeles, and as director of special projects for the Manetti Shrem Museum of Art. The latter is the first project I have been involved in where the intended audience played a role in shaping the design of the building.

## Davis, California: a legacy of community building and mavericks

The City of Davis, California, is located 15 miles from the state capitol building in Sacramento and about an hour's drive from the San Francisco Bay Area. The University of California, Davis, one of 10 public institutions in the University of California system, functions as a leading center for research and education in the sciences, humanities and liberal arts.

The university was created in 1908, and it was formerly known as the College of Agriculture for UC Berkeley before becoming a general campus in 1959.

A spirit of community involvement and resourcefulness extends to running the UC Davis campus where students are empowered to drive the public bus system, run the food services areas and even work in the fire department. UC Davis is a minority majority campus, meaning more than half of the student population is non-Caucasian. Many are first-generation college students. The vast majority (95%) of the undergraduate student population are California residents, while the remaining 5% come from out of state or from other countries (UC Davis 2017a). With a student body of 35,000, students at UC Davis can choose from over 100 majors. The most popular are the social and hard sciences and not the arts. Because of this imbalance, the university art museum cannot rely on a self-motivated student audience similar to one found at a focused, liberal arts–oriented institution. Furthermore, many students may have never visited a museum before except in their early school years.

## Jan Shrem and Maria Manetti Shrem Museum of Art

Despite the limited exposure, experimentation in the visual arts is nothing new to UC Davis. The Manetti Shrem Museum of Art's goal is to combine vanguard artistic and curatorial innovation with audience engagement (UC Davis 2017b). Pioneering new means to connect visitors with art and participating in the process of making art are two aspects of the new museum that are at the very center of its vision. 'Art Wide Open', the museum's opening tag line, refers to the free admission and the open interpretation of *art* in relation to collaborations with other disciplines across the campus. The museum's collection was formed when Richard L. Nelson founded the university art department in 1959. Nelson established a place of radical exploration for faculty and students seeking to break away from the artistic conventions of the mid-twentieth century (resulting in work that is now associated with the California Funk Art movement), where 'In a time of social disruption, scientific rationalization, and political instability, the creation of art was an act of dangerous faith' (De Forest 1967: 3).

It is pertinent that at the same time innovations in agricultural research were emerging at UC Davis in the 1960s, the unprecedented growth of its creative arts was garnering just as much attention. This decade in particular marked the birth of new approaches to making art in America. The UC Davis Department of Art was at the center of that movement, giving rise to important American artists such as Wayne Thiebaud, Robert Arneson, Bruce Nauman, Deborah Butterfield and countless artists and visiting artists who would come to Davis to experiment and innovate. Art from UC Davis was once described rather disparagingly by the *New York Times* as 'defiant provincialism' (Kramer 1981: C10), and it is that iconoclasm and unquestioning confidence that defines the work of this period and has left its mark on the contemporary art world (Figure 8.2).

## Perspectives on university art museums

'Equal parts classroom, laboratory, entertainment center and spiritual gym where good ideas are worked out and bad ideas are worked off' (Cotter 2009: C25), the role of the campus museum can be tenuous as it straddles the line between being an academic resource for collecting and preserving objects, and a place for education and public outreach. It is no longer enough for university museums 'to hide behind their scholarship, [they] must actively encourage people to use their collections for education and enjoyment' (Kelly 2001: 12).

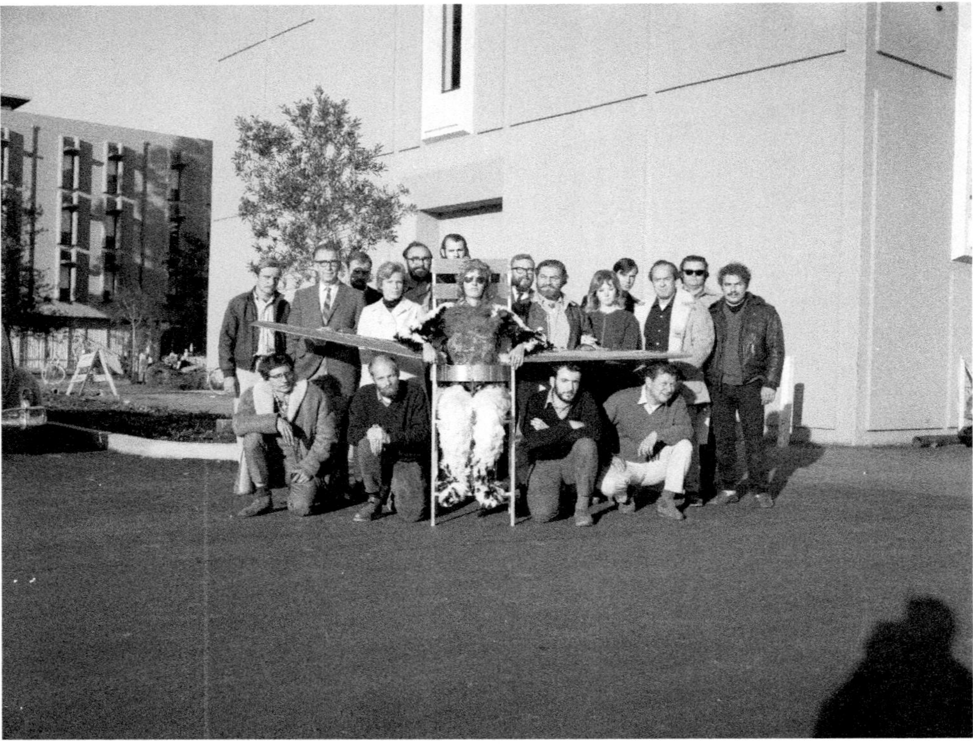

**FIGURE 8.2** Robyn Martin's 1967 M.F.A. thesis project of the *Bird* was one of the many examples by the UC Davis Art Department that led to their work being called 'defiant provincialism'

*Photo:* Photographer unknown. The Jan Shrem and Maria Manetti Shrem Museum of Art. Fine Arts Collection Archive.

Universities have some of the oldest museums and hold many of the most diverse and important collections. Founded in 1683, the Ashmolean Museum at Oxford University is considered to be the first purpose-designed university museum in the world. Art museums, specifically, play a much greater role in the history of American university collections than they did historically in Europe. Harvard University first began collecting portraits as early as 1750, and the Trumbull Art Gallery at Yale University, built in 1832, is widely recognized as the first major museum associated with an American university. The Trumbull has a long history, and much of its story can be told through the unfolding of its architectural additions. From the Gothic-styled Street Hall to Louis Kahn's modernist masterpiece, the design of each successive building testifies to an evolving and enhanced educational interaction with the campus community.

After World War II, there was a boom in the creation of new university museums in the United States. Almost half of the 1,100 university museums in the United States were opened between 1945 and 1995 (Danilov 2011). These new museums, a large majority of them art museums, continued the tradition of amassing collections that existed primarily for the education and scholarship of the students and professors at their institutions. The historical lineage of university art museums continues today and with renewed purpose, serving socially networked students and readying them for the twenty-first-century workplace. A report from the Cultural Policy Center on 'Campus Art Museums in the 21st Century' (Shapiro 2012: 15) states that a university's 'traditions of object-based inquiry match well with new research on multiple learning styles. And their grounding in open inquiry, experimentation, and intellectual tolerance provides a solid foundation upon which to build'.

There is no shortage of new high-profile university art museums being built in the United States: Eli and Edith Broad Museum, Michigan State University, Zaha Hadid (completed 2012); UC Berkeley Art Museum and Pacific Film Archive, Diller Scofidio + Renfro (completed 2016); and Virginia Commonwealth University's Institute for Contemporary Art, Steven Holl Architects (opening 2018). This multimillion-dollar investment in culture is fueled by several factors that include college administrators who recognize that the arts can promote nimble thinking, student demand and donor cultivation (Sheets 2017). University museums talk about inclusion and have a mandate to serve their community, but are they canvassing their constituents and allowing them to participate in the design development process for these new museum building projects?

## Planning a museum for the twenty-first century

Key stakeholders from the Davis community were consulted during the early planning process for the Manetti Shrem Museum of Art. Interviews with students, faculty and administrators, as well as community and art leaders, captured a range of opinions to inform a preliminary vision for the new art museum. The resulting report captured key phrases to describe what the museum should be and offer: 'interdisciplinary', 'informal and comfortable', 'community mindedness', 'distinctiveness', 'visibility for arts', 'student involvement', 'learning laboratory', and 'plenty of outlets, wifi and coffee'. Campus voices coalesced around statements like 'Our culture has to be central – collaborative, participatory, land-based, sustainable and connecting to the community and making it welcoming and inviting'. External feedback argued that 'It needs to have a real resonance . . . exploring new narratives, convening difficult conversations, challenging traditional thinking', and 'A museum should reflect the arts at UC Davis today – adventurous, cutting edge, something different. Highlight the benefits of an art museum at a research university; look critically at design, architecture and landscape architecture' (Lord Cultural Resources 2012: C1–4).

A highly managed and controlled feedback process is not unusual within the museum field and is often the primary work of professional museum consultant groups resulting in rather predictable visioning statements, stakeholder briefing documents, and an internal design project proposal that goes out for architectural tender or RFP (request for proposal). The Manetti Shrem Museum of Art project team decided to go beyond this stage, taking an approach that was in line with Davis's community roots, doing away with what usually gets determined behind closed doors and facilitating an open community forum for the selection of the museum building design.

## The democratic design process

In her paper 'The Role of University Art Museums in the 21st Century' (2006), Shirley M. Tilghman posed the question: should university art museums focus their attention on those audiences most likely to gravitate to the galleries, or should they also embrace non-traditional audiences that may be harder to attract but have more to gain in terms of artistic awareness? Reaching out to diverse audiences has been the illusive cornerstone of museum policy for decades, driven by a need to be relevant and financially sustainable. Yet often the demographics of art museum audiences do not reflect those of the surrounding community. The reason for a museum's inability to attract and resonate with its core community is frequently laid at the feet of specialized staff producing esoteric exhibitions with educational outreach initiatives that are overly ambitious or lacking relevancy. While to some degree this is true, it is the design of the building that creates the first impression leading to 'Threshold Fear' (Heumann Gurian 2006: 365). With imposing building façades that lack transparency, grand entrances with multiple steps, and unfamiliar white voluminous cube galleries, museums are seen by many as 'church-like and stoic' and an 'intimidating space' (Samis and Michaelson 2017: 9).

On the upside, museums are seen as trusted, reliable and the voice of authority. On the downside, many audiences view them as imposing and exclusionary. A sense of importance and grandeur leads to

> an easier correlation with both traditional and contemporary architecture than does the mission to create a welcoming, inclusionary museum . . . especially if visitor needs are seen to interfere with artistic vision, architects create museums that are difficult to use.
> *(Heumann Gurian 2006: 366)*

Buildings that incorporate intimidating architectural features have little in common with our personal and everyday notion of friendly and welcoming, and serve to reinforce the perception of inaccessible and 'not for me'.

An open and democratic design process serves to mitigate this self-perpetuating approach and cultivates museum designs that resonate with, and are meant for, the community while still keeping the 'contemplative' aura of specialness, the very ingredients that make museums notable and distinctive in the first place. The best architecture combines beautiful form with beautiful function. A democratic design approach forces senior museum personnel to listen to ALL of their constituents and understand the architectural process sufficiently, so that the museum's strategic direction and its architectural development don't diverge.

## Architectural competition

In a rather tongue-in-cheek blog post about the prototypical way to launch a new museum, the American Alliance of Museums' Center for the Future of Museums quipped: (1) raise a ton of money; (2) commission an architect to build a posh building (sometime this comes before step 1); (3) open to the public; (4) see if it works – often people are surprised and disappointed when the attendance projections fall short (AAM 2015). Missing from this list, despite its irony, is an additional step at the beginning: consult and listen to your community and constituents, and obtain their buy-in before you embark on the project in the first place.

In the fall of 2012, UC Davis initiated an open RFQ (request for qualifications) invitation to envision a new art museum. The building site had already been selected and the environmental impact reports were submitted and approved. An international roster of architect and contractor teams responded. Having interviewed seven of the most promising and qualified teams, the internal committee representing the museum, campus planning and community then invited three finalist teams to participate in a formal four-month-long design competition.[1]

Museums are notorious for commissioning a substantially greater number of building designs and design revisions compared with other cultural sectors. Architectural plans are approved, scrapped prior to building, or heavily edited or 'value engineered' after breaking ground. These amendments frequently incur additional costs and add significantly to the construction schedule. The average budget escalation for museums during the design phases is 46% (Woronkowicz 2008: 21). Multiple changes to design and construction specifications are a huge risk for museums with set budgets, especially one that involves the community in the design process and is accountable to a state-funded public university (the land was owned by the university, but all of the design and construction cost was funded using private philanthropic sources).

To keep a lid on costs and meet a tight schedule, the Manetti Shrem Museum of Art was classified as a design/build project. Each of the three finalists was required to work with a California state-licensed contractor who controlled the schedule and budget and monitored the architect's work. This arrangement is highly unusual for the design of an art museum, where creative freedom and over-budget modifications are considered part of the process. A thorough and detailed project proposal worked in the project's favor, as did an experienced client team (with museum building experience) to guide it through the creative and construction process and steer it through any stakeholder attempts to meddle with the strategic planning.

The three design teams were charged with creating a building that was appropriate for the display of the university's Fine Arts Collection. Each team was chosen because it made a persuasive pitch for how the architecture would serve as a stage for connecting art with the multidisciplinary research and pedagogy across campus, and capture the irreverent experimentation that defined the work of the legacy art faculty. It was this spirit of inquiry and inclusiveness that was celebrated through the building's democratic and open design competition. Even the much maligned design/build process (architects dislike the lack of control) represented a greater level of transparency with the community.

## Imagine! A conversation with 2,000 people

As the three competition designs for the museum were unveiled in early 2014, so began a rigorous process to solicit community feedback on the proposals. The first was an on-campus exhibition, *Imagine! Three Museum Designs Revealed*, displaying a range of scale models, materials, renderings and drawings associated with each proposal (Figure 8.3). An active call was released to local and regional communities to participate in the selection process. The exhibition captured a range of both complementary and critical community concerns and preferences. Open town hall forums with each of the three architects provided members of the public with the opportunity to ask questions and probe the design teams' visions. The results from the *Imagine* exhibition were extraordinary, with constructive ideas from around the world suggesting how the new museum might take shape:

- The architect's presentation forum for the general public had more than 200 attendees.
- Two receptions and 18 working sessions with the community were held, bringing more than 1,000 people into the conversation.
- The designs were posted to Facebook, Twitter and the UC Davis home page. In total, roughly 1,100 in the social media community commented, shared and participated in giving feedback.

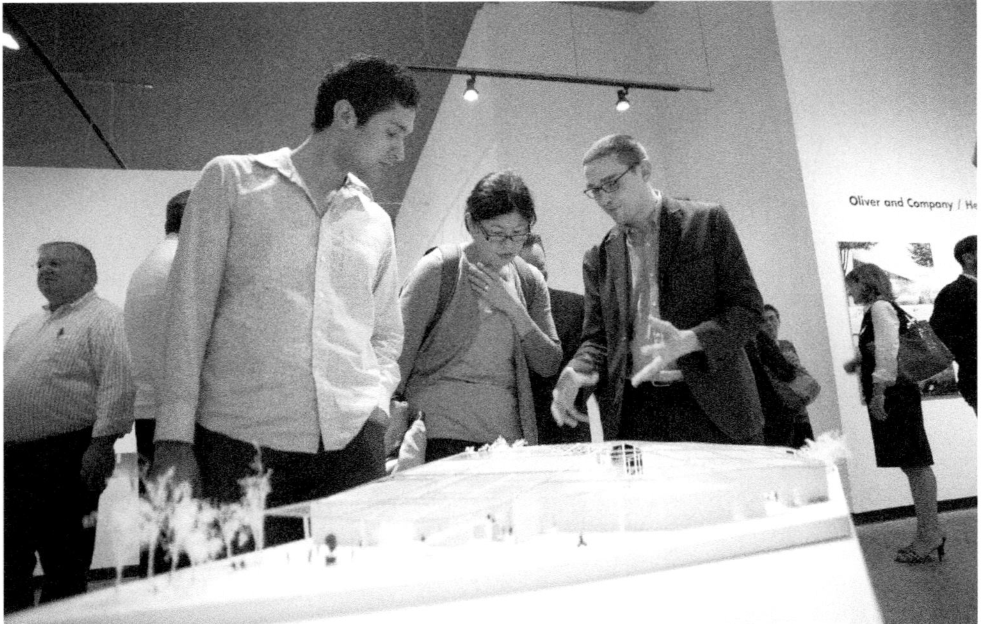


FIGURE 8.3 'Imagine! Three Museum Designs Revealed' displayed a range of scale models, materials, renderings and drawings associated with each design proposal. Over 2,000 community members participated in the selection process

*Photo:* Gregory Urquiaga, University of California, Davis

Engaging audiences with architecture-themed exhibitions can be difficult. Technical plans, elevations and drawings can alienate visitors who may not be familiar with how to read the language of design visual representation. These drawings play a decisive role in selling a scheme to a non-expert viewer. The *Imagine* exhibition was carefully staged to include the community in a celebration of the ideas and proposals. A brief look at the three proposals, and some of the primary words that were used by the community to describe their designs, is included in the accompanying illustrations (Plates 10, 11 and 12).

Over 2,000 community members participated in the conversation and provided feedback about the building designs. Public gatherings and events like this provide opportunities for community inclusion and create a buzz around a project. Community members genuinely appreciated the opportunity to be involved in the selection process: 'Thank you for inviting me to see the drawings, photos and scale models – prepared by three highly qualified architectural teams'. People became more vested in the project: 'Looking forward to the process, outcome and a great art museum at UCD'. Passionate pleas for taking into account the hot summer Davis weather featured regularly, and people were surprisingly informed and brutally honest about the architecture: 'Does not seem to be just an outrageous vehicle for making the architect famous' and 'Both the footprint and the shell of the building are impenetrable' typified some responses to the three schemes. Other voices were more cautious in their approval and the impact of a non-expert audience making the decision: 'My main concern is your method of choosing the building, your professional staff at the museum should weigh in most heavily'. When all was said and done, the 'control' or the 'professional staff' were always there from the outset. The openness of the competition was genuine and led to a consensus for the winning design.

## Site specificity: the winning scheme

> The Canopy activates the Museum's thresholds and interiors. In so doing it transforms the function of a museum from an inert receptacle to a lively, multi-faceted landscape of exploration.
>
> *(Idenburg* et al. *2013: 89)*

'Risky' may be the best way to describe an open invitation to the community to help select the design of a multimillion-dollar museum building and site. Yet the public forums yielded a range of positives and negatives for each of the three designs. However, there was a level of uniformity to the sentiment expressed by the participants for the chosen design and it fortunately mirrored the leanings of the donor and museum team. 'The Canopy is by far the most likely to draw students to it . . . The whole concept is fresh, artistic and human-scale, innovative while still intriguing and welcoming' was how one of the community participants summed up their feedback about the design. 'I have talked with others who agree that we will be very disappointed if the Grand Canopy is not built!' and 'This design places the least emphasis on the architecture. It is most accessible to the most people, it is more comfortable to occupy' was the general sentiment categorically stated by many of the participants.

In the winning design, SO-IL and Bohlin Cywinski Jackson create a 50,000-square-foot permeable cover – a 'Grand Canopy' over both site and building (consisting of three pavilions: education, administration and galleries) (Figure 8.4). The canopy works in two important ways: first, to generate a field of experimentation, an infrastructure and a stage for events; and second, as an urban device that 'creates a new locus of community activity and center of gravity on campus' (Idenburg *et al.* 2013: 91). The surrounding Central Valley has long inspired artists, influenced by the sweeping views over the flat plains beyond to the horizon, and the low-slung building becomes an extension of this plane. The canopy's metal infill beams are arranged in furrows that mimic the surrounding agrarian landscape. Unlike traditional museum buildings that establish identity with hard vertical surfaces, the Grand Canopy offers no imposing façade.

> As a welcoming and public-minded gesture – the roofline reaches out toward the sidewalk, ringing the museum site and bringing visitors beneath its protective embrace – it has real power. The remarkable, shifting shadows cast by the beams above and the peaked opening at its center are also suggestive of a range of successful metaphors, endorsing the idea of a fluidity, permeability, and difference as opposed to the fixed canon of both architectural and art-historical ideas that once shaped most museums.
>
> *(Hawthorne 2017: 36)*

The building equally puts art, education and community up front, all connected around a central lobby and courtyard. Design qualities exude inclusivity, accessibility and site-specificity.

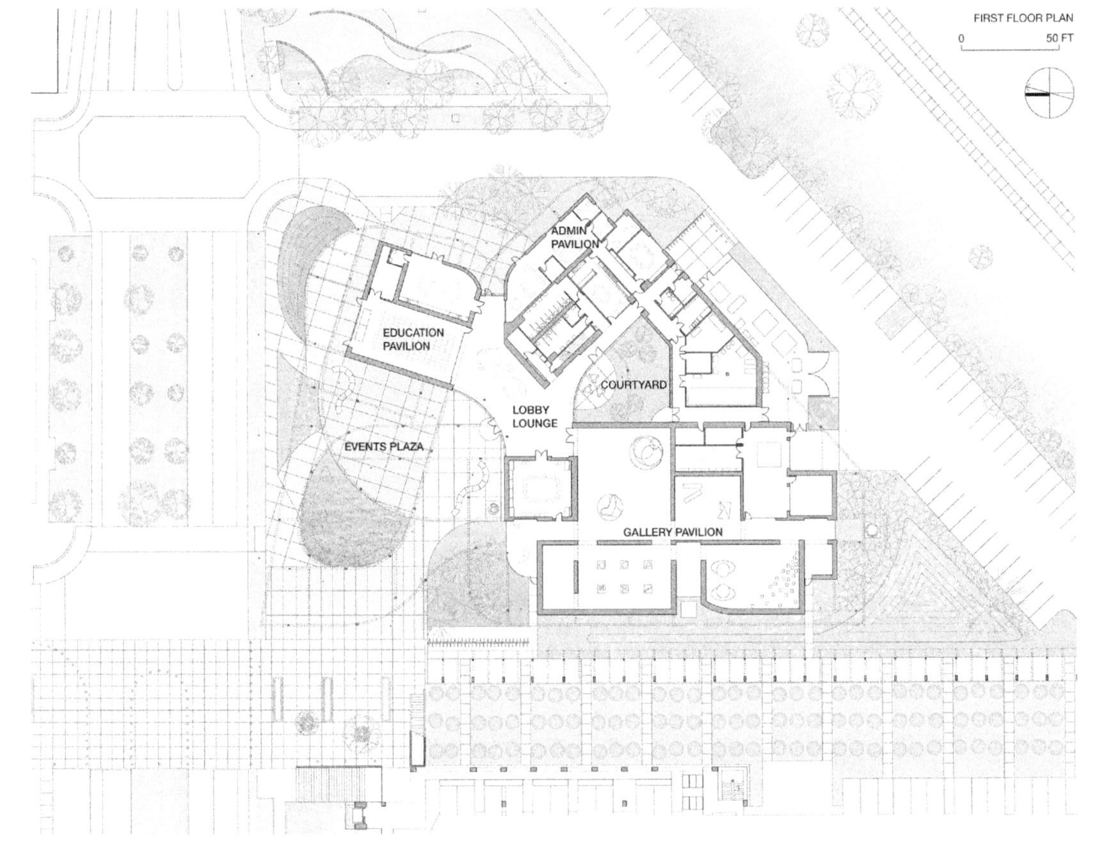


**FIGURE 8.4** Museum plan, Jan Shrem and Maria Manetti Shrem Museum of Art, UC Davis, California, showing of 8,900 square feet of gallery space; 6,450 square feet of event and education spaces; 29,410-square-foot state-of-the-art museum; 50,000-square-foot steel canopy overlaying interior and exterior spaces; 75,000-square-foot site, with outdoor spaces to maximize the experience of art, education and outdoor sculpture landscape

*Photo:* Courtesy of SO – IL, Bohlin Cywinski Jackson, Lutsko Associates

It is these traits combined with aesthetic prowess that resonated with the community: no grand entry steps, with a single-story structure; main lobby and public entrance edged by curving floor-to-ceiling glass that invites transparency to the inside and to the outside; multiple flexible spaces for art, gatherings, and events; art that can be seen as soon as one approaches and enters the building (art up front); plenty of seating for lolling, lounging and loitering; intuitive wayfinding with obvious sightlines to the educational and instructional spaces (education up front), galleries and amenities such as restrooms; a portfolio of exhibition spaces that are human in scale; and a museum building that excels in environmental sustainability (LEED Platinum), important for the local eco-minded community.

## Making choices, understanding and experimentation

During the first months of building construction, the typical milestones of a groundbreaking and then a topping-off ceremony became open events and opportunities that also included the community (not just the primary stakeholders and funders). A second public exhibition on campus was developed and installed to inform the community about progress and keep them engaged in the ongoing design decisions for the project. *MAKE: A New Museum for UC Davis* was part-exhibition, part-forum. Visitors learned more about the Grand Canopy design and how the museum would connect to the broader campus and regional community. Visitors participated in guiding decisions about the museum's furniture, approach to gallery interpretation, and other aspects of the museum experience.

*MAKE* was about choices, understanding, and experimentation. Exhibits informed visitors about the choice of the state-of-the-art LED museum lighting – controlled through adaptive (motion-activated) technology – and a comparison was made between LED and traditional halogen light sources. As to the selection of chairs for the public spaces and lecture room, several options were available for sitting in, and visitors were encouraged to vote for their favorite ones and say why, even sketch a new design if they had a better solution. Various tools were available for visitors to provide feedback and leave comments. If campus art museums are to continue to reposition themselves as laboratories or test sites (Shapiro *et al.* 2012), then *MAKE* was very much in this vein of experimentation and open inquiry. The forum tapped into the 'changing cultural milieu of students, whose generational ethos is ever more participatory, interactive, and focused on non-hierarchical social networks' (Shapiro *et al.* 2012).

## Designed by students for students

University museums are fortunate to have access to a large cohort of motivated students to assist with projects. UC Davis students were instrumental in the design process and expanded the notion of community engagement as 'today's students seek "insider" access to the process as well as the products of culture' (Shapiro *et al.* 2012: 10). Early on, in conjunction with the architectural competition, students envisioned museum building proposals for the site. And faculty used the opportunity to weave the museum into course assignments and envision the building as a teaching tool for the future. In this regard, it was important that the building and all of its designed elements reached an exemplary standard. 'I can teach architecture from this design – it is the only design that gives faculty a pedagogical tool and provides architectural leadership for the campus', wrote one faculty member in the *Imagine* exhibition comments.

*MAKE* celebrated this pedagogical connection by featuring students' work from the various cross-disciplinary courses offered in the UC Davis department of design curriculum – what choices they made as they designed and created furniture, graphic identity, signage, visitor amenities, and other museum-related projects – elements that eventually became part of the museum environment. Above all, *MAKE* encouraged all participants to be part of the process of a museum in the making.

## Convergence and exchange

> Art Wide Open describes a museum that is open inside and out – a museum where all are free to discover new art, and with it, new ideas
>
> *(Teagle in Jones and Kitura 2016)*

Can we conclude that the new museum has succeeded in welcoming community audiences, facilitating learning, and serving as a platform for convergence and exchange? Because a public university has a mandate to be transparent and open, is a democratic design process a viable approach to follow for private and non-university museum projects? Critics have come out strongly in favour of the Manetti Shrem Museum of Art's design 'as a work of architecture, the most thoughtful, the least predictable, and the most encouraging about the trajectory of American architecture', and the building has been called one to 'boost your faith in American architecture' (Hawthorne 2016: E1). This says a great deal about its sense of purpose and human connectedness beyond being simply a museum for the twenty-first century.

Early success metrics point to visitors who love the building, are engaged in the exhibits and feel very welcome in the museum space. From November 2016 to March 2017 the museum welcomed nearly 50,000 visitors and hosted over 90 classes, events, talks and workshops (Figure 8.5). Unlike museums in major cities that are labeled as must-see destinations, university and non-metropolitan museums by their very nature and geographic location can't rely on throngs of sightseeing visitors. Without the default of tourism, these museums tend to take bigger risks with their exhibitions and programming in order to attract audiences (Samis and Michaelson 2017). I would argue that this leads to a level of greater civic-mindedness and more community-focused museums. It also reinforces the notion of the museum as platform, where the architecture facilitates visitor interaction and experience. The physical space is only a means to an end and it is the programming and outreach that will sustain the museum in the long run. In the example of the Manetti Shrem Museum of Art, involving the community in the design of the building legitimized the work of the architect and their winning scheme, encouraged the client (donors and university) to embrace community engagement, made the museum's design concept welcoming and, ultimately, made the design team more accountable (they came face-to-face with their users). It resulted in highly responsive design solutions that informed the creation of accessible museum features and inclusive visitor experiences.

Exposing the community to design thinking and making, activating learning, social exchange and engagement, the architectural design process became demystified and a form of pedagogy – entirely fitting for a university campus. Community participation encouraged the exploration of interpreting architecture and design, and allowed for a real-time evaluation of its success in an exhibition format. Revealing the process also cast the architect/designer in a less authoritarian role. It served to expose the design team as the bridge (or conduit) between

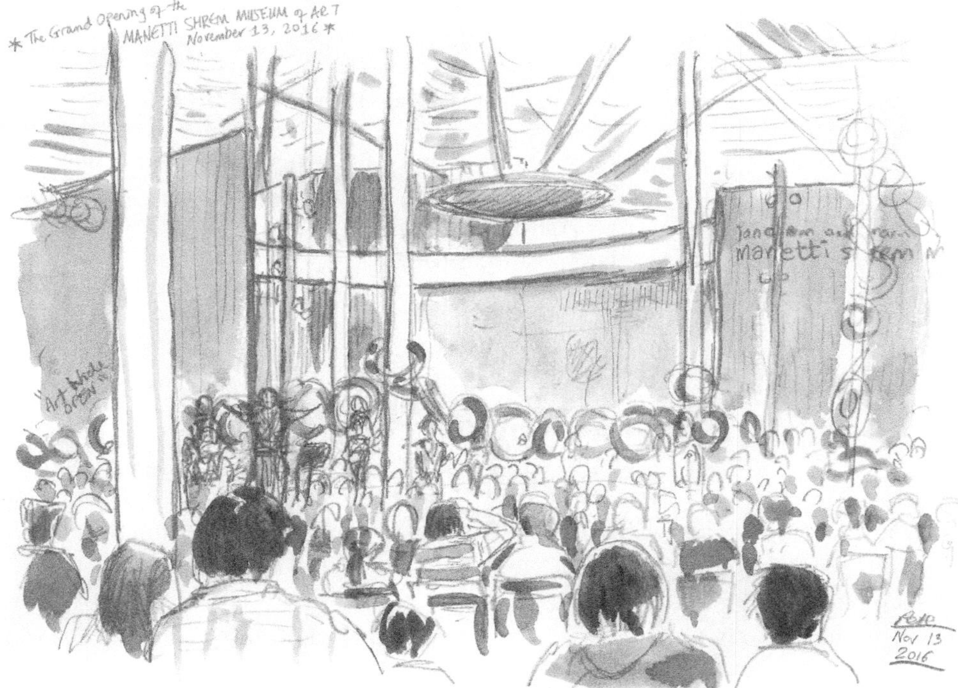


**FIGURE 8.5** Local community sketch-crawler Pete Scully captured the crowds during the opening event and ribbon cutting. Over 2,000 UC Davis students attended the pre-opening party, and 11,807 people attended the opening events in the first week, demonstrating the power of community networking and social media

*Image:* Pete Scully

the museum client who supplies the content, the contractor who implements the vision, and the visitor who interacts and engages with that vision. Adding a community engagement component was additional work within a tight schedule, but the gain was worth it. The following lessons learned may be helpful to other projects:

- All community stakeholders must be involved in the process and develop a shared vision.
- The community's voice must be trusted and the team must remain confident and be willing to act on this input.
- The planning conversation should be focused on designing the experience and not just the architectural form.
- Multiple strong design proposals ensure a favorable outcome regardless of selection.
- It is important to tap into the expertise and resources around you. Don't doubt that the community will enthusiastically participate in the process.
- Rather than seeking community input during the early planning phase, wait until the completion of the architectural competition. This way the community can respond to something tangible, allowing for informed feedback and heightened involvement.

- University museums can offer non-university museums insights and strategies about engagement, inclusiveness, welcoming, and risk taking.
- If at all possible, make the museum admission free to the community. Not only does it encourage repeat visits and casual drop-ins, it fosters incredible community goodwill.

Lastly, a democratic approach to designing that encourages community involvement leads to a 'future art museum [that] is neither isolated nor exclusive, but open and permeable; not a static shrine, but a constantly evolving public event' (Idenburg *et al.* 2013: 89). The Manetti Shrem Museum of Art is open and evolving for the Davis community, and adds significantly to the lexicon of institutions that are defining the design of the twenty-first-century museum.

## Note

1 This speculative design period was accompanied by a paid stipend to cover a proportion of the fees. The RFQ selection process avoided any personal preferences or onerous approvals from an established museum board, since the selection process fell to a committee consisting of university and external members representing various areas of expertise and the community.

## References

American Alliance of Museums (2015) 'Center for the Future of Museums' blog. Monday Musing: Prequel to a Museum, 26 October 2015. Online. Available HTTP: http://futureofmuseums.blogspot.co.uk/2015/10/monday-musing-prequel-to-museum.html. Accessed 27 October 2015.

Cotter, H. (2009) 'Why University Museums Matter', *New York Times*, 19 February 2009, p. C25.

Cotter, H. (2015) 'Toward a Museum of the 21st Century', *New York Times*, 28 October 2015, p. F10.

Danilov, V.J. (2011) *America's College Museums* (2nd edition), Amenia, NY: Grey House.

De Forest, R. (1967) *UC Davis Art Studio M.F.A. Catalogue*, Davis, UC Davis Department of Art Studio.

Gurian, E.H. (2006) 'Threshold Fear: Architecture Program Planning', in Gurian, E. (ed.) *Civilizing the Museum: The Collected Writings of Elaine Heumann Gurian*, London and New York: Routledge, pp. 364–75.

Hawthorne, C. (2016) 'Architecture's Top 10 for 2016', *Los Angeles Times*, 18 December 2016, p. E1.

Hawthorne, C. (2017) 'What SO-IL's Shrem Says About the Future of Museum Design', *Architect*, 2 January 2017, p. 36.

Idenburg, F., Baccus, K. and Stackalis, J. (2013) 'The Grand Canopy', Architectural Competition Proposal For the Jan Shrem and Maria Manetti Shrem Museum of Art, Whiting-Turner, SO-IL, Bohlin Cywinski Jackson, pp. 89, 91.

Jones, D. and Kitura, C. (2016) 'New UC Davis Art Museum Welcomes Thousands', University of California NEWS, 16 November 2016. Online. Available HTTP: www.ucdavis.edu/news/new-art-museum-welcomes-thousands/. Accessed 16 November 2016.

Kelly, M. (2001) *Managing University Museums*, Paris: Organization for Economic Cooperation and Development.

Kramer, H. (1981) 'Art View: Ceramic Sculpture and the Taste of California', *New York Times*, 20 December 1981, p. C10.

Lord Cultural Resources (2012) 'Perspectives on an Art Museum, Key Findings From Student Workshops, Administration, Faculty and Staff Interviews, and Community Interviews', *Exploring the Potential: Jan Shrem and Maria Manetti Shrem Museum of Art, University of California, Davis, Project Advisory Committee Briefing Document*, pp. C1–4.

Samis, P. and Michaelson, M. (2017) *Creating the Visitor Centered Museum*, New York: Routledge.

Shapiro, T., Linett, P., Farrell, B., and Anderson, W. (2012) *Campus Art Museums in the 21st Century: A Conversation*, Chicago: Cultural Policy Center at the University of Chicago. Online. Available HTTP: http://culturalpolicy.uchicago.edu/sites/culturalpolicy.uchicago.edu/files/campusartmuseumsreport_0.pdf. Accessed 19 October 2015.

Sheets, H.M. (2017) 'Why US Universities Are Investing in their Art Museums', *The Art Newspaper*, 5 January 2017. Online. Available HTTP: http://theartnewspaper.com/news/museums/why-us-universities-are-investing-in-their-art-museums/. Accessed 15 February 2017.

Tilghman, S.M. (2006) 'The Role of University Art Museums in the 21st Century' presented at 'Creator, Collector, Catalyst', a symposium sponsored by the Princeton University Art Museum and The Wolfsonian-Florida International University.

University of California Davis (2017a) *Student Profile*. Online. Available HTTP: http://admissions.ucdavis.edu/profile/. Accessed 6 November 2015.

University of California Davis (2017b) *Give UC Davis*. Online. Available HTTP: https://give.ucdavis.edu/SHRE. Accessed 8 February 2017.

Woronkowicz, J. *et al.* (2008) *Set in Stone: Building America's New Generation of Arts Facilities, 1994–2008*, Chicago: The University of Chicago Cultural Policy Center Report. Online. Available HTTP: www.norc.org/PDFs/setinstone%20FINAL%20REPORT.pdf. Accessed 26 October 2015.

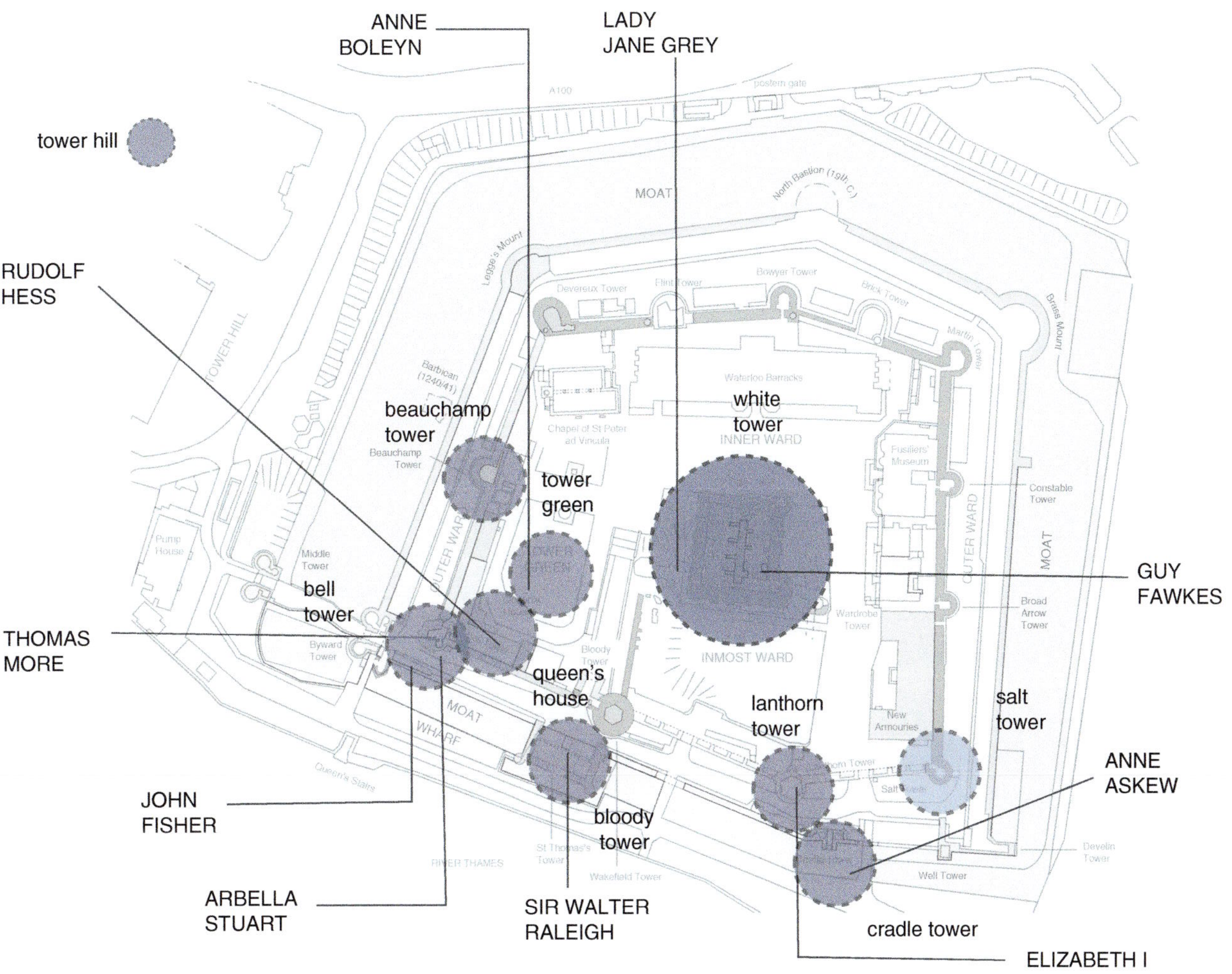


**PLATE 1** People and place: using interpretive design to map people and place

*Illustration:* Tom Duncan. Reproduced with the kind permission of RCMG. Plan by Edward Impey © Historic Royal Palaces.

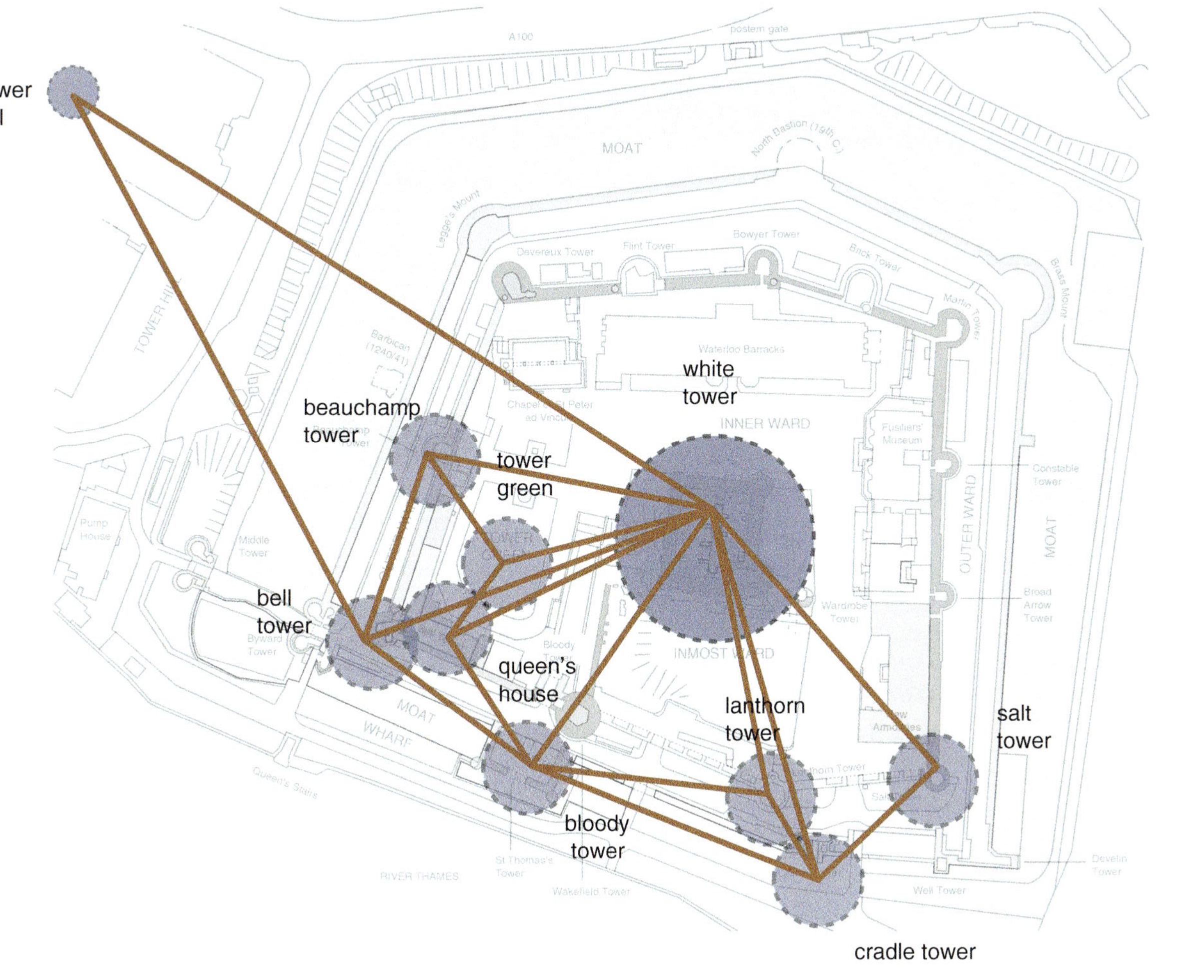


**PLATE 2** Imagining a central hub from which visitors might go off to explore stories around the site in the places they unfolded

*Illustration:* Tom Duncan. Reproduced with the kind permission of RCMG. Plan by Edward Impey © Historic Royal Palaces.

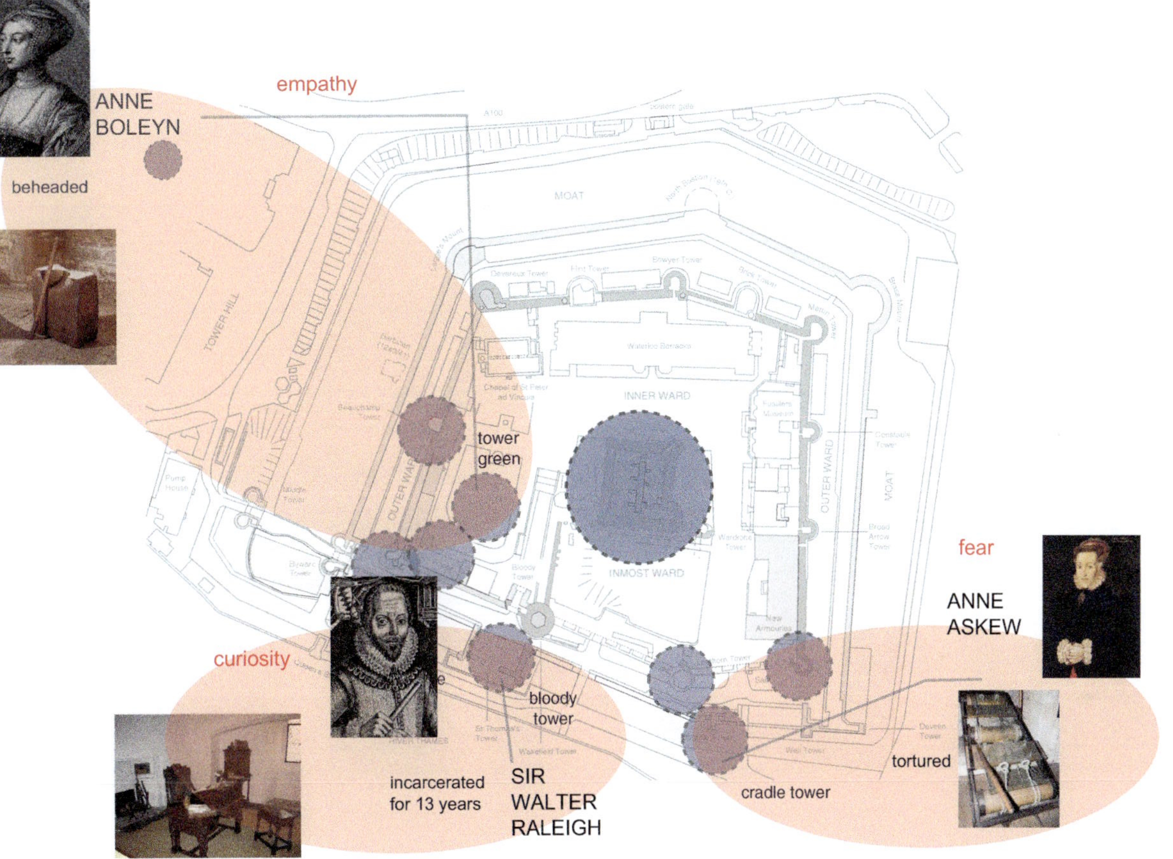


**PLATE 3** Imagining the potential for a range of emotional responses at the Tower of London

*Illustration:* Tom Duncan. Reproduced with the kind permission of RCMG. (Plan by Edward Impey © Historic Royal Palaces. Hans Eworth Portrait of a Lady called Anne Ayscough, Wikimedia Commons, the free media repository, *https://commons.wikimedia.org/w/index.php?title=File:Hans_Eworth_Portrait_of_a_Lady_call_Anne_Ayscough.jpg&oldid=252731449*. Portrait of Anne Boleyn by Hans Holbein and Sir Walter Raleigh, line engraving by R. Vaughan, Wellcome Library, London, CC BY 4.0. Execution block © Royal Armouries. Torture rack photographed at the Tower of London, Wikimedia Commons, the free media repository, *https://commons.wikimedia.org/wiki/File:A_Torture_Rack.jpg*. The Bloody Tower, Wikimedia Commons, the free media repository, *https://commons.wikimedia.org/wiki/File:Bloodytower_interior.jpg*.

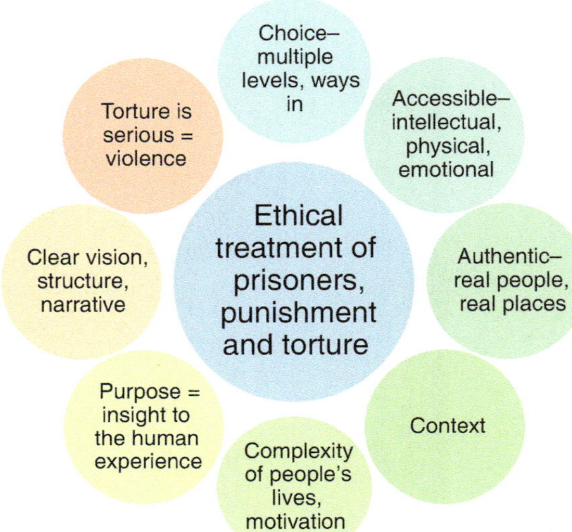


**PLATE 4** Framework for the Ethical Treatment of Prisoners, Punishment and Torture at the Tower of London

Reproduced with the kind permission of RCMG.

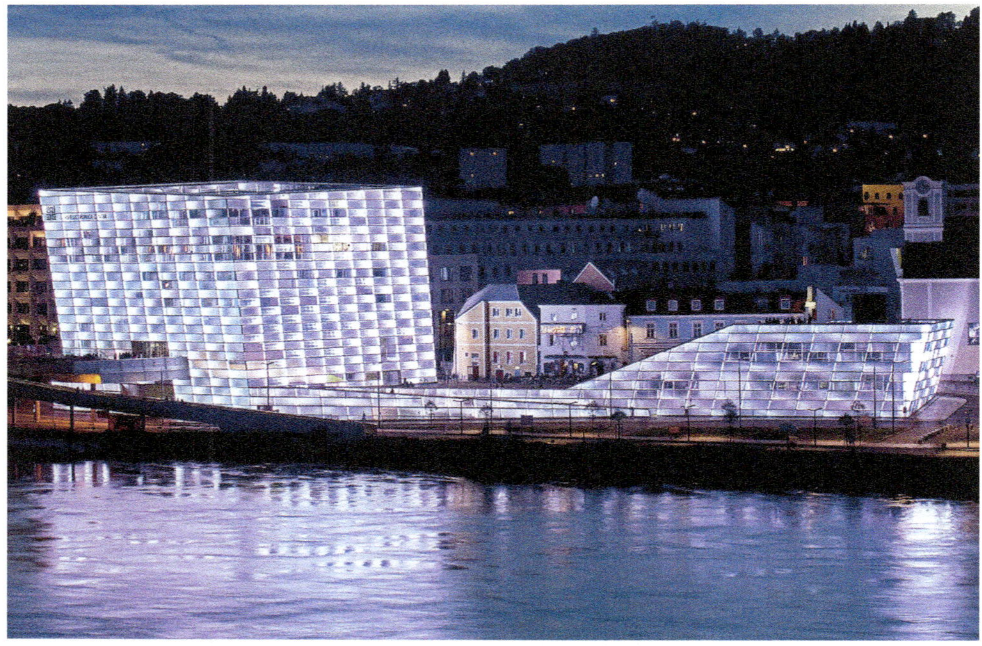

**PLATE 5** Ars Electronica Center, Linz, Austria

*Photo:* Ars Electronica Center Creative Commons 4.0.

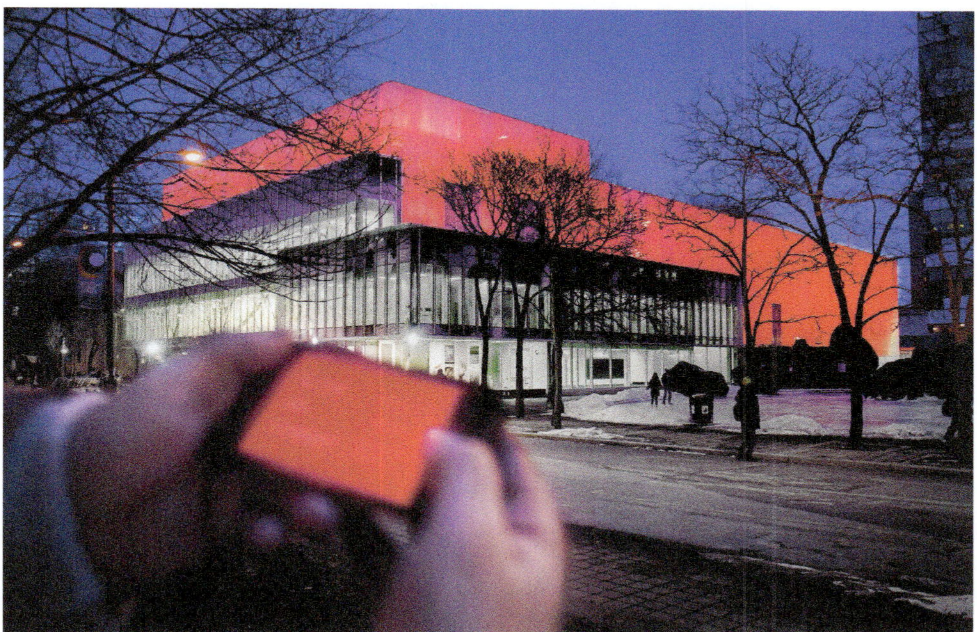

**PLATE 6** *In The Air, Tonight* (2014–2016), Public Visualization Studio

*Photo:* Public Visualization Studio. Reproduced with kind permission of the Artists.

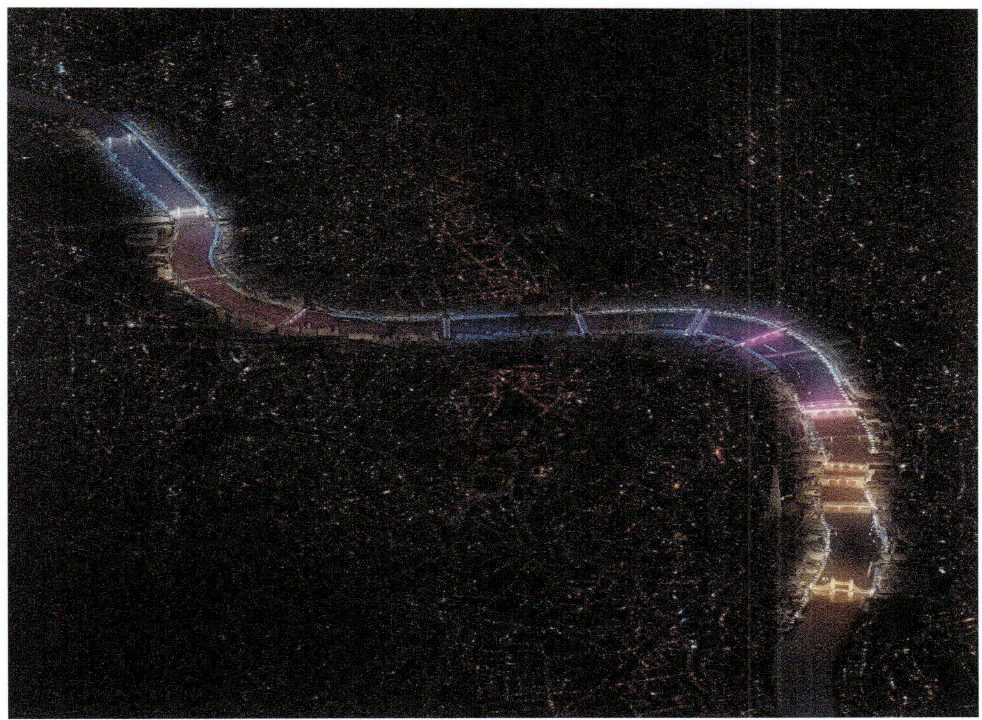

**PLATE 7** *The Illuminated River*, 'Current', Leo Villareal with Lifschutz Davidson Sandilands and Future\Pace

*Photo:* Leo Villareal with Lifschutz Davidson Sandilands and Future\Pace. Reproduced with kind permission of *The Illuminated River*.

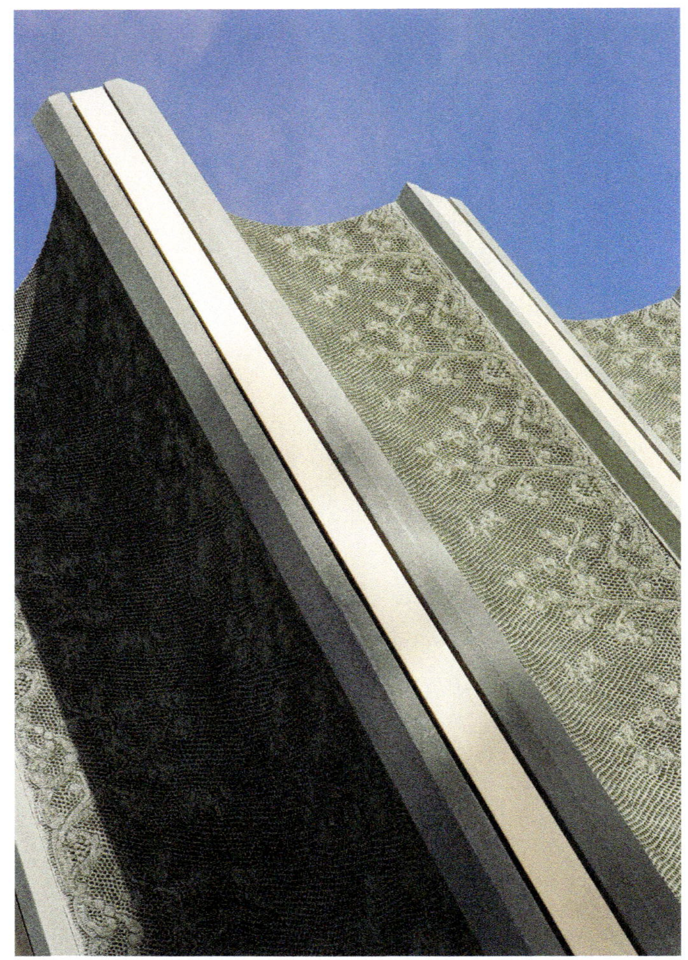

**PLATE 8** Nottingham Contemporary's lace pattern façade detailing

*Photo:* Martine Hamilton Knight. ©Nottingham Contemporary.

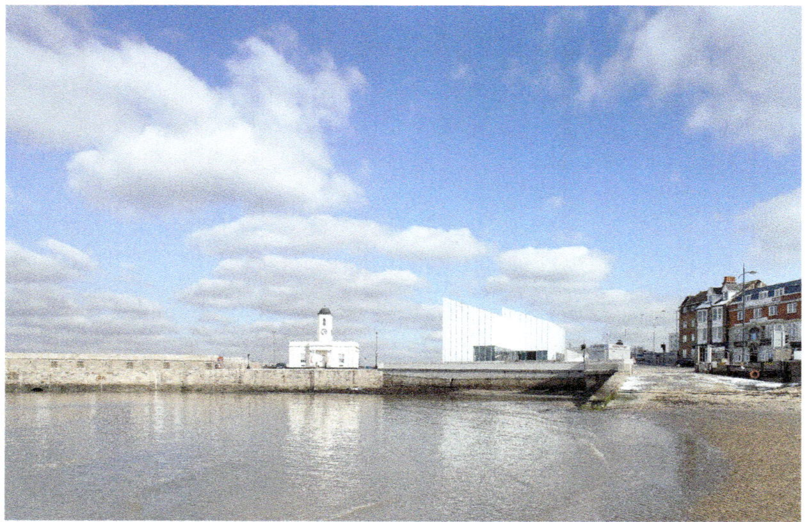

**PLATE 9** Turner Contemporary, Margate

*Photo:* Hufton and Crow.

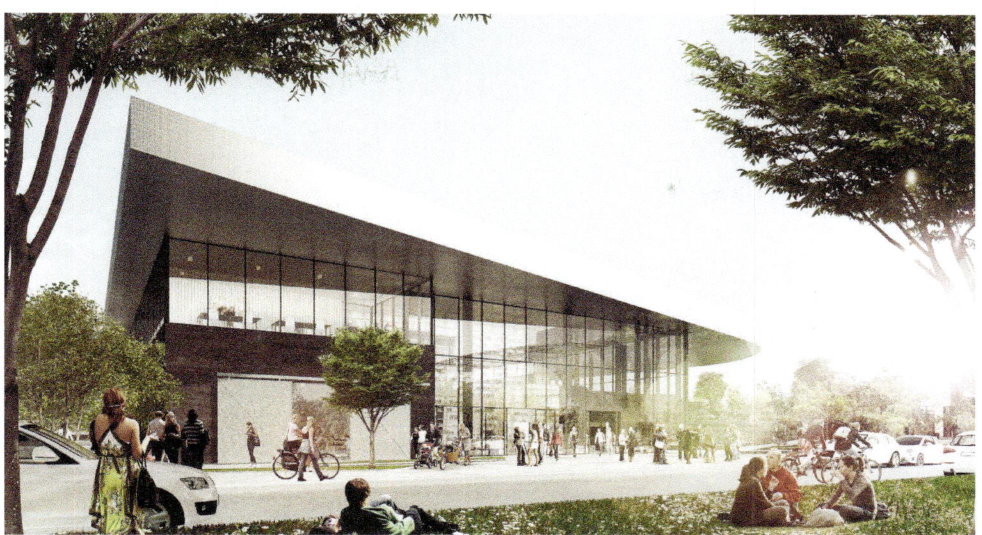

**PLATE 10** The Leaf, Henning Larsen. Competition entry for the Jan Shrem and Maria Manetti Shrem Museum of Art, UC Davis, California

*Design Architect:* Henning Larsen. Executive Architect: Gould Evans. Contractor: Oliver and Company. Project name: The Leaf. Community comments: iconic, hang-out, flexible, corporate, liability, stairs, empty, non-museum, social spaces, coffee shop. Photo: Courtesy of Henning Larsen.

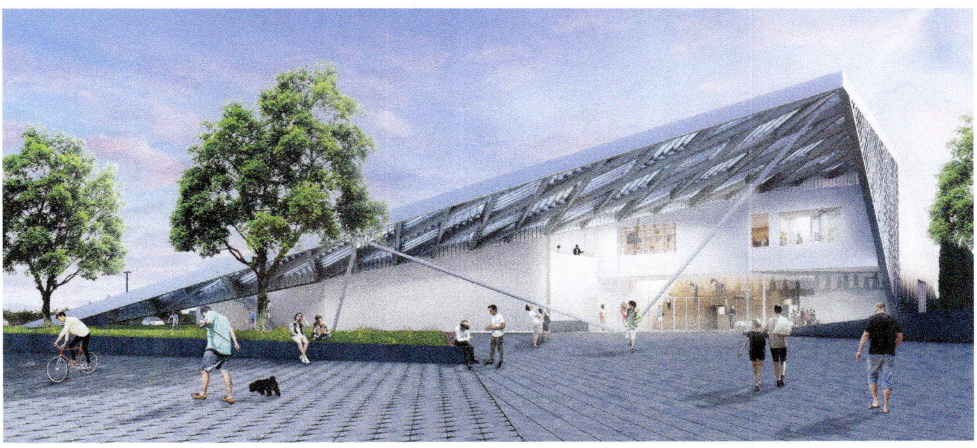

**PLATE 11** The Slant, WORKac. Competition entry for the Jan Shrem and Maria Manetti Shrem Museum of Art, UC Davis, California

*Design Architect:* WORKac. Executive Architect: Westlake Reed Leskosky. Contractor: Kitchell. Project name: The Slant. Community comments: cold, alien, exciting, showy, too architectural, palm trees, impenetrable, Las Vegas, form driven, beautiful but austere. Photo: Courtesy of WORKac.

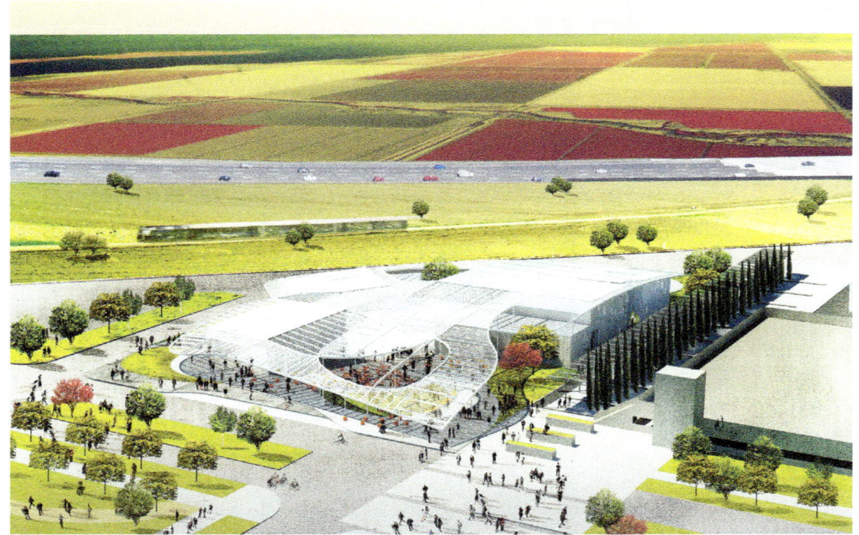

**PLATE 12** The Grand Canopy, SO – IL and Bohlin Cywinski Jackson. Winning design for the Jan Shrem and Maria Manetti Shrem Museum of Art, UC Davis, California

*Associated Architects:* SO – IL and Bohlin Cywinski Jackson. Contractor: Whiting-Turner. Project name: The Grand Canopy. Community comments: rollercoaster, welcoming, friendly, open, active, distinctive, too informal, accessible, site specific, best 24/7 experience, pedagogical tool, human-scale. Photo: Courtesy of SO – IL and Bohlin Cywinski Jackson.

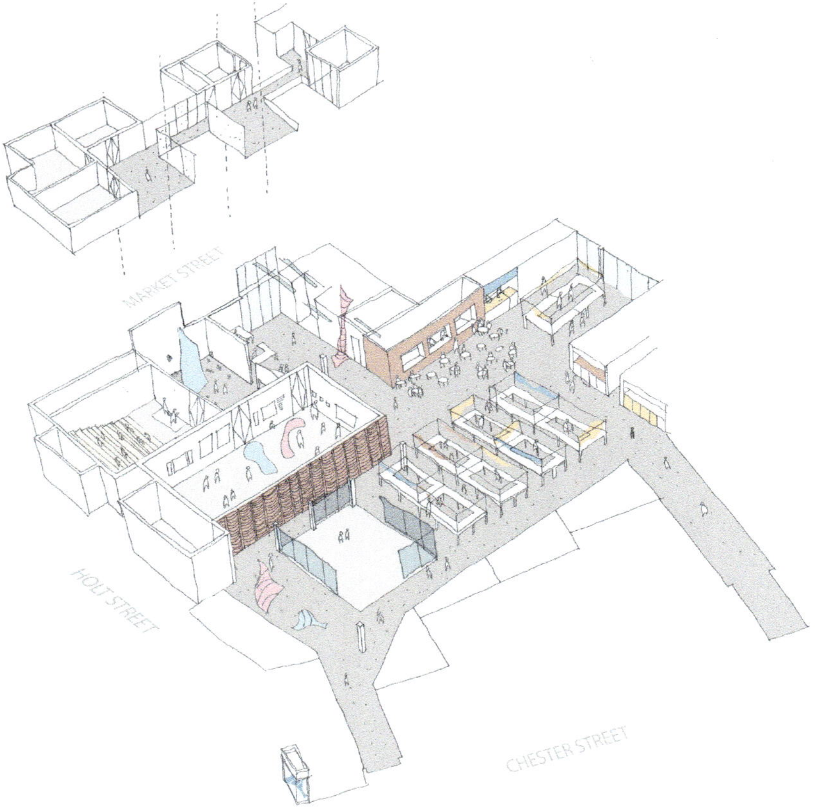


**PLATE 13** Proposed Oriel Wrecsam People's Market exploded axonometric

*Image:* Reproduced with kind permission of Featherstone Young.

# PART II

# Process

## Collaboration, experimentation and participation

Part II of *The Future of Museum and Gallery Design* focuses on Process, with chapters from China, Denmark, Germany, the US, and the UK. All the chapters purposefully set out to challenge conventional processes by exploring a range of contemporary projects and discussing novel visitor-centred and critical approaches to both museum making and museum-design research. The chapters are written by experienced designers, design researchers and PhD students who provide arguments, analyses and exemplar case studies of new galleries and exhibition strategies. Part II emphasises experimentation, participation and collaboration where designers, visitors, a range of museum specialists and researchers work together in various formations to find new ways of both doing museum design and reimagining the future of museums. A number of the chapters point to the need for revised management structures to enable these open and exploratory processes.

Part II starts with a chapter from leading American exhibition designer Kathleen McLean who has, over the last 20 years, continuously called for museums to experiment with their processes in order to stay relevant to their audiences in our rapidly changing world. Here, McLean makes an argument for revolutionising museum exhibition design through the prototyping process. She critiques linear design development processes and describes strategies, methods and examples of 'rapid prototyping' or whole-body experiences of complete exhibitions. She argues that although much has been written about team expertise, roles, and the power politics in exhibition design, there has been very little exploration of the actual process that shapes the outcomes of the work of these teams. McLean describes how she developed the 'Altered State: Marijuana in California' exhibition at the Oakland Museum of California, making three-dimensional mock-ups in the exhibition hall, integrating space, form, images, objects and text simultaneously so that the development team, stakeholders and end users could make judgements through situated sensory experience and full-scale spatial orientation. McLean offers several other examples of exhibition prototyping and concludes by reflecting on and updating her 2010 *Manifesto for the (R)evolution of Museum Exhibitions*.

Part II continues with an introduction to the notion of 'baggy space' from architect Sarah Featherstone and curator Jo Marsh. Together they engaged with the civic role of cultural organisations in the development of the Oriel Wrecsam People's Market gallery in Wrexham,

Wales. The site of the new gallery, a former multi-storey car park and market, offered an opportunity to create a new model of experimental space driven by socially engaged art programmes. This approach reverses the 'exhibition first, engagement second' convention. Rather, architects Featherstone Young designed generous, non-programmed 'baggy spaces' where townspeople can determine for themselves what kind of activity takes place. The location of the building suggested it could be a shortcut to the centre of the town and attract audiences who might not normally visit an art gallery or a city centre market. As a response, Featherstone Young redesigned the entrance to facilitate the shortcut and took inspiration from the everyday character of the streets in Wrexham to create a familiar space for habitual use that functions as an inclusive part of the public realm instead of an exclusive art environment.

Mette Houlberg Rung's discussion of innovative interpretation co-developed with visitor groups at the Statens Museum for Kunst in Copenhagen follows in Chapter 11. Art interpreter and researcher Houlberg Rung uses the idea of 'collective creativity' to define the principle of inviting users and other external stakeholders to be design partners in different projects and describes how this approach has been applied in temporary exhibition and display, educational and interpretational initiatives, and digital projects. She argues that museum design processes can shape the future of the museum through situational, context-orientated, user-centred collaboration. She acknowledges that, while this new type of design process may disrupt existing hierarchies within museum organisations, it has the potential to bring into play new forms of knowledge, and that museums may benefit considerably from a more inclusive, creative and co-productive design process.

In Chapter 12, Tony Butler, executive director of Derby Museums, Hannah Fox, project director, and Suzanne MacLeod introduce Derby Silk Mill – Museum of Making which will, when it re-opens in 2020, be the first major museum in the UK to have been developed, in its entirety, through participatory processes. The chapter explains how the process of human-centred, experimental design and the specific conditions of place were used at every stage to drive the project, to disrupt long-established organisational practices and to enable a process of co-production and collective problem solving with local people. Importantly, the chapter draws attention to the way in which a values-led approach to museum making, which seeks to reinvent the notion of the civic institution fit for the twenty-first century, was used to anchor and direct the human-centred design methodology. The project stands as an example of the importance of visitor-centred, socially aware approaches to museum making and provides a much-needed model of how this work can be taken forward in a mainstream museum.

In Chapter 13, exhibition designers Bill Haley and Oriel Wilson describe leading-edge approaches to inclusive design through a case study of The Museum at the Gateway Arch, one element of The Gateway Arch National Park in St Louis, Missouri, USA, developed with the National Park Service. Haley and Wilson explain how the principle of 'equality of experience for all' (as opposed to 'equality of access for all') was placed at the heart of creative and technical design for all exhibition spaces and media. During the four and a half year process of development, advice was sought from a large number of disability groups, and specialist disability rights advocates were integrated into the design decision-making process. This created a multi-dimensional collaboration where all partners were united by a cohesive approach to universal access. Haley describes how this enabled a fundamental shift away from incorporating piecemeal accessibility devices towards an overall holistic, human-centred design. Rather than simply 'ticking the box' of worldwide disability discrimination legislation, which can often lead to specially made 'alternatives' to exhibits, the process sets new standards in accessible design in its quest for equal experience for all and offers a number of new insights into what the future of museum and gallery design might entail.

In Chapter 14, curator Annette Loeseke draws attention to the institutional buy-in necessary to support experimental and reflective exhibition making processes as well as the need for institutions to allow the learning from experimental museum making to impact institutional hierarchies and processes. Loeseke focuses on the innovative Humboldt Lab Dahlem in Berlin, established to support the development of the new Humboldt Forum which will create a centre for world cultures on Berlin's Museum Island in a reconstruction of a lost royal palace. Discussing a number of focus groups undertaken with students to explore the visitor experience in three of the Lab's experimental exhibitions and keen to see the ambition of the Lab deliver concrete outcomes, Loeseke makes a case for a far greater focus on reception and a far deeper engagement with visitors in the development of new, boundary-crossing exhibition models. In the final stages of the chapter, Loeseke also draws attention to what she sees as unanticipated experiences of the planned architecture of the Forum, restating her call for colleagues in Germany to engage more fully with visitor research in the development of new spaces for culture.

The next chapter in Part II shifts its focus to China. In Chapter 15, researcher Sipei Lu discusses the dilemmas and potential of re-presenting socially engaged art, deeply rooted in its context, in the white box space of the museum. She recounts the difficulties of showing Nanting Research, an education project applying anthropological and art methods, in 'Civil Power', the opening exhibition of Beijing Minsheng Art Museum. Lu makes the point that exhibitions are not just an opportunity for display but a ground for social action. The chapter pays particular attention to the perspectives of socially engaged artists in China explaining how their voices are often overlooked or are assumed to correspond to the overarching curatorial theme. She argues that a rethinking of the way artists engage with the curatorial process would facilitate a deeper understanding of socially engaged arts among curators and audiences, and she points to a new role for museums in China not just as vehicles of display but as active agents of social change.

In Chapter 16, exhbition designer Clare Brown introduces the methods of experience design for products and services from which she distils key principles for exhibition design in large-scale history museums. Brown summarises three interviews looking at Service Design, User Experience Design, and Agile Software Development. She explains that service designers Peer Insight enable their clients to become first-hand witnesses to the customer feedback, which helps the clients come to the solutions on their own. As a result, Peer Insight facilitates solutions rather than provides predetermined propositions. Brown then interviews User Experience (UX) designer Jason Ulaszek, who worked on the Kigali Genocide Memorial. He reflects that the key to UX is sharing tools that not only elicit empathy but convert empathy into meaningful and sustainable action. Finally, Brown describes how Agile places less importance on a specific process, and more importance on the values and principles which enables flexibility and the capacity to react to unexpected changes.

In Chapter 17, Jona Piehl and David Francis, researchers with professional backgrounds in museum graphic design and interpretation, respectively, explore how practice and newly emerging museum-making research might work together. Both authors undertook a forensic analysis of 'Defining Beauty: The Body in Ancient Greek Art' at the British Museum London, 2015, providing a detailed analysis of the exhibition from their own critical standpoint. The analyses, taken together, revealed interesting inconsistencies in the design of the exhibition and opened up questions about how these inconsistences might be addressed in future. Piehl and Francis also found the analyses illuminated their different readings of narrative theory and prompted reflection on how their different practice-based backgrounds contribute to their respective analytical frameworks. They argue that a transparent dialogic or discursive approach to research, in other words a process where researchers from different backgrounds share their insights, has the potential to provide a deeper analysis of the object of study but also to bring about a productive and reflexive critique of the scaffolding of the research process itself.

Part II concludes with Tom Duncan's examination of filmic models and structures that he applies to his museum-making practice to both reflect on and design more engaging visitor experiences. Duncan argues that with the integration of powerful narrative and experiential elements into the museum, the understanding of the overall narrative structure of the visitor experience is perhaps more important than it has been before. He describes how visitors, moving through the museum, perform a kind of choreography. He makes the point that the timing of the sequence of spaces – in other words the design of the choreography – is as important as other architectural qualities such as adjacency, materiality or atmosphere. Duncan describes three case studies where he shows that a knowledge of narrative theory and film structures can be applied as a design tool to map and plan the spatio-temporal, physical and emotional journey of the visitor experience.

# 9

# EXAMINING PROCESS IN MUSEUM EXHIBITIONS

## A case for experimentation and prototyping

*Kathleen McLean*

### Abstract

If museums are to survive the major irreversible social changes brought on by technological advances, globalization, political unrest, and shifting public expectations, we will need to radically evolve our museum practices over the coming years. And we will need to examine outdated assumptions about museum exhibition 'best practices' in design, content development, creation, and management. This chapter elaborates upon potential approaches and strategies for revolutionizing museum exhibition design methods and processes, and includes examples of this work in several museums.

### Introduction

> Good societies need places where trust takes root and our common humanity comes first. Convivial museums are staging grounds where trust and human bonds can grow.
>
> *(McLean and Pollock 2010)*

With hostilities and intolerance on the rise around the world, we urgently need places in which to meet face-to-face and converse with strangers, to appreciate the traditions, beliefs, and values of others while examining our own, and to work together to develop visions for the future around our common humanity. We also need, more than ever, to learn to appreciate, share, and care for this planet we call home. As organizations designed to celebrate and interrogate the human spirit in all of its permutations, museums are uniquely positioned to support these urgent needs. But to my mind, most contemporary museums are still light years away from fulfilling their transformative potential.

Outdated assumptions about museum practice, particularly 'best practices' in exhibition design, content development, and management, prevent museum professionals from keeping pace with technological change, modes of learning, and public expectations, interests and needs. In the last few years, our world has changed considerably. Our visitors have changed, their expectations have changed, and we have changed. But most museums are still organized to conduct their core work of managing collections and creating exhibitions in the same ways and with the same assumptions that they have done for decades.

When I was asked to reflect on the evolution of methods and philosophies in museum exhibitions over the past 50 years and to speculate about their future in the Fiftieth Anniversary Issue of *Curator: The Museum Journal*, I found written evidence of deep stasis. As I read the first volume of the journal, published in 1958, I found it quite disconcerting that articulate museum professionals were presenting perspectives, proposing ideas, and describing visitor experiences that still are considered forward-thinking or even disruptive today (McLean 2007). Of course museums have changed over time, pressured by external forces and internal personalities. But many of these new ways of doing things have been less about visitors and access and more about efficiency, capital, and prestige. In the museums I have worked in, or with, throughout my practice, I have experienced a strong and steady resistance to reconsider or shift assumptions about professional roles, visitor necessities, and exhibition development processes.

## The current design development process

The exhibition development and design process most US museums use today in some form grew out of 1970s and 1980s power politics, when museum exhibition designers and educators were feeling like second-class citizens and not as 'professional' as their curator colleagues. For the most part, designers were treated as 'preparators' or the people who built and painted the walls. Educators were hardly considered at all and usually were treated as schoolteachers or babysitters by their curator colleagues. Consequently, educators began to claim their roles as 'interpreters' and 'visitor advocates', emphasizing models of learning theory that had been missing from previous exhibition development projects, and designers looked to other design professions for a process model that could codify and promote design expertise.

Much has been written about these shifting roles and power politics, from who should lead the project and have final say in decision-making to what types of expertise should be brought to bear in exhibition teams. Even today, in most discussions and documents about the process of making museum exhibitions, emphasis is placed on the roles of the makers, their relationships, and their domains of influence, and very little attention is given to the actual *process* that shapes the outcomes of the work of these teams. In fact, when some museum professionals describe a 'linear model' of exhibition making, they often are referring to a situation in which:

> One individual (generally a curator) [has] sole responsibility for development and implementation and, under his or her supervision, the exhibition move[s] sequentially from one support professional to the next. In the linear model, still common in some natural history and many art museums, the curator has both authority and responsibility for the exhibition.
>
> *(Neves 2002)*

But there is another linear model inherent in exhibition making that creates even more problematic constraints: the design development process.

In the early 1980s, many museums began to adopt the general architectural and engineering design development process with its clear-cut phases, moving from idea and conceptual or schematic design to 50% and 100% design development, then on to construction documentation, construction and fabrication, and finally to installation, all the while getting reviews, approvals, and sign-offs to move from one phase to the next (McLean 1993). This phased architectural process still works for some exhibitions, particularly for collections of statically displayed and showcased objects, trade shows designed to sell products, and infrastructure-intensive exhibitions at sites like aquaria, with their need for reliable life-support systems. And it is a perfectly good process if you are designing an office building, an apartment complex, or a wastewater treatment facility. These constructions can last for hundreds of years, they must support a variety of functions, and most importantly, they must provide long-term safety and usability for their inhabitants, thus the need for inspections, sign-offs, and approvals at the end of each phase of design and construction.

These same constraints apply to the construction of new museum buildings, but with at least one additional complication. Usually, new museum buildings are expected to open their doors with new exhibitions housed within, and exhibition creators are expected to keep pace with the architectural and engineering processes by moving quickly through idea development and conceptual or schematic design, and completing exhibition design plans and elevations in time to inform the architectural design of gallery spaces.

But by its very nature, the linear, phased design development and approvals process does not support the iterative elaboration of ideas, the creation of participatory environments, and the flexibility to evolve and change as a result of public engagement and visitor input. Museum exhibitions, and their juxtapositions of ideas, objects, images, digital media, and phenomena, are dynamic environments that ideally can change over time, and are designed to engage the mind and body, in order to inspire reflection, provoke dialogue and debate, and invite participation.

Exhibition makers must choreograph dozens of ideas and their resultant instantiations, but not all ideas are born fully formed. Some ideas emerge early in the conceptual development of an exhibition, and they can be strong and compelling and have a life throughout the whole project. Other ideas need more nurturing, refining, and time to develop. Some ideas can't survive the scrutiny and elaboration that a rigorous creative process can bring to bear. Some ideas, maybe even the best ideas, can be late bloomers, unfolding at the eleventh hour. But if that eleventh hour is after the 100% design development phase – what some managers call the 'pencils down phase' – these ideas will never see the light of day.

## Prototyping is design

Museums need an exhibition development process that is more fluid, more nurturing of creative idea development, and that enables design and content to evolve *together* and *iteratively*. We need a process that supports the creation of the full-body experiences that are exhibitions, not by sitting at our computers selecting collection objects from tiny images on a database, or using CAD programs and white models to simulate three-dimensional environments, or writing exhibit texts in a two-dimensional vacuum. We need to design our exhibitions in three-dimensional space, to experiment with different forms of mock-ups and prototyping with stakeholders and end users as an essential element of the design process, and to develop ideas, texts, and spaces *simultaneously*.

In industrial design and business domains, prototyping is defined as 'the activity of making basic models of designs for a machine or other industrial product' (Cambridge Business English Dictionary 2011). I prefer instead the etymological roots of the word 'prototype' which, in Greek, means a primitive form or a first impression, because they convey the sense of giving shape to nascent ideas, of starting at the beginning. Prototyping *is* design, and it affords a unique kind of haptic, three-dimensional creativity and spatial orientation that raises different kinds of questions and affords different ways of looking at design problems. It allows us to begin our work quickly as initial ideas emerge, and can be as simple as using a humble design palette of object photocopies, handwritten words, and paper walls. This process is quite different from the image walls and storyboards seen in most design studios, which display a variety of images that can include 'look and feel' references, examples of materials and finishes, outlines of narratives, and images of objects.

I was first introduced to the practice of testing exhibit components with visitors by Chandler Screven and his work in exhibit evaluation beginning in the 1970s. Screven (1974) focused on formative evaluation as an exhibit design technique and proposed a set of experimental questions and evaluation practices to iteratively improve exhibits during design. But it was not until 1994 when I joined the staff of the Exploratorium in San Francisco that I began to understand the potentially transformative power of prototyping during exhibit development and design. Frank Oppenheimer, the Exploratorium's founder, believed that the whole organization was a work in progress, and that the exhibits were 'working prototypes' that could be continually tinkered with and improved over time (Oppenheimer and Staff of the Exploratorium 1986). Over the years, a variety of museums, particularly science museums, have incorporated formative evaluation and some form of prototyping, usually of individual exhibits and components, into their development process.

Today, some museums are exploring prototyping techniques in professional development workshops in a classroom or studio setting, which allows the freedom to try a variety of approaches without immediately impacting the organization, and allows time for staff to consider which projects or exhibits in the organization might best be informed by prototyping efforts. Some museums are using their permanent galleries as temporary labs for this work, since the activity, once completed and reviewed, can be taken away quickly without impacting visitors' experiences in the actual galleries over time. A few museums are creating or relying on innovation labs or incubator spaces that encourage open-ended exploration of new methods and processes, and some are prototyping exhibit elements to incorporate into new exhibitions (McLean 2015). A few museums are prototyping whole exhibitions, which allows creators to examine the effects of adjacencies, the interplay of ideas across space, and some environmental factors, although some effects, such as those of material finishes, lighting, pacing, and the conceptual experience of the exhibition, might not be apparent until final installation.

When the Oakland Museum of California, for example, decided to create and present the exhibition, 'Altered State: Marijuana in California', I was contracted to be exhibition lead, with the expressed understanding that this was an experimental project with a potentially controversial topic and with less funding and less time than is usual for their temporary exhibitions. We needed to move quickly, test our ideas with visitors, and challenge our own assumptions about what was appropriate and effective. After a few months of gathering data, establishing scope, and articulating goals within a team structure of meetings and discussions, we shifted to a major prototyping effort in which we created the entire exhibition with as much content material and as many ideas as we were able to gather at that point.

This first iteration, which took several weeks to create, was rough and messy, with butcher paper, handwritten texts and diagrams, and photocopied images and articles taped to the walls. Once visitors entered the prototype, everything changed. The team dynamic, which was contentious and difficult when sitting around the table and discussing goals and content in the abstract, shifted to a much more collaborative and creative effort when watching visitors engage with the material. Exhibition content, based on what we assumed would be interesting to visitors, expanded to include more data in some cases, since visitors were asking for it, and shifted emphasis and focus throughout the process. New ideas for exhibit elements sprang up from conversations and were some of the most compelling visitor experiences in the long run. The pace of decision-making and design development quickened, since visitor reactions provided the team with evidence of conceptual and experiential strengths and weaknesses that could be enhanced or ameliorated quickly.

Over the next three months, the prototype grew and morphed, and remained as messy, as we revised the installation after every major visitor event. Through conversations and cued interviews with visitors, staff, and stakeholders, the exhibition content evolved until it was ready for final design and fabrication. In looking back at the overall process after the final exhibition opened, staff articulated valuable learning experiences (Seiter 2016), and the exhibition won several national awards of excellence. Arguably, the prototyping could have continued through final design and installation, but the museum shifted at that point back to its traditional design development process as more production and fabrication staff were incorporated into the project and deadlines were closing in.

The Autry Museum of the American West in Los Angeles, California, was faced with a different set of opportunities during its final year of development of a major organizational initiative called 'California Continued', which was designed to incorporate more Native Californian perspectives into the galleries and to showcase objects from its spectacular Southwest Museum collections. The initiative consisted of a building renovation, the creation of a Native California garden, and two exhibition galleries – one for temporary exhibitions and one for a more long-term exhibition called 'Human Nature', about living Traditional Ecological Knowledge in Native California communities and the value of that knowledge for the people of California today.

While the building renovation, the garden, and the temporary exhibition were all moving forward as planned, the 'Human Nature' exhibition was behind schedule for a variety of reasons, including major staff changes over time. With only one year to go before opening, the museum agreed to develop and design the exhibition through a prototyping process in order to incorporate more Native California voices and traditional wisdom in the design process, and to test out exhibit ideas quickly with visitors and stakeholders. When construction of the new gallery was completed, the exhibition team moved in, and created an entire 15,000-square-foot exhibition out of cardboard and paper, beginning with clusters of concepts and images of objects. Text labels were written on the walls and several visitor events brought people into the space for discussion and questions. Exhibition staff worked in the gallery space, developing ideas and designing exhibit components simultaneously. As new material became available, it was worked into the physical space in a continually shifting dance of ideas and elements that evolved quickly.

Some staff openly embraced this new way of working and felt a creative liberation of sorts. For others, who were used to writing and working from comprehensive research documents, or having months to process and prepare collection objects, or designing with digital software that emphasized measurements and standardization, the process was extremely difficult. The prototype essentially took the place of most of the working plans for fabrication, lessening the need for the usual construction drawings and documentation, which created uneasiness with some fabricators and installation crews. Despite the extremely tight time frame, the installation opened on time, with some elements still considered prototypical and slated for change. The conversations that evolved during the prototype formed the basis for future changes.

In my experience, the most powerful contributions prototyping can make in creating exhibitions are the depth of the dialogue among colleagues, stakeholders, visitors, and exhibition creators and the powerful influence those dialogues can have on the evolving ideas, designs, and experiences. This iterative contributory process requires only a few elements to get started, elements that provide a simple set of initial conceptual and physical structures that grow and change over time, as more people participate. Interacting with these structures is what urban planner William Whyte (2001) calls the 'triangulation' effect, which encourages people, even strangers, to come together comfortably to focus on, talk about, and engage with the material at hand. It also helps exhibition creators to focus on three-dimensional ideas and experiences rather than roles and responsibilities. The beauty of this kind of experimental and creative work is that it can happen almost anywhere and at any time, particularly when museums are considering embarking upon new change efforts in uncharted territory. It requires very little planning to get started, and more than anything else, it requires a willingness to be open to new ideas and new ways of working.

## Learning to experiment

In 2010, The Pew Center for Arts & Heritage created a professional development project to help museum practitioners explore creativity and risk-taking in their exhibitions and programs. Over the years, despite an ongoing call for experimental proposals in their funding initiatives, staff at the Center were finding that traditional approaches and predictable plans restrained many of the proposals they received. One of their project publications articulated the challenge:

> We believe that the future of public history practice . . . depends on our willingness to take risks – to challenge audience expectations, push beyond hushed reverence and nostalgia, wander outside our comfort zones, and allow for healthy organizational dissonance.
>
> *(Adair, Koloski and Liu 2010)*

Their professional development project, called 'No Idea Is Too Ridiculous: An Experiment in Creative Practice', encouraged cultural and museum professionals from the Philadelphia region to apply in teams of two or three and propose an experimental project with a public impact that they wanted to undertake at their museum or site. Those selected, from a wide range of cultural organizations in and around Philadelphia, attended an intensive two-day kickoff workshop at the Center, were given $1,000 exclusively for hard costs, and then had eight weeks to plan and implement their projects. The intentionally small amount of money, the short time frame, and the funder's encouragement to push toward the 'ridiculous' forced participants to expand beyond their palette of traditional materials and techniques, to try things out quickly, and to refrain from self-censorship and statements like 'we don't do that here'.

If not totally supportive of the processes and the projects, management at most of the participating museums were, at least, comfortable with this experimental approach because of its temporal nature and the backing of a funder like the Center. Conceived as a one-time workshop, the Center continued the project for five years, and dozens of organizations participated, including history and art museums, science centers and historic houses, botanical gardens and theater companies. 'No Idea Is Too Ridiculous' focused less on actual outcomes and more on creative practice, the processes of rapid idea generation, and working responsively with communities and audiences. Projects ranged from public programs and events to new processes for creating exhibitions, including the creation of a 'Musical Finding Aid' for the archives at the Historical Society of Pennsylvania, which explored how music could contribute to the emotional information about a collection, and 'Bartered Goods', an exhibition at Bartram Gardens that revisited the eighteenth-century Bartram plant trade, by bartering plants with local community residents in exchange for objects and stories about their histories that were exhibited in the gallery.

As consultant and facilitator of the project, what struck me most were participants' deep hesitations to loosen up their methods and practices and to try something new and unusual for fear of how their managers might respond. More often than not, the projects did, indeed, experience the 'healthy organizational dissonance' the Center staff encouraged, particularly when projects didn't conform to organizational norms. At the same time, most participants described a sense of unleashed creativity as they were given permission to experiment, and at the end of the project, most echoed the sentiments from the Historical Society of Pennsylvania:

> Trying something new has shown us that there are no limits in what our cultural heritage materials can be used for, and that we cannot predict how users may benefit from these materials. Breaking from typical professional conventions has shown us how new doors can be opened with just a little extra thinking.
>
> *(Adair, Koloski and Liu 2010)*

## Embracing a new kind of change

Despite a reluctance to alter traditional practices, many museums and galleries are in the midst of major change, often because of external pressures, such as decreases in attendance, membership, or government funding; changes in community demographics and psychographics; termination of leases; or promises of renewal through new funding opportunities. Internal pressures, like changes in boards and leadership, are also an impetus for some to reposition themselves.

Exhibitions, along with museum buildings, the most prominent and distinctive of a museum's public offerings, are usually a major focus of these change efforts and initiatives. Aging infrastructure, worn materials, and outdated technologies most often give the impetus to change, as new exhibitions completely replace older ones, usually with more state-of-the-art technology embedded within them, much like buying a new automobile. While exhibition presentation and furniture styles change, often quite dramatically, underlying assumptions about exhibition creation often do not, because changing the fundamental ways we work is quite difficult.

In 2009, in order to provoke a dialogue about prototyping and experimentation as methods for increasing visitor engagement in exhibitions, I drafted the *Manifesto for the (R)evolution of Museum Exhibitions*. Over the years, it has evolved into a specific set of actions aimed at changing museum exhibition making, with input and critique from a wide range of colleagues, and even some museum visitors along the way (McLean 2010). Some of the actions in the current iteration of the Manifesto, such as 'think of visitors as partners', 'collaborate with others', and 'acknowledge the real-time world around us', are broad philosophical behaviors that are in consideration today at museum conferences and in more forward-thinking museums, even if they have not yet fully taken hold in practice.

Some of the actions, such as 'provide more amenities', 'advocate for what you believe in', and 'strive for sustainability', are common-sense values in the public service realm, yet even today, they are not as evident in museums and exhibitions as one might assume. Some of the actions, like 'pay more attention to the ideas', 'leave room for the imagination', and 'acknowledge that exhibitions are essentially and uniquely about evidence', are ongoing reminders that museum strengths need continual reaffirmation as the forces of the marketplace privilege profits and efficiencies over ideas, imagination, and evidence.

Six of the Manifesto actions, described next, are arguably the actions most critical to fundamental change in museum exhibition practice, and support frames of mind that are essential to the more fluid, dialogical, iterative process of prototyping as exhibition design.

### *Strive for mutations*

In a biological context, mutations create variations in the gene pool. The less favorable mutations tend to disappear from the gene pool through natural selection, while the more favorable ones tend to accumulate. This is called evolution. Although characterizations of mutants in popular culture have led many people to consider them undesirable creatures, they are essential to any evolutionary process. By proactively creating mutant or anomalous elements within an exhibition, whether or not they are beneficial in the long run, we intentionally push ourselves beyond comfort zones and familiar territory. Even in the most conservative museums, small mutant-forming actions can destabilize traditions and provide learning opportunities for exhibition makers. If not worthy of employing in another exhibition, they can disappear.

For example, as an exhibition designer, I am often annoyed by the formulaic approach to object labels and their tidy rectangular shapes. In one installation, I hand-cut all the case labels into irregular-shaped pieces of paper and arranged them with the objects in the cases, which created a lot of discussion among museum colleagues and exhibition design students, many of whom thought the labels to be 'tacky'. Most visitors, on the other hand, did not comment on them in any of the visitor studies we undertook.

### *Experiment*

Unlike mutations, which can pop up as anomalous or spontaneous elements within an exhibition, experiments require an intentional hypothesis or supposition, made with some modicum of evidence, as a starting point for further investigation. Formative evaluation is a good example of a process that underpins one type of exhibit experimentation, particularly related to design factors that afford comprehensibility and usability. For example, during the renovation of the Oakland Museum of California's Gallery of California Art, education staff created a prototyping lab in the center of the gallery to test a variety of interpretive techniques, using cued interviews, surveys, and other formative evaluation methods to collect visitor experiences and code those responses as data. Interpretive elements that met articulated learning objectives and experiences were developed further. The prototyping lab was an uncomfortable intervention for some of the art curators, who saw the messiness of the lab as detracting from the aesthetic refinement of the gallery. Nevertheless, almost four years of messy prototyping ultimately led to one of the most popular and compelling elements in the new gallery, a digital interactive portrait station called 'You Are Here', in which visitors can draw their own portraits and submit them for instant display in the gallery amongst portraits from the museum's collection (Faria and Nelson 2010).

All aspects of museum exhibition making, from idea development and label writing to final design and fabrication, can benefit from experimental processes without necessarily employing evaluation protocols and formal data analysis. Experiments can be as simple as showing visitors several styles of exhibit label writing before selecting one to employ throughout a gallery, or placing several objects together and asking potential visitors to converse with exhibition creators about the connections they make. We need to identify common assumptions in our own museum cultures, articulate hypotheses that reflect these assumptions, and conduct experiments to determine if the outcomes are as predicted. We need to consider these experiments 'feedback loops' that improve our exhibition knowledge and practice.

### *Design for flexibility and change*

Keep things fresh and up to date. Embrace the incomplete. There is no such thing as permanence. As the pace of change accelerates around the globe, museums still retain their sedentary reputation as places with 'the same old stuff'. We need to develop ways to keep exhibition content current, and find new, sustainable ways to continually refresh our technologies. We need to shift assumptions away from the old and outdated paradigm of 'permanent galleries' that only change every 20 years to the new realization of museums as convivial public spaces that respond to and change with public engagement (McLean and Pollock 2010). At the core of experimentation and prototyping is the ability to try out new ideas and ways of doing things, and the ability to change things if they are not working as planned, or if new, more compelling ideas arise, or if exhibit information is outdated or inaccurate. People today have continual access to radically current, minute-by-minute content from unlimited sources using the latest technology, and they expect the same from museums and exhibitions.

### *Work smaller, quicker, and cheaper*

Don't invest so much time and money that you lose your sense of adventure. Major barriers to experimentation in exhibitions are the long time frames required for an exhibition to move from conception to installation, the prevalent notion that small exhibitions have little or no marketing and advertising value, and the assumption of a baseline prerequisite of high production values and 'museum quality' levels of finish. Most exhibitions are elaborate affairs. Museum professionals often are so enthusiastic to share what they know about a given body of knowledge, with so much to tell, that exhibitions can easily turn into mega-projects no matter how simple the intentions. The desire for comprehensiveness tends to tie up all the loose ends of ideas with a finality that leaves little for the imagination to take hold. Issues of comprehensiveness aside, the phased exhibition development process exacerbates the problems of time and expense. Content developers and designers are expected to operate within fixed phases, and produce completed work at some point in the process (which tends to slow them down and strive for perfection before handing off their work to others). Prototyping allows us to be nimble, to employ simple materials, to try out methods and ideas quickly, and revise, improve, and iterate until we reach the 'sweet spot' of engagement. In the long run, prototyping can even *reduce* the amount of time and money it takes to create exhibitions.

### *Mix things up*

Museums tend to operate in a realm of silos, divisions, and many degrees of separation. Staff are separate from visitors, and they sometimes even work in buildings far away from the public galleries; art, history, and science are explored in distinct, bounded disciplines, and usually even reside within different types of museum; and content and ideas are considered separate from design and environment. As a result, different exhibition maker roles are considered separate and often impermeable: curators still assume the role of content authority, responsible for articulating and refining ideas, elaborating upon them in wall texts and catalogues, and then passing off these ideas to designers who will design an exhibition around them. Even the alternative 'team approach' to exhibition development, with its advocacy model of people representing different disciplines, often has reinforced silos, as territory is claimed and roles defined. This multidisciplinary world requires us to cross boundaries, create mash-ups, and emphasize connections.

### *Design exhibitions as if they are programs*

Exhibitions are not static products. Instead, like theater, film, dance, and music, exhibitions are creative endeavors that require artistic vision, diverse talents, and ongoing interactions and relationships with active audiences. Most excellent exhibitions, exhibitions that are memorable and powerful, are created by ensembles of exhibition artists who know a great deal about many aspects of exhibition creation – from idea development, object display, and storytelling to sensory learning, spatial writing, and haptic environments – and they look to their audiences for feedback that helps shape the final experience.

## Conclusion

I have been told repeatedly over the years that museums are not very nimble organizations: they are conservative, cautious, and backward-looking by their very nature, and they change at a glacial pace. With such an ironic metaphor to spur us on, it is time to push for a different kind of change. Since museums, like glaciers, change more rapidly around the edges and contain anomalies in their interstices, I prefer to explore and work in these regions, where there is a bit more room to try things out and the freedom to be more experimental. I have found that when colleagues and stakeholders can experience evidence of the effects of simple experiments and actions, they can much more easily embrace and support a new idea and/or process. In my experience, concrete evidence of visitor engagement inspires change and an eagerness to try new methods of exhibit making. And the ability to change might well be the most important skill of the 21st century.

## References

Adair, B., Koloski, L., and Liu, J. (2010) *No Idea Is Too Ridiculous: An Experiment in Creative Practice*, Philadelphia: Pew Centre for Arts and Heritage.

*Cambridge Business English Dictionary* (2011) Cambridge: Cambridge University Press. Online. Available HTTP: http://dictionary.cambridge.org/us/dictionary/english/prototyping Accessed 22 July 2017.

Faria, M. and Nelson, K. (2010) 'How We Learned to Listen: Research and Evaluation', in Henry, B. and McLean, K. (eds) *How Visitors Changed Our Museum*, Oakland: Oakland Museum of California.

McLean, K. (1993) *Planning for People in Museum Exhibitions*, Washington, DC: Association of Science-Technology Centers.

McLean, K. (2007) 'Do Museum Exhibitions Have a Future?', *Curator: The Museum Journal*, 50(1), pp. 109–21.

McLean, K. (2010) 'Manifesto for the (R)evolution of Museum Exhibitions', *Exhibitionist*, 29(1), pp. 40–50.

McLean, K. (2015) 'Learning to Be Nimble: Museum Incubators for Exhibition Practice', *Exhibitionist*, 34(1), pp. 8–13.

McLean, K. and Pollock, W. (2010) *The Convivial Museum*, Washington, DC: Association of Science-Technology Centers.

Neves, C. (2002) *The Making of Exhibitions: Purpose, Structure, Roles and Process*, Washington, DC: Smithsonian Institution Office of Policy and Analysis.

Oppenheimer, F. and Staff of the Exploratorium (1986) *Working Prototypes: Exhibit Design at the Exploratorium*, San Francisco: Exploratorium.

Screven, C. (1974) *The Measurement and Facilitation of Learning in the Museum Environment: An Experimental Analysis*, Washington, DC: Smithsonian Institution Press.

Seiter, S. (2016) 'Prototyping for "Altered State: Marijuana in California" at OMCA', *Western Museums Association Blog*. Online. Available HTTP: www.westmuse.org/articles/prototyping-altered-state-marijuana-california-omca Accessed 22 July 2017.

Whyte, W. (2001) *The Social Life of Small Urban Spaces*, New York: Project for Public Spaces.

# 10

# DESIGNING AND PROGRAMMING IN 'BAGGY' SPACE

## A case study of the Oriel Wrecsam People's Market project

*Sarah Featherstone and Jo Marsh*

### Abstract

The 'baggy space' concept is about touching an environment just enough, or as little as possible, to enable others to fill the gaps, to garner ownership and create a place that can be used habitually, and open up the potential of useful, meaningful experiences. At Oriel Wrecsam People's Market in Wrexham, Wales, local people questioned the worth of a new art gallery and what it can offer them both socially and economically. This chapter describes how the project team working on the new art gallery responded by thinking deeply about the civic role of cultural organisations and challenging the traditional art gallery environment with its rigid, dedicated spaces and exhibition-led programmes in order to create a new model that offers looser and more experimental space and socially engaged programmes that surpass public expectations.

### Introduction

The use value of the arts, particularly contemporary art, has long been a topic of polarised debate, perhaps never more so than during the current period of 'global crisis and great uncertainty' (Artsnight 2016). In the UK, local authority arts provision across the country has diminished since 2010 as a result of austerity measures and cuts to public services, and the pressure on remaining provision to justify its place, both to audiences and elected council members, has increased. Publicly funded arts projects are ever more frequently measured against outcomes, such as reducing unemployment, requiring quantitative results. Concerns are often raised over the validity of spending public money on cultural activities, when budget cuts have meant, for example, closure of key services: 'All that money wasted! No money for youth centres and day care centres for the elderly, but they can waste millions on this white elephant. I could cry!' (Wrexham.com 2017). As these comments indicate, some people understandably question the validity of money being spent on cultural developments they see as being aimed at wealthy tourists, when locally, services they need are cut.

In this context, we see a growing shift towards socially engaged art practice that is largely happening outside of a gallery setting or cultural institution. These are grass-roots, bottom-up activities that seek direct impact on people's lives. One example is the *Arte Util* movement, which translates as the Useful Art movement, initiated by artist Tania Bruguera. Bruguera worked with curators at the Queens Museum, New York; the Van Abbemuseum, Eindhoven; and Grizedale Arts in Coniston, UK, to devise a list of criteria for what constitutes Arte Util. The list includes the statement that projects should 'Pursue new uses for art within society' and 'have practical, beneficial outcomes for users' (Arte Util 2017). Another example is the 2015 Turner Prize, which was awarded to the art, design and architecture collective Assemble for their urban regeneration project in collaboration with Granby Four Streets Community Land Trust. Through the project, Assemble established the Granby Workshop, which was conceived as 'a social enterprise making handmade products for homes. . . [and] training and employing local people' (Assemble 2015). The project has been described as 'a far cry from other winners such as Damien Hirst's bisected cow and calf in formaldehyde, or Martin Creed's light going on and off' (Brown 2015). Other indicators of a cultural shift include the 2016 launch of the Gulbenkian Foundation's *Inquiry into the Civic Role of Arts Organisations* as well as the work of Middlesbrough Institute of Modern Art (mima), the self-appointed 'Useful Museum'.

However, there is arguably still an overall deficiency in the way that socially engaged art practice is represented within gallery settings. In 2015, Axis web commissioned a piece of research called *Validation beyond the Gallery* in response to the problem that 'Artists operating outside the gallery have come to play an essential role in society, yet these activities appear misunderstood, poorly profiled and simply not valued at the level of practice supported and promoted by the gallery sector' (Smith 2015). In institutional terms, engagement and public programming generally take their lead from exhibition programmes; they are planned around them and in response to them. There is some logic to this, given that exhibitions take a great deal of logistical forward planning, where public programmes by their nature have the capacity to be more responsive. However, the traditional 'exhibition first, engagement second' model is arguably not wholly suitable in a context where the arts are increasingly required to operate across disciplines, making a tangible contribution to civic life. It could be reasoned that exhibition programmes need to 'catch up' and that new models of engagement-led programming are now needed.

In the current UK socioeconomic and political climate, it is clear that the arts have potential to address pressing issues and to positively impact on daily life. This was reinforced by Baroness Kay Andrew's report of March 2014, *Culture and Poverty: Harnessing the Power of the Arts, Culture and Heritage to Promote Social Justice in Wales* (Welsh Government 2014a), and later by the Welsh government's report of December 2016, *Light Springs through the Dark: A Vision for Culture in Wales*, which states that:

> At a time like this it would be easy to say that we cannot afford to invest in culture, that it is some kind of 'luxury spending' that can no longer be justified. To adopt that approach would be a serious mistake. Culture is important, and has intrinsic worth. But we should also recognise its growing value to our economy, and the vital contribution that it can make in the effective delivery of other areas of public policy.
>
> *(Welsh Government 2016)*

What kind of cultural setting and associated programming can respond to and support this socially embedded, civic role for the arts, becoming not only aspirational and challenging but also useful and habitual?

This was the main question the project team at Oriel Wrecsam People's Market (OW People's Market)[1] in Wrexham, North Wales, asked as they considered how to approach the design of a new home for the town's art gallery. Originally imagined as a stand-alone building, this chapter describes how the project team, galvanised by feedback from local people, began to rethink the project and design spaces and programmes that prioritise usability and engagement, promoting a new civic role for cultural institutions. It describes how the development of the new OW People's Market incorporates public programming as a starting point rather than subordinate to the exhibition programme, how the 'baggy' space concept supports and inspires these goals, and how cultural activities are changing in Wrexham as a result. In 2018 the gallery will move into the People's Market building. The building is a vast, open-plan space, which offers an opportunity to imagine a new cultural setting, incorporating arts and markets within the same footprint.

## The project team, 'baggy' space and socially engaged arts

The core project team is the client, Wrexham County Borough Council (WCBC), the architects Featherstone Young and the main funders, Arts Council for Wales. The WCBC were led by Oriel Wrecsam, under the umbrella of the regeneration team, and in the early stages, the creative director was Steffan Jones-Hughes. He was later succeeded in December 2016 by Jo Marsh, Oriel Wrecsam's former learning and engagement officer. This appointment reflected a shift in aspiration to an engagement-driven approach. Featherstone Young Architects were appointed in July 2015. Both Oriel Wrecsam and Featherstone Young have strong social agendas that have come to play a large part in forming the spatial and programming strategy for the new arts centre.

Featherstone Young's work draws inspiration from the more informal, non-prescribed spaces used habitually, such as foyers or streets. They think these types of space offer far greater opportunities for people to make their mark and take ownership of a place. Non-prescribed spaces can support unplanned and unimagined social activity. Featherstone Young refer to these spaces as 'baggy spaces', and the foyers of the Royal Festival Hall are good examples (for similar concepts, see Pallasmaa 2000; Hill 2003; Till 2009; Franck and Stevens 2007). More than just stairs and corridors, these are generous, fluid spaces. The delight of stumbling across an impromptu activity is an unexpected one that draws people into an experience neither they nor the architect had expected to happen. One example of this would be coming across people spread out on the floor in a drawing workshop. This is something that happened frequently when the Royal Festival Hall's education department had to borrow space because they had no dedicated room of their own. As such, these spaces take on a 'looseness that enables people to participate in publicness' (Lefebvre 1974).

In the 1960s, the visionary and influential architect Cedric Price argued that architecture should not determine human behaviour but rather enable possibility. Whilst Price supported the idea that buildings should be demolished when they no longer serve their purpose, Featherstone Young is interested in how little an architect/designer needs to touch an environment to create a 'baggy' space where other people can fill in the gaps. Arguably there is no such thing as a completely loose, 'baggy' space and constructed space exists all around us. For

Featherstone Young, the minimal touch can come from observing and identifying existing social frameworks and choreographing them to create new ones. A spatial language using familiar forms, objects and materials that mean something to people already, emerges from these observations at a small-scale, everyday level. This is rarely a literal representation of familiar forms, and is usually an appropriation where a degree of ambiguity is introduced so that different people can have more subtle and varied experiences.

Ralph Erskine's architecture is influential in this respect. He used a strong social agenda to develop an architectural language that borrowed from the everyday. Through a process of community engagement, the work he did at Byker Estate in Newcastle saw him retain popular buildings and landmarks in and amongst new housing rather than a wholescale demolition. He also reused salvaged material from well-known architectural relics in the city and re-appropriated familiar objects, such as bird boxes, which he turned into ventilation shafts and chimney flues. His use of a language of familiarity helped people identify with and take ownership of their new environment.

Oriel Wrecsam have an engagement-led philosophy and since 2015 have developed an extensive off-site engagement programme, working with a variety of local communities. The team is interested in the transformative potential of the arts, particularly how this can manifest in tangible ways in Wrexham. Alastair Hudson, director of mima, has said that 'not many places are like London, New York or Paris . . . if you're going to find a way for art to work in society, surely you should try it in ordinary places' (Artsnight 2016). In line with this, Oriel Wrecsam are interested in how arts programming can be locally responsive and tailored to serve its specific context, rather than replicating delivery models and programmes from institutions in major cities. Just as Featherstone Young's principle of 'baggy space' introduces scope for people to determine for themselves what kind of activity takes place, similarly a key objective for Oriel Wrecsam is designing projects which allow participants to direct processes and shape outcomes. This means that whilst it is always necessary for projects to have parameters, it is important to build in scope for flexibility and responsiveness, to make space for unknown outcomes to emerge and for project participants to feel ownership – in effect, building in 'baggy space' for engagement programming.

## Oriel Wrecsam People's Market

For centuries Wrexham has been known as a market town. Newspaper reports from as early as the 1600s describe weekly market days and annual market fairs including 'Dydd Llun Pawb', which translates into English as 'Everybody's Monday'. In more recent years, shoppers travelled long distances to visit Wrexham's 'Beast Market'. Markets of all types and sizes proliferated in the town centre, some open air and others covered. As such, Wrexham's historical centre was, and still is in parts, made up of both open and covered streets and squares embedded amongst the houses and shops. There are two surviving covered markets, the Butchers Market and the General Market, and also two narrow, covered streets, Overton Arcade and Central Arcade. These covered spaces, suited to the North Wales weather conditions, are as much a part of the townscape as the open streets and squares, providing loose places for people to pause, shop, chat, and carry out their everyday lives. The importance of this street pattern and market typology is discussed further in the chapter, particularly how they inspired the spatial propositions of the new design emerging from the 'baggy space' concept.

In an attempt to reinvigorate the town centre in the 1990s, a new market, the People's Market, was built comprising a market hall, shops and a multi-storey car park. It is one of the tallest buildings in the town and is strategically located on the edge of the historic town centre and close to the more recent out-of-town supermarkets and shopping malls. However, in 2013 the Quarterbridge report, commissioned by Wrexham Council, stated that the town could only support two, not three, of the remaining markets. The two historic market buildings, the Butcher's and the General, were recommended to remain; the People's Market was identified as the least viable and therefore most suitable to be considered for alternative use.

Like many towns, Wrexham has been affected by changes in shopping habits. There has been a significant drop in footfall in the town centre as the trend towards out-of-town shopping has been exacerbated by the advent of online shopping. In addition, several significant town centre buildings, such as the Hippodrome, have been knocked down. The former Beast Market is now a small Monday market with approximately 10 stalls. Combined with the closing of the town's coal mines and leather, brick and steel works in the second half of the twentieth century, there is a significant sense of loss of identity in Wrexham. This insight was confirmed by a project commissioned by Oriel Wrecsam in 2015, when artists Lisa Heledd Jones and Marc Rees carried out research for a potential large-scale event around Wrexham's identity, as part of the launch celebrations for the People's Market development. The artists discovered the previously mentioned 'Dydd Llun Pawb', and this discovery shaped their research around the feasibility of resurrecting the event in a huge carnival and parade to celebrate both the centre opening and Wrexham's unique identity. In speaking to local groups and individuals, Lisa and Marc learned of a widespread feeling that the town's identity had disintegrated as a result of the decline in markets and loss of industry.

Statistically, Wrexham has high levels of poverty and deprivation. In the 2014 Welsh Index of Multiple Deprivation, part of Wrexham came third in the ranks of Overall Most Deprived Lower Super Output Area (LSOA; Welsh Government 2014b). High levels of unemployment and a high percentage of children receiving free school meals also reflect growing levels of poverty. Service cuts in the town have seen the closure of council-run youth clubs and care homes, and the town centre is experiencing ongoing problems with drug and alcohol abuse.

In March 2015, the Council commissioned a Masterplan for town regeneration and public realm improvements, and AECOM produced a report, *Wrexham Town Centre Public Realm Strategy*, detailing existing and future needs for the town centre. The People's Market was identified as a key building ideally located to help reinvigorate and link centre and edge locations. In 2015, the future of the People's Market was secured when funding was awarded from the Welsh Government's Vibrant and Viable Places project, Arts Council of Wales and Wrexham Council to expand Oriel Wrecsam Gallery and create a new arts and cultural centre within the building.

Oriel Wrecsam Gallery is council-run and is the primary delivery vehicle for Wrexham Council's arts service. Formerly Wrexham Arts Centre, it was housed in the same building as the town's central library from 1974 to 2015. The two council-run services coexisted easily: visitors walked through the entrance and turned left for the library or right for the gallery. Over the years, Oriel Wrecsam built a reputation for high-quality programming, exhibiting artists including Rose Wylie, Joseph Beuys and Helen Sear. Over time, the gallery building was identified as being no longer sufficient in size or facilities to house a developing contemporary arts and cultural offer and the council began seeking an alternative setting, with a feasibility study for extending the existing site being carried out in 1997.

By 2015, with the People's Market identified as Oriel Wrecsam's new home, the gallery's future was secured and the work required to transform the People's Market into a new cultural centre began. Having moved out of their former site, in April 2015 the Oriel Wrecsam arts team moved into two shop units adjoining the People's Market building. Here they created a temporary pop-up gallery shop and a flexible workshop/event space with makeshift offices above. This temporary arrangement meant they had no fixed gallery space, and so the arts programme had to change and adapt.

During this interim period the programme focused on socially engaged projects and building links with local communities. Examples include a project which involved local young people working with artist Antonia Dewhurst to build a full-size shepherd's hut, which will eventually be sited within the People's Market development as a useable miniature space (Edwards 2016). The project was featured in the Arts Council Wales and Welsh Government report *Culture Shifters: Artists Making Change* in 2016, and was designed to enable development of practical skills for the participants (Smith 2016).

Alongside the changes to Oriel Wrecsam's arts programming, other grass-roots arts initiatives were simultaneously emerging in Wrexham. In July 2013 the Leeds-based charity East Street Arts facilitated the opening of Undegun, a pop-up arts space within an empty sports store in the centre of Wrexham, run by the local partnership THIS Project. The emergence of Undegun, in addition to the monthly Wrexham Street Festival, and smaller local initiatives such as 'tWig', the Wrexham Independent Gallery, demonstrate a growing cultural momentum led by local people. The development of Oriel Wrecsam and the People's Market programme is situated in the context of this momentum. Therefore dialogue between the arts team and key stakeholders is significant and is considered essential if the project is to be genuinely locally rooted.

This emphasis on socially engaged projects began to see Oriel Wrecsam extend its appeal to new audiences and apply a more democratic way of making contemporary art accessible to the broadest possible audience. The programme included 'The Make Trips Project', whereby local unemployed adults took part in skills-based workshops at locations across the county, as well as 'Art Vend', whereby commissioned artist multiples are sold for £1 each from vending machines at locations around the county and beyond. These and a number of other engagement projects are detailed on a website specifically profiling the first year off-site (Oriel Wrecsam 2015–16; Sedgman 2016). However, not everyone in the town supported the new arts centre moving to the People's Market. There was a loud message locally that 'This has nothing to do with Wrexham'.

## Combining art and market – understanding the context

The results of official consultation were encouraging: a public consultation event led by Dallas-Pierce-Quintero took place in the summer of 2014 as part of an Arts Council Wales–funded Ideas People Places project (Wrexham Borough Council 2015). This took the form of a pop-up garden in the town centre, a piece of socially engaged practice designed to gain information from visitors to Wrexham town centre and provide Wrexham Council with information gathered in a sociable way and designed to feed thinking on the development of Creative Wrexham (Wrexham Borough Council 2015). Additional consultation took place with plans displayed for comment in the town centre library and the market arcade. Results, however, were mixed. As one of the Oriel Wrecsam gallery assistants involved in the consultation said:

> Responses were extremely varied, there was a great deal of excitement about the forthcoming changes from some, but equally many people expressed concern for the future of the market traders and confusion over why a new arts centre was needed in Wrexham.

Aside from these official consultations, significant additional feedback came in the form of local press and social media responses to the plans. One notable article in the local newspaper was headlined '"No Demand for a Cultural Hub" at Wrexham Market's Expense' (Grieve and Sheehan 2015). Similarly, online discussion forums, such as those on Wrexham.com, an independent local news platform, have hosted many debates about the project which revealed negative feelings from many with comments including: 'What a waste of bloody money . . . The town centre is falling to pieces . . . and all that money is being wasted on "Airy Fairy" Arty stuff' (Wrexham.com 2016). Supporting these views, an anonymous poster was created and pinned up around Oriel Wrecsam's pop-up space, declaring that '90% of people in Wrexham do not want an Art Hub' (Figure 10.1).

In the context of service cuts, the decline of the markets and high street, and high unemployment, negative local reactions to the People's Market development are certainly understandable. When local people are feeling the effects of austerity measures in their lives, it follows that the prospect of an arts and cultural centre that they feel has nothing to do with them is a misdirected use of public money. However, despite opposition from local people, it was apparent to the project team that situating a new arts facility in an everyday market environment could bring opportunities for both to play a more meaningful role in civic society. This coexistence provides a habitual, useful environment and an ideal setting for an arts programme which responds to the concerns of local people in meaningful ways. In order to respond to local concerns and move forward, the project team were tasked with developing a setting and a programme which can be useful to the town. Not without its challenges, it was against this backdrop that a new cultural model for Oriel Wrecsam People's Market began to emerge.

## Designing for 'baggy space'

The decline of the markets in Wrexham has brought about a loss of identity in the town. The financial pressure to retain the old market buildings and their functions is one facing many traditional market towns and is symptomatic of our current political and economic climate. The project team looked at other examples where markets have had to re-think their civic role in order to survive, bringing in new uses such as art galleries, museums, music venues and restaurants to reinvigorate their offer. Markets are vast open-plan spaces that offer looseness and a good setting for public activities. At Altrincham Market, Manchester, for example, the old grade II listed market house has been reinvigorated into a food hall which has helped regenerate the adjacent covered market and town centre. The Time Out Market in Lisbon converts half of the old Mercado da Ribeira into restaurants, bars and event spaces with the other half still housing the food market to create new food and cultural experiences. The current transformation of London's Smithfield Market into the new home for the Museum of London can also be counted among these innovative projects. One of its architects, Asif Khan, speaks of making a 'democratic city square' and 'a resource for creativity' inside the old General Market building (Moore 2016).

From an arts point of view, the market's openness, usefulness and hospitality helped develop Oriel Wrecsam's new approach to programming, with the arts team developing ways to incorporate these principles into all its work. The Useful Museum model as championed by mima became a key reference point for the Oriel Wrecsam People's Market development. Wrexham and Middlesbrough both have diverse demographics and a similar industrial history, similar issues around poverty and unemployment, and in both places there is a feeling that, as with Assemble's Granby Four Streets project, the arts need to make 'a tangible difference to wider

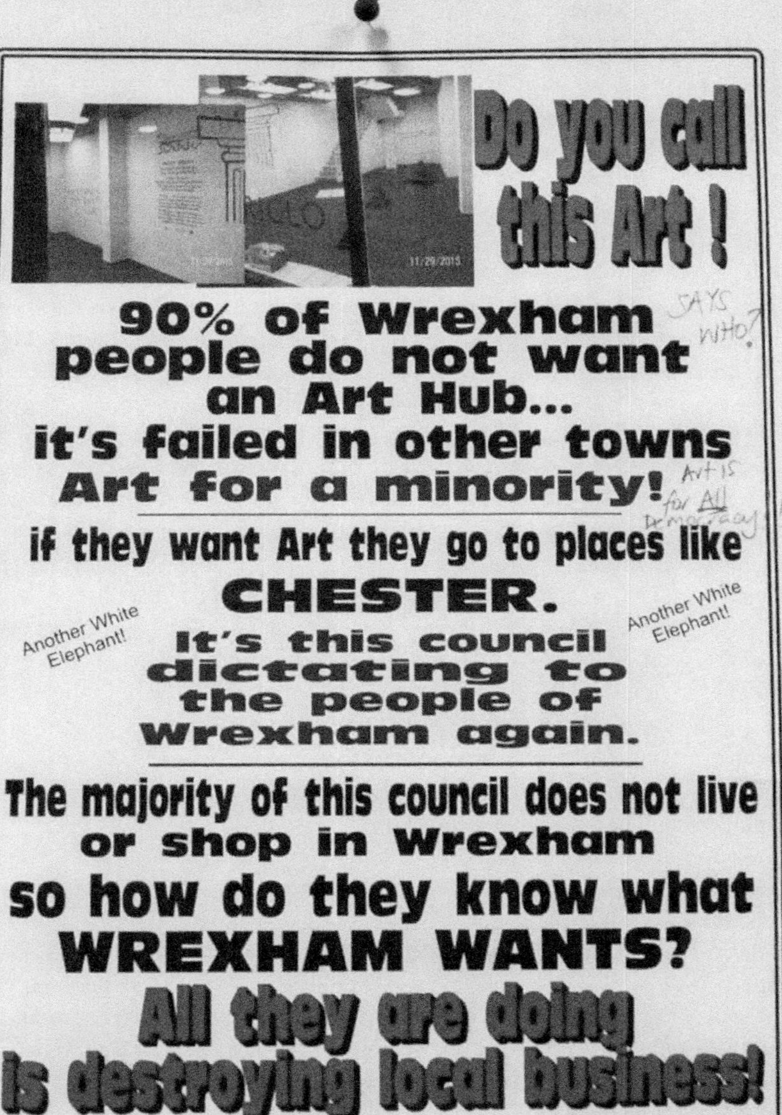


**FIGURE 10.1** Anonymous protest poster

*Photo:* Oliver Stephen

society' (Brown 2015). So within the People's Market development, the coexistence of market and art gallery has the potential to make a broader cultural offer, which addresses Wrexham's loss of identity and change the traditional cultural setting to one that is embedded in the everyday.

In this context, it was apparent that Oriel Wrecsam's original brief given to the architects in 2015 needed to be revised. Parachuting in a complete new arts facility with its own separate spaces would have created a divisive barrier between the art gallery and market use and effectively gone against the spirit of the useful model and socially engaged arts. Rethinking the role of the market and art gallery was to have a significant impact on the brief and spatial propositions within the building. It was clear that the starting point was to strip back the specialist art spaces in order to free up areas in which to situate baggy space.

To create the baggy space, an understanding of what form the minimal touch, spatial propositions might take was needed. Initial research looked for narratives and frameworks already in existence in and around the People's Market. Clues were found in small-scale, everyday observations, and these were used to develop the spatial propositions. The 'shortcut' was one of the initial design clues that emerged, derived from analysing the habitual routes people took across the town. It was observed that people would invariably take the shortest route from their parked car, bus stop or train station to get to their intended destination. If that meant crossing through a department store or down a narrow alley, that would not deter them. It was found that the strategic location of the People's Market between edge and centre of town attractions meant it was next to the route of a well-used shortcut. With more future developments planned along this route, it was recognised that People's Market could embrace this as an opportunity to bring the shortcut through the building and attract an audience who might not normally visit an art gallery or a city centre market.

To make this shortcut attractive and welcoming, Featherstone Young proposed a new main entrance on the out-of-town side of the building to strengthen the link to the other entrance on the town centre side. The building's huge scale and height make it a prominent and familiar sight on the skyline, so this was also used to encourage the use of the shortcut by marking the key corners of the building with painted slashes and supersized graphics above the two main entrances (Figure 10.2).

Featherstone Young's study of Wrexham's historical street pattern led to another important design clue. The street pattern of the historic market quarter – a network of narrow streets, covered markets and arcades – gives the town a strong identity and spatial quality. Applying Featherstone Young's own version of the Nolli map to Wrexham's town centre showed these spaces were part of people's well-trodden routes and meeting places (Figure 10.3). A Nolli map documents the accessibility and flow of spaces within a city and more importantly includes public space inside buildings as part of the urban realm. There is no distinction between inside and out, only space and mass, deepening the comprehension of the neighbourhood fabric. In this frame, the People's Market is part of this public realm and was once itself a network of routes and small streets linking it to the Fruit and Beast markets on either side.

Both the shortcut and street pattern observations link with Featherstone Young's interest in the habitual everyday, and together they have the potential to set up a language of familiarity which can support the baggy space concept. In developing this, Featherstone Young proposed extending the public realm into the ground floor of the People's Market, introducing notional streets, squares and market places. This device is used to help re-establish Wrexham's historical identity and to give a framework for lightly touching the space. Furthermore it breaks up the enormous internal space which would otherwise be difficult to occupy (Plate 13).

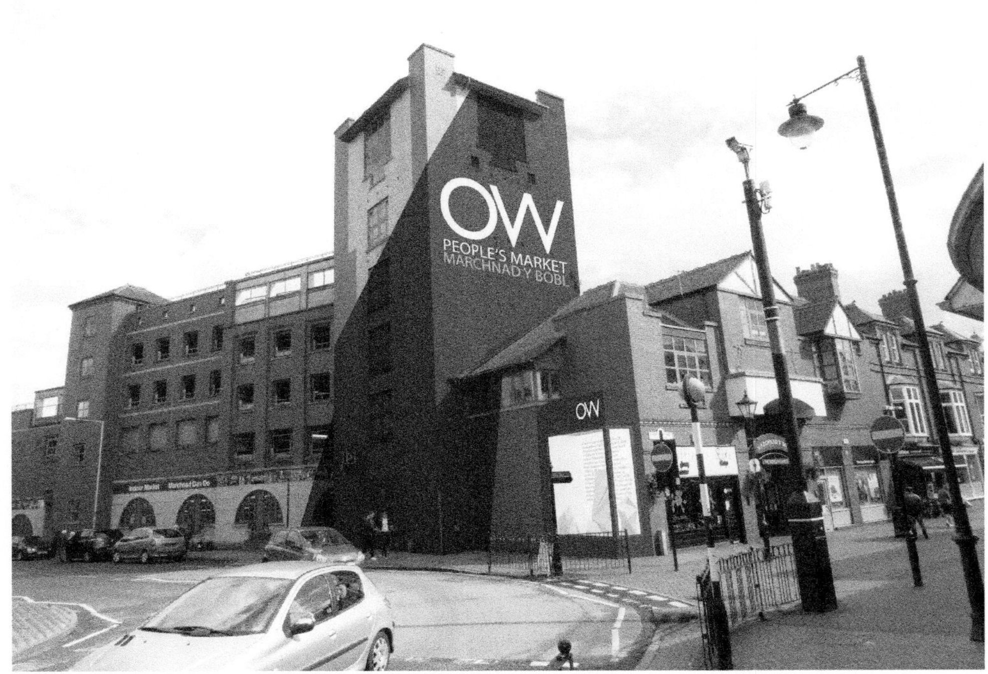


**FIGURE 10.2** Marking key corners of the existing People's Market building

Reproduced with kind permission of Featherstone Young

Within the People's Market building, the shortcut and other subsidiary routes pass through and open out into larger loose spaces, effectively town squares which with small prompts such as street furniture, mesh screens and industrial curtains invite a range of everyday habitual activities and ad hoc, unplanned activities. One of these larger new convergence spaces is Sgwar y Bobl, translated as 'People's Sguare', which has capacity to accommodate a combination of arts, markets and other events, for example, weekly tea dances, pop-up markets, project spaces, performances, temporary exhibitions and so on. It is strategically located on the shortcut route through the building and is an open space defined only by the ability to screen it off with industrial, semi-transparent plastic curtains. The curtains are configured to allow a variety of ways to subdivide the space and can be operated by the people who choose to use them.

Other small-scale elements within this streetscape borrow from the same language to help broker relationships and invite community engagement. Pop-up street furniture, co-designed with maker artist Tim Denton and local community groups, line some of the street walls within the People's Market. Like the curtains, people can take these and use them for impromptu events in the Sqwar y Bobl or elsewhere in the baggy space. This street furniture adds another layer of local meaning by taking playful cues from the traditional Welsh stick chair. People are invited to reinterpret the carved spindles and seat backs, carving their own shapes in organised community workshops, to create a recognisable family of furniture within

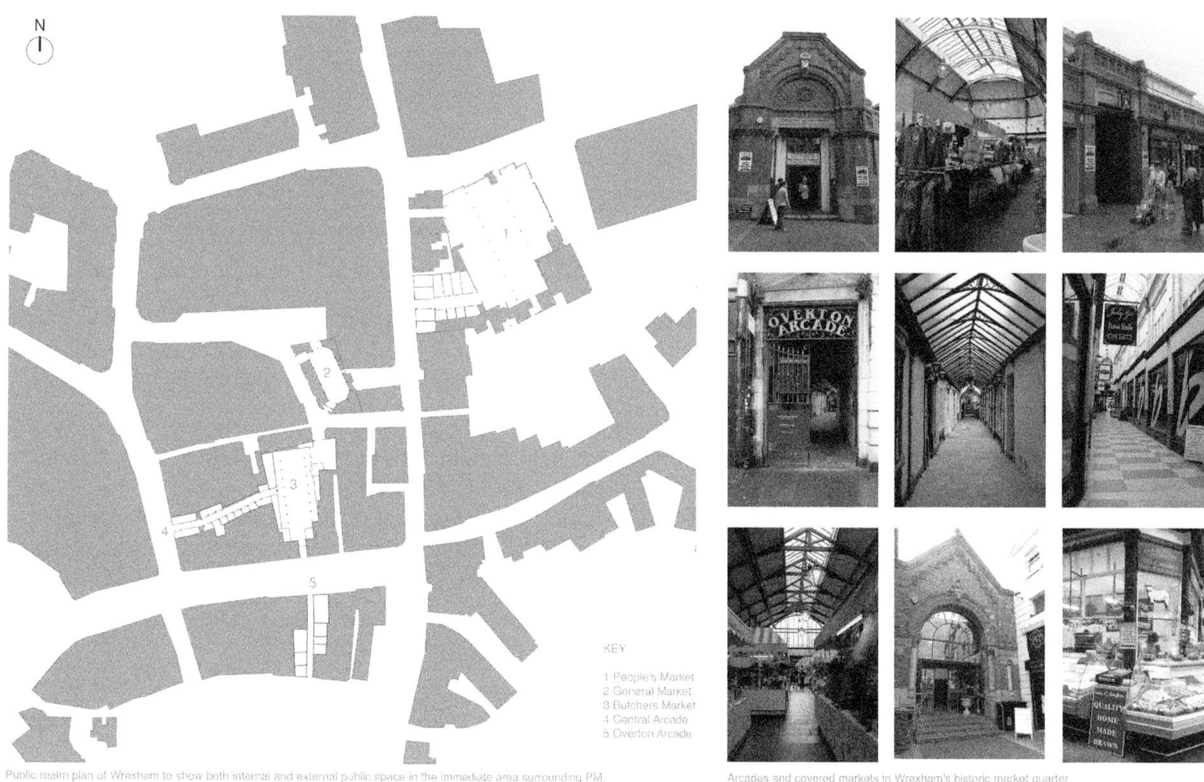


**FIGURE 10.3** Nolli plan of Wrexham's historic core with images of old markets and arcades

Reproduced with kind permission of Featherstone Young

the baggy space. In a second square, the same street furniture is configured to create a social space for communal drinking and eating. Similarly, wayfinding through the building will mark the shortcut and other key spaces using the recognisable street signage found elsewhere in the town.

Careful choreography of spatial elements is needed to invite interaction and ensure continuity without compromising the openness and fluidity of the spaces. Large cuts are proposed in floors and walls to open up the spaces and put all activities on view. Loose sub-divisions are used, such as the semi-transparent curtains and robust mesh screens, so boundaries are blurred and people can adapt their surroundings to suit their use of the space. Barriers and closed doors are avoided so that the building is fluid and welcoming. Wal Pawb, translated as 'Everybody's Wall', is a good example of changing what could have been a large dividing wall between the market and main gallery into an interactive element that mediates between the two. It is a large street billboard that will feature an annually changing public art commission. The brief to artists states that the Wal Pawb artwork should have engagement with both the arts and market communities of Wrexham at its core. In consequence, the market traders and arts team will both be involved in the commissioning process, from shortlisting to interviewing candidates to appointing the successful applicants.

In spatial terms, this new streetscape forms the framework for the baggy space. Its light touch has the potential to support a democratic space where all are on an equal footing, an experimental space which allows for the growth and adaptation of new arts and cultural models. This process has already begun, via Oriel Wrecsam's temporary relocation next to the People's Market as Siop//Shop, engaging with the community and starting the process of establishing an art presence in this location. This has been beneficial in terms of developing trust for the arts, in the context of the local reception to the proposal. The presence of the arts team has fostered neighbourliness, with small gestures such as delivering each other's post, setting out common ground and forming the basis of a community.

Their presence has also presented opportunities to embed ongoing off-site engagement programmes within borrowed spaces in and around the building during its development and in to the future. The shepherd's hut is an example of a current programme which the baggy space can accommodate. It has served as a miniature event space on the Caia Park estate where it was built, and will finally be located within the People's Market as a usable miniature space not unlike a mobile library kiosk found in the street.

The arts team's interim mission statement for the centre is as follows:

> The OW People's Market Development will be a cultural community resource, bringing together arts and markets within the same footprint. This coexistence will celebrate the significance of markets within Wrexham's cultural heritage and identity.
>
> The development will be a new space for dialogue around subjects including social and civic issues, the environment, health, cultural identity, sustainability and education. We will present a contemporary programme of welcoming and inclusive exhibitions, socially engaged projects and live performance. The programme will emphasise skills and craft, working with emerging and established artists from all backgrounds.

Featherstone Young's notion of baggy space as a physical, spatial concept provides a helpful way to articulate Oriel Wrecsam's approach to exhibition programming for the new centre. Rather than a conventional institution schedule that is fully planned two years in advance, the gallery's new exhibition programme will feature its own baggy spaces. In between commissioned exhibitions and national touring exhibitions, these slots in the programme will make the two gallery spaces in the new centre available for experimental and more immediate, locally responsive activities. Initially lasting from two weeks to one month in duration, the baggy space slots could be filled by any number of activities led by local groups or individuals looking for a showcase. Speculative examples could be intensive music or dance rehearsals; conversations around topics that are important to a group or community; exhibitions of artwork; temporary shops; and sharing or teaching of skills. The baggy spaces will be locally advertised via open call with a set of criteria, and slots will be allocated as little as three months in advance.

Rather than a traditional exhibition-first approach, the arts programme will operate via three equal, reciprocal components – public programme, exhibition programme and retail programme – with each taking the lead at different times. In practice, this means that the agenda of the public programme will inform the exhibition programme. This approach is also reflected through the staffing structure and job roles. The entire staff will be an engagement team, as opposed to having one member of staff responsible for engagement. Oriel Wrecsam's off-site retail gallery Siop//Shop will be moving into the People's Market, not only as a shop but a vehicle for programme delivery staffed by the arts team, taking an equal role alongside the public and exhibitions programmes. As well as driving and delivering projects, Siop//Shop will serve as an important intersection between the arts and markets functions of the centre. It will be a for-profit trading unit in a community of trading units.

The Oriel Wrecsam team believe that it is possible to develop a programme that is locally rooted and responsive, engaging with pressing local concerns, but which equally draws audiences and interest from beyond Wrexham and even beyond the UK. The vision is for the centre's rootedness in its local community to be its distinguishing feature, and makes it of interest to external audiences.

## Conclusion

In the current socioeconomic and political climate in the UK, the role of the arts is changing, and cultural institutions have potential to function as a habitual component of daily life like never before. In order for this potential to be fulfilled, it is necessary that visitors and participants are able to have genuine autonomy and input into how cultural spaces are used, and into how cultural programmes develop. Through working in reciprocal dialogue with local people, cultural institutions have the potential to be genuinely embedded in the communities they inhabit, rather than a standalone embellishment, separate from local concerns and daily life. The baggy space model creates capacity for this to take place. In both spatial and programmatic terms, the baggy space model creates capacity for the rhythms and concerns of daily life to become fundamental within the cultural institution.

The baggy space concept has emerged as a key ingredient in the design of both spaces and programmes for the new People's Market development. Based on the views of local people, it was necessary for the project team to move away from traditional models in order to create a cultural setting that seeks to meet the needs of the local community. Going forward into the new development, the focus will be on creating a space that can be used habitually, to provide useful, meaningful experiences. Throughout the design and development process, the project team have recognised their civic responsibility is to surpass public expectations, by serving the community in ways that they can recognise as valuable, relating to their interests and stemming from their involvement. The baggy space concept will enable visitors to have a more direct input into the programme and the building,

Whilst developed in the specific context of the People's Market project, Wrexham's situation is not unique and the baggy space model has potential to be implemented not only in cultural buildings but also in a wide variety of other settings and scales, such as housing and urban planning. In programme terms, the baggy space model has potential to be applied in galleries across the UK and beyond, placing the public programme and engagement programme on an equal footing with exhibition programmes and creating space to be genuinely responsive to current local concerns.

> This is a viable proposition affording new and exciting opportunities to a much wider audience than traditional arts centres. . . . and should provide an exciting model for others to follow.
>
> *(Harry James, Architect Assessor for the Arts Council for Wales)*

## Note

1 The project's name has now changed to Ty Pawb, meaning Everyone's House.

## References


Artsnight (2016) *Nicholas Serota* [Television programme]. Online. Available HTTP: https://subsaga.com/bbc/arts/artsnight/series-3/2-nicholas-serota.html Accessed 28 July 2017.

Arte Util (2017) 'About Arte Útil'. Online. Available HTTP: www.arte-util.org/about/colophon. Accessed 16 July 2017.

Assemble (2015) 'Granby Workshop'. Online. Available HTTP: http://assemblestudio.co.uk/?page_id=1524. Accessed 16 July 2017.

Brown, M. (2015) 'Urban Regenerators Assemble Become First "Non-artists" to Win Turner Prize', *The Guardian*, 7 December 2015. Online. Available HTTP: www.theguardian.com/artanddesign/2015/dec/07/urban-assemble-win-turner-prize-toxteth. Accessed 16 July 2017.

Edwards, J. (2016) *Oriel Wrecsam Shepherds Hut Project* [Video]. Online. Available HTTP: https://vimeo.com/165791406. Accessed 16 July 2017.

Franck, K.A. and Stevens, Q. (eds.) (2007) *Loose Space: Possibility and Diversity in Urban Life*, London and New York: Routledge.

Grieve, J. and Sheehan, R. (2015) '"No Demand for a Cultural Hub" at Wrexham Market's Expense', *The Leader*, 7 August 2015. Online. Available HTTP: www.leaderlive.co.uk/news/151191/-no-demand-for-a-cultural-hub-at-wrexham-market-s-expense.aspx Accessed 16 July 2017.

Hill, J. (2003) *Actions of Architecture; Architects and Creative Users*, London: Routledge.

Lefebvre, H. (1974) *The Production of Space*, Oxford: Blackwell.

Moore, R. (2016) 'Smithfield General Market: The New Museum of London Sets Out Its Stall', *The Guardian*, 31 July 2016. Online. Available HTTP: www.theguardian.com/artanddesign/2016/jul/31/new-museum-of-london-smithfield-market-stanton-williams-asif-khan. Accessed 31 July 2016.

Oriel Wrecsam (2015–2016) *Oriel Wrecsam: One Year Off-Site* [Website]. Online. Available HTTP: www.ow1516.com. Accessed 16 July 2017.

Pallasmaa, J. (2000) 'Hapticity and Time: Notes on Fragile Architecture', *Architectural Review*, 207(1239), pp. 78–84.

Sedgman, K. (2016) *Just Being Really Nice to People: Investigating Cultural Value in Oriel Wrecham's Year Offsite (2015–16)*, Wrecsam: Oriel Wrecsam.

Smith, F. (2016) *Culture Shifters: Artists Making Change*. Wrexham: Wrexham County Borough Council. Online. Available HTTP: www.wrexham.gov.uk/assets/pdfs/oriel_wrecsam/culture_shifters_2016.pdf. Accessed 16 July 2017.

Smith, M. (2015) 'Validation Beyond the Gallery', July 2015. Online. Available HTTP: www.axisweb.org/archive/news-and-views/beyond-the-gallery/validation-beyond-the-gallery/. Accessed 16 July 2017.

Till, J. (2009) *Architecture Depends*, Cambridge, MA: MIT Press.

Welsh Government (2014a) *Culture and Poverty: Harnessing the Power of the Arts, Culture and Heritage to Promote Social Justice in Wales*. Online. Available HTTP: http://gov.wales/docs/drah/publications/140313-culture-and-poverty-en.pdf. Accessed 16 July 2017.

Welsh Government (2014b) *Welsh Index of Multiple Deprivation (WIMD) 2014. Revised*. Online. Available HTTP: http://gov.wales/docs/statistics/2015/150812-wimd-2014-revised-en.pdf. Accessed 16 July 2017.

Welsh Government (2016) *Light Springs through the Dark: A Vision for Culture in Wales*. Online. Available HTTP: http://gov.wales/docs/drah/publications/161213-a-vision-for-culture-in-wales-en.pdf. Accessed 16 July 2017.

Wrexham Borough Council (2015) 'Dallas Pierce Quintero – Wimbourne Gate Project 1 November 2014–17 January 2015: Oriel Wrecsam Archives'. Online. Available HTTP: www.wrexham.gov.uk/english/community/arts_centre/archive/dallas_pierce.htm. Accessed 28 July 2017.

Wrexham.com (2016) 'Millions to be Spent on Arts Hub', 24 February 2016. Online. Available HTTP: www.wrexham.com/forums/topic/millions-to-be-spent-on-arts-hub. Accessed 28 July 2017.

Wrexham.com (2017) 'Video: First Look Inside "OW" People's Market – The New Arts Hub' [Facebook post]. Online. Available HTTP: www.facebook.com/wrexhamdotcom/posts/1191775697543844. Accessed 16 July 2017.

# 11

# COLLECTIVE CREATIVITY IN THE ART MUSEUM

*Mette Houlberg Rung*

## Abstract

"Collective Creativity in the Art Museum" examines different types of collaborative design processes taking place at the Statens Museum for Kunst (SMK), Denmark. Discussing the theoretical backgrounds in 1970s participatory design and user-centred product design, the chapter argues that museums have not only moved from being about something to being for someone – they are now also by someone. The participatory and user-centred focus is analysed across SMK, showing the potential, but also the challenges, of collective creativity.

## Introduction

Museums and galleries are continuously involved in a number of different design processes: they design buildings, spaces, environments, exhibitions, furniture, brochures and a range of other products. The design process itself has traditionally been a question of museums providing an external designer or architect with a brief and, if necessary, some content. The designer then incorporates this into a design she delivers to the museum. This chapter explores how Statens Museum for Kunst (SMK), the National Gallery of Denmark, is experimenting with what I term 'collective creativity', inviting users and other external stakeholders to be design partners in different projects. The chapter presents a brief overview of user-centred and participatory design and its use in relation to museums, followed by an overview of the different ways in which SMK works with this new agenda, forging novel repertoires. Finally, an analysis of the process of creating 'MatchSMK', a family board game situated in one of the permanent galleries at SMK, serves as a case study, demonstrating how museum design processes can shape the future of the museum through situational, context-orientated, user-centred collaboration. It is argued that while this new type of design process may threaten existing power structures within museum organisations, it may also draw on new forms of knowledge, and museums may benefit considerably from a more inclusive, creative and co-productive design process. Applied collective creativity can inspire not only more creative museums, it may also make them more diverse, representative and ensure high-quality experiences.

## Participatory design and user-centred design

Since the 1950s, users have been drawn increasingly closer to both the development and design of all types of products. The primary background for this development is twofold. First of all, the social, political and civil rights movements of the 1960s and 1970s gave people the opportunity to claim a stronger voice in decision-making. Designers responded to this by inviting different voices into their practice, and thereby participatory design was born. This tradition was particularly evident in Northern European countries (Robertson and Simonsen 2013: 1). Another origin can be found in the fact that products were becoming increasingly complex. New technologies, global distribution and large production systems demanded different design approaches. An awareness of the actual use of a specific product became more important and knowledge about the context of use proved vital for both the development and design of products. As American information architect Jesse James Garrett argues, we must look beyond the traditional dimensions of form and function when designing: 'Product design has to be supported by user experience design' (Garrett 2010: 9).

Garrett explains that when the products we deliver become increasingly complex, the context of use and the user experience itself become progressively central issues (Garrett 2010: 8). Put simply, we have to move from product design to experience design. This has slowly led to an inclusion of users into the design process (Sanders and Stappers 2008: 5–8; Robertson and Simonsen 2012: 3). In the early years of this development, the users were passive. Designers and researchers studied them and incorporated the results of these studies into the design. Later, the users were drawn into the design process at an earlier stage, and other stakeholders and specialists from different areas were invited to engage in the development and design in order to provide innovative ideas and new perspectives.

Today, more often than not, users play a key role in the early phases of idea generation and conceptualisation of products. As Sanders and Stappers (2008: 6–13) maintain, users have become experts in their own future use of a product, collaborating and co-creating with both researchers and designers. This user-centred and, in more recent years, participatory approach to design has led to a 'collective creativity' in design, which is argued to hold the power to generate new understandings and solutions that can transform the world far beyond the scope of traditional design (Sanders and Stappers, 2008: 6–13). Sanders and Stappers's notion of 'collective creativity' is defined as a creative process that encompasses two or more people from either inside or outside the field of design. For this chapter, I adapt this definition and use 'collective creativity' as an umbrella term for the different ways of engaging users and other stakeholders in museum design processes. This means that both user-centred design and participatory design are seen as types of collective creativity, but importantly each serving different purposes.

Several variations of both user-centred and participatory design exist and are merged under labels such as 'participatory design', 'co-design', 'UX' and 'user-centred design'. Common among them are the engagement or involvement of users and other stakeholders in the design process, but as Robertson and Simonsen (2012: 5) underline:

> While many areas of design now pay at least lip service to people's participation, the question of how participation is being negotiated and defined (and by whom) is fundamental to distinguishing Participatory Design from the more common user-centred approaches. Participatory Design projects are always driven by ongoing and systematic

> reflection on how to involve users as full partners in design and how the involvement can unfold throughout the design process.

This means that there is an ethical consideration regarding plural voices and representation within participatory design, a dimension which is less important in other dimensions of user-centred design. This highlights a need to distinguish and reflect upon the different ways of working with users, both in relation to what they have in common, but also in terms of what goals are embedded within them. This is particularly necessary for an institution such as a public museum, since today museums are embracing an agenda that is not just ethical, but also commercial.

## Collective creativity in the museum

In 2015, the Cooper Hewitt, Smithsonian Design Museum presented an exhibition on the theme of user-centred design. The exhibition, titled 'Beautiful Users', explored the changing relationship between designers and users. In the catalogue, curator and designer Ellen Lupton (2014: 21) states that: 'The phrase "designing *for* people" is giving way to "designing *with* people" as creative teams seek more egalitarian relationships with an increasingly well-informed public'. These lines echoed a much-quoted statement made by the American museologist Stephen E. Weil (1999), who said that museums had developed 'From being about Something to being for Somebody'. Lupton just took this a step further: design is now produced *with* users. The same development can be seen within museum practice: museums have developed from being *about something* and *for someone* to now also being *with someone*.

The user-centred and participatory wave has influenced museums in numerous ways and on different levels. Nina Simon, director of Santa Cruz Museum of Art and History in the United States, summed this up in her book *The Participatory Museum*. Here Simon (2010: ii) encourages us to view the museum as a platform for interaction, sharing and exchange. She argues:

> The social Web has ushered in a dizzying set of tools and design patterns that make participation more accessible than ever. Visitors expect access to a broad spectrum of information sources and cultural perspectives. They expect the ability to respond and be taken seriously. They expect the ability to discuss, share, and remix what they consume. When people can actively participate with cultural institutions, those places become central to cultural and community life.

Simon describes how museum users can contribute to museum practice and co-create with museums: from simple feedback opportunities to testing exhibitions, developing digital solutions and interpretative material and onwards to co-curating and co-designing exhibitions and permanent displays. Simon, it can be argued, creates a scale upon which the degree of participation can be assessed. Here traditional didactic museums represent one end of the scale while initiatives such as the Open Museum in Glasgow, where objects are available for community groups and other museum users to make their own exhibitions, represent the other. In between these poles, numerous projects and practices exist which involve users in some way or another.

When focusing more exclusively on user involvement in design processes in the museum, Simon debates the differences between a participatory process and a participatory product and the dilemmas and challenges of both. She argues that participatory projects can result in non-participatory products and non-participatory processes can result in participatory products. A similar point was made more than 10 years ago when Gustav Taxén (2004: 205–6) reflected on the emerging practices of empowering visitors to influence the design of the exhibition that they visit. He stated: 'Visitors today are asked to assume the roles of user, tester and informant, but they are very seldom invited to become design partners', and continues:

> Visitor 'representation' has increased through the inclusion of educators, evaluators and designers in most exhibition teams, but the fact that visitors have expert knowledge too – they know what it means to be a visitor – is still not acknowledged enough to allow them to take active part in exhibition design.

Both Taxén's and Simon's assertions highlight the meticulous nature of participatory design and the need to be both reflective and precise when considering engaging users in museological design practices. This is crucial in order to be aware of the actual role the users will have, and to understand how their contribution will impact the design. Combined with the issues concerning the fundamental ethical differences between user-centred approaches and participatory design, it is possible to draw up a list of three key questions to reflect upon when planning to work with collective creativity in the museum:

- Why are we working with our users and other stakeholders? Has the desire derived from an ethical perspective, where plural voices and more inclusive representation are important? Or is it because we acknowledge that visiting a museum is a complex situation where many agendas merge and we therefore need users to help in order to design better experiences? Is it both? And if so, how do these issues relate to each other?
- Is it the process or the product we wish to be participatory, or perhaps both?
- How are the users invited to participate? Are they informants or do they work as equal partners? Or if in between these positions, how can users' and other stakeholders' participation be defined?

## Involving users in design practices at Statens Museum for Kunst

Statens Museum for Kunst (SMK) is the National Gallery of Denmark. Located in the centre of Copenhagen, the museum houses the largest art collection in Denmark, with art dating from 1300 until today. The history of the museum is reminiscent of many other national art galleries in Western Europe, albeit with its own national characteristics. The collections date back to the 1500s and are based on the royal collections which in 1849 were handed over to the state. Over time the collections and the physical building have expanded, and in the past 20 years SMK has, like most Western art museums, taken on the challenge of working within a changing agenda where user experience is increasingly becoming central to museological practice. Therefore, SMK is in the process of moving from being *about something* to *being for someone*, and to a certain extent also to being *with someone*. Alongside increasing research into who the users of SMK are (and who they are not) and why they visit the museum (and why they do not), the museum has also begun to embrace user-centred and participatory concepts. This practice can be found in three areas within SMK: user input in regards to the development of exhibitions and events, educational and interpretative initiatives, and digital projects.

### *Temporary exhibitions and displays*

When planning temporary exhibitions or changes in the permanent displays, focus groups are often used at SMK in order to develop and test ideas concerning content, exhibition titles and interpretative material. Here, users are asked to provide information and to guide the museum in relation to how they would perceive a certain exhibition. In these forms of engagement, the users are not equal participants or design partners, nor are they contributing in terms of plural voices or ensuring representation. In contrast, they are drawn into the design phase as experts on their own experience, giving feedback on ideas and material already developed. Consequently, the approach is a user-centred approach that helps the in-house museum team to develop the exhibition with the user in mind.

Another type of collective creativity takes place when working with temporary exhibitions and displays. Over the past decade, SMK has, when designing exhibitions and permanent displays, worked collaboratively across different departments to ensure a strong presence of different professions within the exhibition team. This means that when, for example, designing a temporary exhibition, a curatorial group consisting of a researcher, an interpreter, a spatial designer and a marketing officer is put together. They are jointly responsible for the exhibition and work closely together from start to finish – each ensuring that their professional background is reflected within the project.

Both the focus groups and the establishment of a curatorial group challenge the traditional hierarchies within the museum – hierarchies which can be strong in large and old institutions such as SMK. Giving users a voice in the planning of exhibitions acknowledges that the museum specialists are not the only ones with valid knowledge about how an exhibition should be developed. The next step would be to work more continuously with users or community groups on the design of an exhibition. To a certain extent, this has been tried out in specific children's exhibitions, but not in larger ones. In the curatorial group, the different professions work as equal collaborative partners with a shared responsibility. This has transformed the way in which temporary exhibitions and permanent displays are being developed. Professions such as design, interpretation and marketing are drawn into the project from the very beginning and are thus much more integrated in the finished exhibition. The result is considerably more diverse and varied exhibitions, where experiments and research in historical art content, but also in spatial, communicative and interpretative approaches, exist side by side.

### *Educational and interpretative initiatives*

In educational and interpretative projects users are also increasingly involved in the development and design phases. In some cases, they actually design the project with support from the museum. Some examples of this are the projects carried out in SMK's Art Labs for Young People.

In 2006, 'Unges Laboratorier for Kunst' ('Art Labs for Young People') opened at SMK. It was a project aimed at young people aged 12 to 25. The idea for the Art Labs was developed by 45 young Art Pilots recruited by SMK with the aim of having young people communicate art to other young people. The Art Pilots created exhibitions and workshops targeted at young people in collaboration with museum staff, and as the first project manager Tine Nygaard explained: 'They [the young people] contribute their knowledge. We contribute ours. And

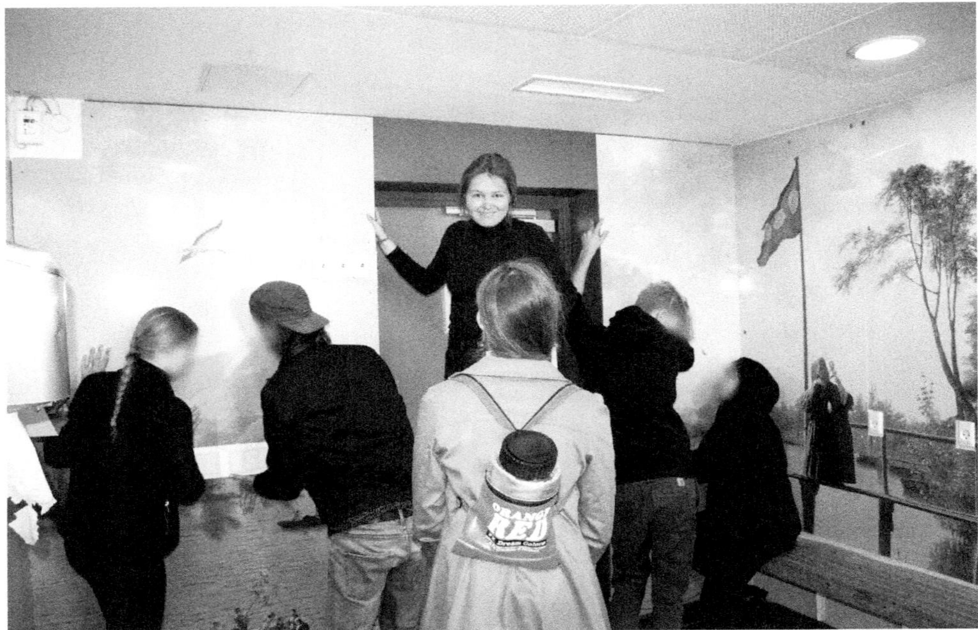

**FIGURE 11.1** 'Skyen' ('The Cloud'), Copenhagen, 2015

*Photo:* SMK Foto

there in the middle of it all, new knowledge is created. And that is what the Art Labs are about, creating new knowledge' (Borello 2008). The Art Labs are still running today. Each season new Art Pilots are recruited and they are continuously involved in both internal and external projects in relation to SMK. In 2015, for example, they contributed to an audio guide for the Royal Cast Collection and conducted a design project with 'Skyen' ('The Cloud'), a safe public space for drug taking in Copenhagen (Figure 11.1). Here the Art Pilots in dialogue with 'Skyen' used images and collages of artworks at SMK to create an inviting and friendly environment for drug addicts.

The work in the Art Labs always has a genuine participatory design approach as outlined by Robertson and Simonsen (2012: 5). Supported by museum staff, the Art Pilots develop ideas, are in charge of the process, design and take ownership of the project, and through this become a representative voice within the museum. In conversations with museum staff, they are perceived as equal partners. There are, however, still opportunities to be explored in relation to drawing the Art Pilots closer to the museum's core functions such as display and exhibitions; the audio guide is an example of how their voices can now be found within more established types of interpretation.

## *Digital projects*

The third area where SMK engages with users is in digital projects. Just as with exhibitions and displays, users are involved as informants in focus groups and in testing and evaluating the digital projects, but there are also digital areas where users become much more engaged. In the last five years, SMK has become increasingly concerned with open access to digitised cultural heritage and the creative re-use of digital images of artworks. As a consequence, SMK has allowed a large number of high-resolution images of older artworks to be freely available for download on www.smk.dk and through projects such as the Europeana collection, available from www.europeana.eu. In itself, this is not participatory or user-centred, but a range of projects evolve out of these free images. The Art Labs have used the images for several projects, but another example is the pop-up exhibition 'Mix It Up!' which was developed for an SMK Fridays event in May 2015. Here, 13 designers and artists created new works based on images of artworks in the SMK collection. Their new works were exhibited in the SMK galleries for a short while. The project included, for example, a jogging suit by designer Mette Geisler Dragelykke, covered in prints showing Harald Slott-Møller's 'Danish Landscape' from 1891, and a ceiling covered with 22 digital Golden Age skies taken from paintings in the collection (Plate 14).

Another example of digital user participation is 'Hint Me', a Twitter-based collaboration between nine Danish museums including SMK. Here, users can become involved in conversations about selected artworks on their smartphone, tablet or computer using hashtags and the website www.hintme.dk. 'Hint Me' distributes user-generated knowledge about the artworks and thus contributes additional voices that supplement traditional interpretative material in the galleries. To date, most of the digital projects initiated have been primarily concerned with participatory products, that is. SMK staff design projects or platforms that have a participatory element with which the users can engage. The users have not been part of the design of the project. There is, however, a great deal of potential within this area.

The three areas of temporary exhibitions and displays, educational and interpretational initiatives, and digital projects apply very different ways of working with users and display not only the broad range of collective creativity taking place at SMK, but also the different positions that users can take in different projects. Each project relates differently to whether users are invited to provide information, take part in the design process as equal partners or engage in a participatory framework made available by the museum. However, in all instances new voices are introduced into SMK, and because of this museological practices are changing, new audiences are developing, different knowledge is emerging and hierarchies are being broken down. The projects working in this manner are sometimes smooth and straightforward, but they can also be difficult. Inviting users and other stakeholders into the design process requires trust and also the ability to accept the loss of a certain amount of control. In addition, working with collective creativity necessitates that the museum becomes aware of its own position and voice and that it is precise in the framework it offers. In the following, I will discuss one design project in more detail, highlighting the different choices, challenges and opportunities that are a natural part of working with collective creativity.

## 'MatchSMK' – a family board game

In 2011, SMK launched a new experimental interpretative initiative called 'MatchSMK' within its permanent galleries. Put simply, 'MatchSMK' is an easily recognisable and simple board game consisting of a board and related playing cards that are used to play a game with storytelling and artworks from the room as its main components. The game is built into a large wooden structure that runs across the centre of a large exhibition room in the collection of European Art 1300–1800. On the wall around the game, large Northern European history paintings are on display – the same paintings which can be found on the game board

(Plate 15). The design of the board game was determined through a collaborative and explorative process between designers, art interpreters, a game developer and museum users. However, a few decisions had already been made before the design group was formed.

## *Background: social interaction, plural voices and a magic circle*

The background for developing 'MatchSMK' was that, in recent years, many studies have shown that museum visits are fundamentally social. Fewer than 10% of the visitors at SMK visit the museum alone, while the majority state that the main reason for visiting SMK is to enjoy a pleasant experience with their friends and family. They also explain that their preferred way of engaging with artworks is to discuss them. This inherent social dimension stands in contrast to the traditional contemplative way of engaging with art and therefore calls for new ways of displaying and interpreting art collections (Rung 2013). The social aspect of a museum visit is widely acknowledged (Falk and Dierking 1992; Leinhardt and Knutson 2004; Silverman 1990; Tröndle *et al.* 2012). However, in practice, a significant amount of interpretative material, particularly in art museums, still supports and encourages an individual art experience. How is it possible to facilitate, support and encourage social interaction in the museum?

While acknowledging the social dimension, interpreters also felt the need to reflect upon the visitor profiles of SMK. Around half of SMK's visitors belong to the privileged 8.1% of the Danish population that hold a postgraduate degree (Danmarks Statistik 2015). This is a typical problem addressed by museologists and sociologists alike. For example, as early as 1969 Bourdieu and Darbel (1990), followed by numerous studies, confirmed that it is the well-educated social groups who visit art museums (Gallup 2009; Kulturstyrelsen 2013). In order to encourage a broader visitor profile, a more diverse and varied approach to communication within the museum is required. One of the ways to achieve this is to include plural voices in the interpretative material in the collection and thereby signal that the historical interpretation of art is just one of many ways to engage with it.

However, it is not enough to introduce varied voices into the collection. Recent research at SMK has confirmed that the users who visit the museum the most are also the ones who feel most comfortable about breaking the rules and conventions of the art museum, that is those who appreciate a non-art historical voice. In contrast, it is the users who know the least about art museums who are most concerned about adapting to the art historical frame (Rung 2013). Therefore, the task was to develop an interpretive activity which encouraged social interaction and plural voices, but at the same time created a safe environment where new users would feel comfortable enough to explore art in a new way. The target group was primarily families with children between 6 and 12, though a broader audience was kept in sight, bearing in mind that frequently a wide range of visitors will use the interpretative material presented in the gallery.

From here the idea of a game emerged: to create a physical board game where museum users could play together and interact. When a game is played, a specific situation is constructed which stands outside or beside the real world. In achieving this, unique systems and rules exist. When we play, in opposition to non-play, it does not (normally) have any consequences if we win or lose, and it is also permissible to comment and reflect on the game as it unfolds. In the book *Homo Ludens – A Study of the Play Element in Culture*, Huizinga (1955: 10) argued that to play a game is to step inside a so-called magic circle. All play, he states, takes place in a separate time and place – 'in a temporary world within the ordinary world'.

Sometimes the game has a physical component, sometimes not, but inevitably a boundary is created around the players. A game becomes a social and psychological space (Juul 2008: 58).

However, to claim that the game exists completely independently from the world would be to overlook its potential as a learning site. Here we can draw on the psychologist Gregory Bateson's ideas of play. He explains that play is characterised by referring, on the one hand, to situations outside play, while on the other hand it is understood and communicated that it is only play. Therefore, in the broadest sense, play is a framework within which actions can be tested (Keiding and Laursen 2005: 54–72). Reality is, in this framework, imitated in the sense that a world is built on recognisable forms of interactions, yet simultaneously refers to its own rules. It is a free space where experimentation with other rules is born.

Following these inputs, to conduct a gamification of an interpretative activity by developing a game inside SMK was to create a magic circle whereby it would be possible, following easy supportive instructions, to test out a new way of engaging with art. It would be a safe situation where users were allowed to fail. Moreover, the game would still relate to the real world, hopefully encouraging users to test strategies from the game during the rest of their museum visit.

## *Designing, testing, prototyping and realising the game*

Accordingly, even before the design team was set, a framework for the interpretative activity was proposed: it should be a game which encouraged social interaction, cut across age groups and invited a pluralistically voiced approach to interpreting art. This clear framing was both a strength and weakness in the design process. First of all, because the project was defined from the beginning, it was easy to invite relevant users and stakeholders into the design group and it was also easy to develop a structure which would drive the project forward. If the project had been less defined, perhaps this would not have been so easy. In addition to two interpreters and two architects from SMK, the design group included four families and game professional Jeppe S. Christensen from Tankespil, who had practical and theoretical experience of developing board games. Nonetheless, it is also clear that the fixed definitions may have limited the creativity within the group. Perhaps the families could have come up with more suitable and relevant activity than a game board? Perhaps they would have been more equal partners if they had been involved in the process earlier? The concept of the game, as well as the design, did however change significantly through the different phases; therefore, despite the fact that the project was not completely open, the external collaborators still had significant impact on the actual design process.

The design process involved a research and development phase that was followed by testing, prototyping and realisation. The families and the game developer were part of the process discussing, responding to and testing the design. The art interpreters and the architects, who in a more traditional design process would have taken on the task of translating the users' needs into a design, now took on the role of facilitators – helping the families and the game developer to respond to the game and devise new suggestions for its development. As Sanders and Stappers (2008: 13–14) describe, this facilitating process entailed 'leading' the actual process, 'guiding' the participants though the process, 'providing scaffold[ing]' to support the user's creative ideas as well as 'offer[ing] a clean slate', making space for new ideas to be brought to the table.

The process lasted six months, and during this time the entire design group was involved in idea generation, workshops and decision-making. Design meetings with mock-ups as well as material testing would also take place inside the SMK collection. The design of the actual game was developed alongside the design of the furniture which houses the game.

## 'MatchSMK' – playing with art

'MatchSMK' was ultimately designed to be about art and storytelling. It was clear that the families needed it to be entertaining to be attracted to it, so the game was based on humour and imagination and no prior knowledge about the artworks was required. Moreover, the activity positions both adults and children as equals – this is not an activity where adults have an advantage over the children from the outset. Therefore, in the game there are no right or wrong answers; instead the best and most imaginative story wins. The game consists of two main components: one game board with an image of one of the artworks in the room and a selection of cards with contemporary images. Each player gets three contemporary cards and in turn players tell a story about how the contemporary card connects with the artwork. For example, how does a mailbox fit with the painting *Fall of the Titans*? Then the players vote for the story they think is the best. The person who gets the most votes wins.

'MatchSMK' ended up being based on the more strategic and complex adult board game called 'Match!', developed by the game developer who took part in the design process, Jeppe S. Christensen, and his company Tankespil. That game had no connection to artworks, but the essential idea about connecting different images with inventive stories was drawn from there. It was not originally intended that the SMK game should be inspired by 'Match!', but as the design process progressed, this made sense for families, SMK staff and Jeppe S. Christensen. This means that the involvement of a game developer had a significant impact on the development of the game.

The families responded to different versions of the game, for example on the question of what image should be printed on the game board. One version had a contemporary image on the board game and the artworks printed as small playing cards. It was clear, however, when working with the families that this was much harder, especially for children. It was difficult for them to come up with stories looking at the contemporary image, envisioning how the artworks connected to them. However, testing showed that it was much easier the other way around. This also made sense for the interpreters as the board game then kept the artwork in focus.

Through working with the families, it became clear their focus was not on strategic issues or complex rules; instead, it was on each other. The game was seen as a supplement and an expansion of an already existing social situation. This meant that the rules had to be repeatedly simplified and that the instructions to the game had to be rewritten several times. The families also added an extra dimension to the project. Through the workshops, families became increasingly curious about the 'real' story behind the artworks. For example, after telling their own stories about *Fall of the Titans*, they were inspired to find out more about the mythology. This led to the development of a series of wooden plates where the myths and biblical stories connected to the artworks were written in language that could easily be read aloud to children. The plates were integrated into the wooden structure alongside the game.

## Making space for people – and design for use

The physical design of the game and the furniture which housed it were intertwined with the development of the content of the game. The game could simply have been placed in a box and the museum could then provide a table and chairs. However, in order to integrate the game into a social situation and relate it to the specific context of the room, a special piece of furniture was custom-made for the situation. From this perspective the physical design informs and sets the framework for the social *and* mental space that unfolds when users inhabit the collection and play the game.

There were a number of practical considerations for the designers to consider: the game needed to be easy to clear away, not be messy, and have only a limited number of small parts that could be lost or taken away. Throughout the workshops with the design group, these situational and practical aspects of the physical design were developed and tested.

The physical design also had a communicative and emotional dimension. In order for the game to function, the physical design had to be quick to comprehend and easy to use. The design needed to be inviting, draw people in and to be built on a shape which would be recognisable and familiar to users so they would feel comfortable. The architects' design research took its starting point in furniture used in traditional game situations. While playing, visitors should be able to sit in front of each other and remain comfortable while playing. Inspiration came from, for example, dining situations, train carriages and picnic tables. The design group worked with different sitting positions and seating heights. In the final design, a backrest surrounds the table; this provides better comfort and creates a more private space around the gaming situation, which supports the mental space mentioned earlier (Juul 2008: 58) (Figure 11.2).

The furniture was sized so there was room for four to six visitors around a game table and the height adjusted to the bottom of the paintings to ensure proper viewing conditions in the

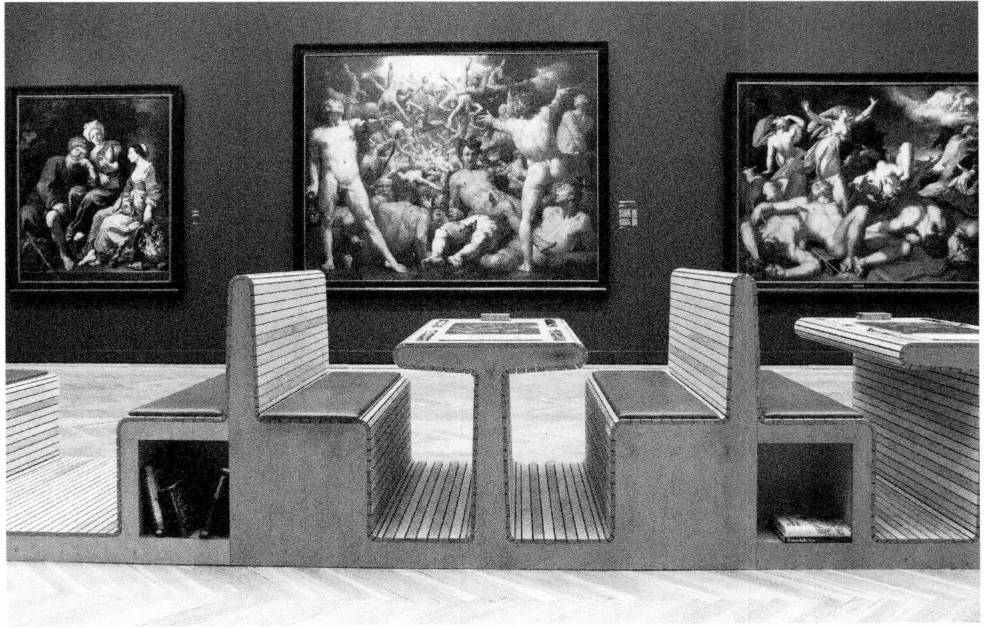

**FIGURE 11.2** 'MatchSMK', permanent collection, SMK

*Photo:* SMK Foto

room. The material chosen was plywood divided into small slats, which gives the furniture a lighter look. The slats also provided the opportunity to work with round shapes, which are more welcoming and comfortable for seating. Following different attempts to paint the plywood, this idea was disregarded; colouring would attract too much attention and compete with the artworks. The design of the furniture had to strike a balance between being a strong visual object in itself, but at the same time not overpower the artworks. Moreover, the plain plywood had a modern feel to it and its colour matched the floor in the room, working almost as an extension of it.

While the game and opportunity for seating were the main components within the structure, it also had to accommodate books and other written materials concerning the artworks in the room, and therefore a multifunctional piece of furniture was designed. The result was a wooden structure enticingly placed in the centre of the room, which aims to attract attention and stimulate the curiosity of the visitor. It is a mixture of a bookcase, bench, sofa, gaming table, dinner table, diner and train carriage with references to the informality and humour seen in children's furniture. Visually it completes the room, sets the scene and makes it a special setting where social interaction can take place.

## *'MatchSMK' – a case of collective creativity*

With 'MatchSMK', SMK wanted to test a new way of conducting collaborative design, one which was based on collective creativity involving external stakeholders as equal partners in the design process. The result was an experimental gamification of an interpretative activity which could work as a catalyst for social interaction and pave the way for new ways of engaging with art. The idea was that the game format itself created a magic circle within the permanent display where a new, more free, and imaginative approach to engaging with artworks could be tested. Nonetheless, 'MatchSMK' was not supposed to function in isolation. The point was that values and ideas from the game could be transferred from the game directly to the visit to the collection. The power of the game lies in the fact that it punctuates and negotiates the traditional rules of engagement with artworks in an art museum. Instead of the traditional historical art approach, the narration of the artwork is liberated and becomes a space for associative and imaginative storytelling. In this way, the magic circle of the game introduces a hack into the context of which it is a part of and, by example, shows how art can be experienced in various ways.

The design process of 'MatchSMK' was more user-oriented than participatory as a number of decisions had already been made before the external stakeholders entered the design group. The clear framework did, however, provide the project with the ability to recruit relevant stakeholders and to develop a structured design process. Nonetheless, what was evident was that working with users and a game developer provided SMK with new types of knowledge which the museum could not have developed on its own. To apply and work with this new knowledge required trust and willingness to experiment on behalf of the museum. As Johannessen and Ellingsen (2012: 33) state: design becomes 'an activity that is collectively negotiated among many stakeholders. Here, the roles between designers and users are not automatically given or fixed but depend on the mutuality of the relationships among the stakeholders'. However, if the museums decide to trust users and other professions and include the practices of facilitation and listening when engaged in designing products, they have the opportunity to be more inclusive and diverse and to provide high-quality experiences that are relevant to their users. Indeed, Sanders and Stappers (2008: 15–16) go even further, suggesting that use of collective creativity will change the *how*, *what* and *who* of design. They argue that design and research will mix, that teams will be more diverse and new tools for design will be needed. Seen from this perspective, design and innovative design practices hold the potential to play a significant part in shaping future museums.

## References

Borello, M.H. (2008) 'Kunst for Fremtidens Generation', *Information*, 11 February 2008. Online. Available HTTP: https://translate.google.co.uk/translate?hl=en&sl=da&u=www.information.dk/kultur/2008/02/kunst-fremtidens-generation&prev=search. Accessed 20 May 2017.

Bourdieu, P. and Darbel, A. (1990) *The Love of Art: European Art Museums and Their Public*, Cambridge: Polity.

Danmarks Statistik (2015) 'Befolkningens Uddannelse 2015', *Nyt fra Danmarks statistik*, København: Danmarks Statistik.

Falk, J.H. and Dierking, L.D. (1992) *The Museum Experience*, Washington, DC: Whalesback Books.

Gallup (2009) *Den Nationale Brugerundersøgelse – Rapport Statens Museum for Kunst*, København: Kulturstyrelsen.

Garrett, J.J. (2010) *Elements of User Experience: User-Centred Design for the Web and Beyond*, Berkeley: Pearson Education.

Huizinga, J. (1955) *Homo Ludens: A Study of the Play-Element in Culture*, Boston: Beacon Press.

Johannessen, L.K. and Ellingsen, G. (2012) 'Lightweight Design Methods in Integrated Practices', *Design Issues*, 28(3): 22–33.

Juul, J. (2008) 'The Magic Circle and the Puzzle Piece', in Günzel, S. *et al.* (eds) *Conference Proceedings of the Philosophy of Computer Games 2008*, Potsdam: Potsdam University Press.

Keiding, T.B. and Laursen, E. (2005) *Interaktion og læring, Gregory Batesons bidrag*, København: Unge Pædagoger.

Kulturstyrelsen (2013) *Den Nationale Brugerundersøgelse*, København: Kulturstyrelsen.

Leinhardt, G. and Knutson, K. (2004) *Listening in on Museum Conversations*, Walnut Creek, CA, London and New Delhi: Altamira Press.

Lupton, E. (2014) *Beautiful Users: Designing for People*, New York: Princeton Architectural Press.

Robertson, T. and Simonsen, J. (2012) 'Challenges and Opportunities in Contemporary Participatory Design', *Design Issues*, 28(3): 3–9.

Robertson, T. and Simonsen, J. (eds) (2013) *Routledge International Handbook of Participatory Design*, New York: Routledge.

Rung, M.H. (2013) *Negotiating Experiences – Visiting Statens Museum for Kunst*, unpublished PhD thesis. Online. Available HTTP: https://lra.le.ac.uk/handle/2381/28913. Accessed 20 May 2017.

Sanders, E. and Stappers, P.J. (2008) 'Co-Creation and the New Landscapes of Design', *Co-Design*, 4(1): 5–18.

Silverman, L.H. (1990) *Of Us and Other 'Things': The Content and Functions of Talk by Adult Visitor Pairs in an Art and a History Museum*, unpublished PhD thesis.

Simon, N. (2010) *The Participatory Museum*, Santa Cruz, CA: Museum 2.0.

Taxén, G. (2004) 'Introducing Participatory Design in Museums', in PDC 04 *Proceedings of the Eighth Conference on Participatory Design: Artful Integration: Interweaving Media, Materials and Practices*, New York: ACM.

Tröndle, M. *et al.* (2012) 'A Museum for the Twenty-First Century: The Influence of "Sociality" on Art Reception in Museum Space', *Museum Management & Curatorship*, 27(5): 461–86.

Weil, S.E. (1999) 'From Being about Something to Being for Somebody: The Ongoing Transformation of the American Museum', *Daedalus*, 128(3): 229–58.

# 12

# PLACING CITIZENS AT THE HEART OF MUSEUM DEVELOPMENT

## Derby Silk Mill – Museum of Making

*Tony Butler, Hannah Fox and Suzanne MacLeod*

### Abstract

When it opens in 2020, Derby Silk Mill – Museum of Making will be the UK's first major museum to have been developed, in its entirety, through participatory processes. This chapter explores the conditions within which the project emerged, the way in which human-centred design was used as a process to disrupt established assumptions and practices within a long-established museum service, the importance of an agreed set of values and principles which would drive the project and anchor the human-centred design methodology, and the ways in which the learning from the process of co-producing the new museum with local people is now impacting the wider organisation. Providing an important case study of participatory and located museum making, the project also illustrates the need in museums for progressive professionals with diverse and complementary skill sets if they are to truly explore new forms of being civic and sustainable.

### Introduction

Derby Silk Mill – Museum of Making is a new museum currently under development in the UK. At the time of writing, the second stage applications for £9.4 million Heritage Lottery Fund and £2.5 million Arts Council England funding support towards the £16.4 million budget have been submitted, and the project team are waiting to find out whether they will be able to complete a project which has occupied their time and energy for the last five years.[1] To an outsider looking in, it is clearly a project which should be funded for its potential to make a significant contribution to the lives of the people of Derby but also to our understanding of participatory approaches to museum making and routes to sustainable development. For the growing number of people who consider themselves insiders to the project, the large number of people who have invested time and energy in its planning, the project is a labour of love told through anecdotes of human contact and learning.

In many ways, the project feels entirely familiar. Derby Silk Mill is the site of the world's first factory and it sits at the entrance to the Derwent Valley Mills UNESCO World Heritage Site (Figure 12.1). Redevelopment will protect a major heritage asset from decline and

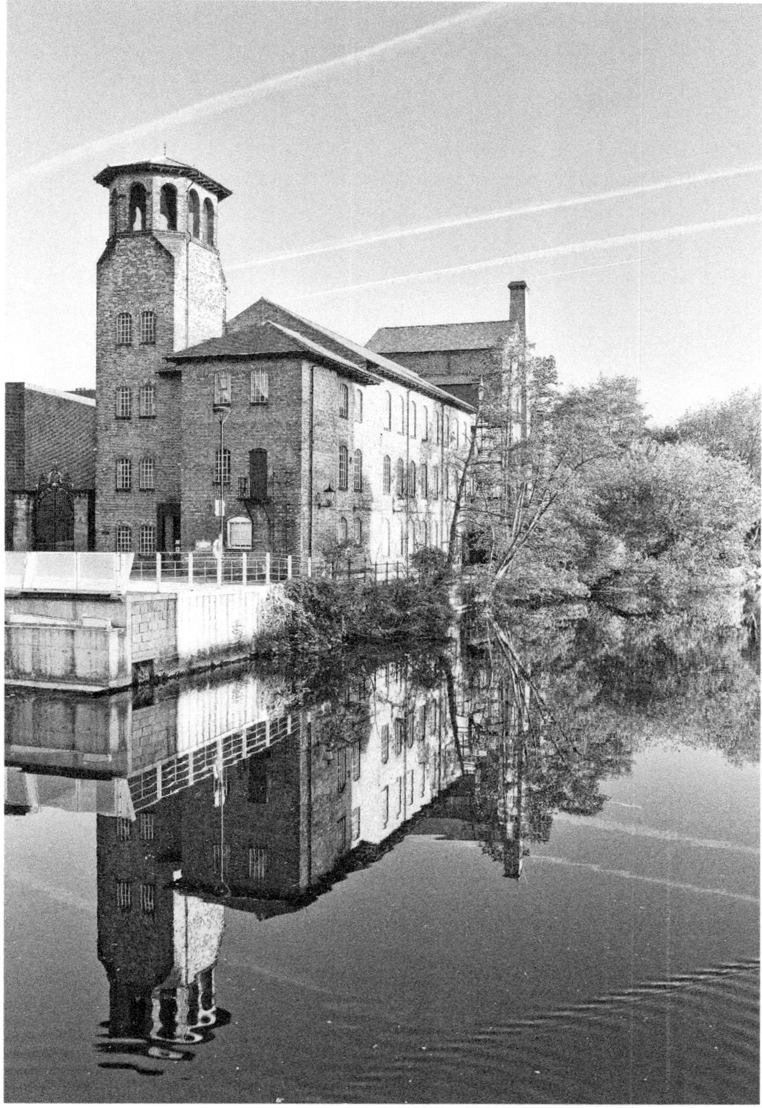

**FIGURE 12.1** Derby Silk Mill is the site of the world's first factory and sits at the entrance to the Derwent Valley Mills UNESCO World Heritage Site

Reproduced with kind permission of Derby Museums Trust

will be a means for people to learn more about their shared pasts. As with so many heritage projects, plans to redevelop the Mill have been welcomed by funders, trustees, residents and local politicians alike. The project, like all other large-scale capital projects, follows the standard development framework and funding model, and expectations are, as with all projects of this type, high.

In terms of the design and construction process however, the project is a wholly unfamiliar story. Once complete, it will be the UK's first major museum to have been developed in its entirety through participatory processes. Derby residents have been directly involved in the preparation of collections, the updating of information systems, the identification of interpretive frameworks and, importantly, both the design of the physical museum and the development of its programmes (Derby Museums 2011–2017). The project has demanded that those responsible for facilitating this process, the architects and the exhibition designers, explore new routes to participation and develop appropriate human-, citizen- and community-centred approaches to delivering a new museum. The project team have embraced risk and their work is characterised not by contracts and the potential for litigation but by collaboration, shared values, open exploration, collective problem-solving and huge amounts of energy.

The project follows a twofold logic: first, that a co-produced, human-centred museum will result in experiences more responsive to the needs and desires of its visitors; and second, and even more importantly, that by involving the public in the making of the Museum of Making and drawing on ideas such as asset-based community development – a methodology for the sustainable development of communities based on their strengths, potentials and resources – Derby Museums Trust will revitalise the notion of a civic institution shaped by the actions and shared interests of its citizens, a process which, if successful, will be made manifest in the occupation and ownership of the new Museum by Derby residents.

This chapter sets out the background to this highly innovative project, looks at why and how those involved have sought to push at the boundaries of museum design, explores the detail of the co-production process and discusses some of the key contributions and positive challenges that the project offers to the future of museum and gallery design. The final section of the chapter explains the ways in which the project is feeding back into ongoing work across Derby Museums Trust as the team seeks to expand perspectives of what a museum can be, transform the ways in which museums are made, position citizens and co-production at the centre of museum development, and reflect on the contemporary challenges faced by UK cultural organisations in becoming socially, environmentally and economically sustainable.

### TONY BUTLER, DIRECTOR, DERBY MUSEUMS TRUST

Prior to being appointed to Derby Museums Trust in 2014, I was director at the Museum of East Anglian Life (MEAL) where I developed the idea of the museum as a social enterprise, using heritage, landscape and arts as a basis for community development for socially excluded groups (long-term unemployed, mental health service users, learning disabled adults). I was influenced by the concept of asset-based community development. The methodology involves assessing the resources, skills and experience available in a community and organising the community around issues that move its members into action.

Programmes were developed with civil society groups such as Mencap and Suffolk Wildlife Trust as well as with individual volunteers. The museum became a hub for the generation of social capital through cultural heritage programmes developed for mutual benefit with its collaborators. The museum behaved much more like a civil society organisation than an authoritative civic institution with all the answers.

## Disruption – a time for new ideas

Like many large regional cities in the UK, Derby's public museums date back to the first half of the nineteenth century and were, from the 1870s up until the establishment of Derby Museums Trust in 2012, run by the borough or city council. By the early 2000s, the future of the city's museums was increasingly uncertain as cuts in public funding and a growing sense amongst service leaders that the service was not necessarily fit for purpose began to coalesce. In 2011, under the insightful leadership of the then head of museums, Stuart Gillis, the decision was taken to close one of Derby's three main museums, the Industrial Museum in Derby Silk Mill, as a route to change.

The Silk Mill had been home to the industrial museum since 1974, though by the time discussions about the establishment of the Trust were underway, the museum was lacking in visitors, supporters and ideas and a number of initiatives to reinvigorate the site had failed to gain traction or funding; a 2008 bid to Heritage Lottery Fund was rejected on the grounds that it lacked ambition and strong partnerships. Subsequent feasibility studies had made a whole series of suggestions for the reuse of the Mill, from a museum of science and technology to a museum of costume and textiles. However, closure, or 'mothballing' of the Museum – leaving the Museum intact but closing it to visitors – was identified as a short-term measure intended to free up the resources needed to create the new Derby Museums Trust and allow time to reconsider its future. Although controversial at the time, the closure proved to be enormously helpful, creating an opportunity for fresh thinking about the most appropriate use for the Mill in the context of Derby and the changing economic climate.

In order to drive this process, Gillis approached Hannah Fox, a specialist in human-centred approaches, to generate a new way forward for the Silk Mill. Over the following months and putting the feasibility studies to one side, Fox used human-centred design to explore the opportunities the Silk Mill offered and the needs it might meet. Drawing on community networks and utilising the local media, she opened the doors and invited people to contribute their ideas in a 'Project Lab' environment of experimentation and play. She asked: What do you need? How might we use this space? What stories could we tell here? These questions formed the basis of new discussions and relationships leading to rapid prototyping of ideas in the form of co-produced events and activities. While most were generous in their engagement, many people turned up ready to confront the core project team over the closure of the Industrial Museum. An empathetic response to these passionate confrontations more often than not resulted in active engagement in the project. Working hard to enable a fresh approach unencumbered by the service and its existing practices, over this period Gillis would purposefully hold the project at arm's-length from the rest of the organisation. Difficult to manage at the time, senior staff in the Trust today are clear that Gillis's courageous strategy was key to driving necessary change.

As discussions with stakeholders continued, two intellectual strands began to converge: human-centred design and the notion of a more participatory civic institution. Attracting support from Arts Council England, in 2012 three temporary job roles (project manager, programme and participation manager, and project assistant) were created to take the project into the next stage. Along with an impending process of organisational change, this led to considerable disruption for existing staff, many of whom were unsettled by the prospect of new ways of working and unhappy about the changes underway. Navigating this disharmony was made all the more difficult when Gillis left just three months into Trust status and Nick Dodd was appointed as interim director. Dodd would play a key part in maintaining the space for experimentation opened up by Gillis; on appointment, he immediately reallocated resources providing Fox with a hand-picked project team. Dodd would also play a key part in the appointment of a new director for Derby Museums Trust, supporting the selection of Tony Butler, a museum leader with a track record in community-focused leadership as the right person to drive the change forward.

### HANNAH FOX, PROJECT DIRECTOR, DERBY SILK MILL

After graduating in design and visual communication, I worked in various roles, including as graphic designer for a large advertising agency and a photo-library manager. These often hard-nosed creative business environments were the ideal way to develop my skills and introduced me both to the positive and negative aspects of the design industry; the positive aspects included using creativity to problem-solve and inspire people into action, the negatives focused on the sense that sometimes those resulting actions didn't align to the social impacts I was interested in helping effect.

As a result, I started developing collaborative side projects that focused on meaningful community engagement. This led to a new business, developing and delivering creative projects for education, culture, heritage, and health clients, using co-production and human-centred approaches to create programmes and brands that felt connected to, and owned by, their communities. Through one such project I met the then head of museums, Stuart Gillis, who asked me to develop an approach for the Silk Mill. The lack of boundaries in this initial commission, albeit in often challenging circumstances, provided an incredible opportunity to apply co-production and human-centred approaches to a project that has grown exponentially through its iterations and is shaped by its social purpose. What was originally a short-term contract to develop some ideas for a museum has grown into a full-time role in a new organisation working hard to re-imagine its role in Derby's life.

## Human-centred design and co-production in the context of Derby

Today, human-centred design is used by organisations all over the world to develop products and services closely allied with the needs and desires of users. Developed in the 1980s as a route towards enabling users to directly influence design decisions, human-centred design utilises deep contextual research, an empathy with users, the iteration of multiple ideas and ongoing prototyping and testing to develop new products and services which, as a result, exhibit a tighter fit to human needs. Reaching across a vast spectrum from consultation with users through to the deep involvement of end users in design decisions and what we might call co-production, human-centred design is focused on making something new. As a concept, it sits comfortably in the museum sector where 'change' has been a defining characteristic of professional debates and academic study for the last four decades.

Open to criticism as far too readily and heavily tied to consumerism and the production of capital and possibly an explanation for its slow take-up in the cultural sector, at Derby the methodology has been adopted creatively and pragmatically and put to work as a route to instilling an outcomes and impact-oriented approach in all projects, supporting staff to adopt new people-centred ways of working, drawing thousands of local people into design processes, and at times working with smaller groups of people to explore and prototype the new museum together. Key here, and of central importance to adapting the methodology to the museum context, has been the unshifting focus on the idea of the civic organisation as a necessary and shared public resource given over to benefiting the lives of citizens and produced through community involvement and action. In Derby, human-centred design has been harnessed to mobilise the human, intellectual, physical and cultural assets in the community as a route to tending and nurturing that community.

Communicating these values and social ideals as well as the human-centred design methodology to citizens, funders, partners and staff alike was essential in supporting them to be understood and embraced. Central to these aims, Hannah developed the Derby Museums' Human-Centred Design and Co-production framework and, in 2014, wrote the first version of a staff handbook with Tony and colleagues to position human-centred design as the latest iteration in a history of innovative thinking in Derby (Derby Museums 2016). Derby was one of the centres of the Midlands Enlightenment during the eighteenth century, and this spirit of discovery and curiosity is exemplified by the paintings of Joseph Wright of Derby. The team invoked five Joseph Wright of Derby works to illustrate the design process:

*Define and Understand.* 'A Philosopher by Lamplight'. We identify the issue we are trying to solve or change and understand the context. Then we agree a set of guiding principles. We ask: Who is involved? What does success look like? What are the available resources/ constraints?

*Think and Imagine.* 'The Alchemist in Search of the Philosophers Stone Discovers Phosphorus'. What are our ideas? How far can we push them? What might we find if we are willing to take risks?

*Model and Prototype.* 'Blacksmiths Shop'. Which ideas are strongest? Can we combine, expand and refine our ideas and make a low cost, low risk prototype or pilot?

*Test and Evaluate.* 'An Experiment on a Bird in the Air Pump'. How are we going to know it has worked? What improvements do we need to make? What did people think, feel, do?

*Produce and Share.* 'The Orrery'. What resources do we need to make it happen? Who else needs to be part of it? Who should we be telling about what we are doing? How does this feed into our other work or the work of others?

## Project overview

To date, the project has comprised three distinct phases. Phase 1 (2011–2013) asked local people to share their hopes and aspirations for the Silk Mill. Following an opening 'Shaping the Vision' weekend, over 100 workshops and activities were co-produced with enthusiastic community volunteers and partners, with no core budget. This enabled over 30,000 people to participate in programmes that fed directly in to a new vision statement for the Silk Mill.

It also resulted in a very clear sense that encouraging experimentation and creativity were essential ingredients for individuals and industry in Derby alike. In particular, the national educational focus on STEM (Science, Technology, Engineering and Maths) needed to be broadened to include Art (STEAM) and it became clear that for participants, the narrative of the Silk Mill and of Derby should focus on an ongoing story of making. The view of the team, that everyone should feel entitled to participate in the Museum, strengthened throughout this phase.

## DERBY SILK MILL – MUSEUM OF MAKING, VISION STATEMENT

How might we use the making of the Museum of Making, to engage people's heads, hearts and hands – empowering them to be the creators, innovators and makers of the future?

Seed-funding from Derby City Council and Arts Council England enabled the engagement of architects Bauman Lyons Associates in 2012, who were asked to develop costed options for the site – from a phased approach to the full redevelopment. Stakeholders encouraged the team to go 'further faster', and the plan to fundraise £16.4 million began. Meanwhile, the project team, encouraged by Bauman Lyons, agreed that the seed-funding created an opportunity to prototype the concept of 'making the museum' through creating a community workshop that could co-produce the curation and display of objects as well as the furniture requirements (Derby Museums 2014). Following a strip-out of the ground floor of the Silk Mill, along with installation of new doors, toilets and kitchen facilities, Phase 2 of the project – Re:Make – launched in November 2013. Re:Make involved the co-production of a prototype of the museum with a whole range of partners, including Makers-in-Residence Studio Tilt, tasked to support the fit-out project; and Artists-in-Residence Seiko Kinoshita and Paul Matosic, who developed new co-produced works in response to the challenges of encouraging people to enter the building and displaying multiple objects in open storage (Plate 16).

Many of the partners and communities who engaged with Re:Make had connected with the project in Phase 1, but new people also arrived ready and willing to help. As a result, rather than spend money on external fabrication and new display infrastructure, Derby Museums Trust invested in employing a workshop supervisor and creating a workshop equipped with laser cutters, CNC machines and IT with open source software where the project team, makers/artists-in-residence, audiences, staff, stakeholders and volunteers might create new ways to 'make the museum of making'. Participants learned new skills in the workshop, made new friends and could be creative in an environment unconstrained by notions of formal learning.

The results of the experimental phase have been unexpected and have breathed new life into what was a fairly uninspiring industrial museum. Working with the project team and 'makers-in-residence', members of the public have made things using Raspberry Pi, a CNC router, 3D printer and laser cutter alongside more traditional tools and techniques. Volunteers have made museum display cases and furniture, designed a mobile kitchen and told new stories about Derby's cultural heritage. They have encouraged and looked out for each other as part of a collective enterprise, volunteering and co-producing on an informal, mutually beneficial basis. They've given time to create fixtures and fittings and solve problems for the museum, in return often using the equipment or developing skills for their own endeavours. For example, one volunteer used the workshop to develop his ideas to make bespoke skateboards. In return he taught coding to year 6's from local primary schools during the Wednesday afternoon Code Club.

As a result of Phases 1 and 2 and the 'Museum of Making' project vision, in 2015 Derby Museums received first round passes for £12 million from Heritage Lottery Fund and Arts Council England, along with a commitment of £4 million from Derby City Council. This investment enabled the recruitment of new team members, including a curator of making and a co-production volunteer co-ordinator. The investment also ensured the funding of Phase 3 – Re:Imagine – which saw the reconceptualisation of the entire project based on Phases 1 and 2 and the submission of the Round 2 funding applications. The team was extended to include the re-appointment of architects Bauman Lyons and the addition of exhibition designers Leach Colour – both bring experience of co-design and an open approach which has been fundamental to achieving the growth of this iterative process – along with a framework of industry, education and community co-production partners and volunteers.

During this phase, the project vision was defined further through a series of workshops, events and activities delivered in the ground floor 'Project Lab'. These included *Art of Artefacts*, a programme led by Leach and the team which set out to discover how the public interact with objects; *Prototyping the Museum*, a series of ideation and prototyping workshops led by architects Bauman Lyons and the team to understand the various needs of the users and the activities intended to take place in the new museum; *Makers/Artists in Residence*, a series of creative responses to the museum's collections and stories; and *Silk Mill Conversations and Design Charettes*, where people could come together and discuss current sustainability considerations in relation to the new Museum. Some 19,000 participants engaged with the project during Phase 3.

As the project moves into the Delivery Phase, emphasis will shift from reimagining to realising the Museum of Making as a place to learn and make. Stakeholders will continue to play an essential part as collections are decanted, outreach programmes are developed and the fit-out of the new museum is fabricated on site. The construction phase will also be characterised by an experimental methodology based on co-production deeply rooted in an agreed set of core values and commitment to the larger project. The IPI (Integrated Project Insurance) model is a cutting-edge procurement model named in the UK government's procurement route aims. The Museum of Making will be the second test case and first heritage project to use this model. By encouraging a no-blame culture, IPI aims to eliminate potentially damaging individual and organisational agendas, encouraging all involved to focus on finding solutions that are best for project.

## The minutiae of the workshopping and design processes

At Derby Silk Mill, the ambition to co-produce the Museum with visitors in its entirety meant that established approaches to museum design had to be abandoned. Design here would be a facilitator, a filter for a whole range of thoughts and ideas provided by others. Rather than producing concepts and detailed designs relatively quickly and early on in the project, in Derby it has taken approximately five years for design concepts to begin to take shape as priority was given to the workshopping processes of relationship building and learning about the needs and desires of others (Plate 17). The roles of Bauman Lyons as project architects, and Leach as exhibition and interpretation designers, went well beyond the traditional 'consultancy' and demanded a belief in this open, iterative process and the ability to invest the time and energy required. Through the Re:Imagine phase, this meant holding back on the desire to jump into design and instead co-creating an extensive programme of workshops that could continue the prototyping of ideas with co-production partners (stakeholders and organisations), regular volunteers and occasional participants.

## Art of Artefacts

Leach engaged with diverse audiences in a bid to inspire narratives, find new ways to display the collection, explore the building and inspire making and self-enquiry. Activities focused on some of the biggest challenges when aspiring to display 100% of the collection. They asked visitors:

1. How might we group our artefacts? Here, Leach displayed 65 artefacts from the collection on a bespoke, flexible display system. A set of cards provided minimal interpretation about each object – made in, made by, made where, made from and made for. Participants were asked to group the objects as they wanted and were then asked how they had grouped the objects, why they had chosen this method and whether the objects meant anything to them.
2. How might we tell our stories? Building on the activities in workshop 1, the team provided a variety of materials, props and resources – including fake smells and musical instruments – to encourage participants to explore how to tell stories that would bring the collections to life. The team gathered a whole range of new ideas which could be used to interpret the city's past, present and future.
3. How might we display our collection? With over 100,000 objects within the museum's collection, participants were asked to work together to explore how 100% of the collection could be made available to people who wanted to see them? Should displays be made up of hundreds of small items or one large item, and how might people engage with the display?
4. How might we inspire visitors to Think, Feel, Do? The final workshop aimed to consolidate the ideas generated from the previous sessions. It aimed to find out what collection items inspired people, and to draw out participants' feelings about the activities being proposed to develop the new displays. What other activities would encourage people to come to the museum and find out more, and what else could visitors do to contribute to making the new museum?

A whole range of findings emerged from the workshops, however, key insights included:

- People enjoyed telling their personal stories linked to an object and relating it to the past, as well as the present;
- Reminiscence was a powerful tool in getting people to be excited about objects;
- Those with more expertise in areas related to the objects were willing to convey further detailed information;
- Many linked the objects to family members – mainly parents and grandparents, but sometimes children;
- People who did not arrive together often talked to each other about the objects and shared knowledge and insight;

- If an object was broken or taken apart, people joined forces to fix it, figure out how it was made or offer suggestions on how it was used;
- People enjoyed offering ideas for the use of unknown objects.

The human element to the stories also mattered – who used it, who made it, who lived/worked there:

- Participants were interested in the life journey of an object once its initial use was redundant, and how it had finally ended up in the museum collection;
- Some people liked the idea of objects with a common connection being displayed together, others liked contrasting and conflicting objects being together;
- The concept of 'firsts' was liked – first made, first used, etc.;
- People liked the hands-on artefact experience, to see items from all angles, and being able to investigate further;
- People were often more interested in how things were made, their materials and manufacture, rather than how they worked.

For the team, working in this way was challenging, not least in relation to the time commitment required which far exceeded the usual amounts of time spent on design. Similarly, the task of synthesising the learning from the workshops into design concepts differed significantly from the usual design process of developing a concept and designing an experience. However, step by step, the findings from the workshops were fed directly into an interpretation strategy and design approach. A number of guiding principles became apparent:

- *Hands-on.* We should enable visitors to investigate and enjoy first-hand, tactile interaction with the collection and displays.
- *Personal and social.* We should provide different spaces, and therefore different opportunities for personal or group activities and reflection.
- *Making, materials, method.* We should tell visitors how and why objects are made or allow them to discover this information for themselves.
- *Individual.* We should support every visitor to create their own experience and define their own level of engagement with a variety of media.
- *Adaptable.* We should plan for regular rotation of the collection and stories.

## Prototyping the Museum

Following directly on from *The Art of Artefacts*, Bauman Lyons Architects developed a series of prototype workshops where participants were invited to develop architectural ideas for the new Museum of Making (Figure 12.2). These workshops continued to 'up-size' the scale of design thinking from the micro-scale of the object, its groupings and narratives, through to how the surrounding spaces and building fabric might be crafted and tailored to enhance visitors' experience and understanding of the collections. Once again, key questions were used to drive this work:

1 How might we design the museum spaces using the collection? Visitors were asked to pick their favourite object(s) from the collection and pair it with an image of an interesting precedent where the fabric or space of a visitor environment has been physically

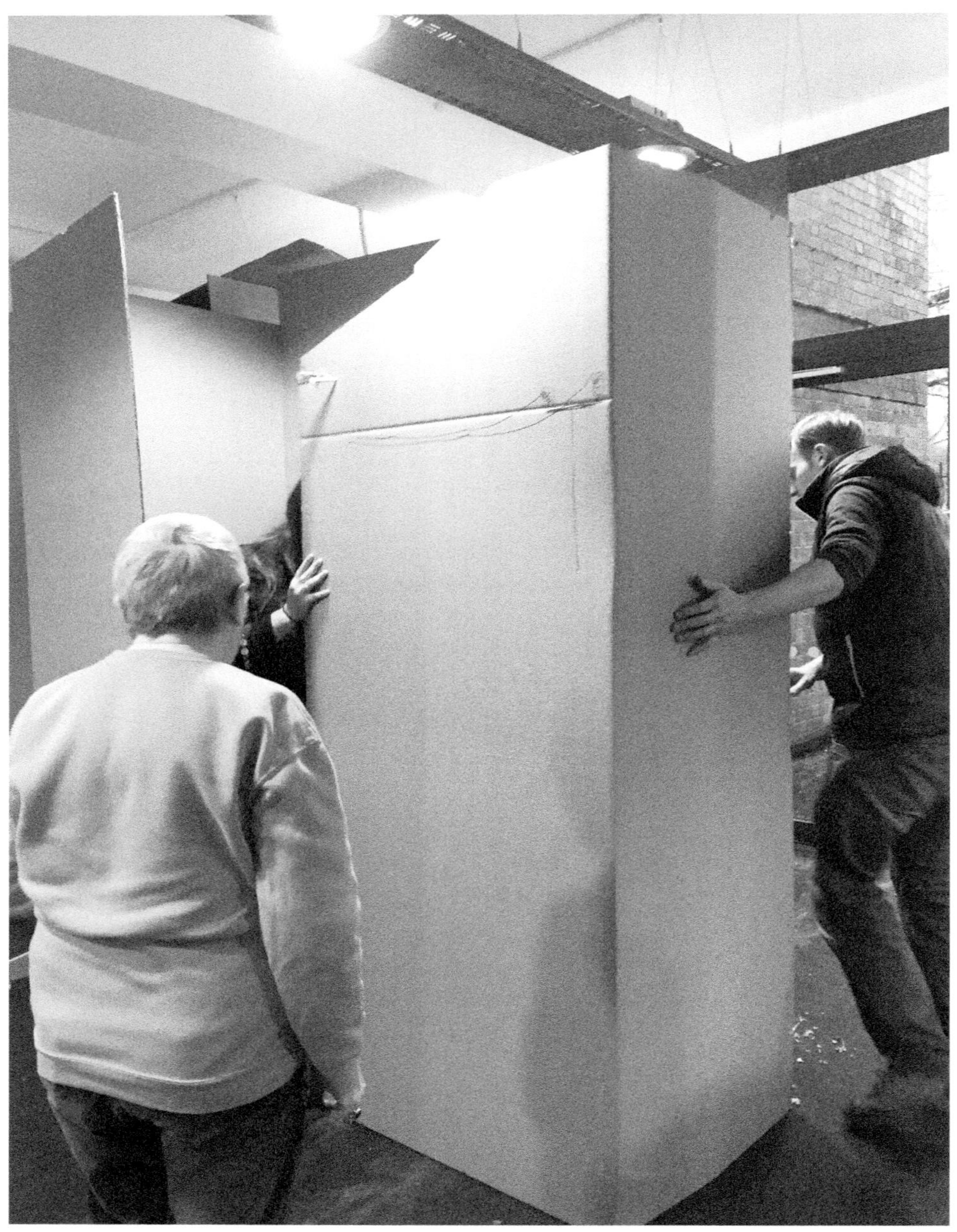

**FIGURE 12.2** Maker-in-residence co-production workshop, Derby Silk Mill. Volunteers participated in a prototyping workshop where they could physically design small spaces around objects from the collection. In this image volunteers are working together to design a small and hidden entrance leading on to the walkway for visitors to discover

adapted to suit the object. The visitor was then asked to find a spot in the Silk Mill where they thought their pairing would work well.

2 How might we create a variety of different spaces for different collections? Volunteers and visitors were invited to select an object or collection of objects and to mock-up 1:1 scale experiential spaces and arrangements inspired by the objects, using large sheets of cardboard and other craft materials and props.
3 How might we select materials for building the museum inside and out? Volunteers and visitors were invited to take a walk around a virtual model of the Silk Mill. They were asked to identify a space and discuss how they would like the new space to feel and how these feelings and atmospheres could be created using materials.
4 How might we refine the design of spaces by creating a full-scale prototype? Participants constructed a series of experimental installations that pulled together the ideas that emerged from the previous workshops. Using materials from the workshop, participants created a more immersive and realistic impression of how these spaces might feel.

The architectural workshop findings were recorded using a photographic method called 'Picture and Story'. This enabled the design team to keep an engaging, personal and visual record of participants and their ideas. It also allowed them to continually review and distill suggestions into spatial principles or 'tools' to inform ongoing design challenges and open up opportunities for new design ideas. These spatial tools were mapped according to architectural scale – from large scale ideas that could be considered across the whole building, to individual room scale, down to micro ideas about how objects and collections might be experienced up close. The spatial tools map enabled the team to identify the ideas that had the greatest potential to be integrated into the ongoing building design and narrative, including:

- Adapting commonly overlooked places such as alcoves, ledges, doorways and windows for object display so that visitors have to pass under and across or look through objects into the next space.
- This idea was taken even further and used to inform the design of the front entrance façade – a three-storey display wall that visitors pass under into the realm of the Museum and can physically experience at upper levels.
- Forgotten places around the building also provide 'one-off' spots to showcase special craftsmanship, experimental maker/artist prototyping or celebrate 'misfit' collections/mystery objects that do not fit easily into curatorial themes. Functional circulation such as staircases could feature an appropriate amount of display to help draw visitors between floors.
- Planning 'Easter eggs' around the Museum to reward visitors who explore the building and chance upon either a hidden object or a special spatial experience.
- Height and distance: a suspended walkway in the Civic Hall (itself the outcome of an earlier workshop) will enable visitors to view the details of the Trent Engine up close, from behind and from the side.

As a result of both the workshops, a shared design strategy named 'Moments of Generosity' will continue to help frame thinking about how the collection and its narratives can be embedded into the physical spaces and fabric of the Silk Mill. The resultant concept designs for the new museum incorporate a vast number of the ideas and approaches explored by participants in the workshops. Utilising the entire space of the Mill for the first time in 50 years,

Derby Silk Mill – Museum of Making will make accessible the entirety of its collection, open up opportunities for browsing and discovery, share its content management system, tell stories, and offer up its space for social exchange and making.

## Embedding disruption

Derby Museums' collections have their origins in the early nineteenth-century philosophical societies (in Derby's case this was driven by a desire to represent the work of its most renowned artist, Joseph Wright of Derby) and, in the late Victorian period, Derby Museum and Art Gallery opened with the support of industrial philanthropists and was maintained for the people of Derby by the local authority. This model sufficed for nearly 150 years. However, social and technological innovation has meant that visitors today demand a more participatory approach to public services. For instance, since the mid-2000s there has been a marked drive for personalisation of social care services, meaning that services are built around user need, the idea being that the 'client' has more agency in choosing services they want, which might improve their quality of life or enable them to live more independently. One of the earliest examples of this was developed by the South London and Maudsley Mental Health Trust who worked with the New Economics Foundation in piloting co-produced services in mental health. For museums, emulating this level of co-production should help stimulate a new kind of civic institution.

Most museums' relationships with their visitors are transaction based. Customers pay an admission fee for an experience which is primarily didactic. This transactional approach belies the social values of 'distanced philanthropy' of the founders of Derby Museums 140 years ago. Outside Derby Museum and Art Gallery stands a statue of Michael Thomas Bass, the brewing entrepreneur and Liberal MP who provided much of the funds for the building of the museum in 1880. He gave over £80,000 to the city over his lifetime (a sum amounting to around £8.1 million today). Bass, like many Victorian philanthropists, was aware that being a successful citizen involved giving something back to the collective, recognising that these assets were for everyone and that citizens have a fundamental role to play in the production of the civic. Today, a new kind of contract between citizens and civic institutions is emerging. If, as Jon Alexander from the New Citizenship Project contends, we see visitors not as consumers but as citizens, then the museums of the future will need to build mutual relationships with the public, be non-hierarchal and be a platform for the free exchange of knowledge and creativity (The New Citizenship Project 2017). Citizens will build institutions.

As a route towards embedding these values and characteristics into Derby Museums Trust, the co-production ethos explored in such depth at the Silk Mill has been systemically embedded across the whole organisation. In 2015 a new natural history gallery, *Notice Nature Feel Joy,* was created involving a phalanx of specialists and experts such as zoologists, entomologists, taxidermists, psychologists and musicians a well as a large group of co-production volunteers. Central to the gallery was the notion of 'your natural world' emphasising that encounters with nature can happen as much from the window of the fourth floor of a tower block, as from a cottage in the countryside. The results are a beautiful melange of specimen, stories and details of the wonders of the natural world, enriched by the voices of many individuals. Never has the maxim that 'no one of us is smarter than all of us' been so true. As we write, Derby Museums is using the same process in the development of a world cultures gallery, *Your Place, in the World,* working with the diverse communities of the city. Co-production is now habitual throughout the organisation.

## Conclusion

The Derby Silk Mill – Museum of Making project is, in so many ways, overdue. As a sector, museums and galleries have discussed the turn to visitors and participatory processes for a long time and over the last decade it has been possible to see the gradual growth in confidence in museums to work in the name of social justice. In the UK, museums, galleries and culture more broadly are now widely recognised as key resources in the drive for democracy, health and wellbeing, learning and human development and, more than this, there is an evident recognition in the sector that for the majority of museums, we need to find new ways of thinking about and ensuring not just the sustainable future of the museum itself but of the social context within which it sits (Crossick and Kaszynska 2016; Thompson and Aked 2011). Yet, it remains incredibly rare to find large-scale museum projects which draw this social awareness into the making of the physical museum (the museum of buildings, exhibitions and displays), which concede their power to shape the museum, its contents and opportunities for experience, and which instead share that privilege with the people who will use the museum in the future and who already fund the museum through their taxes. A significant challenge to any notion of entrenched museum design conventions and processes, the Derby Silk Mill project sets out to be participatory in everything it does, literally tearing up the rule book and writing a new one.

Still ongoing, the project to date has drawn tens of thousands of people into the process, generating wide support for the project and building a core of committed volunteers who have given their time and energy to helping shape the new Museum. The combined time commitment to the project has been both phenomenal and necessary from the initial months of exploration and communication with Derby residents about the future of the Silk Mill through to the detailed work of workshop volunteers and the slow and careful documentation and analysis of the core museum, architecture and exhibition design team. Although often challenging, the design team committed to working together, opening up their practices and staying true to the process. Concrete designs were not committed to paper until five years into the project and even now, as the team await the final funding decision, plans are developing for the continuation of this iterative process of co-production through the detailed design and construction phases. All this work is focused on ensuring that decision-making is shared, responsive and responsible.

The time given to building relationships and trust has also been harnessed to great effect within Derby Museums Trust. The project has utilised human-centred design to drive organisational change – the process provided the disruptive mechanism through which new conversations could be stimulated and new relationships could be forged. In a highly risk-averse sector, human-centred design provided the logic and rigour necessary to satisfy funders and reassure local stakeholders that experimentation and collaboration could also deliver concrete outcomes. However, if the project draws attention to the great significance of design for the cultural sector, it also reinforces an understanding of the need for this work to be undertaken within a values-led framework. In Derby, human-centred design and co-production has been firmly rooted in and shaped by a deep understanding of the value of culture and a desire for museums to act as enablers of the creative lives of citizens. Museums here are a rallying point for community, they are civic belonging in action, they are producers of empowering social relationships and providers of services and experiences adaptable to the lives of diverse people. In Derby the message is clear: museums which generate social capital through genuine co-production are far more likely to be resilient in times of crisis. Linked to this, Derby Museums aim to make all involved far more conscious of the social and cultural value they create every time they use their assets for public good.

Derby Silk Mill – Museum of Making shows how the story of experimentation doesn't need to be a story of swimming against the tide. Rather, an approach of openness and discussion, of speaking to funders, sharing ideas, understanding the needs of stakeholders and, in Fox's words, 'regular, open communication' (the project leaves a wealth of online and printed material in its wake, evidence of the desire of those involved to share, convince and involve), can easily overcome assumptions of difficulty and lack of interest. Those involved in the Derby project have taken responsibility for the risk their project has created and the demands it places on others, recognising that they had a responsibility to explain, ensure rigour and reassure investors. Equally, they are a team utterly committed to their task and to ensuring maximum benefit for the wider public, not least the players of the National Lottery who will be their main funder. Those involved in the project speak of 'holding the space' for innovation, 'holding their nerve and the nerves of others', 'holding their practice' and not allowing the needs of the professional to subvert the process of iteration and learning that will, when all the research and thinking is complete, be translated into a social and physical solution. Demanding a skill set and sensibility quite different to the usual project management role, Derby Silk Mill – Museum of Making offers a glimpse of a deeply human and entirely hopeful future for museum design.

## Note

1 Since writing, the full funding has been awarded.

## References

Crossick, G. and Kaszynska, P. (2016) *Understanding the Value of Arts and Culture: The AHRC Cultural Value Project*, Swindon: AHRC.

Derby Museums (2011–2017) *Derby Silk Mill – Museum of Making, Project Blog*. Online. Available HTTP: www.derbysilkmill.tumblr.com. Accessed 21 August 2017.

Derby Museums (2014) *Re:Make The Museum* [5 minute film]. Online. Available HTTP: https://vimeo.com/93503715. Accessed 21 August 2017.

Derby Museums (2016) *Human-Centred Design and Co-production Handbook* [Version 4]. Online. Available HTTP: www.derbymuseums.org/wp-content/uploads/2017/02/DM-HCD-Toolkit-V4-for-website.pdf. Accessed 21 August 2017.

The New Citizenship Project (2017) *About Us*. Online. Available HTTP: www.newcitizenship.org.uk/. Accessed 21 August 2017.

Thompson, S. and Aked, J. (2011) *The Happy Museum: Reimagining Museums For a Changing World*, London: Paul Hamlyn Foundation.

# 13

# NEW APPROACHES TO UNIVERSAL DESIGN AT THE GATEWAY ARCH NATIONAL PARK

*Bill Haley and Oriel Wilson*

## Abstract

This chapter considers the transformational reworking of the museum design process to reflect a social model of disability. Using the redevelopment of 'The Museum at the Gateway Arch', at The Gateway Arch National Park in St Louis, Missouri, as a case study, the authors demonstrate that both the process *and* outputs of exhibition design benefit from an inclusive methodology. This moves further from merely providing physically accessible exhibition environments, to seeking to facilitate equality of experience for all museum visitors.

## Introduction

Museum designers have long considered and incorporated accessible features into the spaces they create, with varying degrees of effectiveness and usability. Recent trends within the field of museums have witnessed a fundamental shift away from merely adding appropriate accessibility devices, as laid out in disability discrimination legislation worldwide, towards a more ethically nuanced and cohesive approach to universal access and human-centred design. This change moves away from providing accessible 'alternatives' to exhibits, towards the provision of an *equal experience for all* – comparable and simultaneous, regardless of ability or disability.

Technology and digital media also plays into this shifting dynamic – creating opportunities for realising the museum in the virtual world, and diversifying the avenues through which visitors can encounter collections and narratives. Within the physical museum, digital technologies can also support greater equality of experience through 3D printing, soundscapes, virtual and augmented reality devices, apps, immersion rooms and other emerging technologies. However, whilst also enriching the visitor experience for many, these digital media opportunities pose even more complex access considerations that must be addressed to ensure that equitable means of access are provided for all.

Haley Sharpe Design Ltd (**hsd**) is a leading museum design agency. Formed over 30 years ago, the practice has designed and delivered over 500 exhibition schemes globally, working with internationally renowned cultural and heritage institutions. Inevitably, during the company's history, their interpretative design teams have witnessed and responded to changing legal, medical and social constructs of disability, and the consequential impacts of these on the physical and intellectual environment within museums. There has undoubtedly been some outstanding work in museums and galleries where social models of disability have been explored and applied (Dodd *et al.* 2008). However, it is only in very recent years that museum design projects have made a transformative shift, systematically facilitating equality of experience, rather than merely providing some accessible features in a few, select junctures around an exhibit, and usually applied in an ad hoc fashion late in the design process.

This chapter will explore how a cohesive approach to designing accessible environments and creating equitable experiences for all has shaped the emerging creative proposals and design process for the transformed landscape, infrastructure and visitor experience at The Gateway Arch National Park in St Louis, Missouri, USA. Indeed, this project is used to represent the seismic shift away from the piecemeal and selective application of, and adherence to, universal access design guidelines, towards a considered and deliberate design process which envelops inclusivity into the heart of creative and technical design for all exhibition spaces and media. All too often in the past, universal access considerations were included as an afterthought in the design process – with designers conducting stand-alone 'accessibility reviews' of drawing packages at the end of design phases, and usually at a point when many key components of a planned exhibition experience were already set. Thus, the St Louis scheme demonstrates that this fundamental shift in the application of inclusive design is as much about design *process* as a philosophical position – embedding universal design into the planning and conceptual development of a facility and, crucially, involving accessibility advisors and stakeholders intimately throughout the design journey.

## Context

The iconic Gateway Arch, located on the west bank of the Mississippi, commemorates western territorial expansion of the United States (Plate 18). The Monument, which first opened to the public in 1967, and associated visitor facilities is owned and managed by the National Park Service (NPS). The Monument is supported by the Gateway Arch Park Foundation (GAPF), formerly known as the CityArchRiver Foundation (CAR), a non-profit organisation that exists to enhance community usability of the Arch and its surrounding areas for generations to come. The Gateway Arch National Park project seeks to comprehensively renovate the historic 91-acre site and construct new public spaces, substantially enhancing the visitor experience across all components of the landscape, Monument, Old Courthouse and exhibition facilities. The NPS, GAPF, City of St Louis, Great Rivers Greenway organisation and private sector donations are funding the scheme.

The **hsd** team was appointed in 2012 as exhibition designers for galleries at the Old Courthouse, and to develop a new 50,000-square-foot underground museum at the base of the Arch exploring the experience and effects of westward expansion in what is now the United States. The NPS and GAPF were determined to create a world-class exhibit environment which truly delivers an equitable experience for *all* visitors, with exhibits 'accessed, understood and used to the greatest extent possible by all people regardless of their age, size, ability or disability' (CityArchRiver 2016). The focus here would not be equality of access, but equality of experience.

The challenge for designers and architects, who are inclined to think only in terms of architectural and spatial obstacles, was to always consider the *breadth* of visitors' abilities and disabilities, and in particular, the implications for design of neurodiversity and brain-based differences. In the early stages of the project, Gina Hilberry of Cohen Hilberry Architects (CHA), was appointed as an independent consultant to advise on inclusive design and accessibility best practice. Gina recognised that designers assigned to the project needed inclusive design guidance to inform schematic design development. This resulted in the creation of two 'tools' to assist the design team:

1 A set of targeted guidelines for inclusive design. A memorandum, prepared by CHA, authored specifically for the challenges of the Gateway Arch design effort, included dimensional, graphic and tactile requirements. The contents of the memorandum were drawn from a range of best practice inclusive design sources but, significantly, increased the allowances for clearances and movement and stated minimum contrast between materials and colours.
2 A Universal Design Group (UDG) – Working with the city's *Americans With Disabilities Act (ADA) Coordinator*, David Newburger, an advisory group was created, comprising local disability rights advocates experienced with a wide range of disabilities (from visual and hearing loss to physical and mental health needs). The remit of the UDG was to answer questions from designers, to comment and thoroughly review the landscape, building and exhibit designs at each stage of the project. Importantly, the group was empowered to assist in making choices between various design options and to put forward alternative design suggestions throughout the development phases. To further enhance this process, Gina Hilberry's remit was expanded to become the coordinator for the UDG, liaising between the group and the various design teams. Establishing the remit and embedding the input of this UDG at the outset of the schematic design phase was critical to the goal of ensuring that the landscape and the new reconfiguration of the Arch grounds, the interconnectedness of all the physical elements, as well as their relationship with the Old Courthouse, would enhance the overall visitor experience, and would meet the needs of all visitors.

Visitors to NPS sites with any form of disability have legally established civil rights to experience interpretative media in the same way as all other visitors. As a federally mandated organisation, the NPS is legally required to ensure that their interpretative facilities and programmes are equitable in terms of information and context for all visitors, regardless of physical, sensory or cognitive disability. The organisation's mission is stated as follows:

> The National Park Service preserves unimpaired the natural and cultural resources and values of the National Park System for the enjoyment, education, and inspiration of this and future generations. The Park Service cooperates with partners to extend the benefits of natural and cultural resource conservation and outdoor recreation throughout this country and the world.
>
> *(NPS 2016)*

In the context of individual historic sites and natural landscapes, clearly the NPS must consider an array of state, local and site-specific factors when determining the optimal way to facilitate an equitable visitor experience. For the St Louis project, the NPS appointed the US-based National Center on Accessibility (NCA) to advise on specific accessibility requirements and interface with the UDG specifically for exhibit components. Reference was also made to the following guidelines and memorandums throughout the project:

1 Memorandum 'Disability Access in the National Park Service', dated 24 October 2006, issued by the then NPS Deputy Director Steve Martin. This dispatch reflects that 'in spite of the efforts that have been made and the successes achieved, the NPS is falling significantly short of meeting the minimum level of access that is mandated by Federal law' (Martin 2006). The document highlights the need to ensure that all newly constructed assets (visitor centres, events and public programs, exhibits, etc.) comply with appropriate accessibility guidelines, reminding NPS staff that retrospective corrections to projects can be costly.
2 The Principles of Universal Design guidelines, summarised by a working group at the North Carolina State University, based on the term first coined by the architect Ronald L. Mace. The authors of this strategy document included architects, engineers, environmental and product designers, who articulated seven core design principles to ensure that products and environments would be: 'usable by all people, to the greatest extent possible, without the need for adaptation or specialised design' (Connell *et al.* 1997). Widely adopted by North American museum practitioners, the seven principles, when applied to the exhibition environment, can be paraphrased as follows:

   - Equitable Use – Providing the same means of using exhibits for all visitors: identical whenever possible; equivalent when not.
   - Flexibility in Use – Providing choice in how exhibits can be experienced, and being adaptable to the user's accuracy, pace or engagement preferences.
   - Simple and Intuitive Use – Exhibit controls are consistent and easy to understand.
   - Perceptible Information – Exhibits communicate necessary information to visitors regardless of the ambient conditions or user's sensory capabilities.
   - Tolerance for Error – Exhibits minimise hazards or the effects of adverse actions.
   - Low Physical Effort – Exhibits can be used by visitors efficiently, without sustained physical effort.
   - Size and Space for Approach and Use – Exhibits can be approached and manipulated regardless of the visitor's body size, posture or level of mobility.

3 *All In! Accessibility in the National Park Service 2015–2020* (NPS 2014). A strategic plan calling for a cultural shift within the NPS, to enact enduring change and to create a mindset of inclusion. The plan states that: 'The National Park Service will embrace and incorporate accessible and universal design principles when developing all new facilities and programs, so that all completed facilities and programs will be seamlessly inclusive' (NPS 2014).
4 *Programmatic Accessibility Guidelines for National Park Service Interpretative Media* (Harpers Ferry Center Accessibility Committee 2016). Practical guidelines to assist park superintendents, NPS staff, designers and media developers, recommending accessible solutions for a comprehensive range of interpretative exhibits.
5 Universal Design – Design Guidelines & Elements, prepared for GAPF (formerly known as CityArchRiver 2015) and The Gateway Arch National Park (Cohen Hilberry Architects 2013). A memorandum developed by CHA summarising applicable findings and resources collated from experience, NPS requirements, technical requirements included in the International Code Council's 2015 ANSI A117.1, and DeafSpace Guidelines.

Drawing on these various advisory documents, **hsd** embarked on a five and a half year design development journey with GAPF, the NPS, UDG and a large team of consultant architects to create a new visitor experience at St Louis.

## Case study exhibit – the Riverfront Era Wagon

'The Museum at the Gateway Arch' (formerly 'The Museum of Westward Expansion') tells the story of St Louis' role in America's growth and of the Arch which commemorates the 'Gateway to the West'. Multi-generational visitor groups can explore topics that include nation building and identity, immigration and migration, and democracy and civil rights. The story of western expansion is all about the movement of people, ideals and aspirations – it is a dynamic and emotive narrative that visitors can encounter through artefacts, digital media, immersive audio-visual presentations, tactile interactives and graphics spread across nine broadly chronological interpretative zones.

All zones and exhibits have been designed to facilitate equitable access and engagement opportunities. However, to unpack the process of design and creative decision-making required to arrive at an inclusive environment, we will focus on a single exhibit element in just one of the zones: the display of a reconstructed covered wagon located in the 'Riverfront Era' gallery. By exploring this one exhibit, we seek to demonstrate the range of practical design considerations that must be made, as well as the need to constantly review and revisit design solutions to arrive at the optimal approach.

The Riverfront Era thematic area presents St Louis in the mid-1800s when the city was a thriving river port and centre for trade. Displays here explore the practical plans and provisions that pioneers had to make when preparing for the long and arduous journey west. At the centre of the zone is a full-sized replica of a pioneer's covered wagon – essentially a travelling household on wheels – which is surrounded by a variety of interpretative components including tactile models, touchscreens with databases and interactive games, interpretative graphic narratives (including text), specialist active lighting and soundscapes, all of which help visitors to explore different aspects of the preparations emigrants had to make for the journey out west. This dynamic mix of media is arranged around the perimeter of the wagon and is intended to appeal to a wide range of learning styles, ages and visitor interests (Figure 13.1). By circling the wagon, the interpretative media also provides a protective physical barrier to the object itself, which is not suitable for visitors to touch. Protective barriers are covered by US Access Board technical standards, to which we also had to adhere (US Access Board 2014).

### *Design considerations and exhibit media components*

1 *Front access to exhibits and turning radii* – Throughout the museum, and around the wagon, all interpretative media has been designed to be accessed front-on by all users, including visitors in wheelchairs. Guidelines state that visitors must be able to use both hands simultaneously to reach and operate exhibits or touch tactile sections of displays. Through workshop discussions, the touchable and operable area for any exhibit was not to sit beyond a 12" stretch limit from the front face of the exhibit. Therefore, exhibit layouts were prepared to fully reflect these reach requirements, and to avoid overlapping wheelchair access spaces, or bottlenecks in terms of circulation or turning circles (Figure 13.2). Given the central location of the wagon display, our design team had to ensure that

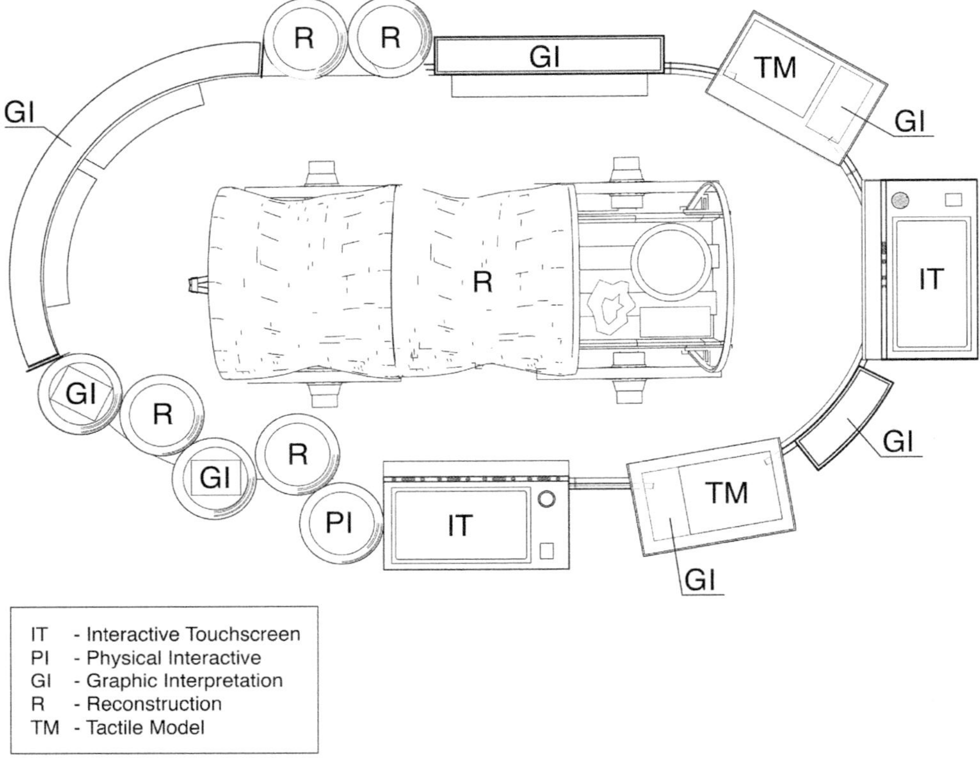


**FIGURE 13.1** General arrangement plan showing the replica covered wagon and associated complex interpretative media components

Reproduced with kind permission of the National Park Service

front-on access to each interpretative component could be achieved without disrupting accessible engagement with other exhibits. Full plans demonstrating this were shared with the UDG for review and comments, which included increasing the turning circles to 72".

2 *Navigational lighting* – The Riverfront Era gallery has relatively low light levels (of between 100–150 lux or approximately 9–13 footcandles) for artefact conservation purposes and to achieve creative and interpretative effect. The wagon itself is also raised up and fixed securely onto a shallow plywood plinth covered with reconstructed cobblestones, with additional barrels used for set-dressing, to hold interactives and to act as a barrier. To ensure that circulation routes are clear, the extent of each exhibit is discernible, and that trip hazards are avoided for visitors with low vision, floor-level detail lighting is embedded around the sections of the wagon plinth. This principle continues consistently throughout the museum around the base of all display cases and other exhibit structures. Again, the UDG reviewed plans showing the precise location and extent of this navigational lighting tool.

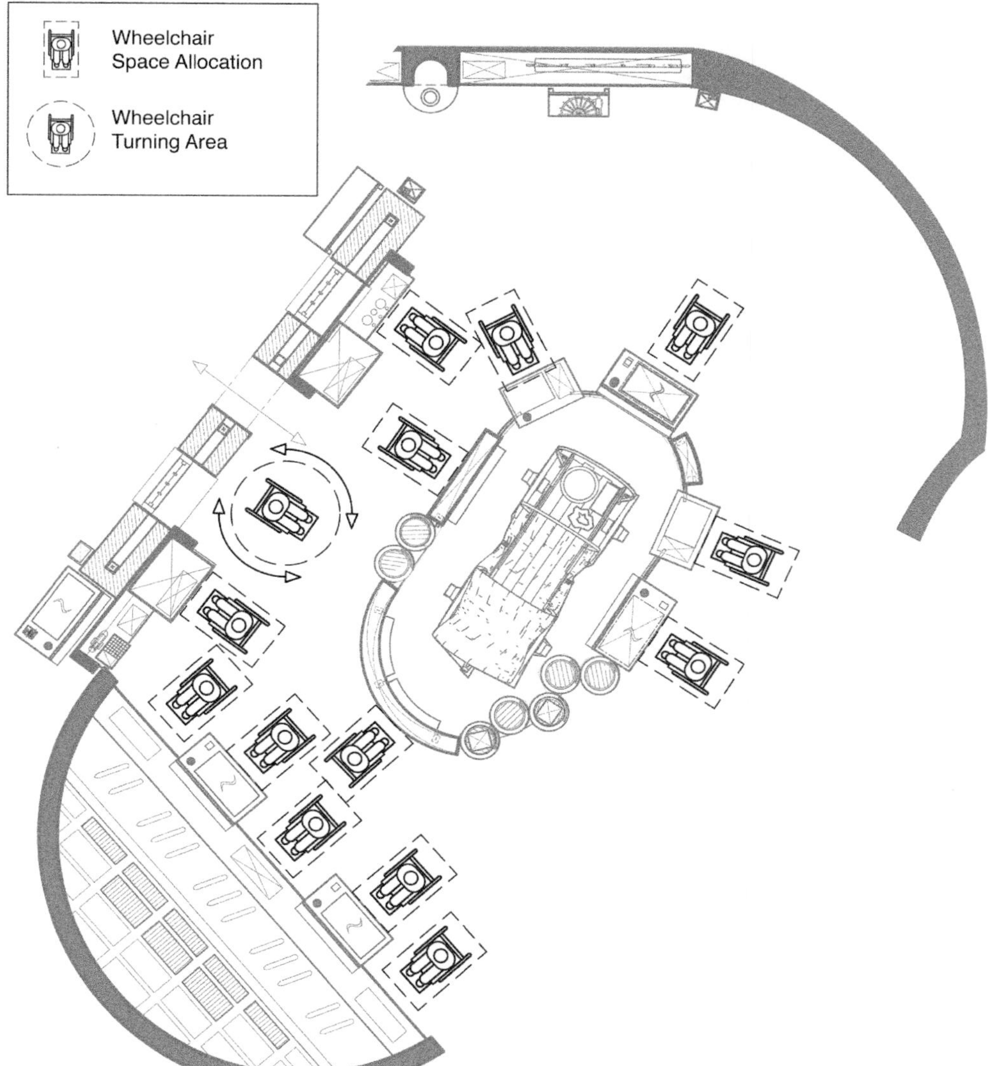


**FIGURE 13.2** Plan showing front-on approach and access for wheelchairs avoiding any potential overlap

Reproduced with kind permission of the National Park Service

3 *Tactile models and replicas* – Haptic exhibits are considered beneficial and highly effective interpretative tools for all visitors. Furthermore, as NPS guidelines point out, tactile models 'are critical to the understanding and perceptions of the elements being interpreted for people with visual impairments and cognitive disabilities' (Harpers Ferry Center Accessibility Committee 2016).

During the design process, it was proposed that replica, 3D tactile models should be created to represent key artefacts from the display cases, maps and 'iconic' aspects of the narrative, such as a Jefferson Peace Medal, a birdman tablet from the Cahokia Mound People, the Eads Bridge, a top hat made of beaver fur and a Creole House. In total this ran to some 61 tactile replicas, produced as bronze resin scaled models, suitable for high levels of touch. Adjacent to the full-size wagon replica in the Riverfront Era zone, a scaled bronze model of the wagon has been included to enable visitors to appreciate the form and structure of this vital component of the emigrants' equipment. The model sits on replica limestone cobbles from the levee to place the wagon in context and to ensure that it accurately reflects that full-scale artefact on display.

Through consultation with the UDG, the scale of the models was found to be problematic, with their relatively small scale not providing sufficient differentiation in textures and surfaces to be clearly discernible by finger touch. As a result, the team increased the size of several models and increased specifications to provide greater contrast in textures and opportunity for detail, to help visitors to understand the entirety and context of each object. Where applicable, people were added to models to provide a sense of scale. The model of the wagon is a good example of where we needed to increase the size of the replica to enhance 'textural readability', giving a clearer sense of its construction style and materials. However, this increase in scale meant that it was harder for visitors in wheelchairs to reach over and touch the back of the wagon model, demonstrating the need to constantly review and reassess access requirements at all stages through the design process and with all UDG members. Through discussion it was agreed that approximately 70% of the rear of the model would be in reach of visitors using wheelchairs.

4 *Typography, graphic design and content* – The wagon display includes seven interpretative graphic panels and labels, set onto reader-rails, the top of reconstructed barrels (used as set-dressing) and as captions adjacent to tactile models. Designing accessible graphics, particularly within the context of low light levels, requires the consideration of numerous factors, including font size, typeface, leading, kerning, tracking, layout, colour contrast, the interplay between illustrations and images and the height and bandwidth of text. Initially drawing upon the *Programmatic Accessibility Guidelines for National Park Service Interpretative Media* (Harpers Ferry Center Accessibility Committee 2016), we used Felbridge, a sans-serif font, at 24 points, with a minimum contrast of 70% between text and background colour for the main body text on all graphic elements.

However, guidelines must always be applied within the specific context of use and tested through dialogue with users and the development of case graphics within the museum provides a useful case study here. Through the graphic styling review workshops, members of the client team and accessibility advisors suggested that, considering the likely viewing distance between visitors and sections of the cases and to increase legibility, all artefact labels (within cases) should be increased to a font size of 36 points. This instruction necessitated a review of case content to reduce the number of artefacts and enable larger labels, which could accommodate the increased font size. However, through further dialogue, members of the UDG with low vision commented that a more flexible approach was preferable to just using a larger font size. In the end, the final solution was to add removable graphic captions tethered to the exterior face of the display cases using the original 24-point font size. This would enable visitors to hold the sheets up to their eyes accommodating individual reading requirements.

With this captioning approach agreed, the design team then had to consider the placement of all external case caption panels and tethering points, adhering to guidelines

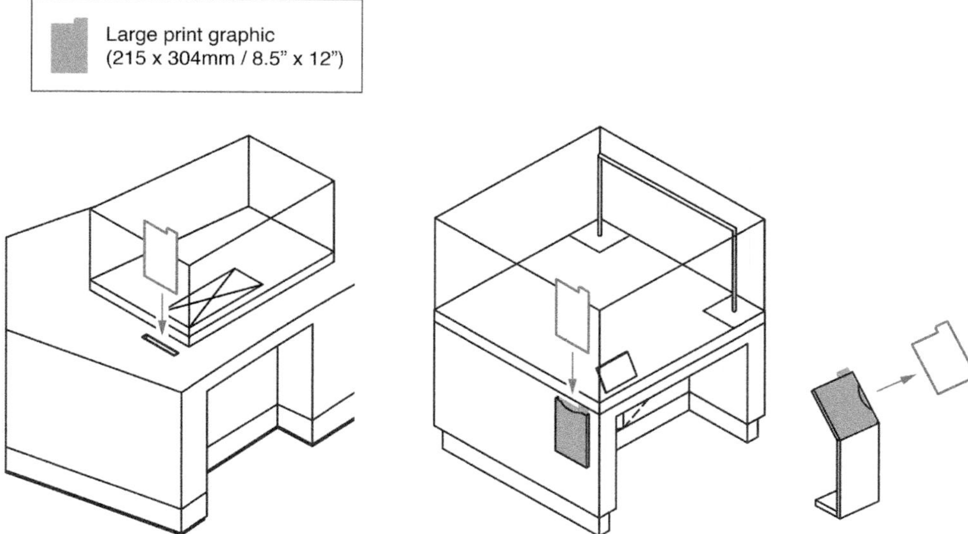


**FIGURE 13.3** Drawing showing the three standard locations for large-print graphic captions

Reproduced with kind permission of the National Park Service

about front-on access and reach. In total, three suitable locations for graphic caption holders were identified, at the front and side of cases, and on freestanding lecterns. These three locations were applied consistently throughout all parts of the museum to ensure that visitors could find information intuitively (Figure 13.3).

Early client team and UDG group discussions also established principles for inclusive writing styles, appropriate reading ages and layered content. The interpretative approach to exhibit texts was deliberately 'expressive' in tone – posing questions and inviting visitors to reflect on the experiences of early pioneers.

5 *Digital platforms and touchscreens* – The challenge of finding devices and solutions that work for all visitors, providing equity of experience, is demonstrated particularly through touchscreen design. For the wagon exhibit there are two interactive games, 'Let's Go' and 'Making the Trip', which encourage visitors to explore the necessary preparation and provisioning for the journey out west, and the experience of being on the Oregon, California or Mormon trails. The interactive games are displayed on angled 46-inch touchscreens set into standard-detail lectern holders. Software, hardware and furniture details must be considered to ensure that the combined exhibit is usable for all, maintaining the 12″ touch zone (i.e. whilst the full screen may be visually available, only the 12″ reach area from the front lip of the exhibit is used for touch activation).

Through the design process, we explored many factors, including how wheelchair users could reach all areas of the screen, the optimal height and position of units for partially sighted users with canes, and what type of touch mechanism was most appropriate for blind visitors or visitors with low vision. For many of these aspects the design process was characterised by debate amongst the UDG workshop participants as to the optimal solutions. For example, during one UDG workshop it was requested that the height from the floor to the lip of the lectern units (under which a wheelchair could be placed),

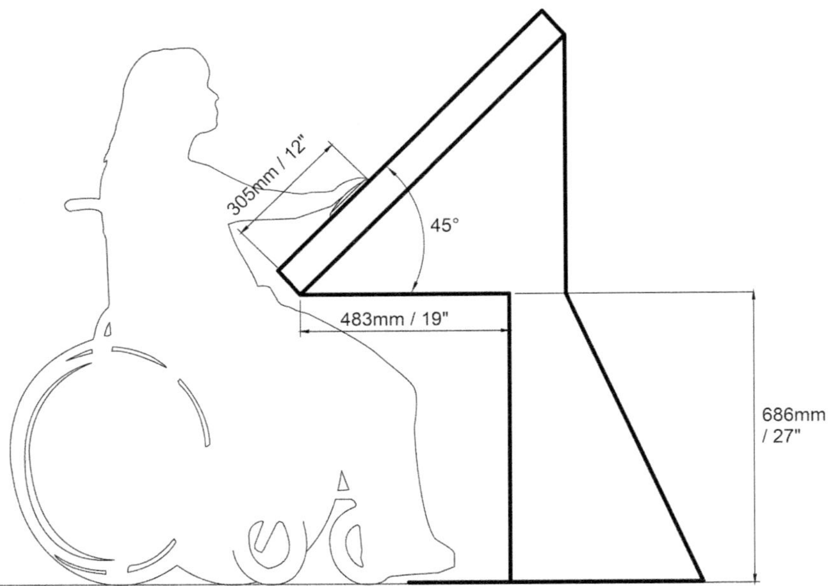


**FIGURE 13.4** Drawing showing the optimal articulation (angle, depth of reach and height) of touchscreen units to maximise usability for wheelchair users

Reproduced with kind permission of the National Park Service

should be a *minimum* of 27″, complying with the Architectural Barriers Act Accessibility Standard (ABAAS) requirements. But whilst that dimension was suitable for wheelchair users, other members of the group, particularly partially sighted users with canes, needed it to be *exactly* 27″, not just a *minimum* of 27″ for a recess of more than 4″. Thus, the final drawings (some 3,000 in total) carried a floor-to-unit height of 2′3″, i.e. exactly 27″, suiting both groups and providing the optimal solution (Figure 13.4).

Audio-enabled EZ-Access Keypads (widely distributed as the Nav-Pad™), were developed in association with the Trace Research & Development Center, with support from the University of Wisconsin. These devices are used as alternative means of accessing touchscreen content for multiple disability platforms (including those with limited hand control, vision loss, limited reading ability, dyslexia, etc.). These simple and visually clear devices provide alternative means for selecting and listening to on-screen content, and making selections on interactive programmes. Debate between the client team, UDG and designers centred upon whether these devices provided the most effective access, with some suggesting that telephone keypads were clearer to use.

6 *Soundscapes and audio descriptions* – Evocative soundscapes, capturing the mood and ambience of each thematic zone, giving an aural picture of each time and place associated with the exhibition storyline, form a core part of the interpretative expression throughout the Museum. To ensure that visitors who are deaf or have hearing loss can appreciate this layer of the interpretative experience, written audio descriptions have been created. Visitors with hearing loss are alerted to this component of the interpretation through informational signs, which encourage visitors to pick up the full written descriptions of those soundscapes should they be interested in finding out more.

Likewise, for visitors who are blind or have low vision, a full audio description of the whole Museum has been produced, which utilises RFID triggers linked to specific exhibit areas. However, the level of detail required for both these accessibility devices was much debated amongst the UDG, as full audio descriptions for exhibitions of this size and complexity can run to over 10 hours of content. The ability of a visitor to independently control the depth and detail of any particular description is critically important.

## Forging an accessible design process

Recent research and best practice guidelines are clear in the necessity to build comprehensive dialogue, consultation and review with representatives from disabled communities and other stakeholders, to maximise the effectiveness of design effort. However, this level of consultation on a project of this scale does not happen automatically but rather, requires sustained coordination, effective organisation and long-term commitment from all parties. Most importantly, embedding UDG input from the outset (for both general architectural and landscaping works as well as the exhibition design component) was a key strength of the St Louis scheme, as well as ensuring that representatives were drawn from more than 25 different disability interest groups, providing a comprehensive reflection of future visitors to the Museum and their likely needs.

Members of the **hsd** design and interpretative teams made presentations to the UDG at key junctures in the design process, usually every two months. Agendas were set in advance to determine what exhibit material would be reviewed at each phase, to correlate and support the wider design development schedule. Material, including large-scale plans, visuals, samples and even some early prototypes, was submitted one week before each meeting along with focused questions relating to specific exhibits for participants to consider prior to arriving at the meeting. The sessions themselves were focused conversations delivered through on-screen presentations. All meetings were signed using American Sign Language (by two people given the length of the meetings), with designers providing clear spoken descriptions of the exhibits being reviewed, accompanied by large-scale illustrations, 3D plans and tactile models where appropriate. Designers developed skills in how to facilitate workshops using 'live' descriptions of 3D models to ensure that all members of the groups could follow which part of the design package was being discussed and be enabled to make contributions accordingly.

At times, different groups and individuals had notably different opinions and reactions to exhibits, highlighting the fact that whilst most accessibility devices and techniques can be used by a range of people, most provide effective solutions for some groups, but not for others. Usually consensus was reached through discussion, with any additional written feedback provided after the meeting, mediated by the UDG chairperson, David Newburger. If necessary, further design work was carried out to explore solutions with drawings resubmitted to the UDG for final comment and approval.

During a four-day workshop to review the final exhibition construction drawings, the client team, Accessibility & Universal Design Consultant and Americans With Disabilities Act (ADA) Coordinator, David Newburger, determined which exhibits required full prototyping by exhibit build contractors during the construction stage, to ensure that accessibility features were fully effective and implemented as intended. Over 70 items were selected for prototyping at full size, from touchscreen lectern stands to tactile models, graphic samples to curved bench seating. This is nearly three times the usual number of prototypes developed for a museum of this size, demonstrating the client team's commitment to delivering accessible exhibition infrastructure.

To facilitate effective review of these prototypes, client representatives and the UDG were invited to a local, 5,000-square-foot warehouse facility where the exhibit fabrication company, Pacific Studio, could demonstrate each element and people could thoroughly review and test the items for usability. This resulted in the robust evaluation of prototypes through discussion and written feedback collated on review questionnaires. Final alterations were made to the articulation and positioning of exhibits to reflect team comments. This included a revision to the angle of touch screens from the base unit, increasing from 30 to 45 degrees to improve usability and to reduce light reflection (Figure 13.5).

## BOX 13.1 DEVELOPING INCLUSIVE EXHIBITS – REFLECTIONS FROM DAVID NEWBURGER, AMERICANS WITH DISABILITIES ACT (ADA) COORDINATOR, ST LOUIS

Three factors made the Universal Design Group's contribution to the St Louis scheme possible and effective:

1 The Gateway Arch Park Foundation and the NPS welcomed the opportunity to address disability issues from the very beginning of the project. It was a factor included in the competition for selecting the designers and continued throughout the project. In other projects, the disability interest was often ignored until a significant number of design and budget decisions had been made. Retrieving lost opportunities in those situations became difficult or impossible.
2 The UDG was composed of private volunteer citizens who had a wide range of disabilities, making the interplay within the group more productive than would have been the case with only one or two disabilities being represented.
3 The lead architectural practice for the scheme (Michael Van Valkenburgh Associates) enhanced the team by contracting Gina Hilberry, who was schooled in accessible design standards and universal design principles. She and her firm were both an advisor for the designers and a close communicator with the UDG. Gina consistently pointed out and posed issues for the UDG to consider, but never made decisions for the UDG or preempted outcomes.

Overall, the UDG's greatest contribution was to allow all the design partners (architects, engineers and exhibit designers) to really see and understand issues through the eyes of people with disabilities. Once achieved, many of the designers increased their sophistication as communicators to a broader audience.

The process of embedding inclusive design in the project was accomplished without fundamental disagreement amongst any of the interests involved. Whilst at times alternative positions were stated between universal design and historic preservation interests, which often required extended dialogue and analysis, all issues were resolved satisfactorily for both interest groups, and wider stakeholders. In short, the project has been a success.

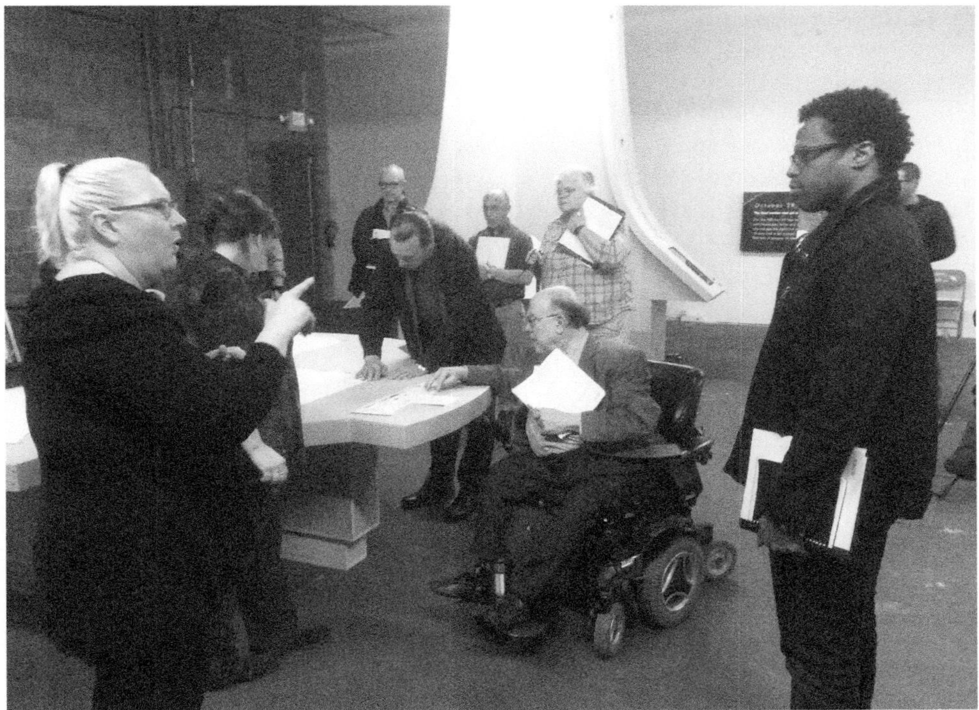

**FIGURE 13.5** Members of the Universal Design Group and Haley Sharpe Design review exhibit prototypes for usability and access

Reproduced with kind permission of the National Park Service

## Conclusion

What makes The Gateway Arch National Park project different to previous accessible design efforts, and in what ways does it represent a true shift towards inclusive design practice? Through this chapter, we have demonstrated the comprehensive and integrated approach taken by all parties involved in the project. All members of the client, design and stakeholder teams worked with a common purpose, striving to create a visitor experience which considers the full range of human diversity whilst seeking to create a comparable experience for all, regardless of age, size, ability or disability. Systematic consideration was given to how all visitors, reflecting an array of abilities and disabilities, would be able to engage with every aspect of the exhibition environment.

Optimal design solutions were developed through a transparent process of discussion and dialogue, democratising both the exhibit development as well as the final exhibition experience. The role of the UDG, contributing from the outset of the project, should not be underestimated, nor should the implications of such a delivery model. Adequate time for dialogue and reviews, effective coordination between all parties, clear and unbiased communication, and a commitment to the process from project leaders are imperative if an equitable experience for all visitors is to be achieved.

The benefits of inclusive environments within museum spaces for every visitor, regardless of ability, should not be overlooked. Through the inclusion of additional tactile components, diversified but equitable means of accessing exhibits, clearly written and presented graphic material and the general streamlining of content to mitigate against the effects of needing increased space for interpretation, the experience for all visitors coming to 'The Museum at the Gateway Arch' is more engaging, dynamic and sensory rich.

Furthermore, as museums consider their long-term sustainability and audience relevance, a holistic approach to accessible exhibition planning is imperative in social, economic and business terms. Statistics vary according to region, however the US Census Bureau gives a figure of approximately 19% of the American population having a disability in 2010 (US Census Bureau 2012). Aside from the ethical obligation to embrace an inclusive design approach, museums and heritage sites lose substantial potential revenues from visitors with disabilities who are unable or choose not to visit as well as from wider parties of family and friends who are dissuaded from visiting due to access barriers.

Overall, we need a new philosophy, a new way of thinking, and a new way to design exhibits to ensure equality of experience for all. It is no longer acceptable to do the best we can, applying piecemeal accessibility solutions on a random basis. If we are to truly achieve the reality of 'All In', embracing all visitors and user needs, clients, stakeholders and design teams must systematically consider access at all points of the design process with continued dialogue, involvement and review by end users.

## References

CityArchRiver (2016) *CityArchRiver, News and Updates*. Online. Available HTTP: www.cityarchriver.org/2016/11/29/gateway-arch-museum-get-new-exhibits-educate-engage-inspire. Accessed 12 December 2016.

Cohen Hilberry Architects (2013) *Universal Design – Design Guidelines & Elements, A Memorandum Prepared for CityArchRiver 2015 & Jefferson National Expansion Memorial*, St Louis: unpublished.

Connell, B.R. *et al.* (1997) *The Principles of Universal Design*, Raleigh: NC State University.

Dodd, J., Sandell, R. and Jolly, D.J.C. (eds) (2008) *Rethinking Disability Representation in Museums and Galleries*, Leicester: RCMG.

Harpers Ferry Center Accessibility Committee (2016) *Programmatic Accessibility Guidelines for National Park Service Interpretive Media, Version 2.2*, Harpers Ferry, WV: Harpers Ferry Center for Media Services.

Martin, S. (2006) *Disability Access in the National Park Service [Electronic Memorandum]*, Washington: US Department of the Interior. Online. Available HTTP: www.nps.gov/dscw/upload/DisabilityAccessNPSMemo_10-24-06.pdf. Accessed 20 May 2017.

NPS (2014) *All In! Accessibility in the National Park Service 2015–2020*, Washington: US Department of the Interior, National Park Service. Online. Available HTTP: www.nps.gov/aboutus/upload/All_In_Accessibility_in_the_NPS_2015-2020_FINAL.pdf. Accessed 20 May 2017.

NPS (2016) *National Park Service, About Us*. Washington: US Department of the Interior, National Park Service. Online. Available HTTP: www.nps.gov/aboutus/index.htm. Accessed 12 December 2016.

US Access Board (2014) *Access Board Technical Guides – Protruding Objects*. Online. Available HTTP: www.access-board.gov/attachments/. . . /protruding%20objects.pdf. Accessed 18 January 2017.

US Census Bureau (2012) *United States Census Bureau, Newsroom Archive*. Online. Available HTTP: www.census.gov/newsroom/releases/archives/miscellaneous/cb12-134.html Accessed 31 March 2017.

# 14

# EXPERIMENTAL EXHIBITION MODELS

## Curating, designing and managing experiments: A case study from the Humboldt Lab Dahlem

*Annette Loeseke*

### Abstract

The chapter discusses the opportunities and challenges of curating and designing intercultural, experimental exhibition projects by exploring three exhibitions commissioned by the Humboldt Lab Dahlem in Berlin. It draws on the analysis of the curatorial concepts and exhibition designs, qualitative empirical findings from a focus group with students, and remarks from keynote speakers at the closing event of the Humboldt Lab Dahlem. It argues that not only should museums become more experimental in curating and designing exhibitions, but correspondingly they should also adopt experimental and performance-centred management models if this work is to be both supported and effect change within the wider institution.

### Introduction

Founded in Berlin as an experimental exhibition-making 'laboratory', the Humboldt Lab Dahlem operated from 2012 until October 2015 in preparation for the future Humboldt Forum in Berlin's reconstructed palace building. Scheduled to open in 2019, the palace building will house the Asian Art Museum and the non-European Ethnological Museum, among others. Three of the most recent exhibitions initiated and organised by the Humboldt Lab Dahlem are discussed in this chapter; 'Object Biographies', 'Enchantment/ Beauty Parlour' and 'Exhibiting Korea'. These exhibitions reflect either intercultural topics, such as the acquisition history of certain parts of the collection, or curatorial approaches to address and communicate intercultural themes, such as the significance of beauty in Swahili culture, or a contemporary re-interpretation of historical Korean artworks of the collection.

The analysis of the curatorial concepts and exhibition designs is informed by qualitative empirical insight into visitor response, drawn from a 90-minute focus group undertaken with 14 graduate and postgraduate students as part of a seminar at the Free University of Berlin in October 2015. The chapter discusses the opportunities and challenges of the experimental design of the three exhibitions. Following recent research which draws attention to the ways in which the reception process evolves through different modes and stages – such as visitors looking for spatial orientation, focusing attention, engaging with the exhibits, reading or listening to information, interactively engaging with material provided, discussing and exchanging ideas with others, contemplating, even interrupting their path through the galleries and finding some rest before re-focusing their attention on the exhibits, and so on – the chapter explores the hypothesis that an experimental and creative curatorial approach and exhibition design should take these different modes of interacting with the setting into account (Falk 2009: 176) and attempt to support a form of visitor engagement that evolves dynamically over the duration of the visit (Loeseke 2012, 2017). Referring to key observations from the closing event of the Humboldt Lab Dahlem, the chapter further argues that not only should museums become more experimental in *curating* and *designing* exhibitions, but also in *managing* exhibition-making processes.

## Humboldt Lab Dahlem and Humboldt Forum in Berlin's reconstructed palace

Since 2012, Berlin's former royal palace has been under reconstruction at its original location in the historical city centre, opposite the museums on Museum Island. The original royal palace was severely damaged during World War II and the ruins were finally demolished in 1950. In the 1970s, the 'Palace of the Republic' was erected in its place, housing the parliament of the German Democratic Republic and the People's Chamber, together with art galleries, a theatre and restaurants. This building was demolished by 2008 and the reconstructed palace is scheduled to open in its place in 2019. Since it will house, among others, the non-European Ethnological Museum and the Asian Art Museum, the intention is to create a 'centre of world culture' (Parzinger n.d., Parzinger 2011), the so-called Humboldt Forum.

The plan to reconstruct the historical royal-turned-imperial palace and the intention to create a 'centre of world culture' has stimulated controversy about Eurocentric museological approaches and postcolonial challenges (Schmidt 2016). In order to respond to these transcultural challenges, the Humboldt Lab Dahlem was founded as a creative 'laboratory' for experimenting with innovative transcultural, intercultural and postcolonial exhibition formats and new forms of exhibiting and programming. The Lab was located at two museums – the Ethnological Museum and Asian Art Museum of the National Museums in Berlin. Initiated and funded by the German Federal Cultural Foundation (Kulturstiftung des Bundes) and the Prussian Cultural Heritage Foundation (Stiftung Preussischer Kulturbesitz), the Lab was led by the directors of the Ethnological Museum and Asian Art Museum as well as a manager, responsible for the contextual concept development of the Humboldt Forum on behalf of the federal government (Kuhl, Schindler and Deuring 2015: 4, 11). The core team running the Lab consisted of a managing director, an assistant to the directors, a communications assistant, a technical coordinator and a project administrator. An international steering committee, comprising seven members, supervised the artistic development of the Lab (Kuhl, Schindler and Deuring 2015: 6). The Lab was intended to discuss ways in which 'the findings achieved [could] be conveyed on a long-term basis, to both the Humboldt Forum and to other institutions'. Throughout the process, a decision was taken not to evaluate the Humboldt Lab Dahlem on the basis of the concrete, often very specific results it achieved. Instead, those leading the Lab considered it more important that the Lab developed experimental ways of working and discussed a multitude of contexts (Kuhl, Schindler and Deuring 2015: 4).

During its four years of operation, around 30 projects were realised by the curators of both museums and invited external curators, artists, scholars, exhibition designers, directors, scenographers and performance groups. Exhibitions presented a wide range of topics and approaches, from 'Layering Meanings' (Wegner 2013) or 'Game of Thrones' (Rosenberg 2013) to 'Man – Object – Jaguar' (Scholz 2013). The individual exhibitions ran between two and seven months, respectively. In addition, the Lab organised public talks, symposia and workshops. All exhibitions and events were documented online and in print (Humboldt Lab Dahlem 2012–2015; Kuhl, Schindler and Deuring 2015). The following sections explore three of the last exhibition projects commissioned by the Lab before it was closed, as scheduled, in October 2015.

## Case study one: 'Object Biographies'

'Object Biographies' presented objects from the African collection of the Ethnological Museum in Berlin and set out to explore ways of addressing the provenance of objects, their interpretation within the new context of an ethnological museum in Europe and the effect that sometimes violent appropriation had on the societies the objects were taken from. The two curators of the exhibition collaborated closely with scholars from the Republic of Benin in Africa. Apart from the collection history, the project focused on the history of exhibiting these objects. It addressed the changing ways of ordering and classifying objects over time, and explored how the circumstances of their appropriation were addressed by exhibitions in the early twentieth century (Rodatus and von Oswald 2015).

The ambition of institutional critique implicit in the exhibition idea was reflected in a narrative exhibition design that sought to mirror the curatorial intention to look behind the scenes. The objects were presented together with files, photographs and videos documenting the whole research process of the project. The objects and other media were presented on the exterior walls of an open and fragmented triangular exhibition space that formed an inner space. The inner space was almost devoid of exhibits, however, 'cut-out' openings in the walls allowed visitors to look, through this inner space, and see the back of the objects and media on the opposite side of the installation.[1] This 'cut-out' exhibition design symbolised both a 'backstage' view of the museum and suggested the idea of institutional critique – an opening-up of the Museum and reflection on its past. The exhibition design was created to represent or symbolise the way the curators not only displayed objects but also critically addressed Western research and classification practices and institutional frameworks that significantly shape the meaning attributed to exhibited objects.

An evaluation of the exhibition was undertaken through a focus group with students as part of a seminar at the Free University of Berlin. The students reported that they walked around the installation and particularly engaged with the objects presented at the exterior of the walls rather than entering the interior space and exploring the inside/outside perspective intended to symbolise a backstage view of the institution. Lack of detailed content in the interior space of the exhibition was cited as the main reason for this lack of engagement; 'You walk around the installation and end up watching the videos. . . . the interior space is nearly empty, nothing draws you in', as one student put it. For some, the cut-outs and overall design were distractions, which undermined concentration: 'The open design is disruptive because you can walk back and forth, enter and leave the space'.

The presentation of the back of some objects triggered some students' curiosity: 'The display of the back of the box makes you want to find out about the front. It demonstrates that the boxes were forgotten in the basement [of the museum]'. For others, the back of the objects did not encourage them to enter the space and get involved: 'The back of the box puts you off. You don't see anything, just the back'. Overall, the curatorial concept of the exhibition remained unclear, at least in part: 'The exhibition design is a good idea; it suggests transparency. However, the idea was not appropriately implemented'. Finally, the placement of most of the objects on the exterior walls and the overall placement of the exhibition in the entrance area to the Africa Department did not encourage students to engage with the exhibits and instead pushed them away from the exhibition, in the direction of the Africa Department.

What was clear from the student feedback was that although the highly symbolic exhibition design was intended to reflect the exhibitionary concept and even shape the content of the exhibition, it did not support the students in interpreting the exhibition or accessing the exhibition concept. On the contrary, the design seemed to hinder some students who felt distracted by the exhibition design. It did not help visitors refocus their attention during their visit or support their sustained engagement and reception. The exhibition design of 'Object Biographies' primarily sought to symbolise and illustrate the exhibition concept as well as key messages of the curators, but it did not fully consider the impact that the exhibition design and spatial layout would have on the attention, level of engagement and reception processes of the visitors.

## Case study two: 'Enchantment/Beauty Parlour'

The second case study analyses an installation called 'Enchantment/Beauty Parlour' which sought to create an experiential, narrative exhibition space through constructing a Swahili beauty parlour installation while at the same time defamiliarising the setting to encourage the audience to take a critical perspective on the topic through highlighting the very construction of the installation (Ivanov and Rostasy 2015). The exterior of the beauty salon was a wooden construction surrounded by a rigid cage constructed from fine black lace.[2] A small number of nineteenth- and twentieth-century objects from the Ethnological Museum's Africa collection that related to 'beauty' (though not directly to a beauty parlour) were presented in niches on the exterior walls of the wooden construction inside the lace cage. Apart from these objects, all materials used to build 'Enchantment/Beauty Parlour' were sourced in Berlin. As Swahili aesthetic combines spiritual and corporeal beauty and addresses all senses, the installation room and, in fact, the whole area around the installation was filled with a distinctive scent. The entrance to 'Enchantment/Beauty Parlour' was placed at the back of the installation and led to an interior designed in the fashion of an African beauty salon. The installation was co-created by a curator of the Ethnological Museum, a director and scenographer, a media technician and a beauty consultant who runs her own beauty parlour in Eastern Africa.

Entering the beauty parlour installation, the visitor was supposed to experience the environment of the production of 'female beauty', especially with respect to wedding ceremonies, as a bride or a female guest, in Swahili culture. The visitor could take a seat in front of a mirror projecting a video that showed a beauty consultant and her client in a beauty salon. The cross-fading of the video projection and the visitor's own mirror image was intended to provide a semi-immersive, 'hyperrealistic' (Ivanov and Rostasy 2015: 220) experience. The installation was intended to 'immerse the visitors in a subjective narrative' of a 'fully equipped beauty parlour, which resembled something between a private ambience and a beauty salon on the street' (Ivanov and Rostasy 2015: 220). The team constructed a 'Beauty Parlour' installation but visibly included elements that were intended to blur the impression of an authentic setting and make the construction visible. Combining the intercultural and interdisciplinary expertise of academic curators, media and stage designers and professional practitioners in the field that is 'exhibited' and through the alienating effect of the exterior installation in particular, the exhibition design of the beauty parlour can be described as fictional and immersive alike – a hybrid between artistic installation and narrative space or quasi-immersive reconstruction of an experiential space. Unlike the self-critical approach of the institutional critique offered by the first case study, 'Object Biographies', the hyperrealistic aesthetic of the 'Enchantment/Beauty Parlour' challenged conventional disciplinary boundaries and analytical interpretative approaches.

'Enchantment/Beauty Parlour' was also evaluated through a focus group discussion with students from the Free University of Berlin which generated the following findings. The response to the installation was controversial: it was well received and appreciated by some students while disapproved of and debated by others. While piquing some students' curiosity ('It is a special experience'), the unfamiliar entry to a secret space irritated others and prevented them from engaging with the installation. The placement of the entrance at the back of the installation was interpreted as a barrier: 'You are not likely to enter when you pass along the installation'. It remained unclear how the objects presented on the exterior walls of the parlour related to the hybrid, immersive experience inside, and the wooden construction and the black lace were not identified as rhetorical means of an aesthetic of alienation: 'The form of a cage is discouraging, it makes it look locked-up' and 'Only on closer inspection you realise that it is not a cage but made of lace'. As 'Enchantment/Beauty Parlour' was presented in the context of an ethnological museum, some students expected it to be an authentic reconstruction of a Swahili beauty salon: 'the concrete floor and the iron door makes the installation look authentic'. Some suggested that in a different museum context, for example a contemporary art museum, they would consider the installation as an artwork: 'You think it is an artwork because it is displayed in a museum'. Overall, it remained unclear to the students whether the 'Beauty Parlour' was an artwork, an authentic reconstruction, a construction for immersive contextual experiences or, in fact, a hyper-realistic installation, as the curator called it.

'Enchantment/Beauty Parlour' sparked controversy. Interpreting an installation that challenged disciplinary boundaries and blurred conventional categories did not come naturally to most students. The complexity and hybridity of the exhibition model remained unclear: 'It is a presentation, nothing innovative'. It seems that this was due to the specific framework of an ethnological museum that was not perceived as a space for experimentation. Engaging with the hybrid experiential space was a complex, non-representational endeavour, since the installation did not represent an authentic setting or reproduce an authentic situation. Instead of reducing a complex phenomenon and adapting it for exhibiting within the specific framework of a European museum setting, the installation in fact raised the complexity of the phenomenon it referred to in the first instance. Instead of analytically separating the diverse intellectual and immersive experiences the installation offered, the visitor to the 'Beauty Parlour' was encouraged, through exhibition design and format, to blend the diverse contradictory and conflicting experiences and interpret them together. Experimental, hybrid, interdisciplinary exhibition design might face challenges in communicating and generating complex ideas and experiences. But stirring controversy about innovative, unfamiliar exhibition models among visitors, as well as curators and designers, also creates opportunities for discussion and reflection, as the focus groups with the students indicated.

## Case study three: 'Exhibiting Korea – Passages'

The third case study describes one of several installations within the exhibition 'Exhibiting Korea' that presented artworks and installations by five contemporary artists. 'Exhibiting Korea' aimed to develop visual as well as narrative strategies for highlighting and interpreting the Asian Art Museum's small collection of Korean artefacts. The exhibition included two video installations and a folding screen, contemporary photographs and sculptures, and historical Korean ceramics. The particular installation 'Passages' referred to the traditional Korean screen that depicts a Korean mountain landscape (Rahman-Steinert 2015).[3] In addition to interpreting the Korean collection, the exhibition set out to challenge Western conventions of exhibition design (Rahman-Steinert 2015).

Discussion in the focus group was organised particularly around 'Passages'. Here, on a wall panel, the artist Inhwan Oh described how he planned to audiotape and videotape a performance in the depicted mountain landscape. Referring to the history of the screen and addressing topics such as migration, journey and movement, the artist intended to encourage visitors to not only engage with the materiality of the object but also to reflect upon the object's journey through space and time. On two videos placed on the floor, he invited the visitor to follow his planned and performed journey through the landscape. While some students found it difficult to identify a clear overall curatorial concept of 'Exhibiting Korea' ('You had to read a lot of text in order to get it'; 'Overall, the exhibition is very text-related'), others found that the curatorial aim to challenge conventional Western exhibition design was not met ('The concept that is described in the introductory text remains unclear, that is irritating'). Picking up on the simple Korean aesthetic of the exhibition, one student commented, 'The concept/design is simple, few exhibits are on display; the focus lies on selected exhibits'.

In terms of 'Passages', the installation generated less controversy than 'Enchantment/Beauty Parlour', even though it offered a complex transhistorical experience of both contemporary and historical artworks: 'The video-performance is an ongoing project and has not yet been completed. However, the project is well explained by the text [on the wall panel]'. This might be due to the fact that the Korean installation could be clearly identified as a cross-media artwork, produced and performed by an artist. Unlike 'Enchantment/Beauty Parlour', 'Passages' did not question disciplinary boundaries, nor did it aim at a hybridisation of categories: 'Some of the exhibits are autonomous artworks, others are not. . . . The curatorial concept to commission contemporary artists as curators works well because the artists present their own artworks'. Unlike 'Enchantment/Beauty Parlour', the video installation 'Passages' was presented, through a lengthy written text on a wall panel, as describing a planned performance, an art form well established in contemporary artistic practice. In addition, and unlike the exhibition 'Object Biographies', the installation 'Passages' and in fact, the whole exhibition 'Exhibiting Korea', did not challenge the way the objects of the Korean collection were acquired. Finally, the design of 'Passages' and 'Exhibiting Korea' proved to be more conventional and familiar to the visitor: 'You have the impression that you move through time when walking through the galleries: The first gallery refers to the present, the second gallery presents historical hanging scrolls, and the third gallery as well'. Unlike the exhibition design of 'Object Biographies', 'Passages' and 'Exhibiting Korea' did not challenge the visitor to take a different, more critical perspective toward the museum as an institution and call into question museological practices and curatorial approaches of the past.

## Key findings from the Humboldt Lab Dahlem

As the description and analysis of the three case studies from the Humboldt Lab Dahlem demonstrate, the experimental development and presentation of innovative exhibitions, in terms of both content and design, raises the need for a distinct reception-centred approach to curating and designing exhibitions. First, while intending to symbolise the exhibition concept, the exhibition design of the 'Object Biographies' needed clarification and adaptation to visitors' reception practice and dynamic reception processes consisting of different stages (Loeseke 2012). This suggests that in order to enhance visitor engagement in complex and hybrid experiences, experimental, creative exhibition design should be reception centred as distinct from primarily content focused. Second, as the case of 'Enchantment/Beauty Parlour' demonstrated, interdisciplinary, collaborative exhibitions that blur disciplinary boundaries and challenge conventional Western notions of exhibitions seem to stimulate reflection upon the constitutive impact of exhibition models, design and frameworks on presentation and reception practice alike.

The case studies presented from the Humboldt Lab Dahlem demonstrate that questioning conventional presentational models, experimenting on a project basis and working in interdisciplinary teams, bears particular challenges but also holds opportunities and that crossing disciplinary boundaries is an effective way of stirring controversy and stimulating debate on frameworks and disciplinary interpretive categories. As findings from the focus group suggest, it would be beneficial if potential contradictions and conflicting perspectives were addressed, exposed and discussed rather than 'resolved' and concealed. Instead of reducing complexity through analytically clarifying interdisciplinary or categorical bias, it is suggested that museums should welcome and integrate creative and experimental processes. These enable complex visitor experiences through cross-disciplinary formats that challenge conventional boundaries and reception practices. The way exhibition developers operate creatively and experimentally, the specific exhibition model, should be foregrounded and indeed communicated and discussed with audiences, as an integral part of 'what' is on display. Museums would benefit from taking risks and actively managing controversial response by visitors, curators and designers (see Heumann Gurian in Part I of this volume).

Finally, as the case studies from the Humboldt Lab Dahlem indicate, the creation of interdisciplinary, collaborative and flexible teams seems an appropriate way of managing the creation of small-scale, varying, experimental exhibitions (Probst and Wegner 2013: 119). Experimental exhibitions can trigger curiosity and get visitors engaged through producing innovative narrative spaces. As the Humboldt Lab Dahlem showed, these exhibitions are enhanced by diverse dialogic formats such as talks, symposia, workshops and performances that actively involved visitors. Visitor response from the focus group about the three presented case studies, especially to the exhibitions 'Object Biographies' and 'Enchantment/Beauty Parlour', strongly indicate that increasingly complex and hybrid exhibition themes, exhibition design and exhibition models as tested at the Humboldt Lab Dahlem need clarification in regards to their experimental, hybrid character and performative exhibition design. Experimental curatorial approaches that either seek to cross traditional disciplinary boundaries or challenge established narratives of acquisition practices in particular benefit from an audience and reception-centred exhibition design that support visitors in structuring their experience and fully exploring the multi-layered themes and designs.

## Findings from the Lab's closing event

This chapter concludes by drawing on a keynote address given by senior staff of the Humboldt Forum at the closing event of the Humboldt Lab Dahlem in Berlin on 15 October 2015. During the closing ceremony, one of the keynote speakers called the reconstructed palace building a 'Hohenzollernhuelle' (royal 'envelope' or 'wrapping', referring to the royal Hohenzollern family that formerly ruled Prussia).[4] Taking the reconstructed palace as a mere envelope does a number of things. First, it overlooks and undermines the aforementioned public controversy about the reconstruction of a long-demolished historical royal-imperial building. Second, interpreting the controversial reconstructed palace as insignificant wrapping for the presentation of non-European ethnographic collections, brought together during colonial times, ignores discussions about Eurocentric museological concepts and more progressive, postcolonial approaches. It also neglects one of the key implications as well as outcomes of the Humboldt Lab Dahlem research: the constitutive impact that the presentational model has on the reception and interpretation of exhibitions.

The speaker further mentioned that after four years, the Humboldt Lab Dahlem had fulfilled its purpose, and the future Humboldt Forum would be run without the Lab. The speaker added that, despite the closure of the Lab, it was expected that the curators and designers at the future Humboldt Forum would continue the Lab's experimental work. They suggested this effort would continue without an appropriate budget and the staff that had managed the Humboldt Lab Dahlem. The statements indicate a certain gulf between the interdisciplinary teams that ran the Humboldt Lab Dahlem and senior management staff at the Humboldt Forum in defining an experimental approach to curating and designing exhibitions and managing museums. The statements suggest that senior staff did not acknowledge the Humboldt Forum's contexts and frameworks, that is its architecture, significant historical location and motivations to reconstruct a historical, formerly royal-imperial building. However, as this chapter has discussed, 'Object Biographies' challenged precisely these institutional contexts and acquisition policies with regard to the collections that will be presented in the reconstructed palace.

The statements further indicate an implicit result-centred approach to innovation and experimentation, as opposed to a continuous process-based one. The suggestion that an experimental 'lab' approach can continue without core curatorial or design staff and without managerial and financial support demonstrates a lack of recognition of the underlying infrastructural systems necessary for innovation. It underestimates the significance of a flexible management model for project-based, collaborative, interdisciplinary teams.

In contrast, this chapter suggests the Humboldt Forum should take account of the curatorial as well as managerial learning acquired in the Humboldt Lab Dahlem. As well as reconsidering exhibition models and programmes, it should also rethink its institutional role if it wishes to become agile, experimental, open, self-critical and an exemplary twenty-first-century institution. In abandoning the experimental apparatus of the Humboldt Lab Dahlem, the Humboldt Forum seems to be reducing its former Lab to a mere technical tool for producing content for its newly built exhibition galleries in the reconstructed palace.

## Conclusion

In this chapter, I have argued that an experimental design approach should not be limited to reflecting the content and symbolising the concept of an exhibition. Instead, a creative, innovative exhibition design should take a distinct reception-centred approach and support visitors in structuring their reception process and practice. As the three case studies from the Humboldt Lab Dahlem indicate, a 'lab' approach needs to be collaborative and interdisciplinary in order to test innovative, experimental exhibition models that cross disciplinary boundaries and challenge conventional exhibition and reception practices. The Humboldt Lab Dahlem operated as a separate, independently funded, project-based management unit. It was provided with an appropriate budget and staff for initiating and coordinating the collaboration between interdisciplinary project team members of different museum departments and external partners at all stages of the management process.

The closure of the Humboldt Lab Dahlem as scheduled after four years of operation and the statements made during the key addresses at the closing event, however, indicate that central implications of the Lab, such as an appropriate management model that corresponds with the needs of a creative, experimental work environment, have not been fully endorsed within the wider organisation. The Humboldt Lab Dahlem was set up to discuss ways of conveying the findings achieved on a long-term basis (Kuhl, Schindler and Deuring 2015: 4). The Lab was to be evaluated on the basis of its 'open-ended working method and heterogeneous contexts' rather than 'the concrete, often very specific results it achieved' (Kuhl, Schindler and Deuring 2015: 4). Considering the closure of the Humboldt Lab Dahlem and drawing on the summarised statements above from the closing event, it seems that the Humboldt Forum ran an innovative, experimental Lab for a limited time period, but that it never fully embraced an overall, sustainable experimental approach to curating exhibitions and programmes, managing institutions and establishing a performance-oriented institutional learning culture.

I have argued that developing and presenting experimental, increasingly complex and hybrid exhibition models requires a clear reception-centred approach and communication strategy that ideally includes regular and active discussions with audiences. As I hope the case studies of the Humboldt Lab Dahlem indicate, museums that intend to meet the transcultural and intercultural challenges and increasingly diverse motivations and expectations of twenty-first-century audiences need to experiment and try new, contemporary, complex approaches. To this end, however, museums rely on the full support from an innovative interdisciplinary, flexible and creativity-led management. It remains to be seen how the Humboldt Forum will define an experimental, self-critical, transparent and participatory approach to running a museum once it opens its doors to the public in 2019. How will the Humboldt Forum define its institutional role and critically address its own raison d'être – the motivations behind the reconstruction, its historical and current contexts such as the reconstructed architecture, historically and politically significant location, its acquisition policies as well as historical and current curatorial strategies – to present its collections and engage audiences? The way it will translate the experimental mission of the Humboldt Lab Dahlem seems crucial for the future role of the Humboldt Forum, in particular how it will address acquisition policies and presentational strategies of the past and present; acknowledge the significance of presentational contexts and frameworks in shaping a narrative; reflect the significance of interdisciplinary collaboration in order to challenge disciplinary boundaries; and reconsider the institutional role of the museum in the twenty-first century.

## Notes

1 Illustrations: www.humboldt-lab.de/en/projet-archive/probebuehne-6/object-biographies/pictures/index.html
2 Illustrations: www.humboldt-lab.de/en/project-archive/probebuehne-6/enchantment-beauty-parlour/pictures/index.html
3 Illustrations: www.humboldt-lab.de/en/project-archive/probebuehne-7/exhibiting-korea/pictures/index.html
4 Also see Probst and Wegner (2013: 112–114) who point to the challenges that the Humboldt Forum faces in its attempt to relate to the reconstructed palace. On the one hand, the authors underline that the palace and Humboldt Forum do not oppose each other, on the other hand, they clearly distinguish between the palace building ('form') and the Humboldt Forum ('content').

## References

Falk, J.H. (2009) *Identity and the Museum Visitor Experience*, Walnut Creek, CA: Left Coast Press.

Humboldt Lab Dahlem (2012–15) *Project Archive*. Online. Available HTTP: www.humboldt-forum.de/en/humboldt-lab-dahlem/project-archive/. Accessed 31 December 2015.

Humboldt Lab Dahlem (ed.) (2015) *The Laboratory Concept: Museum Experiments in the Humboldt Lab Dahlem*, Berlin: Nicolai Verlag.

Ivanov, P. and Rostasy, A. (2015) 'Enchantment/Beauty Parlour/Project Description. Narrative Spaces in Museum Pedagogy', in Kuhl, C., Schindler, B., and Deuring, D. (eds.) *The Humboldt Lab Dahlem: Museum Experiments on the Way to the Humboldt-Forum*, pp. 219–21. Online. Available HTTP: http://d-nb.info/1079569847/34. Accessed 20 May 2017.

Kuhl, C., Schindler, B., and Deuring, D. (eds) (2015) *The Humboldt Lab Dahlem: Museum Experiments on the Way to the Humboldt-Forum*. Online. Available HTTP: http://d-nb.info/1079569847/34. Accessed 20 May 2017.

Loeseke, A. (2012) 'Co-presenting Past and Present: Visitor Studies on the Reception Process', *Engage*, 31, pp. 51–8.

Loeseke, A. (2017) 'Rezeptionszentrierung als zentraler strategischer Managementansatz: Implikationen fuer Forschung, Produktentwicklung und Managementmodelle' [Reception-centred Management Approaches: Implications For Research, Product Development and Management Models], Paper *Zehnte Jahrestagung des Fachverbands Kulturmanagement*, Weimar 2017 (under peer-review).

Parzinger, H. (n.d.) 'Time to Talk about Content, a Q&A Session with Hermann Parzinger', *Humboldt Forum Magazine*, Stiftung Preussischer Kulturbesitz, p. 1. Online. Available HTTP: www.preussischer kulturbesitz.de/fileadmin/user_upload/documents/mediathek/humboldt-forum/rp/TC_Humboldt_komplett_150611_klein.pdf. Accessed 21 August 2017.

Parzinger, H. (2011) *Das Humboldt-Forum: 'Soviel Welt mit sich verbinden als möglich'*, Berlin: Stiftung Berliner Schloss. Online. Available HTTP: www.preussischer-kulturbesitz.de/fileadmin/user_upload/documents/mediathek/ueber_uns/rp/broschuere_humboldt-forum_soviel-welt-mit-sich-verbinden-als-moeglich.pdf. Accessed 20 May 2017.

Probst, B. and Wegner, A. (2013) 'Gut aufgestellt: Stabsstelle Humboldt-Forum und Humboldt Lab Dahlem – Zur Planung und Umsetzung der Konzepte und Projekte', in Stiftung Preussischer Kulturbesitz (ed.) *Das Humboldt-Forum im Berliner Schloss: Planungen – Prozesse – Perspektiven*, Munich: Hirmer Verlag, pp. 112–20.

Rahman-Steinert, U. (2015) 'Exhibiting Korea. The Collection Context as an Opportunity', in Kuhl, C., Schindler, B., and Deuring, D. (eds) *The Humboldt Lab Dahlem: Museum Experiments on the Way to the Humboldt-Forum*, pp. 238–40. Online. Available HTTP: http://d-nb.info/1079569847/34. Accessed 20 May 2017.

Rodatus, V. and von Oswald, M. (2015) 'Object Biographies: Attempted Methods, New Collaborations, and Altered Perspectives', in Kuhl, C., Schindler, B., and Deuring, D. (eds) *The Humboldt Lab Dahlem: Museum Experiments on the Way to the Humboldt-Forum*, pp. 208–10. Online. Available HTTP: http://d-nb.info/1079569847/34. Accessed 20 May 2017.

Rosenberg, A. (2013) 'Game of Thrones', in Kuhl, C., Schindler, B., and Deuring, D. (eds) (2015) *The Humboldt Lab Dahlem. Museum Experiments on the Way to the Humboldt-Forum*, pp. 64–72. Online. Available HTTP: http://d-nb.info/1079569847/34. Accessed 20 May 2017.

Schmidt, T.E. (2016) 'Ein Schloss fuer die Alles-richtig-Macher', *Zeit Online*. Online. Available HTTP: www.zeit.de/2016/02/humboldt-forum-berlin-stadtschloss-kulturpolitik. Accessed 10 April 2016.

Scholz, A. (2013) 'Man, Object, Jaguar: An Approach to Perspectivism', in Kuhl, C., Schindler, B., and Deuring, D. (eds) (2015) *The Humboldt Lab Dahlem: Museum Experiments on the Way to the Humboldt-Forum*, pp. 97–100. Online. Available HTTP: http://d-nb.info/1079569847/34. Accessed 20 May 2017.

Wegner, A. (2013) 'Layering Meanings. Information in Extenso in the Quest for Concentration', in Kuhl, C., Schindler, B., and Deuring, D. (eds) (2015) *The Humboldt Lab Dahlem: Museum Experiments on the Way to the Humboldt-Forum*, pp. 7–11. Online. Available HTTP: http://d-nb.info/1079569847/34. Accessed 20 May 2017.

# 15

# FROM THE 'FIELD' TO THE 'WILDERNESS'

## Translation and creation in curating socially engaged arts

*Sipei Lu*


### Abstract

This chapter explores how museums and galleries in China, rather than being solely places of presentation and display, can become sites for the enactment of socially engaged art. The implications for the future of this kind of exhibition making suggests paying more attention to the perspectives of the artists, whose voices are often overlooked or are assumed to correspond with the overarching curatorial theme. The chapter argues that an examination of the artists' engagement with the curatorial process would facilitate a deeper understanding of socially engaged arts. It also identifies the opportunities and challenges of the curation of socially engaged arts for museums as public spaces in China.


### Introduction

Researching exhibition histories serves not only to investigate the details of artistic and curatorial practice, but also to examine the complexities of exhibition making. Researcher Lucy Steeds (2014: 13–14) argues that scrutinising the relationship between art, curation, and design research can reveal, critique, and develop an understanding of art and the role of museums:

> Consideration of contemporary art's exhibition means prioritising its becoming public – its moment of meeting a public or, rather, plural publics . . . Emphasising art's exhibition in this way usurps the privilege previously accorded, in modernist thought, to the artist's subjectivity or to art's so-called autonomy and its putatively universal appeal . . . the aim is to shift and widen the focus in order to take in the multiple agencies responsible for exhibitions. . . . aspects such as design or interpretation materials and more broadly the role of the institutional or alternative context.

This chapter follows this view and draws art into the conversation on the future of museum and gallery design through a focus on the exhibition making of socially engaged arts in China. It analyses a case study of transporting Nanting Research, a socially engaged arts education project developed in and for a very specific community, into an exhibition titled 'Civil Power' held at the Beijing Minsheng Art Museum from 25 June to 10 October 2015. The chapter pays particular attention to the perspectives of socially engaged artists, whose voices are often overlooked or are assumed to correspond to the overarching curatorial theme. First, the chapter argues that an examination of artists' engagement with the curatorial process facilitates a deeper understanding of socially engaged arts. Second, the chapter argues that the inclusion of the artist(s) in the curatorial process enhances the agency of museums in working with socially engaged arts.

It is often assumed that exhibitions of socially engaged art can be understood as simple presentations of projects, often undertaken elsewhere. However, in group exhibitions where artists play a major role in the conceptualisation and design of their individual exhibition spaces, some socially engaged artists adjust their exhibition-making strategies to enhance project goals and to facilitate future actions, both in the field and in the museum. For these artists, every exhibition is different. Interpreting a project as having the same function in different exhibitions ignores artists' strategic objectives. Furthermore, artists' construction of their own narratives through exhibition design and initiating discussions, site-specific projects, and associated programmes of events offers new possibilities to the curatorial process. Disregarding the details of exhibition making may oversimplify or even misrepresent the politics of exhibiting by focusing on the themes of exhibitions without looking into the specifics of interaction and negotiation taking place in the exhibition-making process. These aspects of exhibition research have not yet been fully explored in the museum making literature, although there are many elaborations of general curatorial conceptions (Lu 2012; Wu 2014; Judah 2014; Wu and Xia 2015).

Reflecting on issues such as spatial relations and spatial construction, the inter-textual relationship within an exhibition, interpretive devices, and exhibition graphics, this chapter does not aim to propose a design model for curating and exhibiting socially engaged art – every exhibition and project is different and there can be no formula. Furthermore, the objectives of socially engaged arts projects may vary at different stages, and artists may position themselves differently in relation to diverse exhibitions, including considering questions of whether to hold exhibitions at all. The case study below offers only a partial view of the variety of implications embedded in the exhibition of socially engaged arts. Nonetheless, it does begin to identify diverse approaches which could be used to examine and evaluate exhibitions of socially engaged arts practice as well as socially engaged arts projects, and attempts to inform future practices by advocating collaborative exhibition design, long-term research, and acknowledgement of the complexities of curating socially engaged arts in China and within the institutional context of the museum.

## Exhibiting socially engaged arts in art institutions

Recent years have seen a growing presence in China of long-term art projects which are often based on specific locations and use art-making as a medium to attract public participation, opening up of discussions and the potential for acting on pressing social issues. These range from community projects aimed at enabling sustainable civic participation, to science-art collaborations treating patients with brain injuries, to individual or networked endeavours to address issues of social justice. In China, there are several terms associated with such practices, such as *shehui jierushi yishu* (社会介入式艺术, the literal English translation of which is 'socially engaged arts'), *zaidi xiangmu* (在地项目, 'on-site/site-specific projects'), or *shehui shijian* (社会实践, 'social practice') (He and Shen 2013; Sheng 2007; Wang 2010; Sun 2011; Bao 2016; Ni 2015; Ou 2016). These projects and the language used to describe them resonate with practices in the West that are termed socially engaged arts, dialogical art, critical practices, or social cooperation (Kester 2004; Thompson 2012; Finkelpearl 2013; Marstine 2017). For the convenience of this article, I use 'socially engaged arts' to refer to the projects in the research, which is the English translation of *shehui jierushi yishu* (Zheng 2010; Wang 2017).[1]

The museum space is a 'wilderness' for socially engaged arts for two reasons. First, the majority of socially engaged arts in China are artist-initiated projects. There are not many projects of this type commissioned by galleries, biennials, and other institutions where the conditions of working are often predetermined. Second, socially engaged artists have only recently begun to view the museum as a ground for action. Many socially engaged arts practitioners develop projects as a critique of the art system and deliberately choose to keep a degree of independence from the institutional realm by, for example, undertaking self-organised initiatives (Bao 2014).

However, the relationship between socially engaged arts practitioners and art institutions is not antagonistic. Many institutions, in an age of transformation, are responsive to emerging socially engaged arts practices, viewing them as a new thread of contemporary Chinese art practice. Many museums see the exhibition of, and events related to, socially engaged arts as an opportunity to deepen their engagement with the public. Indeed, many players in both camps share the same goal of developing new identities and agendas for museums in China. For many practitioners, the institution of the museum increasingly provides a ground for action, facilitating a progressive process, integrated into their overall practices. In addition, the museum platform is seen as an important opportunity for practitioners to communicate with colleagues and visitors on specific issues emerging in their projects.

Museums in China use various forms to engage the wider public with socially engaged arts such as lectures, forums, and exhibitions. There are curatorial programmes that are dedicated to individual socially engaged arts projects, as well as group survey exhibitions where curators put forward propositions and socially engaged arts projects are presented among a wide range of other works. This chapter focuses on the latter. In these group survey exhibitions, one issue that troubles some socially engaged artists is that the interpretation of their work is often subjected to the framing of the wider exhibition and the architectural space of the museum itself, which can result in their projects being historicised and de-politicised. For many artists who choose to participate, exhibition making becomes an attempt to maintain the politics of their projects despite such institutional conditions. The following analyses the experience of displaying Nanting Research in the 'Civil Power' exhibition in order to illustrate the kinds of design strategies socially engaged arts practitioners deploy to maintain the active nature of their work and create opportunities for conversations. The wider implications of this project for exhibition making will also be explored.

## Project context

Nanting is a village in Guangdong Province, South East China, 11.7 km away from the centre of Panyu District, Guangzhou, the capital city of Guangdong. It is one of four villages that remain on Xiaoguwei Island following the construction of a university complex in 2003. The construction of the university complex changed the economic model and lifestyles of the villagers greatly. Most of the rural land was expropriated. At the same time, student-oriented businesses developed very fast in the village, for example house rentals, restaurants, and hotels. Many educational organisations also rent places in the village to offer art training classes (Liu *et al.* 2015; Lee 2015).

Initiated by Chen Xiaoyang, associate professor of fine arts at Guangzhou Academy of Fine Arts (GAFA) in 2012, Nanting Research is a series of educational programmes and exhibitions for undergraduate students in the Sculpture Department at GAFA. Students receive basic training on fieldwork methods and ethics at the start of every year and then conduct research for five weeks in Nanting. They work in groups to collect oral histories, pictures, and other materials, and interview residents as well as previous student researchers. These resources are held in a Nanting database which has been developed to document and store the ongoing research. At the end of the project each year, every student is required to submit a research report, and artworks made and research materials collected in the project are shown in the local ancestral hall of the Guan family in Nanting. The project has two aims. One is to encourage students to make research and artworks based on the public concerns in the village, to work outside the confines of the academy, and develop artistic languages through interaction with social reality. The other aim is to use art as a means to initiate discussions and to bring changes to Nanting. Listening to the villagers is key to the project.

A consideration of the local villagers as the main audience is embedded in the use of the Guan ancestral hall as the exhibition site. The hall is located in the centre of the village and functions as the community centre of Nanting village, an arrangement which makes the exhibitions accessible and easy to visit. Village ceremonies and big events, such as new-born baby celebrations, wedding ceremonies, and mourning rituals, are held there. Ping-pong tables, book corners, and mahjong tables are also available for entertainment. A wall in the hall posts news and information on issues of concern to the villagers. Villagers use the hall regularly for discussing village matters. In this familiar environment, villagers feel at ease in having conversations and responding to, and interacting with, the artworks and the issues reflected in them (Figure 15.1).

In December 2014, the curatorial team of Beijing Minsheng Art Museum (BMAM) invited Chen to exhibit Nanting Research in 'Civil Power', the opening group exhibition of the Museum to be held in the middle of 2015. Nanting Research was identified by the curatorial team as a suitable project to reflect its broad theme, 'presenting works that are rooted in the social reality and among the people; that reflect current thinking and emotions of society; and that demonstrate a concern and responsibility for society' (Minsheng Art Museum n.d.).

On receiving this invitation, there was a moment of hesitation among the project team members, who had not considered showing artworks outside of the 'field', that is the Guan ancestral hall, as the artworks of Nanting research are oriented to have real-time communications with villagers. As a result, the Nanting project team proposed to make the Nanting Village an off-site exhibition location of the 'Civil Power' exhibition. Unfortunately, this plan could not be realised due to logistics and so, in the end, the Nanting research collaborative decided to accept the invitation from the Museum to be part of the larger group exhibition. Heading into its fourth year, the Nanting Research project had previously benefited from exchanging ideas with the public and with researchers from other projects by sharing its work through museum platforms; thus the project team decided to use the exhibition as an opportunity to share the project's research data and artworks with a broader public. The Beijing exhibiton also offered an opportunity to generate discussions among colleagues on

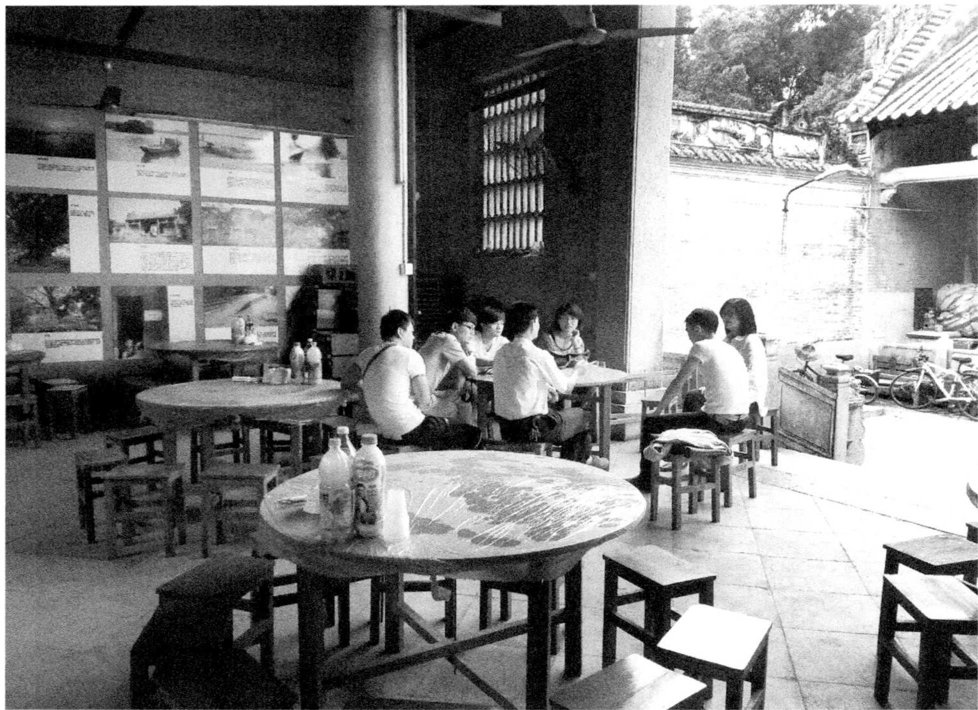

**FIGURE 15.1** Students discussing the project at a corner of the Guan Temple of Lineage, 2012
*Photo:* Nanting Research

developmental issues common in China, which might prompt further research and actions in Nanting Village.[2] As a result, in addition to making a display of project artworks in the exhibition, the team agreed to present documents collected over the years, through electronic devices, seminars and public discussions.[3]

The question of how to communicate the project's emphasis on process and local participation was the first challenge identified by the Nanting project team. There were other problems, such as constantly changing working conditions and differing expectations between the Nanting project team and the museum curators. To address these challenges, the project team explored the possibilities of the visual display of exhibitions. This encompassed the choice and design of existing works and documents, and how they would be constructed in the exhibition in relation to other exhibits. It also included a growing interest in the exhibition itself as a site of creation.

## Maintaining and creating identity in a 'hotchpotch'

The invitation to Nanting Research came from the Invitation Unit of 'Civil Power' which aimed at presenting works from what the curatorial team regarded as iconic artists from the past 30 years. Alongside the Invitation Unit, there were two other channels through which the exhibition curators solicited works: the Competition Unit and the Fieldwork and Art

Projects Unit. These aimed, respectively, to select works via public submission and directly commission others.

When the Nanting Research team was asked to offer an exhibition plan in early 2015, the final list of artworks and layout for the overall exhibition in Beijing had not been issued. However, the curators characterised the exhibition as a large display with around 200 works, most of which were object-based individual pieces, in the 8,200 m$^2$ space of the museum; the Competition Unit alone would include 100 pieces of work (Minsheng Art Museum n.d.). These conditions became the starting point for the Nanting Research project team strategy. As art historian Carol Duncan (1995: 12) establishes, audiences experience exhibitions through the 'arrangement of objects, its lighting and architectural details [that] provide both the stage set and the script'. These non-human elements have been considered by many design researchers and curators, as discussed by Tricia Austin (2012: 109), who states:

> the physical and cultural context of the museum or gallery, the architecture, the collection, the curators, the layout, the lighting, the typography, the materials, colour, forms chosen for the design, the media, the sound and the visitors expectations and behaviours all have a part to play in producing and sustaining the meaning of the place.

It is useful to think of the exhibition design strategies of the Nanting Research project team as responding to Austin's idea of a complex environment. As the team's motivation for participating in the exhibition was to exchange ideas, generate discussions, and enact further research and social action, it was clear to the team from the beginning that the exhibition should present the project as a whole, rather than highlighting specific works made in the process of the project. The team wanted to maintain the project's focus on interaction and its constantly changing and growing nature. To avoid the artworks in the project being read as autonomous artworks and 'getting lost in the immense scale and large number of works in the overall exhibition', as Chen stressed in a group meeting, the team proposed to have an independent space for the project making a replica of the Guan ancestral hall to 'transfer' the original exhibition space, and its relationship between artworks and viewers, into the Beijing exhibition.

The emphasis on a 'transfer' of the hall was to construct the sense of the space, rather than a detailed reproduction. The project team's initial plan was to have a 400 m$^2$ space and build a wooden structure, with the key elements of the hall, such as the sloped roof and some of the furniture including the wooden tables and the ping-pong table, and to add a water installation surrounding the hall structure to give the audience a better sense of the landscape of Nanting. Artworks were to be shown according to their original setting in the hall. However, the curatorial team of the Museum thought the size of the space required for this plan was over-ambitious, considering the number of artworks in the exhibition.[4] It also became clear that the original plan to present documents through electronic devices and hold seminars in the exhibition space to generate discussions about the complexities involved in the project could not be achieved. In one of the team meetings in May, one month before the opening of the exhibition, Chen Xiaoyang suggested, 'It is impossible to do everything now. We need the presentation of our project to be more focused'. The limited conditions presented a major challenge to the team: they had to consider the exhibition design in a more creative and integrated manner to make the artworks and documents that reflected the research process complement one another in the limited space available.

In the final plan, the team used an independent room as a 'framework', and devised an alley at the entrance to create a sense of Nanting and the hall. In the alley, they employed bamboo screens, similar to those seen in the Guan ancestral hall, printed with photos of Nanting and the exhibition scenes in the hall. Upon entering the exhibition entrance, the audience would see a bamboo screen with a picture taken facing the hall. Thus, the alley prepared the audience with a sense of place by leading them through representations of the 'Guan ancestral hall' and the 'streets of Nanting'.

While the design ideas for the independent space of the project were conceived at a very early stage, it was not until the day of installation (two days before the opening of the exhibition) that the team was able to consider the project's relationship with other artworks. Located at the end of a long corridor, both walls of which were installed with individual works of photography and paintings, the space for the Nanting Project was not obvious to visitors. The team attempted to address this issue by moving some red lanterns from the work of one of Chen's students, hung inside the Nanting Research space, to the doors of the space and walls outside the space. The team also arranged a desk with ink and brushes at the entrance to the space. The lanterns were made from shrimp cage commonly used in Nanting. In the 2012 exhibition at the Guan ancestral hall, visitors wrote down blessings for themselves and others on the cages and hung them in the hall. In the Beijing exhibition, however, the shrimp cage functioned in a different way. It was no longer a familiar object to the audience and did not necessarily trigger similar emotional responses or aesthetic appreciation. Nonetheless, it served as an indicator of the site specificity of the project and, in the whiteness of the exhibition, caught visitors' attention, even 'intervening' into the inviolable white wall space (Figure 15.2).

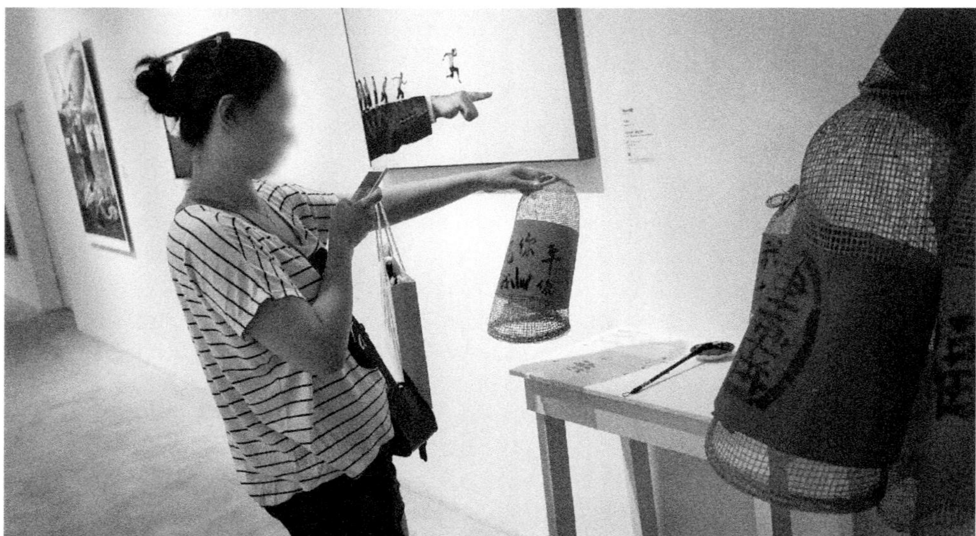

**FIGURE 15.2** Red, installation by Liufu Weitong, Xu Wenshi and Wang Xinming, 2015, outside the Nanting section of the 'Civil Power' exhibition Beijing

*Photo:* Nanting Research

## Communicating the invisible through adaption and creation

> The risk museum audiences, scholars and critics run with process-based art, which itself creates social spaces (often temporary and far from the museum), is to engage not with the artwork itself, but with its documentation and residuum.
>
> *(Siegenthaler 2013: 746)*

As suggested by social anthropologist Fiona Siegenthaler, effectively communicating socially engaged arts projects in museums is a challenge. There are innovative practices, where artists and curators tell the stories of socially engaged arts projects, make new works, or put aside the representational function of exhibitions and use exhibitions as a communication platform, such as through offering access to databases and documents produced by their projects. In 'Civil Power', a large-scale, mainly object-based group exhibition, the Nanting Research team decided to differentiate their project by highlighting its site-specific, process-based character. In so doing, there were three major issues to work through.

First, as it was not possible to arrange the artworks according to their original settings, the team had to think of another approach to present the relationships between artworks and between artworks and Nanting in the space. The team decided to arrange works by themes. Video works which depict general scenes in Nanting were placed at the beginning of the main exhibition space to serve as an introduction; as the viewer moved around the main exhibition space, additional themes focused around specific issues in Nanting were introduced.

Second, both the research and exhibition stages of Nanting Research are designed to enable real-time communications with villagers. Many works exhibited in the Guan ancestral hall were research materials and were part of an ongoing communication process. However, given the different audiences in Beijing, it was necessary to add additional background information. For example, when undertaken in Nanting, *Nanting Calligraphy* started with three students' curiosity over why there were 'No Garbage' signs in the village. The students, Pan Danqiong, Feng Yongfeng, and Su Yongqiang, carried out a detailed survey of the source and circulation of garbage in Nanting and found lots of miscommunication between villagers, temporary tenants, and cleaners, who blamed each other for the unsightly environment. The students set up an online discussion group, involving different stakeholders in a discussion about possible solutions. During the discussion, problems such as the unreasonable locations of trash bins were identified. In the exhibition in the Guan ancestral hall, students used banners they collected from the streets, which said 'No Garbage' and were also covered with curse words, such as 'Don't Be a Litterbug', and displayed them in art frames. The group also printed some of the records of discussions on misunderstandings over the garbage problem and attempts to solve the issues, and displayed them on the garbage bins and wooden tables in the installation. In addition, the students produced QR codes so audiences could access more detailed records of the survey on the rubbish problem and participate in the discussion.

Residents of Nanting were familiar with the garbage issue, and many of them had been interviewed by the students and taken part in the online discussion group, so not much explanation was needed to show the project in the ancestral hall. However, when the works were to be exhibited in Beijing, the team needed to visually embed the background information. For example, the online discussion, originally displayed on the tables in the Guan ancestral hall, was moved to the wall in a poster form, and the framed banners were moved to the wall as well. A short descriptive text introducing the research and art-making process was added.

The third feature is that, because the research stems from an art education course at Guangzhou Academy, students' background and personal interests are the starting point of their inquiry in Nanting Research, and the artwork depends on their encounters and conversations with villagers as they develop their research. It was regarded as key to the Beijing exhibition to present and communicate how the research questions had developed and how the students made use of the research data in the artworks. The focus on students' research was embedded in the wall texts and labels, which introduced the anthropological methods of the project and how the students connected the research findings and their artworks.

The project team's proposal for presenting documents and holding round table discussions was not included in the exhibition loan agreement drafted by the Beijing exhibition curatorial team, which only listed artworks. To make up for the lack of documents and background information on-site, the project team released an online website before the opening of the exhibition, describing the Nanting Project. The website QR code was displayed in the exhibition so audiences could access the research project information and read the opinions of the participants. Online information included a transcript of a conversation that took place in early 2015 between Guan Weiguang, a member of the management team of the Guan ancestral hall, and students Li Peixuan and Li Peishan, who participated in Nanting research in 2012 and 2013, respectively. In the conversation, Guan talked about his views of the project and the cultural continuity in the Nanting Village. In preparing for the exhibition, six students (Li Peixuan, Cai Shuaiwei, Zhang Yuan, Li Peishan, Chen Shuting, and Pan Danqiong) initiated a conversation among themselves, where they talked about their research approaches and reflections, as well as villagers' changing attitudes towards student research. Students also talked about how works produced by previous students inspired and challenged their own strategies, and how they drew on their participation in the project in their further study and work. The record of the conversation was intended to provide the viewer with an additional perspective to interpret the development of the project over the years.

Undoubtedly, in the Beijing exhibition, it was impossible to reveal the interaction between artworks and the architecture and the space of the Guan ancestral hall that characterised the original exhibition setting, and it was difficult to convey the participatory element of the project through design techniques alone. As a result, many works became 'silent' (Monti and Keene 2013: 1). For example students' long-term interaction with villagers, and how the students' learning progressed, not only through conversations but also observation in the field, were not fully evident in the exhibition. Nonetheless, the exhibition experience helped the project team gain experience of exhibition design in communicating the process-based nature of the project, and prompted the team members to contemplate the other possibilities that museums can offer, within and outside of exhibitions. Reflecting on the exhibition preparation, what was lacking, perhaps, was a consensus between the project team and the curatorial team on the inseparability of exhibition content and presentation (Gurian 1991). As Piehl and MacLeod (2012) and Sandell (2005) suggest, though exhibition making cannot guarantee a certain interpretation among all audiences, graphic designs, spatial strategies, and arrangements of works can facilitate certain ways of reading and thinking, contextualise the story and foster intellectual engagement. As a result, curators, architects, designers, and educators all have a role to play in addressing the gap between the messages the museums intend to convey and public understanding.

## Conclusion

This chapter explores the rarely discussed complexities involved in the processes of curating and 'translating' socially engaged arts in the museum exhibition context. As Steeds (2014: 13) notes, 'focusing on exhibitions of contemporary art does not risk collapsing into study of the messenger rather than the message: art remains in the foreground, to be studied in its foregrounding', where the 'meaning and import' of artworks 'are collectively debated'. As an understanding of socially engaged arts is something that cannot be realised easily, communicating them via curated exhibitions is one way forward. It does, though, demand the evolution of a process and model of museum making that emphasises the discursive and dialogical nature of the work. To understand the thinking behind a particular decision, including artists' concerns, could help us to identify the priorities of projects whilst also expanding the practice of exhibition making. As a result, a focus on curatorial practice and exhibition design are a necessary component of knowledge about socially engaged arts practices.

Presenting socially engaged arts in the museum setting plays an important role in producing knowledge of and participation in socially engaged practice. By inviting groups of socially engaged arts practitioners to participate in its opening exhibition, Beijing Minsheng Art Museum introduced, not without controversy, a critical lens by which to examine these art practices. It demonstrated its efforts to be responsive to 'new practices' and become 'a public social space' and 'a platform to facilitate social interactions and inspire creative imagination' (Minsheng Art Museum 2015: 30). It could also be inferred that the museum wants to be more than a stage of presentation; it wants to be a project initiator, a space for discussion, and a site of active social and political engagement. This is borne out by the fact that the curatorial team also commissioned four projects from diverse communities in China, the works of which were exhibited in the Fieldwork and Art Projects Unit. The museum also initiated a series of discussions on topics related to the theme of the exhibition, 'Civil Power', during the exhibition period, with a tight preparation schedule and a restricted budget.

While the impossibility of attending carefully to every art project is clear in large-scale watershed exhibitions in China, and those involved will always anticipate and understand the requisite last-minute alterations and compromises, the need for socially engaged arts exhibitions to reveal project processes and invite participation makes effective artist and curator collaboration an essential component in exhibition making. Both artists and curators need to ensure that audiences have the tools to engage with the projects contextually and politically. In exhibition design terms and in curatorial terms, this demands more than the presentation of a series of autonomous objects for aesthetic consumption. One question to consider is how exhibitions can, through their design, effectively address the differences among projects in a large exhibition of this nature and facilitate communication between the range of practitioners and their projects. In the 'Civil Power' exhibition, the curators missed an important opportunity for mutual exchange between the various artists and groups exhibiting their work.

Last but not least, there is an unrecognised opportunity for museums to act as responsive 'stages' for the diverse modes of socially engaged arts and needs of socially engaged arts practitioners, and to promote reflexive and ethical thinking among artists and audiences. Important issues concerning socially engaged arts arise, such as the ethical complexities of taking critical representation into the gallery, beyond the site-specific boundaries and contexts within which they were conceived (Finkelpearl 2013). The lack of codes of conduct for commissioning projects where socially engaged arts are working with marginalised individuals, means these questions are often left to artists to identify and examine. One text description in the exhibition states, 'The project team's research process caused many inconveniences to the local people. We would like to offer our apologies here'. This is the reflection of the project team. What is absent here, however, is the museum's voice as a framing device or any attempt to draw visitors into the discussion and debate. As a result, it is difficult for visitors to position themselves as part of the discussion.

While art institutions in China have begun to consider their role as public institutions, curating socially engaged arts offers an important opportunity to frame a conversation about the public responsibilities of museums in China, how they can position themselves as sites for social learning and exchange, and how they can challenge established modes of museum making. The 'wilderness' of the exhibition space could be transformed into a place where the complexities of socially engaged arts are collectively addressed, an arena for discussing and implementing research. This requires thinking beyond the museum as a mere space of display. Such a reformulation requires, instead, greater and more effective collaboration between artists and curators in the curatorial process, increased sensitivity to audience needs, and new models of exhibition making. Such new thinking could challenge our now automatic tendencies to characterise socially engaged arts as 'artworks' and instead allow the diverse facets of socially engaged arts to be acknowledged in their own right for their civic agency.

## Notes

1 It should be noted that while theoretical developments in relation to these terms have an impact on socially engaged practices in China, including the discourses used to critique them and the formats some practices employ, using any of them as a 'standard' English translation might incur misunderstandings and simplification of the history, agenda and variety of practices in China.
2 Email communication between Chen and the curatorial team. 10 January 2015.
3 Core members participating in the curatorial process of the project's presence in Beijing include the project leader Chen Xiaoyang, other staff and students of GAFA who have been involved in the project, such as Zhan Yan, He Yixiang, Fan Lin, Liu Jiajing, Li Shuting, among others. I conducted participant observation in the team's online discussion group during the preparation for the 'Civil Power' exhibition and in the museum during the exhibition's installation, from 22–25 June, 2015. The data of this research also came from meetings the team had before and after the opening of the exhibition, interviews with members of other exhibiting projects and curators of the exhibition, as well as Email communications between the curatorial team and the project team.
4 I had a few conversations with Guo Xiaoyan, the Chief Curator of the 'Civil Power' exhibition, from 2015 to 2017. Similar ideas were also evident in publications, such as Guo (2015), where Guo comments on the challenges of organising an exhibition of such scale, including unexpected changes in the curatorial process,

> There is a great number of artworks in the exhibition. On one hand, we want to present as many important contemporary art works as possible for audiences. On the other hand, this is the opening exhibition of our museum. 'How to present so many works in an ideal manner' is the most difficult issue. We had numerous discussions with our design team and changed exhibition planning for several times.

## References

Austin, T. (2012) 'Scales of Narrativity', in Macleod, S., Hanks, L.H., and Hale, J. (eds) *Museum Making: Narratives, Architectures, Exhibitions*, London: Routledge, pp. 107–18.

Bao, D. (2014) 'Rethinking and Practices Within the Art System: The Self-organisation of Contemporary Art in China, 2001–2012', *Journal of Contemporary Chinese Art*, 1(1), pp. 83–95.

Bao, D. (2015) 'The Return of Class: Confronting the Social Nature of Art', *Leap*. Online. Available HTTP: http://www.leapleapleap.com/2016/01/the-return-of-class-confronting-the-social-nature-of-art/. Accessed February 7, 2016.

Duncan, C. (1995) *Civilising Rituals: Inside Public Art Museums*, London and New York: Routledge.

Finkelpearl, T. (2013) *What We Made: Conversations on Art and Social Cooperation*, Durham, NC: Duke University Press.

Guo, X. (2015) '"Civil Power": Initiating and Calling For Power in the Public', *Artron*. Online. Available HTTP: http://gallery.artron.net/20150623/n752733.html. Accessed 5 January 2016.

Gurian, E.H. (1991) 'Noodling Around with Exhibition Opportunities', in Karp, I. and Lavine, S.D. (eds) *Exhibiting Cultures: Poetics and politics of Museum Display*, Washington, DC: Smithsonian Institution Press, pp. 176–90.

He, C. and Ruijun, S. (eds) (2013) *Pulse Reaction: An Exchange Project on Art Practice*, Beijing: Central Compilation and Translation Press.

Judah, H. (2014) 'Disobey!', *Art Review*. Online. Available HTTP: http://artreview.com/features/summer_2014_feature_disobey. Accessed 8 February 2015.

Kester, G. (2004) *Conversation Pieces: Community + Communication in Modern Art*, London: University of California Press Ltd.

Lee, P. (2015) *A Discussion about Site-specificity From the View of New Museology: A Case of Nanting Research* [undergraduate dissertation], Guangzhou: Guangzhou Academy of Fine Art.

Liu, Y., Chen, H., Lin, Z., and Wu, D. (2015) 'The Spatial Evolution of Informal Economy and Its Influence on Land Use in Urban Village: A Case Study of Nanting Village in Guangzhou College Town', *Economic Geography*, 35(5), pp. 126–34.

Lu, P. (2012) 'Invisible/visible: Examining the Power of Cultural Action at the Plum Tree Creek', in Wu, M. et al. (eds) *Art as Environment: A Cultural Action at the Plum Tree Creek*, New Taipei City: Bamboo Curtain Studio, pp. 301–15.

Marstine, J. (2017) *Critical Practice: Artists, Museums, Ethics*, Abingdon and New York: Routledge.

Minsheng Art Museum (n.d.) *Introduction to Civil Power*. Online. Available HTTP: www.minshengartcompetition.cn/AboutExhibition.aspx?model=work. Accessed 17 December 2016.

Minsheng Art Museum (2015) *The Civil Power*, Beijing: The Minsheng Art Museum.

Monti, F. and Keene, S. (2013) *Museums and Silent Objects: Designing Effective Exhibitions*, Aldershot: Ashgate.

Ni, K. (ed.) (2015) *Under-Construction/Reconstruction as the 'Imagination' of Social Practice*, Shanghai: Rockbund Art Museum.

Ou, B. (2016) '2016 Forecast: Interdisciplinary Research is the New Direction of "Art Into Society"?', *Art Express*. Online. Available HTTP: http://artexpress.artron.net/app/wapnews/index?id=103914&from=groupmessage&isappinstalled=0. Accessed 14 February 2016.

Piehl, J. and MacLeod, S. (2012) 'Where Do You Want the Label? The Roles and Possibilities of Exhibition Graphics', in Macleod, S., Hanks, L.H. and Hale, J. (eds) *Museum Making: Narratives, Architectures, Exhibitions*, London: Routledge, pp. 257–66.

Sandell, R. (2005) 'Constructing and Communicating Equality: The Social Agency of Museum Space', in MacLeod, S. (ed.) *Reshaping Museum Space: Architecture, Design, Exhibitions*, London: Routledge, pp. 185–200.

Sheng, W. (2007) 'The Sociological Turn of Contemporary Art', *ARTLINKART*. Online. Available HTTP: www.artlinkart.com/cn/article/overview/5c7hrwl/genres/critique/D. Accessed 13 November 2013.

Siegenthaler, F. (2013) 'Towards an Ethnographic Turn in Contemporary Art Scholarship', *Critical Arts*, 27(6), pp. 737–52.

Steeds, L. (2014) 'Introduction/Contemporary Exhibitions: Art at Large', in Steeds, L. (ed.) *Exhibition (Documents of Contemporary Art)*, London and Cambridge, MA: The MIT Press, pp. 12–23.

Sun, D. (2011) 'The Year of Interventions', *Leap*, 7: 82–5.

Thompson, N. (ed.) (2012) *Living as Form: Socially Engaged Art From 1991–2011*, Cambridge, MA: MIT Press.

Wang, C. (2010) *Art Intervenes in Society: A New Artistic Relationship*, Hong Kong: Timezone8 Limited.

Wang, M. (2017) 'The Socially Engaged Practices of Artists in Contemporary China', *Journal of Visual Art Practice*, 16(1), pp. 15–38.

Wu, C. and Xia W. (2015) 'Awaken Vegetable Human by Personalised Film and Sound: Responses to Huayu ART SANYA/Project Reflections', *Life Observations and Hypothesis*. Online. Available HTTP: www.wuchaoart.com/wu0284/Style_Ten/en_article_596389.shtml. Accessed 27 December 2015.

Wu, J. (2014) 'How Can Voices Be Heard? Issues of Display in "ALTERing NATIVism"', *ITPARK*. Online. Available HTTP: www.itpark.com.tw/people/essays_data/646/1938. Accessed 2 May 2015.

Zheng, B. (2010) 'Creating Publicness: From the Stars Event to Recent Socially Engaged Art', *Journal of Contemporary Chinese Art*, 9(5), pp. 71–85.

# 16

# UNBOXING HISTORY EXHIBITIONS

## Experience design in museum practice

*Clare Brown*

### Abstract

The term 'unboxing', drawn from the realm of technology marketing, refers to the act of revealing a new product for the first time. This chapter introduces 'unboxing' as a metaphor for uncovering new perspectives on the exhibition development and design process at large-scale history museums. The aim is first to begin to consider exhibition design as a discipline within experience design, as defined by fields such as service design, user experience design and Agile software development. Second, the chapter identifies what principles from existing experience design disciplines can be applied in large-scale history museums as a route to more effective and relevant visitor experiences. Drawing from interviews with practitioners from three experience design fields, this chapter proposes a set of mindsets, methods and modes of collaboration useful for evolving exhibition development and design.

### Introduction

When unboxing the latest technology purchase such as a mobile phone, tablet, Google Home™ or Amazon Alexa, many people feel emotions of anticipation and delight as they uncover something new and wonderful – the newest gadget that will improve their lives. Consider the experience of unboxing a new phone or tablet, from opening the graphically appealing outer packaging to pulling the tabs which locate an ingenious seam where the clamshell box opens, to the first reveal of the actual device nestled in a precisely formed cavity, and finally to the simplicity of the instructions on how to initiate use of the device. Each part of this experience has been carefully crafted to give the most enjoyable kinesthetic and emotional satisfaction.

Is there an equivalent experience of sensory and intellectual satisfaction in history museums each time a museum visitor is welcomed into an exhibition? As the exhibition experience unfolds, does the visitor engage with the environment in a kinesthetic and emotional way akin to unboxing a product? Does the experience itself communicate the exhibition's messages? Can you 'unbox' a museum? As a designer with 20 years of experience working in theatre, graduate education and museums, I have collaborated extensively with others working in digital technology and commercial design. My experience of these different fields has prompted me to ask and reflect on the questions above.

In the case of unboxing a product, multi-disciplinary teams of designers have planned and tested every aspect of this experience. Industrial designers have created the ergonomic shell of the device. Ingenious packaging designers have refined the appearance and functionality of the box. Interface and interaction designers have developed the welcoming start-up and home screens. User experience designers have developed the intuitive functionality and tested the ease of use of the digital architecture. Service designers have kept in mind the continuity of experience as a whole: from the moment people see an advertisement and imagine buying the device, to the anticipation of making the purchase, to the cathartic moment of unboxing, through the satisfaction of the initial use of the device.

The designers tasked with creating each part of this product experience have been trained in user-centered design, using iterative and incremental methods to move from idea to final product. By contrast, the teams which create large-scale history museum exhibitions often use project management methods for exhibition development that are top-down and linear, with limited opportunities for iterative and incremental development of content, concept and design. During my career designing for large-scale history museums in the United States, I have observed that the concept of 'experience' is either missing or treated as a secondary factor in the planning and design of these exhibitions. I have participated in exhibition project teams where learning and storytelling through experience is considered secondary to learning and storytelling through didactic texts. Linearly sequenced and content-led project management results in exhibitions that repeat the same design strategies despite varying content.

This chapter aims to consider the methods and processes of 'experience design' used in fields outside of museums as models for creating innovative experience-based history exhibitions for future museum visitors. Drawing on interviews with practitioners from service design, user experience design, and Agile software development, the chapter explores the differences and commonalities among the variations of design thinking. Although the practitioners interviewed are not working primarily in museums, they have been chosen because of their understanding of how their disciplines can be used as models of method and process outside of their own fields. For the purposes of this chapter, these disciplines will be grouped under the heading 'experience design'. The aim is first to begin to consider exhibition design as a discipline within experience design and second to identify what principles from experience design can be applied in large-scale history museums as a route to more effective and relevant visitor experiences.

## Experience design starts with design thinking

One can look at design thinking as the foundation for the different disciplines in experience design. Design thinking is an overarching framework for problem solving which is grounded in iterative and collaborative processes, with an emphasis on user research. In recent years, design agencies such as IDEO, most prominently, have formalized the vocabulary and processes of design thinking, making it a marketable and scalable methodology to create innovation across a variety of corporate, governmental, and not-for-profit sectors (IDEO 1999). IDEO uses, promotes and distributes a 'toolkit' of design thinking mindsets and methods called human-centered design.

The methods include ethnographic forms of user research and structured sequences of ideation, framing of design challenge questions, iteration, rapid prototyping and testing of solutions with users. Mindsets that allow this process to work well include 'embracing ambiguity', 'empathy' and 'learning from failure', and the entire process sits within a methodology of 'divergent and convergent thinking' (IDEO 2015). Importantly, design thinking suggests that solutions to challenges should not be predetermined by the designers because an appropriate solution can only be determined through a process of understanding the user. When designers and stakeholders embrace ambiguity and rely on building empathy before determining solutions, failure is less likely, but failure is still a normal part of the process. When project teams practice many cycles of ideation and iteration, it is appropriate and natural for failure to occur because so many potential solutions have been generated. However, learning from what fails enables design teams to home in on the most appropriate and successful solution.

## Design thinking and service design for innovation: Natalie Foley[1]

Natalie Foley is the vice president and chief operating officer at Peer Insight which, she states, is a 'strategic innovation consultancy'. She goes on to say that Peer Insight 'merge[s] the creativity of design thinking with the smarts of business strategy to guide companies down the path of sustainable growth' (Foley 2017). Clients of Peer Insight include large corporations such as Nike, Intel, Memorial Sloan Kettering Cancer Center, DTE Energy, AARP, and Baker McKenzie. Despite the fact that none of these clients is a museum, it is important to note that these large corporations may be similar to large history museums in their scale of bureaucracy and established modes of working. When I spoke with Natalie in June 2017, I asked her to describe the work of Peer Insight and to explain how they help their clients to understand service design through a process of design thinking.

Peer Insight, as described by Natalie, works primarily with established organizations to create new services and experiences for their customers. She says, 'we work with big clients who already do their core business well. We help them to create new things – a new service, or making a current experience better'. However, their work does not stop at a completed service design. Where it excels is in bringing design thinking to the design and testing of the business model around a service. 'Many [companies] will know how to design a service', muses Natalie, 'but testing it [against the business model] is critical'. Peer Insight encourages their clients to 'play with the business model, test it out; all the things you would do with your user research'. Natalie says Peer Insight encourages their clients to understand that 'the success of a new service is to ensure you don't separate the end user experience from the business model that delivers and sustains the service'.

Peer Insight's own business model includes transparency in their process, with several books and toolkits published to help others with design thinking strategy for innovation. Peer Insight's methods include involving the client in the user research by bringing the client along when customer research is taking place (Liedtka and Ogilvie 2011). The client is trained and given a listening guide to use during customer interviews. Natalie explains,

> It is so important that the client is there, because if they don't hear directly from the customer, it's harder to develop that sense of ownership around the process and, therefore, the end result. Involving the client this way makes sure that they are not surprised by, but in fact they drive, any pivots in the direction of the project.

The clients become first hand witnesses to the customer feedback, which helps the clients come to the solutions and pivots on their own. This first-hand information helps a client to navigate the ambiguities of a project. It also allows Peer Insight to become facilitators to the process rather than becoming the providers of solutions. While maintaining responsiveness and creative flexibility, Peer Insight ensures strong project management with goal-oriented tasks and schedules, which helps a client manage ambiguity. Natalie says 'We may not know what will come out of the project, but at least we will know what type of information we will have and by when'.

According to Natalie:

> Peer Insight is strongest when we can help a client learn by doing – taking on a project, using it as an example. Do a project first, then build the strategy, then train everyone. Design thinking is best taught through a project.

Natalie described an example of such a project when their client Kimberly-Clark, the health care paper goods company, sought assistance in developing a deeper relationship with their customers through the creation of a service. Kimberly-Clark, which is primarily a product-based company, understood that services drive additional revenue and allow for deeper data collection than products. While the initial task at hand was to create a service that would help with problems associated with hospital acquired infections, with the main user being the patient, the customer and business research led the team in another direction. The most viable, needed, and usable service was determined to be one that offered training and support to the family caregiver post-surgery.

The discussion with Natalie revealed that organizational restructuring is sometimes necessary to allow innovation, or the introduction of a new service. 'One condition of an innovation project is that you don't know what you are creating when you start and if you do, you may not be innovating, but rather just executing an existing idea'. This is not the standard way of working, however. Sometimes clients, including large scale government agencies, build the solution into the 'request for proposal', which communicates to any vendor that those are not projects well-matched to an innovative/design thinking-driven approach. She goes on to explain that in a traditional consulting model a client might agree to pay a certain fee in exchange for three solution options, and a recommendation as to which one is best to implement. The mindset of 'embracing ambiguity' does not exist in the traditional model. To help clients accept this approach, Peer Insight puts time brackets around their work. Proposing this to a client Natalie might say 'We are going to work with you for five months and then stop, evaluate if we are on the right path, see if strategically you think we should move forward'. Typically, at that point, Peer Insight would present the client with research from the field and evaluation criteria that cover both customer desirability and business model feasibility. Peer Insight presents these findings as a cross-check between these two areas of criteria.

In addition to gaining a new marketable and innovative service, clients seeking innovation have an opportunity to experience a new way of working, potentially leading to an internal shift in the organization as a whole. Natalie reiterates that 'Design Thinking is an incredibly powerful toolkit to change the ways that organizations work – let's get off the "PowerPoint", let's stand up in the room, everybody's voice is heard'. The inference here is that in the context of large-scale history museums an evolution of exhibitions from linear and didactic to experience based may not be as simple as asking the exhibition designer to create something innovative. The development of any history exhibition is impacted greatly by the team dynamic, by the hierarchies among the team, and by the ways in which the team communicate with each other. Design thinking for services, as practiced by Peer Insight, incorporates more than just the creation of the end service; it also changes the team dynamic and the process by which the service is created. This way of working, as proven effective for large corporations, is a useful model to consider for innovation in large-scale history museum exhibitions.

## User experience design at the Kigali Genocide Memorial, Rwanda: Jason Ulaszek[2]

Jason Ulaszek, a user experience (UX) designer, is the co-founder of 'UX for Good', a non-profit organization which applies the principles and methods of user experience design to global social challenges. When Jason and I spoke in June 2017, I asked him to discuss the meaning of UX design, the application of UX design to social challenges, and the potential application of UX methods and mindsets in the context of museum environments and visitor experience.

Jason began his career in the late 1990s, at a time when the Internet and the 'web' were first taking off. At that time the term 'user experience design' did not exist in the form it does today. There were disciplines such as graphic visual design, information architecture, interaction design and design research, most of which were focused on digital design, and tied to the dot-com boom. According to Jason, in the early 2000s, boutique digital agencies around the world and the disciplines listed above, began using the term 'user experience' to describe the complex assortment of work they were doing. With the advent of Silicon Valley this term grew in popularity, but it also became conflated with visual design for digital platforms, otherwise known as user interface (UI) design. Jason bemoans this conflation, saying,

> I don't believe user experience exists solely at the interface level. UX is more along the lines of a mindset. It is an approach we take that puts people at the center of our decision making and looks to the motivations and frustrations of those we are helping to solve problems. UX draws from a variety of disciplines to move [a design] from an initial hypothesis or abstract notion all the way through gaining understanding, evaluating ideas, and to developing a concrete response. Sometimes that response is a digital app or website, but sometimes it is not. The response might be a new understanding of people, or a new workflow, or a new process.

The systemic approach of human-centered design in the creation of a total experience is an area of overlap between user experience design and service design. Both disciplines, according to Jason, share an emphasis on 'lower[ing] the bar to participation' for both the customer and the client. Like the approach taken by Peer Insight, Jason emphasizes the importance of integrating the client and stakeholders in the process of understanding the user. This is a valuable way to make the process of experience design accessible to a client or stakeholder. He says it is essential to:

> define for the client what empathy means, and to help the client understand how they can serve people better through empathy . . . The designer can help the stakeholder or client to develop critical thinking, develop an ability to synthesize data, and an ability

> to derive or extract insight to [create a useful and compelling narrative for the user experience].

Jason's work with the Kigali Genocide Memorial is a useful example for understanding the practical application of experience design with clients and stakeholders in a museum-like environment (Inzovu 2017). According to the memorial's website:

> The Kigali Genocide Memorial includes three permanent exhibitions, the largest of which documents the 1994 Genocide against the Tutsi. There is also a children's memorial and an exhibition on the history of genocidal violence around the world. The Education Centre, Gardens, and Genocide Archive of Rwanda form part of a meaningful tribute to those who perished and provide a powerful educational tool for visitors.
>
> *(Kigali Genocide Memorial 2017)*

The UX for Good Design Challenge in 2014 brought Jason and a team of user experience designers to Kigali to consider the following challenge:

> Virtually every visitor to a genocide memorial or holocaust museum can attest to overwhelming feelings of sympathy, sadness and outrage. Schoolchildren and world leaders alike leave speechless. But most visitors can also attest that they did nothing substantively differently as a result. The profound feelings genocide memorials elicit are a powerful fuel. What can we do to convert them into meaningful and sustainable action?
>
> *(UX for Good* et al. *2014)*

Through over 500 hours of research, the UX for Good team gathered observations and data about the existing visitor experience of those people attending the Kigali Genocide Memorial and the on-site exhibitions. Jason outlines the research tasks including visitor interviews, observations of educational programs, evaluating the existing digital assets for memorial outreach and marketing, interviews with genocide survivors, and genocide subject matter experts, and interviews with other leading museum/memorial curators and directors.

This design research was also informed by the work done by Tania Singer, a neuroscientist who has studied the distinction between empathy and compassion. As Jason explained, 'too much empathy leads to one of two outcomes – either a "burn out" or a "shutdown"'. This problem revealed itself in the UX for Good research at the Rwandan Genocide Memorial. The team observed that visitors experienced a significant emotional trough when confronted with the difficult narrative, collections, first-person accounts and artifacts associated with the genocide. Despite being receptive to the memorial's request for donations, visitors left overwhelmed. Interestingly, notes Jason,

> stories of hope and reconciliation had been built into the educational workshops held at the memorial, and into the sustainable peace-building curriculum of the Rwandan national education system. But these more hopeful elements were not present in the memorial or the exhibitions.

The UX for Good team found that the hopeful elements needed to be part of the Memorial and exhibition experience in order to move visitors from a place of despair to an emotional state capable of, and compelled to, action. The result of this finding is the 'Inzovu Curve', a diagrammatic curved line which represents the evolution of the visitor experience, from interest and curiosity, down through emotional hardship, and deep into despair. The curve then turns upward, like the elephant's trunk, from which the word 'Inzovu' is derived, as the visitor is presented with elements of hope and reconciliation, allowing the visitor experience to change from an emotional state of 'burn out' to an emotional state capable of action.

The framework presented in the Inzovu Curve demonstrates a model in which the Kigali Genocide Memorial can more effectively achieve its mission: sustainable peace-building and the prevention of future global genocides. As Jason concluded, 'the curve helped with lowering the bar to participation because that model illustrated both the problem and a solution that could be evolved'. Changes that have followed this study include the museum constructing a new reception center to welcome visitors to the memorial. This welcome center now presents a film created by Sundog Pictures which captures stories from genocide survivors. Modest investment enabled new text panels to be added to the existing exhibitions to discuss hope and reconciliation. Second phase funding will allow further redesign over the next few years including the development of new forms of visitor activation such as a new website to facilitate a more comprehensive 'prior-during-after' continuum of the visitor experience. Jason aims to apply user experience design methods and principles to envisage what will become of the Kigali Genocide Memorial in 20 years. He says,

> If the mission [and teaching and learning messages] of the memorial continue to exist, will there be a point in time when the physical memorial in Kigali is not needed? Rather, could the form of the memorial become, for instance, pop-up experiences around the world to generate action . . . Rwanda has cracked the code for sustainable peace building, they can be facilitators globally, on the global stage, not just at the memorial. They have the antidote or the thinking that can be applied to the south and west side of the city of Chicago, or elsewhere.

It is possible to infer that user experience design could help lead the exhibition project teams in a direction where the principles of a museum are retained, but the form of the experience might not look like a traditional 'four-walled' exhibition. Large-scale history museums currently conceive exhibitions according to fairly narrow parameters evident in the regular use of a sequential narrative defined by arrangements of objects, didactic texts and contextual imagery. Given this rigid definition of what constitutes an exhibition, it would require these museums to embrace ambiguity and to evolve the collaborative working methods to enable exhibition teams to consider new forms of physical exhibitions. As described below, the methodology of Agile software development holds key values and principles which could be useful to history museums wishing to generate innovation in exhibition design.

## Agile software development and Agile coaching for project teams: Matthieu Cornillon[3]

Matthieu Cornillon is the Agile coach at Amplify, a New York-based education company which provides curriculum, assessment and learning products and services for primary and secondary education. Agile, an 'incremental and iterative' method of software development, is based on values and principles outlined in the *Manifesto for Agile Software Development* (Beck *et al.* 2001). As Agile coach, Matthieu guides individuals and teams in the mindsets and methods of Agile, for improved collaboration, workflow and innovative product/service development. In speaking with Matthieu in June 2017, I asked him to define Agile, what the use of Agile is in the context of his work, and how he sees the potential for Agile to be used in contexts other than software development.

Agile, Matthieu explained, begins with a set of four value statements and 12 principles. In diagrammatic form, one can see values as the base of a pyramid. Then come the principles, which help you live the values. At the top is process: the specific things you do to enact the principles. Unlike other methodologies, Agile specifies nothing about specific process. This, Matthieu believes, means that Agile is incredibly adaptable to any given situation, which is key to the sustainability of the methodology.

> In other methodologies the only thing defined is process. That's fine if everything goes exactly as you expect, but the world isn't like that. If you encounter a situation not provided for in the process, the lack of defined values and principles leaves no basis to make decisions.

There seems considerable potential to apply this approach in the museum field because exhibition teams are continuously dealing with situations that quickly become more complex. For example, at any moment exhibition project teams could be faced with changing exhibition parameters such as new object lists, new space constraints, changes to the budget, unexpected requirements by donors and new ideas from a museum director or board of trustees. Agile begins with understanding values and principles before determining product. In thinking about my experience designing exhibitions for large-scale history museums, I recognize that there is very little emphasis placed on establishing exhibition, or museum-specific values and principles at the outset of a project. I have witnessed numerous exhibition projects that begin without a foundation of shared values and principles. My experience has been that exhibition teams work under the assumption of shared values. I have also observed that without making those values explicit there is a significant risk that projects will lose direction. Making those values explicit, perhaps by creating a manifesto to define what the exhibition will or will not be, should reduce risk and strengthen the foundation from which content and design decisions are made.

What are these values and principles in Agile? The 'Agile Manifesto', created by 17 software developers in 2001, begins with the following statement:

> We are uncovering better ways of developing software by doing it and helping others do it. Through this work we have come to value:
>
> **Individuals and interactions** over processes and tools
> **Working software** over comprehensive documentation
> **Customer collaboration** over contract negotiation
> **Responding to change** over following a plan
>
> That is, while there is value in the items on the right, we value the items on the left more.
>
> *(Beck* et al. *2001)*

Matthieu remarks that it is important to note that the opening phrase of the manifesto is:

> 'We are uncovering' not 'we have uncovered'. It's continually evolving. . . . They didn't say they had conceived or theorized or predicted that these ideas would work. [Rather,] they had discovered approaches proven to work in the real world. The manifesto shares the essential commonalities they found between those approaches.

The 12 Agile principles are:

1. Our highest priority is to satisfy the customer through early and continuous delivery of valuable software.
2. Welcome changing requirements, even late in development. Agile processes harness change for the customer's competitive advantage.
3. Deliver working software frequently, from a couple of weeks to a couple of months, with a preference to the shorter timescale.
4. Business people and developers must work together daily throughout the project.
5. Build projects around motivated individuals. Give them the environment and support they need, and trust them to get the job done.
6. The most efficient and effective method of conveying information to and within a development team is face-to-face conversation.
7. Working software is the primary measure of progress.
8. Agile processes promote sustainable development. The sponsors, developers, and users should be able to maintain a constant pace indefinitely.
9. Continuous attention to technical excellence and good design enhances agility.
10. Simplicity – the art of maximizing the amount of work not done – is essential.
11. The best architectures, requirements, and designs emerge from self-organizing teams.
12. At regular intervals, the team reflects on how to become more effective, then tunes and adjusts its behavior accordingly.

(*Beck* et al. *2001*)

According to Matthieu, these principles reflect an:

> embrace of iterative and incremental processes. Instead of saying 'I know what will work, I will write it down, plan it, and execute it' they are saying 'The world is too unpredictable and complex for that. Therefore I must find my way toward the finish line by steps. After each iteration I will adjust course as necessary and repeat'. Once you accept the world's unpredictability, some really interesting things happen. One of them is this: a customer can't just ask for what they want and expect it to be delivered some time later; because there are too many unknowns that would change the plan. Since you can't plan everything out with certainty, the customer, the one paying the money, is in effect saying 'Hi, Person I Don't Know, I want you to build me something, but I don't really know what it is. But I am going give you a bunch of money and trust you and we will figure out what I get for my money when we get there'. That is a huge leap of faith for people, and it is a fundamentally different way of approaching product development.

It is evident that the approach of embracing ambiguity and iteration is one which Agile shares with design thinking, service design, and user experience design. Each of these disciplines value an emphasis on the 'leap of faith' referenced by Matthieu.

## Agile vs. waterfall: considering new modes of exhibition development and design

Matthieu explained that Agile is often viewed as the opposite of a linear working method called 'waterfall'. The waterfall software development method is akin to the project management method used for exhibitions in large-scale history museums. Waterfall is described as 'a single-pass sequential, document-driven, gated-step approach' (Larman and Basili 2003). The term 'waterfall' is drawn from a diagram showing a cascading series of steps. It starts at the top by defining the solution to a problem, followed by a linear sequence of implementation towards completion at the bottom. While this project management sequence seems logical, it does not account for the need for responsiveness to real-world conditions. The pervasiveness of waterfall-like project management is a real factor to contend with, however, and it persists in large-scale history museums as the framework for developing and designing exhibitions. Large-scale museums, especially those which operate with rigorous contracting procedures are more likely to embrace and perpetuate waterfall-like project management for exhibitions. Larman and Basili, who have written about the history of 'iterative and incremental' software development, the broader category in which Agile sits, note that waterfall software development was an appropriate response to US federal contracting procedures which required milestone deliverables for project-based work. They acknowledge reasons for the pervasiveness of waterfall-type project management, some which resonate in large-scale history museums:

> It's simple to explain and recall. 'Do the requirements, then design, and then implement'. [Iterative and Incremental Development] is more complex to understand and describe . . . It gives the illusion of an orderly, accountable, and measurable process, with simple document-driven milestones (such as 'requirements complete').
>
> *(Larman and Basili 2003: 3)*

Interestingly, Larman and Basili trace how engineers and designers, as early as the 1950s, working with major US government agencies and initiatives found ways to circumvent the waterfall-like project management process despite US federal contracting requirements. Evidence of Agile-like iterative and incremental methods of working can be found in Project Mercury, the 1960s NASA initiative for the first US human spaceflight. Larman and Basili cite Gerald M. Weinberg, who worked on Project Mercury, saying 'All of us, as far as I can remember, thought waterfalling of a huge project was rather stupid, or at least ignorant of the realities. . . ' (Larman and Basili 2003: 10). They also cite other governmentally scaled projects such as software development for the Canadian Automated Air Traffic Control System, and for the US Department of Defense, which utilize iterative and incremental development methods.

Exhibitions may not be a matter of life and death in the way that air traffic control or national defense may be, however, exhibitions *are* experiences created for and by humans, with human-based complexities and unpredictable factors. Iterative and incremental methods of design such as Agile have been proven to yield the success in creating effective experiences and products for and by humans, despite rigorous contracting systems, and in response to real human needs (Larman and Basili 2003). The appeal of Agile, when considering the development and design of exhibitions, is that it allows for responsiveness to real-world conditions of a given project. The nature of large-scale history museums in the United States is that millions of dollars and thousands of hours of work are at stake for permanent or semi-permanent exhibitions. The variables of these projects are ever-changing, and the risk of failure is extremely high. Agile has been proven to reduce risk by maintaining a method of working which is responsive to changing factors, and which incorporates iteration, testing and evaluation throughout. In addition, Agile promotes collaborative modes of team interaction which would greatly benefit the exhibition teams who experience pressure to reach success on these high value projects.

## Conclusion

Through three interviews this chapter has explored how industry-specific experience designers have developed methods applicable to exhibition development and design for large-scale history museums. While each interview was intended to focus on a discussion about the industry-specific disciplines of user-centered design, the topic of organizational change management rose to the fore. It became clear that while innovation and improvement are generally considered desirable by both corporate and cultural organizations, many large companies and organizations are not set up for change. What this means is that although they may seek innovation and improvement, those tasked with creating innovation are also faced with the challenge of organizational change management. Large-scale history museums are often entrenched in organizational structures and modes of working which pose barriers to innovation in exhibition experiences. If large-scale corporations or government agencies who seek innovation can benefit from iterative and incremental, user-centered design to evolve their organizational structure and modes of working, so, too, might large-scale history museums. This systemic change could result in large-scale history museums evolving new formats and definitions of 'exhibition' which are more likely to be relevant and accessible to future audiences.

To achieve this change, key principles for an experience design-based model for exhibition development and design are proposed. In contrast to the waterfall-like exhibition development and design process used currently at many large-scale history museums, an experience design-based project management system might emphasize a series of mindsets, methods, and modes of working. Rather than defining, at the outset, content organization, educational messages, gallery parameters, and design strategies, and then progressing in a step-like fashion through implementation, an experience-design based model would begin by establishing values and principles, and then allow the final form of the exhibition to evolve through a human-centered, iterative development process.

Experience design mindsets which are critical to successful exhibition development and design include: building empathy to the visitor, embracing ambiguity, willingness to learn from failure, and an understanding that the values and principles of a museum or project are the baseline for making decisions about exhibition design strategies and solutions. The methods of experience design which are most applicable to exhibition design include: establishing values and principles at the outset of each exhibition project, iteration cycles as a practice for exhibition content and design development, shorter timescales for each cycle of iteration, incorporating user and stakeholder testing regularly throughout iteration cycles, and a regular practice of divergent and convergent thinking throughout iteration cycles. Lastly, the modes of collaborative working which are essential for productive exhibition teams in large-scale history museums are drawn directly from Agile. These include working together daily, face-to-face is better, and engaging the client, which might include the museum director, stakeholders or the curators, in user research to regularly evaluate the direction of the project.

Overall, this experience design-based model for the development and design of large-scale history exhibitions is underpinned by a willingness to change course if necessary. Regular evaluations of progress are benchmarked against the project's established values and principles, which inform any decision to move forward or to change course. Although large-scale history museums may seem like difficult environments in which to effect change, the demonstrated success of experience design-based methodologies outside of museums indicates that evolution and innovation are possible in large-scale organizations, and the potential results may benefit the museum functionality and the overall visitor experience.

## Notes

1 Content based on a Skype interview with Natalie Foley, 9 June 2017.
2 Content based on a Skype interview with Jason Ulaszek, 23 June 2017.
3 Content based on a Skype interview with Matthieu Cornillon, 9 June 2017.

## References

Beck, K., *et al.* (2001) *Manifesto for Agile Software Development*. Online. Available HTTP: http://agilemanifesto.org. Accessed 8 August 2017.

Foley, N. (2017) *Natalie Foley*. Online. Available HTTP: www.linkedin.com/in/natalie-foley-5149292. Accessed 18 July 2017.

IDEO (1999) *Reimagining the Shopping Cart*. Online. Available HTTP: www.ideo.com/post/reimagining-the-shopping-cart. Accessed 8 August 2017.

IDEO (2015) *The Field Guide to Human-Centered Design* [1st edition], San Francisco: IDEO.org.

Inzovu (2017) *Fixing Social Systems by Design*. Online. Available HTTP: http://inzovu.co/. Accessed 18 July 2017.

Larman, C. and Basili, V.R. (2003) 'Iterative and Incremental Developments. A Brief History', *Computer*, 36(6), pp. 2–11.

Liedtka, J. and Ogilvie, T. (2011) *Designing for Growth: A Design Thinking Tool Kit for Managers*, New York: Columbia Business School Publishing.

Kigali Genocide Memorial (2017) *Kigali Genocide Memorial*. Online. Available HTTP: www.kgm.rw/memorial. Accessed 1 August 2017.

UX for Good, Insight Labs and Aegis Trust (2014) *The Inzovu Curve Booklet*, Kigali, Rwanda.

# 17

# UNTANGLING EXHIBITION NARRATIVES

## Towards a bridging of design research and design practice

*Jona Piehl and David Francis*

### Abstract

Museum design research draws on a variety of existing disciplines from fields as diverse as architecture, graphic design, learning, theatre, animation, film, and museum studies. As an emerging area, museum design research has many characteristics that other fields aspire to but find hard to create, including 'genuine cross-sector links, a deep desire to join forces to create new ways of working, new knowledge, and importantly contributions to real and positive change' (MacLeod *et al.* 2015: 314). In the spirit of this multidisciplinary approach, this chapter brings together perspectives from different areas of museum design research – graphic design and interpretation, respectively – in a dialogue that examines exhibition narratives. As the body of knowledge about museum design research grows, it will provide methods, frameworks and questions to advance the field. This chapter points to the need for exhibition analysis to reflect the collaborative nature of exhibition making by approaching exhibition narratives from a variety of different perspectives – spatial, textual, visual – to reflect the multimodal nature of the medium. It also underlines the potential for exhibition-making practice to work with the existing body of narrative theory to further develop a vocabulary of exhibition storytelling.

### Introduction

Both authors, Jona Piehl and David Francis, are researchers with professional backgrounds in museum graphic design and interpretation respectively. Our starting point for this chapter was a joint analysis of the exhibition 'Defining Beauty: the Body in Ancient Greek Art', which was on display at the British Museum in London from March to July 2015 (Figure 17.1). We use this collaborative analysis to tease out to what extent our respective perspectives are shaped not only by our theoretical frameworks but also our professional disciplines as practitioners. As such, our analysis is not only concerned with the detailed reading of one particular exhibition but a wider reflection on the relationship between different actors and their practices that come together in the making of exhibitions.

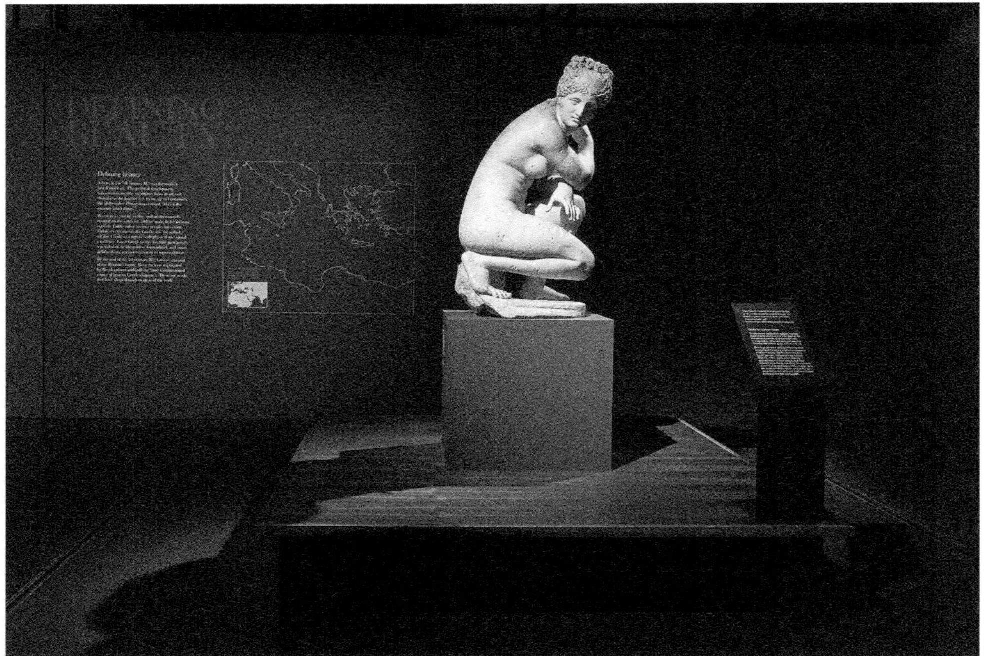

**FIGURE 17.1** Exhibition view of 'Defining Beauty'

*Photo:* Trustees of the British Museum

The chapter is aimed both at those who analyse and those who make museum exhibitions. It not only brings together two researchers with different perspectives on exhibition narratives, but it also encompasses the intersections between the dual identities we both hold of researcher and museum practitioner and the way in which these complement and, at times, contradict each other. In developing the chapter, tools we use in the making of exhibitions, such as schematic plans and diagrams, became powerful methods for analysis, allowing us to reveal the different structures underlying the exhibition narrative that shape how visitors engage with the content and make meanings in the space, while our respective narratological frameworks emerged as potentially productive for the planning of exhibitions. In exploring the space between analysis and practice, we are interested in the creative tension that exists between the two and championing the possibilities of being both.

In adopting this dialogic approach, we are situating ourselves within a wider body of cultural communication theory that includes the Russian literary theorist Mikhail Bakhtin (1981), who viewed all texts as composed of multiple voices, and the philosopher Martin Buber (1958), who argued that dialogue is a special type of human relationship that requires high-quality contact. This dialogic approach is a particularly appropriate lens through which to analyse museum exhibition narratives, because unlike the novel – with its singular author figure – exhibition narratives cannot occur without the collaboration of a number of practitioners from different disciplines. Exhibitions, an inherently collaborative practice (Davies 2010), are created through the dialogues between curators, designers, interpreters, project managers and, increasingly, the exhibition's audiences themselves. We argue that the dialogic approach can be adopted for the analysis of exhibitions and museums, that bringing together a range of analytical perspectives will yield new insights and that in the tensions between alternate readings, we are able to identify the key issues for both exhibition analysis and exhibition-making practice. An experiment into how a dialogic approach to research might look, our critical dialogue aims to harness the creative energy that exists within the collaborative process of making an exhibition, resulting in a richer reading, both of the exhibition and our own critical frameworks.

The chapter first discusses the insights gained from the examination of the exhibition narrative itself, which was focused specifically on the concepts of narrative structures and narrative voice. Following that, we reflect more broadly on the implications of applying narrative analysis to museum exhibitions. Our dialogue illustrates the potential of narrative theory in the analysis of exhibitions. It also underlines the potential opportunities and challenges of how exhibition research may feed into exhibition-making practice.

## Analysing 'Defining Beauty'

In our joint analysis of the exhibition narrative of 'Defining Beauty', we considered the exhibition partly on our own and partly in conversation with each other; we exchanged observations, discussed the data generated and shared insights. While common themes emerged in these conversations, such as the structure of the narrative in the exhibition space or the nature and manifestation of the narrative voice(s), our approaches to a narrative analysis of exhibitions are distinctly different. They are rooted on the one hand in conceptions of literary narratives (for example Freytag 1997 [1863] and Barthes 1990 [1974]) and on the other in transmedial narrative theory (for example Ryan 2006 or Herman 2002). Furthermore, while analytically we approach the exhibition in its entirety as a 'narrative text', we nevertheless approach it from different disciplinary perspectives, one that begins with the interpretive texts and one that begins with the spatial-visual experience.

There are a number of definitions of what constitutes a narrative, ranging from the very narrow that only admits literary narratives, to wider definitions that allow for a discussion of degrees of narrativity in different media (Richardson 2000; Austin 2012). One concept that is shared across these definitions is the idea of an event taking place, a change in state, and the connecting of these events together to create a sequence. In a museum exhibition, the sense of sequence is created by arranging exhibitions according to an underlying logical system, for example chronological, typological or thematic; the division of individual units of the exhibition into rooms or sections; and by the visitor's own bodily movement through the space. Depending on your focus, different structures come to the fore, and in 'Defining Beauty' a focus on the textual components yielded different readings of structure than a focus on the visual components.

Beginning with a reading of 'Defining Beauty' based on the interpretive texts and object constellations in the gallery space itself, we can see that there is a structure made up of ten sections. These are indicated by an introductory text and title to delineate a new section, for example 'Rites of Passage' or 'Beauty and the Beast'. Looking at the way in which each of the individual sections is connected to create a sense of progression within a thematic sequence, we can further group the sections into three acts – to borrow a term from drama and film theory (see floor plan in Figure 17.2). Act one (containing sections 1 to 4) introduces the key concept of the exhibition: how beauty and thought were interlinked in the form and ideas that informed the creation of Ancient Greek sculpture. This space was arranged as a series of

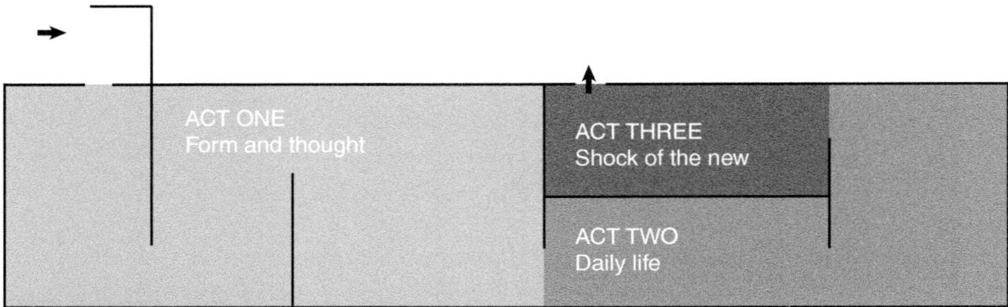


**FIGURE 17.2** Narrative structure in three acts. Act one: Form and thought; act two: Daily life; act three: Shock of the new

striking vistas in which visitors encounter large sculptures positioned to create intellectual and aesthetic juxtapositions. Act two (sections 5 to 8) can be read as providing a counterpoint to act one's focus on the ideal male body, contrasting it with depictions of everyday life, women and the non-Greek 'other'. The spaces in act two become narrower, the objects smaller and the density of objects in cases increases, here the change in the visual display reflects the change in the focus of the interpretive text. The third act (sections 9 to 10) introduces the legacy of Greek sculpture, and features objects from later periods such as the Belvedere torso and Renaissance works by Michelangelo. This section returns to the strategies of display of the exhibition's first act, creating a final vista centred around two key sculptures – the Belvedere Torso and the reclining Dionysus from the Parthenon.

Within 'Defining Beauty's' three-act structure, we can identify two clear object climaxes where objects are grouped together to create striking vistas that are effectively high points of the exhibition. These are the trio of sculptures by Myron, Polykleitos and Phydias in section one, and the pairing of the Parthenon Dionysus and the Belvedere Torso in section 10. The label text alerts the visitor to the particular significance of these objects both as iconic works of art in themselves but also their importance within the exhibition as one of the narrative climaxes, as the text panel 'Shock of the new' states: 'Presented in this room, for the first time, are two sculptures that at different times have been considered to be perfection in ancient art'.

There is also what might be called a conceptual climax in section 4, 'Giving form to thought', in which the question posed by the exhibition's title, 'How did the ancient Greeks define beauty?' is addressed. In the words of the introductory panel to this section: 'the works in this room present a series of encounters with the ideas that shaped the body in Greek art'. These encounters are clustered around a series of key themes, including the male, female and divine body, abstraction, idealism and realism, and sculpture and the use of drapery. Anticipation for this intellectual climax is built up by the preceding three sections, which, through displays on colour and material, provide visitors with some of the key information required to prepare them for these encounters. The German dramatist Gustav Freytag expressed plot in the form of a diagrammatic line, dubbed Freytag's pyramid (1997 [1863]). We can do the same with 'Defining Beauty' expressing its climaxes with three clear peaks, a conceptual climax, bookended by two object climaxes (Figure 17.3).

Turning our attention to the visual expressions of narrative structure through the exhibition graphic design, a different reading of the exhibition structure emerges. As a narrative medium, exhibitions draw on a wide range of semiotic resources to tell their stories.

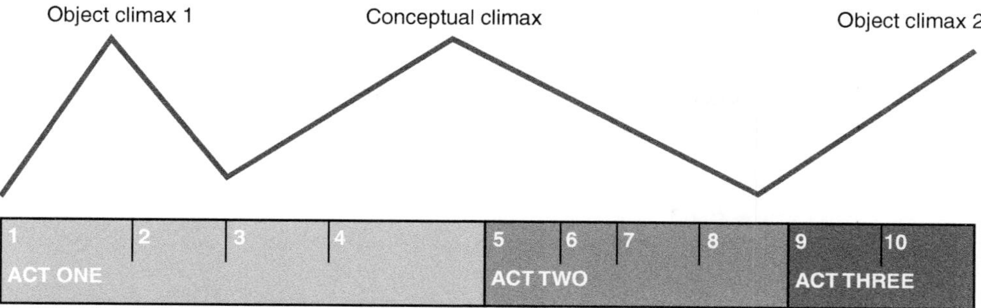


**FIGURE 17.3** Expressing the plot in diagrammatic form. Object climax one: Vista of three sculptures, conceptual climax: giving form to thought; object climax two: Shock of the new vista

Exhibition graphics, providing visual cues through the features of their graphic language, that is the choice of typeface, their typographic design or the images used as part of a graphic object, can be examined for their contributions to the construction of the exhibition's storyworld, the conceptual model of where and when the story takes place (Herman 2002).

Considering the exhibition graphics of 'Defining Beauty' in terms of a sequential unfolding of events, concentrating on the graphic objects in the gallery space, it is immediately apparent that their graphic language is static rather than progressive. The set of graphic objects, the gallery texts, the artefact labels and wall quotes, are introduced at the start of the exhibition and used consistently throughout. The design of these graphic objects, the materials, the presentation and constellations with other exhibition elements remain the same across the exhibition. While the graphic design expresses the vertical structure of the exhibition text via hierarchies of graphic objects, from the large exhibition title to the small object label (Velarde 2001), there is little evidence in the exhibition graphic design of a sequential structure; the graphic language neither changes nor develops in response to the narrative and its events. An exception are the colours used on the exhibition walls that change from space to space. Not only demarcating the succession of physical spaces, these colours also visually establish a sequence of thematic sections and it is in the use of colours that the exhibition content is structured horizontally, that is, as it is presented over the course of the gallery space.

This visual-narrative structure differs from the three-act structure identified above on two accounts. First, in the visual structure the narrative is extended to include the introduction outside of the main space as the first encounter with the exhibition narrative when moving from the wider museum space into the gallery. Second, considering the sequence of colours and their repetition over the course of the exhibition, the visual structure suggests a narrative in four parts (Figure 17.4a), in which there is a close relationship between the beginning and the end of the narrative where the use of blue acts as visual bookends to the warm colours in the middle sections of the exhibition.

Questions arise here with respect to the alignment of the different dimensions of the exhibition narrative and, further, its legibility: what narrative structures are created through the words, the objects, the design and what is their relationship to each other? Furthermore, what is made visible, legible, to the audience, what narrative sequence(s) are offered

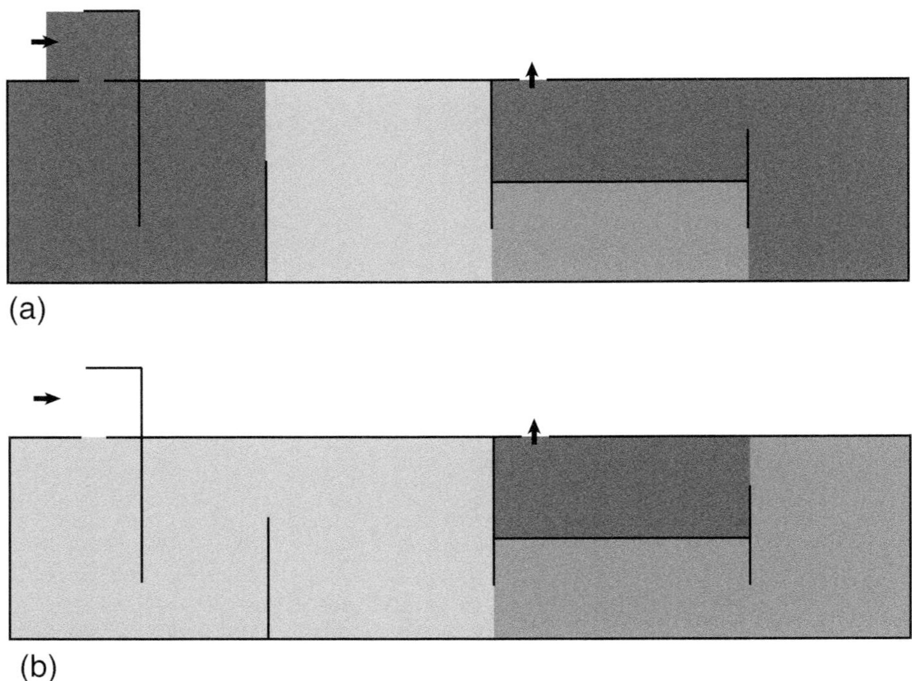


**FIGURE 17.4** Comparison of structure established by sequence of wall colours (a) and three-act structure according to text (b)

to the exhibition visitor? In 'Defining Beauty', the structures established visually do not align with the act structure that can be identified in the written texts. While on the one hand, this raises the question of why the visual is not supporting the written (and whether it should do). If we consider the object climaxes and conceptual climax on separate layers, perhaps the colour sequence can, in fact, be seen to support the expression of the object climaxes? On the other hand, it raises the question of intent: to what extent is the exhibition crafted with a narrative structure in mind? Furthermore, we analyse the multimodal exhibition text in its entirety but with a focus on different dimensions of interpretive texts or visual elements and, equally, visitors may choose which dimension of narrative they prioritise.

Alongside structure, one of the key elements of narrative is who is speaking and where does this voice manifest itself. This notion of narrative voice is relevant both in terms of who is speaking and what they are saying, but also in terms of how they are saying it and in what relationship different voices appear to each other and the reader (Aczel 1998). The narrative voice may include the voices of the narrative's characters, the protagonists populating the world of the story, and the voice of the exhibition's narrator, in other words, the voice of those who are telling the story. In film, the idea of narration is often extended to include the point of view provided by the camera, and in museum exhibitions voice can be found not only in the exhibition text but also its visual manifestation. The narrator is a narrative device and as

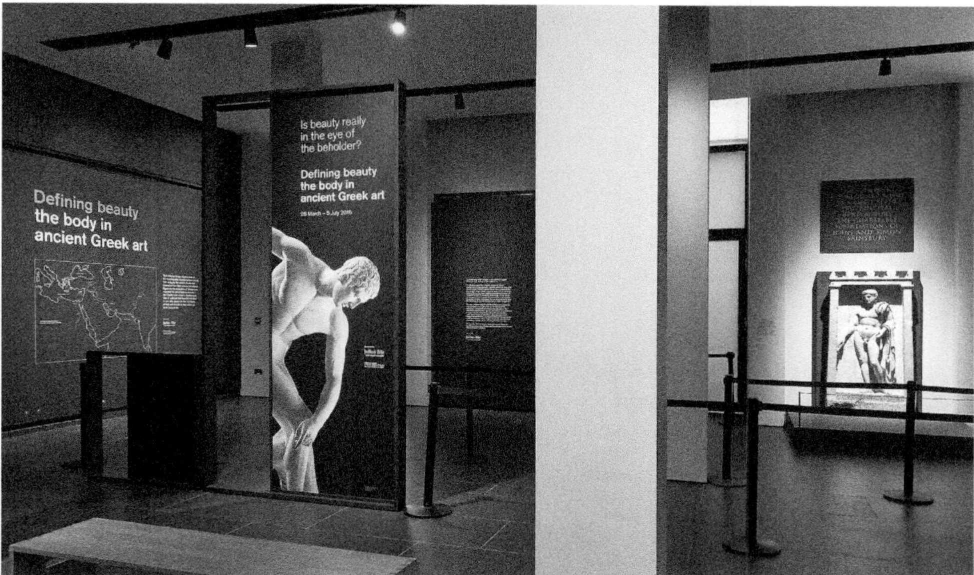


**FIGURE 17.5** Graphic language in the British Museum and in 'Defining Beauty'

*Photo:* Trustees of the British Museum

such it is not identical with the author, but in museum exhibitions the two are often conflated: despite the multiple authors collaborating in the making of exhibitions, the museum institution as the host of the exhibition, is perceived to be the author-narrator of the exhibition narrative (Arnold 1998).

In 'Defining Beauty', this author-narrator is visually present in the exhibition through the exhibition graphics (Figure 17.5). The graphics align closely with what might be described as genre-typical codes of display, the artefact label that provides verbal information about the object on display, or the section texts at the beginning of a new topic. Furthermore, the exhibition graphics use the same set of typefaces that can be found across the museum, in permanent galleries as well as on marketing material. Through the features of their graphic language the exhibition graphics not only confirm the situation as 'exhibition' they also visually position the narrative as a British Museum narrative: the narrator visually adopts the tone of voice established as that of the British Museum. There are other voices present in the exhibition; for example the texts incorporate direct citations from literary and historical sources. This multiplicity of voice is visualised on the level of the individual texts, for example through the use of a combination of several typefaces and typographic signals such as quotation marks. However, while this serves to delineate different sources of information, the graphic language overall is closely aligned with the institutional voice.

This does not mean that the exhibition does not have its own distinctive voice, created through the collaborative text-writing process between the curator and the interpretation officer. This narratorial voice is characterised by texts that directly address the viewer, that take the point of view of the visitor viewing the objects, and personify the sculpture, effectively encouraging a two-way encounter:

> Approached from behind, Aphrodite glances over one shoulder, while her fingers appearing over the other seem to beckon us to view her from all sides. Our curiosity leads us around her body to confront finally her divine and dangerous stare.
>
> (Defining Beauty, *2015, label text, 'Aphrodite' exhibit)*

The titles given to these objects also differ from typical British Museum labels in that they often take the form of a playful pun – for example, 'Sexual animal' rather than the more typical 'Ceramic pot with an image of a satyr'. This approach was a deliberate tactic employed by the exhibition to defamiliarise potentially well-known objects that many British Museum visitors would have seen before in the permanent collections. At the same time, the strategy of removing the name of the object from the label's title, as, for example, calling Iris from the Nereid Monument 'Spirit of the sea', can be seen as a wider strategy of decontextualising objects from their original (archaeological) settings. Instead, visitors are encouraged to approach the objects as works of art.

Yet, the potential of this particular, exhibition-specific voice, and with this the possibility of emphasising a multiplicity of voices in the exhibition, was not carried through in its visual manifestation. Rather, the graphic language homogenises the multiple voices that are present in the narrative and institutionalises the exhibition's distinctive narratorial voice. In other words, the exhibition is not only told in a visually coherent voice, it also visually appears to be fully integrated into the larger narrative of the museum. While a strong visual identity, as one component of its 'brand', is a valid concern of the contemporary museum that has to establish and maintain its profile against other institutions, here, its expression throughout the exhibition takes precedence over the potentially diverse voices in the exhibition. As a result, rather than 'showing their hand' to the visitor (Bal 1996) by making visible who is speaking and on what authority, the exhibition hides behind an institutional monologue and the graphic language supports the construction of the museum institution as author-narrator of the exhibition narrative. It is noteworthy that the sponsor panel at the entrance of the exhibition, where the exhibition's main sponsor conveyed a supporting message to the exhibition audiences, also uses the museum's graphic language. As such, its textual content is both visually positioned as part of the exhibition narrative, as content, and the institution and its commercial sponsor visually appear to be aligned.

Here, our critical dialogue of narrative analyses not only draws attention to questions of narrative structure and alignment in the relationship between the verbal, material and visual dimensions of the exhibition narrative but also to the multiple voices that are present in the exhibition and how they are (or are not) made visible. This raises questions not only regarding the multiple authorial instances that are involved in the creation of exhibitions, and the different authors' intentions but also regarding the power dynamics of exhibition making and the ways these manifest themselves in the text and the design of the exhibition.

## Critical dialogues in research and practice

Taking a step back from the text 'Defining Beauty' and the detail of its narrative construction, we can group the questions that emerge – both around the exhibition itself and exhibition narration more generally – into three aspects that we consider relevant in thinking about future practice in exhibition making and exhibition design research. The first concerns the exhibition as a narrative medium, the possibilities and challenges of what might be described as developing a 'narratology of exhibitions'. Key to this project is the need to explore such questions as what specific qualities are unique to exhibition narratives: what concepts developed in the context of literary narratives are useful in the analysis of exhibition storylines, and what concepts need to be adapted when addressing the complex, multimodal, spatially and institutionally specific narratives of exhibitions?

The second aspect concerns the practice of exhibition making: how can narrative theory provide productive tools for the creation of exhibitions, where can a narrative perspective be challenged, how does it relate to other approaches, for example, the focus on objects and the encounter with the object? The third aspect concerns the dialogic approach itself and how it brings together different actors involved in the making of exhibitions: how is the multimodality of exhibitions acknowledged in the theory and practice of exhibition making, how are the different disciplines such as design, curation, education, articulated, and how may we actively seek to move beyond these disciplinary confines?

In the first instance then, the dialogic analysis throws up questions about the relationship between narrative theory and exhibitions as a narrative medium and one of the main challenges of conducting the dialogue was establishing the overlaps and tensions between our respective critical frameworks. Concepts adopted (and adapted) from the field of narrative theory appear in many different guises in exhibitions and museums practice as well as in the discourses of exhibition analysis and museum studies (Piehl 2017). Terms such as narrative or the narrator are used in practice to describe exhibition content, its format in the gallery and in discussions of the nature of content, in other words, in discussions of whose stories are brought on display (for example, Hooper-Greenhill 1992, 2000; Macdonald 2005; Knell *et al.* 2007). They are also used in the theorisation of exhibitions to conceptualise the way in which exhibition content is constructed. Here, the variety and richness of the field of narrative theory is reflected in different models and concepts adopted in the discussion of exhibitions, while some draw on classic literary concepts in their analysis (Buschmann 2010, Hanks 2012), others approach exhibitions as a distinct narrative medium and with this query what theoretical concepts can become productive in their analysis (Thiemeyer 2013).

Questions that arise from our dialogue in particular concern the way in which concepts are made productive in the context of exhibitions, and how do they capture the medium-specific features, where do they fall short unless they are adapted, in other words, how might we conceive of a 'narratology of exhibitions'? The manner in which textual models of narrative have been adapted for the analysis of narrative in film provides a potential way in to such a discussion. Drawing on Deleyto's (1996: 217) distinction between the narrator ('who speaks?') and focaliser ('who sees?'), we can argue that though narration and focalisation can appear in both the novel and film; one mode of telling tends to be emphasised at the expense of the other. The novel favours the textual, while the film with its 'camera eye' (Black 1986: 4) emphasises the visual. Both mediums also have a primary mode by which they are consumed: the novel through the act of reading, while the film is centred around the viewer and the gaze. Museum exhibitions are less clearly aligned with either narration or focalisation, but rather exist on a spectrum that incorporates the textual, visual and spatial. Some exhibitions, particularly museum exhibitions, are heavily reliant on texts, while on the other end of the spectrum contemporary art exhibitions in a white-cube setting may eschew all text in order to emphasise the visual qualities of the artwork on display. This range of narrative expression surfaces, for example in the work of Mieke Bal who takes a primarily textual-spatial approach to analyse the colonial discourses latent in the panels and displays of the Met and the Natural History Museum in New York (Bal 1996). This contrasts with her decidedly cinematic approach to the contemporary art exhibition 'Partners' (Bal 2007), where she explores the parallels between the display of contemporary art with filmic devices such as the montage, dissolve and close-up.

However, if exhibition narratives are characterised by their multiple tracks of narration, the question is how these multiple tracks of text, objects, spatial and visual components (as well as lighting or sound) are considered and how the exhibition in its entirety can be analysed as a 'text'. Our analysis of the graphic language in 'Defining Beauty' revealed not only who is speaking but also how the different voices are made legible in the exhibition, or rather how the graphic language served to visually homogenise the multi-voiced narrative, including the visual conflation of the institution and the exhibition's commercial sponsor that seeks to draw the sponsor into the museum and into the exhibition narrative. In other words, the examination of the narratorial voice across the verbal and the visual dimensions of the exhibition narrative underlined the impact of the exhibition graphic design on the exhibition narrative, and in doing so shifted its role explicitly beyond its functionality as a means of display.

Such an acknowledgement of the wide range of semiotic resources of exhibitions that extend beyond the textual components of the interpretive texts and the materiality of objects to include visual and spatial elements chimes with the points Marie-Laure Ryan (2006: 30) makes with respect to the notion of medium-specificity. She argues that each narrative medium has distinct characteristics, and that it is vital to understand these characteristic features in order to avoid mere transpositions of narratives from one medium into another. In other words, in order to enable both analyses that capture the full scope of exhibition narration and to promote the further development of 'original' exhibitions narratives, rather than, polemically speaking, 'books on the wall', it is necessary to consider the specific nature of exhibition narratives and their complex, multifaceted multimodality (Piehl and MacLeod 2012).

Here, a direct transfer of concepts developed in the context of literary narratives, that is, in relation to verbal narratives, may prove limiting. For example, it may be queried to what extent the concept of the narrator as defined in the context of literary prose applies to exhibition narratives or how it may need to be adapted in order to become analytically productive. Is there a narrator or narrators in the literary sense in exhibitions and if so, how are these expressed visually and spatially? The field of transmedial narrative theory adopts a wide definition of what constitutes a narrative, promoting the consideration of a broad range of cultural objects as narratives. In the case of multimodal texts such as exhibitions, transmedial narrative theory extends the subject of analysis to explicitly include aspects such as exhibition design and draws attention to the complex construction of the narrative across the semiotic resources.

The concept of the storyworld as articulated by Herman (2002) is particularly productive to examine exhibition design as a constituent part of the exhibition narrative. According to Herman, the storyworld is constructed in the minds of the reader (or the audience) on the basis of the cues that a text provides them with. Taken to the context of exhibitions, these cues include not only verbal and material cues but also spatial and visual cues. For example, exhibition graphics may be analysed for the visual cues they provide to evoke a sense of the spatiotemporal setting of the narrative, to express a visual tone of voice or to support the underlying structure of the narrative.

As shown above, such an analysis can reveal factors shaping the exhibition narrative that remain unacknowledged by perspectives derived from literary narrative theory, which primarily focus on the written word in the exhibition. Therefore, Ryan's (2014) notion of a 'media-conscious' narratology, a narratology mindful of the specific features of its respective medium, speaks to key questions raised during our dialogue. These questions concern the acknowledgement and negotiation of the distinct qualities of exhibition narratives. For example, in addition to an understanding of the interplay between the different elements brought together in the exhibition space, the embodiment of the exhibition narratives in the visitor's journey through the space needs to be taken into account when moving towards a narratology of exhibitions (Brawne 1982; Bal 1996, 2007; Boon 2011; Lyotard 1996).

Following on from the discussion of how we might develop an understanding of exhibitions as a narrative medium, or perhaps, in fact, preceding it, is the question of how narrative theory might inform or play out in future practice or exhibition making. During our analysis, the notion of the act borrowed from drama and film theory emerged as a key idea and it provides a useful case study to explore how a concept taken from narrative theory might be used as a tool to aid in exhibition making (Greenberg 2012; Hanks 2012; Francis 2015; Piehl 2017; see also Duncan in this volume).

In dramatic theory, an act is defined as a series of scenes brought together and delineated by the lowering of the curtain (Lanouette 2012). The number of acts a play has varied historically. Aristotle famously observed that a Greek drama should have a beginning, a middle and an end – or three acts. Conversely the Roman dramatist Horace argued that a drama should have five acts, and this view prevailed until well into the nineteenth century, until the plays of Eugene Scribe (Lanouette 2012) advocated the use of a tripartite structure. This three-act structure remains very much the model for the Hollywood blockbuster today and is advocated by script-writing theorists such as Robert McKee (2006).

As well as being a unit of time, an act refers to the dramatic function of the collective sequence of scenes, but does not necessarily imply a chronological telling of events. McKee (2006) defines an act as a series of sequences that peaks in a climactic scene that causes a major reversal of values, more powerful in its impact than any previous sequence or scene. Aristotle referred to this moment of revelation as anagnorisis: a change from ignorance to knowledge in relation to one's true character and their situation, which forms the climax of the drama. For example, in Sophocles' Oedipus Rex, this moment of revelation is when Oedipus realises what the audience already knows, that he has slept with his mother and killed his father. Freytag (1997 [1863]) places this moment of revelation at the climax of his pyramid.

Another explanation for what drives us to read a story comes from Barthes (1990 [1974], 75) who identifies five narrative codes by which narrative is compromised. Two of these specifically relate to the sequential function of narrative in time. The proairetic code refers to the series of sequential actions and events that move the story along, while the hermeneutic code is the mystery that lies at the heart of a story that builds in the reader an expectation and desire for a solution.

One of the potential uses of the dividing exhibitions into acts is that it could change how their structure is perceived, from being flat to building a sense of anticipation, climax and resolution in the visitor. Certainly an exhibition like 'Defining Beauty' can be seen as having a hermeneutic mystery at its heart suggested by its title: how did the ancient Greeks define beauty? Sections 1, 2 and 3 of the exhibition explore different aspects of this question with the culmination of these ideas reaching their climax in section 4. At the same time, what is unique to exhibition narratives is the role played by the object, and in 'Defining Beauty' we see the exhibition's most iconic objects bookending the exhibition.

Much has been written about the 'affective weight of things in museums' (Harrison 2013b: 5), about their charismatic (Wingfield 2010), or enchanting (Harrison 2013a) qualities. This leads us to the critique of a 'narrativisation' of exhibitions, namely that the application of linguistic or discursive theory to museum exhibitions fails to capture the inherent materiality of things or the apparent agency things may have in object-human encounters suggested by the material turn and actor-network theory (Harrison 2013b: 36). Another criticism of approaches that foreground the creation of narratives is that objects are reduced to mere props that illustrate the story rather than acting as something in their own right (Scholze 2004).

It is with this need to look at exhibition narratives from a variety of perspectives and listen to the multiple disciplines involved in their making that we return to the premise of this dialogue about the analysis and practice of museum design. Adopting a dialogic approach to exhibition analysis delivered more than simply exposing the discrepancies of the textual and visual structures of the exhibition, rather, the dialogue helped to draw out the richness and unique qualities of exhibition narratives. In making you aware of your own disciplinary position, it actively moves you beyond disciplinary boundaries. In so doing it draws the research into a wider body of dialogic theory, established by thinkers such as Mikhail Bakhtin and Martin Buber, which rejects the primacy of an autonomous self in favour of a model of being that locates communication with others at its centre.

Bakhtin (1981) regarded human life as intrinsically dialogic, shaped by the many language-mediated relationships that make up our social worlds. For Bakhtin every text comprises many voices, and a text is never comprised in isolation, but always in dialogue with previous texts and their multiple voices. It is easy to see how this idea might be applied to museum exhibitions, which contain the many voices of an exhibition's multiple makers, as well as the objects in the exhibition itself. In museums a dialogic approach has played an important aspect in their reorganisation with the goal of widening access and engagement, this has included the incorporation of indigenous groups and visitors in the curatorial process (Harrison 2013b: 12; Macdonald 2011). In analysing the exhibition and bringing together interpretation and design, we attempted to draw out the dialogue between the different dimensions of the exhibition narrative and argue for their closer integration in the future.

Buber (1958: 18) stated that 'in the beginning is the relation' to advocate the primal nature of communication in shaping the self. He championed communication as a state of mutual recognition, openness and responsiveness, to only attempt to change the other, if you are open to be changed by the other as well. In utilising a dialogic approach that draws on both critical theory and museum practice we hope the two disciplines will modify one another. Our findings show the value of moving beyond our natural disciplinary focus by entering into a dialogue between disciplines that enabled us to share perspectives on the exhibition. As researchers, we can learn from the collaborative methods and processes we use as museum professionals, and that drawing on each other's specialist skill sets leads to a more creative and rewarding research process. Moreover, the iterative exchange of ideas made for a more reflexive approach, raising awareness of what our respective approaches exclude or downplay, challenging the assumptions that underlie our research. We believe that it is through this interdisciplinary exchange that a new terminology for the analysis of exhibition narratives can be forged, while at the same time moving beyond the diagnostics of exhibition narratives towards greater theoretical, conceptual insights also for exhibition practice.

## Acknowledgments

For their respective travel support, Jona Piehl would like to thank the University of the Arts, and David Francis would like to thank the AHRC.

## References

Aczel, R. (1998) 'Hearing Voices in Narrative Texts', *New Literary History*, 29(3), pp. 467–500.

Arnold, K. (1998) 'Birth and Breeding: Politics on Display at the Wellcome Institute for the History of Medicine', in Macdonald, S. (ed.) *The Politics of Display: Museums, Science, Culture*, London: Routledge, pp. 183–96.

Austin, T. (2012) 'Scales of Narrativity', in MacLeod, S., Hanks, L., and Hale, J. (eds) *Museum Making: Narratives, Architectures, Exhibitions*, London: Routledge, pp. 107–18.

Bakhtin, M. (1981) *The Dialogic Imagination*, Austin: University of Texas Press.

Bal, M. (1996) *Double Exposures*, London: Routledge.

Bal, M. (2007) 'Exhibition as Film', in Macdonald, S. and Basu, P. (eds) *Exhibition Experiments*, Oxford: Blackwell, pp. 71–94.

Barthes, R. (1990) *S/Z*, Oxford: Blackwell.

Black, D.A. (1986) 'Genette and Film: Narrative Level in the Fiction Cinema', *Wide Angle,* 8(3/4), pp. 19–26.

Boon, T.A. (2011) 'A Walk in the Museum with Michel de Certeau: A Conceptual Helping Hand for Museum Practitioners', *Curator: The Museum Journal*, 54(4), pp. 419–29.

Brawne, M. (1982) *The Museum Interior: Temporary + Permanent Display Techniques*, London: Thames and Hudson.

Buber, M. (1958) *I and Thou*, New York: Scribner.

Buschmann, H. (2010) 'Geschichten im Raum: Erzähltheorie als Museumsanalyse', in Baur, J. (ed.) *Museumsanalyse: Methoden und Konturen eines neuen Forschungsfeldes*, Bielefeld: Transcript Verlag, pp. 149–69.

Davies, S.M. (2010) 'The Co-production of Temporary Museum Exhibitions', *Museum Management and Curatorship*, 25(3), pp. 305–21.

Deleyto, C. (1996) 'Focalisation in Film Narrative', in Onega, S. and Garcia Landa, J.A. (eds) *Narratology*, London: Longman, pp. 217–33.

Francis, D. (2015) '"An Arena Where Meaning and Identity Are Debated and Contested on a Global Scale": Narrative Discourses in British Museum Exhibitions, 1972–2013', *Curator: The Museum Journal*, 58(1), pp. 41–58.

Freytag, G. (1997) 'Die Technik des Dramas', in Garland, H. and Garland, M. (eds) *The Oxford Companion to German Literature*, 3rd edition, Oxford: Oxford University Press.

Greenberg, S. (2012) 'Place, Time and Memory', in MacLeod, S., Hanks, L., and Hale, J. (eds) *Museum Making: Narratives, Architectures, Exhibitions*, London: Routledge, pp. 95–104.

Hanks, L. (2012) 'Writing Spatial Stories: Textual Narratives in the Museum', in MacLeod, S., Hanks, L., and Hale, J. (eds) *Museum Making: Narratives, Architectures, Exhibitions*, London: Routledge, pp. 21–33.

Harrison, R. (2013a) *Critical Approaches*, London: Routledge.

Harrison, R. (2013b) 'Reassembling Ethnographic Museum Collections', in Harrison, R., Byrne, S. and Clarke, A. (eds) *Reassembling the Collection: Ethnographic Museum and Indigenous Agency*, Santa Fe, NM: SAR Press.

Herman, D. (2002) *Story Logic*, Lincoln NE: University of Nebraska Press.

Hooper-Greenhill, E. (1992) *Museums and Shaping of Knowledge*, London: Routledge.

Hooper-Greenhill, E. (2000) *Museums and the Interpretation of Visual Culture*, London: Routledge.

Knell, S.J., MacLeod, S., and Watson, S. (eds) (2007) *Museum Revolutions: How Museums Change and Are Changed*, London: Routledge.

Lanouette, J. (2012) 'A History of the Three-Act Structure', *Screentakes*. Online. Available HTTP: www.screentakes.com/an-evolutionary-study-of-the-three-act-structure-model-in-drama/. Accessed 9 May 2017.

Lyotard, J.F. (1996) 'Les Immateriaux', in R. Greenberg *et al.* (eds) *Thinking about Exhibitions*, London: Routledge, pp. 159–73.

Macdonald, S. (2005) 'A People's Story: Heritage, Identity and Authenticity', in Corsane, G. (ed.) *Heritage, Museums, and Galleries*, London: Routledge, pp. 272–90.

Macdonald, S. (2011) 'Expanding Museum Studies: An Introduction', in Macdonald, S. (ed.) *A Companion to Museum Studies*, Malden, MA: Wiley-Blackwell, pp. 1–12.

MacLeod, S., Dodd, J., and Duncan, T. (2015) 'New Museum Design Cultures: Harnessing the Potential of Design and "Design Thinking" in Museums', *Museum Management and Curatorship*, 30(4), pp. 314–41.

McKee, R. (2006) *Story: Substance, Structure, Style, and the Principles of Screenwriting*, New York: Regan Books.

Piehl, J. (2017) 'Visualizing Storyworlds', in Black, A., Luna, P., Lund, O., and Walker, S. (eds) *Information Design: Research and Practice*, London: Routledge, pp. 577–90.

Piehl, J. and MacLeod, S. (2012) 'Where Do You Want the Label? The Roles and Possibilities of Exhibition Graphics', in MacLeod, S., Hanks, L., and Hale, J. (eds) *Museum Making: Narratives, Architectures, Exhibitions*, London: Routledge, pp. 257–66.

Richardson, B. (2000) 'Recent Concepts of Narrative and the Narratives of Narrative Theory', *Style: Concepts of Narrative*, 34(2), pp. 168–75.

Ryan, M.-L. (2006) *Avatars of Story*, Minneapolis: University of Minnesota Press.

Ryan, M.-L. (2014) 'Story/Worlds/Media: Tuning the Instruments of a Media-Conscious Narratology', in Ryan, M.-L. and Thon, J.-N. (eds) *Storyworlds across Media*, Lincoln, NE: University of Nebraska Press.

Scholze, J. (2004) *Medium Ausstellung: Lektüren musealer Gestaltung in Oxford, Leipzig, Amsterdam und Berlin*, Bielefeld: Transcript Verlag.

Thiemeyer, T. (2013) 'Simultane Narration: Erzählen im Museum', in Strohmaier, A. (ed.) *Kultur – Wissen – Narration: Perspektiven transdisziplinärer Erzählforschung für die Kulturwissenschaften*, Bielefeld: Transcript Verlag, pp. 479–88.

Velarde, G. (2001) *Designing Exhibitions*, 2nd edition, Aldershot: Ashgate Publishing.

Wingfield, C. (2010) 'Touching the Buddha: Encounters With a Charismatic Object', in Dudley, S. (ed.) *Museum Materialities: Objects, Engagements, Interpretations*, Routledge: London, pp. 53–70.

# 18

# BEYOND THE MUSEUM

## A comparative study of narrative structures in films and museum design

*Tom Duncan*


### Abstract

The medium of film, with its narrative structure and spatial qualities, has an affinity to the museum experience. This chapter proposes that by analysing the language and structure of narrative in film, we can inform the physical experience of the museum or exhibition visit. Comparisons are drawn between example exhibition projects by the studio Duncan McCauley and three identified types of narrative structures in films: collage, repeat structure and reverse chronology. The analysis suggests that looking at the form of structures beyond the medium of the museum can benefit the design and development of innovative museum experiences.


### Introduction

This chapter sets out to investigate the narrative structure of the museum visit, and how thinking about narrative and the progression of the museum visit can be part of the planning process for a museum. Using studies of narrative structures in specific films, this chapter proposes that looking beyond the typology of the museum can benefit the development of innovative museum experiences. Museum experiences have always been spatial, dynamic and time based, as visitors have always made a physical journey through the museum. However, museum professionals and designers now understand more about the way physical designed forms in combination with audio-visual media are implicated in shaping experience. As a result there is more emphasis on utilising a whole range of media and spatial qualities to create highly affective and dynamic experiences, which support the context and content of the museum and open up opportunities for meaningful visitor experiences.

For example, Duncan and McCauley (2012: 291) describe the visitor journey as traversing both the architecture of the spaces and that of the digital media, acknowledging that the space and the different media together make up a complex whole. This chapter aims to contribute to the understanding of the design of the visitor experience, and in particular how the structure and duration of the journey can contribute to the visitor's perception of the narrative, leading to new interpretive possibilities. Through an understanding of narrative theory and dramatic structure, the chapter draws comparisons between the experiential compositions in the language of film and their counterparts in exhibitions and museums. With the increasing integration of powerful narrative and experiential elements into the museum, understanding of the overall narrative structure of the visitor experience is perhaps more important than it has been before.

The first half of the chapter introduces some of the key ideas and theories that sit behind the arguments set forward. First, some elemental understanding of the viewer and the visitor experiencing the mediums of film and exhibition respectively are provided, with the idea of movement in Sheets-Johnstone (2009) and Bergson's theory of the perception of time (Guerlac 2006). Following this, the writings of Bal (2009) and Herman (2009) support the suggestion that the theory of narrative is applicable across the different mediums of film and exhibition. Finally, Eisenstein et al.'s (1989) essay *Montage and Architecture* and Corbusier's ideas on the Architectural Promenade (Samuel 2010) are introduced in order to reflect further on the comparison between the dramatic structure of the experience of film and that of architecture.

In the second half of the chapter and following a brief outline of the research methodology, case studies of exhibition projects draw on the possibilities of the definitive structures of film in order to demonstrate how the recognition and application of these structures can be useful for designing frameworks for museum experiences. Three different types of filmic narrative structure are defined and their forms and theories are then applied to both ongoing and completed exhibition projects by the studio Duncan McCauley.

## Movement, time and narrative

The spatial qualities and narrative structure of film have an affinity to the museum experience. In *Reshaping Museum Space*, Greenberg (2005: 230) describes how exhibition designers borrow methods from film, such as the creation of a dramatic structure to create engaging narrative experiences as in the example of 'The Holocaust Exhibition' at the Imperial War Museum, London. Also referring to a masterplan project for the Victoria and Albert Museum, Greenberg (2005: 235) considers the museum as 'moving and filmic rather than static and monumental'. When watching a film, the viewer's attention is carried by the sequential presentation of narrative fragments embedded in a spatial context. Similarly, visitors to a museum perceive the content as they move sequentially through the spaces of the museum environment. The museum experience differs, however, in that the spatial qualities are more prominent and the experience itself is dependent on a physical engagement and choices by the visitor. The visitor to a museum moves through spaces with views and axial relationships but also juxtapositions, contrasts and spatial conflicts to confront or to avoid.

Jonathan Hale (2012: 197) describes how the dancer and philosopher Maxine Sheets-Johnstone talks of our possibility to think with movement, suggesting movement is one of our primary modes of engagement and communication with the world. In her book *The Corporeal Turn*, Sheets-Johnstone (2009: 40) gives the example of a dancer or dance group performing contact theatre, a type of spontaneous, improvised dance. She argues that the decision of where and how the dancers move in space, with and around each other, occurs through the physical act of movement. The same approach can be applied to the visit to an exhibition because it is a physical experience. The visitor navigates through the exhibition environment, their body reacting to the signs of the objects and images and the other visitors. Following Sheets-Johnstone's logic, the movements visitors make between the objects and the exhibits are a type of museological choreography. The timing, the sequence and the rhythm of the overall experience, although ultimately controlled by the movements of the individual visitor, is a necessary part of the museum planning. Understanding the timing of the sequence of spaces in the museum is as important as other architectural qualities such as adjacency, materiality or atmosphere.

The philosopher Bergson's theory of time is also valuable in investigating the experience of the museum visit. His thinking deviates from the conventional understanding of the perception of time, which he describes as spatial, where past, present and future are positioned along a line in space, present being positioned somewhere between past and future. As the scholar Suzanne Guerlac (2006) explains, to strengthen this point, Bergson describes how we count spatially, where the numbers we have recited are held in space in our minds adjacent to those that are to follow. For example, the recited number two proceeds number three, and the not yet recited number four is positioned somewhere on the other side of three.

Bergson's radical departure from the conventional idea of time was to see time not only in the context of space, but also in our inner consciousness. In his essay 'Time and Free Will', he differentiates between two different types of consciousness: 'reflective consciousness' is always held in a spatial framework because it refers to outside bodies or influences that are somehow positioned relatively in space. 'Immediate consciousness' is how an experience feels to us without any kind of thought about it to ourselves or without trying to communicate it. 'Immediate consciousness' does not relate to space as 'reflective consciousness' does. 'Immediate consciousness' is what Bergson refers to as 'real or pure duration'. Guerlac suggests that duration implies a mode of temporal synthesis that binds temporal dimensions together as a melody does. The melody is detached from the linear narrative development of past-present-future, it evolves as if the notes were inside one another. The temporal nature of the complex entity of the melody experienced by a listener evolves over time. The visitor to an exhibition, like the listener to a melody, resonates between immediate consciousness and reflective consciousness; being both immersed emotionally and reflecting and communicating on the fragments of narratives, as they are experienced.

## Narrative theory

An understanding of the theory of narrative is useful to give some grounding to the way the term narrative is used in the context of the museum environment. Mieke Bal (2009: 5) introduced the three-level model of narrative consisting of narrative text, story and fabula. In literature, the narrative text are the words, while cinema uses moving images in combination with sound and spoken word. The story is the way and the order that the events are presented. Finally, the fabula is the straightforward and chronological account of the events according to narrative logic. In the museum, the narrative text is the navigable exhibition experience consisting of sequences of spaces, images, written words and objects, in combination with different media. The story is how the designer intends the visitor to experience the exhibition; in other words, how the multiple elements and media are presented and organised. The fabula is the chronological account of events, not necessarily in the order in which the visitor experiences them.

The diagram Text, Story, Fabula illustrates Bal's three-level model applied to the example of the 'Botticelli Reimagined' exhibition at the Victoria and Albert Museum, March–June 2016, where the reverse chronology of the presentation demonstrates the difference between the fabula and the story (Figure 18.1). The four different exhibition rooms are the four main stages of the narrative text. The fabula is the chronology of events starting with

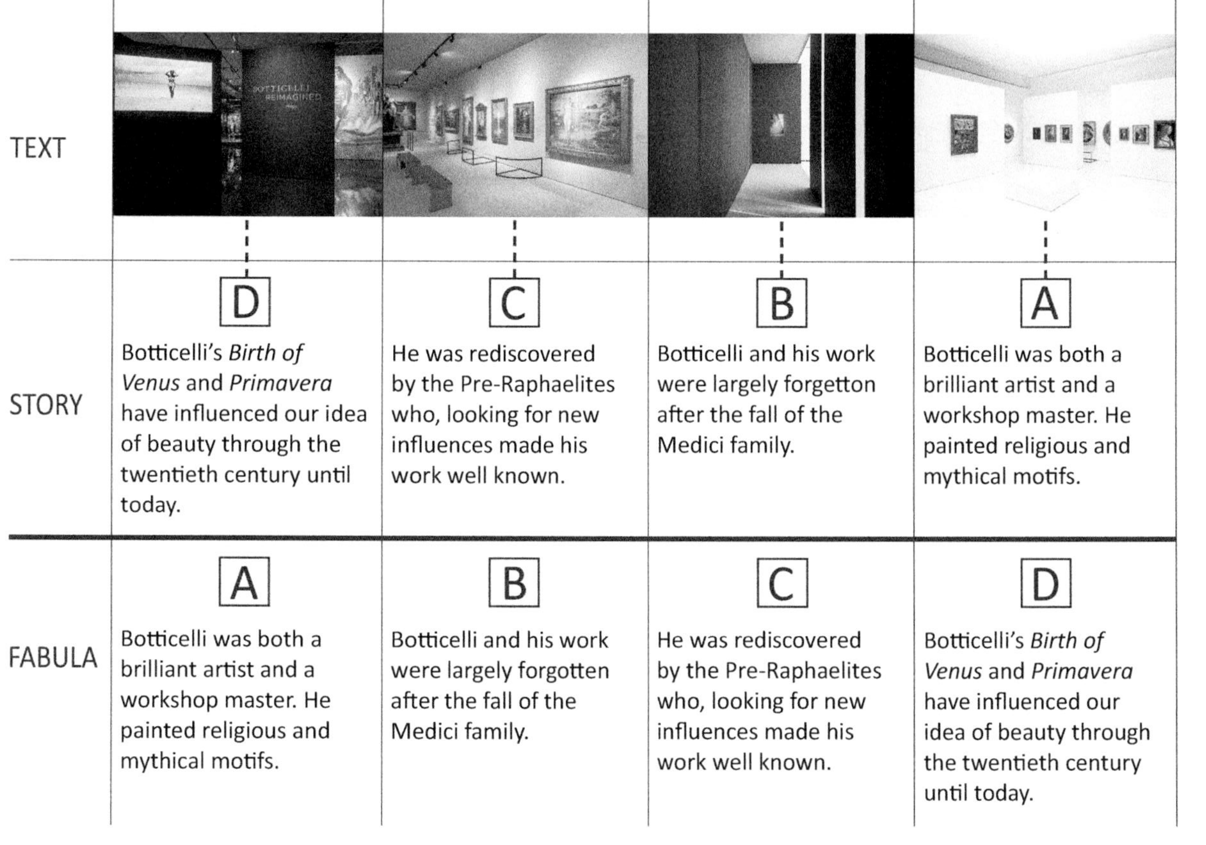


**FIGURE 18.1** Text, story, fabula diagram representing Bal's three-level model of narrative theory, for the exhibition 'Botticelli Reimagined'. Victoria and Albert Museum, 2016

*Photos:* Philipp Obkircher. Reproduced courtesy of the V&A. Image: Tom Duncan.

Botticelli as a successful artist in fifteenth-century Florence, his reputational decline and the rediscovery of his works by the Pre-Raphaelites in the nineteenth century, through to the present-day influence of his work on the idea of beauty. The story is the organisation of these events in reverse order, as developed by the curators and the exhibition design team, to create a compelling visitor experience.

Where Bal provides us with a structuralist approach to the theory of narrative, the narratologist Herman (2009: 105) introduces the idea of the immersive qualities of narrative storyworlds. He defines storyworlds as 'the worlds evoked by narratives'. The power of the storyworld is to transport the reader/viewer/visitor to, and immerse them in, the world of the narrative. The storyworld exists not just in the description of place but is a result of the narrative discourse, in other words how the story is expressed. In a feature film, representations of place help us to construct the storyworld, but the storyworld is also formed by what is implied and what we don't see. The viewer is positioned within the storyworld for the duration of the discourse.

Herman (2009: 112) goes further to say that 'Story openings prompt interpreters (readers) to take up residence (more or less comfortably) in the world being evoked by a given text'. He explains that narrative has an immersive quality and the ability to form worlds that occupy the reader or the viewer.

> Interpreters of narrative do not merely reconstruct a sequence of events and a set of existents but imaginatively (emotionally, viscerally) inhabit a world in which, besides happening and existing, things matter, agitate, exalt, repulse, provide grounds for laughter and grief, and so on.
>
> *(Herman 2009: 119)*

The idea of the storyworld applied to the context of the exhibition environment is the world suggested by the physical space of the exhibition in combination with the imaginary worlds created through the visitor's interpretation of the objects, written words and media. It would be a misreading to consider the physical exhibition environment as a storyworld. The storyworld exists in the mind of the visitor and is imagined through the visitor's interaction with the space and content of the exhibition.

## Dramatic structure in film and architecture

Considering the narrative qualities of navigable space, the filmmaker Eisenstein acknowledges that the physical and visual experience of architecture plays an important role in our appreciation and understanding of the language of film. In the essay 'Montage and Architecture', inspired by the writings and drawings of Auguste Choisy, Eisenstein et al. (1989: 3) describe the sequence of images as a visitor moves around the Acropolis in Athens, referring to this experience as a cinematic one: 'it is hard to imagine a montage sequence for an architectural ensemble more subtly composed, shot by shot, than the one that our legs create by walking among the buildings of the Acropolis'.

Discussing interconnections between architecture and film, the visual theorist Giuliana Bruno (2002: 55) refers to the paper by Eisenstein as a 'pioneering meditation on film's architectonics'. Like the architectural theorist Anthony Vidler (2002), Bruno concentrates on Eisenstein's use of the word 'path'. The path is what connects the real spaces and the images as the visitor moves through the spaces of the Acropolis, but the path is also that which connects the spaces and time frames of the different scenes of the film, as perceived by the immobile viewer in the cinema. Eisenstein's analysis of the diagrammatic representation of the sequence of views of the Acropolis by Choisy (1899a; 1899b) makes a connection between the language of architecture and the language of film. This chapter will later demonstrate how through an analysis of the diagrammatic representation of the narrative structure of films it is possible to make a connection back to architectural space, reinforcing Eisenstein et al.'s (1989) claim that the experience of architecture is the precursor to experiencing film.

The architect Le Corbusier (1991: 128) used the phrase 'Architectural Promenade' to describe the path of a visitor through the sequential spaces of his architecture. The architect Flora Samuel (2010) proposes that the experience of the sequence of spaces in the architectural promenade could have similarities to a narrative structure developed by the nineteenth-century novelist Gustav Freytag (1894). Based on Aristotle's theory of narrative, Freytag's dramatic structure, also known as Freytag's pyramid, consists of five stages: (1) exposition, (2) rising action, (3) climax, (4) falling action, and (5) resolution. Samuel refers to Le Corbusier's architectural promenade and its different stages as a design tool for structuring the experience of the architecture, remarking however that most of Le Corbusier's journeys in the Villas can be described as a 'Jacob's Ladder' type of journey. Starting low down in the dark and working their way up through the building to the sky, the culmination of the 'architectural promenade' is usually either with light coming into the space from above such as the library in Villa La Roche or with a framed view over the landscape from the roof as in Villa Savoye. Le Corbusier's design approach encompassing movement and visual framing illustrates his interest in timing and sequence in the experience of his architecture. Samuel's analysis of the architectural promenade indicates that patterns are readable in the dramatic structure of the experience of Le Corbusier's architecture, supporting the idea to develop patterns of dramatic structure in the design process for a museum environment.

## Methodology

This chapter proposes that by analysing the language and structure of narrative in film we can inform the structure of the physical experience of the museum or exhibition visit. This research attempts to go beyond a purely theoretical approach by using a comparison of the narrative structures of both films and concrete exhibition examples where a direct correlation can be made between both the narrative theory and the practical application of the narrative structure. Eisenstein's musings on architectural space bring the media of film and the spatial and time-based qualities of architecture into close proximity. There is a connection between the movement of the viewer or the visitor and what they see and hear both in the physical world, such as moving around the Acropolis, and in a film where the static viewer is taken on a journey through the spaces in the images.

Using a graphical representation analogous to an orchestra score, Eisenstein produced a diagram (Figure 18.2) to analyse a scene of the film *Alexander Nevsky* (1938). The diagram presents the correlation between visual and aural elements of the film and their effect on the viewer over time. In the top line are the frames of the film. The second line shows the musical score and the individual musical phrases. The third line shows how the image is composed. The bottom line refers to a subjective response to the scene, a gestural emotive reaction of the viewer to the image. He describes that in shots III and IV, the visual diagram of the images is

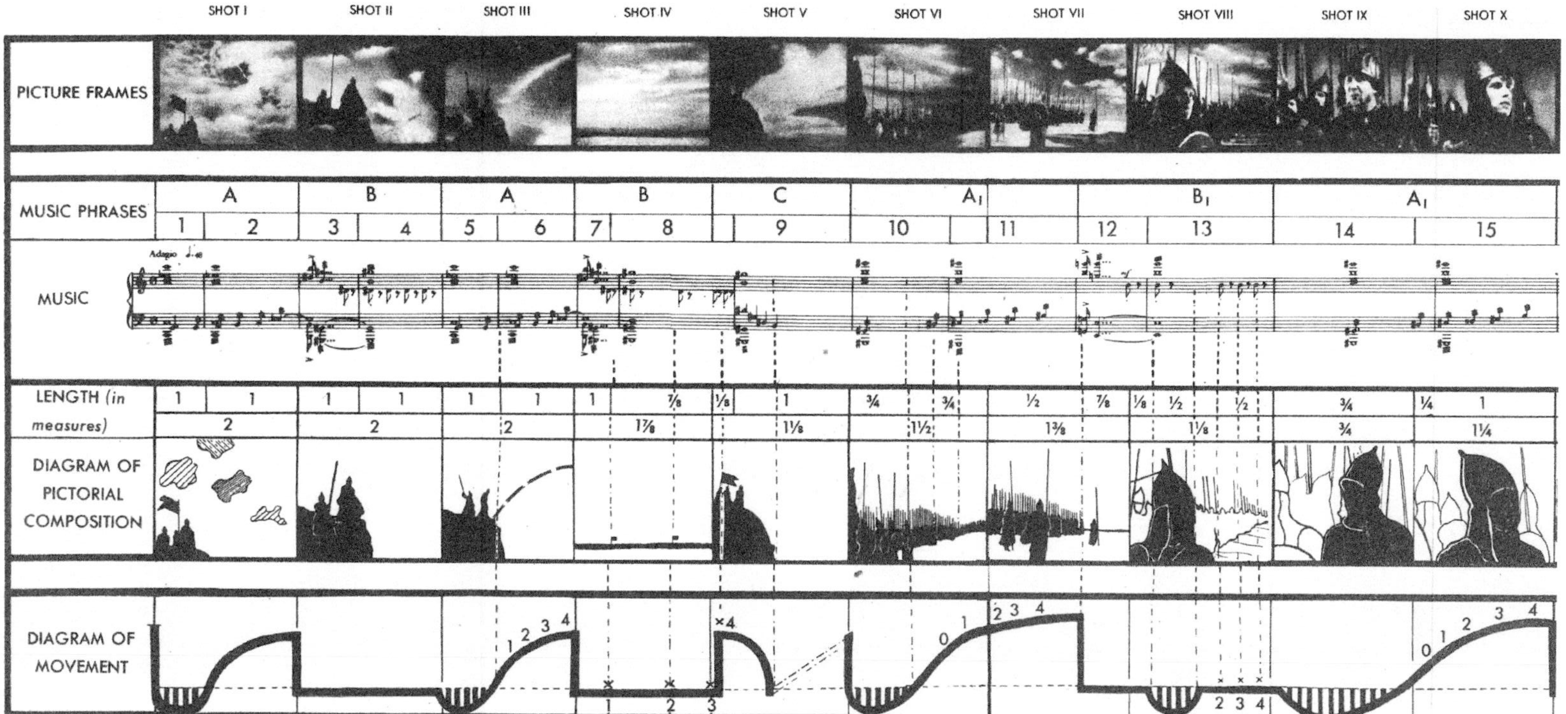


**FIGURE 18.2** Sergei Eisenstein, *The Film Sense* 1938. An analytic diagram of a sequence from the film *Alexander Nevsky* [excerpt]

*Image:* Courtesy of Houghton Mifflin Harcourt

the same as that of the music. The parallel emotional movement depicted in the bottom two lines is the reason why the shots III and IV are the most powerful in the sequence.

The separation of the different components of film, image, pictorial composition and sound over time in the diagram by Eisenstein has been an inspiration for analysing and investigating the composition of different media in the museum and how these together make up the sequential experience of the visitor. This chapter argues that the different elements of film stills, image, sound and pictorial composition can be substituted with those of a museum visit. For this research, diagrammatic representations of the narrative structure of the analysed films present the lengths and positioning of the scenes within the narrative text. Similar diagrams are created for the imagined visitor journey through the museum projects. It is suggested that the comparison of the narrative structure diagrams of the films with those of the imagined visitor experience can strengthen our understanding of sequence, time and the experience of narrative in the museum and prove useful during the design process.

Three different types of narrative structure of film have been chosen that are appropriate for comparison with the exhibition projects. These are repeat narrative structure, reverse chronology narrative structure, and collage. Repeat narrative structure is where an element of the film is repeated with different outcomes, such as in *Run Lola Run* (1998) by Tom Tykwer, or is shown from different viewpoints, such as in *Mystery Train* (1989) by Jim Jarmusch. Reverse chronology is a narrative structure that begins with the end of the story. The viewer is then taken on a journey 'backwards in time' to discover why these events happened. Examples of this type of narrative structure can be found in the films *Memento* (2000) by Christopher Nolan and *Irréversible* (2002) by Gaspar Noe. The term 'collage', described by film theorist David Bordwell (1985: 187), is widely used to describe the style of films made by Jean-Luc Godard, such as *Made in USA* (1966), which deny a cinematic unity and are visually and stylistically fragmented. A fourth narrative structure, not included in this chapter but that would be appropriate for further study, is described by Verstraten as 'ensemble' (2009: 5), where the narrative tells parallel stories, connected through their proximity of place and time with chance meetings between the protagonists. *Short Cuts* (1993) by Robert Altman is an example of this type of narrative structure.

The museum projects have been chosen because their narrative structures or elements are somehow comparable to the narrative structures of the film projects. The duration and structure of the museum visit are not as finite as that of the film but consist of many variables dependent on the visitor's movement and choices. The aim of the comparative analysis is to identify some moments in the sequence of events in the narrative structure of film that could be useful in structuring the museum visit. The selected exhibition projects and their corresponding films are as follows: repeat narrative structure of the visitor experience at Vischering Castle, Germany, is compared to the film *Run Lola Run*; reverse chronology narrative structure in the exhibition 'Botticelli Reimagined' at the Victoria and Albert Museum, London, is compared to the film *Memento*; the idea of a collage structure is used for the exhibition project 'Luther and the Princes', Torgau, Germany, and the film *Made in USA*.

The comparison between the narrative structure of films and the case studies of exhibition projects has been conducted at different stages in the design. For the exhibitions 'Botticelli Reimagined' and 'Luther and the Princes', the comparative analysis took place after the design of the exhibitions had been completed; the investigation enhanced the understanding of the narrative structure of the completed exhibitions but did not influence the design of the visitor experience. In Vischering Castle, however, the comparative analysis of the narrative structure of the film took place at the feasibility phase in the project, allowing the research to feed into some of the decisions about the placing of thresholds and moments of decision-making in the visitor journey.

## Comparative narrative structures in museum and film projects

### *Repeat narrative structure*

The film *Run Lola Run* is the story of Lola, who has to find 100,000 Deutschmarks within 20 minutes in order to save her boyfriend's life. The narrative structure differs from a classical Hollywood structure in that the main action part of the story repeats three times with different happenings and different outcomes. Between each of the main action scenes of Lola running through the city is a reflective scene of Lola and her boyfriend, Manni, having a conversation in bed. The tempo of the film changes in these interstitial scenes. The opening scene is a telephone conversation between Lola, played by Franka Potente, in her room at her parents' home and Manni, played by Moritz Bleibtreu. Manni, a small-time criminal, has just finished a job selling stolen cars and has accidentally left the money in a bag on the underground train. If he doesn't find the money by the time his boss arrives in 20 minutes, his boss will kill him. At the end of the opening scene, we experience the start of Lola's adventure as she decides to run out of the house in an attempt to save her boyfriend's life. This moment is an important threshold in the storytelling structure. The structure diagram of the film helps us to visualise the framework of the narrative composition over time (Figure 18.3).

Comparing the narrative structure diagram of the film with the narrative structure diagram of the museum visit, it is possible to identify similarities between the narrative experience of the viewer and the visitor. At Vischering Castle, the visitor enters through a gateway to the outer courtyard (Figure 18.4). From the introduction in the outer courtyard, the visitor is invited to cross a bridge over a moat and to enter the inner courtyard and the main museum. For the visitor, this is the most important threshold. They have had time to orientate themselves and now they have decided to commit and take part in the adventure. The museum is on three floors in the castle building. The visitor route is designed so that the visitor has to repeatedly re-enter the courtyard as they move between floors. The museum experience on each floor of the castle has a similar role to the repeating action sections of the film and the experience in the courtyard is a moment of reflection, as is the interstitial scene of the conversation between Lola and Manni in bed.

At this stage in the planning process for the museum, our aim is to identify key thresholds and shifts in the narrative. One of the planning discussions has been where to place the ticket control. If we define the outer courtyard as the equivalent to the introductory storytelling section, its role is to set the scene. In the film, the introductory section is the scene of the telephone conversation between Lola and Manni. In the same way that Lola has to make a decision as to who and where she runs to, the visitor needs to make a decision at this moment in their journey whether to buy a ticket in order to cross the bridge and pass into the inner courtyard of the castle. The identification of the point of the beginning of the adventure in the museum journey has helped to confirm the position for the placing of the ticket control before the bridge leading to the inner courtyard. In the site plan, these findings start to give a structure and to strengthen the elements of the narrative journey that are already part of the museum site. The analysis of the film *Run Lola Run* and its comparison to the planned

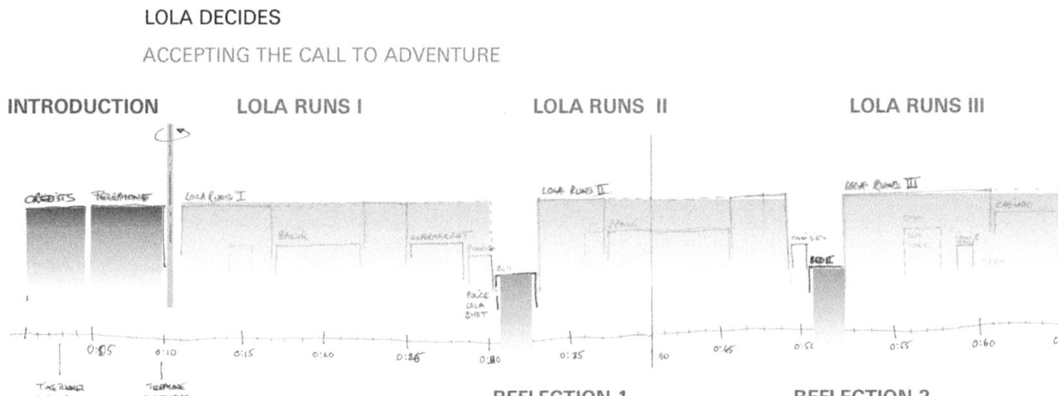


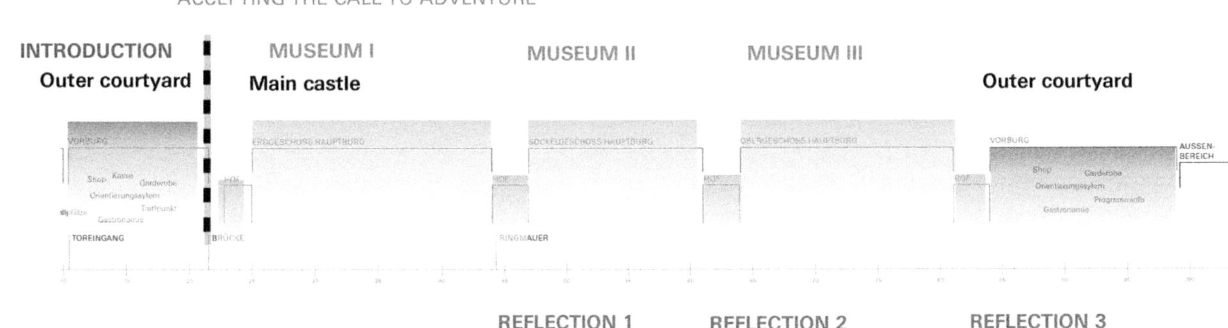


**FIGURE 18.3** Narrative structure diagram comparing the film *Run Lola Run* and the visitor experience at Vischering Castle

*Image:* Tom Duncan

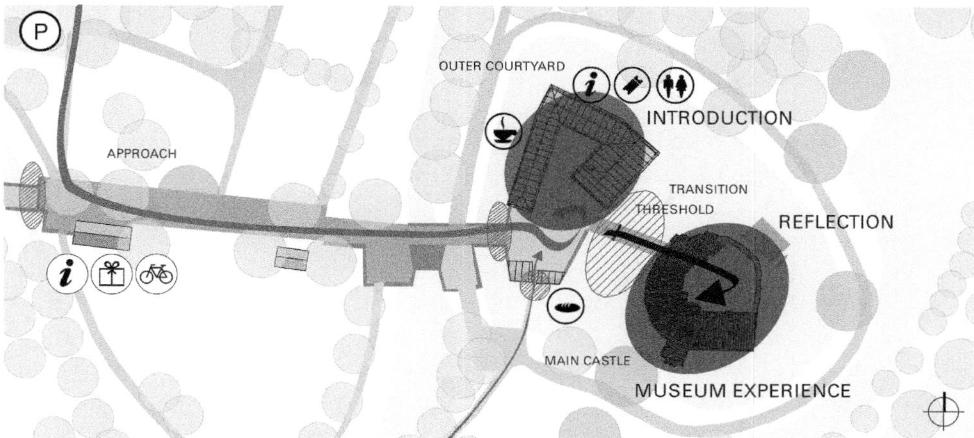


**FIGURE 18.4** The site plan of Vischering Castle for the feasibility phase of the project

*Image:* Duncan McCauley

visitor experience at Vischering Castle helped to inform the design team of some of the key moments in the overall visitor experience, including the relevance of the repetition of the place for reflection in the courtyard as well as the definition of the start of the adventure.

## *Reverse chronology narrative structure*

The film *Memento* is the story of Lenny, who has lost the ability to form new memories and is seeking revenge for the murder of his wife. In the first scene, Lenny kills a man. The narrative travels back through time, unravelling the story of why and how he came to do this. In order to create a reverse chronology, and because each scene has to run forwards for the viewer to make sense of it, the beginning of each scene is the same as the end of the following scene. Therefore, when two scenes connect, there isn't a correlation in the story between the end of one scene and the beginning of the next. To help the viewer follow the film, there are stylistically different clips, shot in black and white telling a parallel story, cut in between the reverse narrative scenes. The 'in-between scenes' contain flashbacks to the past and create fragments of a chronologically forward-moving story. On first viewing, the film appears to have a highly complex narrative structure with multiple storylines. However, the analysis shows that the structure repeats itself throughout the film. The apparent complexity of the narrative structure implies that the process of recalling and assembling fragments of a story in a reverse narrative structure is more challenging for the viewer than a conventional Hollywood structure.

In the exhibition 'Botticelli Reimagined' at the Victoria and Albert Museum, the narrative starts in the present and takes the visitor on a journey back in time from the reception of Botticelli's image of beauty and the influences of his work on twenty-first-century and twentieth-century art, to his rediscovery in the nineteenth century, to the final room where the original Botticellis are displayed (Plate 19). To assist the visitor to imagine where the story has come from, contextual images placed throughout the exhibition give a view back into the past to the original works of Botticelli. The contextual images help the visitor to understand the relationship between the original Botticellis and the artworks from the twentieth or nineteenth century. They have a similar narrative function to the black-and-white 'flashback' scenes in the film *Memento*. They create chronologically forward moving narrative fragments, allowing the visitor to compare what was with the time of the artwork they are looking at. These narrative fragments also help the visitor to comprehend the overall structure of the exhibition. A corridor between the nineteenth century and the Renaissance represents omitted time. In film narratology terminology an ellipse takes place, a jump in time breaching the temporal continuum (Verstraten and Lecq 2009: 35) as the visitor moves down a grey corridor towards an image of a self-portrait of Botticelli. The corridor represents the time where Botticelli was forgotten. Botticelli's paintings are installed in the final room at the end of the exhibition experience. The visitor has to recall experiencing the other objects and spaces in order to be able to perceive the end of the exhibition as the beginning of the story.

The comparison between the narrative structure of the film *Memento* and the exhibition 'Botticelli Reimagined' highlights the similarity in the narrative structures between the filmic flashbacks of Lenny's past and the contextual images depicting the original works by Botticelli. Both the flashbacks and the contextual images are forward-moving narrative fragments within an overall reverse chronology helping the viewer/visitor to understand the story. Being able to identify the role of the contextual images within the narrative structure of the exhibition is a technique to structure the anticipated visitor experience.

### *Collage structure*

To mark 500 years since the Reformation, the exhibition 'Luther and the Princes' in Hartenfels Castle, Torgau, Germany, tells the complex story of the Reformation with objects, the portrayal of the characters, and the authentic place. The town of Torgau is described as the political centre of the Reformation. The presentation of the objects in combination with the authenticity of the site create a spectacular window into the story of the development of the modern world. The curatorial intention was to display the objects in the foreground and to respond to the site of the castle and the town as objects in the context of the exhibition, rather than to attempt to create a strong linear narrative. The task of the exhibition architecture was to form a framework for the objects and to express the power of the Reformation encompassing the architecture of the rooms of the castle. The time before and after the Reformation is expressed with a change of materiality and feel of the rooms. In the exhibition, the time before the Reformation is expressed with a red textile covering the surface of the walls and exhibition elements; it represents the pomp and extravagance of the Catholic Church. In the time after the Reformation, the exhibition architecture is stripped back to its substructure, symbolising transparency and a reduction in the value of material wealth in Luther's religious revolution. The exposed timber framework carries the objects and displays the stories of the German princes who supported or opposed the Reformation while allowing the architecture of the castle to be visible. The display of objects, paintings and documents engages the visitor with the complexities of the protagonists' stories through political differences and family ties.

The visitor experience is dependent upon the individual movements of visitors through the spaces and their 'reading' of the objects (Plate 20). Visitors to an exhibition are used to applying associative thinking in the way that they piece together the fragments of narrative. Causal connection in an exhibition is usually made by the spatial proximity of the objects or the themes. The visitor is expected to recognise the spatial cues and move from one object to another. The spatial proximity can also define the chronological or time proximity in that the visitor will see an object next, directly after the previous object. The sequencing of the narrative elements in a novel or a film is sufficient for the viewer or reader to make the causal connection. The spatial causal connections in an exhibition are more difficult to define as they are dependent on the movement and choices of the visitor in the space. Referring to Bal's three-level model of narrative theory mentioned earlier, the 'text' of the exhibition at Hartenfels Castle could be described as a complex layering of authentic architecture, exhibition architecture, graphic representation, objects and their relationships to each other and written text. Collage is perhaps an appropriate term to describe how the visitor interprets the spatial/causal connections of the multi-layered combination of media, form and authentic site as they move through the exhibition environment.

In the movie *Made in USA*, Jean-Luc Godard's cinematic language is open to interpretation because the film structure departs from our typical understanding of narrative logic in the cinema. Susan Sontag (1969: 163) refers to Godard, in a positive sense, as a destroyer of cinema due to his lack of regard for rules of coherence and mise en scène. As she says, 'the narrative of Godard's films is regularly broken or segmented by the incoherence of events and by shifts in tone and level of discourse'. Although the storytelling is vague and the narration fragmentary, the introduction, the main action section and the conclusion are recognisable. However, after the introduction there is a 15-minute scene showing the main character, Paula, in a café. The dialogue with the barman and a worker has no direct reference to the story and doesn't comply with our expectations concerning narrative structure. The fact that Godard's films don't follow strict rules of cinematic narration opens them up for a broader analysis regarding concepts of space and narrative. Godard's cinematic discourse could be compared to the experience of moving through a museum where the attention of the visitor or viewer wanders between themes, details and vistas.

Bordwell (1985: 317) states how critics often referred to Godard's film style as collage and makes an analogy with the artworks of the Parisian cubist artists Picasso and Braque. The fragmentation of the unity of the image in the artworks could be compared to Godard's lack of coherence described by Sontag. Bordwell's analysis leads him to suggest that Godard 'works towards a "spatialization" of narrative'. By inserting images and narrative fragments whose meanings are perhaps not immediately obvious to the viewer, there is a widening of possible interpretations and a less defined telling of the story.

Following Bordwell's analysis of Godard and applying this to the exhibition narrative, the 'spatialized' quality of the narrative is inherent in the physical experience of visiting an exhibition. The narrative style of Godard's films can be an inspiration for thinking about alternative narrative structures that are applicable for museums. The open narrative structure of his films and the lack of importance of causal relationships between scenes and events perhaps have a stronger relationship to the exhibition as a medium than they do to classic Hollywood films. Appropriate perhaps both for the experience of the exhibition in Hartenfels Castle and for the viewing of the Godard film, Mieke Bal would say the narrative is 'under construction', and this is part of the process of viewing (Macdonald and Basu 2007: 75).

## Conclusion

Macdonald and Basu (2007: 9) suggest that to make exhibitions, assemblages of different people, things, ideas, spaces and media have to be brought together. The multidisciplinary nature of the design, and the complexity of understanding how a visitor experiences it, demands that we look beyond the museum for inspiration to further develop the design process and to better understand the possibilities of narrative structures to guide the visitor experience.

The comparative analyses between films and exhibition projects have proved beneficial to understanding the relevance of narrative structures for the visitor in exhibitions where a specific sequential structure and timing of events is necessary for the narrative of the exhibition. The findings also emphasise the importance of key moments of choice, both for the characters in a film and for the visitors of an exhibition. The positioning of these moments of choice for the visitor of an exhibition can be better understood by an analysis of the position of the moments of choice for the protagonists in the narrative of a film.

Exhibitions have a less rigid narrative structure than films due to the variables in the choices the visitor makes regarding their physical movement through the space and their selective process in choosing content and assembling narrative fragments as they move through the exhibition. Although narrative in film plays a different role than narrative in the physical space of the exhibition environment, some elements of the narrative structure in films are relevant for thinking about the visitor experience of exhibitions. Films that have a narrative structure that differ from a classical Hollywood film may offer more possibilities for comparison, as they invite the viewer to make multiple readings. Investigating narrative in films has provided an awareness of narrative structure that can influence the design process, encouraging the designer to think about the sequence and timing of visitor experiences of an exhibition analogous to the viewer of a film.

The research can also assist the practice of museum design in developing new cross-disciplinary collaborations in the area of design, storytelling and narrative theory to create more powerful visitor experiences. The study of the repeat structure of *Run Lola Run* gives an insight into how different story outcomes can be connected by moments of reflection. The reverse chronology of *Memento* reinstates our spatial perception of time and informs us of the challenges we ask of the viewer in assembling narrative fragments in reverse order. The disruptive detours of the story in *Made in USA* denies traditional cinematic discourse of continuity and suspense and invites the viewer to make multiple interpretations of the meaning of the story. This meandering quality of the narrative is itself perhaps more similar to that experienced by a visitor to an exhibition.

The narrative structure of a film is fixed; a film is a product. The sequences and their relationships to each other, defined through the editing process doesn't change and is part of the way the viewer understands the story. The interpretation of the narrative in a museum visit is more varied and is dependent on the relationship of the visitor to the objects, images, space and media, defined by their movement over time. An understanding of the narrative structure of film can suggest reference points for a narrative framework and enable the designer to identify key thresholds and moments of decision in the open, temporal structure of the experience of the museum visit. Feature films offer an experience with an overall length similar to that of a museum visit. Film is a popular medium. Awareness of the experience of watching a film can help us to create more accessible museum experiences looking beyond the museum to broaden the potential of what the museum could be.

## References


*Alexander Nevsky* (1938) Sergei M. Eisenstein [Film] Soviet Union: Mosfilm.

Bal, M. (2009) *Narratology: Introduction to the Theory of Narrative*, 3rd edition, Toronto: University of Toronto Press.

Bordwell, D. (1985) *Narration in the Fiction Film*, Madison, WI: University of Wisconsin Press.

Bruno, G. (2002) *Atlas of Emotion: Journeys in Art, Architecture, and Film*, New York: Verso.

Choisy, A. (1899a) *Histoire de l'architecture. T. 1*, Paris: Baranger.

Choisy, A. (1899b) *Histoire de l'architecture T. 2*, Paris: Baranger.

Duncan, T. and McCauley, N. (2012) 'A Narrative Journey: Creating Storytelling Environments With Architecture and Digital Media' in Macleod, S., Hanks, L.H., and Hale, J. (eds) *Museum Making: Narratives, Architectures, Exhibitions*, Abingdon: Routledge, pp. 288–97.

Eisenstein, S.M. (1948) *The Film Sense*, London: Faber and Faber.

Eisenstein, S.M., Bois, Y.-A., and Glenny, M. (1989) 'Montage and Architecture', *Assemblage*, 10, pp. 111–31.

Freytag, G. (1894) *Freytag's Technique of the Drama: An Exposition of Dramatic Composition and Art* [Translated and edited by E.J. MacEwan], Chicago: Scott, Foresman and Company.

Greenberg, S. (2005) 'The Vital Museum', in MacLeod, S. (ed.) *Reshaping Museum Space: Architecture, Design, Exhibitions*. Abingdon and New York: Routledge, pp. 226–37.

Guerlac, S. (2006) *Thinking in Time: An Introduction to Henri Bergson*, Ithaca, NY: Cornell University Press.

Hale, J. (2012) 'Narrative Environments and the Paradigm of Embodiment', in MacLeod, S., Hanks, L., and Hale, J. (eds) *Museum Making: Narratives, Architectures, Exhibitions*, Abingdon: Routledge, pp. 192–200.

Herman, D. (2009) *Basic Elements of Narrative*, Hoboken, NJ: Wiley.

*Irréversible* (2002) Gaspar Noé (DVD) France: Nord-Ouest Productions/Studio Canal.

Le Corbusier and Schreiber Aujame, E. (1991) *Precisions on the Present State of Architecture and City Planning: With an American Prologue, a Brazilian Corollary Followed by the Temperature of Paris and the Atmosphere of Moscow*, Cambridge, MA: MIT Press.

Macdonald, S. and Basu, P. (2007) *Exhibition Experiments*, Malden, MA: Blackwell.

*Made in USA* (1966) Jean-Luc Godard [DVD] France: Anouchka Films, Rome Paris Films, S.E.P.I.C.

*Memento* (2000) Christopher Nolan [DVD] USA: Summit Entertainment, Team Todd.

*Mystery Train* (1989) Jim Jarmusch [DVD] USA: Mystery Train Inc, Victor Company of Japan, MTI Home Video.

*Run Lola Run* (1998) Tom Tykwer [DVD] Germany: X-Filme Creative Pool, WDR, Arte.

Samuel, F. (2010) *Le Corbusier and the Architectural Promenade*, Basel: Birkhäuser.

Sheets-Johnstone, M. (2009) *The Corporeal Turn: An Interdisciplinary Reader*, Exeter: Imprint Academic.

*Short Cuts* (1993) Robert Altman [DVD] USA: Fine Line Features, Spelling Films International, Avenue Pictures.

Sontag, S. (1969) *Styles of Radical Will*, London: Secker & Warburg.

Verstraten, P. and Lecq, S.V.D. (2009) *Film Narratology*, Toronto: University of Toronto Press.

Vidler, A. (2002) *Warped Space: Art, Architecture, and Anxiety in Modern Culture*, Cambridge, MA: MIT Press.

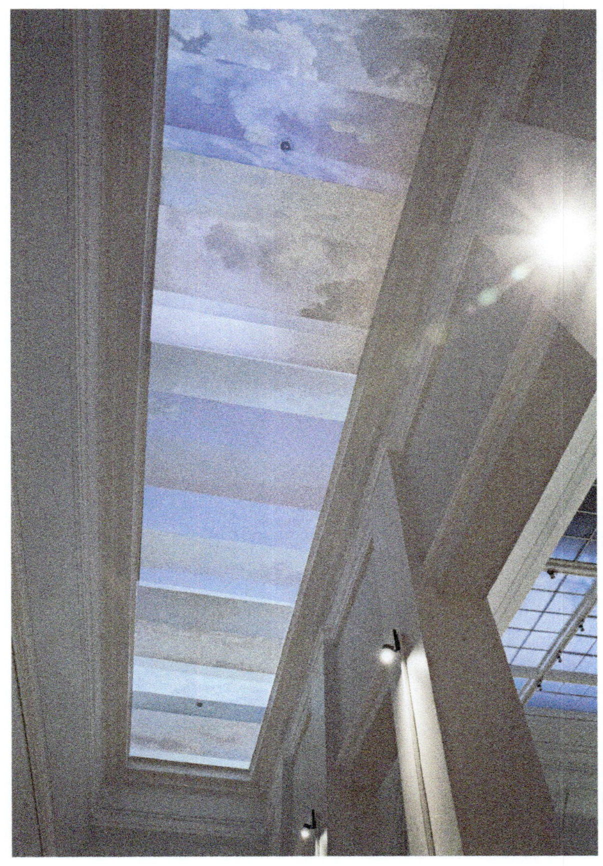

**PLATE 14** '22 Skies' by Filip Vest, *Mix it up*, SMK, 2015

*© Filip Vest. Photo:* Lisbeth Holten.

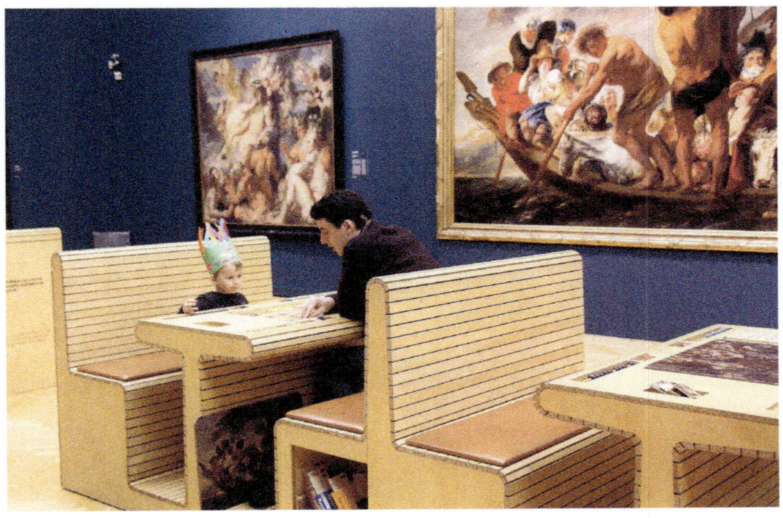

**PLATE 15** 'MatchSMK', permanent collection, SMK

*Photo:* Jenni Fuchs.

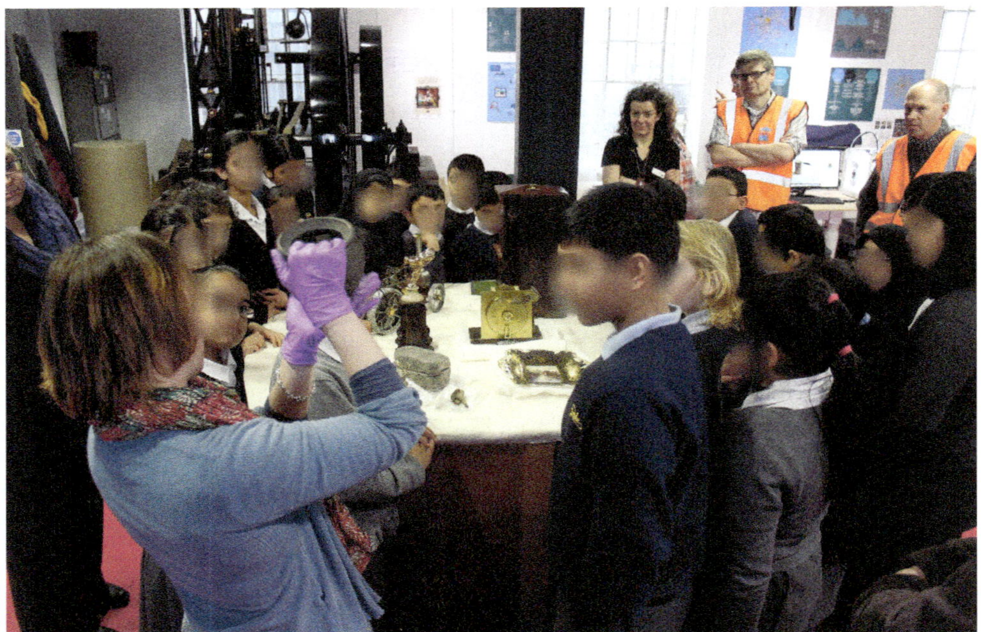

**PLATE 16** Working through the display considerations of objects with young people as part of the Re:Make Phase in 2013

Reproduced with kind permission of Derby Museums Trust.

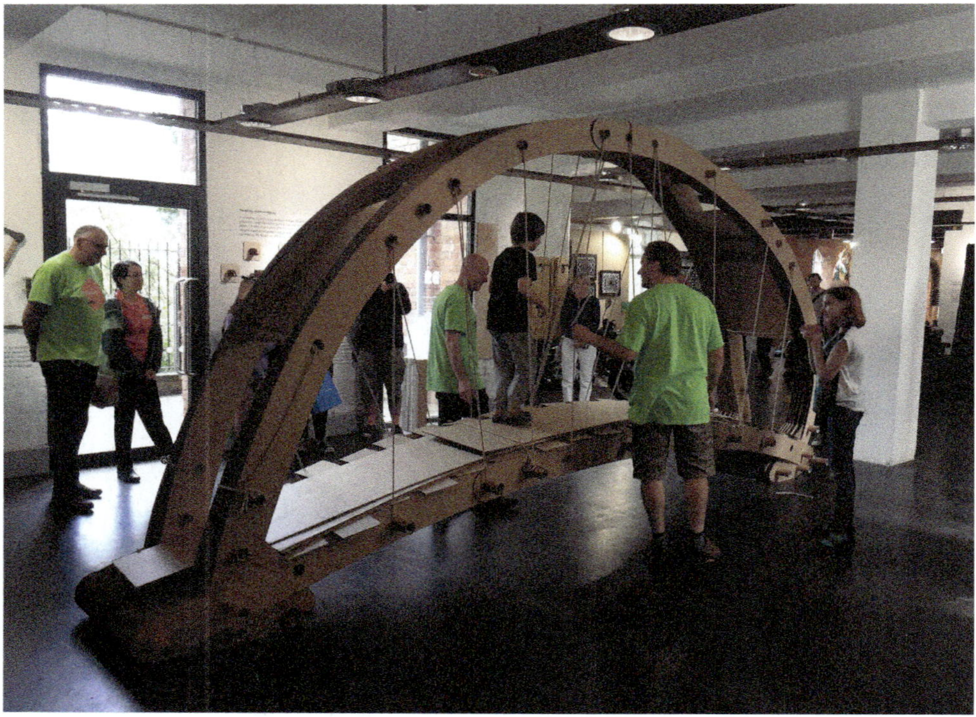

**PLATE 17** A bridge-building workshop with Leach Colour, part of the pilot programme FIGMENT, 2016

Reproduced with kind permission of Derby Museums Trust and Leach Colour.

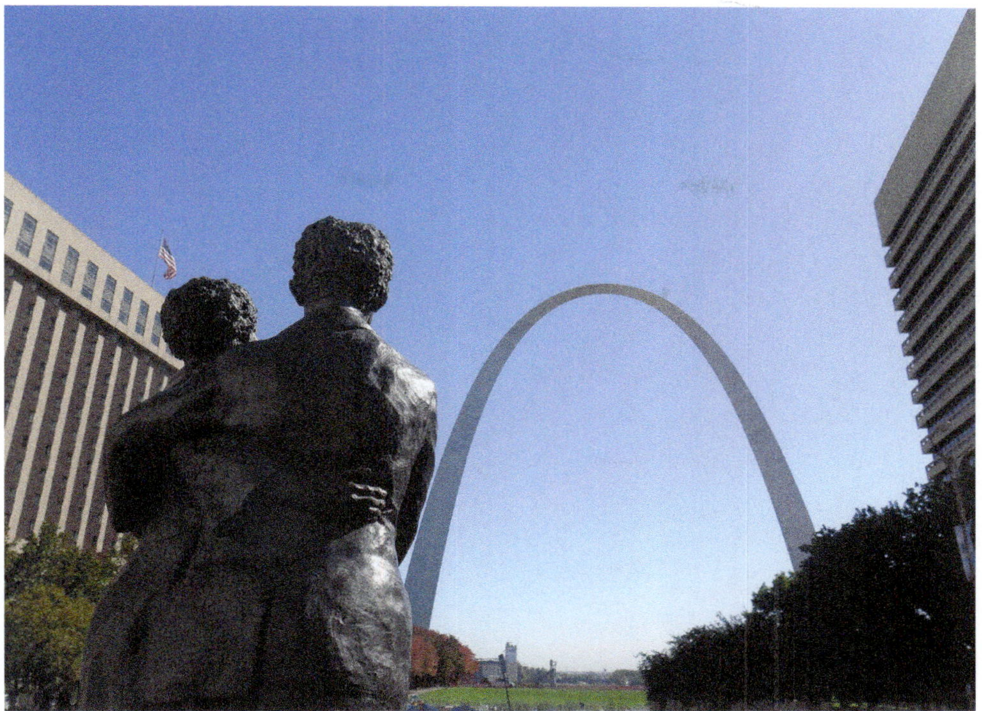

**PLATE 18** Statue of Dred and Harriet Scott located outside the St Louis' Old Courthouse gazing towards The Gateway Arch National Park and across the Mississippi River

*Photo:* Bill Haley.

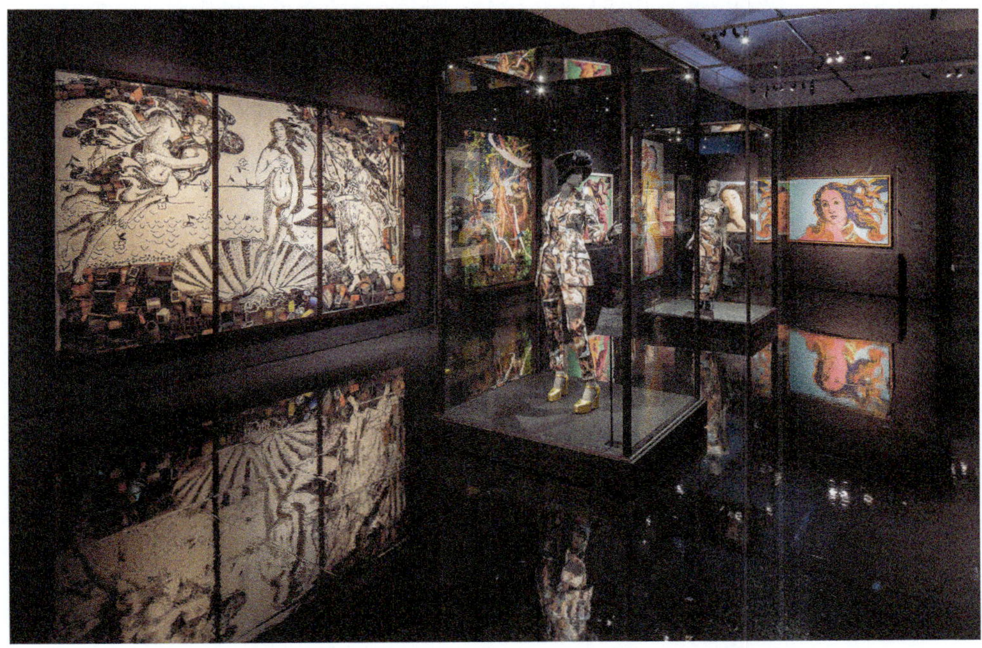

**PLATE 19** The first room of the exhibition 'Botticelli Reimagined, showing twentieth-century art'. Victoria and Albert Museum, 2016

*Photo:* Philipp Obkircher. Reproduced courtesy of the V&A.

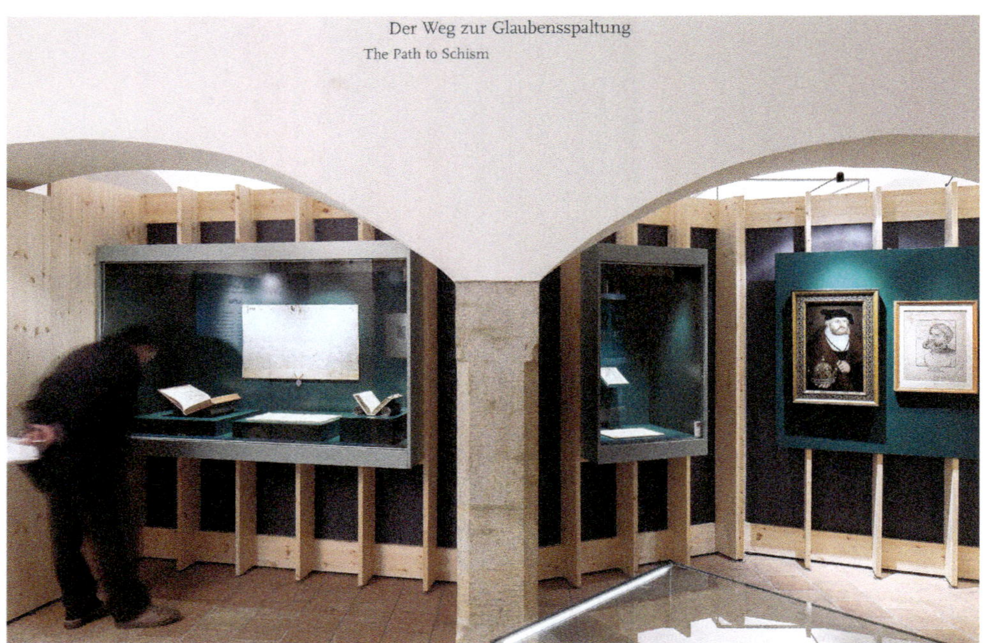


**PLATE 20** An image of the exhibition 'Luther and the Princes', showing the collage-like representation of the multiple layers of media; authentic architecture, room graphic, object, text and exhibition architecture. An exhibition by the Staatlichen Kunstsammlungen Dresden in Hartenfels Castle, Torgau, 2015

*Photo:* Philipp Obkircher.

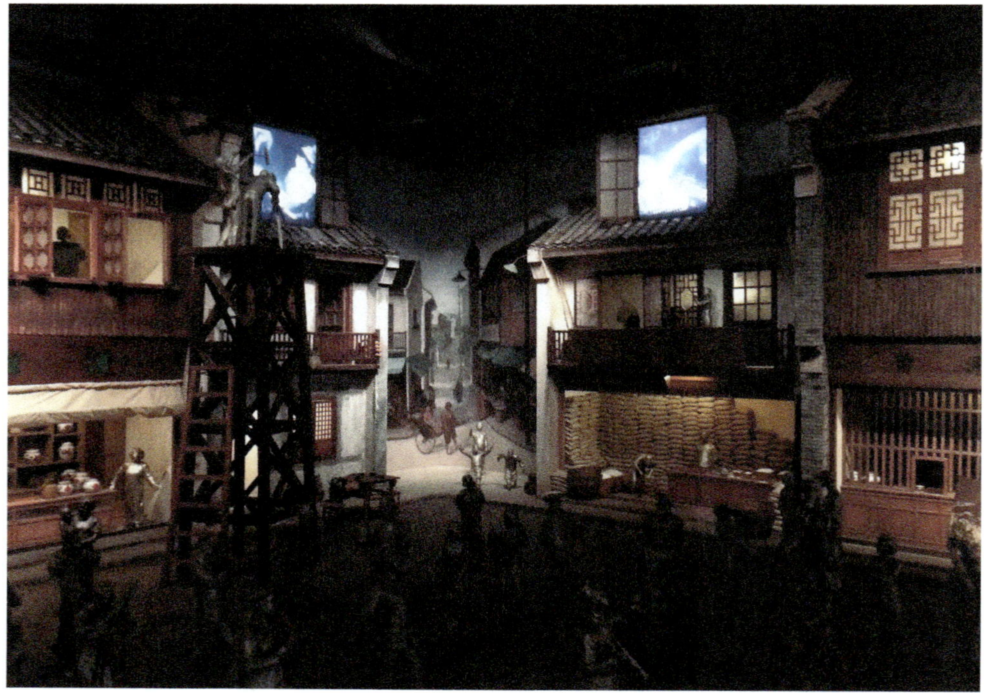

**PLATE 21** Street Angel, *Malu tianshi* (1937) diorama

*Photo:* Author's own, 2014. Reproduced with kind permission of Shanghai Film Museum.

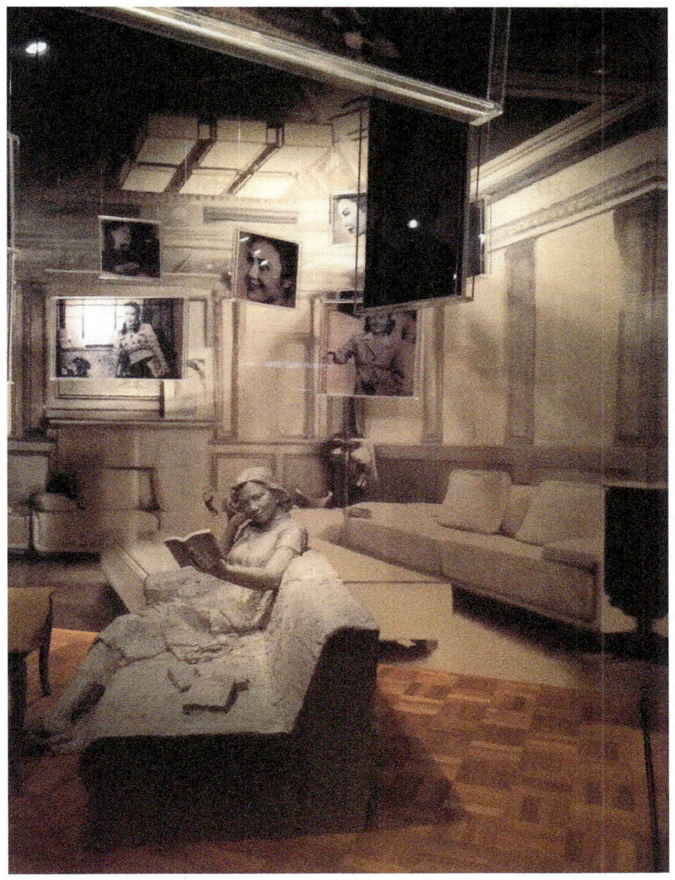

**PLATE 22** Bai Yang diorama

*Photo:* Author's own, 2014. Reproduced with kind permission of Shanghai Film Museum.

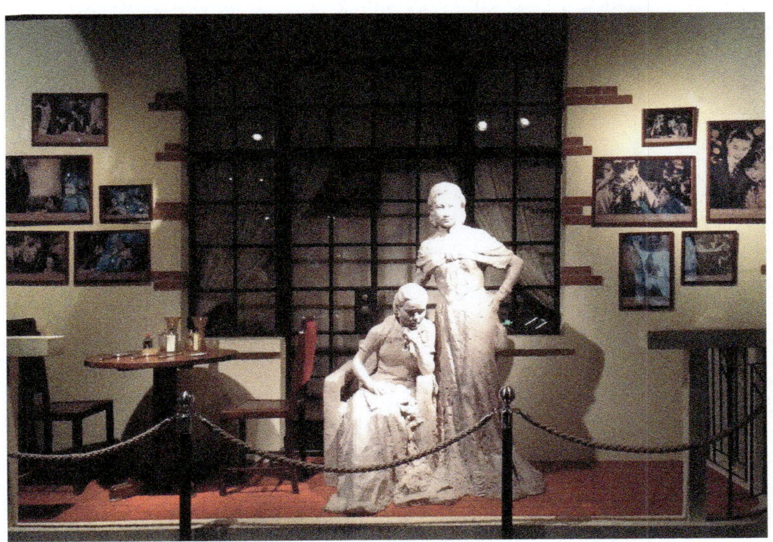

**PLATE 23** Ruan Lingyu and Hu Die diorama

*Photo:* Author's own, 2014. Reproduced with kind permission of Shanghai Film Museum.

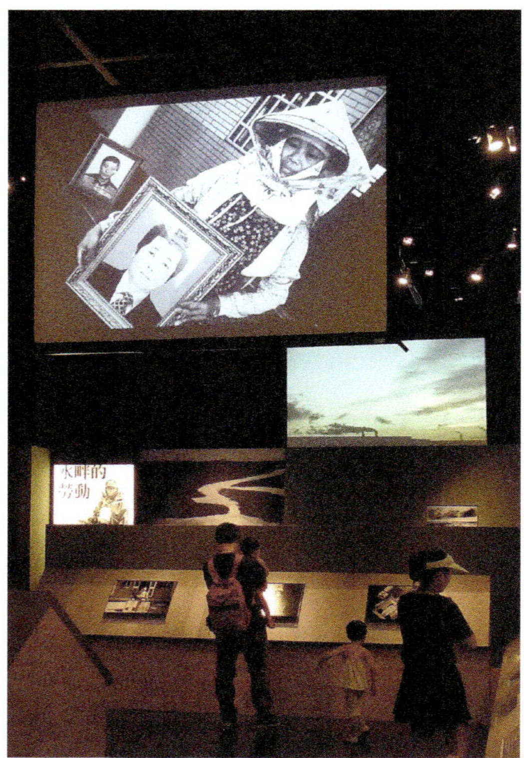


**PLATE 24** The slideshow of photographs of Taixi residents holding photographs of relatives lost to cancer that was screened in Zone D provides a stark foreground for the video playing in Zone E, which shows the Sixth Naphtha Cracker as seen from Taixi's Embankment

*Photo:* Hsu Huang.

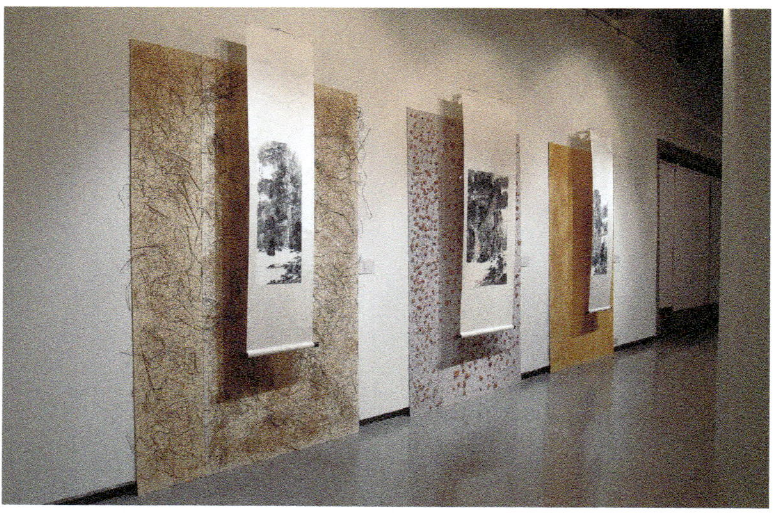

**PLATE 25** In the Yellow Box exhibition, painting scrolls are suspended away from the wall and shown against backdrops made of different materials to highlight the delicate texture of the ink works. 'The Yellow Box: Contemporary Calligraphy and Painting in Taiwan', gallery 3A of TFAM

*Photo:* TFAM.

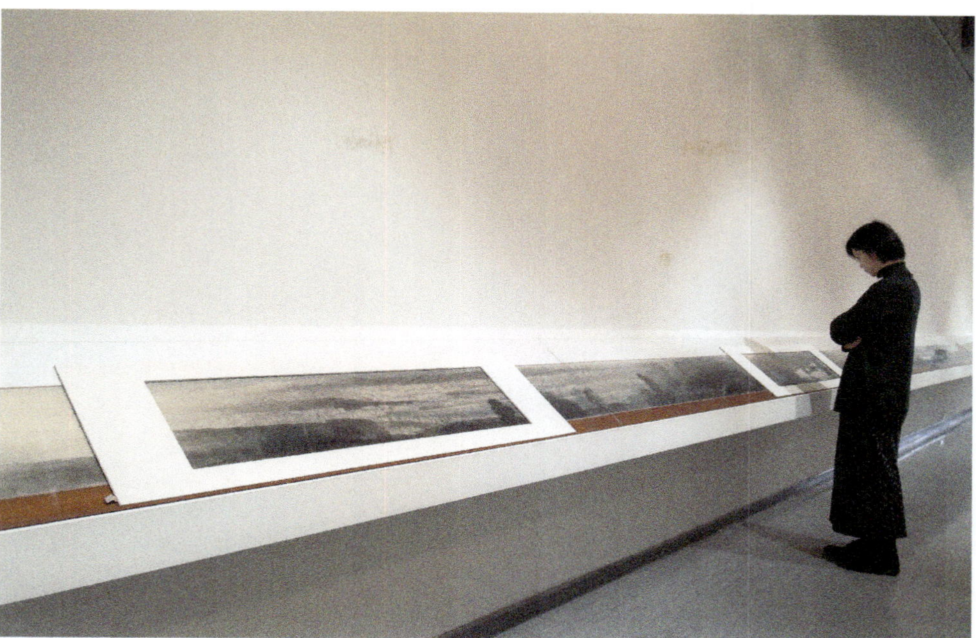

**PLATE 26** Movable viewing frames are installed to encourage viewers to re-frame the handscroll and foster more dynamic interactions with the work. 'The Yellow Box: Contemporary Calligraphy and Painting in Taiwan', gallery 3A of TFAM

*Photo:* TFAM.

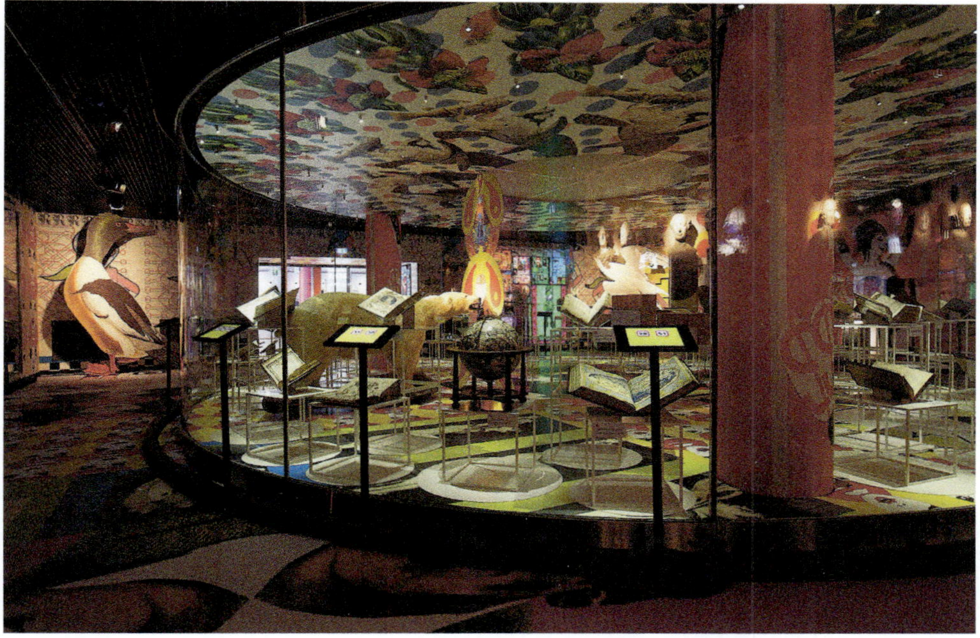

**PLATE 27** 'Treasures' from the Royal Danish Library. Staged by Andrey Bartenev, 2012

*Photo:* Christian Nygaard. Reproduced with kind permission of the Royal Danish Library.

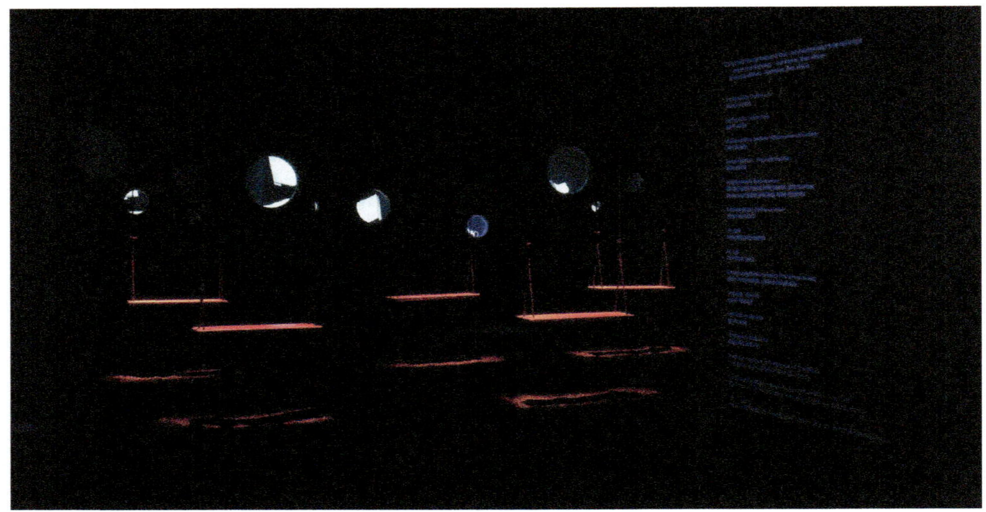

**PLATE 28** 'Everything you can think of is true – the dish ran away with the spoon'. Staged by Robert Wilson, 2008–2009

*Photo:* Lesley Leslie-Spinks. Reproduced with kind permission of the Royal Danish Library.

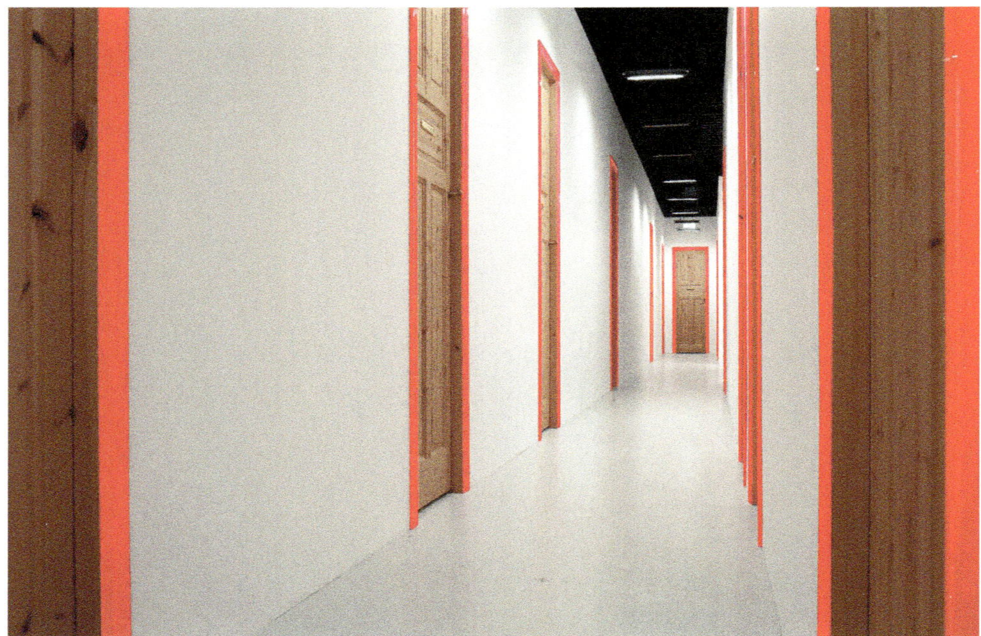

**PLATE 29** 'The Original Kierkegaard'. Designed by Christina Back, 2013

*Photo:* Sidsel Becker. Reproduced with kind permission of the Royal Danish Library.

# PART III

# Perception

## Embodiment, experience and narrative

The chapters in Part III of the book focus on Perception: the nature of the museum experience in all of its sensory, bodily and intellectual richness. They do this in order to consider how the broader notion of design thinking might creatively contribute to new forms of visitor engagement that draw on the full range of spatial and material experience that the museum as a multi-sensory medium uniquely offers. While some chapters draw on historical precedents, such as the Chinese tradition of the 'literati gathering', others reach out to learn from the display strategies employed in other visual disciplines such as filmmaking and installation art.

In Chapter 19, the Hong Kong–based curator Tsong-Zung Chang offers the traditional Chinese *yaji* garden event (literally an 'elegant gathering' of artists and collectors) as a model for a new kind of viewing experience. Opposed to the typical Western museum with its strict separation between object and audience, Chang describes a more participatory experience where artists and collectors met to inspect and discuss their favourite objects. In the case of artworks such as ink drawings and scroll paintings, owners would even add their own appreciative annotations in the form of seals and colophons, which then became part of the 'original'. By directly handling the objects the viewer achieved a more intimate encounter with the work, while at the same time enjoying the distinctive atmosphere of a carefully designed naturalistic environment. As a deliberate provocation to the ingrained Euro-American model of the so-called white cube gallery, Chang coins the term 'yellow box' to describe this alternative scenario.

Chapter 20 focuses on the moving body of the visitor as the key vehicle of museum experience. Linda Johnson describes how the immersive installation format of the diorama has been used to present a cinematic history of Shanghai's modernist period (1911–49). The exhibition transforms what could superficially be seen as simply a nostalgic look back at the films of Shanghai's 'golden age' into a future-oriented vision of a recurring and continuing modernist spirit of revolution, a spirit that still seems so characteristic of the city's identity today.

In Chapter 21, Hsu Huang and Chia-Li Chen – curator and academic, respectively, both based in Taipei – explore the potential of the exhibition as a multi-sensory, multimedia, narrative environment, showing how design can be harnessed to enable visitors to science museums to enjoy active and ongoing engagements with contemporary issues. Purposefully seeking to draw attention to contentious issues and highlight the relations between science, politics and the lives of ordinary people, 'When the South Wind Blows' (shown at the National Museum of Natural Science in Taiwan in 2014) displayed the sufferings of the residents of Taixi Village as a result of polluting chemicals from a nearby industrial plastics factory. The team harnessed interpretive design approaches to create an immersive and symbolic setting which provided a number of contextual cues for a highly structured narrative and a collection of documentary images. The emotional impact of these immersive elements was assessed through an extensive analysis of visitor comments generated as part of the exhibition experience. The analysis also considers the installation's effectiveness in raising people's political awareness – especially regarding the potential ideological conflict between short-term economic profit and long-term environmental protection.

Chapter 22 broadens the palette of the exhibition formats further into time-based experience, this time inspired by the metaphor of the museum-as-theatre. Maja Gro Gundersen and Christina Back of the Royal Danish Library in Copenhagen present a detailed case study of an experimental video installation which was situated within an exhibition of photographs titled 'Imprints of War' (2014). A single enlarged black-and-white landscape image was presented at one end of a 'stage-set' black-box viewing space which was separated off from the main display. This image was then overlaid with a projected video sequence, accompanied by an enigmatic but emotive musical soundtrack. Visitor research again demonstrated the emotional and intellectual impact of highly interpretive gallery design, where a carefully controlled immersive environment provides a set of contextual cues for the viewer's 'reading' of the artwork – though this time without reliance on gallery text and labels.

Ariane Karbe's chapter takes the theme of cinema to consider the effect of suspense on the experience of the museum visitor. By drawing on the techniques of Hollywood scriptwriters and dramatists who attempt to draw film viewers into a suspenseful story in the hope of retaining their attention throughout the length of the movie, in Chapter 23 Karbe suggests that much can be learnt about how to structure a museum visit in a way that similarly invites the visitor to speculate creatively about the 'outcome' of the story. Through a careful analysis of the design of a historical exhibition of her own devising, she echoes some of the findings reported earlier in this book in the chapter written by Tom Duncan.

In the penultimate chapter and speaking back to Chapter 19, Vivian Ting, a curator and academic based in Hong Kong, presents a detailed explanation of the driving principles behind exhibitions that aim to translate the traditional *yaji* experience into a contemporary 'yellow box' exhibition format. Even when the artwork is too precious or fragile for visitors to handle directly, Ting suggests various ways in which a more physically interactive encounter can still be achieved. This might involve, for example, movable viewing devices as a way of engaging the visitor's bodily interaction in an extended process of looking. Drawing attention to a lack of detailed visitor research, Ting highlights the need for more research if we are to really begin to understand the role of these devices in multiple and complex experiences.

Finally, in Chapter 25, Jonathan Hale and Christina Back continue to explore the broader question of the role of bodily experience in the visitor's engagement with the objects and spaces of the museum. Drawing on the philosophy of Maurice Merleau-Ponty and recent research in neuropsychology on so-called embodied cognition, a theoretical framework is proposed for interpretive design as a way of better understanding the contribution that the architectural setting can make to the experience of the exhibition within it. This framework also takes account of the current revival of interest in embodied, sensory engagement in museums, alongside the increasing significance of materiality, such as in the paradigm of the 'Yellow Box'.

# 19

# YAJI GARDEN

## Art under the sky

*Tsong-Zung Chang and Shiming Gao*

### Abstract

This chapter proposed the Chinese *yaji* garden event (literally an 'elegant gathering' of artists and collectors) as a model for a new kind of viewing experience. Opposed to the typical Western museum with its strict separation between object and audience, Chang describes a more participatory experience where artists and collectors met to inspect and discuss their favourite objects. In the case of artworks such as ink drawings and scroll paintings, owners would even add their own appreciative annotations in the form of seals and colophons, which then became part of the 'original'. By directly handling the objects, the viewer achieved a more intimate encounter with the work, while at the same time enjoying the distinctive atmosphere of a carefully designed naturalistic environment. As a deliberate provocation to the ingrained Euro-American model of the so-called white cube gallery, Chang coins the term 'yellow box' to describe this alternative scenario.

### Introduction

With often-used sobriquets such as 'White Cube' (canonized by Brian O'Doherty in his seminal series of essays first published in *Artforum* in 1976 and reproduced in O'Doherty 1999), it is inevitable that in the popular imagination the idea of art and its context of display have been entwined with its architectural site. Indeed, celebrity museum architecture has become the norm for contemporary times, and art spaces are acknowledged prestige projects for architects. It was symptomatic when the brilliant visionary (but much vilified) Thomas Krens made it one of his first endeavors as director of the Guggenheim Museum to restore the original architecture by Frank Lloyd Wright, and continued to collaborate with celebrated architects to develop successful offspring of architecturally defined Guggenheim affiliates in places as unlikely as Las Vegas and Bilbao. In modern society, the 'fine art museum' (modern or contemporary) is recognized all over the world as a necessary institution for a civilized, developed society, even in countries where a history of fine art has long been celebrated without such an institution. In China it is claimed that hundreds of new museums are on course, either just recently opened or in the process of being built. In this context, the concept of *yaji garden* is proposed as a reminder of the historical form of art site in China, existing outside the walls of architecture and constituting a different approach to the engagement with art and the notion of exhibition.

What the emphasis on architecture points to is the necessity for an art site to be identified as a public place promising special experiences. Concomitantly, this site is the place where the transformation of an artifact into 'art' is recognized. The power of endorsing what qualifies as art is what makes the museum/art site so special, especially today when the idea of art is changing so rapidly that many of the new artistic practices are unrecognizable to the public. There are no clear processes through which the 'art-ness' embodied in an artifact reveals itself. However, the institutional construct of art (bringing together the edifice of the museum, the historical study of art, and critical and endorsement mechanisms) assures us that certain things are 'art things' and others are not.

A principal instrument for this assurance is the physical museum, the container of exhibitions and the repository of artworks, which through its architecture proclaims itself as a serious work of art worthy of (or even loftier than) its contents. The comparison often made here is with the religious temple, but there is a critical difference between the two institutions: the temple contains powers already recognized by the public, and its content has no need for endorsement, whereas the intrinsic worth of the 'art thing' is not self-evident. As O'Doherty states,

> A gallery is constructed along laws as rigorous as those for building a medieval church. Walls are painted white. The ceiling becomes the source of light. . . . In this context a standing ashtray becomes almost a sacred object.
>
> *(O'Doherty 1999: 15)*

The *yaji garden* diverges from this presumption from the start. It is not a public institution, as it consists of private spaces, and in principle does not represent the ideological order of the state; and yet as a site of display and connoisseurship, the *yaji garden* is a historically recognized institution. One might call it an institution endorsed by 'custom'. The *yaji garden* is a physical embodiment of the traditional Chinese mode of art connoisseurship. Meaning 'elegant gathering', *yaji* also has the implications of a 'literati gathering': the meeting of learned and refined scholars.

Traditionally, the *yaji* is a communion of artistic friends and associates who meet to enjoy art and performances in private gardens attached to private residences. The gardens typically contain artificial mountains and brooks created in the spirit of Chinese landscape painting. Ideally, one would prefer to build a garden around an actual idyllic site in nature instead of constructing artificial rockery. As the Ming dynasty scholar Wen Zhenheng (1585–1645) suggested in his celebrated book about refined taste: 'The preferred choice is to live amidst mountains and waters; country village living is second best, and living outside an urban town is the third' (Wen 1984). For the example of ultimate extravagance for the concept of a garden, there exists a first-person account by the missionary Jean Denis Attiret (1702–1768), who in 1743 spent several months in the imperial garden Yuan Ming Yuan in Beijing, as official painter under the employ of Emperor Qianlong (Attiret 1749).

The origin of *yaji* is ancient, and the concept and practice have had a continuous history until the present day; even in modern times this practice continues within Chinese society, albeit in mode and style adapted to the present. In general, *yaji* may justifiably be identified as the archetypal 'exhibition practice' of pre-modern China. Historically, the most celebrated *yaji* event is probably the 'Gathering at the Orchid Pavilion' in 353 CE, at which Wang Xizhi (canonized in the seventh century as the Sage of Calligraphy by Emperor Taizong of the Tang Dynasty) wrote the famous calligraphic text *Preface to the Anthology of Orchid Pavilion*. This piece of calligraphy by Wang Xizhi was beloved by Emperor Taizong, who invited leading scholar-calligraphers of his day to make interpretative copies of the original. Until this day, Wang's text (through its seventh-century copies) remains the paradigmatic copy model for every serious student of calligraphy (Figure 19.1). For a modern audience unfamiliar with the *yaji* tradition, it is important to first examine the questions of what precisely happens during the 'literati gathering'. What are its implications for the experience of art, and in what ways does it differ from the modern museum?

There are two components that constitute the *yaji garden* experience: the *yaji* activity and the site of the garden. If we translate this experience to the modern museum, these components would correspond to the visitor's experience and the architectural edifice containing the exhibition display. Here one sees a fundamental difference in emphasis: the success of a *yaji* experience is contingent on the gathering, therefore the success of the event depends as much on the dynamics generated by the participants as on the art being displayed. For the museum, the emphasis is on its function as an edifice of material display. Today the museum is also open to occasional participatory events and 'happenings', and it collects records of ephemeral activities that appear within and outside its domain demonstrating various art 'processes', but its main concern is clearly with collecting, whether actual artworks or archives, and visitors are there to be educated, and share a discourse shaped by the institution. As museum historian Tony Bennett has suggested:

> The exhibitionary complex was a response to the problem of order, but one which worked in seeking to transform that problem into one of culture – a question of winning hearts and minds as well as the disciplining and training of bodies. . . . Through the provision of object lessons in power – the power to command and arrange things and

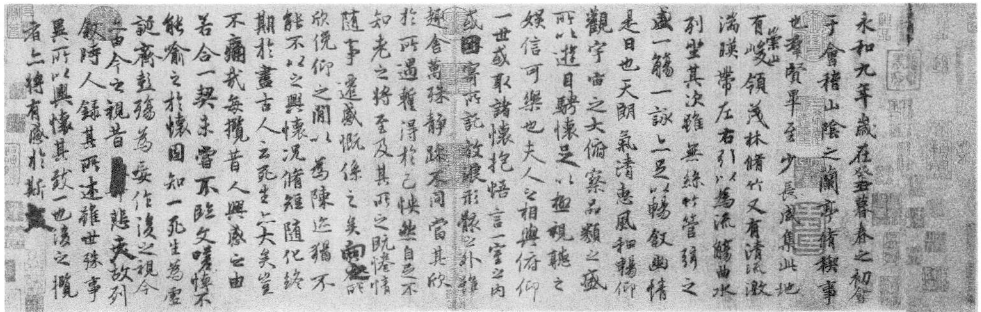

**FIGURE 19.1** Copy by Feng Chengsu (c. 627–50) of Jin-dynasty (265–420) calligrapher Wang Xizhi's (c. 303–61) original calligraphic masterpiece Lantingji xu (Preface to the Anthology of the Orchid Pavilion). Collection of the Palace Museum, Beijing

Illustration courtesy of the Palace Museum, Beijing

> bodies for public display – they sought to allow the people, and *en masse* rather than individually, to know rather than be known, to become the subject rather than the objects of knowledge. . . . to become, in seeing themselves from the side of power and what power knows, and knowing themselves as (ideally) known by power, interiorizing its gaze as a principle of self surveillance and, hence self regulation.
>
> *(Bennett 1988: 76)*

## Play and connoisseurship

Seen in the light of the modern museum, the salient feature of the *yaji garden* is its role as a site for 'playing' (*wan*, or play, is a word commonly used in place of more formal words for connoisseurship), and for providing an apparatus for engendering the 'aesthetic moment'. The Chinese word for such a moment of inspiration is *xing* (pronounced 'shing'); *xing* means to be inspired or lifted to creativity.[1] Typically, a *yaji* gathering starts with an invitation from a host who provides a pretext for the event, which may be a seasonal holiday, appreciation of a seasonal flower, sharing of antiques or new (or newly acquired) artworks. The guests would be expected to share their own art, and take part in the connoisseurship by artistic responses such as composing poetry and commentary, or simply engaging in conversation.

In a *yaji* gathering, play is fundamental. Through the enjoyment of art the *yaji* gathering brings participants back to the primordial cultural experience of playing, a feature that defines and creates human society. Johan Huizinga surmised that for *homo ludens* 'play is older than culture, for culture, however inadequately defined, always supposed society, and animals have not waited for man to teach them their playing' (Huizinga 1949: 1). He went as far as to claim that '[civilisation] arises *in* and *as* play, and never leaves it' (Huizinga 1949: 173). In the *yaji garden* play has been guided by a particular cultural regime of connoisseurship to encourage 'players' to share the experience of inspired art making. The words *wan* (play) and *shang* (appreciation/connoisseurship) are often used in the compound form *wan-shang*, 'play-connoisseurship', to indicate the integral link between playing and appreciation. In other words, connoisseurship is conceived as a form of engaged playing, with the intention of arriving at an inspired lifting of the spirit (*xing*) (Chen 2002).

Playing is necessarily participatory, therefore the terms of contemporary participatory art might be one way to conceive the *yaji* experience. However, the *yaji garden* is a participatory experience specifically defined by a history of art that melds literature, painting and critical writing. It also presumes a cosmology that views mountains and the natural world as offering direct access to a transcendent experience, and providing a context for the inspired lifting that leads to personal connoisseurship/creativity.

## Power of display and spontaneity of play

The *yaji* event takes place in a garden and its attached residence, usually accompanied by music and other cultivated activities like the appreciation of incense, seasonal flowers and teas. In such an ambient surrounding, participants are expected to be alert to form an immediate artistic engagement. Unlike the emphasis of the modern museum on passive visuality, *yaji* is a tactile, immersive experience: the Chinese traditional painting format of hanging and rolled scrolls, which requires handling by the viewer, is indicative of the spirit of tactile corporeal involvement. The demand on both host and guest to articulate their aesthetic response dispels passive spectatorship, and conspires instead to bring out the 'aesthetic moment'.

Major historical *yaji* gatherings are remembered by anthologies of poetry and essays that result from the events, which arguably form a loose record of China's 'history of exhibition' before the age of exhibition (in the modern sense) arrived in China in the first decades of the twentieth century. Unlike private salons and cultural gatherings in the West, which have been replaced by the paradigm of museum exhibition, the *yaji* has continued to form the recognized locus of connoisseurship and display of 'literati art' in China.[2] One major reason for this is the continuity of its format, which is tied to a specific type of site, the *yaji garden*. A legitimate art institutional site presupposes the power to endorse and legitimise 'art', which is also the function served by the *yaji garden*. However, unlike modern institutions, the *yaji garden* has no official status and it is only defined as an art site by the activities that happen within its walls. Not only is the garden at most times a private space for pleasure, but literati gatherings do not actually guarantee recognition of artworks apart from the private circulation of opinions that might or might not build their public reputation. In what ways, then, is the *yaji garden* 'institutional' in a way that may compare with the white cube museum?

The modern museum is a social institution created to serve the modern 'public', a creature of the civic urban world endowed with its own social regime and benefits. A 'citizen', as a member of the public, is entitled by right to modern institutions of social services, and this right is exactly the term of democracy not granted the pre-modern Chinese. However, there is a trade-off with this right of access as it presupposes a new form of social regime that requires the modern public to defer to a new authority of knowledge, who speaks and negotiates on behalf of the uninitiated individual. In the modern museum system, the public does not share in the legitimation of artworks; this right is reserved for the art professionals. By contrast, the *yaji* gathering is a private event, and the audience is invited guests. The relation between the organiser and participants is 'host' and 'guest'. Historically the artistic authority of *yaji* gatherings relied on the reputation of the participants, much like the consensus of today's art circle and, like the modern art circle of cultural intellectuals, they shared a common knowledge base and held comparable social status as 'literati'. But there is a fundamental difference between the modern critical intellectual and the pre-modern literati: whatever their occupation or social circumstance, the literati were of the same 'class' of the learned (here referring to those sharing a similar worldview) that constituted the cultural critical sector as well as those wielding political power in office. In China's pre-modern days, up to the first decade of the twentieth century, artistically minded scholar-officials would host *yaji* parties, and a common villager would expect his district governor to be proficient at writing poetry as part of his claim to office. In the pre-modern *yaji garden*, through the constituency of its members, art and politics met on the ground of aesthetics.

Although the *yaji garden* is not an official institution, within its walls the quality of artworks are judged and legitimated by participants who represent the cultural order of Chinese society. The *yaji garden's* legitimacy as 'institution' is more by right of customary practice than right of law, and events hosted in the garden might be called 'institutionalized happenings', wherein artworks are deemed to perform their function as 'art' through evoking aesthetic responses from the participants.

The above described process of legitimation of art has a distinct pre-modern character: not only is it independent of an institutionalized class of professional experts, the reliance on a mode of connoisseurship that depends largely on cultivated taste and personal practice lacks the theorized form of rigor to which moderns are accustomed. Here it is instructive to compare a parallel aesthetic sentiment in Europe that met its demise in the eighteenth century, through an analysis by Bernard Stiegler (2016). Stiegler's interpretation of a famous debate between the Amateur and the Expert highlights an issue that is usually overshadowed by the understandable enthusiasm for the democratization of social power. Stiegler's attention was on two different processes of knowledge acquisition, one developed through critical connoisseurship by 'copying' and cultivation of personal sensitivity, and the other developed through the analytical faculty. Underlying the original conflict between 'natural taste' and 'theory' is the former's claim to authority of artistic judgment based on non-utilitarian passion for art and personal skill in analytical 'copying', a sign of the true Amateur. The Amateur involved in this particular debate in 1759, the Comte de Caylus, emphasized the importance of analytical copying as a form of close 'reading' (*graphein*), upon which 'natural taste' was founded. On the other hand, the Expert, represented by Denis Diderot of *Encyclopaedia* fame, champion of the epoch of the Republic of Letters, claimed that the new reading public could judge art through their individual sentiments without such privileged cultivation. Stiegler sees symbolized in this dispute an epochal shift in the way that knowledge is transmitted: from the corporeal practice of copying/writing (*graphein*) through which one's own critical judgment is formed, shifting to a reliance on another form of 'writing' that is speculative and 'professional', which later in the epoch of cultural industries molds a public that relinquishes its capacity to judge to the critical intellectuals. Stiegler calls this modern public the 'proletarized consumers'.

A comparable quarrel in the case of China's literati did not emerge until the beginning of the twentieth century, when the urban 'public' arrived with China's revolutionized National Republic, established in 1911 with the overthrow of the Qing dynasty (and by extension the dynastic system).[3] Although the technological and social turn that created the new public did, over the past century, eventually go the way of Stiegler's 'proletarized consumers', memory of the Amateur in the form of the literati has lingered in China. Today, artists who carry on the tradition of literati art continue to shun the label of 'professionalism' and seek the endorsement of connoisseurs whose tastes are formed through the deep reading of classical literature and personal practice of *shuhua* (calligraphy/painting), even though the literati class itself has disappeared with modernization.

However, as regards the notion of copying/writing propounded by the Comte de Caylus, there is a fundamental difference between European and Chinese art history. In the case of Caylus, his copying/writing would secure his authority as a connoisseur and recognized arbiter of artistic taste, but never as an artist in his own right. In China's literati history, not only were the critical connoisseurs Amateurs in the sense of Caylus, but established artists also insisted on labeling themselves literally as Amateurs (*yeyu*), and prided themselves on their insights derived from the practice of copying the ancients. For the literati, copying was not just the connoisseur's training tool, but the very foundation for inspired lifting and inventive improvisation, out of which original art of exceptional aesthetic quality could arise.

The site of the *yaji* gathering, the garden, is constructed to be conducive to the experience of art, suitable for 'teasing out' the 'aesthetic moment'. What this implies is not only should the garden embody the terms of aesthetics of Chinese fine art, but it is also designed as a site for opening up the artistic imagination. The traditional term for aesthetic imagination is *yijing*, meaning literally the 'intentional realm', or 'aesthetic realm'. As a secluded site removed from the humdrum life of the mundane world, the garden's realm of aesthetics liberates the mind to partake in the livingness of nature and dynamics of the cosmos. The garden is built to evoke an idyllic natural site, the same principle used in landscape painting. In an ideal situation, the garden should be a catalyst for linking with the cosmos. As the Ming dynasty literatus Ji Cheng wrote in the chapter 'Yuan shuo' (Garden Theory) of his treatise *Yuan ye* (Creating Gardens):

> Gardens can be built in villages or in towns. It is best if sited away from urban centers, with plants cut from wild groves. Sceneries should be created according to the site, and orchids cultivated where there is a living brook.
>
> *(Ji 1988)*

## The time for aesthetics

One might loosely claim that the aim of literati art represents a pursuit of the cosmic realm through connecting with nature and great artworks of the past and present. Art is experienced in the garden with the garden as witness and reminder that livingness means the pleasure of communion with creatures and things of the world. As a famous fourteenth-century poem by Weng Sen says, 'birds on the branches are my friends, petals drifting on the pond resemble fine literature' (Weng c. 1350). The *yaji garden* is a site for art that aspires to communion with nature among friends who share this appreciation. The culture of interactive connoisseurship is reflected in the attitude towards the treatment of antiquities: old masterworks are not simply venerated as objects of the past, but brought 'up to date' through the tradition of continuous commentaries and poetry that are written in elegant calligraphy and attached as addenda to the original artwork. This is the reason for the numerous collectors' seals on old Chinese master paintings and calligraphy. By contrast with the modern museum, which hastens to historicize (or museum-ize) artworks, the literati treated artworks as living projects. The incorporation of fresh critical responses into old artworks demonstrates an implicit resistance against museum-ization. With each fresh colophon the artwork's story continues, pending commentary from the next deserving connoisseur.

A famous example of this process can be found in the history of the Yuan-dynasty masterpiece *Dwelling in the Fuchun Mountains*, by the literati artist Huang Gongwang (Figure 19.2). On the original scroll are inscribed many seals and colophons added by artists, collectors and connoisseurs over the centuries. This celebrated painting is also one of the most important paradigms of Chinese landscape painting history, and it has been studied, copied and imitated by countless artists over the centuries, with painstaking copies and interpretations undertaken by such illustrious traditional masters as Shen Zhou (1427–1509) and Wang Yuanqi (1642–1715). The illustration of Huang Gongwang's painting (shown here in two sections, as it was damaged by fire in the seventeenth century and remained in two pieces ever since, each owned by different collectors) is accompanied by two copies of the handscroll by two modern artists: one by the twentieth-century master Wu Hufan (1894–1968) and the other by contemporary painter Zheng Li (b. 1964) (Figure 19.3). Wu Hufan was also an important collector, and in 1938 he acquired the first section of Huang Gongwang's scroll, a short section that was detached from the original. In 1939, Wu Hufan made a photographic print of the two sections of the painting and in 1954 he painted a copy of the fully reconstructed painting, adding in his own interpretation of small sections missing because of fire damage. The other imitation of Huang's scroll illustrated here is by the contemporary painter Zheng Li who, as a technical challenge, copied the work by painting the entire composition in reverse,

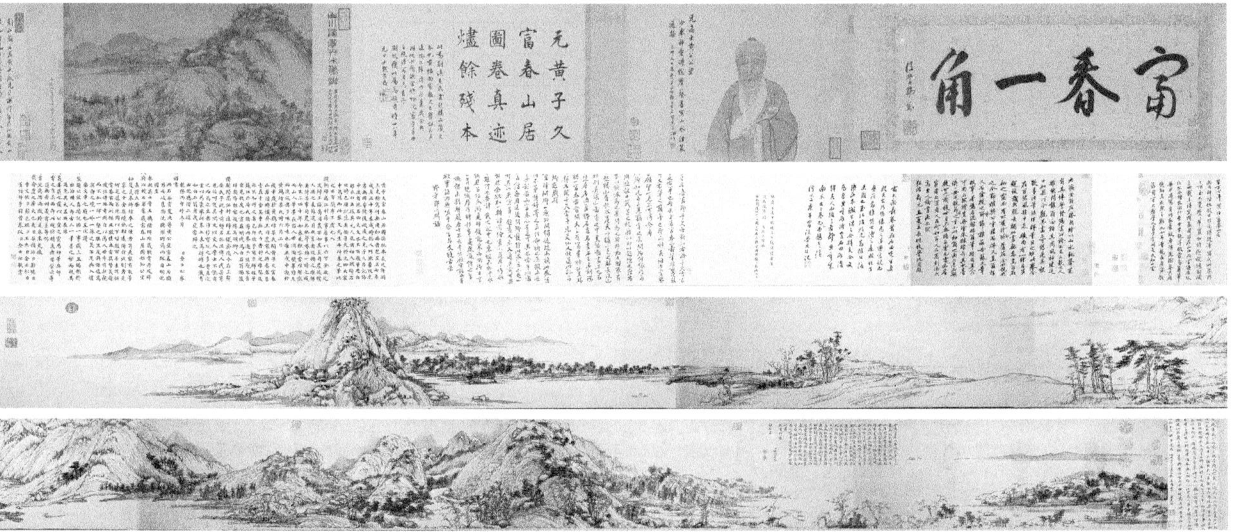


**FIGURE 19.2** Yuan dynasty masterpiece *Dwelling in the Fuchun Mountains*, by the literati artist Huang Gongwang. In the collection of the Zhejiang Provincial Museum, Hangzhou and the National Palace Museum, Taipei

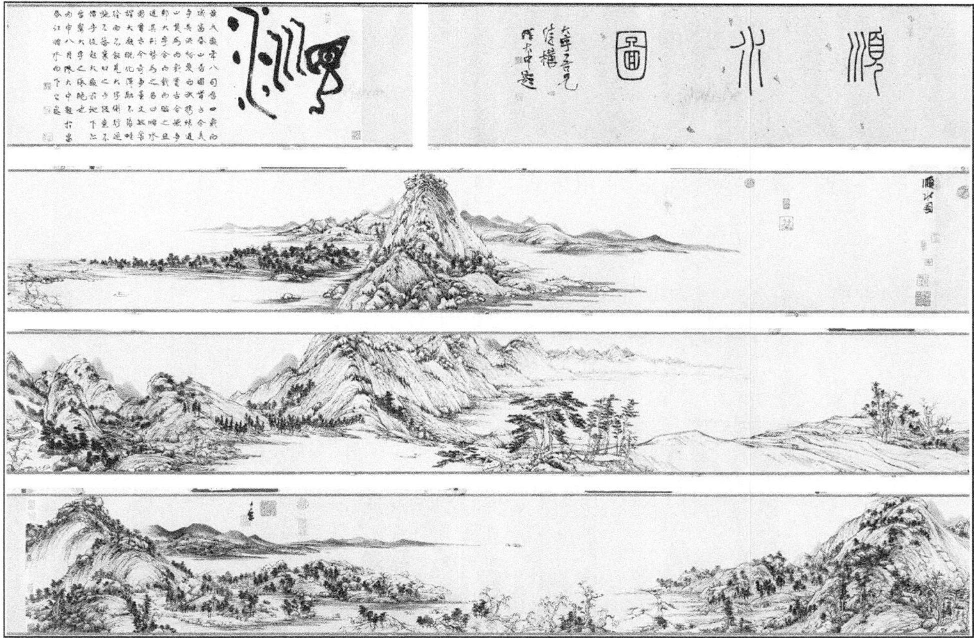

**FIGURE 19.3** Zheng Li (b. 1964), *Downstream*, 2016. Handscroll: ink and colour on paper, 35 cm × 696 cm

Courtesy of the artist, Zheng Li

so that the viewer is confronted with scenery going downstream instead of upstream; thus the painting turns into a mirror image of the original. In this version Zheng Li also gives his own interpretation of the section lost in fire. Both Zheng Li and Wu Hufan also add new elements to the handscroll, including colophons and seals.

In a spirit comparable to the writing of colophons and copying old masters, contemporary artist Yeh Wei-Li (b. 1971) pays tribute and also offers contemporary significance to the work of the late modern painter Yeh Shih-Chiang (1926–2012) by restoring and photographing his derelict studio. He archives and reworks the old painter's discarded rubbish as museum-ized relics, and adds them to the installation of Yeh Shih-Chiang's paintings so that the old artist comes alive in the contemporary exhibition context (Figure 19.4). The additional interpretations become the younger artist's personal artworks, while at the same time they give a new lease on life to the art of Yeh Shih-Chiang. In the meantime, Yeh Shih-Chiang's restored and reinterpreted studio at its original site in Taiwan gradually emerges as a re-energized contemporary site for encounter, engagement and gatherings of both an aesthetic and scholarly nature, within a context of continuity and congruity with the past.

Implicit in the *yaji garden*'s practice is a view of art fundamentally different from the traditional European aesthetics of re-presentation. The artistic pursuit of *yijing* (intentional/aesthetic realm) implies self-discovery as integral to unveiling the mystery of the world. The *yaji garden* experience is designed to provide a congenial condition to evoke the intended *yijing*, so as to draw its strength from powers greater than the isolated artwork, and return art to the cosmic (natural) context from which it arose. In his celebrated text *Renjian cihua* (A Study

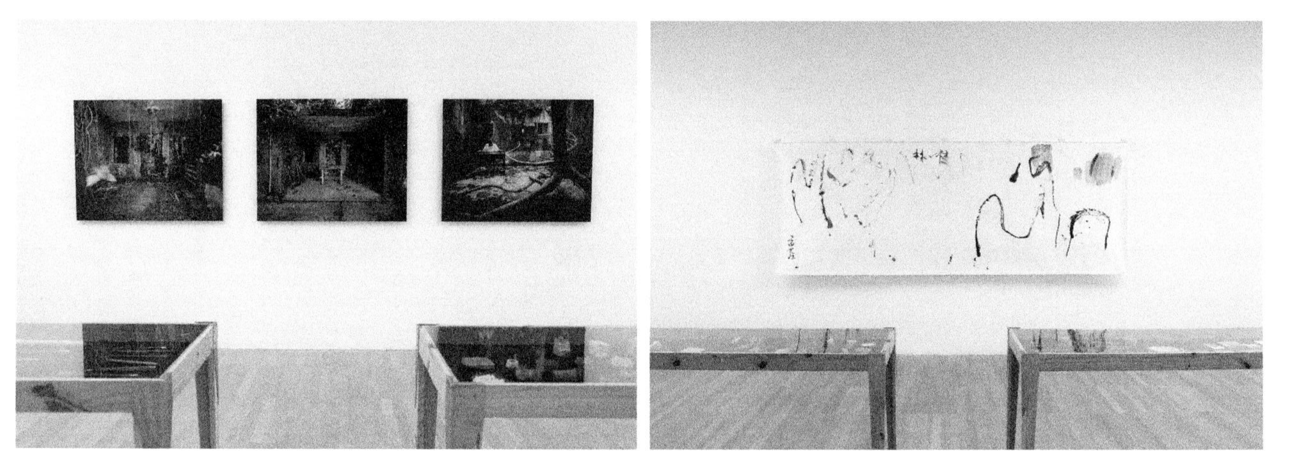

**FIGURE 19.4** Left: Installation view of one part of *Illuminated Presence* project featuring photographs and installation of artefacts by Yeh Wei-Li (b. 1971). Right: Painting by Yeh Shih-Chiang (1926–2012). Shown at International Triennial of Slovenia, 2016

*Photo:* Kokyi Chan

on Literary Criticism), published in 1909, the literary theorist Wang Guowei (1877–1927) proposed another term for *yijing* or 'intentional realm': this was *jingjie*, which can be loosely translated as the 'realm of the inner landscape'. As Wang wrote: '*Jing* (scene, realm) is not simply a scene, as human temperaments are also scenes in the mind. Therefore whoever is capable of depicting authentic scenes and articulating authentic temperaments may be said to have attained *jingjie*' (Wang 1981: 2).

'Art under the sky' comes from a long historical memory of mountain worship. A visit to Mount Tai, or 'Taishan' (a sacred mountain which Confucius praised as standing like a lord above the surrounding plains) revives the memory of art as worship, as veneration of the cosmos (Figure 19.5). It was at an altar on this mountain that ancient emperors made offerings as an act of acceptance of the Mandate of Heaven, which gave legitimation to their rule. Han dynasty historian Sima Qian (145 or 135–86 BCE) recorded 72 such major ceremonies since the prehistoric kings, and the practice continued until the end of the Song dynasty (960–1279). Here the mountain itself forms a magnificent site of display. A single ascending path leading to the Dai Temple at the top is lined on either side with calligraphy carved onto boulders and rock faces. A veritable 'gallery' exhibition on a grand scale, the aura created by these monumental calligraphies testifies to the majesty of the mountain display.

To enjoy 'art under the sky' is the principal pleasure of the *yaji garden*. Traditional painting and calligraphy are in formats designed for the library rather than the wall, mostly mounted as rolled scrolls or book albums, made for handling by the viewer. On fine days the artworks would be brought outside into the garden for a *yaji* gathering. The format presumes fine art connoisseurship to be a personal reflective process referencing the experience of literature; it is symptomatic that Chinese terminology for art appreciation uses terms such as 'reading' or 'playing' (*du, wan*). To bring this art into the garden is like bringing a good book into the park to share with friends. Time of day and seasonal elements make the experience particular; in contrast to the religiosity of a modern museum, where the halo of spotlight (intimating eternity) both fixes the artwork as an icon of worship, and transfixes the respectful viewer, light in the *yaji garden* is dependent on the sky. The natural condition and delight of the garden not only direct the viewer to art but also to the cultural memory of transcendent Heaven and spirituality associated with mountains. The mountain as a 'realm of the immortals' (in written form the Chinese word for immortal is a composite of the characters for mountain and person) is the metaphor for garden rockery and also for landscape art. Viewing a landscape painting within the garden's landscape is not the equivalent of studying a portrait painting in the company of the person depicted; the point here is not to re-present or idealize, but to seek to engage and enter the mystery of nature.

One of the main advantages of the White Cube is to have established a uniform viewing mechanism that can be reconstructed at different sites. The exhibition space is therefore transportable, and may be universally applied for diverse types of exhibitions. The *yaji garden*, on the other hand, provides unique exhibition situations, and each garden is an individually structured set of viewing devices. The visitor is guided through a garden by way of paths and corridors that lead to what can be described as curated encounters with the natural world. Windows and doors frame views designed to arrest the visitor's attention, and hint at surprises waiting to be disclosed. Like an art gallery, every displayed view intends to offer an aesthetic delight. The classical *yaji garden* is both the site where art is enjoyed, as well as a device that illustrates how nature might be appreciated from the point of view of *shanshui* painting ('mountain and water', i.e. the Chinese concept of 'landscape'). It aestheticizes the natural world by attuning it to human perspectives, and directs the mind to the livingness and power

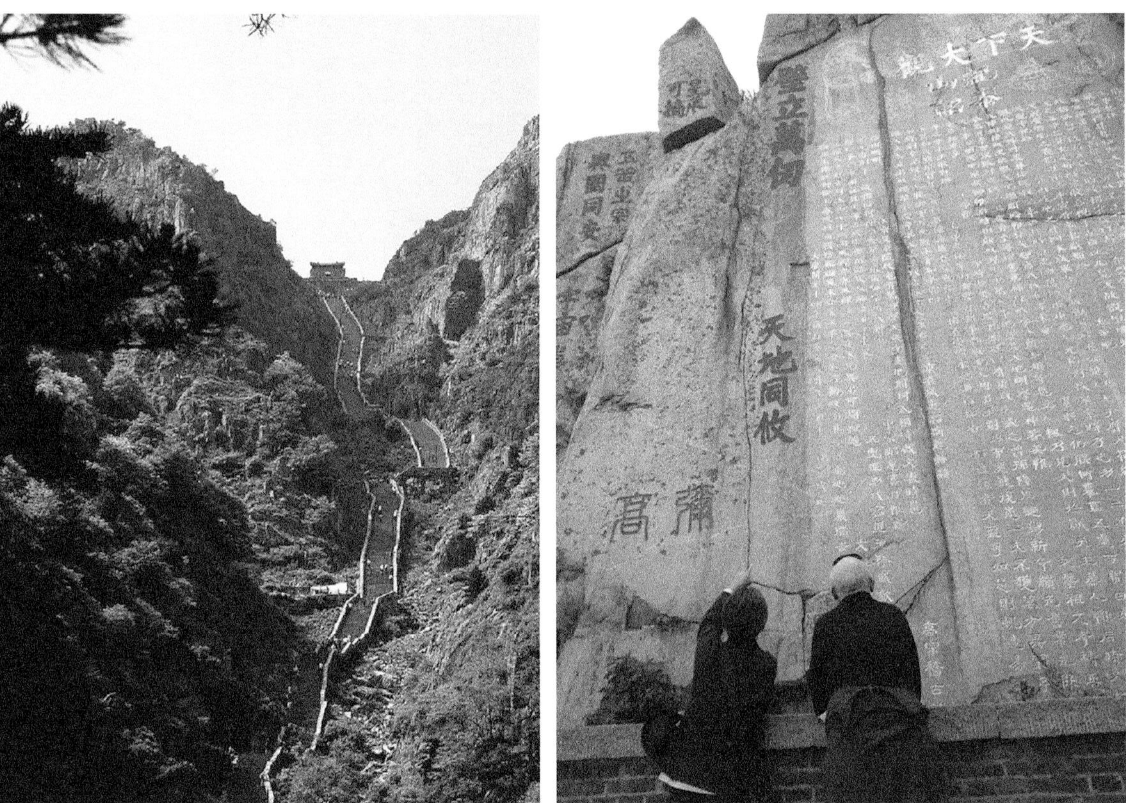


**FIGURE 19.5** Left: The South Gate to Heaven at Mount Tai, Shandong, China. Right: Calligraphy on cliff of Mount Tai from the Tang dynasty (618–907)

*Photo:* Charlie Fong (left); Gu Fei (right)

of nature. Of the various viewing devices employed in the *yaji garden* the principle of *jie*, or borrowing, best illustrates its spirit of openness.

The metaphor of *jie* (borrowing, lending the strength of), used liberally in the literature of art, suggests the fleeting pleasure of borrowing from powers beyond (which includes exemplary works of early masters). Perhaps it is because to access the aesthetic realm (in order to go beyond the mundane) an artist/connoisseur requires the help of powers beyond his ken, and illicit borrowings, such as the garden designer's 'borrowing sceneries from beyond the walls' (*jiejing*) and the artist's 'borrowing the moon's reflection in the pond', prompt him to return to the 'scene of the crime'. The word *tou*, 'to steal', is used in literature in a spirit of secret delight to congratulate oneself on one's luck in getting more than one's fair share from the workings of the Heavens. In this sense, the landscape of the garden for the artist/creator could be interpreted as a site of transgression where the boundary of hidden secrets is trespassed. It is a repository of literary references and a site of cultural mnemonic.[4] In the chapter '*Xingzao lun*' (Initiating Construction) of his text *Yuan ye* (Creating Gardens), the Ming-dynasty scholar Ji Cheng (b. 1582) wrote:

> Garden construction should be clever in *yin* (responding) and *jie* (borrowing), and sophisticated in being appropriate in its form. . . . A garden may partition its inside from the outside, but with *jie* (borrowing), it matters not how distant the actual scenery is [the view is still brought into the garden]. Whether it is green woods emerging from clear rolling hills, or blue sky reaching the heavens, one decides whether to include or exclude it according to its beauty. All views are treated as mirage, and that is the meaning of being both clever and appropriate.
>
> (*Ji 1988*)

## Art and power

Given its particular characteristics in the practices of connoisseurship and display, how may the *yaji garden* be compared to contemporary art institutions? Or asking the question in reverse: how may the contemporary museum be problematized by the *yaji garden*? The contemporary museum is complex and rich in implications as it takes inspiration from multiple historical institutions, and today its voracious creativity also prompts it to gradually take over functions served by other types of cultural institutions.

The religiosity of the modern art museum experience is a legacy of the Christian church, and artworks are made sacred through apparatuses borrowed from European ecclesiastical experience. The predilection of the white cube toward visuality is also derived from a religious mode of spiritual worship. Christian eschatology finds its way quietly into the museum of history, and ideas about ethos of history are transformed into assumptions about temporal linearity and progress. The implication of art as a source of knowledge production finds kinship with the Enlightenment, especially its institution of the *wunderkammer*, further advances the idea of linear progress and pursuit of the new. What has been most criticised by post-colonial analysis is the hidden hegemonic agenda symbolized by nineteenth-century museums of world cultures. Like the ancient museums of imperial conquests, which imposed cultural order on civilizations of the conquered, the museum of loot merged with modern science in the nineteenth century to create the early museums of anthropology and of world cultures, which in an oblique way endorsed the Eurocentric modern museum of art, even as the latter thrived on its legacy of iconoclastic avant-gardism. Today the museum of contemporary art not only critically embraces the richness of its diverse ancestry but also, through sustained efforts to resolve the legacy of imperial history, has evolved into a platform of creative richness and openness, so much so that the contemporary museum finds itself being adopted globally.

How the *yaji garden* may thrive in contemporary times remains a challenge for practitioners. As a contemporary institution the *yaji garden* also requires a critical appraisal of its apparatuses, especially its cultural specificity, and an exploration of how to situate itself within the scope of a new global institution open to the world. The special dynamism and openness of contemporary art museums benefits from a particular European tradition of iconoclasm, which emphasizes the new and the radical. And as an open forum for negotiation of ideologies, the contemporary platform keeps alive the memory of the Greek agora, emphasizing democratic participation. How the *yaji garden* may offer fresh possibilities while maintaining dialogue with its historical legacy will depend on the creative adaptability of its adherents.

One way to start is by revisiting the definition of 'art' in the *yaji garden*. It is well known that Chinese fine art is heavily prejudiced towards the written word. After painting and calligraphy, seal carving is probably the only legitimate addition to traditional fine arts in recent centuries. But the *yaji* gathering also brings together diverse artistic activities: music, performance, appreciation of antiquities and curiosities, poetry writing, enjoyment of incense and tea, and, importantly, lively conversation. In other words, the experience encompasses the intellect and all sensible faculties. This suggests a perimeter of art that is expandable through creative interaction. Chinese interest in antiquities is an old tradition and, like the museum of archaeology, is bound to its obsession with cultural-historical narrative. The literati also had a predilection for curiosities, manifest in the connoisseurship of exotic rocks and roots, and in the literati studio, a natural object transforms into 'art' if it is deemed to be endowed with powers of the cosmos. This wide interest in things intellectual and sensible gives the *yaji garden* great flexibility in embracing aesthetic experiences, a quality that is especially useful in rapidly changing times and fluctuating sensibilities such as ours today. Theoretically, one may imagine future *yaji* to be a platform that does not start with artworks but, like a performance stage, embraces all that happens within its compound as part of the *yaji* aesthetic experience.

Unlike the museum of modern art, the *yaji garden* is an art site without an archival collection. The power of the modern art museum is partly derived from its authority over archival history: additions to the museum collection are justified by the assertion of novelty and departure from earlier art. Implicit in the authority to endorse new art is therefore the legitimation of 'novelty' as a necessary criterion for 'art', which accompanies a teleological bias towards historical linearity. The *yaji garden* is not concerned with novel originality; its claim to authority comes from its metaphoric relation to cosmos/nature. It is true that Chinese literati art constantly refers to art history, but the emphasis is not on evolution and development; rather it is a look behind the shoulder towards exemplary historical models. The neglect of archival history means the *yaji garden* is not dependent on the principle of accumulation and progression for artistic authority; its success as an institution is contingent upon the interactive dynamics and social influence of its current participants. The *yaji garden*'s openness and freedom from the tyranny of 'the new' is an advantage on the one hand, but also a disadvantage on the other, as it lacks the stability of an independent historical narrative that comes with the process of archiving.

The exclusive nature of the traditional *yaji*, often criticized today in comparison with modern institutions, needs to be addressed in contemporary times, and mechanisms for a selective inclusion of members of the public is essential for *yaji* practice to flourish as a legitimate institution for society at large.

## Boundary of the site of aesthetics

It is a moot point to speculate on the *yaji garden*'s potential as a platform for politically engaged art, a role in which the contemporary art museum distinguishes itself. The contemporary art museum ventures forth to negotiate sensitive ideological-political issues that other cultural institutions do not feel entitled to address, and this openness is a major attraction of this hugely successful modern institution. In the European context the historical institutional structure of parallel, and contesting, governmental powers of state and religion opened up a space of negotiation beyond secular law. In the early modern era Enlightenment science also took up the challenge to state power. Given this history it is tempting to speculate how the radicality of the modern western museum has benefited from the legacy of the church, which has always claimed a position above that of secular law, and offers the space of spirituality for political critique. To be placed above the law, metaphorically if not legally, allows the contemporary art museum to become the platform for sensitive ideological and cultural issues.

How may one understand this modern role of the museum in terms of the *yaji garden*? The contestation between God and Caesar is not a Chinese tradition, but between scholar-officials and the court there is a continuous history of power brokering. It is important to note that the nature of the literati in China was different from that of modern intellectuals; the former were by training devoted to public affairs, but unlike the critical intellectual, scholars who succeeded in public examinations could move on to official administrative positions. There was the theoretical possibility for the literati to move from critique on the outside to the inside, and be granted an official role to realize their social-political ideals. This means the scholar class, artists included, shared a common worldview and looked upon affairs of the state to be their personal calling, and their critical attitudes arose from a shared ideology of Chinese civilization. The *yaji garden* provided a site where the literati gathered outside of the worries of worldly affairs, but worldly affairs were never far from their concerns. Although the cosmic reference of a garden's 'mountain and water' (*shan shui*) carries no political weight, it offers a legitimate refuge that keeps worldly affairs in perspective. One may say mindfulness about the cosmic order keeps the human order in check, and in contemporary terms, mindfulness about the natural world also makes a sympathetic partner of today's environmentalist green movement. While in Europe God and country administered the soul and the state separately, in pre-modern China the literati formed a common link for both.

Many well-known political activities did actually happen in the garden, a late dynastic example being the nineteenth-century revolutionary group *Xiao Dao Hui*, who in the 1850s plotted rebellion against the Qing dynasty in the famous Yuyuan Garden adjacent to Shanghai's City Temple. However, purely as a site, the garden carries only faint memories as a space outside the law; if one must look for historical examples of transgression, the clearest reference to this privilege can be traced to the epoch of the famous Orchid Pavilion gathering in 353 CE. This special space that stood at the edge of state law was the imperial garden Hualin Yuan, situated at the northeast corner of the imperial palace (incidentally the layout of palace grounds in the third century was similar to that of the Forbidden City in Beijing today). Between the third and sixth centuries CE, Hualin Yuan served as a private garden of pleasure for the emperor, and here he held relaxed meetings with his ministers. But incongruously, it was here in the garden that the emperor also customarily exercised his sovereign right of granting royal pardon to convicted criminals – a special privilege that put imperial verdict above national law. There are no records explaining the choice of the imperial garden as the site for exercising this supra-judicial power, particularly as Hualin Yuan was situated just to the north of the imperial court of justice, but it does hint at the haloed position of Hualin Garden as a site above secular rule, prompting comparison with the transcendent position of sacred mountains (Tsuji 2005).

## Professing art

Apart from its democratic appeal to the public, the modernity of the museum institution depends equally on the rationalization of its profession. Increasingly in recent decades, compartmentalized professionalism in the art system has reduced the holistic experience of art to specialized knowledge. The art world has been rationalized into diverse fields that include 'artist', 'critic', 'curator', 'audience' and 'market', with the implication that aesthetic authority rests with the critics and curators who represent the aesthetic professionals. The need for professionals in aesthetics also reflects today's globalized realities; with increasingly accelerated expansion of the art field, the proliferation of exhibitions makes it impossible for the layman to get adequately acquainted with the latest developments, and the curator now ironically also takes on the role of art's professional audience.

The historical model of the *yaji garden* offers a perspective to reflect on the art of contemporary times (Figure 19.6). The phenomenon of the recent proliferation of international

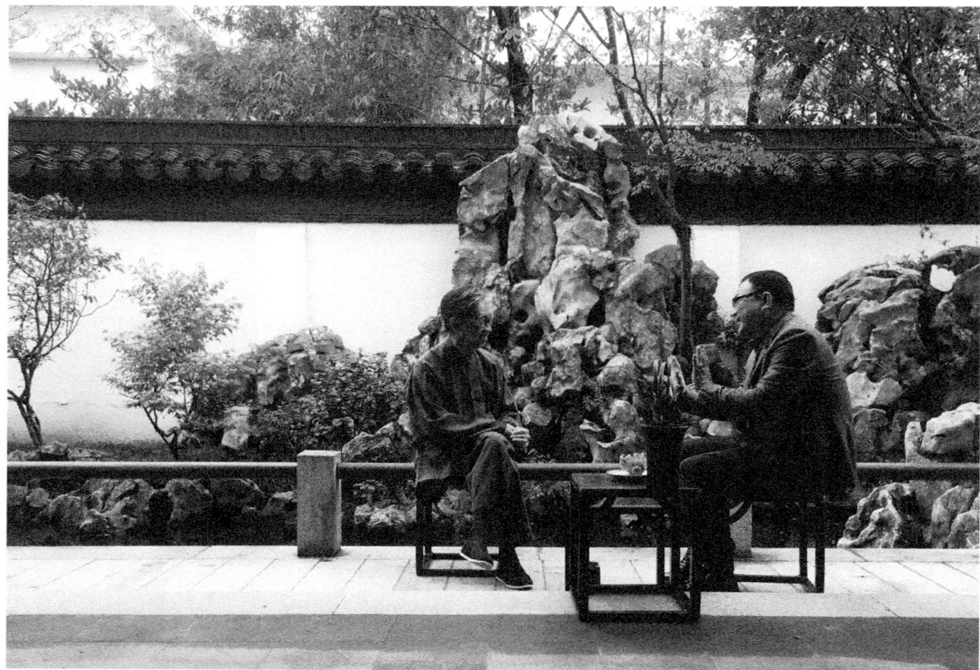

**FIGURE 19.6** Photograph of contemporary *yaji* gathering and landscape at Jia Yuan Hall in Suzhou, China, October 2016

*Photo:* Chen Xue

biennials is an interesting case. New biennials hosted by urban centres from around the globe are event-based, and they are formed principally around the aesthetic interaction between international artists, curators and specialists, who take precedence over the authority of the typical modern museum. Although the public is welcome and encouraged, they still mainly participate as adjunct spectators. But this is already an important step in moving beyond the monolithic museum to offer event-based exhibitions with a global perspective. Looking forward to the international biennial as sites where the 'moment of aesthetics' may be instituted, one might look upon these events as future possibilities of a form of mega-*yaji* where the platform of art becomes truly participatory for the audience, and lifting as personalized aesthetic experience.

While the *yaji garden* continues to evolve within its traditional confines, it hopefully brings a fresh context for thinking about dynamic, event-based practices of display and art. As a laboratory for aesthetic sensibilities and incubator of artistic imagination, the ongoing project of the *yaji garden* should remain an open invitation.

## Notes

1 *Xing,* or inspiration, was identified as one of three principal modes of writing poetry as early as the third century BCE, in the preface written for *The Book of Poetry*, the sixth-century BCE anthology originally edited by Confucius (551–479 BCE).

2 The term literati painting (*wenren hua*) was first formally used by the artist and critic Dong Qichang (1555–1636), who identified the Tang dynasty painter Wang Wei as the progenitor of the style. The contemporary art historian Shih Shou-chien writes that

> The so-called "literati artists" for the most part can be described as artists who created outside of the imperial court system: they did not paint in the service of the court, or for political or religious purposes, or for any other than artistic reasons. As artists, they were responsible only to themselves, and their creative practice was undertaken for the sake of individual expression and spiritual cultivation.
>
> *(Shih 2010)*

3 In January 1918 the modern thinker and founder of China's Communist Party Chen Duxiu (1879–1942) published an explosive essay in the journal *The New Youth,* urging 'a revolution in art'. As he wrote: 'If we want to renovate Chinese painting, the first thing we must do is rebel against the Four Wangs. This is because no renovation of Chinese painting can do without the spirit of realism of Western painting' (Chen 1918). The 'Four Wangs' to whom Chen Duxiu refers are four celebrated artists of the Qing dynasty, with the same surname Wang, who represented orthodox landscape art. The pioneering scholar reformer Kang Youwei (1858–1927) promoted the concept of Renovating Chinese Painting as an integral part of his political ideals. Kang believed that jettisoning the freestyle methods of literati art would help Chinese art to return to its original roots, and also open the doors to learning from Western realist techniques, in order to generate China's own modern tradition.

4 Ideas about the significance of the concepts of *jie* (borrowing) and *tou* (stealing) in Chinese garden aesthetics were developed in casual discussions between this author and the contemporary Hong Kong scholar Chiu Kwong-Chiu, spring and summer 2016.

## References

Attiret, J.-D. (1749) 'Letter to M. d'Assaut in Paris', 1 November 1743, in *Lettres édifiantes et curieuses écrites des missions étrangères par quelques missionnaires de la compagnie de Jésus*, Paris: Guérin, 27, pp. 1–61. English translation (1752). Online. Available HTTP: http://inside.bard.edu/~louis/gardens/attiret account.html. Accessed 19 August 2017.

Bennett, T. (1988) 'The Exhibitionary Complex', *New Formations* (4) (Spring), pp. 73–102.

Chen, C. (2002) *Shuo yuan* [On Gardens], Shandong: Shandong Pictorial Publishing and Tongji University Press.

Chen, D. (1918) 'Meishu geming [Art Revolution]', in *Ershi shiji Zhongguo meishu wenxuan shang*, [Selected Writings on Art in China in the Twentieth Century], Vol. 1. Shanghai: Shanghai shuhua chubanshe, pp. 29–30.

Ji, C. (1988) *Yuan ye zhushi* [Annotated *Yuan ye*] (annotation by Chen Zhi), Beijing: China Architecture and Building Press.

Huizinga, J. (1949) *Homo Ludens: A Study of the Play-Element in Culture*, London: Routledge & Kegan Paul.

O'Doherty, B. (1999) *Inside the White Cube: The Ideology of the Gallery Space*, Berkeley and Los Angeles: University of California Press.

Shih, S-C. (2010) *Cong fengge dao huayi: fansi Zhongguo meishushi* [From Style to Expressiveness in Painting: a Rethinking of Chinese Art History], Taipei: Shitou chubanshe.

Stiegler, B. (2016) 'The Quarrel of the Amateurs', Lecture Given at the China Academy of Art, Hangzhou, China, April 2016. Online. Available HTTP: www.s-i-m-a.org/site/?p=1572. Accessed 30 April 2016.

Tsuji, M. (2005) 'A Basic Study on the Judicial Reviews and Inspections of Cases by the Emperors in Medieval China' in *Tijdschrift voor Rechtsgeschiedenis* [Legal History Review], 55.

Wang, G. (1981 [1909]) *Renjian cihua* [A Study on Literary Criticism], Chengdu: Sichuan People's Publishing House.

Wen, Z. (1984) *Changwu zhi jiaozhu* [Annotated 'Treatise on Superfluous Things'] (annotation by Chen Zhi), Jiangsu: Jiangsu Science Technology Press.

Weng, S. (c1350) *Pleasures of Reading in Every Season (Sishi dushu le)*.

# 20

# SCREENING TIMES

## Dioramas at the Shanghai Film Museum

*Linda Johnson*

### Abstract

The dioramas at the Shanghai Film Museum (SFM) provide visitors with an experience of Shanghai, not of the nation. The city's distinctive past, with its intimacy with foreign influences, was inscribed onto its films of the modernist period (1911–1949) and is visualised in SFM through its recreations of the form of the city alongside the people and film scenes that embodied Shanghai's engagement with the new. In this chapter I argue that the story this museum tells is not one of a past left behind but of a continuing, recurring modernism rooted in the early twentieth century and integral to contemporary Shanghai. In its representation of the history of film, the museum reflects an alternative way of visualising time and brings the city's Golden Age into Shanghai's future, principally through its use of dioramas. Drawing on recent scholarship from outside museum studies, I will examine the potential role of the museum's dioramas within the context of contemporary Shanghai.

### Introduction

Theatrical visual experiences have been part of museums since the mid-nineteenth century, most obviously in natural history dioramas and ethnographic tableaux (Griffiths 2003). The aim of these installations was to provide visitors with an emotionally engaging experience by recreating reality as object through skilfully painted backgrounds, taxidermy, wax figures and authentic objects (Wonders 1993). At Shanghai Film Museum (SFM), the subject of the dioramas is not natural reality, but film; there are no physical traces connecting their content to the real. Barthes saw the chemical reaction between subject, light and the photographic surface as giving photographs their essence, their 'that-has-been' authenticity essential to engage the audience emotionally (Barthes 1981: 76–82). Michelle Henning (2007: 665–6) has used the same approach to see animals' skins in taxidermy providing physical traces of the real. This 'reality effect', they argue, distinguishes photography and taxidermy from other types of visual representation by allowing viewers to take what they see as reality, making the encounter with spectacle haptic, touching their lives.

The capacity to move the visitor to SFM lies in her recognition of the past living on in the present and future of Shanghai. According to Barthes, where the representation is simply iconic it can still appear real to the viewer under certain circumstances such as where the viewer is shocked by making the connection between looking at something that is dead and gone, yet is seen before her as a present sign of a dead thing. In *Camera Lucida* (1981: 94–6) he sees the viewer of a photograph experiencing two points in time simultaneously: 'that is dead' (past) and 'that is going to die' (present) so that the index operates in the present even though the subject is a past event. It is this juxtaposition between past and present that is key to the experience of the visitor to SFM, not only providing the opportunity for haptic experience, but also reflecting a particular view and interpretation of time.

## Film in the museum

Opened in 2013 by the Shanghai Film Group, SFM is a purpose-built 15,000-square-metre space housing over 3,000 exhibits. Part of the gigantic wave of museums opening across China (Jacobson 2013), it was included within a commercial re-development to provide an old studio site with cultural cachet while fulfilling the requirement for state-owned enterprises to use their property within defined purposes. Film museums have received relatively little attention in museum studies and where they have been examined interest has largely focused on either their value as repositories of film or as exhibitors of film (Bottomore 2006). SFM has no publicly accessible film archive, and whilst it contains three cinemas and visitor access to a discrete collection of old films, its main objective is to present the history of Shanghai film alongside visitors' interactive and visual experience of the process of filmmaking. It ties the past, present and future together in a complex relationship in which the craft of the past is part of the technology of the future, with the built environment of Shanghai displayed as an essential part of the aesthetics of film past and future. Film is written into place and place into film. The story told by the museum, most effectively through its dioramas, is not about looking at linear history but about film as part of an evolving Shanghai, a living history of place that is not only seen but felt and experienced.

The technology in the museum, its installations, display screens and interactive terminals dominate the design of the space. Engaging and modern, their impact reinforces the presence of the contemporary world and a futuristic Shanghai. Whole rooms are filled wall to ceiling with screens, with flashing motion-activated lights and, perhaps most dramatically, 55 snaking waist-high, motion-activated horizontal blue screens, telling the story of film from 1950 to 2011 (1965–1978 excepted). These are environments of movement; the visitor is encouraged to walk and move from one interactive to the next; the walls are screens imbued with movement and light, like film itself. Movement through the multi-level galleries is further encouraged by the use of arrows embedded in the floors, overhead signage and motion-sensored escalators. Most of the spaces are vast, containing different visual elements punctuated by interactive screens: the atmosphere is one of perambulation not contemplation, reinforcing connections between seeing and moving.

More traditional forms of screen do play a role. The 'Original Seeds of Cinema' section plays an introductory video across three vast walls every 25 minutes filling the space with panoramic images of the early history of Shanghai film, engaging the visitor as if she were present at its defining moments. A small viewing area with a terminal and a projector screen allows the visitor to make a choice from a range of pre-1949 films and watch an entire film in Chinese. There are occasional films playing on screens around the museum, usually shown according to a schedule but without seating.

Film has physicality but, unlike other objects, must be animated by light and projection onto a screen to be viewed. Just as museums and art galleries provided for private, intimate, emotional experience of the material world in buildings of public exhibitionary space, cinemas did the same using film. Museums had walls, whilst cinemas had screens and both incorporated movement and the capacity to intimately move an audience within a public space (Bruno 2014). Museum scholarship has extended our understanding of materiality beyond physicality to the cultural and historical information that gives objects their meanings. By re-emphasizing interactions between object and audience, this work has recognised the phenomenological impact of the object on the senses (Edwards 2010), yet also reasserts the need for an object around which visitor experience takes place (p. 23). A roll of film or the disc that contains it however provides no opportunity for experience of a film's content. To encompass film, materiality needs to be seen as a set of material relations rather than as requiring material existence (Bruno 2014: 8). Using this approach, projected images have materiality through their relationships with their audience and how the visual is experienced, that is to say projected images have materiality through the act of exhibition. As work in visual media has established, experiencing film is not solely visual, but as with most experiences is multisensory (Mitchell 2005). Capturing film within other material objects, such as photographs, video screens and dioramas works as a cipher, allowing an audience to relate to projected images by having those projections adopt a particular materiality. A diorama of a film scene is an exhibition of the film itself as it acquires materiality from that particular surface (Bruno 2014).

## Experiencing dioramas in the museum

The Achievement of Masters section of SFM houses 14 dioramas showing a frozen glimpse into the lives of the most well-known directors, actors and cinematographers of the day. Their layout encourages the visitor to feel that there is much more ahead, prompting movement through the displays. Each display contains a mix of sculpture, objects, enlarged photographs and painted backdrops. A sense of realism comes from the backgrounds whilst their representativeness is acknowledged in the use of monochrome (revealing no distinction between flesh and clothing), rough-surfaced, but detailed human figures. Maintaining this tension between reality and representation frees the visitor to engage with the display, in the same way as film frees its audience to become immersed in the world and characters on screen (Bordwell 1986, Mulvey 1975). The filmmaker Xie Jin, for example, is cast larger than life against a realistically painted perspective background of the location of one of his most celebrated films, *Hibiscus Town, Furong zhen* (1986). The intention here is not to deceive or to claim reality but to suggest, reinforce or persuade. The walk through this area, with its glimpses of technology, historic streetscapes of Shanghai and other surprises provides an opportunity for engagement of the emotions, engendering responses to what is seen, felt and heard. There is no expectation for the visitor to sit and contemplate these exhibits as objects. Rather the visitor is expected to roam, evoking the city of Shanghai where everything is in motion.

As the visitor roams, the dioramas reassert connections between Shanghai's visual and physical identity then and now. Visitors, particularly local visitors, are able to recognize themselves and their city, shifting their viewpoint as the past intertwines with the future of

Shanghai, grounding their contemporary experience of a rapidly changing city. This capacity to incorporate movement and intimately move an audience links museums with cinemas and by reasserting connections between the physical and visual identity of Shanghai's past with its present and future, the dioramas enhance the hapticity of the encounter.

In a 1991 circular, the Chinese government pointed out the importance of museums and cultural sites to present exhibitions that allowed visitors to perceive history 'directly through the senses' (Denton 2014: 4), and it is not unusual for museums in China to use a limited number of authentic objects alongside contemporary models, enlarged photographs and modern installations to achieve this. The first priority has often been to preserve the essence of an object or event through reproduction or representation rather than the object itself (Li 2005). In looking at the form of display here my aim is, however, not to see it as distinctively Chinese, essentialized and ahistorical, but as a visual practice that results from ideas translated, modified and disseminated across time and space for a range of purposes across cultures, what Martin Powers (1995) refers to as 'a fractal network, permeated by patterns from all over the globe'. Related to currents in museological practice in contemporary Shanghai, these dioramas are informed by a wide range of influences and ideas that include the history of dioramas in museums, the use of social realism in visual culture and the significance of film culture in the context of Shanghai. For the purposes of this chapter, of central importance is the alternative way these dioramas can be seen to conceive time as they freeze motion.

What is generally significant about the use of this type of three-dimensional representation is how they appear to manufacture reality, re-creating a reality to advance a narrative (Griffiths 2002). These display forms, like films, create a representation that captures time and manipulates the field of vision to emphasize particular aspects that would otherwise be lost in motion, whilst downplaying others. Suited to a modern way of seeing, by fictionalizing reality yet seeming to reproduce it, they yield ideological meaning in a way not dissimilar to propaganda (Miller 1996: 53). As a spectacle, dioramas offer a simulacrum of reality that gives their audience the experience of visual engagement with the past, allowing a current relationship with it (Groys 1994: 148–50). Lacking the capacity to overawe the visitor that the size, complexity and hyper-reality of nineteenth-century panoramas had, these contained dioramas do not inspire wonder at their content. As with film, the audience is not involved in an experience of the real, but engaged with a particular visual to tell a particular story. In Guy Debord's words, 'the spectacle's job is to cause a world that is no longer directly perceptible to be *seen* via different specialized mediations' (1994: 17).

The authentic reconstructions manufactured in nineteenth-century panoramas re-enacted a reality only available in the museum (Griffiths 2003), providing visualizations that improved on the original with their multiple perspectives and types of encounter, transporting visitors to the time and place depicted (Griffiths 2002). Within the dioramas at SFM, the function of their reconstructions of the environment of Shanghai is rather one that reinforces temporal connections, bringing the vignettes of past Shanghai into the present. Their allusions to architecture are not exotic or unusual, but streetscapes still visible in contemporary Shanghai, and a visitor's memory of that connects the visitor and the city to its past.

Dioramas, miniatures and wax models featured in natural history and ethnographic museums have been criticized for their failure to represent science authentically, for sensationalizing cultures (Quinn 2006), promoting discourses of nationhood and encouraging imperialist and colonialist narratives (Duncan 1995). By transforming nature or a cultural moment into an exhibited object, they have been seen as doing violence to the reality, erasing it (Henning

2006, Varutti 2011). This is a very different result from the tableaux in SFM, which involve a remembering or a reassertion of the historical significance of what is displayed to celebrate it and to cement their associations with contemporary Shanghai. The purpose is not to colonize or to advance nationhood, erasing difference, but to promote the distinctiveness of Shanghai and its glorious past. What is erased in the museum is what came next, not the circumstances that produced what is displayed in the dioramas.

The other major criticism of mimetic or illusionistic displays in museums comes from their association with edutainment, yet seeing them as voyeuristic and comparing them negatively with exhibits that anticipate a visitor's participation (Sandberg 2001) fails to adequately take account of the movement towards engagement on which they were based. Changes in exhibition design brought about by modernism challenged the exclusivity of art in favor of engagement, changing the relationship between museum and visitor (Henning 2006: 58–69). This idea of inclusivity pushed installations into the foreground and made the exhibition a place of movement and interactivity (Henning 2006: 63). By using methods seen in department store windows, including dioramas, and incorporating utilitarian objects and popular culture allusions, they turned the everyday into museum exhibitions, replacing focus on the unique object with reproductions, models and multiples (Hein 2000: 105). As Henning argues (2006: 69), display essentially overcame the object, promoting the idea of a mediatic museum where what was required of the visitor was movement without the contemplative gaze.

## Time and the city

I use a particular approach to time to suggest that at SFM the purpose of the historical exhibits is not to present a politicized history, a theme park 'edutainment', or nostalgic revelling, but to present a spectacle of Shanghai by revisiting a past that is embedded in the city and its future. This approach to Shanghai's relationship with its pre-revolutionary past is not unusual in scholarly work on the city (Abbas 2000; Greenspan 2014; Lagerkvist 2013) but scholarship on museums has generally adopted a linear view of time with the past left behind and the future up ahead. Seeing time differently affects not only how the past is perceived but also how it is presented in the museum and SFM dioramas are supportive of a view of time that sees the past in the present. Not as a line or as a circle, but as an advancing spiral (Chang 2009; Greenspan 2014: 208–9). Shanghai is not simply leaving its past behind, but is preserving elements of its past so that it can move with them into the future.

There are parallels here with Zygmunt Bauman's work on modern life, which he sees as characterized by 'an inclination to constant change' with no endpoint of perfection (2012: viii). Within the classic Chinese text, the *Yijing*, time is also described as an aspect of perpetual change, without any final destination (Chang 2009). The text explains a worldview that sees change as a way of life, providing a process for negotiating a dynamic world by accumulating experience and aligning change with the right time to preserve personal and universal harmony. In classic Western philosophy time moves forward whilst space stands still whereas here time and space are indivisible; spatial perception is concurrent with time and colours, smells, fluids, emotions, orifices, planets are all linked to space-time. On this reading change and time are fundamental aspects of all things and every event. All are in the process of self-realization or self-creation through change and the right time for change is gauged through accumulated experience, or from gained momentum.

The world, then, is expressed as a series of constantly rotating dualisms, each gives rise to the other, each supports the other, providing strength, and it is the movement from one to another that produces time. These dualisms are popularly displayed as *yin* and *yang*, light and shadow. In the built environment of Shanghai *yin* appears as the contemporary spectacle of the glitz and drama of futuristic Pudong together with the renovation of its past glory in Puxi (Wasserstrom 2009; Greenspan 2014). The Bund and Shanghai's monuments to Art Deco, an aesthetic movement which itself integrated the past to create the modern (Wood 2003: 38–41), stood for Shanghai's economic strength and interest. Investment in this past is visible all over Shanghai as the city seems to be reviving an earlier potential stunted by the circumstances of its history. The *yang*, balancing this ostentation, is the private that lies behind in the *lilong* or residential laneways. These quintessentially Shanghai developments, adaptations of European lane houses, are synonymous with Shanghai and its modernizing identity emerging out of its Imperial past, part of its movement through time (Liang 2010). A percentage of *lilong* have escaped demolition, some restored, others famously turned into shopping centres, making them part of the landscape now and then.

This view of the world, as in Confucianism and Zen Buddhism, contains the idea that returning to the past brings with it the production of the new and that the new contains the past (Chang 2009, cited Greenspan 2014: 12). This dynamic and creative relationship between past and future visualizes constant revisits to the past not merely as nostalgia, but a necessary, integral aspect of both present and future. As Abbas observes, 'in Shanghai, the past allows the present to pursue the future' (2000: 780); or on Greenspan's formulation, 'As a future city, Shanghai. . . (re)-emerges in a temporal spiral out of which the future city reaches back to the past in order to construct itself today' (2014: 209). She argues that what is being re-experienced is the sense of being poised on the edge of the new (2014: 3–4); a sense that was captured in the dominant aesthetic of the films of Shanghai's Golden Age where the distinctive spatial characteristics of the *lilong* (des Forges 2010) contrasted with the space and opulence of foreign-built villas (Hong 2009). The museum visitors' promenade through a rematerialized vision of these films loops time in on itself, as the city loops time in its own spaces, making their experience not one of nostalgia but of contemporary Shanghai (Lagerkvist 2013).

The environment of the *lilong* is captured by an extensive diorama of the opening scene of the film *Street Angel*, or *Malu Tianshi* (1937), still considered by many to be China's greatest ever film (Plate 21). An open diorama edged by a cordon and occupying a large corner space, it reconstructs a Shanghai laneway, with a painted background showing the laneways receding into the distance. Realism of the streetscape is enhanced through many object details, such as baskets, jars and furniture. In contrast, the foreground is peopled with miniaturized actors, crew and filming equipment painted silver grey, making them seem ephemeral; unreal or temporary, representational. At the rear, two screens play an extract of the film showing the stars of the film, Zhou Xuan and Zhao Dan, singing to each other across the lane from opposing windows, a form of communication emblematic of the *lilong* where close and intensely populated living spaces generated private sounds, smells and sights to be shared by neighbours (des Forges 2010).

The film itself opens with a frenetic montage chronicling the competing foreign interests in Shanghai: neon lights in English and Chinese, give way to scenes of the foreign built architecture, foreign modes of transport, leisure, religious buildings and the decadent lifestyle of the city with intermittent images of clocks on buildings, showing Western time as ruling over Shanghai. Once the montage ends, the film plunges the viewer into the Chinese laneways of Shanghai as a band enters the lane heralding the arrival of a traditional Chinese wedding procession. It is this scene that is the subject of the diorama and the film's themes, migration and social oppression are brought into contemporary Shanghai through the realism of the laneway. The visitor to this display is an onlooker, separated by the cordon and watching the screens, while Zhou Xuan's voice provides another form of sensory distance. *Street Angel* is probably the best example of a Shanghai film spatializing modernity, exploring socially stratified relationships and social issues through the spaces people occupy. Spaces materialized to restate the continuing presence of Shanghai's distinctive identity, recognizable to visitors from the city outside the museum, where migration and poverty continue to be key social issues.

## Aesthetics, from film to museum

Shanghai Film itself was part of the city's distinctive identity throughout the Republican Period. The undisputed centre of film, the first film being shown in the city within a year of the technology going on public display in Paris (Zhang 2003), by the late 1930's Shanghai had the most cinemas showing Hollywood films of any city in Asia (Lee 1999b: 75) and its own filmmaking companies (Zhang 1999). The movies, together with the print media that grew around them, formed an important mass media spreading ideas about modernity, fashion and innovations for a new way of life that valued leisure and incorporated foreignness.

The visitor encounters a range of visual references to Shanghai's distinctive cultural identity in the museum through the presentation of a series of curated elements from the city's golden age of film that reassert its modernity and its departure from the traditionalism and conservatism of its alter-ego Beijing. This is produced at first sight through the aesthetics of the display, which take on a form familiar to local audiences. As in natural history dioramas, the recreations of frozen moments in time at SFM place three-dimensional forms before a panoramic background, many of which recede endlessly into the distance. Lynn Pan in her book *Shanghai Style* (2008) discusses the development of *haipai* during the Concession Period as the expression of the city's culture 'constituted as much by an attitude, a context, a way of living and behaving as by an aesthetic or a set of definable formal features' (p. 6). This term came over time to encapsulate Shanghai's distinctive character: a 'proud defiant banner' (Pan 2008: 11) of all that was and is fashionable and modern. A cosmopolitan space, a gateway port at the head of a convergence of rivers, Shanghai stood in a unique position for a distinctly modern culture to emerge within a rapidly changing environment. The seas (or '*hai*') flooded the city with foreign ideas, innovations, and peoples making them part of Shanghai's new identity as the country struggled with its transition out of Imperial rule.

As Pan explains, *haipai* was encapsulated in the image of the ubiquitous 'calendar girls', hyper-realist paintings of fashionably dressed beautiful young women that became emblematic of Shanghai as modern, new, eager for profit and open to foreign influences. Used to advertise cigarettes, alcohol, make-up and other modern wares, artists in Shanghai perfected both the luminescent, touchable, healthy glow to their skin and finely detailed panoramic backgrounds. The women stood apart from this background, as if it were a studio photograph or a stage or film set, making them seem more real than their surroundings, typically a Shanghai landscape, a site of leisure or a fashionable interior. The same aesthetic persisted through the Mao Period, with some of Shanghai's most famous commercial 'calendar girl' artists joining Mao's communist soviet in Yan'an before 1949, where they painted and taught their skills. Reproduced in propaganda posters, with the clothing changed and industrial features added to the landscapes, the women became imbued with Soviet realist muscles but the aesthetic was popularized. Re-imagined in the dioramas that place a three-dimensional body against a realistic background, connections are forged linking *haipai* and its modernity, full of promise, with contemporary Shanghai.

Iconic women of Shanghai Film feature prominently in the dioramas. Like the laneways of the built environment and the calendar girls of the print environment, the newly constructed star system within film was part of *haipai* (Pan 2008: 179ff.) and was infused with Shanghai's search for modernity (Hong 2009; Zhang 2005). The leading actress Bai Yang (1920–1996) is captured within a huge glass case, not in one of her many famous roles nor alongside a film crew, but seated in a domestic setting (Plate 22). This intimate view, showing her seemingly relaxed and imagining her past roles, as blown-up still photographs appear to float above her, projects a vision her fans would have liked to see. This is the material of the print culture that grew around the stars, revealing their real life, lived in parallel to the roles they played, reinforcing the characters they projected on the screen. The actress, her books and the sofa on which she sits are all sculpted from the same rough-textured clay, whilst the classic Shanghai parquet flooring, the fashionable modernist furniture and her living room walls appear as realistic through a combination of painted and photographic images. Other real details are provided by objects from her home and items of print media, labelled as museum exhibits. Housed behind glass, what is displayed is a protected world that a visitor can only look into and not enter, but the arrangement allows that visitor to see the complete private scene. Containing it within glass fetishizes the scene, adds to its reality whilst ascribing it with its own temporality, apparently without time (Henning 2006: 8; 2007: 670). Her surroundings present a story of an archetypal Westernized Shanghai lifestyle, with the star at leisure, engaged in refined and elegant activities, and the form of the display conveys an aura of frozen reality. This, however, is denied to Bai Yang herself as the form she takes proclaims her unreality and this complicates the temporality of the scene. A historical figure, the form of her representation acknowledges her death, leaving the surroundings and its *haipai* as enduring elements.

The adjacent diorama takes intimacy a stage further in its open display of Shanghai's first generation of leading film stars, Hu Die (1908–1989) and Ruan Lingyu (1910–1935) (Plate 23). They are portrayed in a fictionalized moment of affection at Ruan Lingyu's lane house, Hu Die apparently comforting Ruan Lingyu. They were both symbols of fashionable modernity in their day, regularly appearing in print culture and film as models for the correct way for young women to be modern. These actresses were iconic markers of a sea change that allowed women in entertainment to be seen as smart, strong willed social actors with moral values (Zhang 2005). The urban legend of Ruan Lingyu's tragic love life and suicide are the subtext of the display, reinforced by photographs of her funeral and a commemorative magazine labeled and displayed alongside in a glass case. Her death shocked Shanghai: an estimated 100,000 people took to the street to join her funeral procession, as it not only meant the death of one of its greatest stars but also made a striking statement of the problems inherent in colonial modernity. Within the museum she appears as an icon of modernity, but also as a reminder of the need to make Shanghai's future its own rather than a replica of the West.

The statement the tableau makes about modern women and how that idea was performed distinctively in Shanghai reinforces this. Whilst the figures of Hu Die and Ruan Lingyu convey the visual idea of fashionable femininity, that idea is patently situated in Shanghai and not in Hollywood. The tableau reproduces an aesthetic from magazines, films, and calendar girl posters of the day to convey the idea that modern fashionable Shanghai women felt no shame to be seen in public (Lee 1999b: 82). This was about possessing a character defined in part by female stars who 'served to instruct the female viewer on how to become correctly modern' (Hansen, 1994: 15). A fashionable qipao and carefully drawn eyebrows were part of the modern Shanghai look, but character was indivisible from modern-ness, character that displayed a 'rich knowledge, lofty thinking, and a strong will' (Lee 1999b: 82). This marked a turning away from seeing women in the entertainment industry as prostitutes and, in a sense, reinstated them with the status educated courtesans possessed in Imperial times. Femininity in modern Shanghai required an inner virtue amongst this generation of society's iconic women (Chang 1999) and, as a result, photographs of Ruan Lingyu always show her dressed in a long qipao looking introspective or thoughtful. As Zhang Zhen has observed (2001: 242) 'the figure of the actress embodies not so much the glamour of stardom as the multiple and concrete social roles available to women at the time, both in the domestic and public sphere'.

This aesthetic is evident here and motion-sensor spotlights directed at the actress figures enhance the relationship between the visitor and the tableau (Griffiths 2002). The spotlighting gets slowly more intense as the visitor approaches referencing cinema and the roles Ruan Lingyu played as allegory for modernism and its social injustices. The key drama within her later films, like in many of the 'leftist' films of the period, pose Shanghai's modernity as a question of how to overcome a range of dualities with which the city was presented: old or new, traditional or modern, East or West, national or colonial time (Lee 1999a: 3). In some, like *Goddess, Shennu* (1934), Ruan became a metaphor for the city, trying to be modern but simultaneously rejecting the foreign (Hong 2009). The film was a call to arms for the people to take action so as to ensure China's modernity. As the most intimate diorama in the space, the visitor is not only connected to Ruan as a screen personality but to her image and all it represents (Zhang 2005). The figures, again constructed in roughcast clay, are posed against a realistically constructed replica of a lane house wall with original windows and distinctive rendering, situating her in an enduring image of the city. What is displayed here is not glamour, but embodiments of the modern woman of the day, battling against such negative aspects of modernity as migration, poverty, and social oppression: themes still resonant with contemporary Shanghai.

The nearby diorama of Zhou Xuan (1918–57) known locally as 'golden voice', intensifies this message with sound. Another open diorama but with no human figures, Zhou Xuan's famous voice is disembodied, pervasive and unconstrained. More of an installation than a diorama, visitors can encircle the display of objects used or owned by the singer, including a piano, microphone, gramophone and music, as backlit photographic images of Zhou Xuan circle above, reinforcing the lack of her physical presence. Within the museum her music, still used in contemporary film to evoke 1930's Shanghai, provides another sensory connection to the city and *haipai*.

## Conclusion

Time, space and movement have a particular significance in SFM where the concept of the museum and the concept of film are brought into the same domain. Shanghai was the Hollywood of the East during its modern age and is today, as a city once again on the brink of being new, faced with considerations of how to be modern. By asserting a familiar aesthetic in its displays that reproduce the human form, the museum allows visitors to see themselves in a present imbued with the past and imagine its contemporary Golden Age. The aim of the dioramas is not to remove the intervening years between past glories and current claims to greatness through wonder, but to demonstrate how the past is woven into the present and the future through recognizable and definitively Shanghai elements that still define the city today. Displayed in a landscape they bring a sense of mobility, enhanced by their sheer number, the size of the spaces, and the regular reassertion of the domain of the street. The expectation is for an attentive yet roaming visitor, connected to the huge city outside that is restated in the exhibits themselves and the film narratives to which they relate.

## References

Abbas, A. (2000) 'Cosmopolitan De-scriptions: Shanghai and Hong Kong', *Public Culture*, 12(3), pp. 769–86.

Barthes, R. (1981) *Camera Lucida: Reflections on Photography*, New York: Hill & Wang.

Bauman, Z. (2012) *Liquid Modernity*, 2nd edition, Cambridge: Polity Press.

Bordwell, D. (1986) *Narration in the Fiction Film*, London: Routledge.

Bottomore, S. (2006) 'Film Museums: A Bibliography', *Film History: An International Journal*, 18(3), pp. 327–49.

Bruno, G. (2014) *Surface: Matters of Aesthetics, Materiality, and Media*, Chicago, IL: University of Chicago Press.

Chang, M.G. (1999) 'The Good, the Bad, and the Beautiful: Movie Actresses and Public Discourse in Shanghai, 1920s and 1930s', in Zhang, Y. (ed.) *Cinema and Urban Culture in Shanghai 1922–1943*, Stanford, CA: Stanford University Press, pp. 128–59.

Chang, W. (2009) 'Reflections on Time and Related Ideas in the Yijing', *Philosophy East and West*, 59(2), pp. 216–29.

Debord, G. (1994) *The Society of the Spectacle*, New York: Zone Books.

Denton, K. (2014) *Exhibiting the Past: Historical Memory and the Politics of Museums in Postsocialist China*, Honolulu: University of Hawai'i Press.

Des Forges, A. (2010) 'Shanghai Alleys, Theatrical Practice and Cinematic Spectatorship: From Street Angel (1937) to Fifth Generation Film', *Journal of Current Chinese Affairs*, 39(4), pp. 29–51.

Duncan, C. (1995) *Civilizing Rituals: Inside Public Art Museums*, London: Routledge.

Edwards, E. (2010) 'Photographs and History: Emotion and Materiality', in Dudley, S.H. (ed.) *Museum Materialities: Objects, Engagements, Interpretations*, London: Routledge, pp. 21–38.

*Goddess, Shennu* (1934) film, Lianhua Film Company, directed by Wu Yonggang.

Greenspan, A. (2014) *Shanghai Future: Modernity Remade*, Oxford: Oxford University Press.

Griffiths, A. (2002) *Wondrous Difference: Cinema, Anthropology and Turn of the Century Visual Culture*, New York: Columbia University Press.

Griffiths, A. (2003) '"Shivers Down Your Spine": Panoramas and the Origins of the Cinematic Re-enactment', *Screen*, 44(1), pp. 1–37.

Groys, B. (1994) 'The Struggle Against the Museum, or, the Display of Art in Totalitarian Space', in Sherman, D.J. and Rogoff, I. (eds) *Museum Culture: Histories, Discourses and Spectacles*, Minneapolis MN: University of Minnesota Press.

Hansen, M. (1994) *Babel and Babylon: Spectatorship in American Silent Film*, Cambridge, MA: Harvard University Press.

Hein, H.S. (2000) *The Museum in Transition: a Philosophical Perspective*, Washington, DC: Smithsonian Institution Press.

Henning, M. (2006) *Museums, Media and Cultural Theory*, Maidenhead, UK: Open University Press.

Henning, M. (2007) 'Anthropomorphic Taxidermy and the Death of Nature: The Curious Art of Hermann Ploucquet, Walter Potter and Charles Waterton', *Victorian Literature & Culture*, 35(2), pp. 663–78.

*Hibiscus Town, Furong zhen* (1986) film, Shanghai Film Studio, directed by Xie Jin.

Hong, G. (2009) 'Meet Me in Shanghai: Melodrama and the Cinematic Production of Space in 1930s Shanghai Leftist Films', *Journal of Chinese Cinemas*, 3(3), pp. 215–30.

Jacobson, C. (2013) *New Museums in China*, New York: Princeton Architectural Press.
Lagerkvist, A. (2013) *Media and Memory in New Shanghai: Western Performances of Futures Past*, Basingstoke, UK: Palgrave Macmillan.
Lee, Oufan L. (1999a) *Shanghai Modern: the Flowering of a New Urban Culture in China, 1930–1945*, Cambridge, MA: Harvard University Press.
Lee, Oufan, L. (1999b) 'The Urban Milieu of Shanghai Cinema, 1930–40: Some Explorations of Film Audience, Film Culture, and Narrative Conventions', in Zhang, Y. (ed.) *Cinema and Urban Culture in Shanghai, 1922–1943*, pp. 74–96.
Li, R. (2005) *Quiet Brilliance: Analysis on Exhibition Form of Shanghai Museum*, Beijing: Cultural Relics Press.
Liang, S.Y. (2010) *Mapping Modernity in Shanghai Space, Gender and Visual Culture in the Sojourners' City, 1853–1898*, London: Routledge.
Miller, A. (1996) 'The Panorama, the Cinema and the Emergence of the Spectacular', *Wide Angle*, 18(2), pp. 34–69.
Mitchell, W.J.T. (2005) 'There are No Visual Media', *Journal of Visual Media*, 4(2), pp. 257–66.
Mulvey, L. (1975) 'Visual Pleasures and Narrative Cinema', *Screen*, 16(3), pp. 6–18.
Pan, L. (2008) *Shanghai Style: Art & Design Between the Wars*, San Francisco, CA: Long River Press.
Powers, M.J. (1995) 'Art and History: Exploring the Counterchange Condition', *The Art Bulletin*, 77(3), p. 382.
Quinn, S.C. (2006) 'The Worlds Behind the Glass', *Natural History*, 151(3), pp. 48–51.
Sandberg, M. (2001) 'Ibsen and the Mimetic Home of Modernity', *Ibsen Studies*, 1(2), pp. 32–58.
*Street Angel, Malu tianshi* (1937) film, Mingxing Film Company, directed by Yuan Muzhi.
Varutti, M. (2011) 'Standardising Difference: The Materiality of Ethnic Minorities in the Museums of the People's Republic of China', in Dudley, S. (ed.) *The Thing About Museums: Objects and Experience, Representation and Contestation*, London: Routledge, pp. 297–309.
Wasserstrom, J. (2009) *Global Shanghai, 1850–2010: A History in Fragments*, New York: Routledge Curzon.
Wonders, K. (1993) 'Habitat Dioramas as Ecological Theatre', *European Review*, 1(3), pp. 285–300.
Wood, G. (2003) 'The Style and the Age', in Benton, C. and Wood, G. (eds) *Art Deco 1910–1939*, London: V&A Publications.
Zhang, Y. (1999) *Cinema and Urban Culture in Shanghai, 1922–1943*, Stanford, CA: Stanford University Press.
Zhang, Y. (2003) 'Industry and Ideology: A Centennial Review of Chinese Cinema', *World Literature Today*, 77(3–4), pp. 8–13.
Zhang, Z. (2001) 'An Amorous History of the Silver Screen: The Actress as Vernacular Embodiment in Early Chinese Film Culture', *Camera Obscura*, 16(3), pp. 229–63.
Zhang, Z. (2005) *An Amorous History of the Silver Screen: Shanghai Cinema, 1896–1937*, Chicago IL: University of Chicago Press.

# 21

# DISPLAYING AND INTERPRETING INDUSTRIAL POLLUTION

## A study of visitor comments on 'When the South Wind Blows'

*Hsu Huang and Chia-Li Chen*

### Abstract

This chapter explores how narrative-led, highly interpretive exhibition design was utilized at the National Museum of Natural Science in Taiwan as a route to exploring how natural science museums might engage in contemporary issues and, more specifically, play a part in raising contentious social issues and generate deep reflection on environmental protection amongst visitors. 'When the South Wind Blows' displayed a series of documentary photographs capturing the lives and suffering of the residents of Taixi Village affected by the pollution broadcast from the plant of the Formosa Plastic Corporation. Purposefully seeking to prioritise human stories above more conventional forms of scientific narrative and to target adults as opposed to children, the exhibition team sought to create a media rich environment which could potentially open visitors to emotional encounters with the stories of Taixi village and provoke deep reflection on the personal and environmental sacrifices bound up in industrial development in Taiwan. The chapter describes the rationale for the design of the exhibition and presents an analysis of 1,780 visitor comments which suggest that the exhibition successfully stimulated visitors to reflect upon the costs of economic development and the importance of protecting the environment.

### Introduction

Taixi Village is located in southwestern Changhua County, Taiwan, on the northern bank of the Zhuoshui River estuary. Similar to many rural areas in Taiwan, the steady outflow of residents to major metropolitan centers since the 1970s has burdened Taixi with chronic problems that include a disproportionately large population of elderly people, a high ratio of households where grandparents are caring for young children as their parents seek work elsewhere, and a steady decline in the value of agricultural production. However, the 398 smokestacks of Formosa Plastic Corporation's Sixth Naphtha Cracker, completed in 1998 and easily visible from the village across the Zhuoshui River, make the problems faced by Taixi uniquely grim. The seasonal South Wind that blows through the summer months carries smokestack emissions northward and directly across Taixi Village, forcing residents to live not only with the smell of chemical plant emissions but also with the risk of health hazards brought by the many toxic compounds in these emissions. A survey conducted in the area in 2014 identified a frighteningly long list of chemical compounds and heavy metals, many of which are known to harm human health and cause cancer (Chan 2014).

Health is a basic human right. The International Covenant on Economic, Social and Cultural Rights ratified by the United Nations specifically mandates the responsibility of all governments to create conditions whereby everyone may enjoy physical, material, social, and economic wellbeing. But in a world where the rights of ordinary citizens are often placed second to economic development and where the gap between the scientific literacy of the public and their political choices seems to be widening (Conn 2006), what role might museums of natural science play in raising the profile of contentious social issues, providing public forums for debate, and raising a broader visitor awareness?

With these questions in mind and with the explicit aim to move away from the non-contentious and often rather abstract approaches to exhibition making in science museums, in 2014 the six-month special exhibition 'When the South Wind Blows: the Documentary Photographs of Taixi Village' (hereinafter the South Wind Exhibition) opened at the National Museum of Natural Science (NMNS) in Taiwan. The exhibition, which focused around a body of documentary photographs of Taixi Village by Sheng-hsiung Chung and Cheng-tang Hsu, set out to prioritize stories of human suffering as a route to drawing attention to the plight of Taixi residents whose protests had gone largely unheard; advocate for a public forum within which Taixi residents could put their view to government and industry; and utilize interpretive design in order to both activate the documentary photographs and create the conditions for emotive as well as reflective and critical experiences amongst adult visitors. This chapter describes the South Wind Exhibition before going on to share some of the findings from the opportunities for visitor reflection which were built into the exhibition itself.

## The narrative of the South Wind Exhibition

The primary exhibits in the South Wind Exhibition were a collection of 102 black-and-white photographs taken by Sheng-hsiung Chung and Cheng-tang Hsu, augmented by written information, documentary films and video clips. The role of the exhibition design as Huang (2015: 87–8) analyzed was 'through the deployment of the different media, to reinforce the message and meaning behind the images and to bring the forces of the documentary photography into action'. The documentary photographs were also accompanied by significant amounts of descriptive text. Skolnick (2005: 120) and MacLeod (2005: 3) have both suggested that text significantly affects the concept, planning, and design of exhibitions and that this text may rightly be considered an 'engine' of the exhibition design process in narrative-led exhibitions, which helps structure the exhibition space and contextualize its content. In what follows, the narratives and design concepts of the South Winds Exhibition will be briefly discussed.

### *Concepts of exhibition design*

The environment in and around Taixi Village was the principal design focus of the South Wind Exhibition. Hoping to give visitors the impression of a physical visit to Taixi and to evoke something of the realities of the place, the exhibition planning and design teams conducted field research to select three elements that signify the environment of Taixi Village and then translated these elements into the primary spatial images and framework of the exhibit. These elements included the main Taixi canal, the seaside Embankment, and the traditional courtyard houses. The decision to select the canal, embankment, and traditional homes as the primary spatial images of the exhibition was further confirmed by their being regularly mentioned in interviews with Taixi residents and by their frequent appearance in the documentary photographs.

As shown in the South Wind Exhibition floor plan (Figure 21.1), visitors walked into an irregularly shaped 'central axial zone' immediately after entering the exhibition area (Zone L). Lacking an exhibit-related theme, this zone was simply an elongated hallway leading to the exhibition area intended to orientate visitors and convey something of the exhibit's primary spatial images. In the real Taixi village, the canal leads visitors from the center of the village to further along both sides of the waterway. A blue-coloured floor with floor lighting bordered

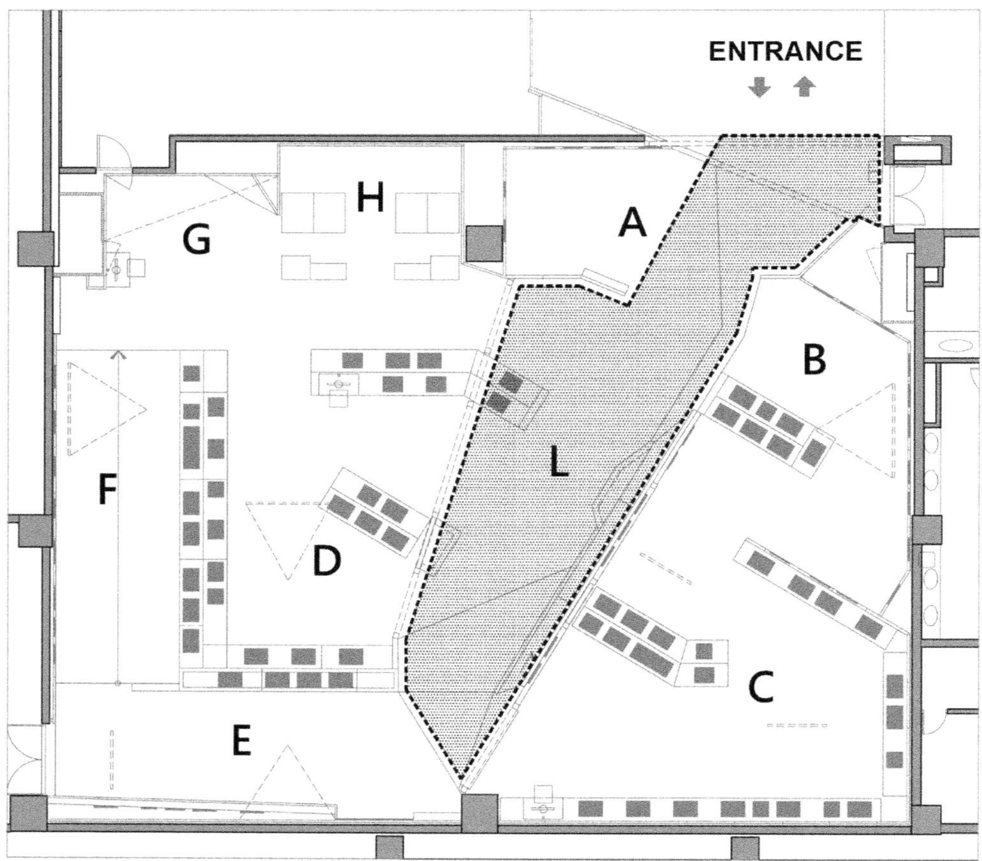


**FIGURE 21.1** Floor plan of 'When the South Wind Blows: The Documentary Photographs of Taixi Village', National Museum of Natural Science, Taiwan, 2014

*Design credit:* Hsu Huang and Ting Hsu Huang

by a gray-painted mock-up of a small river dike was designed to guide visitors through the exhibition. Looking outwards from the central axial zone gave visitors clear views of the exhibition's two other symbolic elements. The first of these were mock-ups of the village's traditional red brick and black-tile roofed courtyard houses that lined both sides of the walkway and served a practical purpose as exhibit cabinets. The second symbolic element, located at the far end of the central axial zone, was a high, gray-coloured angular wall topped by a silhouette sketch of a gazebo that was meant to represent Taixi's embankment. Set into this installation and working to establish a direct relationship for visitors between the imagined context of Taixi village and the issue of pollution, was a screen that played a video of the Sixth Naphtha Cracker, showing how the residents of Taixi village regularly see this sprawling petrochemical complex within their daily lives.

## *The narratives and themes*

Most of the photographs displayed in the South Wind Exhibition were from the 2013 photography compilation book titled *South Wind* (Chung and Hsu 2013). After carefully analyzing and classifying the photographs, curators selected and distinguished the photographs into six categories:

1 'The Stories Blowing in the Wind' (Zone A): Six photographs which highlight the physical position of Taixi Village and describe its geographical relationship with the Sixth Naphtha Cracker in neighbouring Mailiao. Zone A tells visitors how the seasonal southerly Winds of summer regularly sweep polluted air from the Sixth Naphtha Cracker complex across Taixi Village and influence the residents' health. This statement is further supported by academic studies, which link pollution from the plant to the incidence of cancer in surrounding communities. These panels thus set the overall tone for the exhibition's central narrative.

2 'Visiting Taixi Village' (Zone B): Twenty-two photographs focusing on Taixi Village's elderly and very young residents to underscore the chronic problems of an ageing population and the forced absence of younger adults. A preponderance of old and young and a corresponding scarcity of young adults is one of the first impressions gleaned from a visit to Taixi.

3 'The People of Taixi Village' (Zone C): Most of the 28 photographs in this category feature images of individual Taixi residents. While most reflect the hardships borne by their subjects, a few images showing happy smiles simply exacerbate the overall pall of despondency.

4 'Portraits in the South Wind' (Zone D): Twenty-one photographs examining the effects that cancer has wrought on Taixi Village. Over half of the images here depict the family members of cancer victims holding pictures of their lost relatives and staring directly into the lens of the camera.

5 'Working along the Water' (Zone E): The nine photographs in this category show the residents of Taixi earning their living along the capricious shores of the Taiwan Strait in winter. The narrative descriptions that accompany these photographs highlight the worries of residents about the environmental impact of the Sixth Naphtha Cracker on local eel fry populations and on coastal wetland wildlife.

6 'The People and the Land' (Zone F): Most residents who do not fish for a living in Taixi cultivate rice, vegetables, and watermelon. The latter was once a widely prized speciality crop of the area. The 16 photographs in this category document the agricultural wisdom and hardships of Taixi residents as well as shifts in agricultural crops over time.

The exhibition included a further two theme sections in addition to the six that were photograph related. The first, 'Wetland Park' (Zone G), described the diversity of the wetland areas in Dacheng Township, the area around Taixi village. The second, 'South Wind Theatre' (Zone H), featured a regular rotation of three films. Thus, together with the central axial zone (Zone L), the South Wind Exhibition embraced a total of nine distinct themes. Using a justified permeability graph (j-graph) to organize and analyze the relationships among these units (Hillier and Hanson 1984; Huang 2008) revealed that the spatial arrangement of the exhibit partitioned the story of Taixi Village into three distinct parts. The first part synopsized the exhibit; the second part described the sociocultural threats facing Taixi Village; and the third part explored concerns regarding the threats to human health and the natural environment from the Sixth Naphtha Cracker. This strong narrative would structure the exhibit space and contextualize the exhibit content. Further still, the spatial structure created new relationships among the various exhibition themes and allowed the narrative of each theme to form interrelationships of varying degrees of strength, which created the potential for visitors to select from several different narratives and different paths through the museum.

## Documentary photographs on display

> Because each photograph is only a fragment, its moral and emotional weight depends on where it is inserted. A photograph changes according to the context in which it is seen.
>
> *(Sontag 1977: 105–6)*

In the exhibition, most of the photographs use common documentary techniques to portray daily life and work. However, those in the 'Portraits in the South Wind' section show residents purposefully posed in a desolate family courtyard or house holding pictures of a deceased relative. The images of the deceased that were shown in these photographs were the images used for their funeral – their final farewell to the mortal world as well as a bitter condemnation of how industrial pollution robbed them of their health and life. Most of the photographs in this section are accompanied by a narrative description, provided by the photographers and edited by the exhibition curator, of how cancer took the life of the individual. These sentences anchor the photographic content (Barthes 1993) and provide to visitors a clear linkage between industrial pollution and the village's high rates of cancer and cancer-related deaths. For example, the description that accompanied the photograph of Mei-chue Chen and her deceased husband (Figure 21.2) reads:

> Mei-chue Chen's husband Shun-shih Hung died in 2009 of colon and lymphatic cancer. Shun-shih was a farmer, a shoreline fisherman, and a harvester of eel fry. Mei-chue reminisces about how he used to head to the sea wrapped in fishing nets. The eel fry and clams were once abundant, and the clams especially, she says, were unforgettably sweet and succulent. However, after the naphtha cracker, the air took on a rancid, sour

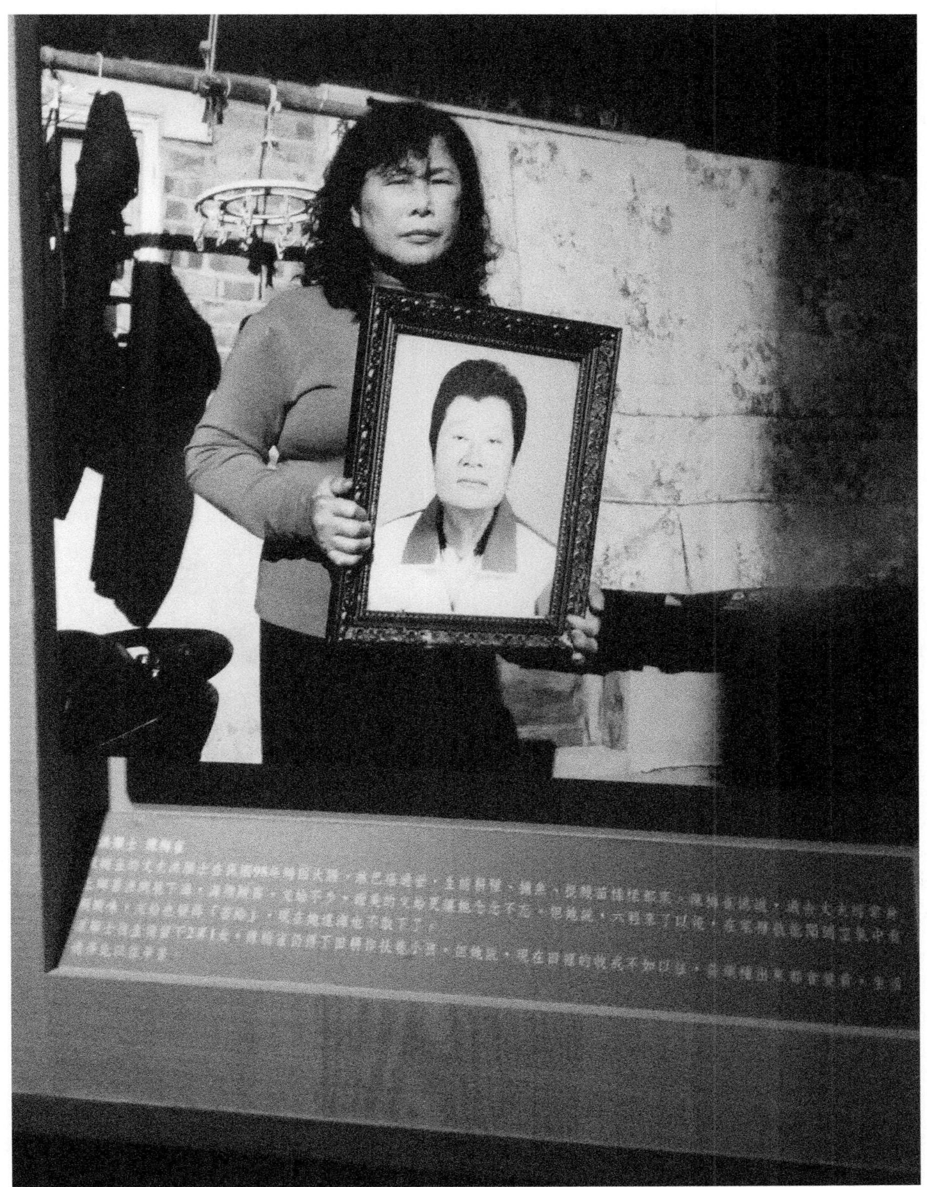

**FIGURE 21.2** Photograph of Mei-Chue Chen and her husband exhibited with text panels describing their suffering, 'When the South Wind Blows: the Documentary Photographs of Taixi Village', National Museum of Natural Science, Taiwan, 2014

*Photo:* Sheng-Syong Jhong

smell and the clams, once so sweet, became 'bitter clams'. Today, because of the Sixth Naphtha Cracker, she dares not go down to the sea anymore.

Shun-shih left behind two sons and a daughter. While Mei-chue still farms the land to support her children, she says harvests are not what they used to be. The garlic now often turns yellow in the field. Mei-chue's life is much harder than before.

*(Chung and Hsu 2013: 173)*

Another photograph displayed in the 'Portraits in the South Wind' section is *Cai Cai-feng and Su Wei* (Figure 21.3):

Cai's hands are swollen, her edema a sign of her continued dialysis over the past 10 years. She is now 79 years old. Her late husband, born in the same year as Cai, passed away in 2011 from lung cancer following many years of pain and suffering.

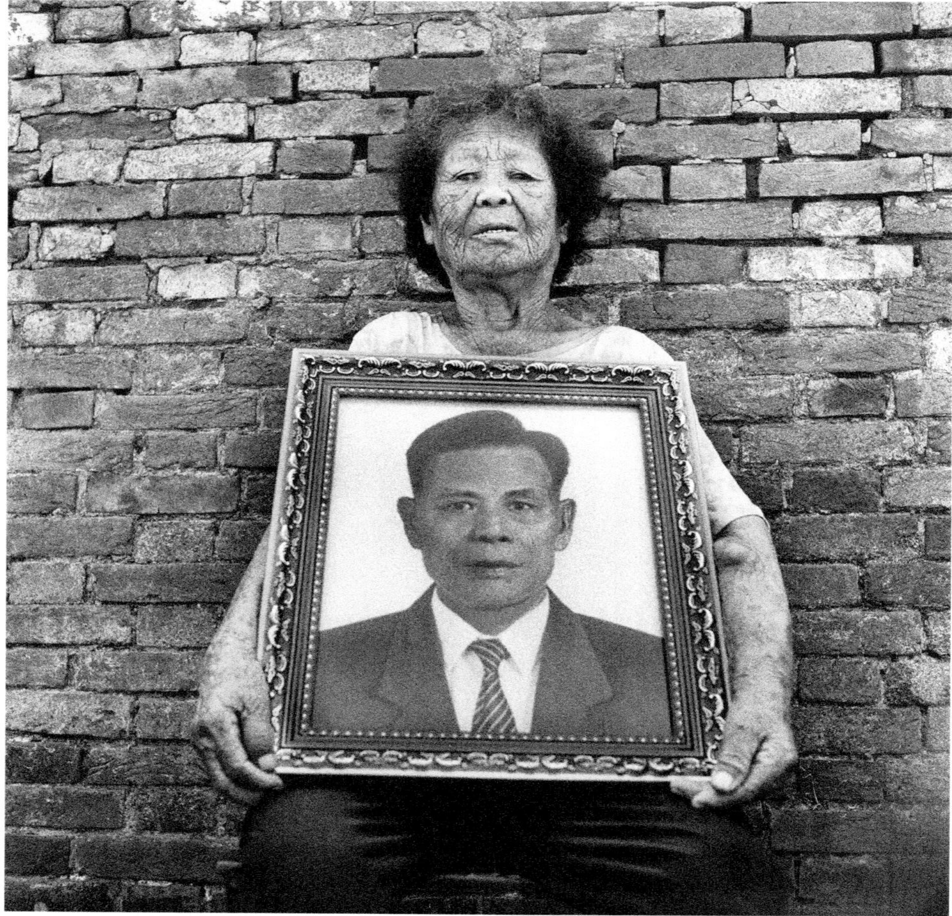

**FIGURE 21.3** Photograph of Cai Cai-feng and Su Wei, 'When the South Wind Blows: the Documentary Photographs of Taixi Village', National Museum of Natural Science, Taiwan, 2014

*Photo:* Sheng-Syong Jhong

In addition to the careful display and interpretation of the documentary photographs, a large (2.4 m × 1.4 m) projection screen suspended from the exhibition's nearly 5-metre-high ceiling in Zone D displayed 10 photographs on a continuous loop. Reflecting the 'portraits' theme of this zone, most of these pictures depicted surviving family members holding portraits of their cancer-stricken loved ones. These looming, larger than life-size images created a natural focal point for the 'Portraits in the South Wind' section of the exhibition and accentuated its message of human suffering. Moreover, the juxtaposition of Zone D with Zone E (Working along the Water) established for visitors an intuitive, emotionally heart-rending 'face-to-face' dialogue between these two zones (Plate 24).

Zone E recreated the look and feel of Taixi's embankment. The video that was screened here of the Sixth Naphtha Cracker as seen from this embankment showed a constant stream of pollution emanating from the plant's smokestacks from late afternoon into the evening. The slideshow in Zone D, in which family photographs fade in and out every 10 seconds, was designed to provide a visual link between the troubled faces of these individuals and the smokestacks in the video, highlighting for visitors the deep-set concerns of Taixi villagers about the possible connection between their failing health and Sixth Naphtha Cracker operations.

In addition, two other videos were shown in 'Visiting Taixi Village' (Zone B) and 'People and the Land' (Zone F), respectively. Both short video clips, filmed in black and white, follow an older man on his travels around Taixi Village by bicycle, which remains an important form of transportation in the village today. The video was produced so that the cyclist maintains the same pose and position throughout, as the landscape scrolls by in a streaming series of Taixi Village scenes. Visitors thus accompany the cyclist as he tours the village in the gallery. Cheng-tang Hsu's cyclist photograph, which was enlarged and featured in Zone B, provided the inspiration for the films. Trees in the foreground aesthetically frame the old cyclist and his bike as he travels from left to right. These trees in the foreground and the buildings in the distance naturally reflect different levels of light, giving the image its rich depth. Inspired by *The Walk to Paradise Garden* by US photographer Eugene Smith and its message of hope in the face of oppressive pain and troubles and to persist in times of despair, the halo of light that surrounds the cyclist sets him at the metaphorical crossroads between darkness and light as he peddles in earnest to extricate himself from the darkness and emerge into the light.

The exhibition utilized these highly interpretive approaches to underscore and activate the tremendous power that photographs hold with the explicit aim of deeply affecting how people understand their world. In order to better understand the impact of 'When the South Wind Blows', the researchers conducted a comprehensive analysis of visitor comments made as part of the exhibition experience. This analysis and its results are described in the following section.

## Visitor comments: analysis and methods

On the subject of viewer reactions to photographs depicting contemporary disasters, Sontag (2003: 91) indicated: 'one could feel an obligation to look at these pictures, gruesome as they were, because there was something to be done, right now, about what they depicted'. The question remains, then, as to how visitors reacted and responded to the human and environmental narratives within the South Wind Exhibition. Furthermore, is it possible for a museum to stimulate visitors to think introspectively on these topics and then to take relevant action? Macdonald (2005) discussed using written visitor comments to conduct visitor research, saying that these comments were freely given and not subject to the inherent limitations of

**TABLE 21.1** Comments from the South Wind Exhibition: categories and percentages

| *Category* | *Comments on Exhibition* | *Answers to Given Question* | *Provision of Information* | *Unrelated to the Exhibition* | *Total* |
|---|---|---|---|---|---|
| Number of Comments | 817 | 308 | 64 | 591 | 1780 |
| Percentage of Total | 45.9% | 17.3% | 3.6% | 33.2% | 100% |

formatted interviews and questionnaires. Thus, visitor comments may be expected to more fully express visitors' subjective thoughts and opinions. However, a drawback to using visitor comments is that these comments typically lack critical demographic information on the respondents such as level of education, gender and age.

The exhibition curators developed a visitor comment strategy that used three computer stations installed in different exhibition sections to elicit visitor responses to a total of three questions, which were designed to better understand visitors' thoughts about the exhibition and environmental issues. This approach also ensured that the questions and the reflection they encouraged was a core part of the exhibition experience. In the first stage of analysis, the authors reviewed all of the comments and assigned each to one of several classification categories. A total of 1,780 comments were received from visitors to the South Wind Exhibition. Of these, around 70% of comments addressed the exhibition topic, exhibition content, or questions posed by curators. This relatively high valid-response rate demonstrates the effectiveness of the computer installations and questions in attracting visitor interest. Furthermore, nearly half (46%) of the comments were related to the exhibit content or design. Meanwhile, 33% of the comments were unrelated to the exhibit, 17% responded to curators' questions, and 3.6% either responded to other commenters or provided relevant news and information (Table 21.1).

## Comments on exhibit content

Nearly half of the visitor comments dealt with the content and design of the exhibition and expressed the impressions and thoughts of the commenter. These comments and thoughts are categorized and analyzed in the following subsections.

### *Evincing empathy and sadness*

Many of the comments, especially those that addressed the photographs in the 'Portraits in the South Wind' section, conveyed the emotional sentiment of the commenter. This finding highlights that many visitors, especially female visitors, perceived strong feelings of empathy following their visit. Some even expressed being moved to tears:

> Seeing everything like that, the sorrow of it all made me cry. The camera lens led me through so much helplessness and heartache.
>
> *(Ms Chen)*

> Each of those photographs of the dead is a denunciation of the earth by mankind.
>
> *(Ms Yeh)*

### *Criticism of the government and expectations of museums*

Apart from stimulating empathy, the exhibition encouraged visitors to reflect critically on the actions of government and industry:

> High-pollution industries are the most profitable. While profits flow into the pockets of corporations, locals are left to suffer the consequences of this pollution.
>
> *(Mr Chan)*

> I wish to thank the NMNS for holding this exhibition. I was born and raised in the city and thus have a hard time imagining what life outside the city is like, especially in poor rural areas that are affected by industrial pollution. I am wondering if the content of the exhibit will be organized into a report format and submitted to local governments so that they can take a more serious and proactive approach to this problem!
>
> *(Ms Lan)*

Although the NMNS did not submit a report to the government, the curatorial team issued formal invitations to local officials and representatives to visit the South Wind Exhibition in hope that the exhibition might inspire them to address industrial pollution and environmental protection more seriously.

### *Inspiring civic responsibility and action*

The visitor comments also highlighted that everyone has a right and responsibility to guide Taiwan's destiny. Thus, a number of comments called on everyone to fulfill their responsibility by drawing attention to and rectifying injustices:

> I live in Mailiao and the situation is just like it said at the end of the film. Our beautiful island of Taiwan is one, unified ecosystem. Today, no one can afford to stand dispassionately on the sidelines. We must take responsibility not only for what has been said but also for what has not been said. We can no longer be silent citizens!
>
> *(Ms Tseng)*

Importantly, a good number of these comments drew attention to the relationship between this call to action and the media of the exhibition:

> The south wind that was supposed to be warm and delighted, is now becoming smelly and harmful because of the plastic corporation . . . The enlarged photographs of the relatives who passed away are showed on the projection screen above. I stop to watch these photos above again and again. These photos seem peaceful, but they strike into my heart strongly. Without reading the text, tears are already in my eye only by looking at these enlarged photos . . . Riding the bicycle and keep on riding, riding through the houses, riding through the paddy field and the seashore . . . Taiwan is a beautiful island, we need to protect our environment and society. I will keep on being concerned about the environment and society. Act up, citizen.
>
> *(Ms Chang)*

In general, visitor comments revealed empathetic expressions of regret and sadness. Even more significantly, the comments suggested that many visitors perceived themselves a part of the problem and were taking the next step to consider how to change things for the better.

## Answers to curators' questions – reflection and debate

Aside from thoughts and opinions related to the exhibition content, around 17% of visitor comments addressed one or more of three questions posed by curators.

### *From economic development to environmental protection*

Question 1 was: 'How have you experienced the Sixth Naphtha Cracker in your everyday life?' A total of 58 visitor comments addressed this question. This relatively low response rate indicates that most visitors had a low awareness of any relationship with the plant and that most perceived the problem largely in the context of economics:

> I was born in Mailiao and once saw the Sixth Naphtha Cracker primarily as an engine of national prosperity and growth. But this growth comes at the cost of ecological and environmental destruction. Balancing prosperity with environmental health is one of the most difficult problems for our generation. As we progress forward, we should in all good faith ask – What sort of future are we preparing to leave for our children?
>
> *(Vivian)*

At the end of their visit, many visitors no longer considered the Sixth Naphtha Cracker in exclusively economic terms, but also in the context of environmental protection and sustainability. Many visitor comments revealed a negative questioning of the plant:

> I feel that the Sixth Naphtha Cracker has greatly harmed this village. It's terrible. No one should sacrifice the happiness of an entire village for profit.
>
> *(Berry)*

> Although it (the plant) has done damage, it has sustained a lot of families.
>
> *(Wen)*

> While the Sixth Naphtha Cracker does bring jobs for some families, are you willing to be the one asked to sacrifice? 'Men should not do to others what they would not wish done to them'. . . . This exhibition encourages us to examine how we choose to live and offers the chance to construct a better way to live together as a society.
>
> *(Tsang-Kai)*

The visitor comments suggest that the exhibit inspired many visitors to ponder the price of economic prosperity and to adopt a critical approach towards the Sixth Naphtha Cracker. The small minority of comments that reflected positively on the economic contributions of the plant tended to attract derogatory comments and criticism from other visitors, turning the visitor comment station into a lively center of debate.

### *Reflection on environmental protection and economic development*

Question 2 was: 'Which do you feel to be more important – economic development or environmental protection? Are these two necessarily mutually incompatible?' A total of 145 visitor comments addressed this question. The higher response rate for this question likely reflects its clarity of meaning and thought-provoking nature. Further analysis revealed that 66 (45.51%) of the 145 comments valued environmental protection over economic development and 41 (28.28%) gave equal weight to both. Furthermore, 36 (24.83%) either stated that more thought was needed on this issue or did not provide an opinion. Only two comments valued economic development over environmental protection. The primary argument for valuing environmental protection over economic development was centered on the close relationship between the environment and human survival. A 'good' environment was argued to be a basic human right and the environmental destruction caused by corporations was roundly criticized.

> Many people willingly prioritize economic concerns in exchange for short-term material gain. However, I feel that sacrificing our good environment will make life for humanity miserable indeed. At that point, material pleasures will be out of the question. Placing a high value on the environment is not necessarily a moral act. It is the choice that protects our own interests. This is why I choose environmental protection.
>
> *(Huang)*

Additionally, 44 comments indicated that economic development and environmental protection were equally important. The comments in this category tended to advocate for a change in the current approach to economic development using legal strictures to strike a more equitable balance with environmental concerns.

> The two are of equal importance. We just need to use legal means to set the relevant moral boundaries. In facing problems of environmental protection, it's the indifference of those on the sidelines that allow the destruction to expand and spread.
>
> *(Ms Peng)*

> Economic development and environmental protection are not mutually incompatible. The problem lies in our 'generally limited understanding of economics'. The key lies with who's economics and who's development are we talking about? Our understanding of economics has long hinged on the quick, easily measured GDP aggregate measure of performance. This has narrowed our perception of economic development drastically. . . . Environmental protection can absolutely thrive alongside economic development.
>
> *(Mr Chan)*

Twenty-two comments stated the opinion that this issue deserved further deliberation, including the gathering of more scientific evidence and the encouragement of more scholarly debate.

> I feel this is a very important problem that can only be addressed with sufficient scientific evidence and social debate. What is most important for humankind? I strongly

> support the NMNS continuing to organize exhibitions on environmental and social issues of Taiwan.
>
> *(Ms Chen)*

Though the majority valued environmental protection, two of the comments expressed a preference for economic development over environmental protection. The main sentiment underlying these two comments is that human life is short and advantage should be taken of the opportunities for pleasures and enjoyment. These two comments are presented below:

> I think that money is more important.
>
> *(Daniel)*

> As long as the profits are big enough, who in their right mind cares about the environment? The environment is protected by poor people with so-called 'ideals'. It's useless to talk about doing things that end up harming yourself. How long do we have to live anyway? As long as the apocalypse doesn't come in my lifetime, I look forward to spending my life enjoying all the wealth and splendor that I possibly can.
>
> *(Dumbstruck)*

In summary, aside from the very small number that advocated economic development over protection of the environment, the vast majority of visitor comments in this section echoed opposition to Taiwan's former pursuit of economic growth at the cost of the environment and quality of life. Furthermore, these comments illustrated that visitors were reflecting and expressed the hope that various measures could be taken to achieve an equitable balance between these two choices.

### *Environmental protection and activism*

The South Wind Exhibition further referenced recent environmental issues and protests. In 2008, wetlands in the Zhuoshui River estuary in Changhua County's Dacheng Township were approved for use by the Kuo Kuang Petrochemical Corporation. Supporters of the project, known as the 'Economic Development Faction', included the then county magistrate and various national legislators. Those opposed to the zoning decision, including environmental groups, artists, and health professionals, were known as the 'Environmental Sustainability Faction'. Opposition to the Kuo Kuang Petrochemical project eventually grew into a substantial national movement. In the face of this concerted public effort, Taiwan President Ma formally announced his opposition to Kuo Kuang's plans in Changhua County on Earth Day 2011 (22 April) and designated the Dacheng wetlands as an ecological area of national importance. At the third computer station, visitors were asked to comment on the environmental-protection movement and related protests. The question was: 'Do you feel that the Zhuoshui River estuary should be protected? How should this protection be implemented?' A total of 104 visitor comments addressed this question. Of these, 101 (98%) of the comments acknowledged the importance of protecting the Zhuoshui River estuary. Examples of practical suggestions for achieving this protection included:

> Put decision-making authority in the hands of the local residents. They're the only ones who can understand the best way to proceed. (Ask 'experts'? Be very wary that they'll cast their lot with big money.)
>
> *(Mr Huang)*

> The Zhuoshui Estuary Wetlands should be protected because the ecological value of not developing this area is higher than the economic value to be gained from development. Start from education and change the mindset. Only after this is done can concrete measures related to protection have a chance of success.
>
> *(Mr Chen)*

A large majority of the comments relating to this question were in favor of wetland protection. Some went further to suggest practical measures and other suggestions for protecting wetland ecosystems, including the ideas that everyone shares responsibility for ecological protection, that education is key to achieving fundamental change, and that local residents should be allowed the right to choose.

## Conclusion: towards museum exhibitions grounded in social practice

The analysis of comments showed that the exhibition successfully led visitors to walk into the remote Taixi village, observe the environment through the eyes of residents and connect with their life stories. In discussing photography, Barthes (1993: 41) referred to two distinct concepts: *studium* and *punctum*. Studium refers to the cultural and historical connotation of photographs. Thus, studium is interpretable by the viewer. Conversely, punctum refers to the elements of a photograph that are emotionally provocative and disturbing and thus not interpretable. For Barthes, the substance of documentary photography is clear, which leaves the genre devoid of disturbing 'punctuation' and other surprising or emotionally painful elements. Thus documentary photographs normally belong squarely in the realm of studium. Despite the documentary nature of the photographs in the South Wind Exhibition, the comments analyzed indicate that these photographs, supported by the highly interpretive environment and highly emotional narrative, elicited strong, even emotionally painful, reactions from visitors. Moreover, the three questions posed by curators successfully stimulated visitor thinking on the difficult contemporary issues of economic development and environmental protection leading visitors to offer practical strategies and actions that may be used to achieve environmental protection goals.

In addition to raising the levels of public concern over industrial pollution and environmental protection, the South Wind Exhibition elicited a range of follow-on effects. When the exhibition toured to Taipei, some of the affiliates of the exhibition, including the Taixi community, civic groups, politicians and exhibition curators, went together to the Office of the President of Taiwan to protest. In addition to holding up images of loved ones, a number of the protestors held up images of the South Wind Exhibition. Also among these effects was the promise made by Yunlin County Magistrate Chin-yung Lee in March 2015 during his visit to the South Wind Exhibition to take effective measures to improve the problem of air pollution in the county. Soon afterward, the Yunlin County Council expeditiously passed a ban on the burning of soft coal and petroleum coke in a majority vote that united legislators across party lines. The new regulations banned plants in Yunlin County from these two fuel sources as a first step toward improving air quality. However, the regulations were rejected by the central government as contravening national regulations and were declared invalid by the Environmental Protection Administration (EPA). These actions spurred the Yunlin county government to protest, to petition the Legislative Yuan directly, and to submit a written explanation of its actions to the Judicial Yuan under the Local Government Act (Chen 2015). This flurry of information and news, shared with visitors in the comment area through the exhibition, encouraged a significant and public outpouring of support for the actions of the county magistrate, who became widely known as 'Uncle Brave'.

In addressing the question raised by the NMNS curators – 'What can a museum of natural science do to further the cause of environmental protection?' – it may be helpful to refer to Conn's (2006) exploration of the development of the American Museum of Natural History. He found that museums continued to focus on presenting only non-controversial scientific evidence to avoid the various issues and social responsibilities that had accompanied the development of the sciences. Moreover, Conn (2006) noted a trend during the twentieth century that reoriented natural science museums to the interests of children and abandoned the needs of adult visitors. This trend ultimately widened the gap between the scientific literacy of the public and their political choices. Therefore, Conn stated that only by re-embracing adult visitors and making science part of daily life would museums of natural science be able to provide to the public the scientific information and up-to-date research findings that are necessary to make clear and informed political choices. We would add to this that museums of natural science can move firmly into the realm of emotions and get involved in promoting and seeking social justice.

The visitor comments analyzed in the present study demonstrate that museums of natural science can harness exhibition design as one important resource as they strive for social relevance. At NMNS, the painful landscape created by documentary photographs and panel texts was transformed into an experience that touched visitors' emotions, stimulated reflection, encouraged action, and fostered the potential to change society for the better. Exhibitions may be used to give a public voice to the formerly neglected shouts and sorrows of the disadvantaged and of the marginalized. Exhibitions also hold the potential to rouse the public to focus attention on environmental and human rights issues. After showing in NMNS, the South Wind Exhibition will continue to tour and display around the country. Therefore, apart from eliciting sympathetic responses from the Yunlin county government and the general public, the exhibition holds the potential to realize the vision of its curators – to blow its messages nationwide, as well as to the central government, recruiting an increasing number of citizens and public officials to take actions towards protecting the environment and safeguarding human rights.

## References

Barthes, R. (1993) *Camera Lucida: Reflections on Photography* (trans R. Howard), London: Vintage.

Chan, C.-C. (2014) *Environmental Epidemiological Cohort Study in Yulin County (2013–2014)*, Taipei: National Taiwan University. Unpublished Report Commissioned by Yulin County.

Chen, Y.-L. (2015) 'Controversy over Fuel Burn Ban, Yunlin County Government Submits Explanation of Actions to Judicial Yuan', *United Daily News*. Online. Available HTTP: https://video.udn.com/news/367442. Accessed 10 September 2015.

Chung, S.-H. and Hsu, C.-T. (2013) *South Wind*, Taipei: Acropolis Publisher.

Conn, S. (2006) 'Science Museum and the Cultural Wars', in Macdonald, S. (ed.) *A Companion to Museum Studies*, Oxford: Blackwell, pp. 494–508.

Hillier, B. and Hanson, J. (1984) *The Social Logic of Space*, Cambridge: Cambridge University Press.

Huang, H. (2008) 'Mapping of Knowledge in the Natural History Museum', *Collection and Research*, 21, pp. 51–78.

Huang, H. (2015) 'Concealment and Disclosure: Dialogue between Documentary Photography and Exhibition Design', *Museology Quarterly*, 29(4), pp. 87–109.

Macdonald, S. (2005) 'Accessing Audiences: Visiting Visitor Books', *Museum and Society*, 3(3), pp. 119–36.

MacLeod, S. (2005) 'Introduction', in MacLeod, S. (ed.) *Reshaping Museum Space: Architecture, Design, Exhibitions*, London: Routledge, pp. 1–5.

Skolnick, L.H. (2005) 'Towards a New Museum Architecture: Narrative and Representation', in MacLeod, S. (ed.) *Reshaping Museum Space: Architecture, Design, Exhibitions*, London and New York: Routledge, pp. 118–30.

Sontag, S. (1977) *On Photography*, London: Anchor Books.

Sontag, S. (2003) *Regarding the Pain of Others*, New York: Picador.

# 22

# SPATIAL MEANING-MAKING

## Exhibition design and embodied experience

*Maja Gro Gundersen and Christina Back*

### Abstract

This chapter reports on an exhibition experiment in which a highly staged environment of a single exhibit was intended to serve the function usually performed by other interpretation and learning initiatives – most often exhibition texts. The chapter explores the workings, perspectives and challenges associated with this specific case, and does so by reflecting on a qualitative reception study. The experiment was carried out at the Royal Danish Library, Copenhagen, drawing on years of practice working with the spatial design of exhibitions at this institution.

### Introduction

This chapter explores the potentials in working with the exhibition space and its design, with embodied encounters and moreover with a high level of trust in visitors' meaning-making as it may unfold in a scenographically staged environment. The chapter reports on an exhibition experiment that explores premises, possibilities and challenges connected to the use of spatial staging and a sensory-based mode of interpretation. Over the past century, increasing recognition has been given to the fact that our being in this world relies on our physicality. As suggested by architectural theorist Jonathan Hale in the anthology *Museum Making*, recent years' influential work in social and cultural studies along with inspiration from phenomenology may be an important influence on this development (Hale 2012: 193, 195).

A similar preoccupation with the body and affective aspects of human experience can be seen in the practice and priorities of museums as well as in the field of museology. Especially within recent decades, traditional modes of display have been re-worked by means of experimentation (Macdonald and Basu 2007) and museum collaborations with curators and exhibition designers rooted in fine arts, theatre, filmmaking and the like have contributed to an increased orientation towards the sensorial and the scenographic (Heinich and Pollak 1996; den Oudsten 2011; Skolnick 2012; Crawley 2012). The exhibition environment and the physicality of visitors' encounter with objects appear to be attracting greater attention (den

Oudsten 2011; Skolnick 2012; Crawley 2012; Hale 2012; Candlin 2010; Dudley 2010, 2012). All this seems to reflect a marked prioritization of the point of contact between exhibitions and their audiences that takes place as sensing bodies move through a physical space.

This chapter reports from a case-based study of the spatial anchoring of the exhibition medium, a study that looks into visitors' experiences of a physical encounter with an exhibition. More specifically, the study employs an experiment where a handful of test visitors were invited to visit a small exhibition fragment, displaying only a single object – a photograph – that appeared in a highly staged set-up (Figure 22.1). After visiting the space, the visitors participated in a qualitative interview to afford insight into their perception and the formation of narratives[1] resulting from the encounter.

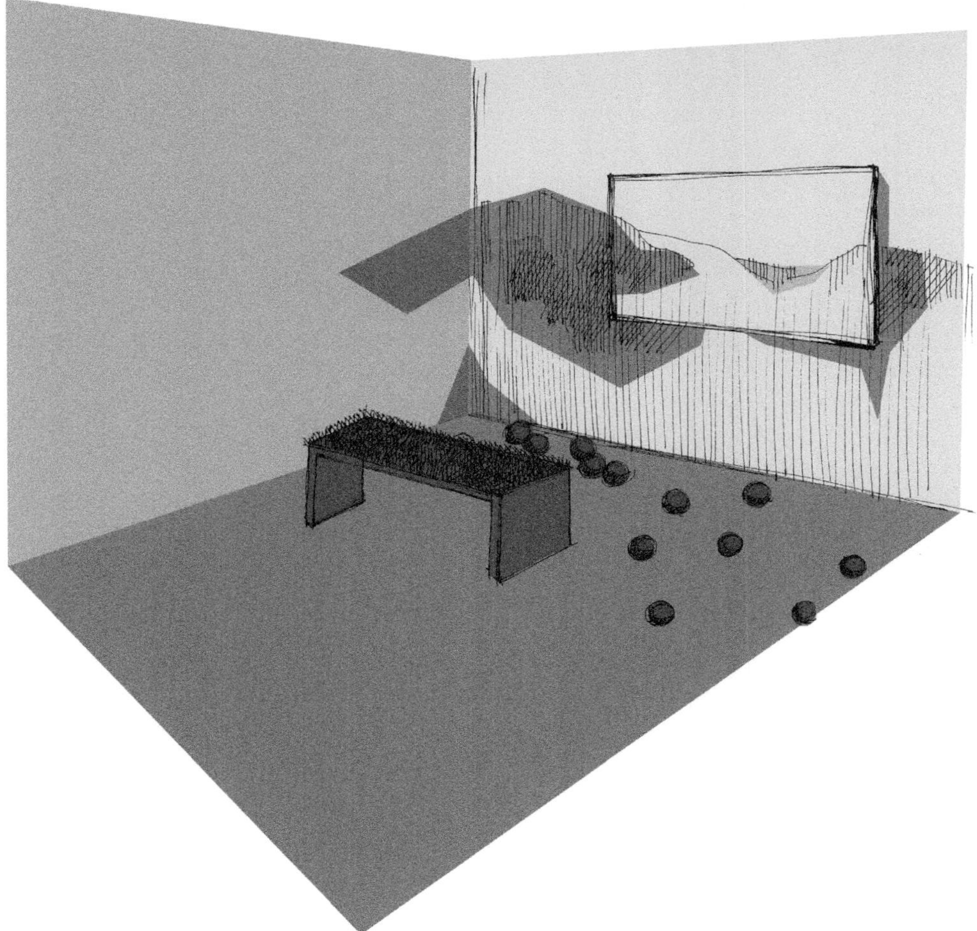

**FIGURE 22.1** 'Imprints of War – Photography from 1864', the National Museum of Photography, Royal Danish Library, Copenhagen, 2014. Staged by Christina Back

*Illustration:* Mette Ørnstrup. Reproduced with kind permission of the Royal Danish Library.

## The design

The exhibition space considered here was a fragment of the larger exhibition, 'Imprints of War – Photography from 1864', shown at the National Museum of Photography (June to September 2014), which is housed within the Royal Danish Library.[2] A single exhibit was displayed alone in an enclosed space; a black-and-white 1.5 × 2.2 m photograph showing a bare landscape from southern Jutland, where a well-known gory battle took place during the Danish-Prussian war in 1864. The image was staged as the center of a dynamic installation that included filmic projection, light, sound and tactile physical objects, all contributing to a nine-minute course of shifting (and at some points moving) 'tableaux'. These were composed to offer different views of the image and point to a range of perspectives of relevance to its history.

The design did not address the historical background by way of lifelike installations, depicting realistic scenes from a different historical time. Instead it had a more abstract feel, offering scenes of a metaphorical nature. Central to the strategy employed in the set-up was a desire to encourage bodily/sensorial approximation to the landscape and to let this play a considerable role in the visitors' approach to the historical content addressed.

Taking on the role of interpretation, the staging was loaded with what we will refer to in the following as a set of 'clues' hinting at a narrative in relation to the image. The notion of clues in this context may be seen as parallel to that of 'affordances' introduced by J.J. Gibson, that is as covering latent possibilities for action in the specific surroundings (Gibson 1986, 1979). In this case, however, the reference is rather to an intended communicative latency in the staged environment, represented by a panoply of more or less open constellations of meaning that were incorporated into the design.

The staging held nine such clues, the primary one of which had to do with linking the impression of the image – which appeared rather strange and anonymous – to the war actions that had once taken place in the landscape depicted, and having the visitors see the landscape as a battlefield. In that regard, the absence of war elements in the image was highlighted in the initial tableau by placing real cannonballs on the floor in front of the image. In addition, a bench was put in the middle of the space, with artificial grass mounted on the seat, the tactility of which was meant to form a connection to the grass in the image.

In order to evoke the dramatic presence of the battle, a moving-image projection was gradually, and *very* slowly, applied to the image, creating a filmic course of shifting lights in the landscape in combination with dark cloud formations drifting across the sky (Figure 22.2). A gloomy sound element emphasized the sense of eeriness. As the projection merged with the image it gave the impression of movement within it, bringing cinematic conventions into play that added a sense of leaving the here-and-now in favor of a narrative sphere.

At a point in this scene the sound of lark song was heard. This was a specific reference to a recently published book on the war in which soldiers' diaries demonstrated that several soldiers remembered having heard a lark sing just before the battle began. Towards the end of this 'tableau', the projection gradually expanded to cover the entire wall, using the larger scale to enhance the sense of presence and immersion (Figure 22.3). When the projection shrunk again, clouds and music disappeared, and the image reappeared without modifications. The set-up had now returned to that of 'the opening scene', except at this point the visitor was lit from above in order to break the point of immersion, to cause self-awareness, and to let the image reappear as an object again. In a final tableau, the black-and-white image gradually gained colour, the grass turning green, prompting awareness of time and of the landscape as a

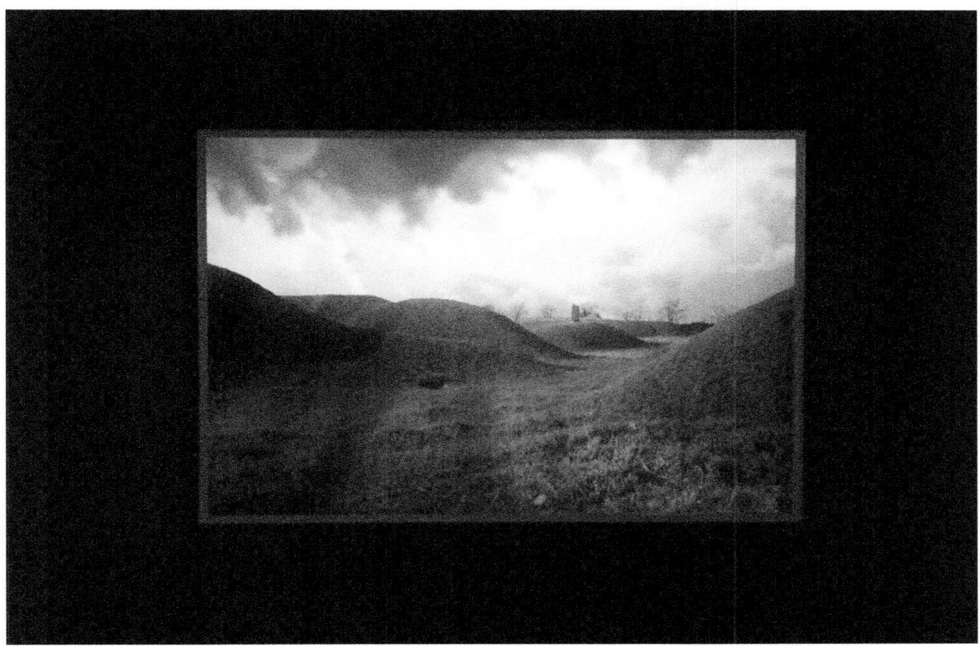

**FIGURE 22.2** 'Imprints of War – Photography from 1864', the National Museum of Photography, Royal Danish Library, Copenhagen, 2014. Staged by Christina Back

*Photo:* Tobias Ebsen. Reproduced with kind permission of the Royal Danish Library.

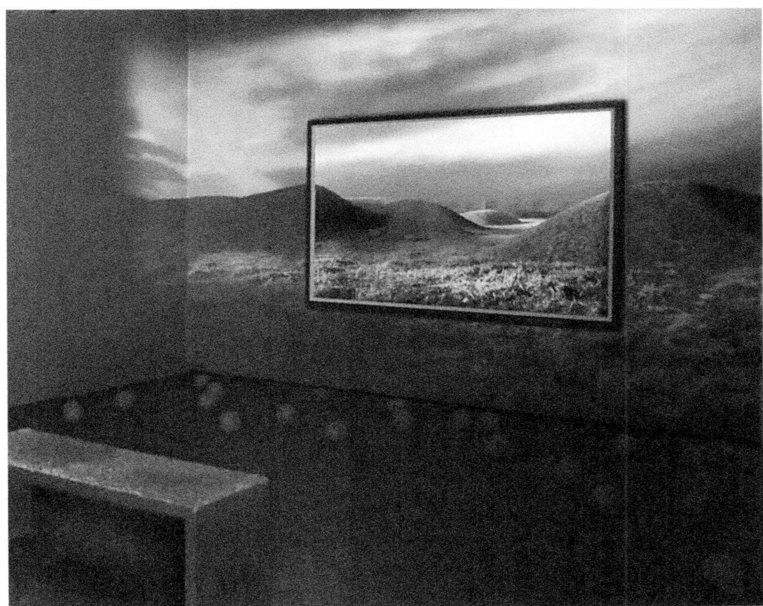

**FIGURE 22.3** 'Imprints of War – Photography from 1864', the National Museum of Photography, Royal Danish Library, Copenhagen, 2014. Staged by Christina Back

*Photo:* Tobias Ebsen. Reproduced with kind permission of the Royal Danish Library.

real and still-existing place.[3] A video documentation of the staging can be seen on YouTube (Ebsen 2014).

## The inquiry

This composition was subjected to a reception study in which a small sample of five visitors participated in an in-depth interview following a visit to the space. The results suggest that a certain set of dynamics were crucial to their experience, and the following is a reflection on the nature of their involvement in the process of consumption. The participants are considered to be likely visitors to the exhibition as they were recruited among followers of the Royal Library's Facebook pages and members of its culture club. In composing the group, we strove for variation in terms of age, occupation and sex. It consisted of:

Kai (male, 72), management consultant
Jesper (male, 30), journalist
Sille (female, 34), student/museum conservation
Pernille (female, 47), unemployed, legal background
Susanne (female, 70), retired upper secondary teacher.

It may be noted that the inquiry is somewhat reminiscent of a laboratory experiment, mostly due to the particular conditions of the respondents' visit compared to a supposed 'natural' visit. The respondents were, for example, requested to visit alone, and were only exposed to this limited space, thus not facing the urge to move on to other parts of the exhibition, as might be a factor when navigating in a larger exhibition context. The spatially demarcated set-up combined with solo visits and the exposure of only one single object was chosen in order to be able to compare parallel experiences with a high level of detail. Exhibition texts and other kinds of language-based interpretation were omitted so as to focus exclusively on the space and its impact on the visitor experience, exempt from the influence of language-based exhibition content.

The interviews took place shortly after the respondents' exhibition visits, following a five-minute writing exercise where the respondents jotted down their first thoughts on the experience in response to the pre-written phrases: 'Describe your visit with four words'; 'How do you interpret the image at this point?'; 'Describe the image with four words'; and 'The visit to the exhibition made me think about. . . '. Interviews were conducted back in the exhibition space in order to support the respondents' recollection of their first visit and allow them to link their statements to specific aspects of the space. The written notes worked as a starting point for the interview, and they are quoted in the following alongside excerpts from the interviews.

The interview method is comparable with, for instance, 'photo elicitation' in terms of its use of photography as a means to trigger memory (Harper 2002). The interviews being conducted within the exhibition space parallels the social anthropologist Sarah Pink's description of a method called 'walking with video' (Pink 2007). A method building on the assumption that co-experiencing 'body to place' may reveal insight into another person's meaning-making as taking place in connection to bodily, multisensory engagement with a physical environment.

## A wake-up call to the senses

The study was concerned with the respondents' sensibility to the staged exhibition environment as an important prerequisite for its ability to function as an interpretation and learning element in itself. The interviews, however, revealed clear indications that the five respondents had been attentive during their visit and were finely attuned to the whole situation.

Within a museological context, architectural theorist Jonathan Hale has suggested that the interplay between aspects of 'familiarity' and 'novelty' in an exhibition space is an important factor when working with visitors' level of attention. He points to a balancing act where aspects of familiarity are required for the space to be decipherable and manageable, while occurrences of novelty might function as triggers of attention (consciousness) needed for the exhibition to have an emotional and intellectual impact (Hale 2012: 199). A similar argument is seen in sensory geographer Paul Rodaway's theory on the interplay between sensory perception and the physical surroundings. Distinguishing between different states of the physical being in an environment, Rodaway argues that what he calls 'simple contact' with the surroundings (largely defined as 'generally passive touching or rubbing against or simple co-presence') may shift to a more conscious state of 'exploratory activity' as a result of breaks with the taken-for-granted in how one perceives the surroundings (Rodaway 1994: 45). However, this exploratory state is likely to decrease again along with 'habituation' with the things that have caused it (Rodaway 1994: 12, 37).

In accordance with these perspectives, the reports of some respondents indicate that perceived aspects of novelty – in terms of changes happening and breaks with the expected and the familiar – had affected their level of attention while visiting the exhibition space. These all used the word 'surprising' when invited to describe their visit using four words.

Kai (male, 72) said of his visit that he was 'very present throughout' and remarked that 'when first something dynamic started to happen [. . .] I suddenly didn't feel it was difficult to hold on to the experience'. Jesper (male, 30) recounted a similar experience, stating that:

> When [the image/projection] suddenly began to move, music was added, and the light changed, and it turned completely *widescreen* it all became a completely different experience than just looking at a photograph. [. . .] That was when I was sucked in, and that was when I suddenly became totally focused, and acquired an eye for more details because it all became something else.

Breaks with the taken-for-granted thus played a role in relation to Jesper's heightened sensibility to the image and its appearance. Sille (female, 34), the last one to explicitly address the subject, described being in a state of immersion while she was in the exhibition: 'Just as soon as the 'film' [. . .] started, I felt that it was tremendously meditative just to sit there waiting for what was going to happen. It was very beautiful indeed'.

## An embodied sense of connectedness to the image

Each respondent pointed to one or a few elements in the staging that particularly affected their experience. Most of them referred to these elements as eye-opening points in terms of an intensification of the sensorial experience (which seemed to be appreciated in itself) and in terms of direct engagement with the realm of the image as well as the process of meaning-making. The 'trigger' aspects were things like touching the grass; the vast expansion of the image; the experience of the sound element while watching the image/projection; being lit by spotlights while viewing the image; and the slow pace of the changes happening to the image. Exactly what affected each individual appeared to have been influenced by various factors such as prior interests and experiences (e.g. being an amateur landscape photographer and feeling like taking mental photographs during the course of the experience), sensorial and artistic preferences (e.g. being very much into music and audio experiences in general) and an emerging logic of the narrative being pieced together by the individual.

Especially in two cases, quite simple kinaesthetic experiences of the respondent's individual body, interacting with other environments than that of the exhibition space, appeared to affect the approach to the staged image. One of these cases was Kai, and the experience occurred when he touched the artificial grass mounted on top of the bench:

> and then I put my hands down into *this,* and that was really good. Then the experience changed. [. . .] I felt I was present. Close to the picture, right? [. . .] I suppose it's meant to represent grass. Even though it's perfectly obvious that it isn't. But it has a kind of texture that reminds you of grass. I get out into nature a lot, and it's great to plunge your fingers into real grass.

The encounter with the artificial grass appeared to add a sense of touch to the impression of the image, enabling an imagined sense of direct bodily contact with the landscape depicted. This instance seems to address a synaesthesia of the senses where visual perception, touch and embodied familiarity with a certain type of situation intertwine and result in a felt proximity to the image. In this case, *tactile* stimuli affected the visual impression of the image. But in another example visual stimuli appeared to trigger a sense of touching or rather inhabiting the landscape depicted. With Jesper, the combined image/projection, and in particular its expansion across its borders, marked a point of significant sensual engagement, causing him to imagine what it might be like to stay in the landscape as a soldier waiting for an attack:

> It creates a completely different feeling of those great expanses where one's simply lying there, and the enemy is in some direction or other. And can come at any moment.

He further recounted:

> The whole animation of the picture means that suddenly you . . . feel that you *are there.* And especially when it becomes so wide, you are sort of standing in the middle of the landscape. [. . .] It's this that makes it so captivating. It suddenly feels very real.

Jesper's visual impression of the projection of moving images is likely to have actualized kinaesthetic experiences, causing him to image being there physically, and consequently to empathize with the mental state of imagined soldiers. The sudden lifelike scale of the expanded image seems to have helped evoke this body-to-landscape imaginative experience.

This occurrence of sensory synergy in the exhibition set-up aligns with a perspective seen within cinematic theory, where Laura U. Marks has looked into the ability of film and video to activate a broader sensual register. In *Touch – Sensuous Theory and Multisensory Media* (2002), she explores what she calls 'haptic visuality' and 'haptic vision' within cinema, both being characterized by the evocation of a sense of bodily proximity to something by means of visual and audio stimuli (Marks 2002). Such a view on vision marks a contrast to critical perspectives on so-called ocularcentrism (implying a distanced and disembodied form of cognition), a notion which has been used as part of a critique of museum displays where supposedly eyes are more welcome than bodies (e.g. O'Doherty 1986; Candlin 2010; Dudley 2010; Golding 2010). Marks, however, refrains from regarding vision as an isolated sense, relating it instead to a whole body. This perspective is shared with Paul Rodaway, who for instance introduces 'imagined touch' as a mode of haptic experience which might occur on the basis of visual impressions while drawing on memory and expectation (Rodaway 1994: 54).

## Emotional involvement

For three of the respondents, the affective aspect of their experience appeared to influence their attribution of meaning to the image. One of them, Susanne (female, 70) referred to the exhibition fragment as both 'incredibly effective' and 'moving' in the writing exercise. To her, the interplay between the sound element (which she referred to as 'music') and the clouds appearing in the image/projection marked a point of increased immersion and narrative engagement. She particularly delved into the sound element accompanying the changes of light and the sky in the landscape:

> it intensifies the feeling of horrors that have taken place, because it's so threatening [. . .] Suddenly there are lots of feelings that well up with the music and the dark clouds drifting past.

Susanne ascribes the impact of the sound to its mood-setting qualities, which charged her view of the image with markedly emotional elements. The experience seemed to reinforce her prior conceptions of the historic battle, which she knew of in advance. Her imagination was thus directed towards the horrors of the battle, and accordingly she empathised with 'the cruelty the soldiers were exposed to'; an empathy which led to further personal considerations like, 'we just go on producing more generations that wage war on each other – it's quite hopeless'.

Generally speaking, the appeal to sensorial engagement with the physical environment appeared to play a pivotal role for the respondents as a source of the emotional aspects of their experiences. Similar conclusions have been seen in prior visitor studies. In sociologist Gaynor Bagnall's study of visitor consumption practices at two British museums, she detects a significant 'interconnection between the physicality of the experience and the emotions and imagination engendered' (Bagnall 2003: 88). Bagnall's study further indicates that the emotional engagement was of great influence to the visitors' ability to imagine at the sites (Bagnall 2003: 93).

This question of appeal to emotional engagement may call for a certain level of interest: psychology research on the relationships between emotion and attention indicates that emotionally charged information (e.g. perceptual stimuli) tends to be selected and gain more attention than neutral information, and to attract more attentional resources to be spent on them (Yiend 2010: 256). However, for one respondent, Pernille (female, 47) the evocative aspect of the staging was also subject to critical reflection. She saw herself as a pacifist and found that 'there was perhaps too much pathos with that solemn music' and further, 'I think it is morally suspect to link too much pathos to war'. She explained her reservations by comparing the sound element to the pushy rhetoric of film music and canned laughter:

> the filmmakers want to communicate a certain feeling. I would like to be able to decide for myself if I am to feel something, and what that something is.

Thus she points out a challenge for museums in working with affective content, as visitors may feel that they are being told what to feel – and think – also about potentially problematic issues.

## The 'real' and the realm of 'fiction'

In order for the staging to be able to function as interpretation, the visitors needed to engage in a creative dialogue with the set-up. This creativity was evident in the reports of the five respondents, who charged the set-up with various symbolic, metaphoric and more personalized and associative fragments of meaning. Susanne for instance identified the sound of breathing in the audio element, associating it with the films of David Lynch:

> It's just like breathing . . . that's what I thought while I was sitting there. The dead soldiers' breathing. Just listen: it'll come in a moment. . . [both listened.] It's very effective – like 'Haaaee'. It's completely David Lynch–like. They were here – they *are* here, somewhere or other, right? Uh! [Both laughed.]

The sound is placed in a poetic sphere and laden with an extraordinary kind of meaningfulness. And thus a certain mode of decoding seems to be at stake that bears similarities with a description of the nature of theatricality offered by dramatic researcher Josette Féral. With Féral the term has been freed from the physical constellations of theatre: it occurs when a spectator enters a certain mode of perceiving where the things perceived are ascribed to both a 'real' reality and to another sphere of representations. Entering this dual mode of perceiving, things and actions may be charged with meaning in an extraordinary way as 'the spectator [. . .] becomes aware that in this space, signs signify differently, being part of this secondary structure, the fiction that is being built' (Féral 2002: 10).

This description seems to apply to the respondents' reception, as they all clearly 'poeticise' what they perceive while being aware of the premise that whatever meaning they have ascribed to the image has partly taken form in the realm of the imagined. A further question concerns what role the staging might have played in suggesting such an approach? According to Féral, the theatrical mode of perceiving has to do with the spectator 'pick[ing] out a series of cleavages that allow him to infer theatricality in the object or event represented' (Féral 2002: 10). These cleavages may be ones 'inscribed by the artist and recognized by the spectator [. . .] aimed at making a disjunction in the systems of signification, in order to substitute more fluid ones' (Féral 2002: 10). That kind of intention surely applies to this staging.

The respondents seem to have most significantly entered a liberated sphere of meaning-making while in the process of sensing and testing narrative possibilities. When it came to forming a coherent narrative, the realm of 'otherness' apparently did not prevent the respondents from pursuing (to a greater or lesser extent) a link to historical 'realism' and the perceived realities of present time. Thus Kai's impression of the image as 'a meaningless, radically transformed landscape' that expresses a state of 'waiting' and 'emptiness' was transposed into being about 'the emptiness of war'. Hence, the creative exploration and the imagined were rendered positively useful as a means of approaching something of the real world as well.

There appeared to be a distinct pleasure associated with the creative activity of constructing a narrative (as is evident in Susanne's example of finding the soldiers' breathing in the sound element). And generally, the theatrical dynamics of perception appeared to be an important driving force behind the respondents' narrative engagement in the set-up, allowing them (or providing them with 'cleavages' encouraging) a quite creative and freestyle process of meaning-making.

## Specific communication

The perspectives applied to the photograph seemed to a great extent to match the communicative intentions behind the design. Most of the clues incorporated in the design were addressed by the five respondents (taken as a group), as they spoke of their experience in the exhibition. Some were even brought up by all five of them. It was, however, clear that each individual added his or her own layers of meaning to the clues, 'versionized' them, and adapted them to fit individual lines of thought. Clues not calculated within the design were added as well. This mediating, versionizing and selective behaviour depending on the individual can also been seen in prior research on how visitors make use of museum exhibitions (e.g. Goulding 2000; Bagnall 2003; Falk and Dierking 2012). This seems to actualize a premise put forward by the scenographer Frank den Oudsten, who has stated that 'a staged exhibition space holding a narrative potential does not imply that the narrative will necessarily unfold completely in all its dimensions' (den Oudsten 2011: 25). And clearly what the French phenomenologist Maurice Merleau-Ponty has referred to as 'one's own body' (Merleau-Ponty 1997 (1945)), encompassing lived physical experiences of sensorial and kinaesthetic involvement with the surroundings, appeared to exert a considerable influence on the appeal found by the respondents in the different tableaux and sensorial aspects of the space.

Looking to how the design was able to successfully communicate certain clues, a perhaps quite obvious prerequisite appeared to be the aspects of redundancy in the staging. In other words the inclusion of well-known references to moods and meaning seemed to matter. Among the most effective parts in this study were the dark clouds and sombre sound element, which are seen similarly in the tradition of cinema, as working as signifiers of drama and lurking danger.

## The individual reception

For two of the respondents, the meeting between the exhibition set-up and their expectations of a museum setting left them with a feeling of uncertainty, which addressed the division of authority between author and recipient. To look more closely into this, we will look into the rhetoric of the design, which deliberately combined a semantically defined aspect with a high degree of open-endedness in terms of intended meaning in the clues that were incorporated. Regarding its communicative aspects, the staging might be comparable to certain forms of visual-artistic expression, and in light of this comparison, Umberto Eco's concept of 'the open work' (Eco 1989) has offered an analysis of relevance as regards the communicative aspect of modern art (which is contrasted with 'traditional' art). The latter he largely characterizes as having been created with a view to being accessible and intelligible in a fashion analogous to the intentions of the sender, while the modern, open work of art makes use of a combination of a narrative structure and a simultaneously marked aim of intentional semantic openness that leaves behind various possible choices and a semantically unfilled space for its onlooker. So we are not only dealing with the fact that the work, as a more general condition, was susceptible to countless different interpretations according to the individual addressee and his or her particular background and prerequisites for interpreting. It is a question of the work – the exhibition design in this instance – balancing specific intentional semantic structures with multiple meanings (more than one possible semantic track to follow as a recipient) and what, within art history, is often referred to as 'blanks' or 'Leerstellen', where the perhaps most prevalent examples are the unfilled fields of the painter on the canvas which leave room for the onlooker's own projections. This means that the communicative aspects of the design included an appeal to the exhibition visitor to fill in meanings, as well as to 'complete its sentences'.

The semantic openness and possibility to interpret somewhat freely was judged quite positively by three of the respondents. This was apparent, for example, when they were asked how they felt about the absence of the usual exhibition text. Susanne then called it 'completely irrelevant' and felt that a text 'would only confuse me, I think. Because it is a mood picture that one enters into'. Kai, who didn't miss a text either, humorously remarked: 'if you were to have a text for that space [. . .] it ought to say be patient!' Sille, for her part, said she would have read a text if one were available, but nevertheless appreciated not having the option. What she liked was:

> that surprise effect, where you don't know what's going on, and you don't know what you are looking at – you simply have to take things as they come. And relate to them. If I had read the text, I think I would have been told a story that I would have applied to it, instead of just taking it as an experience.

These three generally seemed quite content with their unconfirmed narratives. For Jesper and Pernille, however, the aspect of the unconfirmed marked a point of uncertainty. This had to do with their awareness of opening themselves up to an individual interpretation, and doubting its accordance with 'reality' or the communicative intention that lay behind the staging. By abandoning traditional linguistic interpretation methods – such as written labels, handouts, or wall texts – the staged set-up left its visitors without an opportunity to have their own narrative outcomes 'verified'.

Jesper, who had otherwise enjoyed his experience, mentions a pent-up feeling of:

> questions and doubts, because the story I built into [the image/staging] . . . is not complete in any way. [. . .] I mean, you could also invent a *different* story [. . .] *I* think more about that soldier angle. And it's so . . . it's pretty unresolved. There's no real *pay-off* on the expectation and the mood I *myself* have built up.

Pernille's experience was affected by much doubt. She did engage in extracting fragments of a narrative, but was obstructed in this process by a wish to make sober assumptions about the image, and to see it as a documentation of facts in relation to the historical past addressed. As the image dealt with a war theme, she felt ethically obliged to not just *assume* things. Several times throughout the interview she expressed a reluctance to 'give in' to the narrative impulses felt, saying for instance: 'I think it shows greater respect for those who are affected by war that nothing metaphysical and symbolic, etc. is woven into it'. She explained her dilemma:

> You don't of course want to operate with any list of answers, and then it's difficult to find . . . then you never get an answer as to what is a reasonable level of ambition for an interpretation, and what in actual fact you yourself are projecting into it.

Pernille and Jesper thus found it difficult to navigate within the dual sphere of the imagined and their own individual and provisional narrative on the one hand, and the reality expected to be revealed or reflected on the other.

## Conclusion

On the basis of a small-scale qualitative reception analysis, we have proposed a range of reception dynamics in relation to the staged exhibition fragment, stressing aspects of the embodied encounter with a multi-sensorial space. A common denominator of a number of the proposed dynamics is that they place the staging in a field where the museum as 'sender' does not define or control the 'narratives' resulting from the visit. The physical, emotional and sensory aspects of reception stood out as important mediating factors in relation to the communicative intentional stratum of the exhibition. In light of this, the exhibition design in question may be said to imply an empowerment of the exhibition visitor in terms of determining the content of the exhibition. Pointing in the same direction, we find the open-ended rhetoric used, as well as the appeal to what we have called a theatricalizing mode of perceiving. These aspects seem to pave the way for a particularly creative and associative mode of decoding. But as on the one hand, the study indicates that the design enabled an open rhetoric, letting the audience step in as co-authors, on the other hand it also indicates that the design was effective in suggesting certain perspectives or 'readings' of the set-up (as clues were picked up by the respondents). Thus the narrative put forward by the museum, however open, still appeared very present in the workings of the design.

An issue identified in the study is the fact that for some respondents, the sense-borne form of interpretation seemed to clash with their expectations of a didactic exhibition premise; one in which their own interpretations would be either confirmed or corrected by the museum as the ultimate authority. This issue might designate a significant premise potentially at stake when employing spatial exhibition staging to function as interpretation (at least in cases where exhibition texts are omitted, which may of course be seen as a radical use of staging), namely that museum visitors' appreciation of such a set-up may depend on a toning down of a horizon of expectation linked to more didactic types of exhibition. What visitors might have to appreciate as a valuable outcome of an exhibition visit, to fully embrace it, is a sense of material or otherwise bodily proximity to exhibits; attaining a felt relationship with them as well as a sense of guided, tentative meaning and raised curiosity, perhaps leading to further reading or exploration elsewhere. In any case, the present study points to a potential for awakening the senses and encouraging a sensorially driven engagement in the realm of exhibits by way of spatial staging, and thereby to encourage deeper engagement in exhibition subjects.

## Acknowledgements

The research project is a part of the research network *The Prism of Sustainability* funded by the Danish Agency for Culture. The network is based on a research collaboration between four Danish museums, focusing on interpretation and learning in museums.

## Notes

1 The term 'narratives' used here does not refer to perfectly progressive 'stories' with clear meanings alone. It will be used to describe all that the respondents piece together in terms of forming a set of impressions, ideas, approaches and maybe also some questions about the image. Thus the term will be broadened to include unfinished, fragmentary narratives at a stage that precedes the clearly meaningful.

2 The exhibition was curated by Sarah Giersing, with whom the spatial staging was developed.

3 A video recording of the staging can be seen at full length here: www.youtube.com/watch?v=ponAUfKqWFI&list=UUPYYQwMYGrAfJhyO3t4n-Mg

## References


Bagnall, G. (2003) 'Performance and Performativity at Heritage Sites', *Museum and Society*, 1(2), pp. 87–103.

Candlin, F. (2010) *Art, Museums and Touch*, Manchester & New York: Manchester University Press.

Crawley, G. (2012) 'Staging Exhibitions: Atmospheres of Imagination', in MacLeod, S. *et al.* (eds) *Museum Making: Narratives, Architectures, Exhibitions*, London & New York: Routledge, pp. 12–20.

Dudley, S. (2010) 'Museum Materialities: Objects, Sense and Feeling', in Dudley, S. (ed.) *Museum Materialities: Objects, Engagements, Interpretations*, London & New York: Routledge, pp. 28–57.

Dudley, S. (2012) 'Encountering a Chinese Horse: Engaging With the Thingness of Things', in Dudley, S. (ed.) *Museum Objects: Experiencing the Properties of Things*, London & New York: Routledge, pp. 1–15.

Ebsen, T. (2014), 'Entrenchment III'. Online. Available HTTP: www.youtube.com/watch?v=ponAUfKqWFI&list=UUPYYQwMYGrAfJhyO3t4n-Mg. Accessed 18 March 2018.

Eco, U. (1989) *The Open Work*, Cambridge, MA: Harvard University Press.

Falk, J. and Dierking, L. (2012) *The Museum Experience Revisited*, Walnut Creek: Left Coast Press.

Féral, J. (2002) 'Foreword', *SubStance*, 31(98/99), pp. 94–108.

Gibson, J.J. (1986) *The Ecological Approach to Visual Perception*, New Jersey: Lawrence Erlbaum Associates.

Goulding, C. (2000) 'The Museum Environment and the Visitor Experience', *European Journal of Marketing*, 34(3/4), pp. 261–78.

Hale, J. (2012) 'Narrative Environments and the Paradigm of Embodiment', in MacLeod, S. *et al.* (eds) *Museum Making: Narratives, Architectures, Exhibitions*, London & New York: Routledge, pp. 192–200.

Harper, D. (2002) 'Talking about Pictures: A Case for Photo Elicitation', *Visual Studies*, 17(1), pp 13–26.

Heinich, N. and Pollak, M. (1996) 'From Museum Curator to Exhibition *Auteur* – Inventing a Singular Position', in Ferguson, B.W. *et al.* (eds) *Thinking about Exhibitions*, London: Routledge, pp. 231–50.

Macdonald, S. and Basu, P. (eds) (2007) Exhibition Experiments, London: Blackwell Publishing

Marks, L. (2002) *Touch: Sensuous Theory and Multisensory Media*, Minneapolis: University of Minnesota Press.

Merleau-Ponty, M. (1997) *Kroppens fænomenologi*, Copenhagen: Det lille Forlag.

O'Doherty, B. (1986) *Inside the White Cube: The Ideology of the Gallery Space*, California: University of California Press.

Oudsten, F.D. (2011) *Space.Time.Narrative*, Surrey & Burlington: Ashgate.

Pink, S. (2007) 'Walking With Video', *Visual Studies*, 22(3), pp. 240–52.

Rodaway, P. (1994) *Sensuous Geographies: Body, Sense, and Place*, London: Routledge.

Skolnick, L.H. (2012) 'Beyond Narrative: Designing Epiphanies', in MacLeod, S. *et al.* (eds) *Museum Making: Narratives, Architectures, Exhibitions*, London & New York: Routledge, pp. 83–94.

Yiend, J. (2010) 'The effects of emotion on attention: A review of attention processing of emotional information', in De Houwer, J. and Hermans, D. (eds) *Cognition and Emotion*, Hove: Psychology Press, 211–75.

# 23

# THE FEAR OF POPCORN

## Drawing inspiration from Hollywood for curating suspenseful exhibitions

*Ariane Karbe*


### Abstract

This chapter offers a method for sharpening the curators' dramaturgic tools in order to apply them more specifically. Concretely, it explores the potential of creating suspense in cultural historical exhibitions following the example of classical Hollywood films. Based on scriptwriting manuals and the writings of David Bordwell and Noël Carroll, suspense is described as uncertainty which invites the viewer to hypothesize, torn between hope and fear, about the protagonist's destiny. The chapter describes how these insights are being utilized by the author in the creation of a permanent exhibition for a house museum in Merano, South Tyrol.


### Introduction

The greatest fear of Hollywood scriptwriters is that spectators of their films leave the screening room during the performance to buy popcorn. It would mean they had failed to attract the attention of the audience, to make them anxious enough not to miss any single story item provided. Of course, classical Hollywood films[1] are unlike cultural historical exhibitions. Whereas the filmmakers try to create a world as 'true' and plausible as possible, museum curators should – according to a widely held view – not pretend to represent 'objective knowledge' and 'truth' but communicate to the exhibition visitors that a 'narrative', a specific perspective and crafted story, is presented (Roberts 1997; Martinz-Turek 2009). But despite the profound differences between popular films[2] and cultural historical exhibitions, the severe struggle of the scriptwriters to reach the audience – their 'fear of popcorn' – can serve as an inspiration for curating. Storytelling is understood in this chapter as a core function of curators, and this implies first that this task should not be delegated solely to designers, and second that it is crucial not to back off from the emotional components of stories but to deal with them and especially their apparent inconsistency with research – another core function of curators. But what does this mean in concrete terms? Can the modes of operation of Hollywood authors not only serve as an inspiration for curating but also as a technique to adopt? Or are the distinctions between films and exhibitions too strong after all? This will be discussed in what follows, using the example of suspense techniques which are highly important for the scriptwriter's toolbox. For that purpose I describe how my research about suspense has influenced an exhibition curated by me. But first the phenomenon of suspense has to be specified – with the aid of Hollywood films.

## The phenomenon of suspense

### *Hope and fear*

Scriptwriting manuals have proved a valuable source to explore how scriptwriters assess and explain suspense. Such guidebooks have been published broadly at least since the introduction of the sound film in 1927 because writing good dialogues became a much-needed skill (Eidsvik 1992: 181). Even if the approaches vary, the focus of the authors is to explain how to write a successful (i.e. marketable) movie; the most famous representative is probably Syd Field (1979). To publish a guidebook for a 'film d'auteur' would be a contradiction in terms; still, writers who plead for greater openness describe common patterns. Christoph Vogler (2007: xviii), whose idea to model scripts after a 'Hero's Journey' has been highly influential, states: 'Artists who operate on the principle of rejecting all form are themselves dependent on form. The freshness and excitement of their work comes from its contrast to the pervasiveness of formulas and patterns in the culture'.

What makes the manuals so instructive in respect to suspense is the fact that this phenomenon plays such a pivotal role for classical Hollywood movies. Scriptwriting teacher Frank Daniel's famous definition of a good script boils down the essence of such films: 'Somebody wants something badly and is having difficulty getting it' (cited in Howard and Mabley 1993: 22). David Howard, whose manual *The Tools of Screenwriting* was heavily influenced by Daniel's approach, elaborates this concept: 'Thus a good story could be said to be about a character with whom the audience has some measure of empathy, who strongly wants something that is very difficult, yet possible, to achieve' (Howard and Mabley 1993: 22). Following Howard's further explanations, the link between a 'good' (i.e. successful) story and suspense becomes evident: the audience adopts the – exciting – conflict of the hero or heroine:

> So what is the trick behind keeping the audience participating in the story and creating in itself the emotional response that drama depends upon? In a word, uncertainty. Uncertainty about the near future, uncertainty about the eventual turn of events. Another way of stating this idea is hope versus fear. If the filmmaker can get the audience to hope for one turn of events and fear another, where the audience truly does not know which way the story will go, this state of uncertainty becomes a very powerful tool indeed. We often find ourselves riveted to a story that has a strong component of hope versus fear.
>
> *(Howard and Mabley 1993: 37–8)*

Ari Hiltunen, author of *Aristotle in Hollywood*, explains that feeling fear and hope is crucial for experiencing suspense. To him Aristotle's concept of the 'proper pleasure' seems to be the key to successful storytelling. He refers to the Greek philosopher's *Poetics* which remains, up to today, a central reference point for scriptwriting (Eick 2006: 38–9), as well as to his *Rhetoric*.

Following Hiltunen (2002: xiv), the proper pleasure a good story evokes, is for Aristotle a conglomerate of fear, pity and catharsis. The philosopher defines fear as the anticipation of evil, anxiety and unrest, caused by the notion of impending danger, which nevertheless includes a pleasurable element: the hope for safety. Fear can only be felt by the spectators if the danger is imminent and connected to goal-oriented action because only then are they able to anticipate what might happen (Hiltunen 2002: 8). Pivotal for creating 'proper pleasure' and suspense on the side of the audience, is therefore that hope and fear are attached to future events and potential undeserved misfortune.

> The audience heed the evil forebodings, begin to anticipate the possible dangers and catastrophes that threaten the hero, and start to look for hopeful solutions. The plot provides the audience with opportunities for considering ways of avoiding the catastrophe and so become involved in the events of the drama.
>
> *(Hiltunen 2002: 10)*

## *Questions and gaps*

This characterization of suspense found in scriptwriting literature corresponds with the description of this phenomenon in film theoretical literature. But whereas the Hollywood authors and scriptwriting teachers emphasize the emotional components of suspense, the film scholars David Bordwell and Noël Carroll, whose approaches will be introduced briefly in what follows, address themselves primarily to its cognitive aspects. Both scholars are regarded as important representatives of cognitive film theory but this does not mean that they ignore and underestimate feelings triggered by specific story features. Their main attempt is solely to understand how a viewer *comprehends* the film narrative.

Noël Carroll's explorations of suspense are inspired explicitly by Vsevolod Illarionovich Pudovkin's *Film Technique and Film Acting*, first published in 1929 (Pudovkin 1960). Carroll explains that the Russian director and scriptwriter suggested that 'the relation of earlier scenes and events in a film narrative to later scenes and events can be generally understood on the model of the relation of a question to an answer' (Carroll 1988: 171). One scene provokes – albeit in most cases subconsciously – a question on the audience's side which is answered in one of the following scenes. Carroll calls this relation 'erotetic'. In his opinion this narrative connective is even more important, that is more common than causal connections. This is an important aspect to note because other film scholars consider causality as *the* decisive feature of narratives. Edward Branigan (1992: 216), for example, states: 'If I were forced to use a single word to characterize a narrative organization of data, that word would be "causality"'. It could be argued that linking two story events by cause and effect (because!) or by a question and answer (why?) is not so different as it may seem at first sight, but the point is that this shift in focus ascribes to the spectators a more active role. According to Carroll (1988: 172–3), crucial for creating suspense is that posing a question means raising 'a structured set of possibilities' and that the spectators are challenged to keep track of various lines of action and their possible outcomes until one alternative is actualized. And the confidence to get these questions answered – in case of linear film narratives – is an important factor for doing so.

> Given the erotetic model, we can say what it is that audiences expect: they expect answers to the questions that earlier events have made salient – will the shark be

> destroyed, will the jumbo jet crash, will Johnny Gray win Annabelle? It is a general feature of our cognitive makeup that, all things being equal, we not only want but expect answers to questions that have assertively been put before us, this explains our intense engagement with movies.
>
> *(Carroll 1988: 181)*

David Bordwell considers film viewing, just like Carroll, as an activity in which the spectator plays a far from passive role. He states: 'A film, I shall suggest, does not "position" anybody. A film cues the spectator to execute a definable variety of *operations*' (Bordwell 1985: 29). Even though he does not address the topic of suspense extensively in his book *Narration in the Fiction Film*, his explanations about how narratives work provide an excellent frame for better understanding this phenomenon's modes of operation. Viewers of popular films, he explains, speculate about the further course of action based on different patterns (so-called schemata) learned from all movies watched so far and, of course, guided by the actual film narrative. Essential for this process is in his opinion the difference between 'syuzhet' (alias 'plot' or 'discourse') and 'fabula' (alias 'story'). The terms go back to the school of Russian Formalists who asked what the literary artwork is. One of the most illuminating definitions is given however by Seymour Chatman (1978: 19) in his book *Story and Discourse*: 'In simple terms, the story is the *what* in a narrative that is depicted, discourse the *how*'.

Interestingly enough, Bordwell (1985: 49) defines 'fabula' taking the viewer's perspective as a starting point:

> Presented with two narrative events, we look for causal or spatial or temporal links. The imaginary construct we create, progressively and retroactively, was termed by Formalists the *fabula* (sometimes translated as 'story'). More specifically, the fabula embodies the action as a chronological, cause-and-effect chain of events occurring within a given duration and a spatial field.

By 'syuzhet' he understands the actual arrangement and presentation of the fabula in the film, again with an emphasis on the constructivist activity of the viewers. He concludes: 'The syuzhet, then, is the dramaturgy of the fiction film, the organized set of cues prompting us to infer and assemble story information' (Bordwell 1985: 52). It becomes clear that the term 'story' designates in the sense of 'fabula' the events in the order they really (even if fictional) happened, but also – quite contradictory – in general use, the creative end product. To avoid misunderstandings, in the following the word 'fabula' will be used when the difference to 'plot/syuzhet' is to be accentuated.

Coming now to the 'concrete narrational work of any film' (Bordwell 1985: 51), it is important to note that while watching a film, for the process of meaning-making, the guiding question is how far the plot corresponds to the logical, temporal and spatial nature of the fabula the spectator constructs. Deviations trigger him or her to look for explanations as do featured gaps. It is impossible for a plot to cover all events implied in a fabula, therefore every plot includes gaps: if they are underlined, then the experienced spectator knows that there may be a reason for this that is worth pondering. Bordwell (1985: 55) explains:

> A flaunted gap may warn us to pay attention: either the omitted fabula information will become important later, or the narration is misleading us by stressing something that will prove insignificant. If a gap is suppressed, however, surprise is the likely result, especially

> if the omitted information ranks low on a scale of probabilities. These are only general indications, but they suggest the range of effects that 'gapping' tactics can achieve. In each case, it must be remembered, the viewer will strive to justify the very presence of the gap by appeal to principles of compositional, realistic, transtextual, and artistic motivation.

To illustrate 'how the syuzhet manipulates fabula information over an entire narrative' detective stories are especially helpful, as Bordwell states, because 'In fact, specific sorts of syuzhet tactics are *the differentia specifica* of the genre' (1985: 64). The structure of the plot is determined by the progress of the investigation and gaps are indicated and underlined by questions asked like 'Who killed X?'. Bordwell writes: 'The genre promotes suspense with respect to the twists and turns of the investigation and plays upon curiosity about the missing causal material' (1985: 64). In summary, exposed gaps invite the viewers to create hypotheses and hypothesizing is essential for experiencing suspense. In fact, Bordwell declares that suspense understood as 'anticipating and weighing the probabilities of future narrative events' (1985: 37) is the *primary* focus of hypothesis forming.

Taking all this together, some important conclusions can be drawn about how suspense is created in classical Hollywood films. First, the spectators' activity consists to a great extent of hypothesizing about the further course of events. They do so by looking for answers to questions (consciously or subconsciously) raised by the action of the film and by observing how far the syuzhet is in line with the fabula. When deviations occur which they are able to interpret as noteworthy signals (based on their internalized knowledge about the modes of operation of popular films), like for example gaps, they begin to weigh possibilities for how the storyline will unfold. Second, this process of speculating about possible story outcomes is closely connected to feelings of hope and fear. These emotions are evoked by establishing a protagonist the recipients are able to empathize with and therefore share the thrill. For this purpose, it is necessary that the viewers are aware of possible outcomes, and this is achieved through equipping the protagonist with a well-defined goal. Last but not least, expectations play a pivotal role for experiencing suspense while watching this kind of film: the recipients' willingness to play such an active part in unfolding the narrative is strongly dependent on the certainty that in the end their efforts will be rewarded because all questions will be answered.

What then, does all this mean for curating cultural historical exhibitions? This will be explored in the next section by describing my attempt to create a suspenseful exhibition narrative for a historical house museum in South Tyrol, Italy.

## The exhibition project

### *Establishing the protagonist*

Five years ago, Rosamaria Navarini (b. 1926) died. She had lived almost her whole life in the villa her grandfather Franz Fromm (1854–1941) had bought in 1921 in Merano, South Tyrol. She devised that a foundation should be established (Fondazione Navarini-Ugarte, based in Merano) and the Villa Freischütz be turned into a museum presenting the collection of fine and decorative art that her grandfather had collected. The development of the exhibition concept (still a work in progress), which I am developing in close consultation with the governing board of the foundation, began with the challenge to choose the period of interpretation to present in the house museum and, closely connected to this, to decide which inhabitants' stories are worth telling.

Even though Rosamaria Navarini succeeded in holding together her grandfather's collection over decades and provided her fortune to the public in the form of the museum, her biography seems of no further interest for future visitors. Moreover, the decades she spent in the villa after the Second World War, first together with her parents and then alone, might be described as times of stagnation. This supported the decision to select as the period of interpretation not her life span but, rather, the years between 1921 when the house was purchased by Franz Fromm and his death in 1941.

Not to foreground the collector was at first encouraged by research about historical house museums in general and the history of this house in particular. Since the vast majority of historical house museums centre around rich and/or famous men, it was advisable to examine intensely if another museum should be dedicated to such a figure. In her introduction to *Interpreting Historic House Museums*, Jessica Foy Donnelly (2002: 1) declares: 'In light of current thinking, however, house museums that disproportionately interpret the heads of their historical households do so at the expense of the other people, activities, and relationships that also distinguish their sites' histories'. And, indeed, both daughters of Franz Fromm played pivotal roles in the history of the Villa Freischütz, as did the governesses who stayed with the family long after the children were grown up, so it was plausible to tell, if not prominently, the story of the villa's female residents (see Reid 2002). This idea was supported by further insights gained through analyzing the documents on the building and its inhabitants, as well as examining the collection, and through doing literature research especially about the town of Merano. All three topics which emerged as central for the universe of Freischütz were characterized by radical changes caused or affected by the First World War: gender concepts, (economic) bourgeoisie, and South Tyrol. And all three topics concentrated in the person of one of Fromm's daughters, Zoila Fromm Hilliger (1892–1982) (Figure 23.1). Her biography seemed to mirror the turmoil of the selected time period the plainest: brought up as a typical daughter of a bourgeois family, she had internalized as chief life goal to marry and have children. But she also felt the urgent necessity to develop her artistic talents, at a time when it became more common for upper-class women to pursue a profession and to stand on their own feet. Her father's struggle to keep his standard of living in the difficult post-war era in South Tyrol affected her immediately and challenged her to position herself in a society where the boundaries between the social classes were becoming more and more fragile.

At this point of the concept development the research results about suspense became important. The knowledge that empathy with the protagonist is used by Hollywood authors to establish strong ties between the story and the audience, encouraged the decision to feature one person, and indeed the daughter, not the father. Her person seemed to provide more connecting factors for future museum visitors because even today everybody is faced with the challenge to realize life plans within specific social constraints. This promised to comprise a more fertile area of conflict and a bigger potential for touching the visitors than foregrounding Franz Fromm who apparently clung to the 'good old days'. This did not mean the neglect of the collection which is so essential for the specific profile of this historical house museum. Admittedly, it was Franz Fromm who had brought together the miniature paintings, snuffboxes, cabinets and precious fabrics (to name only some highlights) during his journeys through Europe, but Zoila was raised in homes decorated and furnished with these pieces and was without doubt strongly influenced by her father's passion for art. The idea of using biographies in order to get audiences 'hooked' and to gain their empathy and interest, is of course not new. To give but one example, at the beginning of the exhibition 'Titanic & Liverpool: The Untold Story', shown in

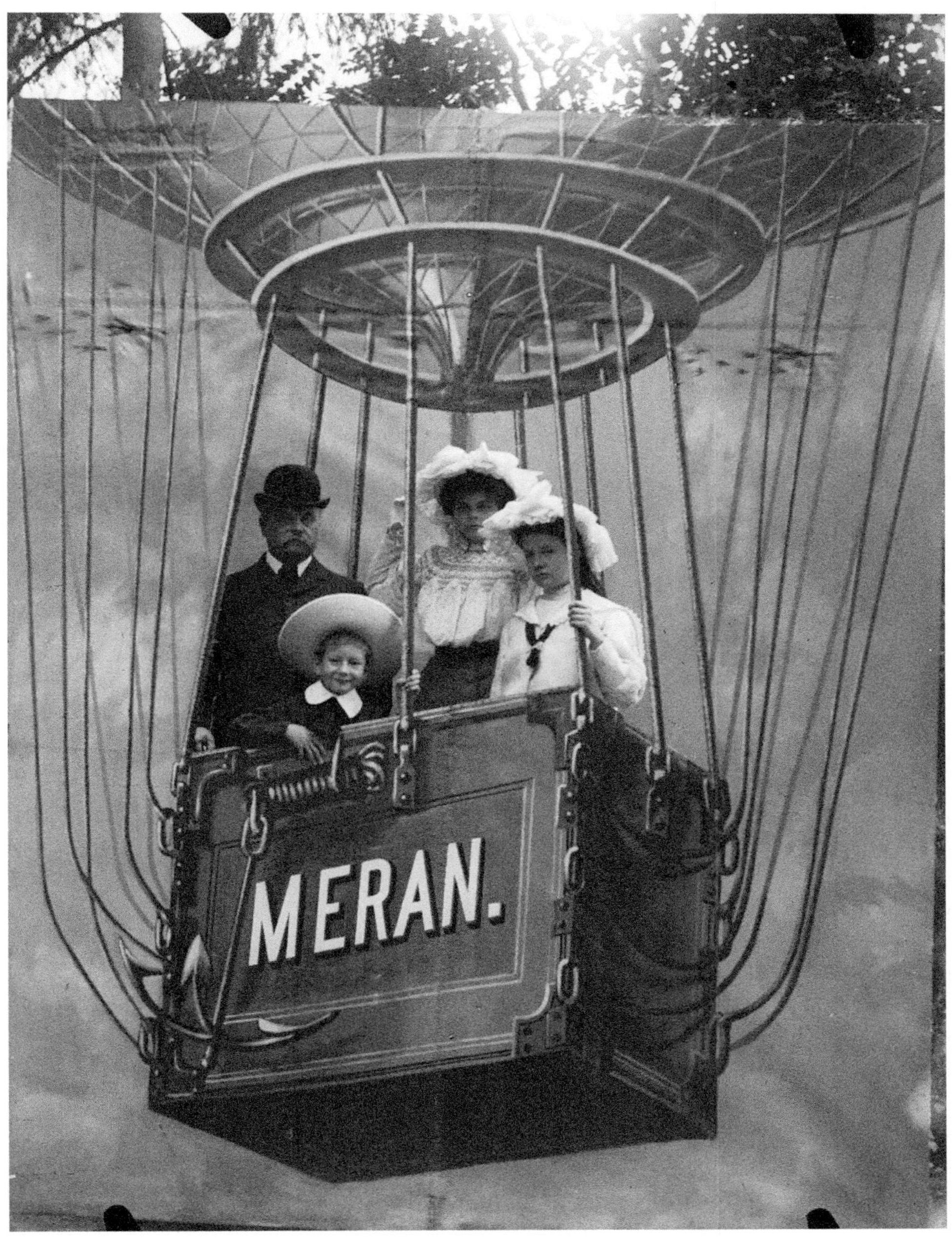


**FIGURE 23.1** Private collector Franz Fromm with son Paco and daughters Luisa and Zoila (on the right), c. 1906

the Merseyside Maritime Museum (30 March 2012 to 21 April 2013), visitors could select one of several cards depicting a passenger. A short text included some personal information and the reason the person had been on the ship, ending with the words 'Discover my fate at the end of this exhibition'. By contrast, the idea was to build in the Freischütz an arc of suspense running through the *entire* exhibition, indissolubly linked to Zoila's story.

## *Challenges in provoking hypotheses*

The aim to attract the audience's attention and to encourage emotional responses was therefore critical for the choice to narrate the years from 1921 to 1941 not from the perspective of the collector but from that of his daughter. Having thus appointed the 'protagonist', the question became relevant if and how it could be possible to provoke feelings of hope and fear on the visitors' side and/or to animate them to hypothesize about the course of the events while following the storyline. This is the point where it became difficult to borrow the modes of operation of suspense typical for classical Hollywood films for this exhibition, and where the differences between both media became evident. David Bordwell's (1985: 74) quote illustrates one of the sharpest distinctions:

> In watching a film, the spectator submits to a programed temporal form. Under normal viewing circumstances, the film absolutely controls the order, frequency, and duration of the presentation of events. You cannot skip a dull spot or linger over a rich one, jump back to an earlier passage or start at the end of the film and work your way forward. Because of this, a narrative film works quite directly on the limits of the spectator's perceptual-cognitive abilities. A gap will be closed only when the syuzhet wants it that way; retarding material, however annoying, must be suffered through; a gap may be hidden so cunningly that the spectator cannot recall how the trick was pulled. It is evident that in cinema many processes of narration depend upon the manipulation of time.

In cinema. But exhibitions work in a different mode because the spatial dimension is so important: moving visitors reshuffle the narrative material constantly and in a highly individual way. Thus, a fixed chronology is difficult to achieve. In this case it seemed especially important not to fix a route the visitors would have to follow. They should not perceive the rooms, like too often in historical house museums, as two-dimensional static pictures but as spaces which can be walked through, lived in and (sensually) experienced. This objective was inspired strongly by the approach of Franklin Vagnone and Deborah Ryan, described in their *Anarchist's Guide to Historic House Museums* (2015). Therefore it seemed impossible to ensure that visitors would perceive *first* a question and *then* its answer while wandering through the villa. But if no question is noticed by the audience, no suspense can be experienced, and if the answer is given too early, suspense cannot unfold because the moment the answer is known, it expires.

Equally obstructive was the fact that classical Hollywood films do not share their erotetic quality (which Carroll ascribes to them) with exhibitions. It is only the knowledge that in the end all questions will be answered, that ensures the viewer's patience while watching these movies unfold and allows for experiencing the meantime as enjoyable. Museum visitors, on the contrary, familiar with the common structure of cultural historical exhibitions, do not expect to find that questions posed early in an exhibition narrative will only be answered later in the visit. Werner Hanak-Lettner (2011: 26) explains in *Die Ausstellung als Drama* that we are used to understanding exhibitions as primarily spatial and not temporal constructions. According to him, exhibition visitors would become frustrated if not given the information at the precise spot where the object in question is displayed. As a consequence, it is highly doubtful that the visitors to the Villa Freischütz would decipher questions as triggers for suspense, as they are not familiar with 'reading' a cultural historical exhibition in this way. In an analogous manner, it seems difficult to induce the exhibition visitors to interpret gaps exactly as they would in a cinematic context, as described by Bordwell. This is mainly because exhibitions in general are characterized by a more or less fragmentary structure, due not least to the importance individual objects play for this medium. Whereas the 'net' of meanings is knitted tightly around the single story events of a Hollywood film, it is only draped loosely on objects deployed in cultural historical exhibitions. Even though curators try to narrow down possible connotations by using additional interpretive texts, the fact that visitors often ignore them in favour of their own personal interpretation (and that objects presented in an exhibition space can be understood in different contexts) accounts for the relative vagueness of the medium. Gaps are therefore considered not as confounding factors but as necessary and desirable components of exhibitions. This specific character of exhibitions is very well described by Annabell Fraser and Hannah Coulson (2012: 223):

> In the museum, there is a space between an image or object and its label, between a narrator and their audience, and between history and our imagination. Though we cannot see it, this space is a key player in the way we construct museum narratives. This space, ripe with possibility, often contains the essence of what we are looking at and can be where the most exciting things are happening.

To put it straight, viewers of popular films understand gaps as invitations to hypothesize, museum visitors perceive them as triggers for associations (Schärer 2003: 109).

All of these factors taken together led to the idea of offering an audio tour based on the biography of the collector's daughter, as an essential part of the presentation in the Villa Freischütz. This would allow for telling a linear narrative while wandering through the rooms and perceiving the atmosphere and engaging with the objects. Choosing a method which shares some essential characteristics with the film medium, would make it possible to pose concrete questions and to express and evoke emotions like hope and fear. For example, the narrative could begin like this: 'When my father bought this villa, I was 28 years old, still unmarried and deeply troubled: would I ever find a husband in this boring, small spa town?'

## Conclusion

Did the attempt to apply the dramaturgic suspense techniques to the exhibition concept fail? Not at all. The precise knowledge about the modes of operation of this phenomenon helped to develop an important guiding idea for the project. Whether the audio tour will actually create an experience of suspense for the audience effectively, this can be assessed only after the museum has been opened. But apart from this specific project, being aware of the potentials and limitations of the exhibition medium concerning suspense can prevent curators in general from labelling an exhibition superficially as 'exciting' and to focus instead on the *effective* points of contact between films and exhibitions.

Furthermore, the research results suggest that, even though it seems difficult to develop an arc of suspense throughout a whole exhibition narrative mainly based on the selection, arrangement and presentation of the objects, it should be possible to build Hollywood-like suspense on a micro level, in an exhibition text or perhaps even a whole section. Last but not least, the precise knowledge about suspense described in this chapter helps to rethink the role of questions for stories told in and with exhibitions. It is interesting to ask for instance if it would be feasible to produce *concrete* questions not by posing them precisely and explicitly like in popular films, but by using staged objects. All this could mean not only creating enthralling and fascinating narrative environments, but also ones which invite visitors to participate actively and deeply in the step-by-step development of the storyline.

There is a broad consensus that a modern exhibition can and should be entertaining, and as the editors of the groundbreaking volume *Suspense* state in their preface: 'suspense is a major criterion for both an audience's selection and evaluation of entertaining media offerings' (Vorderer *et al.* 1996: vii). While this is no plea for the attempt to create suspense in *every* exhibition in the way described – the appropriate way to tell an exhibition's story will vary from case to case – it is a plea for sharpening the curators' dramaturgic tools in order to apply them more specifically.

Finally, it should be mentioned that my intense involvement with the topic of suspense has provoked a fundamental change in my own curatorial attitude. Instead of persisting in a 'neutral' viewpoint and leaving the dangerous, that is potentially manipulative field of emotions to the designers or artists alone, I now appreciate feelings like suspense and take them seriously as an opportunity to engage broad audiences. Probably, it should not be the main objective to simply thrill museum visitors – but making their hearts beat a little bit faster by incorporating pointedly suspenseful elements into exhibition narratives seems to be a promising way forward.

## Acknowledgements

I am very grateful to Suzanne MacLeod for her constant interest and support for the research undertaken. Many thanks to the governing board of the Fondazione Navarini-Ugarte, especially to Herta Waldner, Anntraud Torggler and Karin Pircher for their openness and constructive discussions. I would like to pay tribute to the inspiring vision of 'Historic House Museum anarchists' Franklin Vagnone and Deborah Ryan.

## Notes

1 The term 'classical Hollywood film' is drawn from Bordwell *et al.* (1985). It is used to designate movies not necessarily produced in Hollywood but following a specific narrative pattern which is characterized by linearity and causality.

2 Throughout this chapter, the terms 'classical Hollywood film' and 'popular film' are used synonymously to refer to a type of films written to reach broad audiences and characterized by narrative closure. The term 'popular film' is drawn from Eder (2007: 10).

## References

Bordwell, D. (1985) *Narration in the Fiction Film*, Madison: The University of Wisconsin Press.

Bordwell, D., Staiger, J., and Thompson, K. (1985) *The Classical Hollywood Cinema: Film Style & Mode of Production to 1960*, London: Routledge & Kegan Paul.

Branigan, E. (1992) *Narrative Comprehension and Film*, London and New York: Routledge.

Carroll, N. (1988) *Mystifying Movies: Fads and Fallacies in Contemporary Film Theory*, New York: Columbia University Press.

Chatman, S.B. (1978) *Story and Discourse: Narrative Structure in Fiction and Film*, Ithaca and London: Cornell University Press.

Donnelly, J.F. (2002) 'Introduction', in Donnelly, J.F. (ed.) *Interpreting Historic House Museums*, Walnut Creek, CA: AltaMira Press, pp. 1–17.

Eder, J. (2007) *Dramaturgie des populären Films: Drehbuchpraxis und Filmtheorie*, Hamburg: Lit, 3rd edition. Online. Available HTTP: www.slm.uni-hamburg.de/imk/Personal/eder/dramaturgie_neuauflage.pdf. Accessed 10 May 2012.

Eick, D. (2006) *Drehbuchtheorien: Eine vergleichende Analyse*, Konstanz: UVK Verlagsgesellschaft mbH.

Eidsvik, C. (1992) 'Drehbücher aus der Fabrik: Schreiben für die amerikanische Filmindustrie', in Schwarz, A. (ed.) *Das Drehbuch: Geschichte, Theorie, Praxis*, München: Schaudig/Bauer/Ledig, pp. 173–95.

Field, S. (1979) *Screenplay: The Foundations of Screenwriting*, New York: Dell Publishing Company.

Fraser, A. and Coulson, H. (2012) 'Incomplete Stories', in MacLeod, S. *et al.* (eds) *Museum Making: Narratives, Architectures, Exhibitions*, London and New York: Routledge, pp. 223–33.

Hanak-Lettner, W. (2011) *Die Ausstellung als Drama: Wie das Museum aus dem Theater entstand*, Bielefeld: transcript.

Hiltunen, A. (2002) *Aristotle in Hollywood: The Anatomy of Successful Storytelling*, Bristol: Intellect.

Howard, D. and Mabley, E. (1993) *The Tools of Screenwriting: A Writer's Guide to the Craft and Elements of a Screenplay*, New York: St. Martin's Press.

Martinz-Turek, C. (2009) 'Folgenreiche Unterscheidungen: Über Storylines im Museum', in Martinz-Turek, C. and Sommer, M. (eds) *Storyline: Narrationen im Museum*, Wien: Turia + Kant, pp. 15–29.

Pudovkin, V.I. (1960) *Film Technique and Film Acting*, New York: Grove Press.

Reid, D.A. (2002) 'Making Gender Matter: Interpreting Male and Female Roles in Historic House Museums', in Donnelly, J.F. (ed) *Interpreting Historic House Museums*, Walnut Creek, CA: AltaMira Press, pp. 81–110.

Roberts, L.C. (1997) *From Knowledge to Narrative: Educators and the Changing Museum*, Washington, DC: Smithsonian Institution Press.

Schärer, M.R. (2003) *Die Ausstellung: Theorie und Exempel*, München: Verlag Dr. C. Müller-Straten.

Vagnone, F.D., Cothren, O.B., and Ryan, D.E. (2015) *Anarchist's Guide To Historic House Museums*, Walnut Creek, CA: Left Coast Press.

Vogler, C. (2007) *The Writer's Journey: Mythic Structure for Writers*, 3rd edition, Studio City: Michael Wiese Productions.

Vorderer, P., Wulff, H.J., and Friedrichsen, M. (1996) 'Preface', in Vorderer, P., Wulff, H.J., and Friedrichsen, M. (eds) *Suspense: Conceptualizations, Theoretical Analyses, and Empirical Explorations*, New York and London: Routledge, pp. vii–ix.

# 24

# THE YELLOW BOX AND ITS RHETORIC OF DISPLAY

## Exhibiting Chinese art in a museum

*Vivian Ting*

### Abstract

In considering how to encourage intimate interactions between objects and viewers, this chapter examines *The Yellow Box: Contemporary Calligraphy and Painting in Taiwan* (11 December 2004–27 February 2005), a curatorial experiment developed by Tsong-Zung Chang and the Visual Cultural Research Centre of China Academy of Art, and its implications for museum exhibition design. Held at the Taipei Fine Art Museum, this exhibition offers an institutional critique of a white cube space by considering the exhibition of artworks within their own cultural context and by exploring broader topographies of exhibition in relation to contemporary sensibilities. By enacting a contemporary interpretation of the traditional *yaji* (literally 'elegant gathering'), the Yellow Box project develops exhibition rhetoric – coordinating spatial arrangement with display devices – to cultivate a global appreciation of arts and culture. To curators and museums eager to embrace diverse cultures, the curatorial experiment considers exhibition as a performative space where objects and audiences are involved in co-creating multiple meanings. The experiment proposes new possibilities for bringing a cultural context into the design of an exhibition space and considers how audiences would relate to the artworks and cultures presented.

### Introduction

At the Suzhou Museum, the temporary exhibition *Wu School Painting Series: The Art of Qiu Ying* drew its collection from 12 museums across China and abroad. I was excited to see a wide range of delicate works by Qiu Ying (c. 1494–1552), the master painter from the sixteenth century. When I arrived at the galleries, I could not help pressing my face to the glass cabinets to make a closer inspection of the paintings. Unfortunately, the glass reflections were distracting, the lighting was dim, and the paintings were reluctant to reveal their meticulous details to a casual visitor. Apparently, the paintings would only reveal themselves to 'professionals' who were equipped with viewing devices such as folding magnifiers.

Nonetheless, I was looking forward to having a better view of the showcase object, *Copy after Along the River during the Qingming Festival*, a 9.87-metre-long handscroll. It was Qiu Ying's interpretation of a flourishing cityscape in the Yangtze region and was large enough to accommodate many viewers at the same time. Nevertheless, a long queue had formed outside the gallery, waiting to see the featured piece. Two staff workers were instructing visitors to keep walking along the display case and they promoted the museum's WeChat platform as another venue for appreciating the featured piece. Even with the better lighting, it was impossible to examine how Qiu Ying coordinated the movements of wrist, arm, and brush to document the dizzying action of a metropolis. The distance from the work also hindered viewers from seeing the subtle interactions of ink on paper that conveys the delicate grace of the painting.

Qiu Ying's works would originally have been shown in a *yaji* (literally translated as 'elegant gathering'), where the host would prepare food and drinks, arrange musical performances, display some artworks from his personal collection, and the participants would enjoy each other's company and write poems about the event. In such intimate social settings, the artwork would be shown and appreciated according to the season and the participants' reactions (Wang 2004; Chen 2009; Cahill 1978: 24–5). *Yaji* is an amiable, multi-sensory environment that encourages participants to look at the objects and discuss their aesthetic qualities. Curiously, in a museum exhibition – a public cultural platform meant for the world to see – the objects are enclosed in display cases that limit the sensual interaction between the work and the audience. If the experiences embodied by the ink paintings are impossible to see, how can the exhibition encourage visitors to engage with the objects per se and promote a better understanding of the culture? How can curators learn from *yaji* and begin to transform objects from their mute, static and detached presence into sensual provocations that develop an alternative object-viewer relationship?

## Yellow box and *Yaji* – an elegant gathering

Appealing to the traditional literati notion of *yaji*, the Yellow Box project intends to create a poetic and intimate exhibition space that facilitates meaningful dialogue between Chinese art and museum visitors. According to the curator, Tsong-Zung Chang:

> In order for calligraphy/painting (*shu hua*) to maintain its traditional vantage point it appears to be the duty of curators to act as mediators, so that an intermediate space may be sought within the modern exhibition hall. The concept of the Yellow Box is therefore an interpretation of the spirit of literati art manifested in physical spatial installations. In other words, the Yellow Box is a buffer zone, a filter made for a particular culture of connoisseurship.
>
> *(Chang 2005: 8)*

The curatorial team is concerned about whether or not the Chinese ink works (usually in the form of scrolls or albums) seemed incongruous in a conventional white cube setting. Being exhibited against clean white walls with theatrical-lighting, ink works tend to lose their material presence and seem blank in the visual realm. They would not be directly handled, shown as a temporary display in response to mood, or invite viewers to add colophons (Chang *et al.* 2015: 104). As many researchers have pointed out, the white cube converts artworks into 'ceremonial pieces', confining the art experience to a timeless, transcendental realm, isolated from its context (O'Doherty 1986: 41; Duncan 1995: 19; Weibel 2007: 143). It creates a spectacle and asks for admiration, but does not ask how an artwork might be relevant to an individual or how it might speak to the moment.

To highlight the embodied experiences of art viewing, the Yellow Box project rejects a passive notion of spectatorship in favour of more active engagement, recreating and responding vigorously to what has been shown. It sets out to define artwork as an active agent engaging viewers with an ongoing dialogue between the artist and his or her cultural tradition. That is, artwork is seen as a process of expression which shows viewers how the artist's bodily actions work with the medium within an aesthetic tradition. Technically, the making of objects is a bodily reflection of materiality in relation to the object's function and cultural values. Historically, the making of an object is also a sensuous dialogue between the artist and his or her predecessors that explores the technical and artistic possibilities for developing a shared pool of cultural resources. By considering artworks as an ongoing process of meaning-making, the Yellow Box invites viewers to co-create new meanings with the works in a contemporary context. Curatorial interpretations and the visitors' ways of seeing can inspire infinite aesthetic imaginations and enrich our understanding of the arts and cultural traditions – the very notion that sits at the core of the Yellow Box exhibition.

*Yaji* is an intimate social network where like-minded literati shared a similar aesthetic sensibility and cultural repository, bringing different approaches to the appreciation of objects in relation to personal experience and collective imaginations (Shih 2010: 385). The white cube, however, in line with contemporary museum thinking is a public platform for accommodating the diverse needs and interests of the anonymous masses (McClellan 2008: 191). The challenge of the Yellow Box exhibition, therefore, lies in transforming a private social event into a public viewing mechanism that celebrates creativity, materiality and interactivity. The curatorial team must therefore develop some forms of presentation that inspire an imaginative association with the artwork and redefine what an exhibition might offer to its audience. In contrast to the white cube, the Yellow Box offers an aesthetic experience that is fully embodied, and not just a visual spectacle that promises intellectual fulfillment but remains essentially detached. That is, the Yellow Box is a kind of discursive space, where visitors interact with a variety of artworks in different ways; for example, by taking clues from the spatial design, sharing ideas with other visitors, or being involved with the creative process. The space can be communal, encouraging intellectual exchanges about the artworks, with artists, and other visitors, or can be for aesthetic contemplation, allowing for intimate moments with the works.

## Suggestive spatial design

To re-enact a contemporary version of *yaji*, it would be easy to fall into a crude imitation of a traditional Chinese setting, such as a scholar's studio or garden where a *yaji* would have taken place. In fact, museums have long used such strategies to empower visitors to experience the past. Most notably, shop-front models, display backdrops and architectural fittings have been some of the three-dimensional exhibition elements used to position objects within a particular scenario. For example, the Minneapolis Institute of Arts reinstalled a seventeenth-century scholar's library and study from Suzhou to illustrate an 'authentic' setting for their Chinese collection (Anon 2005). Contextualising artworks within a 'historical' scene typically transforms the setting into a spectacular tableau, gaining the visitors' attention and admiration of its realistic aesthetics. Nevertheless, these neatly integrated totalities can also distract visitors from engaging with individual exhibits. Ironically, the more details the installation contains, the more spectacularly the effect is magnified, while fewer visitors communicate with each component of the setting (Shank and Tilley 1996: 77). Drawing its power from its apparent authenticity, such scenes often create an awe-inspiring and all-encompassing visual experience that overlooks the individuality and materiality of objects.

Taking a leap from realism, the Yellow Box project proposed three basic rules for designing an exhibition space:

1 Design should be as simple as possible; avoid iconography of traditional Chinese culture;
2 Design should avoid literal imitation of traditional architectural structure. It should avoid stage-like design; and
3 The structure should avoid direct interference of artwork, such as digital enlargements or reduction, or video projections.

*(Chang 2005: 10)*

Clearly, the curatorial team does not aim to revive domestic design from the past, nor try to vacuum temporality from contemporary work and violently re-locate it in a quasi-context of traditional Chinese culture. It is not the physical setting (in its literary sense) that curators learn from the notion of *yaji*, but the unique mode of viewing. In a *yaji*, multiple approaches can be used to interact with the exhibits, and intimate and personal encounters with the objects are always possible. In creating an amicable environment, curators break down the single 'white cube' into smaller zones, each with its particular setting of a 'Yellow Box'. Different Yellow Box units can be connected or separated by windows, partitions or folding screens and the design can also dramatically alter the spatial layers and patterns of light in an exhibition area. The layout of a Yellow Box exhibition is neither a route leading visitors from a point of departure to a destination, nor is it a predetermined formula that makes clear from the outset what people are going to see. Visitors are invited to follow certain lines of thought, yet are welcomed to negotiate the space by themselves. Within the free-flowing, 'matrix-like' space, a different pathway is always an option.

Simplicity is the primary principle in designing an exhibition space or exhibiting spaces. Each standard Yellow Box is a compartmentalised unit with wall height proportional to the scroll; and equipped with a back screen and set of chairs and tea-table (Chang 2005: 12). The fewer the details, the more the aesthetic imaginations will complete the task. Every component is designed to offer suggestive clues for intimate encounters with the artworks and to encourage dialogues among the viewers. By contextualising the artworks in a 'domestic-like' setting, the curators create interesting tensions between interior architectural devices and the implied exterior scenery that entice viewers to go beyond the boundaries of the immediate reality. In contrast to a white cube that highlights nothingness, a Yellow Box offers a rich aesthetic imagination by creating a window with a hint of nature, projecting shadows and light from the outside environment, or simply by arranging a vase or a garden rock near some of the exhibits. The design suggests a sophisticated association between the artworks and their creative sources – *yaji* and the literati tradition. Still, as a contemporary reinterpretation of *yaji*, the intrigue is developed by encouraging viewers to go back and forth among the objects wandering in the imaginative realm of art. In short, the Yellow Box is a world revealed, with each compartmentalised unit being a place of intimate encountering, where every association opened by the viewer leads to countless dimensions of imagination. The simplified design anchors people to their immediate physical reality, while urging them to roam around in their imaginative domain. Turning away from the overall design, I now discuss how objects are shown in the exhibition context.

## Approaches to ink art per se

To *yaji* participants, an ink work would be considered as *wanwu* (object of amusement) that inspires aesthetic imaginations in both sensory and intellectual dimensions. Tang Hou (fl. 1322), the art critic, stated 'Looking at paintings is like judging beautiful women: their spirit and bone structure are more important than their flesh and limbs' (quoted from Bush 2012: 127). His remark suggests that a literati connoisseur would not only look at the formal qualities of a painting, but also at its 'spirit' and 'structure' – the embodiment of the artist's personality, aesthetic expressions and ideas, and his or her response to the medium and the art form. Ideally, the connoisseur's mode of looking would not be an analytical examination, but rather an imaginative experience of the interplay between the artist, subject matter, and medium. For instance, personal associations would be created from the artist's interpretation of an ancient sage that further explores his or her aspiration, or uses poetic language to describe the co-ordination between ink and brush that highlights the artist's bodily movement and passion for the arts. Looking at an ink work as an interaction of materiality and aesthetic ideas transcends into personal interpretations that can be sensuous and fluid, and involving a dialogue with contemporaries and different generations (Ye 1985: 88–94). In any case, the creative act encourages the visitors' personal interpretations of an object, inspired by the artist's unique perspective on the world.

Considering contemporary museum visitors who have diverse interests and experiences, it is almost impossible to develop a set of viewing routines that would describe the connoisseurs' object-viewer relationship in *yaji*. How would curators enable the bodily experiences elicited from an object and empower visitors to connect the objects to their personal experiences? How would exhibition devices such as framing and furniture promote the connoisseurs' mode of viewing? To answer some of these questions, three categories of exhibition devices are used in the Yellow Box exhibition.

### *Free-hanging suspended scroll and materiality*

According to the literati tradition, hanging scrolls are generally shown on specific occasions, and as such, they are seldom put on permanent display (Silbergeld 1982: 13). Regardless of its temporality, a hanging scroll is comparable to a drawing or oil painting and put up on a white wall against a colossally high ceiling in conventional exhibition settings. Under a spotlight, the flimsiness of the paper scroll renders the work weak, flat, and almost unfinished, especially in a gigantic white cube. In some cases, the scroll embarrassingly fails to stick flat onto the wall (reducing its materiality) or is allowed to wobble as if being held by a servant boy among the literati.

In the Yellow Box exhibition, the curatorial team insists that a scroll should be presented as a work of spatial art, not on a plain surface that avoids exposing the subtleness of the paper scroll. Curators recommend that the scrolls should be displayed away from the wall, with the bottom of the scroll secured to the ground to provide stability (Chang 2005: 11). Interestingly, a suspended hanging would cast a shadow onto the wall, bringing out its materiality and three-dimensionality. The space between the scroll and the wall also highlights the contrast between the flat two-dimensional wall and the three-dimensional scroll body. In the Yellow Box, the wall height would be proportionate to the scale of the work, and a suspended hanging would turn the focus onto the delicate texture of the paper scroll to reveal the scroll material and the quality of the ink work. In some cases, the curatorial team suggests creating a backdrop made of a variety of materials such as mud and ash or pulverised bricks and corn husks. By filling the wall space, viewers would be encouraged to compare the texture of the ink works to the rough surface of the backdrop (Plate 25).

Obviously, ink artists have long been aware of how the flimsy scroll may not work well in a white cube environment. During the early twentieth century, when the notion of exhibition – displaying one's works in a public platform – first travelled to China (see Pedith Chan's chapter in Part I of this book), many artists considered re-enacting the monumental style of Northern Song paintings so that the works would be properly seen in a vast, empty space (Shang 2007: 84). This is still a popular method of display in many contemporary art exhibitions. For instance, the Shanghai-born artist Xu Longsen is renowned for making gigantic art pieces larger than 10 metres, which easily occupy a whole exhibition space. His work, *Beholding the Mountain with Awe No. 1* (2008–2009) was shown as a public installation at Art Basel Hong Kong 2015. The enormous work flowed from the ceiling to the ground floor like a pictorial waterfall. The sheer scale of the work dominated the visual experience, and the translucent and free-flowing quality of the scroll interacted with the interior lighting, giving the work a sense of temporality.

For artists who seek less dramatic effects, framing works with different materials, such as glass or steel, can highlight the objecthood of ink works while maintaining a presence of the artist. Conventionally, artists mount works on silk brocades and frame them with wood and glass to protect them from dust and dampness. In museums, traditional ink works are usually put into glass cabinets for the sake of their conservation. Unfortunately, such practices tend to keep the artwork away from visitors, and the formal qualities, especially the delicate texture of the brush work, become even harder to appreciate. Nonetheless, it is not the curatorial intervention – the strategy of suspended hanging – that sets the golden rule for displaying an ink work. Rather, it is the rationale for highlighting the materiality of a work and creating a captivating viewing environment that enables the work to be seen properly. For museums housing traditional ink works, despite their good intentions to safeguard the objects, they will have little meaning if visitors cannot see their subtle and profound qualities. In showcasing contemporary ink works, the concern should be less about their conservation and more about curators and artists working together to explore the different possibilities for rendering the work's unique presence.

### *Handscroll, freestanding screen and temporality*

Besides materiality, Chinese ink art tends to integrate temporality by adopting multiple perspectives and a tempo for viewing. Handscrolls, like a 'motion picture', allow the viewer to unfold the work at arm's length, revealing a series of sub-frames that progress through time and space. The intimate objects allow only one viewer at a time to manipulate the movement of the painting and control the pace of reading (Wu 1997: 57–9). The process of viewing resembles that of painting, where viewers can experience how the 'world of aesthetics' is seen from the artist's perspective. Conventional exhibition practice, however, would have a handscroll lying flat in a glass cabinet, revealing its secrets all at once. Such exposure discourages the viewer's involvement and only weakly shows how individual images are related to the overall composition. More importantly, the essence of 'intimacy' – a rather individual connection with the work – would be lost in the exhibition.

To facilitate viewers taking control of their viewing, the Yellow Box project uses a scroll table for reading works section by section. On top of the table cabinet where the handscroll is completely unfolded, a couple of movable viewing frames are installed to enable viewers to 'frame' the work at will (Chang 2005: 15). While the cabinet properly preserves the work, the viewing frame enables a temporal viewing as if one is surveying scenery while strolling in nature. Thus, visitors can explore a handscroll by physically re-framing its pictorial composition and developing their own approaches to looking at individual images (Plate 26).

Another format for Chinese ink work integrates the elements of time and space in a free-standing screen. In terms of space, a screen sets the boundaries between interior and exterior, and private and public, and defines the nature of the space. Composed of multiple panels, the screen presents a montage of time and space by compiling a series of images taken from different viewpoints (Wu 1997: 15–16). Conventional exhibition practice would consider a multiple-panel screen as a pictorial plane, occupying a considerable proportion of flat wall. Again, this practice offers a 'panoramic' view of the work, but ignores its materiality and the element of time and space embodied by the way of looking. In the Yellow Box exhibition, the curatorial team proposes displaying a multiple-panel screen as a zigzag that breaks the homogenous flatness of the wall (Chang 2005: 18). It provides a temporal viewing that encourages viewers to recognise individual images and their relation to the overall pictorial composition. More intriguingly, while a viewer looks at one surface, the next panel, facing the other direction, engages further exploration of the series.

## *Seating and other exhibition devices*

Set in a comfortable environment, *yaji* offers a sensuous feast of arts and culture, where the participants would enjoy good food and good art. In most exhibition designs, the seating tends to be mundane, though essential for creating a leisure space. Physically, seating provides a relief from navigating in an exhibition. It also encourages viewers to remain engaged with the exhibition by staying in front of an art piece and pondering its formal qualities and relevance to individual experience. In the Yellow Box exhibition, the curatorial team would carefully arrange a variety of furniture to enable the art experience to be relaxed and intimate.

In each unit of a Yellow Box, a set of chairs and a tea table is arranged (Chang 2005: 13). Considered as an essential part of the aesthetic experience, the seating allows visitors to absorb, ingest and digest the ample visual material for an extended period. The seats are positioned against the walls, so that visitors would enjoy some form of privacy, instead of feeling like they were sitting on a pedestal or they were part of the exhibition. The arrangement also encourages visitors to slow their pace and be more contemplative.

To avoid dividing each Yellow Box as a standardised unit, the curatorial team uses a bed platform, known as a *kangyi*, to foster the visitors' interests (Chang 2005: 16). In the past, families from Northern China would invite guests to climb onto a bed platform and sit together with the host. The bed platform creates a sociable and intimate venue for the literati to engage in conversation and entertainment. In the exhibition, it serves as an inviting device that encourages visitors to climb onto the bed and approach the artworks, when the work might otherwise be difficult to see (Figure 24.1). The bed platform can effectively shorten

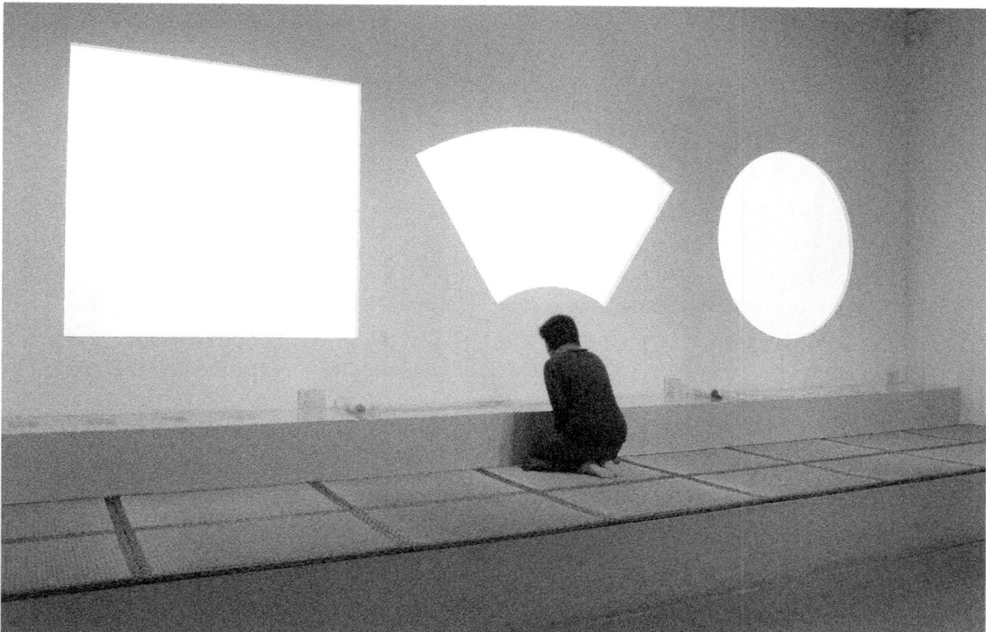

**FIGURE 24.1** A bed platform is designed to shorten the distance between the artwork and the visitor and create a more intimate viewing experience. 'The Yellow Box: Contemporary Calligraphy and Painting in Taiwan', gallery 3A of TFAM

*Photo:* TFAM

the distance between the audience and artwork in a vast exhibition hall. The curatorial team states explicitly that the bed platform is meant to challenge the contemporary phenomenon that artworks must be spectacular to impress the viewers (Chang 2005: 16). Some suggest that competing for attention, a spectacular show of art would nurture a rather mindless art experience that might yield cerebral stimulation but ignore works that are subtle and more thought-provoking. By inviting visitors to sit on a bed platform, a bodily gesture is encouraged to get close to the art and experience something more intimately and personally. For those who are not familiar with art exhibition or might be hesitant to take the initiative, a relaxed and friendly atmosphere could be more appealing than the possibilities offered by the white cube.

Besides seating, the exhibition also offers leaning supports, such as balustrades for looking at the works. Such supports would allow for an aesthetic experience when using the railings to enjoy a scenic view. Again, such structures facilitate the visitors' bodily experiences and their viewing distance. The leaning supports also promote social interactions and encourage visitors to see the works from a specific vantage point. Such socialising spaces help to prevent people from packing tightly together or avoiding all interactions.

Overall, the curatorial team provides direction for the visitors' viewing tempo and distance from different pieces. The variety of furniture, including seating arrangement, bed platforms and leaning supports emphasises different bodily experiences of visitors for interacting with the works and with other visitors. These devices help shape the exhibition as a public, yet private space, where the exhibits can reveal a world of colours, lines and shapes, infused with the artists' ideas, interpretations of traditional culture and contemporary associations.

## Interactions and the amicable atmosphere

Thus far, the discussion has focused on the interior furnishing of a Yellow Box and how spatial design, exhibition installations and devices can be used to shape the visitors' experiences and contribute to their understanding of Chinese ink art. Keeping in mind that the dynamics of a *yaji* not only lie in the venue and furniture, but also in the intellectual interactions among like-minded colleagues, it facilitates a social form of connoisseurship. It is an intellectual pursuit of knowledge, especially cultural history, and is a sensory enjoyment that transforms technicality into culturally defined ideas. *Yaji* may also involve a personal interpretation that transcends individual sensory perceptions to become shared aesthetic images for communicating a repertoire of cultural expressions. For instance, historically, connoisseurs would liken a hue of pale green to colours extracted from 'thousands of mountains', or a soft glow of jade, or a clear sky after rain, in which a sense of lucidity, grace or ingenuity might shine forth (Chen 2003: 2.18B; Xu 1994: 53). These descriptions offer a set of standardised images that allow colours to evoke culturally defined imaginative associations, such as the tenderness captured by the green colour. Interestingly, these images may not be directly related to the colour, but they would remind connoisseurs to look for essence of the materials and create imaginative approaches to interact with the objects (Ye 1985: 88–94). To some extent, it is not unlike what contemporary museums aspire to be – a communicative and inclusive powerhouse that generates enjoyment, creativity and knowledge. In this context, art can be fluid, performative and inclusive, enabling different people to collaborate, interact and negotiate various notions of culture, history and power in an exhibition (Greenblatt 1991: 52–3; Piotrowski 2011: 83–4).

One other question remains: how could the Yellow Box exhibition highlight an interactivity that draws from traditional literati culture and also stays in touch with contemporary ideas? The curatorial team invited artists to develop two participatory projects in exploring new ideas of art making and visitor involvement.

### *Yu Peng and his* Paper Window Project

By mounting paper on a window-pane at the exhibition, the artist Yu Peng developed a *Paper Window Project* as an ongoing process of art making during the exhibition. He invited visitors to paint or write at his platform desk, and possibly incorporated the visitors' ideas into his own creative works (Chang 2005: 19). The artist turned the process of painting into a public performance to re-define the exhibition space to be more than just a venue for art viewing – to also serve as a site of production. Nurturing a form of cultural synergy, it encourages knowledge, skills and ideas to be shared by many people.

### *Project for writing colophons*

To nurture genuine dialogues between visitors about contemporary ink art, the exhibition provided brush and paper for visitors to respond to the artwork. In return, the artist selected visitors to write colophons onto the works (Chang 2005: 19). A colophon is a form of writing inscribed onto a piece of ink work that includes additional information about the work (such as the date of its completion, the artist's professional background or a specific dedication). Colophons can also be creative responses from the artist's friends, patrons or even collectors from later generations. In the long trajectory of an object's life, colophons are seen as a tangible network between the past, present and future of a cultural tradition (Lee 2012: 85). By inviting visitors to write a colophon on an ink work, the project upholds a long tradition of Chinese art to engage visitors into an ongoing dialogue between the past and the present. Viewers are encouraged to reflect on how their personal experiences are related to ink art, and imagine the meaning of art production in contemporary culture.

Community participation is positioned against a mythic form of art experience that is spectacular, contemplative, and in most cases, detached from daily life. These participatory projects encourage short viewing episodes or a continuum of experience that relates the work to personal associations and transforms interactions between artists and visitors to drive art making. Nevertheless, community participation should be further examined in terms of recent misconceptions about participation and community involvement. It should not be seen as a lighthearted component at the expense of artistic integrity or simply a way to allow the 'feel-good factor' to cloud curatorial judgement. Participation is about creating communication and building relationships, and any form of public participation should answer whether or not such involvement helps different groups to communicate ideas (in this case, ideas about ink art), and how this might help people to relate to each other. As the Yellow Box exhibition has not yet undergone any substantial visitor studies research, it is difficult to evaluate the extent to which these projects promote a better understanding of ink art.

## The Yellow Box as a performative space

The Yellow Box exhibition is a curatorial experiment focusing on 'how to look at ink art per se' instead of considering 'what to look at'. Drawing from traditional Chinese connoisseurship, it advocates for a more engaging, affective and sensuous mode of viewing by reworking the exhibition rhetoric that integrates contemporary practices with traditional ideas. To summarise, the exhibition is developed based on three major components:

1. Suggestive spatial design that shapes the exhibition space to be public, yet personal, and contemplative but convivial. It points to the world of art and contemporary culture, while encouraging imaginative associations with the works;
2. A variety of furniture and diverse approaches are used to view the artworks, and to focus on the materiality of Chinese art;
3. The amicable atmosphere encourages dialogues among the visitors in relation to their interaction with the artworks.

The rhetorical devices shape the exhibition area to become a performative space – a social platform that encourages visitors to interact with the artworks through bodily movement and creative inputs. It considers the artworks and the visitors as performers who co-create the meanings of their experience of art. Highlighting interactivity, a performative space aims to foster multi-layered exchanges between the exhibits and the imaginative associations created by visitors.

To further sustain the intellectual vigour of the Yellow Box approach, more research and curatorial experiments should be conducted to understand how different design languages – such as materials, colour, light, and movement – can contribute to visitors' experiences and the locating of artworks within their own cultural context. Without proper implementation, this strategy could easily be seen as an isolated effort to re-enact the historical literati culture, resulting in an experience remote from contemporary society. If it becomes too reliant on simply creating a nostalgic presence, devoid of any contemporary connection, the result could leave an irrevocable gap between daily experiences and traditional culture. However, as I have tried to demonstrate through the examples described above, by referring to the literati notions of aesthetics, behavior patterns and cultural identity, the Yellow Box can also be seen as a thoughtful reinterpretation of traditional *yaji* experiences that points to new possibilities for exhibition design and curatorial practices. Its critical reception also presents a bold statement claiming that traditional culture can be vigorous and inspiring to contemporary audiences.

## Acknowledgements

I would like to express my sincere gratitude to Mr Tsong-Zung Chang who has been very generous in sharing his ideas and aspiration for the continuous development of the Yellow Box project.

## References

Anon. (2005) 'Architecture: Scholar's Library and Study', *The Art of Asia*, Minneapolis Institute of Arts. Online. Available HTTP: http://archive.artsmia.org/art-of-asia/architecture/chinese-scholars-study.cfm. Accessed 14 November 2015.

Bush, S. (2012) *The Chinese Literati on Painting: Su Shih (1037–1101) to Tung Ch'i-ch'ang (1555–1636)*, Hong Kong: Hong Kong University Press.

Cahill, J. (1978) *Parting at the Shore: Chinese Painting of the Early and Middle Ming Dynasty, 1368–1580*, New York: Weatherhill.

Chang, T.J. (2005) *The Yellow Box: Contemporary Calligraphy and Painting in Taiwan*, Taipei: Taipei Fine Arts Museum.

Chang, T.J. *et al.* (2015) 'Inside the Yellow Box: Chang Tsong-Zung (Johnson Chang) in conversation with Lynne Howarth-Gladston and Paul Gladston', *Journal of Contemporary Chinese Art* 2(1), pp. 103–15.

Chen, L. (2003) *Toayao (Pottery Refinement)*, Beijing: Quanguo tushuguan wenxian suowei fuzhi zhongxin.

Chen, Z. (2009) 'Chuantong yaji zhong de shihua hebi ji qi zai shilu shiji de xin bian – Yi mingren hezuo 'yaocao shanfang tuhuan' wei zhongxin' (Poem and Painting created in the Elegant Gatherings and the Changing Trend in 16th Century – A Case Study on the 'Scroll of Medicinal Herb Mansion') in Fan, J. and Cao Y. (eds) *Maishushi yu Guannianshi* (*Art History and Intellectual History*), Nanjing: Chifan daxue chubanshe, pp. 88–101.

Duncan, C. (1995) *Civilizing Rituals: Inside Public Art Museums*, London: Routledge.

Greenblatt, S. (1991) 'Resonance and Wonder', in Lavine, S.D. and Karp, I. (eds) *Exhibiting Cultures: The Poetics and Politics of Museum Display*, Washington: Smithsonian Institution Press, pp. 42–57.

Lee, D.D. (2012) 'Colophons, Reception, and Chinese Painting', *Word and Image*, 28(1), pp. 84–99.

McClellan, A. (2008) *The Art Museum: From Boullée to Bilbao*, Berkeley: University of California Press.

O'Doherty, B. (1986) *Inside the White Cube: The Ideology of the Gallery Space*, Berkeley and Los Angeles: University of California Press.

Piotrowski, P. (2011) 'Museum: From the Critique of Institution to a Critical Institution', in Hansen, T. (ed.) *(Re)Staging The Art Museum*, Berlin: Henie Onstad Art Centre, pp. 77–92.

Shang, Y. (2007) 'Zhongguo huihua de ganshang fangshi yu jindai meizhan yanjiu zhi biyao' (Approaches of Viewing Chinese Paintings and the Importance of Studying Art Exhibitions Held During the Republican Period), *Journal of Nanjing Arts Institute: Fine Arts and Design*, 2, pp. 80–4.

Shanks, M. and Tilley, C. (1996) 'Presenting the Past: Towards a Redemptive Aesthetic for the Museum', in *Re-Constructing Archaeology: Theory and Practice*, London: Routledge, pp. 68–99.

Shih, S. (2010) 'Zhongguo bimo de xiandai kunjing' (Contemporary Predicament of Chinese Ink Work), in *Style to Huayi (Picture-idea): Ruminating on Chinese Art History*, Taipei: Rock Publishing International, pp. 381–94.

Silbergeld, J. (1982) *Chinese Painting Style: Media, Methods, and Principles of Form*, Seattle and London: University of Washington Press.

Wang, H-T. (2004) 'Leisure and Taste: The Management of Daily Life and Culture of Appreciation among the Late Ming and Early Ch'ing Literati', *The National Palace Museum Research Quarterly* 22(1), pp. 69–97.

Weibel, P. (2007) 'Beyond the White Cube', in Weibel, P. and Buddensieg, A. (eds) *Contemporary Art and the Museum*, Stuttgart: Hatje Verlag, pp. 138–45.

Wu, H. (1997) *The Double Screen: Medium and Representation in Chinese Painting*, Chicago: University of Chicago Press.

Xu, Z.H. (1994) *Yinliuzhai shuoci* (*Remarks on Porcelain from the Studio of Wine* Chengdu: Bashu shushe.

Ye, L. (1985) *Zhongguo meishushi dagang* (*Outline of Chinese Aesthetic History*) Shanghai: Renwen chubanshe.

# 25

# FROM BODY TO BODY

## Architecture, movement and meaning in the museum

*Jonathan Hale and Christina Back*

### Abstract

This chapter considers the role of bodily experience in the visitor's engagement with the objects and spaces of the museum. Drawing on the phenomenological writings of Maurice Merleau-Ponty (1908–61), as well as recent research in neuropsychology and philosophy on so-called embodied cognition, the chapter puts forward a theoretical framework for what might be called 'interpretive exhibition design' – the use of space, setting and the active engagement of the visitor in the creation of more meaningful and memorable encounters with museum objects. The first part of the chapter describes several recent examples of 'interpretive' exhibitions at the Royal Danish Library in Copenhagen, showing a range of ways in which architectural space can be deployed as a tool for visitor engagement – transcending some of the inherent limitations of traditional text-based interpretation methods. The central section of the chapter draws on a range of historical and emerging research on the role of bodily movement in the ongoing processes of perception and cognition, in order to develop a more effective understanding of the interpretive potential of immersive 'viewing' conditions available within museums and exhibition spaces. The final part of the chapter considers the role of the visitor's bodily movement within the various viewing practices identified in recent research in museum studies. This includes the current revival of interest in embodied, sensory engagement alongside the increasing significance of materiality.

### Introduction

This chapter emerged from a research project titled *The Prism of Sustainability*, carried out in 2014–15 by a group of four Danish museums: National Gallery of Denmark (SMK); the Medical Museion; Trapholt Museum of Modern Art and Design; and the Royal Danish Library, Copenhagen. With government funding from the Danish Culture Agency, each organization was able to appoint an international research advisor to work alongside the local project leaders. Hence the co-authorship of the current chapter between Jonathan Hale (professor of architectural theory, University of Nottingham) and Christina Back (exhibitions designer, Royal Danish Library). Exhibition staff at the Library were keen to extend their knowledge regarding the potential of the architectural 'staging' of the exhibition environment as a tool for interpretation by drawing on new thinking on the role of the body in the perception of architectural space. The work at the Royal Danish Library carried out within the *Prism* project also involved the design and implementation of two new public exhibitions. One of these was also used as the basis for an in-depth audience evaluation, and this is separately described in Chapter 23.

## Exhibition as installation

The intention in this chapter is to explore the broader theoretical context out of which the initial collaboration developed – essentially a dialogue between exhibition designer and architectural theorist based on a shared interest in the bodily and spatial aspects of the museum experience. The project also aimed to build on an existing design approach already deployed in a successful exhibition programme at the Royal Danish Library, which – since 2008 – has also included a number of collaborative projects involving external artists. In each case the artist was part curator and part designer, working closely with the in-house team to explore the possibilities of the exhibition as an artistic medium in its own right. The semi-permanent exhibition of 'Treasures' from the Library's rare book collection, devised by the Russian artist Andrey Bartenev and installed in 2012 (Plate 27), shows the emergence of one of the central principles of the team's approach: the use of the staging of the exhibition as a mode of spatial – rather than textual – interpretation. Bartenev's contribution towards this idea was to create a vibrant and immersive, pop art–inspired environment, in which the historic books and manuscripts could be gradually discovered. By using a combination of over-scaled and brightly coloured 'super-graphics' along with a number of carefully placed sculptural objects – such as a stuffed polar bear and a series of portrait busts – the visitor would be magically transported into the virtual space of the texts on display. While the books themselves were not always immediately identifiable amid the visual onslaught of multi-coloured 'background' elements, there was an intention to encourage more detailed exploration of the texts via the information presented on a series of fixed tablet computers.

The strategy adopted within the 'Treasures' exhibition can also be seen emerging in a parallel series of temporary installations sited within the main exhibition spaces in the basement of the Library over the period from 2008 to 2014. Broadly speaking, the approach could be described as following the principles of 'installation art', where the emphasis is placed on communicating with the viewer through the overall effect of the space itself, rather than individual objects set off against an apparently neutral background, as is the case with the typical 'white cube' model (O'Doherty 1999). Alongside this there was also the idea of adopting a theatrical metaphor, treating the exhibition design as a form of scenography, and thereby transforming the act of curating into one of 'staging' an exhibition in the literal sense. In this way the visitor is invited to contemplate their own role in the viewing process, even to the extent of becoming an 'actor' in the 'performance' of the exhibition visit, as opposed to a passive spectator.

To assist in beginning to explore the potential for a more performative notion of exhibition making, in 2008 the theatre artist Robert Wilson (perhaps most famous for his operatic collaboration with Philip Glass, *Einstein on the Beach*, from 1976), was invited to guest curate an exhibition of artists' sketchbooks, including examples from painters, poets, playwrights and architects from the eighteenth to the twentieth centuries. Setting a pattern that would later be seen in the 'Treasures' installation, Wilson set out to create an immersive environment that would transport visitors into a kind of virtual 'dreamscape', a darkened space where a series of unexplained objects were dramatically emphasized with theatrical lighting (Plate 28). The central element giving visual structure to the space was a double row of bright red plastic swings – the kind of thing one might expect to find hanging from a tree in a garden or a children's playground, but not normally inside an exhibition space. The main exhibits were partially concealed within display cases built in to the four perimeter walls, requiring the viewer to peer in through a series of circular 'porthole' windows. Some windows revealed sketchbooks and others inscrutable objects, while some contained miniature landscapes which suggested a view into the mental world of the artist or writer; all of which seemed to offer a variety of metaphors for interpreting the books themselves. The slightly surreal and dream-like atmosphere implied that the visitor had entered a highly ambiguous space, where the book becomes a kind of portal into the process of creative thinking.

The other important element of Wilson's approach was to set up the space as a kind of challenge to the typical visitor: presenting the exhibition as a field of opportunities for action, or 'tasks', to be taken up by the viewer as an active participant. In this way, the act of viewing engaged the fully embodied experience of the visitor, who thereby became an active player in the spectacle being witnessed by the other visitors. A more recent example of an exhibition that also took a 'task-oriented' approach to structuring the visitor experience was 'The Original Kierkegaard', part of a programme of events in 2013 celebrating the Danish philosopher's 200th birthday. This time the show was staged by the Library's in-house design and production team, but like the exhibition already discussed above, this one also adopted some of the key conventions of installation art. By dividing the larger space into a series of individual rooms accessed from a central corridor the immediate impression on entering the exhibition was of heightened curiosity about what to expect inside (Plate 29). Each of the rooms was themed according to an episode from the philosopher's life – sometimes a single publication, a significant event or a characteristic of his personality. The visitor was invited to piece together a story by visiting each of the spaces in turn, drawn in to the process of discovery by a combination of features both familiar and unexpected. The wood-paneled doors along the central corridor suggested a familiar domestic interior, but these turned out to be strangely over-scaled, with handles placed at shoulder height. This slightly surreal, 'Alice in Wonderland' feeling continued inside each room, where the display cases of books and papers were each set within an individual 'theatrical' staging. Dramatic lighting, sound effects, and distinctive finishes such as artificial grass and mirrored floors helped to confound the initial impression of intimacy and calmness. Some of the spaces suggested that the visitor might even be a witness to the act of writing, as if these rooms were in some way similar to those in which the philosopher himself might actually have worked.

In the Kierkegaard exhibition, the rooms themselves were at least as important as the individual objects. By creating a contrast or contradiction between the initial visual impression of the space and the subsequent embodied exploration, the visitor was invited to interpret the rooms metaphorically – perhaps even to imagine themselves on a journey through the mental space of the writer. This emphasis on the interpretive power of the scenography, or three-dimensional spatial staging, also had another advantage: relieving what could otherwise have turned out to be a rather monotonous display of printed texts and papers.

An earlier exhibition at the Royal Library which took a more literal approach to the use of space was one that attempted to explain the institution itself by exposing the inner workings of the building. In this show, which also involved a collaboration with the Danish performance artist Kirsten Dehlholm ('Hotel Pro Forma'), visitors were invited to go on a journey to visit six of the specialist departments of the Library. This was achieved by a combination of methods, including opening up direct views from the exhibition gallery into the normally sealed-off 'backstage' spaces as well as projecting videos of library staff onto the six freestanding concrete columns that form part of the permanent structure of the building. By using these cylindrical forms to 'stand in' for the person representing each of the six departments, the installation also restated the anthropomorphic connection between column and body familiar from the history of Classical Greek and Roman architecture (Rykwert 1996). Passing in front of the six 'personified' columns and underneath a directional loudspeaker, the visitor could hear each person talking about their day-to-day experience of working in the various parts of the Library.

## Installation as interpretation

In their shared emphasis on the interpretive function of the architecture of the spatial setting, each of the exhibitions described above borrowed to some extent from the conventions and language of installation art. As the Danish art historian Anne Ring Peterson has recently written, installation art could be said to occupy the space between the worlds of 'image and stage' (Petersen 2015). As a specific genre of artistic activity installation art first emerged as part of the early modernist avant garde, specifically perhaps in the experimental *Proun Room* installation created by El Lissitzky in 1923. By wrapping a series of relief sculptures around the internal corners of a gallery, Lissitzky created a kind of three-dimensional painting large enough to walk around in. As the art historian Claire Bishop has suggested, commenting on Lissitzky's own writings, he appears to have inaugurated a new genre of artistic activity in order to subvert the normal constraints of Renaissance perspectival painting. In opposition to the single ideal viewpoint at the centre of the painter's cone of vision, Lissitzky instead argued that 'space does not exist for the eye only: it is not a picture; *one wants to live in it*' (Bishop 2005: 81). Bishop also highlights an important political dimension to this kind of immersive bodily experience. By questioning what were already seen as complacent and unthinking bourgeois viewing conventions, it was hoped to create a newly 'reactivated' museum visitor who might take this sense of awakened agency back out into the world.

A related but inverted movement to bring the everyday world into the realm of the gallery might also be identified in that other significant anticipation of the emergence of installation art, the 1938 International Surrealist Exhibition in Paris organized by Marcel Duchamp. Here the opulent interiors of the Galerie des Beaux-Arts were almost completely obscured by a combination of black paint, low lighting and ceilings hung with dusty coal sacks filled with newspaper. Nestling among the artworks were other ambiguous elements, such as Louis XV–style beds with rumpled linen and a garden pond with planting devised by Salvador Dalí. Opening night visitors were given torches to illuminate the objects on display, as if to exaggerate the sense of nocturnal wandering within a mystical Freudian dreamscape.

So alongside Lissitzky's activated viewer as a political agent in the outside world, Duchamp's dream wanderers are likewise encouraged to 'take control' – this time of the psychological world inside their own heads. Both of these examples provide evidence of one of the key lessons to be drawn from the experience of installation art: the idea of the viewing subject as an engaged participant, as a politically – and not just an aesthetically – active agent. Bishop also draws attention to Lissitzky's emphasis on the importance of the moving body in the viewing experience, which anticipated the pioneering work on embodied perception by the French phenomenologist Maurice Merleau-Ponty (1908–61). This work also had a formative influence on artists of the 1960s and '70s (Potts 2000: 207–34), particularly those responsible for the kind of formal experimentation that gradually saw the merging of traditional forms like sculpture and theatre in the new medium of performance art.

## Perception and action

In his major work *Phenomenology of Perception* (published in French in 1945 but only translated into English in 1962), Merleau-Ponty laid out a new framework for thinking about the body not simply as an *object in* space but rather as the *origin of* space, at least of 'lived space' as it exists for human beings rather than some post-rationalized mathematical abstraction. By this he meant that it is only by virtue of our own material embodiment – the fact that we are ourselves material things that occupy three-dimensional space – that we can have any understanding of the world of objects arranged in space around us. In other words, it is only because we have experienced 'from the inside' what it feels like to be an object that we can have any sense or 'feeling for' the space and the objects we encounter. One of the most commonly overlooked characteristics of perception is the somewhat paradoxical fact that when we think we have perceived something what we have actually experienced is the relationship *between* our bodies and the thing that we have encountered. For example, if I pick up a tennis ball and squeeze it to test its springiness, what I have experienced is not simply some objective quality possessed by the 'ball-in-itself'. Rather it is a certain degree of resistance that the ball offers towards the squeezing movement of my hand, in other words, what the ball 'feels like to me'. The philosopher David Morris has more recently described this way of understanding perception as 'the crossing of body and world' (Morris 2004: 4–6), which also serves as a reminder of its broader philosophical significance. If all perception begins in this kind of ambiguous state of continuity between the body and the world, then the sense of ourselves as existing independently of the people and things around us must be some kind of illusion. In other words, our emerging sense of the distinction between 'self and other' must be based on a more primal state of 'con-fusion', that is, literally, a state of being 'fused together' with the world of things and others around us that is in fact our natural condition.

Merleau-Ponty's later, unfinished and slightly more obscure writings extend this idea even further into deeper philosophical territory (Merleau-Ponty 1968). In coining the term the 'flesh-of-the-world' to describe this shared fabric of material embodiment (both bodies and things), he provides an opportunity for us to infer at least two significant consequences. The first is *phylogenetic*, relating to the evolutionary emergence of the human species, which must have involved a gradual emergence of the kind of self-consciousness that sets us apart from other living beings. The second is somewhat closer to home and relates to our individual *ontogenetic* emergence, the process by which – from birth onwards – we again become gradually aware of ourselves as 'independent' self-conscious entities. Both of these points suggest that we should understand the self not as a pre-given whole, but rather as an achievement that we strive towards – a continuous, ongoing and ever-unfinished project. Ongoing, because at each moment, for example, as we open our eyes on the scene in front of us we are again offered the challenge of making sense of what we see, and likewise deciding how much of what we are seeing 'belongs to us' and how much belongs to the world. Numerous examples of optical illusions, such as those created by the Lotto Lab, provide powerful evidence of just how often and how easily we can be mistaken in these judgements (Lotto 2017).

Another example of the fluid nature of the boundary between the self and the world results from the skillful use of manual tools which can act as 'prosthetic' extensions of the biological body. Merleau-Ponty's most powerful illustration of this effect involves a blind person navigating by using a white cane. In this case the sensory surface of the hand extends out to the tip of the cane which, with practice, gradually becomes 'invisible' to the user and literally 'incorporated' into an extended definition of the body. As Merleau-Ponty writes, in this case it is the acquisition of a 'habit' or skill that allows the re-combining of body and tool to take place:

> Habit does not *consist* in interpreting the pressure of the cane on the hand like signs of certain positions of the cane, and then these positions as signs of an external object – for the habit *relieves us* of this very task. . . . the cane is no longer an object that the blind man would perceive, it has become an instrument *with* which he perceives.
>
> *(Merleau-Ponty 2012: 152–3)*

Another inference that could be drawn from this scenario relates to the phylogenetic process of emergence referred to earlier. As more recent thinkers such as Bernard Stiegler have suggested (1998: 152–3), the early experience of tool use among non-human primates could perhaps have been the spur towards an emerging self-awareness – what psychologists refer to as 'meta-cognition'. In other words, it could be that the experience of technology actually inspired a process of self-reflection, a dawning awareness of the biological body as also providing a set of tools for reaching out and engaging with the world.

It is important to remember that these early experiences with simple stone tool technologies would also have taken place within a social and cultural context. It is therefore likely that a form of social or group cognition preceded the kind of individual self-awareness that we take for granted as adults today. The importance of this wider context in the healthy development of self-cognition also appears in the concept of environmental 'affordances' as described by the American psychologist James J. Gibson (1986: 127–43). Gibson suggested that our primary mode of perception is functional rather than formal, in other words, things appear to us not so much as 'what they are' but rather as 'what they can do'. Or rather, in Merleau-Ponty's terms, they appear as 'what *we* can do *with* them', according to the possibilities and limits of our own embodiment. The key idea is that the world appears to us in primary perception as a field of opportunities for bodily interaction. As Henri Bergson also nicely summarized: 'The objects which surround my body reflect its possible action upon them' (Bergson 1988: 21). The fact that the world we encounter is already socially and culturally structured should also remind us that while we are drawing on the philosophical resources of phenomenology we are not granting any special privilege to so-called subjective experience. We should think instead of 'self' and 'world' as emergent properties of – or abstractions from – what we typically refer to as 'human experience', as it begins in this in-between realm of what Merleau-Ponty called the 'flesh of the world'.

One further implication of this idea that the world is first encountered as an arena for action, is the fact that the use of tools also transforms our perception of potential affordances.

By enhancing the capacity of our biological bodies to engage with the environment around us, skilled tool use causes new features of the world to begin to 'show up' in perception – simply because they have now become available to us for use or occupation. One illustration would be the difference in outlook that results from the possession of different skill sets, for instance, compare the reaction of a geologist to that of a mountain climber when faced with a vertical cliff face. The former might see it as a potential source of fossils ready to yield to the gentle tap of a rock hammer, whereas the latter would take it as a challenge to her climbing ability and would begin by instinctively assessing the quickest – or perhaps the safest – route to the top.

This example of the climber's initial, intuitive, sense of the rock face as either 'climbable' or 'not climbable' also highlights a key component of what Merleau-Ponty referred to as 'motor cognition'. This is the idea that our primary grasp of the space around us comes from a bodily sense of how to 'cope' with it, which perhaps also helps explain what was described above as the functional or 'task-oriented' basis of perception (Dreyfus 2014: 8). Further evidence of the mechanisms by which this bodily response is orchestrated comes from recent research in neuroscience on the workings of the so-called mirror neuron system. Initial experiments carried out at the University of Parma in the late 1990s showed a significant overlap in the neural mechanisms active during both perception and action (Gallese *et al.* 1996). The neural circuits in operation during the performance of a particular action also become activated when observing someone else carrying out the same movements. While these initial findings involved the direct observation of an action happening 'live', later experiments showed similar results from observations of the physical traces left behind by previous actions. For example, in experiments carried out by Vittorio Gallese and the art historian David Freedberg, participants were shown paintings by Jackson Pollock and Lucio Fontana. In both cases mirror neurons were activated in response to the movements implied by the marks on the canvas, whether the paint dripping actions of Pollock or the canvas-cutting gestures of Fontana (Freedberg and Gallese 2007).

More recent research is beginning to explore the role of mirror neurons in the perception of spatial affordances, for example in the neural responses to objects and spaces that are specifically shaped for bodily actions (Jelic *et al.* 2016). All of these strands of research are now becoming incorporated within a new paradigm in the cognitive sciences known as the '4E' approach, which suggests that perception and cognition are, necessarily, 'Embodied, Extended, Embedded and Enactive' (Menary 2010). The examples referred to already above provide evidence for the first three of these four Es: the idea that experience begins with a biological body that is extendable by technical tools that are, in turn, 'geared into' a pre-structured environment – the continuum of all three equating to Merleau-Ponty's notion of the 'flesh of the world'. Perhaps most importantly, the enactive element relates to the essential role of our own bodily movement, which is also implied by the close connection between perception and action seen in the workings of the mirror neuron system. Historically, this idea is also prefigured in the findings of Gestalt psychology, from which Merleau-Ponty also took direct inspiration. This is the idea that our perception of a three-dimensional object must include an assumption about two things that cannot – at any one moment – actually be seen: the background which is currently obscured by the object, as well as its own hidden sides. When I 'read' the scene in front of me as, for example, a box on a table, I must have already made two unconscious assumptions: one is that the table must be continuous even though part of it is hidden by the box, and the second is that if I walked around behind the table I would see the back of a three-dimensional box, and not some flat 'cardboard cut-out' like a piece of theatrical scenery. This 'enactive' definition of perception as a necessarily ongoing, unfolding process suggests that to 'correctly' perceive a three-dimensional object *as* that thing that it is, I must also have grasped how its appearance changes according to my own movement in relation to it.

Merleau-Ponty also highlighted a normative element in perception that appears to drive this ongoing unfolding of experience, the idea that we are somehow impelled to explore the world around us in order to achieve the best possible understanding of it. Interestingly, he also referred to a museum experience in order to illustrate this point:

> For each object, just as for each painting in an art gallery, there is an optimal distance from which it asks to be seen – an orientation through which it presents more of itself – beneath or beyond which we merely have a confused perception due to excess or lack. Hence, we tend toward the maximum of visibility and we seek, just as when using a microscope, a better focus point.
>
> *(Merleau-Ponty 2012: 315–6)*

Drawn in by the 'solicitations' of the world we are naturally curious to confirm or correct our expectations, and we should therefore think of all our experience as an ongoing process of 'learning' – especially in light of the fact that we will never again encounter exactly the same scene. According to a recent model of the brain as a constantly improving 'prediction machine' – as set out by the contemporary philosopher and cognitive scientist Andy Clark – we are constantly refining and retuning our expectations of what we are about to encounter in experience (Clark 2016). This principle also goes some way towards explaining why the context (both physical and social) of an educational experience is so central to its success, as the educational theorists Jean Lave and Etienne Wenger have so powerfully pointed out (Lave and Wenger 1991; Lave 1988). In other words, it is perhaps more correct to say that when we have really learned something new – even some item of so-called propositional or factual knowledge – we have also learned in what context (i.e. how and when) it makes sense to 'use' it. This idea also echoes the famous attempt made by the philosopher Gilbert Ryle to dismantle the typical distinction between 'knowing that' and 'knowing how', that is between possessing a piece of information (or a belief) about something, and having a practical, bodily ability to perform a particular action (Ryle 1963: 28–32).

## Learning from the body

By engaging museum visitors in a 'learning process' of bodily exploration and discovery, the genre of installation art could perhaps best be seen as an extension of our experience of everyday reality. By presenting the artistic space as a bodily 'task' or challenge to the visitor, this experience taps into a deep-seated force at the heart of what it is to be human. As each of us has grown up in a world pre-structured by others before us, we have had to learn how to come to grips with it on a more or less 'trial and error' basis. Out of this process of largely unconscious and mimetic, or imitative, learning, we have gradually acquired what Pierre Bourdieu famously called an appropriate *habitus* for each situation – sets of rules and habits of behavior deemed acceptable by the culture in which we find ourselves. One of the reasons why these patterns of behavior are so difficult to acquire – and, by the same token, so difficult to change – is the length of time it takes to develop them, through repeated attempts to perform them, followed by continued efforts to 'correct' them. Witness the commonly quoted factoid that it takes 10,000 hours of practice to become an 'expert' at any new skill. Even more significant for a social theorist like Bourdieu is that fact that everyday bodily behaviors are often unconsciously acquired and maintained, like those distinctive styles of speech or fashion that are characteristic of particular professions. By slipping in 'under the radar' of conscious intellectual awareness these habits are also notoriously difficult to resist, even after their insidious workings have been unmasked by the sociologist in the medium of everyday language.

The relative ineffectiveness of the medium of language to 'control' or override this kind of intuitive bodily learning is one the key reasons why art itself is still such a powerful means of communication (Noe 2015). As Bourdieu has written:

> the work of art always contains something *ineffable*, not by excess, as hagiography would have it, but by default, something which communicates, so to speak, from body to body, i.e. on the hither side of words or concepts, and which pleases (or displeases) without concepts.
>
> *(Bourdieu 1977: 2)*

This might even be one of the underlying reasons for the continued popularity of the museum experience, being a fully immersive medium of spatial and bodily communication. While offering something unique that is missing from two-dimensional forms such as books and websites, it seems ironic that so many exhibitions still rely on textual methods of interpretation to reinforce their message. Thankfully, recent years have also seen a broader cultural interest in the significance of embodiment, evident for example in a proliferation of writings in cultural studies on bodies and 'body cultures' (Feher *et al.* 1989; Weiss 1999; Shilling 2003; Turner 2008). This shift is also reflected in the way that museums and galleries increasingly use more embodied forms of interpretation, such as interactive 'hands-on' exhibits, along with task-based – and in-gallery – educational activities.

Many recent exhibitions have also directly addressed the theme of embodiment through a focus on sensory experience, such as those surveyed by curator Madeline Schwartzman in the book *See Yourself Sensing* (2011). These examples draw attention to the unique opportunities offered by the museum as a bodily mode of communication, capable of drawing on all forms of cultural expression while exploiting the full potential of the human sensorium. Perhaps envious of the immersive multimedia work of artists such as Bill Viola and Olafur Eliasson, even veteran film makers like Peter Greenaway have been tempted to present their work in more interactive ways – suggesting that cinemas are no longer good enough for film, but perhaps museums are (Pascoe 1997). Likewise, contemporary dance practitioners are also increasingly attracted to work in museums and galleries, including choreographers like Rosemary Butcher whose work has always moved between visual arts and performance (Butcher and Melrose 2005). While some examples have simply replicated theatre viewing inside the walls of the gallery – and hence stayed within the limitations of the static-viewer/moving-image format – others have attempted to explore the combination of moving performer and mobile audience, the Spanish artist La Ribot being just one intriguing example among many from the genre of performance art. Finally, there are also now many examples of visual and performance artists working as guest-curators within museums, including those where the artist's own live performance also becomes a medium of museum interpretation (Wookey 2015).

## Conclusion

In conclusion, we would like to make brief reference to another recent exhibition, which also involved a more nuanced exploration of the possibilities of 'reactivated viewing'. This example also involved a gallery environment that offered what Merleau-Ponty called 'solicitations' to the spectator, whereby the space offered itself as a challenge to the visitors' active process of interpretation. In some ways, similar to the 'Yellow Box' exhibition described by Vivian Ting in the previous chapter of this book, this final example also attempted to engage visitors' bodies directly in the process of viewing. Staged at the Royal Danish Library in 2015 as part of the exhibition series described above, this show also dealt with the challenge of presenting written texts as a whole-body experience. Titled '101 Danish Poets', the show comprised written compositions from a range of living writers who were each asked to provide handwritten copies of the submitted work. Seeing the work written out by hand gave the viewer an immediate physical link to the individual writer, partly on the basis that the visible trace of a bodily gesture activates the mirror neuron circuits, as described above. As with the Yellow Box exhibition, the viewer was invited to make a certain physical 'investment' in the act of viewing, as each poem was mounted at a different height on the wall requiring an adjustment of bodily comportment. As with Merleau-Ponty's museum visitor searching for the optimum viewing position, either a seat or moveable steps were offered to facilitate this exploration (Figure 25.1).

One lesson from the success of the '101 Danish Poets' exhibition relates to the challenge of creating environments that balance novelty with familiarity. This is something that has often been referred to in relation to the design of learning spaces – a balance of stimulation and reassurance that is characteristic of 'moderately novel' environments (Falk and Dierking 2000: 116). A second, more specific, lesson concerns what we initially called 'spatial interpretation',

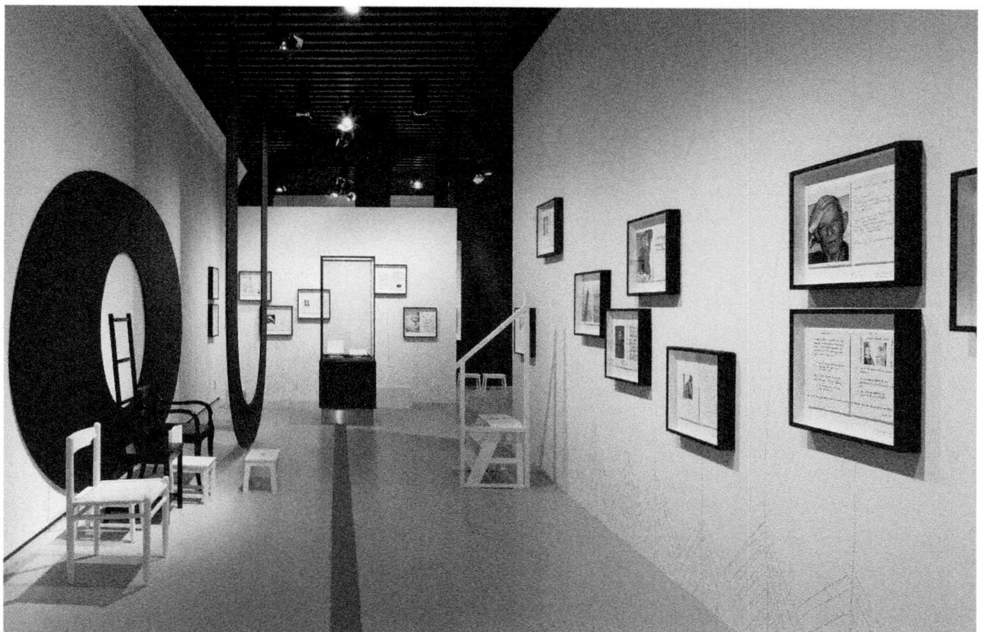

**FIGURE 25.1** '101 Danish Poets'. Designed by Christina Back, 2014

*Photo:* Laura Stamer. Reproduced with kind permission of the Royal Danish Library.

relating to the message that is conveyed by this attempt to actively engage with the spectator. It serves to illustrate that even the process of reading is a necessarily embodied activity, and that to really 'understand' a text is, in a sense, to come to 'inhabit' it and find oneself in it, or – as Merleau-Ponty implied – to 'take it up' like a tool, or as a project of one's own:

> The word has never been inspected, analysed, known, and constituted, but rather caught and taken up by a speaking power, and, ultimately, by a motor power that is given to me along with the very first experience of my body and of its perceptual and practical fields. As for the sense of the word, I learn it just as I learn the use of a tool – by seeing it employed in the context of a certain situation.
>
> *(2012: 425)*

## References

Bergson, H. (1988) *Matter and Memory* (trans N.M. Paul and W.S. Palmer). New York: Zone Books.

Bishop, C. (2005) *Installation Art: A Critical History*, London: Tate.

Bourdieu, P. (1977) *Outline of a Theory of Practice* (trans R. Nice) Cambridge: Cambridge University Press.

Butcher, R. and Melrose, S. (2005) *Rosemary Butcher: Choreography, Collisions and Collaborations*, Enfield: Middlesex University Press.

Clark, A. (2016) *Surfing Uncertainty: Prediction, Action, and the Embodied Mind*, Oxford: Oxford University Press.

Dreyfus, H.L. (2014) *Skillful Coping: Essays on the Phenomenology of Everyday Perception and Action*, Oxford: Oxford University Press.

Falk, J.H. and Dierking, L.D. (2000) *Learning From Museums: Visitor Experiences and the Making of Meaning*, Walnut Creek, CA: AltaMira Press.

Feher, M., Naddaff, R., and Tazi, N. (eds) (1989) *Fragments for a History of the Human Body*, New York: Zone Books.

Freedberg, D. and Gallese, V. (2007) 'Motion, Emotion and Empathy in Esthetic Experience', *Trends in Cognitive Sciences*, 11(5), pp. 197–203.

Gallese, V., Fadiga, L., Fogassi, L. and Rizzolatti, G. (1996) 'Action Recognition in the Premotor Cortex', *Brain*, 119(Pt 2), pp. 593–609.

Gibson, J.J. (1986) *The Ecological Approach to Visual Perception*, Hillsdale, NJ: Lawrence Erlbaum Associates.

Jelic, A. *et al.* (2016) 'The Enactive Approach to Architectural Experience: A Neurophysiological Perspective on Embodiment, Motivation, and Affordances', *Frontiers in Psychology*, 7(March), p. 20.

Lave, J. (1988) *Cognition in Practice: Mind, Mathematics and Culture in Everyday Life*, Cambridge: Cambridge University Press.

Lave, J. and Wenger, E. (1991) *Situated Learning: Legitimate Peripheral Participation*, Cambridge: Cambridge University Press.

Lotto, B. (2017) *Deviate: The Science of Seeing Differently*, London: Hachette Books.

Menary, R. (2010) 'Introduction to the Special Issue on 4E Cognition', *Phenomenology and the Cognitive Sciences*, 9(4), pp. 1–4.

Merleau-Ponty, M. (1968) *The Visible and the Invisible; Followed by Working Notes* (trans A. Lingis). Evanston, IL: Northwestern University Press.

Merleau-Ponty, M. (2012) *Phenomenology of Perception* (trans D.A. Landes) Abingdon, OX; New York: Routledge.

Morris, D. (2004) *The Sense of Space*, Albany, NY: State University of New York Press.

Noe, A. (2015) *Strange Tools: Art and Human Nature*, New York: Hill and Wang.

O'Doherty, B. (1999) *Inside the White Cube: The Ideology of the Gallery Space*, Expanded edn, Berkeley, CA; London: University of California Press.

Pascoe, D. (1997) *Peter Greenaway: Museums and Moving Images*, London: Reaktion Books.

Petersen, A.R. (2015) *Installation Art: Between Image and Stage*, Copenhagen: Museum Tusculanum Press.
Potts, A. (2000) *The Sculptural Imagination: Figurative, Modernist, Minimalist*, New Haven; London: Yale University Press.
Rykwert, J. (1996) *The Dancing Column: On Order in Architecture*, Cambridge, MA; London: MIT Press.
Ryle, G. (1963) *The Concept of Mind*, London: Penguin Books.
Schwartzman, M. (2011) *See Yourself Sensing: Redefining Human Perception*, London: Black Dog.
Shilling, C. (2003) *The Body and Social Theory*, 2nd edition. London: Sage.
Stiegler, B. (1998) *Technics and Time: The Fault of Epimetheus* (trans R. Beardsworth and G. Collins) Stanford, CA: Stanford University Press.
Turner, B.S. (2008) *The Body & Society: Explorations in Social Theory*, 3rd edition. London: Sage.
Weiss, G. (1999) *Body Images: Embodiment as Intercorporeality*, New York; London: Routledge.
Wookey, S. (ed.) (2015) *Who Cares? Dance in the Gallery and Museum*, London: Siobhan Davies Dance.

# TOP 20 PRINCIPLES FOR THE FUTURE OF MUSEUM AND GALLERY DESIGN

## The future of museum and gallery design must . . .

1 Be **inclusive** – museum designers must place visitors at the centre of everything they do.
2 Be **collaborative** – the best museum and gallery design will draw on expertise from design and from research and find **new ways** to merge design knowledge with museum knowledge.
3 Be **non-hierarchical** – true collaboration means teamwork and the museum sector needs **new ways** of doing museum design which remove hierarchies and truly value the expertise of both professionals and the public.
4 Develop **new strategies** for **participation** and **co-curation** – we need a greater understanding of how different modes of museum making can work effectively in different contexts.
5 Be **multi-sensory** – museum experiences must engage the whole human being, body and mind.
6 Prioritise **social interaction** – museum designers must develop and share **new methods** for enabling and supporting interactions amongst groups of visitors and amongst strangers – this is essential to their social role.
7 Be **action-orientated** – museum designers must develop and share **new prototypes** for enabling diverse activities within the physical museum experience, recognising that museums are made through use as much as they are through design.
8 **Trust** museum visitors to construct their own narratives and recognise the role of the museum maker as one of creating opportunities to access new ways of knowing – the exhibition narrative is not the same as the visitor experience.
9 Take account of the **local** – museum makers must understand the local environment and respond to local user's interests and needs.
10 Be **embedded** in its environment – museums must find new ways of blurring the boundaries between the space and experience of the museum and the space and experience of everyday life.

11 Find new and **ethical** ways of working which take account of the role of museums as socially responsible organisations and agents of social change.
12 Be **real** – museum makers must avoid or subvert the tendency in museums to build iconic objects and symbols and instead prioritise real people, real lives and use built forms to provide welcome and stimulate curiosity.
13 Be **human** – museum design must avoid or evolve its tendency towards the spectacular and instead create meaningful content and experiences at a human scale.
14 Be underpinned by high-quality **research** – museum makers must find ways to make use of, direct and consolidate the growing body of museum design research.
15 **Reach beyond** narrow definitions of design – museum design and design thinking can make a positive and significant contribution to organisational change and sectoral change.
16 **Inspire** – we need case studies of excellent practice to inspire us all and open up new possibilities for the cultural sector.
17 **Cross boundaries** – we understand more about the museum as a medium the more we **explore and experiment** beyond the well-established models.
18 Be **strategic, visible, connected and organised** – museum design is fragmented, and the museum, design and research professionals involved in the development of museum design practice and research need to work together and share ideas in order to move the field forward.
19 Be **varied –** we want a diverse museum landscape where difference is celebrated and divergent perspectives are explored and debated as a route to fostering understanding and tolerance.
20 Be **transformative –** design has a key role to play in the democratisation of museums – it can drive as well as enact change. Let's make it matter!

# AFTERWORD

*Adrian Cheng, Founder and Honorary Chairman, K11 Art Foundation*

How should we conceive of the exhibition space of tomorrow? What does it look and feel like? What should we aspire to achieve? These were big questions that we considered during *The Future of Museum and Gallery Design* conference in Hong Kong. Co-presented by the K11 Art Foundation (KAF), we were proud to have facilitated and participated in the conference, which fostered pioneering initiatives and built a network of global connections.

The academic symposium explored models for future museum and gallery spaces. A plethora of issues were dissected from architecture to operation, conservation, digitalisation, archiving, localisation and much more. With a truly international scope and outreach, the conference was successfully held, and we were honoured to have been joined by 150 speakers from universities, galleries, art institutions, museums, and government bodies hailing from over 45 cities and 16 countries.

Exhibition making in the twenty-first century is facing great swathes of change, as the tastes of audiences rapidly evolve across the globe. The advent of technology is one of the main contributing factors to this transformation, the channels through which we are exposed to art continue to grow, and the world has become much smaller and more interconnected than ever before. Contemporary art practices are engaging with these innovations, challenging curators and those at the helm of exhibition spaces. It is within this context that my team and I continue to re-evaluate KAF's visions and values. One of KAF's core missions is to incubate young Chinese contemporary artists and curators, and to promote public art education, by providing a 'glocal' platform to generate broad awareness of contemporary art practices in China.

The three-day conference ultimately resulted in the collaborative promulgation of the 'Top 20 Principles for The Future of Museum and Gallery Design', a set of ideals that future museum and gallery design should aim to accomplish and realise. The principles include notions of inclusiveness, collaboration, social interaction, localisation, experimentation, and connectivity among many others. Moving forward from the conference, we at KAF continue to embody these ideals, as part of our ongoing international collaborations, developing new strategies for participation and co-curation. We have also leveraged new platforms to priotize social interaction, such as the One Minute Film festival, which engages the masses through

Instagram and online participation. In Hong Kong and China, where models of exhibiting are less rigidly embedded, these principles can be seen in the exhibition spaces our team selects. The annual programme is held at a host of spaces across the country, including our K11 Museum retail spaces, seeking to cross the boundaries between the traditional white-cube and the spaces of everyday life. From China to further afield, our vision is to continue to innovate, and create new experiences that are singularly generated for each context, creating new journeys that value the audience at their core.

When launching K11, the first museum retail hybrid, in 2009, we came to the realisation that we would need to create a new model for art appreciation in Greater China, one that was aligned with and tailored to the lifestyle of urban Chinese. The resulting concept was a pioneering project that differed from Western notions of art presentation, successfully introducing modern and contemporary art to Chinese audiences, bridging the chasm between the wider public and art. We are proud to have created an inclusive space which provides welcoming access to art, whilst nurturing audience development.

Similarly, the non-profit KAF was established to defy the conventional framework of exhibition production and presentation. We are a constantly evolving entity, adapting and changing with the shifting cultural ecosystem. Our outreach has formed long-term partnerships with leading institutions across the continents, including MoMA PS1, the New Museum (New York); the Institute of Contemporary Arts, the Serpentine Galleries (London); Centre Pompidou, Palais de Tokyo (Paris); and many more, creating an international platform for Chinese artists to showcase their artworks to a truly global audience. In parallel, a combination of both permanent and pop-up spaces across Hong Kong and Shanghai, allows Chinese audiences to view and discover works by both a new generation of local voices, as well as the most celebrated international masters. Our strategy is to keep bringing this momentum forward, and further develop our outreach with future spaces planned for Guangzhou, Shenyang and more in China to be launched in the coming years. *The Future of Museum and Gallery Design* allowed for us to place KAF in the global context, and provided opportunities to align ourselves with the trajectories of transgeographical development.

My hope is that KAF will continue to innovate, and meaningfully contribute to the art ecosystems both locally and internationally. With our forward-thinking spirit, and alongside the varied range of professionals who make up the cultural sector – demonstrated by the range of contributions to this book – we aim to play a key role in developing the museums and galleries of the future.

# INDEX

4E cognition 346
20 principles 3, 352–3, 354
*2030:Smart City Life 360 View* 62

affordances 20, 54, 65, 306, 345, 346
ageing population 291
Agile software 219–23
*Agora* 272
*In The Air Tonight* 65
AL_A 67
Albert Bridge 66
*Alexander Nevsky* 244
*Altered State: Marijuana in California* 124
alternative vision 1
American Alliance of Museums (AAM) 106
Ames, Michael 41
Anderson, Suze 41
Annabell Fraser 325
*Aristotle in Hollywood* 318
ARS Electronica Center 60
Arte Util 133
Art Labs for Young People (SMK) 151
art of the ordinary 31
Art Pilots (SMK) 151, 152
Arup Foresight and Innovation 45
Assemble 133
audio tour 325
authenticity 18, 20, 21, 24, 76, 259, 277, 331
Axis web 133

Baggy space 117–18, 132, 134, 135, 138, 140, 141, 143–5
Bagnall, Gaynor 20
Bai Yang 284
Bakhtin, Mikhail 226, 236
Bal, Mieke 234, 241, 243
Barthes, Roland 227, 235, 277–8, 301
Bateson, Gregory 155
Battersea Arts Centre 16
Bauman Lyons Associates 166, 168, 169
Bay Lights, The 60, 67
Beijing Minsheng Art Museum 201, 203, 209
Bennett, Tony 261–2
Bergson, Henri 241, 345
Biennial/Biennale 46, 275
*Biografias* 46
Bishop, Claire 343, 344
body 20, 32, 228, 232, 240, 255, 284, 304, 340, 341, 343, 344, 345, 346, 348, 350
Bordwell, David 317, 319, 320, 321, 324, 325
*Botticelli Reimagined* 249–50
Bruguera, Tania 133
Bruno, Giuliana 243
Buber, Martin 226, 236
Burns, Michael 49–50
Butler, Tony 162

Calgary Tower 66
calligraphy 31, 73, 75, 78, 81, 83, 207, 261, 264, 265, 269, 270, 328, 329, 335
Carroll, Noël 317, 319
Caruso St. John 95
Casabianca, Julien de 47
catharsis 319
Central St. Martins (CSM) 52, 53
Certeau, Michel de 90
chaos theory 37
Chatman, Seymour 320
Cheng-tang Hsu 289, 291
Chen Xiaoyang 203, 205
Chinese art xiv, 71–2, 73, 74, 77–8, 80, 83, 84, 202, 264, 275, 328, 329, 337

Chinese University of Hong Kong 9
Christensen, Jeppe S. (Tankespil) 155, 156
*City Insights* 47
civic 11, 26, 59, 69, 88, 90, 91, 100, 133, 143, 144, 160, 165, 173, 210, 297, 301; institution 118, 162, 163, 172, 263; role 45, 117, 132, 133, 134, 138, 201; space 9, 47, 60, 61, 65
*Civil Power* 201, 203, 207
Clark, Andy 347
Clarke, David 32
Clunas, Craig 77
CN Tower 60, 66
co-curation 10, 45, 46, 47, 48, 49, 50, 51, 52, 56, 352, 354
co-design 4, 10, 45, 46, 50, 51, 52–3, 54, 55, 56
Cohen Hilberry Architects (CHA) 177
collaboration 4, 56, 66, 67, 68, 118, 133, 151, 153, 162, 173, 220, 315, 341, 343, 352, 354
collaboration - cross-sector 7, 52, 103, 117, 197–8, 201, 209, 210, 213, 226, 252, 304
collective creativity 6, 118, 147, 148, 149, 150, 151, 153, 158, 159
Colophon 255, 259, 265, 267, 329, 336–7
community-based architecture 100
community engagement 49, 65, 68, 69, 92, 98, 100, 102, 111, 112, 113, 135, 141, 164
complexity 5, 10, 15, 17, 25, 35, 36, 38, 41, 42, 43, 185, 193, 249, 252, 280
complexity - theory 34, 37–9, 41, 42, 43
Constant 59
context orientated 118, 147
co-production 16, 118, 147, 160, 162, 164, 165, 166, 167, 168, 170, 172, 173
*Copy after Along the River during the Qingming Festival* 329
copying 264, 267
Cornillon, Matthieu 219–20, 221, 222
*Corporeal Turn, The* 240
Costa, Arthur L. 35
Cotter, Holland 102
Coulson, Hannah 325
creative: effort 125; lives xviii, 13, 15, 26, 173
*Creative Spaces/A Toolkit for Participatory Urban Design* 52
critical approaches 117, 298
Cuban, Larry 38
curating and designing exhibitions 189, 190, 195, 196
curatorial process 48, 119, 200, 201, 210, 236

Dallas-Pierce-Quintero 137
dance 32, 90, 130, 144, 240, 348
David, Percival 72
David Chipperfield Architects 96, 97
Debord, Guy 59
*Defining Beauty: the Body in Ancient Greek Art* 225, 226, 227–8, 229–30, 231, 232
democracy 2, 10, 32, 35, 64, 68, 173, 179, 263
Deng Yizhe 74
Derby Museums 16, 162, 163, 164, 166
Derby Silk Mill - Museum of Making 160, 161, 163, 164, 166, 172, 173, 174
design: for change 129; process 2, 3, 4, 6, 9, 11, 14, 16, 100, 101, 102, 105–6, 107, 111, 112, 118, 123, 125, 147, 148–9, 153, 155, 156, 158, 165, 167, 169, 175, 176, 181, 182, 183, 185, 213, 223, 244, 246, 252, 289; as a resource 4, 6, 302; sensibility 2, 9, 18, 25; thinking 16, 51, 54, 102, 112, 169, 213, 214–15, 216–17, 222, 255, 353
Deveron Arts 49
Diller Scofidio+Renfro 66, 67
diorama xi, 255, 277, 278, 279–80, 281, 282, 283, 284, 285, 286
discourse 43, 64, 65, 102, 233, 234, 243, 251, 252, 261, 280, 320
disrupt/disruption 103, 163, 172
diverse 4, 6, 9, 13, 15, 16, 17, 25, 26, 56, 68, 98, 104, 138, 147, 151, 154, 158–9, 160, 168, 172, 173, 193, 195, 197, 201, 209, 225, 232, 269, 271, 272, 274, 328, 330, 337, 352, 353
Dodd, Nick 164
Donnelly, Jessica Foy 322
Duncan, Carol 72
Duncan McCauley (DMC) 14, 239, 240
dynamic environments 123

Eco, Umberto 313–14
*Eighteen Scholars, The* 80
Eisenstein, Sergei 243, 244, 246
embodied - cognition 257, 340
embodied - experience 25, 26, 304, 330, 342
embodied - narrative experience 19, 20, 21, 22, 25
emotion 20, 311
empathy 17, 34, 35, 37, 51, 97, 119, 164, 215, 217, 218, 223, 296–7, 311, 318, 322
empathy and political empowerment 6
Empire State Building 60, 64, 66
enactment of socially engaged art 200
*Enchantment/Beauty Parlour* 189, 192–3, 195
environment 20, 36, 41, 52, 54, 132, 169, 280, 282, 289–90, 292, 297, 299, 300, 301, 302, 346, 352
equality of experience 118, 175, 176, 188
Erskine, Ralph 135
ethics 9, 13, 14, 15, 17, 25, 26, 203
Eumorfopoulos, George 72
*Exhibiting Korea - Passages* 189, 194
exhibition narratives: first person 41; layering 39; light framing 40; multi-varied 34, 40; multi-voiced labels 41, 234
experience design 119, 148, 213, 214, 217, 218, 223, 224
experiences: dynamic 239; spatial 239, 244, 255, 336, 341; time-based 239, 244, 256

experiment 10, 103, 117, 123, 126, 158, 165, 197, 227, 304, 305, 328, 337, 353
experimental exhibition-making 40, 119, 189, 195, 197
experimentation 4, 6, 7, 40, 103, 105, 109, 111, 117, 121, 128, 129, 155, 163, 164, 166, 173, 174, 196, 304, 344, 354
Exploratorium (San Francisco) 124

*Fabula* 241, 242, 320, 321
*Fall of the Titans* 156
Featherstone Young Architects 134, 135, 140, 143
Fehn, Sverre 90
Féral, Josette 312
film/movies 90, 91, 120, 219, 225, 230, 233, 239, 240, 243, 244, 246–7, 249–50, 251–2, 277, 278–9, 282–4, 285, 310, 319–20, 324, 325
film museums 277, 278
Foley, Natalie 215–16
*Fourth Plinth, The* 66
Fox, Hannah 163, 164
*Framework for Ethical Interpretation at the Tower* 24
Francis Crick Institute 52, 53, 54, 55
Freedberg, David 346
Freytag, Gustav 227, 228, 244
Freytag's pyramid 228, 244
Fromm, Franz 321–2, 323
full-body experience prototyping 123
Fu Sinian 74
future 5, 10, 11, 14, 17, 26, 45, 66, 121, 126, 136, 172, 173, 201, 272, 275, 279, 282, 284, 286, 319, 321, 337; ethics 13, 25; of exhibitions 53, 122, 200, 233, 235; of museum design 2, 3, 7, 13, 84, 86, 87–8, 117, 118, 119, 147, 159, 162, 200, 352, 354
Future\Pace 67
Fu Zhenlun 75

Gaffikin, Alex 18
Gallese, Vittorio 346
Gallos, Joan 42
Garrett, Jesse James 148
Gateway Arch National Park 175, 176, 187
geomedia 61, 64
Gerard, John 23–4
Gestalt psychology 346
Gillis, Stuart 163, 164
Godard, Jean-Luc 251
Granby Four Streets Community Land Trust 133, 138
Grand Central Parkway 61
graphic language 229, 231, 232, 234
Greenfield, Adam 62
Greenfield, Susan 36
Guangzhou Academy of Fine Arts (GAFA) 203, 208
Guerlac, Suzanne 241
Gurian, Elaine Heumann 106

habit 81, 345
habituation 309
Hale, Jonathan 20, 240, 304, 309, 340
Haley Sharpe Design (hsd) 175, 176, 185
hapticity 280
haptic vision 311
health 38, 50, 51, 143, 164, 173, 177, 289, 291, 292, 295
Herman, David 243
high-quality experiences 147, 158
Hilberry, Gina (CHA) 177
Hilliger, Zoila Fromm 322, 323, 324
Hiltunen, Ari 318–19
Historic Royal Palaces (HRP) 3, 14, 18, 19, 23
*Homo Ludens – A Study of Play Element in Culture* 154
Hooper-Greenhill, Eilean 48
Howard, David 318
Howell, Julie 55
Huang Gongwang 265
Hu Die 284
Hudson, Alastair 135
Huizinga, Johan 262
human-centred design 16, 51, 118, 160, 163, 164–5, 173, 175
human rights 302
Humboldt Forum 189, 190, 196, 197
Humboldt Lab Dahlem 189–91, 195, 196, 197
Hunt, Jamer 17

IDEO 51, 214, 215
illuminated infrastructure 59, 60–1, 62, 63, 64–5, 66, 68–9
*Illuminated River, The* 66, 67, 68, 69
*Imagine! Three Museum Designs Revealed* 107, 108
immersive experience 47, 192, 193, 262, 343
*Imprints of War - Photography from 1864* 305, 306, 307
inclusive: methodology 175; visitor experiences 4, 102, 112
*In Search of Art* 32
installation art 341, 342, 343, 344, 347
institutional: critique 191, 193, 328; role 196, 197, 198
interactivity 281, 330, 337
*International Exhibition (of Chinese Art)(1935)* 71, 72, 83
*Internet of Things (IOT)* 62
interpretation 18, 21, 22, 23, 24, 25, 81, 91, 98, 103, 118, 151, 168, 184, 191, 196, 200, 202, 208, 225, 236, 252, 264, 265, 267, 278, 295, 309, 315, 321, 325, 328, 329, 332, 336, 341, 348
*Interpreting Historic House Museums* 322
interpretive design 18, 19, 22, 23, 25, 27, 256, 257, 289
Inzovu Curve 219

iteration 16, 125, 128, 164, 165, 174, 215, 221, 222, 223

Jacobs, Jane 63
Jan Shrem and Maria Manetti Shrem Museum of Art 11, 100, 102, 103, 105, 107, 112, 114
Ji Cheng 265, 271
Jones, Lisa Heledd 136
Jones, Paul 15

K11 Art Foundation (KAF) 354, 355
Keith Williams Architects 88, 90, 91
Kigali Genocide Memorial 217–18, 219
kinaesthesia/kinesthesia 27, 213, 310
Kluitenberg, Eric 66, 68

Larman and Basili 222–3
*Launchpad* 1
Leach Colour 167, 168
learning 3, 6, 11, 19, 20, 23, 25, 26, 35, 40–1, 42, 50, 102, 105, 112, 121, 122, 125, 126, 128–9, 130
Le Corbusier 244
Lefebvre, Henri 47
Levete, Amanda 67
Lifschutz Davidson Sandilands 67
*lilong* 282
Li Ruinian 76
Lissitzky, El 343–4
Lupton, Ellen 149
Lynch, Bernadette 49
Lynn Pan (*Shanghai Style*) 283

*Made in USA* 246, 251, 252
Ma Hen 74
*MAKE: A New Museum for UC Davis* 111, 112
*Makehistory* 48
MA Narrative Environments (MANE) 54, 55
manifestation of organisational mission 6
*Manifesto for Agile Software Development* 220–1
*Manifesto for the (R)evolution of Museum Exhibitions* 128
Marks, Laura U. 310–11
Martin, Alicia 46
*MatchSMK* 147, 153–4, 156, 157, 158
materiality 90, 120, 194, 234, 250, 257, 279, 330, 332, 333, 334, 337, 340
Mayching Kao 72
McQuire, Scott 59, 63, 64, 68, 69
meaningful experiences 132, 144
Media Architecture Institute 60
media city, the 59
*Memento* 246, 249, 250, 252
Merleau-Ponty, Maurice 20, 313, 340, 344, 345, 346–7, 349–50
Middlesbrough Institute of Modern Art (mima) 133
mirror neurons 346
MOCA Shanghai 9, 30
modernism 277, 281, 285
modes of collaboration 213, 223
Moggeridge, Bill 51
*Montage and Architecture* 243
Moses, Robert 61
mountain worship 269
movement (bodily) 5, 23, 32, 91, 194, 227, 240–1, 244, 246, 250, 251, 252, 278, 279, 280, 281, 285, 329, 332, 337, 340, 346–7
multidisciplinary approach 225
multimodal nature of museums 225
multivalency 86, 87, 88, 91, 95, 96, 98
museum: design research 5, 6, 11, 225, 353; development in China 1, 3, 74, 76; training programmes 39, 42
Museum at the Gateway Arch, The 175, 179
museums as agents of change 45, 46, 48, 50, 56
*Museums in the Digital Age* 45

Nanting Research 200, 202, 203, 204–5, 206, 207, 208
narrative 39, 43, 53, 75, 86, 87, 88, 90, 98, 105, 124, 140, 166, 168, 171, 175, 179, 182, 192, 193, 195, 197, 218, 219, 230, 234–5, 256, 272, 280, 288, 289, 291, 295, 301, 306, 312, 313, 315, 317, 319, 320, 321, 325, 352; embodied 19–20, 21, 22; experience 19, 20, 21, 22, 25, 240, 243, 247; of place 95, 96, 97; structure 120, 227, 228, 229, 230, 232, 239, 240, 244, 246, 247, 248, 249, 250, 251, 252, 292, 314; theory 120, 225, 227, 233, 234, 235, 240, 244, 251, 252; visual 71, 72, 229
narrativity 227
narratorial voice 231, 232, 234
National Center on Accessibility (NCA) 177
National Museum of Natural Science, Taiwan (NMNS) 288, 297, 302
National Museum of Photography, Royal Danish Library 305, 306, 307, 340, 349
*National Trust app* 47
natural history 172, 277, 280, 283
nature 172, 260, 265, 269, 271, 280, 310, 331, 334
Navarini, Rosamaria 321–2
network theory 37
Newburger, David 185, 186
New England Complexity Institute 37
Noah, Trevor 35
*No Idea is too Ridiculous* 126
Nottingham Contemporary 87, 95, 96
Novium, Chichester 87, 88, 91, 92

*Object Biographies* 189, 191–2, 195, 196
ocularcentrism 311
O'Doherty, Brian 259, 260, 311, 330, 341
Oriel Wrecsam 132, 134–44
*Original Kierkegaard, The* 342

Origin Housing Association 52, 53, 54, 55, 56
Oudsten, Frank den 313
Ou Ning 1
*Outings* 47
ownership 17, 53, 54, 56, 60, 69, 78, 83, 132, 134, 135, 152, 162, 215

Papanek, Victor 50
*Paper Window Project* 336
participation 4, 6, 49, 62, 64, 65, 66, 68, 101, 112, 117, 148, 149, 153, 162, 201, 209, 217, 219, 272, 281, 337, 352, 354–5; design 4, 51, 147, 148–9, 150, 152; innovations 3; processes 118, 149, 160, 162, 173
Peer Insight 215–16, 217
Pelliot, Paul 72
People's Market, Wrexham 132, 134, 135, 138, 140, 141, 143, 144
perception 5, 6, 20, 27, 90, 181, 239, 240, 252, 255, 281, 305, 310, 313, 340, 341, 344, 345–6, 347
perceptual acuity 10, 59, 61, 69
performance-centred management models 189
Peterson, Anne Ring 343
phenomenology 304, 344, 345
*Phenomenology of Perception* 344
photography 206, 277, 289, 301, 306, 308
physically accessible exhibition environments 175
Pier Arts Centre, Stromness, Orkney 87, 88, 91, 92, 93, 95
place 86–8, 90, 91, 92, 95, 96, 97–8, 103, 118, 206, 210, 243, 246, 260, 278; identities 86–7, 98; and placemaking 59, 61, 63, 64, 65, 66, 67, 68, 69
planning process 49, 105, 247
play 64, 153, 154, 155, 157, 262
Playgrounding 16
plot 22, 40, 228, 229, 319, 320, 321
pollution 62, 288, 291, 292, 295, 297, 301
Poole, Nick 36, 41
positive social impacts 5, 52
Powell, Kenneth 91
Poy Gum Lee (Li Jingpei) 73
Price, Cedric 134
*Prism of Sustainability, The* 340
progressive 95, 160, 196, 202, 229
*Project for Public Spaces* 63
prosthetic 345
prototyping 16, 40, 49, 51, 117, 123–5, 126, 128–9, 130, 155, 163, 164, 167, 168, 169, 170, 171, 185, 215
public spaces 47, 63, 64, 65, 68, 69, 111, 129, 176, 200
Public Visualization Studio 65
Pudovkin, Vsevolod Illarionovich 319
*Punctum see Studium and Punctum*

Qiu Ying 328–9

RCMG 14, 18
Rees, Marc 136
reflection 91, 123, 149, 185, 191, 195, 208, 210, 225, 252, 298, 299, 308, 311, 330, 345; need for 26, 33, 34, 43, 288; opportunities for 14, 120, 169, 194, 247, 249, 289, 296
Reiach and Hall 92
research-led design 6
*Reshaping Museum Space* 240
Riverfront Era Gallery 179–80
Rodaway, Paul 309, 311
*Role of University Arts Museums in the 21st Century, The* 105
Rothschild, Hannah 67
Ruan Lingyu 284, 285
*Run Lola Run* 246, 247, 252
Ryan, Marie-Laure 234
*#RyeLights* 65, 66, 69
Ryerson Image Arts Building 60, 65

Samuel, Flora 244
Santa Cruz Museum of Art and History 49, 51
Santa Fe Institute 37
scenography 341, 342
Schwartzman, Madeline 348
scratch theatre 16
Screven, Chandler 124
scriptwriting 318, 319
*See Yourself Sensing* 348
self-awareness 306, 345
Sennett, Richard 2, 66
sensory experience 117, 348
service design 16, 51–2, 119, 213, 214, 215, 217, 222
*Shanghai Exhibition (1935)* 10, 71–2, 73, 74, 75, 76, 77, 78, 80, 81, 82, 83
Shanghai Film Museum (SFM) 277, 278, 279, 281, 283
Sheets-Johnstone, Maxine 240
Sheng-hsiung Chung 289, 291
Shishi Xunhao 75
Sidney Estate, Somers Town 46, 53
Siegenthaler, Fiona 207
Simon, Nina 41, 49, 149, 150
Situational 118, 147
Situationist International 10, 59, 60
Sixth Naphtha Cracker (Formosa Plastic Corporation) 288, 291, 292, 294, 295, 298
Sixth Patriarch Huineng 29, 33
smart cities 59, 61, 62–3, 64, 65, 66, 67, 68, 69
social: biographies of space 19, 21; expression 11; model of disability 175, 176
sociality 6, 17, 27, 62, 64
socially engaged art 118, 119, 133, 134, 200–2, 207, 209–10
socially responsive design 51, 52

*Societal Journal of the Museum Association of China* 76
SO-IL, Bohlin Cywinski Jackson 109
spatial staging 304, 315, 342
staging 90, 121, 304, 306, 308, 309, 311, 312, 313, 314, 315, 341, 342
Statens Museum for Kunst (SMK) 147, 150–4, 156, 158
Steeds, Lucy 200
Stiegler, Bernard 264
*Story and Discourse* 320
storytelling 17, 130, 153, 156, 158, 214, 247, 251, 252, 317, 318
strategic design 6, 46, 56
*Street Angel (Malu Tianshi)* 282, 283
*Streetmuseum* 47
*Studium and Punctum* 301
*Superfluous Things* 77
Suspense 252, 256, 317, 318, 319, 320, 321, 322, 324, 325, 326
sustainability 9, 51, 56, 128, 143, 300
sustainable 16, 46, 54, 56, 61, 65, 100, 105, 106, 119, 129, 160, 162, 173, 197, 201, 215, 218, 219, 221
Suzhou Museum 328
Synaesthesia 310
*Synchronizing the City: Its Natural and Urban Rhythms* 67
*Syuzhet* 320, 321, 324

Tai O 31
Taipei Fine Art Museum 328
Taixi Village 288–92, 295, 301
Taxén, Gustav 150
Temple 82, 83, 204, 260, 269, 273
Tilghman, Shirley M. 105
time 19, 68, 84, 88, 239, 240, 241, 246, 249–50, 269, 277, 280, 281, 282, 283, 284, 306, 333, 334
*Time and Free Will* 241
Time/temporality 284, 333
*Tools of Screenwriting, The* 318
*Torture at the Tower* 24
*Touch - Sensuous Theory and Multisensory Media* 310–11
touch/tactility 40, 134–5, 143, 179, 182, 306, 310
Tower Bridge 66
Tower of London 9, 13, 19, 21–4
Transmedial narrative theory 227, 234
Tsong-Zung Chang 328, 329, 331, 334, 336
Turner Contemporary, Margate 87, 96, 97

Ulaszek, Jason (UX for Good) 217–18
Umbrella Movement, the 10, 29, 32
unboxing 213–14
Universal Design Group (UDG) 177, 180, 182, 183, 184, 185–6, 187
user-centred: collaboration 118; design 11, 54, 147, 148–9
user experience design 119, 148, 213, 214, 217, 218, 219, 222

*Validation Beyond the Gallery* 133
Verhoeff, Nana 63
Villareal, Leo 60, 67
visitor studies 128, 311, 337

Wang Chen-hua 73
Wang Shijie 73
Wang Ximeng 80
Weil, Stephen F. 149
wellbeing xiv, 6, 15, 30, 48, 53, 173, 289
Wellcome Collection 52, 53, 54, 55
West Kowloon Cultural District (WKCD) 30–1
*When the South Wind Blows* 288, 289, 290, 291–2, 295, 301
White cube 255, 259, 263, 269, 271, 328, 329, 330, 331, 332, 333, 341
Whyte, William W. 63, 126
Wilson, Robert 341–2
Wright, Joseph 165, 172
Wu Hufan 74, 265, 267
*wunderkammer* 271
*Wu School Painting Series: The Art of Qiu Ying* 328

Xu Beihong 74

*Yaji* 256, 328, 329, 330, 331, 332, 334, 336, 338; garden 255, 259–60, 261, 262, 263, 265, 267, 269, 271, 272, 273, 274, 275
Ye Gongchuo 74
Yeh Shih-Chiang 267
Yellow Box 255, 256, 257, 259, 328, 329, 330, 331, 332, 334, 335, 336, 337, 338, 349
*Yellow Box: Contemporary Calligraphy and Painting in Taiwan* 328
Yu Peng 336

Zhangxi Liu 55
Zhang Zhen 285
Zhou Xuan 282, 283, 285